CIVIL WAR LAWYERS

CONSTITUTIONAL QUESTIONS, COURTROOM
DRAMAS, AND THE MEN BEHIND THEM

ARTHUR T. DOWNEY

CIVIL WAR LAWYERS

CONSTITUTIONAL QUESTIONS, COURTROOM
DRAMAS, AND THE MEN BEHIND THEM

Defending Liberty
Pursuing Justice

Cover design by ABA Publishing.

The materials contained herein represent the opinions and views of the authors and/or the editors, and should not be construed to be the views or opinions of the law firms or companies with whom such persons are in partnership with, associated with, or employed by, nor of the American Bar Association, unless adopted pursuant to the bylaws of the Association.

Nothing contained in this book is to be considered as the rendering of legal advice, either generally or in connection with any specific issue or case; nor do these materials purport to explain or interpret any specific bond or policy, or any provisions thereof, issued by any particular franchise company, or to render franchise or other professional advice. Readers are responsible for obtaining advice from their own lawyers or other professionals. This book and any forms and agreements herein are intended for educational and informational purposes only.

© 2010 Arthur T. Downey. All rights reserved.

No part of this publication may be reproduced, stored in a retrieval system, or transmitted in any form or by any means, electronic, mechanical, photocopying, recording, or otherwise, without the prior written permission of the publisher. For permission, contact the ABA Copyrights & Contracts Department at copyright@americanbar.org or via fax at 312-988-6030.

All photographs and images in this book are courtesy of the Online Catalog of the Prints and Photographs Division of the Library of Congress.

Printed in the United States of America.

14 13 12   5 4 3

Library of Congress Cataloging-in-Publication Data

Downey, Arthur T.
  The Civil War lawyers : constitutional questions, courtroom dramas, and the men behind them / by Arthur T. Downey.
     p. cm.
  Includes bibliographical references and index.
  ISBN 978-1-61632-042-3
  1. Law—United States—History—19th century. 2. Lawyers—United States—History—19th century. 3. United States—History—Civil War, 1861–1865—Law and legislation. 4. Slavery—Law and legislation—United States—History—19th century. I. Title.
  KF366.D69 2010
  973.7'1—dc22
                              2010043418

Discounts are available for books ordered in bulk. Special consideration is given to state bars, CLE programs, and other bar-related organizations. Inquire at Book Publishing, ABA Publishing, American Bar Association, 321 North Clark Street, Chicago, Illinois 60654-7598.

www.ShopABA.org

Contents

Introduction — xi

CHAPTER 1
Prologue: 1776 to 1857 — 1

The Declaration of Independence 2
The Articles of Confederation 3
The Constitution 4
    The Slave Trade 5
    The Three-Fifths Clause 6
    The Fugitive Slave Clause 7
Change and Unimaginable Polarization: 1800–1855 9
The World Changes and the Civil War Era Begins 13

CHAPTER 2
The *Dred Scott* Case — 15

The Facts 15
    The Missouri Cases 17
    The Political Angle 18
    The Federal Case 18
    At the Supreme Court 19

The Decision of the Supreme Court   24
    The Taney Opinion   25
    The Taney Opinion Continues   29
    Concurring Opinions   31
    The Dissents   34
After the Dred Scott Case   37
    Ableman v. Booth   41
    Lemmon v. People   43
    Dred and His Owners   44

CHAPTER 3
Virginia v. John Brown   47

John Brown Before Harpers Ferry   47
The Trial of John Brown and His Coconspirators   53
The Trial as an Event, and the Aftermath   58
Brown's Secret Supporters: Frederick Douglass and the Secret Six   61
Brown's Legacy   65
The Second Trial: United States v. Brown; The Mason Committee   67
After the Mason Report   73

CHAPTER 4
Secession   75

Early "Secession" Activity   76
    The Louisiana Purchase   76
    The Hartford Convention   77
    The Missouri Compromise   78
South Carolina's Nullification and "Secession" of 1832   81
    The Nullification Crisis of 1832–33   83
The Loss of Equilibrium   87
    The Annexation of Texas   87
    The Christiana Riot   92
Seccession   94
    War   95
Black's Opinion and Buchanan's Response   97

Contents   vii

      South Carolina Secedes, Then Others   103
          Reaction and Rallies   105
          Mississippi Secedes   106
   Texas Secedes   108
      The Confederate States of America   108
      Fighting Begins   111
      Virginia's Secession and the Formation of West Virginia   112
   Is Secession Legal?   117
      Texas Secession and the Supreme Court   117
   Secession in Today's World   120

❧ CHAPTER 5

The Conflict Between the Chief Justice and the Chief Executive: *Ex Parte Merryman*   125

   The Beginning   126
      A World of Difference   128
      Their History   130
      The Arrest of John Merryman   132
   The Political Context: The Events Between March and May   138
   Taney's Decision   144
      The Written Opinion   144
      An Unavoidable Confrontation?   147
   Lincoln's Response   149
   The Attorney General's Opinion   151
      The Resolution of Merryman   *156*
      The Habeas Corpus Act   157
      The First Proclamation Under the Act   158
   Aftermath   161

❧ CHAPTER 6

The War at Sea: International Law and Diplomacy   167

   The Privateers   168
   The Savannah *and the* Enchantress   *174*
      The Savannah *Trial   175*
      The Jefferson Davis *Trial   178*

The Different Verdicts   179
Aftermath   181
The Chapman Piracy Project   182
The Blockade   186
The Prize Cases   188
International Relations   189
The Trent Affair   192
The Union's Official Response   198
The Prize Cases in the Supreme Court   201
The Arguments   201
The Decision   203
Aftermath   206

CHAPTER 7
Ending Slavery   209

The English Heritage   210
Slavery and the American Revolution   212
Pre- and Post-Revolution   213
Nibbling Away at Slavery   216
Ending the Slave Trade   216
British Abolition   219
The District of Columbia   220
Southern Worries and Northern Assurances   222
Ending Slavery During the War   225
Fremont's Order   228
The Cameron Report   230
Persuading the States to End Slavery   232
The Hunter Order   234
The Territories and Border States   236
The Emancipation Proclamation   240
The Reaction   244
The Amendments and Final Proclamation   245
Aftermath   249
Emancipation in the South?   253
The Thirteenth Amendment   256

Contents

CHAPTER 8
The Revenge Trials   259

The Trial of the Assassination Conspirators   259
     The Johnson Argument   265
     Speed's Opinion   266
     The Verdicts   267
The Trials of John H. Surratt, Jr.   271
     The Second Trial   273
Dr. Mudd's Legal Efforts into the Twenty-First Century   276
The Trial of Captain Henry Wirz: The Andersonville Trial   279
The Non-Trial of Jefferson Davis   282
     Trial Preliminaries   287
     Double Jeopardy   288
Revenge Turns to Reconciliation   290

APPENDIX 1
Dramatis Personae: The Lawyers   295

APPENDIX 2
Intersecting Lawyers   329

APPENDIX 3
Chronology   335

Notes   357

In Appreciation   433

Index   435

About the Author   463

Introduction

The history of the American Civil War period is often focused exclusively on military events. But other perspectives are clearly relevant: economic, social, racial, feminist, moral. An important component of Civil War history that is sometimes overlooked and has rarely been treated in a comprehensive fashion is the legal issues and the lawyers who addressed those issues.[1] The purpose of this book is to demonstrate how important the law and the lawyers were during that tortured period of United States history. The law, and the lawyers, dominated many of the fundamental elements of American life—social relations, economics, and the conduct of the War itself. Crucial Supreme Court arguments and Executive decisions on lofty constitutional issues, as well as the tense courtroom trials where individual lives were at stake, shaped the War and shaped the legal landscape in all the years that followed.

Some of the broad legal questions of the Civil War period still have relevance today. For example: How expansive are the powers of the Executive in wartime? To what extent may civil liberties be curtailed in light of threats to national security? Can citizens who are not in the military be tried by military commissions when civil courts are available?

Lawyers in the Mid-Nineteenth Century

The leadership in America for the first several generations was composed, to an extraordinary degree, of lawyers.[2] During the first seventy-six years the United States existed, from 1789 to 1865, there were sixteen presidents—twelve of whom were lawyers.[3] In contrast, during the most recent seventy-eight years (1932–2010), the trend was almost completely reversed. There were fourteen presidents during this period, only five of whom were lawyers.[4]

The trend is the same with respect to the Congress. The Thirtieth Congress (1847–1849), in which Lincoln served as a member from Illinois, was composed predominately of lawyers—74 percent. Businessmen constituted 16 percent, farmers 7 percent, and educators and clergymen 1 percent. In 1845, 95 percent of the U.S. Senators had legal training.[5] In contrast, in the One Hundred Eleventh Congress (2009–2011), for the first time, the leading occupation was "public service/politics," and law is the second-ranking occupation, almost tied with business and education.[6] Thus, since the 1840s, the dominance of lawyers in the Congress has vanished, and this is consistent with the sharp decline in lawyer-presidents.[7]

Why is it that lawyers so dominated public and political life during the first third of American history? Some insight is offered in an excellent biography of lawyer-President Andrew Jackson:

> The legal profession, in the 1780s as later, was to American society what the clergy and the military were to certain other countries and cultures: an avenue of advancement for those with talent and ambition but with neither wealth nor connections. Protestant America had no church hierarchy to speak of, precluding the priestly route to success, and it had no standing army, making a military career unappealing. Yet every society requires means for the humble to get ahead, lest their frustrated ambitions destabilize the status quo. In America, the law long served that purpose.[8]

Needless to say, hostility toward lawyers also flourished, especially toward the lawyer-politicians. One Democratic legislator from Massachusetts claimed in 1834 that the lawyers' union deliberately monopolized political office.[9] Years before he became Lincoln's vice president, Andrew Johnson, during his 1851 congressional race, pointed out that all but 23 of the 223 members of Congress were lawyers. Johnson asserted that the "laboring man of America is ignored, he has no proportionate representation, though he constitutes a large majority of the voting population." Johnson felt that lawyers were corrupted by their reading of English law books, which led lawyers to appreciate the British government more than their own.[10]

During the formative period of the United States, and well into the nineteenth century, there were no law schools as we know them today, and there were no bar exams. Lawyers usually learned through apprenticeships with established lawyers. In 1840, only eleven out of thirty states required all lawyers to complete an apprenticeship.[11] Lincoln, for example, was admitted to the Illinois bar without any written examination. He fulfilled the statutory requirements of a certificate of good moral character offered by a county judge, and he then passed a perfunctory examination given by two justices of the state supreme court, and then in 1837, he was "enrolled" by the clerk of the state supreme court, i.e., he was admitted to the bar.[12]

The lives of Americans in the early and mid-nineteenth century, and lawyers in particular, were linked to their own state. The national government was remote, and during much of the first half of the nineteenth century, it was seen as weak. In the 1830s, Alexis de Tocqueville noted that

> the Union executes vaster undertakings, but one rarely feels it acting. The [state] government does smaller things, but it never rests and it reveals its existence at each instant. . . . The Union assures the independence and greatness of the nation, things that do not immediately touch particular persons. The state maintains freedom, regulates rights, guarantees the fortune, secures the life, the whole future of each citizen.[13]

For lawyers, the focus within their state was the county courthouse.

> Lawyers formed a unique kind of community; in some states they traveled in groups, "riding circuit" from county seat to county seat, following a court that was equally peripatetic. They stayed in local inns, sometimes sharing a room and even a bed with their fellow travelers after an evening of food and drink.[14]

As a result of the close relationships fostered by the nature of law practice at the time, many of the lawyers who were prominent during the Civil War period were aware of each other professionally and had also practiced law and tried cases together—sometimes against each other.[15] While they did not reach the same political or legal conclusions, most of them were trained and practiced their craft in a similar fashion: they read Cicero, Blackstone,[16] and Kent, and tried to think dispassionately and analytically. (Appendix 2 sets out a dozen examples of how the professional lives of many of the important lawyers intersected.) The lawyers got to know each other's thought processes, as well as virtues and vices.[17] For example, Chief Justice John Marshall arranged accommodations for the Supreme Court Justices in one boarding house to foster fellowship; when it opened in 1820, the Indian Queen Hotel near Capitol Hill was the most prestigious hotel in Washington, where members of Marshall's Court lived during Court terms, sharing meals and conversation in an atmosphere that encouraged consensus.[18]

In short, the Civil War period was a time when prominent politicians were predominantly lawyers. De Tocqueville in the 1830s found that lawyers in the United States "naturally form a body. It is not that they agree among themselves and direct themselves in concert toward the same point; but community of studies and unity of methods bind their mind to one another as interest could unite their wills."[19] It is not surprising that the key members of Lincoln's cabinet were *all* lawyers,[20] or that Lincoln's key diplomatic appointments were *all* lawyers,[21] or that the five men who tried to end the War at the Hampton Roads Peace Conference on February 3, 1865, were *all* lawyers.[22]

The Legal Issues

This book attempts to explore significant legal issues during the period leading up to and through the Civil War.[23] They are addressed in a variety of contexts, the most obvious of which is in decisions of the Supreme Court. The most significant Supreme Court decision just prior to the War (*Dred Scott*), and the *only* significant Supreme Court decision during the War (the *Prize Cases*), are each reviewed, as well as the dramatic decision of the Chief Justice in *Ex parte Merryman*, dealing with presidential powers.

Courtroom trials—some electric with high drama—also illustrate the role of the law and the lawyers. The courtroom experience of the John Brown trial in Virginia and his "second trial" by a select Senate investigating committee is explored, along with the piracy trials of the Confederate privateers in New York and Philadelphia. And of course, it would be inappropriate not to review the trials of the Lincoln assassination conspirators and other key figures of the time, including the non-trial of Jefferson Davis.

Apart from judicial decisions and courtroom trials, the book reviews the way in which presidents dealt with the legality or constitutionality of their decisions, such as Buchanan's understanding of the limits of his power to confront secession, and Lincoln's understanding of his authority to sign the bill accepting the secession of West Virginia from Virginia or to issue the Emancipation Proclamation. The objective purity of the law during the Civil War period was occasionally overthrown for the sake of expediency. In the *Merryman* case, Lincoln took the position that, despite the rich heritage of the liberty-protecting writ of habeas corpus enshrined in the Constitution, he should suspend the writ in secret, because he felt it was expedient to protect the Union from the adventures of Confederate sympathizers. It proved to be expedient for Attorney General Bates to take no action to accelerate the progress toward the Supreme Court of the cases involving vessels taken as prizes, until Lincoln had sufficient time and opportunity to add his own appointees to the Court. An early decision in the *Prize Cases*—i.e., a decision made at a special term of the Court—without the benefit of new Justices appointed by Lincoln probably would have resulted in an adverse decision, which would have harmed the Union's war effort. Perhaps President Buchanan should have relied on "expediency" during the last several months of his administration, rather than wholly accept the tight legal limits on his room for action—as defined by his Attorney General—in which case he might have been able to act to prevent or at least curtail secession.

The law also shaped and influenced many Civil War era events without directly controlling or determining the outcomes. There were many reasons Lincoln crafted the Emancipation Proclamation to be applicable only in territory controlled by the Confederacy—one of which was to reduce the chances that an aggrieved former slaveholder could pose a court challenge to the constitutionality of the Proclamation. While the fear of war with Great Britain clearly was the deciding factor in Lincoln's successful resolution of the *Trent* affair, the fact that the U.S. capture of the Confederate envoys Mason and Slidell was a clear violation of international law was an influential factor as well.

Finally, the dark side of the law was also revealed during this heated period. The post-assassination revenge trials dishonored sound legal principles and demonstrated that justice may be disregarded in an atmosphere of such enflamed passions. The revenge trials essentially exposed the unfairness of a system of justice that was appropriate for the military, but that was outside the traditional tensions between the law and lawyering in civilian courts. Joseph Holt, a brilliant lawyer and master prosecutor used the law—probably abused the law—to advance the administration's goal of purging the evil of the Confederacy from the nation. At the other extreme, however, the lawyers, the prosecutors, and the judge at John Brown's trial bent over backwards to ensure that Brown would receive a fair trial. Ironically, they ended up giving Brown a platform to spread his message of martyrdom.

Larger-than-Life Lawyers

Civil War lawyers animated, argued, and articulated the law. The legal issues of the day come to life as these lawyers appear and re-appear throughout the period. (Appendix 1 offers brief biographical sketches of one hundred and one lawyers prominent during the period; Appendix 2 sets out a dozen examples of how the professional lives of many of the important lawyers intersected.)

These lawyers could be clever and inventive: Dred Scott's lawyer in Missouri figured out a way to get his case heard in a federal court, after being unsuccessful in the state court system. Ben Butler, a lawyer-turned-political-general at Fortress Monroe, used his legal skills to figure out that slaves assisting the Confederate war effort might legally be taken and protected as "contraband."

Strong and prominent lawyers sometimes took courageous positions representing unpopular individuals. Virginia attorneys Botts and Green (the mayor of Harpers Ferry) took on the task of defending John Brown after he led the attack that killed many of their fellow townspeople. Imagine the fear in the hearts of the defense team representing the CSA privateers in New York when Secretary of State Seward ordered that the lead lawyer, Algernon S. Sullivan, should be arrested and confined as a "political prisoner." Justice Curtis was so disappointed by Taney's opinion of the Court in the *Dred Scott* case that he left the bench. Years later, Curtis took the principled, but unpopular, position that Lincoln had overstepped constitutional bounds with his Emancipation Proclamation and impairment of civil liberties. Reverdy Johnson, perhaps the most prominent constitutional lawyer of the time, unsuccessfully defended Mary Surratt. Charles O'Conor, one of New York's most famous trial lawyers, successfully defended Jefferson Davis.

The legal ethics context in which lawyers worked at that time was not as clear as it is today. Thus, it did not seem wrong when President-elect Buchanan wrote to one of the Supreme Court Justices and asked him to persuade another Justice to move toward a majority position in the *Dred Scott* case. No one seemed to be bothered that one of Dred Scott's lawyers (George T. Curtis), who argued the case before the U.S. Supreme Court, was the brother and former law partner of one of those Justices (Benjamin R. Curtis). Justice Curtis just happened to agree with his brother's legal position. The winning lawyer (David Dudley Field) in the key Supreme Court civil liberties case of the time, *Ex parte Milligan*, was the brother and former law partner of one of the Justices (Stephen Johnson Field) who agreed with the opinion of the Court.

The Unresolved Constitutional and Legal Issues

There were important and broad constitutional issues that surfaced during the War that were *not* selected for close treatment in this book because they were not finally resolved until *well after* the War. For example, at the beginning of the War, the U.S. government was virtually insolvent, and it became necessary, literally, to print money. Constitutional challenges to this step, known collectively as the *Legal Tender Cases*, were not decided by the Supreme Court until February 1870.[24] Another major step in financing the War was the country's first income tax law passed by Congress in August 1861.[25] While its constitutionality was challenged immediately, the Supreme Court did not address the question until its unanimous decision in February 1869.[26] In the end,

Introduction							xvii

the Sixteenth Amendment to the Constitution, ratified in 1913, was required to resolve the constitutional issue.

Even more important than financing the War was supplying the manpower to fight it. The first conscription law, the Enrollment Act of March 1863, was controversial on constitutional grounds, and the draft notices that were issued in July of that year were met with evasion and horrible riots. But the issue of the constitutionality of the conscription law never reached the Supreme Court, in large part because the suspension of the writ of habeas corpus effectively blocked courts from releasing draft resisters. Indeed, it was not until the twentieth century that the Court had occasion to decide—unanimously—that conscription was indeed constitutional.[27]

Apart from broad constitutional issues, there were more purely "legal" developments that had lasting significance, but that also are not treated in this book because they were so narrowly focused. An illustration is the "Lieber Code," approved by Lincoln and published in April 1863.[28] This was America's first code regulating the conduct of its army in wartime, and it led directly to the adoption of the first international treaties on the law of war—the Hague Conventions on land warfare of 1899 and 1907, and later to the Geneva Conventions.[29]

The goal of this book is to demonstrate that the law, and the lawyers, were unusually important during the Civil War period; they were, perhaps, the warp and woof of its fabric.

CHAPTER 1

Prologue: 1776 to 1857

Almost three generations separate the American Founding Fathers from the *Dred Scott* case, which marks the beginning of the Civil War period. The Founding Fathers produced three fundamental legal documents, the last of which—the U.S. Constitution—is the framework within which the great issues of the Civil War period were debated. Following is a brief look at the country and the government these documents helped establish and their use—and abuse—during the Civil War era.

The Declaration of Independence

The ringing Declaration of Independence of 1776 listed the "long Train of Abuses and Usurpations" of the King that created the right and the duty to "throw off such Government" by dissolving "the Political Bonds which have connected them." The immediate purpose of the document was to explain why the thirteen colonies separated from Britain: to gain respect and support from the European Great Powers, especially France and Spain. The goal was to establish international legitimacy, and to assert the right to conclude alliances against Britain.[1]

In 1860–61, many of the seceding states relied on the original "right of revolution" concept to support their acts of secession. In President-elect Jefferson Davis's inaugural address on February 18, 1861, he focused on Thomas Jefferson's revolutionary concept, claiming that the new Southern Republic "merely asserted the right which the Declaration of Independence" declared unalienable.[2] The seceding states tended to view the Declaration as an act of state creation, rather than an emancipatory message.

The Declaration, in its seminal passage, also asserted that one of the self-evident Truths is that "all Men are created equal, that they are endowed by their Creator with certain unalienable rights." In the mid-nineteenth century, those opposed to slavery relied on that assertion in the Declaration to justify, in part, their abolitionist actions—a mandate for the crusade against slavery. Lincoln argued in 1857 that the drafters did not mean to assert the

> obvious untruth, that all were then actually enjoying that equality, nor yet, that they were about to confer it immediately upon them. . . . They meant simply to declare the right, so that the enforcement of it might follow as fast as circumstances should permit.[3]

There was no mention of slavery in the Declaration, though slavery was a fundamental element in American colonial life. On the eve of Independence, the population of the thirteen colonies was 2.5 million, and one-fifth were slaves. The most populous colony (Virginia) had the most slaves (40 percent), but 14 percent of New York's and 8 percent of New Jersey's population was slave.[4]

The Articles of Confederation

The Articles of Confederation was adopted by the Second Continental Congress in 1777 and formally ratified in March 1781 (when Maryland finally endorsed it). The Articles defined the relationship among the states and reflected the structure of a multilateral treaty[5] among sovereigns, "a firm league of friendship," as noted in Article III. As in a treaty, no changes to the Articles could be made unless confirmed by the legislatures of every state. As Professor Joseph Ellis has noted, "the government established under the Articles of Confederation was not really much of a government at all, but rather a diplomatic conference where sovereign states . . . met to coordinate a domestic version of foreign policy."[6]

The term "perpetual Union" is employed five times in the Articles of Confederation; the final Article XIII declares that "the Union shall be perpetual." It is not unlikely that the drafters of the Articles were well aware of the Treaty of Union of 1707[7] by which Scotland and England united and became Great Britain. Before 1707, the term "union" was used in a general sense to mean an association or alliance for any common purpose; but in the 1707 Treaty, the term referred to a new and more narrow concept (at least in English eyes): an "incorporating Union."[8]

In contrast to the apparent notion of equality of all men and their unalienable rights as asserted in the Declaration, the Articles of Confederation explicitly granted all the privileges and immunities of "free citizens" of each of the states only to the "free inhabitants" of each of the states. The words "slave" or "slavery" did not appear in either the Declaration or the Articles, but it was expressly provided in the Articles that only "free inhabitants" had full rights—and the obvious implication is that slaves did not enjoy those rights.

The "perpetual Union" under the Articles lived for only nine years, 1781 to 1790. By 1787, the Confederation was in "shambles."[9] Thus, in that hot summer of 1787 in Philadelphia, thirty-nine men met in secret and proposed a new creation: a Constitution.[10]

The Constitution

The Constitution established a new political order, clearly something more than a mere "league" or treaty-like alliance.[11] The sovereignty of the states that existed under the Articles was now to be limited. In a sense, perhaps Lincoln misspoke at Gettysburg when he suggested that a new, indivisible nation was created in 1776—rather, it was later, in the Constitution, that a new and indivisible nation really was created. Chief Justice John Marshall, who had lived through the Revolution and the Founding, said it clearly in 1824:

> [W]hen these allied sovereigns [the thirteen states] converted their Congress of Ambassadors . . . into a Legislature, empowered to enact laws on the most interesting subjects, the whole character in which the States appear, underwent a change.[12]

The new Constitution was designed to be ratified by "the People"—not by state legislatures, but rather by Special Conventions formed for the sole purpose of ratifying the Constitution. (State legislators might have opposed the new creation because it would reduce their power.) The document was kept short, less than 8,000 words, so that it could be widely read.[13] The arrangement for ratification was one of the most important differences from the old Articles of Confederation. The new Constitution was to come into force when three-fourths of the states ratified it, nine out of thirteen; under the Articles of Confederation, unanimity was required for ratification.[14] Each state could decide whether to join in the formation of a "more perfect union" or to remain fully sovereign and independent. New Hampshire was the ninth state to ratify, on June 21, 1788, by a close vote of 57–47, and the new Constitution came into force. In effect, this new Constitution was a mass secession from the former Confederation of States "united."[15] A new and "more Perfect" union was formed, rather than simply an improved Confederacy.

National security was a central motivation for this new Constitution: a truly "United States" would be more likely to blunt European adventurism, ensuring that European monarchs could not play one state off against another. There were British forts to the north, Spanish ports to the south, and the French occupied the vast region between the Appalachian Mountains and the Mississippi River.[16] The strength of a united America would eliminate the need for a large national standing army (as opposed to state militia) in peacetime. The Founders were worried about an excessive and independent military power. Three generations later, Lincoln also worried about the national security need to preserve unity, and aimed to prevent the emergence of two powerful and hostile regimes that could generate an arms race or a trade war, which might lead to permanent militarization (and economic ruin).[17]

To amend the Articles of Confederation, first Congress had to agree to the amendment, and then the legislatures of every state had to confirm it.[18] Unanimity ruled. In contrast, the new Constitution provided in Article V that two-thirds of both Houses, or two-thirds of the states, could propose an amendment; ratification of the amendment required the assent of three-fourths of the states. Unanimity ceased to exist. (Nevertheless, the Southern states or the small states were numerous enough to block any proposed amendment they deemed unsatisfactory.) There was a single, and very important, exception to the amendment process, and that related to slavery.

Yes, slavery was an issue, but that word did not appear in the Constitution—just as it had not appeared in the Declaration or in the Articles.[19] Slavery was camouflaged; it was orchestrated silence.[20] But that does not mean the Constitution was neutral on the subject: to the contrary, it tilted in a pro-slave direction. Slavery was "the original sin in the New World garden, and the Constitution did more to feed the serpent than to crush it."[21]

The slavery issue was dealt with in the Constitution in three areas: the temporary protection of the slave trade, the role of the slave population in assessing legislative apportionment, and the obligation to return escaped slaves. Even though one-third of the Delegates to the Convention owned slaves, only a few of them (Georgians and South Carolinians[22]) actually defended the morality of slavery.[23]

The Slave Trade

The Constitution, in Article I, Section 9, barred Congress from terminating the slave trade until 1808.[24] In 1808, then, the importation of slaves could be terminated, but termination was not required. Just to be sure that slave trade was really protected for those twenty years, a provision in the Article detailed the one constitutional exception to the amendment process: no amendment could be made to the provision that safeguarded the slave trade.[25] Despite this exception, relatively fewer slaves were imported into the Deep South at the end of the eighteenth century than had been expected, in part because of the slave revolt in Haiti in 1791, which suggested to Southerners that it would be safer for them to deal with domestic slaves than to import insurrection-minded slaves. (And in fact, the Confederate Constitution of 1861 provided for a permanent ban on the importation of slaves.[26])

The Three-Fifths Clause

While the protection of the slave trade established in the Constitution was temporary—only for twenty years—the impact of slavery on legislative apportionment was permanent. The infamous "three-fifths" provision appeared in Article I:

> Representatives . . . shall be apportioned among the several States . . . according to their respective Numbers, which shall be determined by adding to the whole Number of free Persons . . . three fifths of all other Persons.

This "three-fifths" clause had nothing to do with whether a slave was valued as subhuman, a partial person, or even with viewing slavery with disapproval. The purpose of the provision was to strike a power balance among the states: if each slave was fully counted as a whole person, the result would have been more power to the slaveholding states. An antislave approach would have been to not count the slaves at all. The three-fifths compromise was reached on July 12, 1787. John Rutledge of South Carolina and Roger Sherman of Connecticut were leaders in working out the compromise. As one scholar put it, "Connecticut shut its eyes to South Carolina's slavery and slave trade, while South Carolina accepted Connecticut's claim to western lands."[27]

Many Southern delegates, including the South Carolina delegation, had urged that slaves be counted in full. Charles Pinckney, a leading delegate from South Carolina, rose in the House of Representatives more than thirty years later, speaking as the only Member of the House at that time who had been an active member of the Constitutional Convention, and asserted vehemently that the three-fifths provision had been a great concession by the South.[28] Geography, however, did not produce uniform opinions: George Mason of Virginia, one of the Founding Fathers, spoke out strongly and repeatedly against slavery during the debates at the Constitutional Convention, and opposed the move to count slaves for representational purposes, even though such a count would have been favorable to Virginia.[29] For example, although Massachusetts had a larger free population than Virginia, Virginia got five more seats because of its 300,000 slaves.[30] This provision gave the South rough parity with the North in the Congress.

In a sense, the "three-fifths" provision gave the slaveholding South an incentive to produce more slaves, since growth in that population would translate into greater congressional power. Professor Akhil Reed Amar of Yale has speculated[31] what would have happened if the three-fifths provision, like the slave trade, had been formulated to make it temporary, perhaps even on a sliding scale: for example, count the slaves as three-fifths in 1790, two-fifths in 1800, one-fifth in 1810, and zero in 1820. Such a slow phasing out might have provided the South with an incentive to reduce its slave population relative to its free population. Unfortunately, this creative idea was not floated in 1787. Indeed, in early 1860, Frederick Douglass, in a speech in Glasgow, Scotland, held out "to every slaveholding State the inducement of an increase of two-fifths political power by becoming a free State."[32]

The Fugitive Slave Clause

The third key proslavery provision in the Constitution—the fugitive slave clause—was contained in Article IV, Section 2:

> No Person held to Service or Labour in one State . . . escaping into another, shall . . . be discharged from such Service or Labour, but shall be delivered up on Claim of the Party to whom such Service or Labour may be due.

Once again, the term "slavery" was not employed, but in this provision the words make it clear that a person was being "held" and then "escaped," which hardly concealed the ugly fact of slavery. The Northwest Ordinance of 1787, enacted under the Articles of Confederation roughly contemporaneously with the drafting of the Constitution, banned slavery from the territories, but it also provided for the return of fugitive slaves.[33]

The Supreme Court in 1847 dealt with the validity of the 1793 fugitive slave statute[34] and the provision in the Constitution itself. In *Jones v. Van Zandt*,[35] the Court unanimously upheld both the statute and the clause, and noted that the fugitive slave clause was "one of [the] compromises" introduced into the Constitution, and, quoting Justice Story in an earlier fugitive slave case, "the constitution itself . . . flung its shield, for security, over such property [slaves] . . . and the right to pursue and reclaim it within the limits of another state."[36] The question of whether a slave state could demand extradition from a non-slave state, where the accused was charged with having helped a slave to escape—sort of a "fugitive slave clause lite," arose in *Kentucky v. Dennison*,[37] which was argued just before Lincoln's inaugural and decided ten days after Lincoln became president. The case involved a request to the governor of Ohio from the governor of Kentucky for the extradition of a man accused of helping a Kentucky slave to escape. Chief Justice Taney delivered the opinion of a unanimous Court that the Extradition Clause created a duty on the part of the Ohio governor to extradite, although the Court had no power to coerce the governor.[38]

These three "slave" provisions gave the Constitution a proslavery tilt: There is no way to see the Constitution as slavery-neutral. Raw politics dictated this: the South needed guaranteed assurances that its interests would be protected in the unique, indivisible union. The Constitution was sufficiently proslavery to be ratified in the South, and sufficiently not proslavery to be ratified in the North. Professor Joseph Ellis notes that "[a]ny clear resolution of the slavery question one way or the other rendered ratification of the Constitution virtually impossible."[39]

Most of the Founders lived with the belief—or the illusion—that slavery in the United States was dying away and would eventually disappear, especially with the likelihood that the slave trade would be terminated in 1808. During the decade of the 1780s and early 1790s, Virginians were actually relaxing the Black Codes that governed their slaves' lives; Virginians formed anti-slave societies, and manumitted their slaves by the thousands.[40] They thought that slavery was on its last legs and would naturally die away.[41]

Three generations later, in 1861, the new vice president of the Confederate States of America, Alexander H. Stephens, offered his perspective on the work of the Founders in dealing with slavery in the Constitution:

> The prevailing ideas entertained by [Thomas Jefferson] and most of the leading statesmen at the time of the formation of the old [1787] constitution, were that the enslavement of the African was in violation of the laws of nature; that it was wrong in principle, socially, morally, and politically. It was an evil they knew not well how to deal with, but the general opinion . . . was that, somehow or other in the order of Providence, the institution would be evanescent and pass away. . . . The constitution, it is true, secured every essential guarantee to the institution while it should last . . . .[42]

Stephens charged that the "prevailing ideas" in 1787 rested on the assumption of the equality of the races, but that assumption was flawed and "a sandy foundation" for the Union. The "cornerstone" of the Confederate States of America "rests upon the great truth, that the Negro is not equal to the white man; that slavery—subordination to the superior race—is his natural and normal condition." The "cornerstone" of the secessionist states could not have been explained more clearly; the evil was exposed.

The Constitution made no provision for a state to withdraw. A right of secession—today, self-determination—was not expressed.[43] However, the people of the United States could always decide, via amendments to the Constitution, to permit secession; they were then, and are today, free to undo what the people did in 1788, but only as set forth in the Constitution— a two-thirds vote for a proposal and a three-fourths vote for ratification.

Change and Unimaginable Polarization: 1800–1855

For the first decade or two after the Founders' creation, the framework of 1787 worked; its basic assumptions remained valid. But the situation began to change.

The 1803 Louisiana Purchase[44] brought vast new lands into the Union, doubling its land area. While Eli Whitney invented the cotton gin in 1794, it was not until the 1820s that the design was refined and ready for large-scale[45] production, and that made slavery more valuable. America moved due west.[46] Slavery began to dominate the nation's consciousness. However, national security also continued to be a paramount issue. The War of 1812 and the Monroe Doctrine of 1823[47] reflect that concern. European powers still had their eyes on the continent, and the United States was relatively small: Britain was twice the size of the United States, and France was three times larger.[48]

By 1820, the basic political division of the country was no longer large states versus small states; it had become North versus South.[49] A new political compromise was needed to deal with the future of slavery because of the move to the new lands in the west. The Missouri Compromise of 1820 essentially divided the new lands evenly according to the presence or absence of slavery: the free state of Maine was admitted along with the slave state of Missouri. That was also the year of the establishment on the African continent of the new country of Liberia by the American Colonization Society—thought by its members to be the only way to deal with the "problem of the African." The American Colonization Society helped found the colony in Liberia in 1821–1822 in an effort to return freed blacks to what they considered greater freedom in Africa.

Even though there was a general political compromise in 1820, tensions over the slavery issue gradually rose. The 1831 Nat Turner slave rebellion in Virginia terrified Southern slave owners. The decision of the British Parliament in 1833 to abolish slavery in its overseas possessions encouraged the abolitionists in the North and worried the slave owners in the South. In the South's defense, John C. Calhoun declared in 1837 that the relations between the races in the slaveholding states was "instead of an evil, a good—a positive good."[50]

The presidency of Andrew Jackson (1829–37) created a strong national Democratic Party, which had a solid, unifying impact on the nation. National party unity helped to counter the centrifugal forces of the North-South divide. Indeed, twenty-three years after Jackson's presidency, the collapse of the national Democratic Party into sections was the key factor that permitted the election of Abraham Lincoln. His new Republican Party was a Northern sectional party, unlike the former national Democratic Party.

ANDREW JACKSON.

The presidency is a national office and a symbol of the nation's unity. Jackson was a strong president who served for eight years. But when Jackson's presidency was over, the period of powerful and long-serving presidents was also over. All but two of his predecessors served eight years each; none of Jackson's eight successors served eight years.[51] In a sense, the president as a symbol of national unity was also weakened. The post-Jackson presidents were also relatively weak in relation to the great congressional leaders of the period, such as Daniel Webster, Henry Clay, and John C. Calhoun.

The 1840s saw the admission of Texas (1845) as a slave state,[52] and the acquisition of additional vast lands in the west as a result of the 1846–48 war with Mexico.[53] These actions reduced the size of Mexico by more than half and increased the size of the United States by a third.[54] This second great wave of expansion continued to change the nature of the country. Economically, the nation advanced strongly into the mid-century. Great railroads, steamboats, and canals all headed west.[55] This expansion also opened the question of slavery's expansion, which supposedly had been settled by the Missouri Compromise of 1820.

The population grew to the west too, but the North dominated the population growth in relation to the South, and this changed the balance of political power: in 1790, the House had 57 free state members and 49 slave state members; by 1850, there were 147 free state members and only 90 slave state members. However, the Senate, in the late 1840s, was split evenly, 15 slave states and 15 free states—thus ensuring that the Southerners in the Senate could block any legislation adopted by the House. It was this parity, and the issue of the admission of California, that produced the great Compromise of 1850,[56] fathered by Senator Henry Clay[57] and shepherded to passage by Senators Stephen Douglas and Daniel Webster. It was around this time, too, that congressional votes began to divide on geographic rather than party lines.

Clay's Compromise of 1850 was designed to achieve a political settlement by ensuring that the slave state/free state balance of interests was broadly maintained. The Compromise was in fact a series of five laws that balanced North and South interests: California was admitted as a free state; Texas was paid $10 million for relinquishing its claims to the territory of New Mexico; the New Mexico Territory was organized without any prohibition against slavery; the trade in slaves in the District of Columbia was abolished; and a very strict Fugitive Slave Act was adopted. Had the Compromise failed, and had war between the North and South ensued in 1850, it is likely that the South would have won its separation and that two, or perhaps three, independent nations would have been formed; there would have been no United States when World War I began less than two generations later.

The delicate political balance reflected in the Compromise of 1850 would not long endure. In the North, the abolitionists were attacking the slave South with increasing shrillness in sermons and pamphlets. The publication in 1852 of Harriet Beecher Stowe's *Uncle Tom's Cabin* electrified the general population against slavery.[58] In the South, the slaveholders were feeling more aggrieved, threatened, and defensive. By the mid-1850s, the nation was increasingly polarized politically and culturally in ways not imaginable by the Founders.

The Kansas–Nebraska Act of 1854 reflected an effort to refashion the issue of slavery in the vast new lands of the West. It in effect repealed the Missouri Compromise of 1820 as it applied to the territories west of the Mississippi. Thus, the 1820 ban on slavery no longer applied to the territories that make up present-day Kansas, Nebraska, and all or part of the Dakotas, Montana, Colorado, and Wyoming. These territories were now open to "popular sovereignty" over whether a territory should be slave or free. The Kansas-Nebraska Act led directly to the 1856 mini-civil war in Kansas, which became known as "Bleeding Kansas."

The paramount importance of national security—so central to the work of the Founders—was in sharp decline. The United States was no longer merely a small strip on the Atlantic coast threatened by potentially hostile powers; it was a continental country in no serious danger from outside its borders. The pressure to compromise on differences that had been provoked by the national security situation in 1787—and which continued for a couple of generations—was no longer present.

The basic assumptions of the Founders that forged and permitted the 1787 Constitution had fundamentally changed by the mid-1850s. The nation had changed dramatically, but the Constitution had remained unchanged since 1804.[59]

The World Changes and the Civil War Era Begins

The year 1857 witnessed the Indian rebellion against British rule, the first step toward Indian independence; the occupation of Canton by France and Britain; the beginning of the emancipation of the serfs in Russia by Czar Alexander II; Garibaldi's efforts to begin to unify Italy; and the inauguration of President James Buchanan. In early March of that year, the Supreme Court of the United States decided the case of *Dred Scott v. Sandford*. That decision may be said to mark the beginning of the Civil War period.

The Constitution of the Founding Fathers denied Negro citizenship—as would be decided by a 7–2 majority in the Supreme Court in *Dred Scott*—and protected slavery. At the end of the Civil War period, that political/legal compact was re-set with respect to those two issues, not by the courts, but by the process of amendment by vote of the legislatures of three-fourths of the states, reflected in the Thirteenth and Fourteenth Amendments of 1865 and 1868, respectively. The other fundamental legal issue—whether the Union was perpetual or whether there was a right of secession—was also not definitively resolved in a court. It was settled on the battlefield.

CHAPTER 2

The *Dred Scott* Case

The Facts

Dred Scott was born sometime in the late 1790s in Virginia. There is no record clearly providing a more exact place or time.[1] His owner was Peter Blow, a plantation owner. In about 1819, Blow moved his family to Alabama to start a new plantation; Scott and several other slaves accompanied the Blow family. Blow got tired of farming, and in 1830 moved to the booming frontier town of St. Louis, Missouri, and opened a hotel. Blow and his wife became ill, and both died by 1832. Dred Scott was sold by the Blow's estate in late 1833 to an army surgeon, Dr. John Emerson.

In 1834, Dr. Emerson moved due north up the Mississippi River from St. Louis, Missouri, to Fort Armstrong near Rock Island, Illinois (a free state), and he brought Scott with him. Emerson served as the post physician until May 1836. In April or May of 1836, Fort Armstrong was evacuated, and Dr. Emerson moved northward again, further up the Mississippi to Fort Snelling on the west bank of the Mississippi River in that part of the Wisconsin and Iowa territories[2] that would later become Minnesota. This area was north of the state of Missouri and therefore, under the provisions of the Missouri Compromise of 1820, Fort Snelling was located in "free" territory.

After he arrived at Fort Snelling with Dr. Emerson, Dred Scott met another slave, Harriet Robinson, who was owned by another army officer at the fort, Major Lawrence Taliaferro. In 1836, Major Taliaferro

DRED SCOTT.

sold (or gave) Harriet to Dr. Emerson. That same year, with the consent of Dr. Emerson, Dred and Harriet married.[3] In October 1837, Emerson was transferred to the Jefferson Barracks back in St. Louis, but he left the Scotts at Fort Snelling, hiring them out. One month later, Dr. Emerson was assigned to Fort Jessup in Louisiana. While at Fort Jessup, Dr. Emerson met Eliza Irene Sanford, of St. Louis, while she was visiting Louisiana. They married in February 1838, and the following month, the Scotts joined the Emersons in Louisiana, a slave state.

In October 1838, Dr. Emerson was transferred back to Fort Snelling. During the voyage back to Fort Snelling, Harriet Scott gave birth on the steamboat to her first child, whom she named Eliza after Mrs. Emerson. In 1840, during the Seminole War, Dr. Emerson was transferred to Florida, but Mrs. Emerson and the Scotts returned to St. Louis. Then, in August 1842, Dr. Emerson was discharged and returned to St. Louis. Later, Emerson moved to Iowa, but Mrs. Emerson and the three Scotts remained in St. Louis. Dr. Emerson died suddenly in December 1843, when he was only forty years old. He left his estate to his wife and appointed as executor his wife's brother, John F. A. Sanford, a wealthy merchant in New York. Mrs. Emerson "hired out" the Scotts and collected the wages.[4] During part of this time, Scott was rented to an army officer and taken to Texas. When Scott returned from Texas in early 1846, he tried to buy his freedom from the widow Emerson, but without success. In early 1846, Harriet had another daughter, Lizzie, born in St. Louis.[5]

The Missouri Cases

There was a provision in Missouri law by which a slave could petition a court to become free. The "freedom suit statute" was originally enacted in the Louisiana Territory in 1807 and, in 1824, became Missouri law. (Between 1812 and 1865, 300 slaves filed petitions in St. Louis courts, but less than half of them were successful in securing freedom.) In April 1846, attorney Francis Butler Murdock filed papers for the Scotts, under this freedom statute, in the Missouri Circuit Court for the City of St. Louis.[6] In June 1847, the case came to trial, and the jury found for Emerson/Sanford.[7] However, due to a technical error (the use of hearsay evidence), a new trial was ordered. Dred Scott received financial aid for his litigation from the Blow family, his original owners.

The second trial was held in January 1850; both parties had new lawyers, and John Sanford had completely taken over the widow Emerson's affairs. (At about this same time, Mrs. Emerson had married Dr. Calvin C. Chafee of Massachusetts and had moved to Springfield, Massachusetts, with him.) The judge instructed the jury that residence in a free state or territory would destroy the Scotts' slave status, and therefore, if the jury found that the Scotts had in fact resided in such a free area—such as Illinois or the Wisconsin/Iowa territory—they would be set free. The jury found that the Scotts should be set free.

The legal basis for the jury charge was based on Missouri law of many decades, which, in turn was based on a famous 1772 English case, *Somerset v. Stewart*. *Somerset* held that when a master took a slave into a jurisdiction that lacked positive laws establishing slavery (e.g., England), the slave reverted to his "natural" status as a free person. In other words, residence in a free state such as Illinois would have the effect of emancipating a slave like Dred Scott. The *Somerset* rule, however, was modified in 1827 by the English case of *The Slave Grace*, which held that residence in England only suspended the slave status. If a slave returned to a slave jurisdiction, the law of England would no longer be applicable, and the person's status would again be determined by the laws of the slave jurisdiction. Courts in the United States were slow to adopt the concept in *The Slave Grace*.

John Sanford, on behalf of Irene Emerson Chafee, appealed to the Missouri Supreme Court. The State Supreme Court, on March 22, 1852, reversed the decision of the Circuit Court, and held that Scott was still a slave.[8] The Supreme Court noted that Missouri was a slave state, and slavery was perfectly legal within its borders; Scott and his family were still slaves of the defendant. The decision was inconsistent with decades of Missouri law on the subject, which had been based on the 1772 *Somerset* case; however, the 1852 Missouri Supreme Court's decision was consistent with the concept articulated in the 1827 English *The Slave Grace* case.

The Political Angle

Apart from the strictly legal underpinnings, at least one scholar has argued that the Missouri Supreme Court's decision to overturn the Circuit Court was "frankly political," quoting Missouri Chief Justice William Scott:

> Times are not now [in 1852] as they were when the former [Missouri] decisions on this subject were made. Since then, not only individuals but States have been possessed with a dark and fell spirit in relation to slavery, whose gratification is sought in the pursuit of measures, whose inevitable consequence must be the overthrow and destruction of our Government. Under such circumstances, it does not behoove the State of Missouri to show the least countenance to any measure which might gratify this spirit.[9]

Chief Justice Scott's remarks reflect the rising tensions in the country over the slavery issue. This was underscored by the slave state of Missouri's geographic position: contiguous to the free state of Illinois and the free territory of Iowa, only a river separated those free areas from the slave state of Missouri.

The Missouri Supreme Court, in the years prior to its 1852 decision in *Scott v. Emerson*, repeatedly signaled that its approach to determining a slave's freedom was contingent on the acceptance in free states of slaveholders' rights to pass through free states when traveling from one slave state to another. This was based on the northern states' recognition of slavery's legitimate place in the Union.[10] During the 1840s, however, the position of courts in Ohio and Illinois became increasingly murky and ambiguous.[11] This quid pro quo context makes more understandable the rejection by the Missouri Supreme Court of years of precedent in the *Dred Scott* decision: indeed, the "times were not [in 1852] as they were" when those earlier decisions were made.

The Federal Case

The case was sent back to the lower court for the issuance of a final order—though the parties agreed that the case in the lower state court would be continued to await the possible judgment of the U.S. Supreme Court.[12] However, Justice William Scott crafted his opinion in a manner that would avoid review by the U.S. Supreme Court—he did not challenge the constitutionality of the Missouri Compromise, which would have permitted federal court review.[13] In the meantime, the Scotts remained in the technical custody of the Sheriff of St. Louis County, who had been renting Scott out and retaining the money in escrow until the case was finally settled.

The Scotts' new lawyer, Roswell M. Field, a leading member of the Missouri bar, then figured out a way to try to bring the issue to the federal court system. Now that the former Mrs. Emerson was living in Massachusetts with her new husband, and since her brother, Sanford, lived in New York, and since the Scotts lived in Missouri, it might be possible to introduce a case into federal court on the basis of "diversity jurisdiction." The Constitution[14] permits federal courts to exercise jurisdiction when a citizen of one state sues a citizen of another state. "Diversity" refers to the different state citizenship of the plaintiff and the defendant. Roswell Field filed a new case in November 1853, this time in a federal court. (Four years later, Chief Justice Taney expressed his worry that this new route to the U.S. Supreme Court would be, in effect, a way to maneuver around disagreeable state court rulings.[15]) The technical basis for the lawsuit was based on the legal argument that the Scotts (and their daughters) of Missouri were assaulted and falsely imprisoned by John Sanford of New York.[16]

This third lawsuit brought by the Scotts, the first in federal court, went to trial in May 1854. The case was heard in a rented room on North Maine Street in St. Louis, due to overcrowding at the federal court. Sanford's lawyers argued—in pleas in abatement, i.e., asking the court to stop (to abate) the case immediately—that while Scott was a resident of Missouri, he could not be a "citizen" of Missouri because he was a Negro of African descent.[17] Judge Wells rejected Sanford's plea, based on the notion that Scott or any free black was entitled to minimal rights, including the right to sue, and thus the idea of "citizen" for purposes of federal diversity jurisdiction meant a full-time resident of a state regardless of race. The case went to trial, and Judge Wells told the jury that Scott's status was to be determined by Missouri law and, since the Missouri Supreme Court had already decided that Scott was still a slave, the jury ruled in Sanford's favor. Thus, the Scott family remained slaves; Dred Scott at this time was working as a porter at the Barman Hotel in St. Louis.

Having exhausted their local remedies, the Scotts' lawyers filed an appeal to the U.S. Supreme Court in December 1854.

At the Supreme Court

Both sides sought and obtained top lawyers to assist in the argument before the U.S. Supreme Court. The Scotts' St. Louis lawyer persuaded Montgomery Blair to argue the case in Washington—without charging a fee. Blair was originally from Missouri, lived in "Blair House" in Washington (given to him by his father),[18] and was the son of the politically influential Democrat newspaperman, Francis Preston Blair, Sr., and the

MONTGOMERY P. BLAIR.

older brother of Francis Preston Blair, Jr., then of St. Louis and a member of the Missouri House of Representatives. Blair was a member of the "free-soil" wing of the Democratic Party, opposed to the spread of slavery, though not opposed to slavery itself. Joining Blair as co-counsel for the reargument in December 1856 was George T. Curtis, a famous lawyer and writer from Massachusetts, who happened to be the younger brother of Supreme Court Justice Benjamin R. Curtis.

On the other side, Sanford retained proslavery Senator Henry Geyer of Missouri, who happened to have originally practiced law in Frederick, Maryland—where Chief Justice Taney had also practiced. Geyer (a Whig) was a political enemy of Blair's.[19] His co-counsel was Reverdy Johnson of Maryland, a former U.S. Senator and U.S. Attorney General, and perhaps the most renowned constitutional lawyer in the United States; it was said that his mere presence in a case made opposing lawyers apprehensive.[20] Johnson also happened to be a Maryland friend of the Chief Justice.[21]

It is hard to imagine more skilled, or more powerfully connected, legal talent arrayed on both sides.

* * *

The *Scott* case was filed with the U.S. Supreme Court on December 30, 1854, too late for the Court's 1854 term, so the case was held over for the December 1855 term and set for oral argument on February 11, 1856. Arguments lasted four days. The briefs focused on whether Negroes could be citizens of the United States, whether Congress had the power to prohibit slavery in the territories, and whether the Missouri Compromise of 1820 was constitutional.[22]

The paramount national public issue in 1856 was the turmoil—the virtual civil war—in Kansas, and the presidential election among Republican John C. Fremont, Democrat James Buchanan, and Know-Nothing Millard Fillmore. It was in that context that the parties argued before the Court for four days: first Blair, then Geyer and Johnson, with Blair concluding.[23] The Court's chamber was located on the ground floor of the original north wing of the Capitol Building. Completed in 1819, the chamber was likened to an umbrella or a pumpkin; it was a dark, low subterranean apartment, where the lighting was never adequate and the room was dim, dingy, and gloomy.[24]

After several conferences in early 1856 and a month's recess, the Justices were still unsettled on some issues. The Chief Justice noted in his opinion that, since the "questions in controversy are of the highest importance," and since the Court was pressed by "ordinary business," "it was deemed advisable" to continue the case and direct a reargument of some points so that the Court might "have an opportunity of giving to the whole subject a more deliberate consideration."[25] It is also likely that the Justices were reluctant to render a controversial decision during such a contentious presidential campaign.[26] In support of this, Taney noted that Justice McLean at that time was a serious contender for the Republican nomination,[27] but McLean made no objection to a postponement, even though a strong defense of the Missouri Compromise might have enhanced his political chances. One scholar argues that it was more likely that the Court put off a ruling simply because the Justices had reached an impasse over the plea in abatement[28] and citizenship issues.[29] In the same vein, another scholar notes that the Justices were evenly divided on the citizenship question—whether the issue of the Scotts' citizenship was properly before the Court—and Justice Nelson was uncertain—and so the Justices agreed unanimously to have the case reargued.[30]

On May 12, 1856, the Court ordered that the case should be reargued and focused on whether the "pleas in abatement" were legitimately before the Court: whether a free Negro could be a citizen of a state or of the United States and, as such, bring a suit in diversity in a federal court.

The second round of arguments was held on December 15, 1856, after President Buchanan was elected.[31] Each of the nine Justices must have been aware that the Court was handling an explosive package. The Court's chamber was filled with many distinguished jurists and members of Congress. In 1849, the Court had changed its rules to limit oral advocacy to two hours unless the Court granted "special leave."[32] In this highly public case, the Court granted special leave, and so the proceeding took more than twelve hours over four days.[33] The performance of Johnson and of Curtis won most of the public acclaim. By year's end, Dred Scott's name was probably familiar to most Americans who followed national events. (The classic book on *Dred Scott* is Don E. Fehrenbacher's *The Dred Scott Case* from Oxford University Press.)

The Court held its first internal conference on the case on February 14, 1857. At that point, there was a majority of five Justices—Nelson, McLean, Catron, Grier, and Campbell—for a dismissal of the case. They argued that the sole question was whether slaves temporarily residing in a free territory possessed a valid claim to freedom after returning to a slaveholding jurisdiction, and that question was one of state law. In this case, the Missouri Supreme Court had already ruled on that matter. There was no need to rule on the constitutionality of the Missouri Compromise. At the majority's request, Justice Nelson, a Democrat from New York, was asked to prepare the opinion of the Court.[34]

Sometime in mid-February, the Nelson majority got derailed with Justice Wayne leading the rejection, and Chief Justice Taney was asked to write the opinion of Court that addressed the constitutional issues raised by restrictions on slavery in the lands acquired by the Louisiana Purchase.[35] One scholar has suggested that the most plausible explanation for Wayne's move is that he viewed a broad opinion as a step toward restoring sectional harmony: "a solution imposed by the Court as an institution . . . provided the best hope of finally resolving the issue, undermining the arguments of secessionists in the South . . . ."[36]

Nelson's draft opinion finally became his concurring opinion. It is not clear why this rejection of his very narrow approach—that it was purely a state matter—took place. Some suggest that it was because the very public reargument had created a public expectation that "all issues" would be dealt with.[37] This was consistent with views increasingly expressed by members of Congress that the Court ought to handle the seemingly intractable slavery question. Others suggest that the majority was stunned by the strong and broad positions taken by Justices McLean and Curtis in their proposed dissents, and that they now felt that it was incumbent upon the majority to address all those same issues.

On March 4, 1857, the Chief Justice administered the presidential oath of office to James Buchanan.[38] In his inaugural address, Buchanan noted that there was a public issue over whether the people of a territory should decide whether to be slave or free—the issue of "popular sovereignty." But he dismissed that as of "little practical importance" and stated that it was a judicial question "which legitimately belongs to the Supreme Court, before whom it is now pending . . . [and that he would] cheerfully submit" to the Court's ruling, no matter what it was.[39] (Though he obviously had in mind the *Dred Scott* case, the question of whether the people in a Territory should have the power to decide whether it should be free or slave was not exactly the question around which that case centered as it was presented to the Court.)

CHAPTER TWO

The Decision of the Supreme Court

Two days later, on March 6, the Chief Justice—just short of his eightieth birthday—began the reading of opinions in a crowded courtroom in the basement of the Capitol Building, the same low subterranean room where it all began. The Court was composed of nine Justices, all but two of whom (Curtis and Campbell) were born in the eighteenth century. Taney was the oldest, and Campbell was the youngest, at 46. The Court was balanced geographically: two Justices were from the Deep South (Wayne of Georgia and Campbell of Alabama), four were from the North or West (McLean of Ohio, Nelson of New York, Curtis of Massachusetts, and Grier of Pennsylvania), and three from the Upper South (Taney of Maryland, Catron of Tennessee, and Daniel of Virginia). However, the Court was well out of balance politically: there were seven Democrats, one Republican (McLean), and one independent/Whig (Curtis).[40] "Southern Democrats commanded the Court in 1857 because the Democratic Party, with its southern power base, had won five of the previous seven presidential elections."[41]

Though they were out of balance politically, the Taney Court can be said to have been remarkably centrist, dominated by Southern unionists and conservative Northerners.[42] The moderation reflected the judicial selection process, which then, as today, "favors persons with ambivalent, unknown, or centrist views of the hotly contested constitutional issues of the day."[43] As a result, persons with known militant views on slavery (or today, for example, on abortion) are screened out, unless their vote will not be decisive or their supporters have enormous political influence. In 1857, the Court was a bastion of moderation when compared to the Congress: one-third of the Congress would support militant proslavery positions, and another one-third were reliably antislavery voters. In contrast, on the Court there was only one Southern fire-eater, almost a fanatic on slavery (Daniel), and only one Justice (McLean) openly opposed to slavery.[44]

The Decision, as officially reported, is 240 pages long. The Chief Justice's opinion of the Court is 55 pages long; it took him two hours to read it in a low voice that became almost inaudible. Six other Justices wrote concurring opinions of varying lengths; Nelson and Catron read their relatively brief concurring opinions after Taney spoke. Justices McLean and Curtis wrote dissenting opinions, which took them five hours to read the following day. (The remaining four Justices filed their concurring opinions without reading them in Court.) The seven Democrats were on one side, and the Republican and the nonaffiliated Whig dissented.

The *Dred Scott* Case

The official publication of the decision was not until May—a squabble arose between Justices Taney and Curtis over the text of the opinion. Justice Curtis asserted that the Chief Justice held up the printing so that he could add text to his opinion in rebuttal to points that Curtis made in his dissent. Taney asserted that he had only made minor alterations in the nature of adding supporting authorities.[45]

The two dissenters, Curtis and McLean, had released the full texts of their opinions to the newspapers for prompt publication in March when the opinions were read to the public in the Court's chamber. Taney found this step by the dissenters—attacking in the press the opinion of the Court before the readers had had an opportunity to read the Court's opinion first—unprecedented and an undermining of the authority of the Court. This dispute with Taney was probably a factor in Curtis's resignation from the Court within months, although Curtis's stated explanation was that his salary was too little and the travel demands were too much.[46]

What did the Court decide? Taney's opinion concluded: "Upon the whole, therefore, it is the judgment of this court . . . that [Scott] is not a citizen of Missouri in the sense in which that word is used in the Constitution; and that the Circuit Court of the United States, for that reason, had no jurisdiction in the case . . . ." It is clear that seven of the nine Justices decided that Dred Scott was still a slave. Beyond that, it is not clear exactly what the Court held. The jurisdictional and purely legal issues were complex—whether he was a slave was a substantive legal issue, and whether the Court had jurisdiction to hear the case depended on whether he was a slave. The fact that there were nine separate opinions added to the lack of clarity.

The Taney Opinion

The Chief Justice framed the initial issue: "Can a Negro, whose ancestors were imported into this country, and sold as slaves . . . become entitled to all the rights, and privileges . . . guaranteed by [the Constitution] to the citizen . . . ?" He made it clear that the issue was not confined to current imported slaves, but extended to the descendants of such slaves "when they shall be emancipated, or who are born of parents who had become free before their birth." This, then, was the class of persons to which the opinion applied. This class did not include Negroes living in foreign countries who came to the United States and sought naturalization as citizens; Congress had the power to naturalize anyone of color.[47]

Taney was anticipating this question: What about the situation of the Indians?[48] Were they not in the same boat? It is true, Taney noted, that the Indians—like the Africans—formed no part of the colonial communities, and they were uncivilized. But, quite unlike the Africans, the Indians were "a free and independent people."[49] Many Indian tribes—including the Cherokees, Choctaws, Chickasaw, Creeks, and Seminoles—held African slaves.[50] (In 2007, the Cherokees voted overwhelmingly to revoke the tribal citizenship of thousands of descendants of people the Cherokees once held as slaves.[51]) The Indian governments were regarded and treated as foreign governments; they could, like other foreigners, be naturalized and become citizens of the United States.[52]

The ultimate question, Taney said, was whether the Constitution included the African race—apart from any Africans who voluntarily immigrated to the United States—within the notion of citizenship, or did it contemplate that any individual state could make an African a United States citizen, i.e., "introduce a new member into the political community created by the Constitution of the United States." Taney posited that this, as with all Constitutional questions, depended on the interpretation of the words as understood at the time they were formulated.

The Continuing Debate

This touches on the current controversy as to whether a Justice should confine herself or himself to the understanding of the Constitutional language at the time it was created, or whether a Justice may, or should, add to the original language contemporary factors and understanding.[53] The former view is called "original intent"; those who hold this view, "a small, though growing, minority in the legal academy,"[54] argue that it is the "obligation of the judges to keep the times in tune with the Constitution, not to keep the Constitution in tune with the times."[55] On the other hand, "Originalism" is often "dismissed as either hopelessly naïve or as cynical obfuscation."[56]

Taney clearly felt bound to search for the original intent of the Framers. He cleverly "supposed" that no one would want the Court to take into account the great change in public opinion with respect to Negroes—"this unfortunate race"—during the intervening seventy years, in order to "give the words of the Constitution a more liberal construction in their favor than they were intended to bear when [the Constitution] was framed and adopted." Thus, Taney acknowledged that he was fully aware that the political and social advance by freed blacks was significant.[57] But

The *Dred Scott* Case 27

then Taney added the fundamental point: "[I]f any of its provisions are deemed unjust, there is a mode prescribed in the instrument itself by which it may be amended; but while it remains unaltered, it must be construed now as it was understood at the time of its adoption."

In short, Taney's position was: Our conclusion may seem harsh with respect to the rights of the Negro as we may see him today, in contrast to the position three generations ago, but we have no alternative. The only alternative is in the hands of the political authorities, not in the hands of the judicial authorities.[58] If the Constitution needs to be updated to reflect current realities, it should be *amended* to that end,[59] not *interpreted* to that end. Any other rule of construction "would abrogate the judicial character of this court, and *make it the mere reflex of the popular opinion or passion of the day. This court was not created by the Constitution for such purposes.*"[60]

With that framework established, Taney reviewed the language of the founding documents of the nation—the Declaration of Independence, the Articles of Confederation, the Constitution itself, the legislation of the various states before, during and after the adoption of the Constitution, the legislation of the Congress from the time of its establishment, the uniform practice of the Executive departments—all of which, Taney found, led to the same result: citizenship was outside the reach of the Negro. "[T]he legislation and histories of the times . . . show that neither the class of persons who had been imported as slaves nor their descendants, whether they had become free or not, were acknowledged as a part of the people . . . ."[61]

Taney noted that it was "difficult at this day [1857] to realize the state of public opinion in relation to that unfortunate race which prevailed in the civilized and enlightened portions of the world at the time of the Declaration of Independence, and when the Constitution of the United States was framed and adopted." More than a century before the Constitution, Taney continued, Negroes were regarded as "beings of an inferior order, and altogether unfit to associate with the white race . . . ." Then Taney employed a memorable phrase that has been repeatedly taken out of context: for more than a century *before* the Constitution was written, Taney maintained, Negroes had "no rights which the white man was bound to respect . . . ."[62] That opinion was "at that time fixed and universal in the civilized portion of the white race . . . in morals as well as in politics . . . ."[63] As the leading scholar of this case has noted: "Taney was not, in this passage, making a ruling about Negro rights in 1857; he was not expressing his own personal view. Rather, he was talking about the racial attitudes of the founding fathers and their generation, which presumably no longer prevailed."[64]

At the time of the American Revolution, Taney noted, all thirteen colonies had English laws that show that "a perpetual and impassable barrier was intended to be erected between the white race and the one which they had reduced to slavery . . . . And no distinction . . . was made between the free negro or mulatto and the slave . . . ."[65] The Declaration of Independence used words—that all men are created equal—that "would seem to embrace the whole human family, and if they were used in a similar instrument at this day [1857] would be so understood."[66] But in 1776, those words clearly did not carry that meaning.[67] If they did, then "the conduct of the distinguished men who framed the Declaration of Independence would have been utterly and flagrantly inconsistent with the principles they asserted . . . ."[68]

Thus, at the time of the drafting of the Constitution, Negroes were "never thought of or spoken of except as property."[69] In the text of the Constitution, Taney wrote, there are two clauses that point directly to the Negro: in one, the states are given the right to import slaves at least until 1808, and in the other, the states pledge to each other "to maintain the right of property of the master, by delivering up to him any slave who may have escaped . . . ."[70] At the time of the Constitution, no Negro had migrated to the United States voluntarily; "all of them had been brought here as articles of merchandise."[71] Taney acknowledged that by the time the Constitution was adopted, many of the states in the North had moved toward gradual emancipation, but, he argued, this was not because of a change in opinion as to that race. His proof is that many of the same states were actively and profitably engaged in the African slave trade: it was "openly carried on, and fortunes accumulated by it, without reproach from the people of the States where they resided."[72] This was an oblique elbow to New Englanders who were largely against slavery, but who profited from the transportation of slaves.

Taney then reviewed the laws of several states, including all of New England, during the first generation after the Constitution was adopted. He concluded that "in no part of the country except Maine did the African race . . . participate equally with the whites in the exercise of civil and political rights."[73] Then, he noted that the large slaveholding states would never have accepted a Constitution if it had been understood as requiring them to receive Negroes as citizens from other states, since the South would have viewed that as endangering the peace and safety of the state.

Taney noted that Acts of Congress soon after the adoption of the Constitution also suggest that same notion of citizenship: that it only applied to whites. He reviewed several such laws.[74] The most relevant was the 1790 naturalization law, which confined the right of becoming citizens to "aliens being free white persons." He hastened to add that the Constitution does not limit the power of Congress to naturalizing only white persons, but it does show, he argued, that "citizenship" at that time was understood to be confined to the white race.

Finally, the actions of the Executive Branch were similar to those of the colonies, states, and Congress: in an Opinion in 1821, Attorney General William Wirt[75] decided that the term "citizens of the United States" was used in Acts of Congress in the same sense as in the Constitution, and that free persons of color were not citizens within the meaning of the Constitution and laws.[76] More recently, Taney noted, Attorney General Caleb Cushing[77] had confirmed the Wirt Opinion, and, as a result, the Secretary of State refused to grant passports to Negroes as citizens of the United States.

After reviewing all this history—the colonies, the language of the Declaration and the Constitution, the enactments of the States and of the Congress after the United States was formed, and the actions of the Executive Branch—Taney concluded: "the court is of the opinion, that . . . Dred Scott was not a citizen of Missouri within the meaning of the Constitution of the United States, and not entitled as such to sue in its courts . . . ." Consequently, the U.S. Circuit Court had no jurisdiction, and its judgment that Scott should be freed was erroneous.

The Taney Opinion Continues

One might have expected the Court's opinion to end right there, the place where Justice Nelson and the original majority of five for dismissal of the case would have stopped. Without jurisdiction, the Circuit Court case should clearly have been dismissed, and Scott would have remained a slave under the 1852 Missouri Supreme Court decision. Taney, however, went on.[78]

Anticipating that continuing on in his opinion would lead to the charge that anything else the Court might say would be mere irrelevant *dicta*, Taney forcefully rejected that potential objection here: "The correction of one error in the court below does not deprive the appellate court of the power of examining further into the record, and correcting any other material errors which may have been committed by the inferior court. . . . This is the constant and invariable practice of this court where it reverses a judgment for want of jurisdiction . . . ."[79] Taney was acknowledging that the rest of the opinion really made no difference to the parties either in a personal or a pecuniary way, but that this fact would not justify the Court in sanctioning an error.

Taney then reviewed the facts which Scott asserted gave him his freedom; first, that Scott once lived in a territory in which Congress, as part of the Missouri Compromise of 1820, had prohibited slavery. Taney did not take note of the fact that the Missouri Compromise of 1820 in effect was repealed by the Kansas-Nebraska Act of 1854, which created two new territories (Kansas and Nebraska) and provided that the question of slavery should be left to the decision of the settlers themselves—the so-called "popular sovereignty." Counsel for Scott, reported Taney, made much of the fact that the Constitution gives Congress the authority to "dispose of and make all needful rules and regulations respecting the territory or other property belonging to the United States . . . ."[80]

But, Taney argued, that Constitutional clause was irrelevant; it had no bearing on this case, because it was a power confined to territory that then (1787) belonged to the United States—which Missouri did not. That power was not intended to relate to a territory afterwards acquired from a foreign government, such as the Louisiana Territory purchased from France. Taney turned to the question of the powers of Congress to obtain new territory. This was clearly given in the power to admit new states. But the territory so acquired was "not to be held as a colony and governed by Congress with absolute authority." There are no express provisions in the Constitution defining the power of the Congress over the person or property of a citizen in such a territory, but clearly they cannot be "ruled as mere colonists." The Louisiana Territory was acquired by the federal government as trustee of the people of the United States, and it "must be held in that character for their common and equal benefit."

No one would argue, Taney claimed, that Congress could make a law in a territory regarding the establishment of religion or abridging free press. Similarly, one's right to property under the Fifth Amendment could not be abolished by Congress for the territory—e.g., when a citizen is deprived of his property "merely because he . . . brought his property into a particular territory . . . ." The right of property in a slave is

> distinctly and expressly affirmed in the Constitution. The right to traffic in it, like an ordinary article of merchandise and property, was guaranteed to the citizens . . . for twenty years. . . . [N]o word in the Constitution can be found which gives Congress a greater power over slave property or which entitles property of that kind to less protection than property of any other description.[81]

At this point, the Chief Justice noted that some argue that "the laws and usages of nations" reflect the view that there is a "difference between property in a slave and other property." Taney dismissed that idea as irrelevant: "no laws or usages of other nations, or reasoning of statesmen or jurists upon the relations of master and slave, can enlarge the powers of the Government or take from the citizens the right they have reserved. And if the Constitution . . . makes no distinction between [property in a slave and other kinds of property], no [U.S.] tribunal . . . has a right to draw such a distinction . . . ."[82] (Just a few years earlier, the United States had successfully negotiated compensation from Great Britain for having freed the Virginia slaves who had mutinied on the U.S. vessel the *Creole*—the U.S. "property"—from a British colony.[83])

The Continuing Debate

The question that Taney touched on—to what extent, if at all, is it relevant for a U.S. Justice to take into account the views of foreign law or foreign tribunals and jurists—is a hot topic today. The main opponent of the practice of taking into account foreign views is probably Justice Scalia (along with Justice Thomas and the late Chief Justice Rehnquist). Justice Scalia wrote that the Court "should cease putting forth foreigners' views as part of the reasoned basis of its decisions. To invoke alien law when it agrees with one's own thinking, and ignore it otherwise, is not reasoned decisionmaking, but sophistry."[84]

The other side of the current debate is usually taken by Justices Breyer and Ginsburg, and retired Justice Sandra Day O'Connor. Justice Ginsburg, for example, quoted from Chief Justice Taney's opinion in the *Dred Scott* case in a speech to the Constitutional Court of South Africa in February 2006.

Concluding his discussion of the position of Scott with respect to his stay in the territory, Taney said: "it is the opinion of the court that the act of Congress which prohibited a citizen from holding and owning property of this kind in the territory [the Missouri Compromise of 1820] is not warranted by the Constitution, and is therefore void . . . ." This was the first time in United States history when the Court invalidated a major piece of federal legislation—denying to Congress a power it had exercised for thirty-seven years. And so, for another reason, Scott was not made free by having been brought into the territory.

Concurring Opinions

While that was the opinion of the Court as written by its Chief Justice,[85] there were six concurring opinions, all by Democrats, and two dissenting opinions from the single Republican and former Whig.

The first concurring opinion was by Justice Wayne of Georgia. He thought the Chief Justice's opinion was exactly right and expressly concurred in all of it. He did comment on the question of the propriety of addressing whether the Missouri Compromise was constitutional: yes, of course it was proper to address this issue, and those who disagreed simply did not understand the plea system and the difference between an appeal from a state court and an appeal from a U.S. Circuit Court. In the former instance, the Court would be acting extrajudicially if it gave an opinion after it decided it had no jurisdiction. But, the *Scott* case was an appeal from a U.S. Circuit court, and so the Court may correct an error on the merits.

Justice Nelson of New York wrote a concurring opinion on a single point and expressed no opinion on whether the Missouri Compromise was constitutional. He did not focus on Scott's time in the territory, but solely on his time in Illinois. The fact that he was there temporarily and did not acquire domicile there (his domicile remained in Missouri) seemed important to Nelson, though he agreed with Taney's opinion on the basis that the courts of Missouri must control the decision as to the status of Scott. He noted that the question of whether the master has a right to travel with his slaves into or through a free state was not before the Court in this case. But Nelson must have been aware of the *Lemmon* case, which was on appeal from New York state courts, and which presented exactly that issue: a Virginian in transit through New York City with his slaves. (See a discussion of the *Lemmon* case later in this chapter, at pages 49–51.)

Justice Grier of Pennsylvania presented the briefest concurring opinion, agreeing with Nelson, but also going further by specifically endorsing Taney's view that the Missouri Compromise was unconstitutional.[86]

Next came the concurring opinion of Justice Daniel of Virginia.[87] Daniel correctly noted at the outset that there had never been more important questions submitted to the Court—never "a conjuncture of graver import." As a Virginian, perhaps Daniel had some special role in endorsing Taney's view of the Northwest Ordinance of 1787 and the language in the Constitution regarding the power of Congress over "the territory" and other property, because those Northwest lands had been ceded by the state of Virginia. Daniel quoted at length from another Virginian, James Madison, a father of the Constitution and one of the authors of *The Federalist Papers*. Madison wrote a letter in 1819 making it clear that no one at the time of the adoption of the Constitution thought it gave Congress expansive power over territories, and certainly everyone intended to protect the right to bring slaves into the territories.[88] In thirty-three pages, Daniel agreed with Taney's opinion in all respects.

JUSTICE JOHN A. CAMPBELL.

Justice Campbell of Alabama, the newest member of the Court (having joined in 1853), delivered a twenty-five-page concurring opinion.[89] Campbell's is an extraordinarily erudite discussion on all phases of the case,[90] especially with respect to the lack of authority of Congress to enact the Missouri Compromise. Campbell remarked the "disunion between Great Britain and her colonies originated in the antipathy of the latter to the 'rules and regulations' made by a remote power respecting their internal policy. In forming the Constitution, this fact was ever present in the minds of its authors."[91] He concluded: "the claim for Congress of supreme power in the Territories . . . is not supported by the historical evidence drawn from the Revolution, the Confederation, or the deliberations which preceded the ratification of the Federal Constitution." On the other hand, Campbell said, he could not say how much power might be exercised in a territory by Congress (as it was a political, not a judicial, issue), but certainly it did not include the status of persons.

The last concurring opinion was by Justice Catron of Tennessee. In a well-documented and well-reasoned opinion, Catron fully concurred with Taney's, and especially Nelson's, opinions. He focused forcefully on the Missouri Compromise in the context of the equality of the states and their citizens to move freely within the United States, implying that its application prohibits a slaveholder from entering the territory with his slaves, since he would lose his property there. Catron drew an analogy: "Congress [might] have said to those of the North, you shall not introduce into territory south of said line your cattle or horses, as the country is already overstocked, nor can you introduce your tools of trade, or machines, as the policy of Congress is to encourage the culture of sugar and cotton...."[92] Catron concluded that the Compromise of 1820 "violates the most leading feature of the Constitution—a feature on which the Union depends, and which secures to the respective States and their citizens an entire EQUALITY of rights, privileges, and immunities."[93] Catron thus found "the Compromise void, and Dred Scott can claim no benefit under it."[94]

Seven Justices—from the North (New York and Pennsylvania), the South (Georgia, Virginia, Alabama), and the Middle (Tennessee and Maryland)—agreed that Dred Scott remained a slave. Most also agreed that the Missouri Compromise of 1820 was unconstitutional. There were two dissents: McLean and Curtis.

The Dissents

Justice McLean of Ohio had served on the Court longer than any other Justice, having been appointed by Jackson in 1829,[95] seven years before Taney. He was passionately interested in becoming president (his detractors saw only "Machiavellian adroitness"[96]). McLean argued that the Supreme Court was not bound to follow the Missouri Supreme Court's decision in the *Scott v. Emerson* case, because it was inconsistent with earlier Missouri cases[97]—in effect, he decided that despite what a majority of the State Supreme Court said, the U.S. Supreme Court should ignore that and follow earlier decisions of the state. On the larger questions concerning the equal rights of the states—for example, as set out in Justice Catron's opinion—McLean suggested that the state of Illinois also had rights that must be respected: "I can perceive no reason why the institutions of Illinois should not receive the same consideration as those of Missouri." He believed that requiring a slave brought into Illinois to remain a slave there "defies the sovereignty of the free State."

As to the inherent status of a Negro, McLean was clear: "Being born under our Constitution and laws, no naturalization is required, as one of foreign birth, to make him a citizen."[98] Many of the "colored race" were citizens of the New England states and exercised the rights of suffrage when the Constitution was adopted, McLean explained. Then he expanded: "A slave is not a mere chattel. He bears the impress of his Maker, and is amenable to the laws of God and man, and he is destined to an endless existence."[99]

As to the power of Congress to legislate broadly for the territories, McLean said that if Congress should decide that slaves or free colored persons were injurious to the population of a territory—perhaps because their presence would lessen the value of the territory—Congress had the power to prohibit them from becoming settlers on it. McLean concluded that the jurisdiction issue, and only that issue, "was decided by [the majority] authoritatively, but nothing beyond that question." In short, McLean claimed that the constitutionality of the Missouri Compromise was not decided by the Supreme Court.

Finally, there is the main, sixty-nine-page dissent of Justice Curtis of Massachusetts. As with the opinions of most of the other Justices, Curtis spent some time on the technical pleadings, but then he slightly reframed the jurisdictional question: whether any person of African descent, whose ancestors were sold as slaves in the United States, can be a citizen of the United States.

The first step in the process, according to Curtis, was to see whether such persons were citizens of the United States at the time of the adoption of the Constitution. His answer: at the time of the ratification of the Articles of Confederation in 1781, all free native-born inhabitants of New Hampshire, Massachusetts, New York, New Jersey, and North Carolina, though descended from African slaves, were not only citizens of those states, but some could vote. Thus, Curtis concluded that every free person born on the soil of a state, who was a citizen of that state, was also a citizen of the United States: "as free colored persons were [at the time of the Constitution] citizens of at least five States, ... they were among those for whom ... the Constitution was ordained ...." This was in direct conflict with the portion of Taney's opinion that said that a state action making a Negro a citizen of that state does not at the same time create U.S. citizenship. Curtis noted that the right to vote and citizenship were not the same, that many citizens have voting restrictions, e.g., age, sex, etc. (Taney had noted that some states granted voting rights to people who were not citizens.[100])

Having disposed of the question of whether persons of African descent can ever be U.S. citizens, Curtis then dissented from the "assumption of the authority to examine the constitutionality of the ... Missouri Compromise .... [S]uch an exertion of judicial power transcends the limits of the authority of the court ...." Assuming it was constitutionally enacted, the Missouri Compromise "changed the status of a slave coming into the Territory . . . [and] this change of status should be recognized everywhere."[101] (Curtis acknowledged that he might not have so concluded if the Missouri Supreme Court had based its decision on the judgment that Dr. Emerson had never been domiciled in the Territory.)

Curtis rejected the majority position that the broad authority given to Congress was intended only to relate to the territory of the United States in 1787, and that only limited power was given for the governance of territory later acquired. The adoption of the Northwest Ordinance—though adopted by the old Congress under the Articles of Confederation—was proof for Curtis that the framers believed they had broad power, including the authority to prohibit slavery. Curtis concluded that the framers of the Constitution understood that persons who are slaves in a state gain their freedom "when their owners voluntarily place them permanently within another jurisdiction, where no municipal laws on the subject of slavery exist."[102]

For all these reasons, Curtis concluded that the Missouri Compromise was constitutional and valid, and that the judgment of the U.S. Circuit Court should have been reversed and the case remanded for a new trial. One highly regarded scholar, however, found that in "purely legal terms, Curtis's characterization of the status of the discussion of the Missouri Compromise was simply wrong."[103]

After the *Dred Scott* Case

In March 1857, with the press reports of the decision and the publication of the two dissents, the Northern press launched a fierce attack on the decision, although there was some support for it in the North—based on partisan politics, business interests, or racism. In the South, the press was, unsurprisingly, pleased and crowed about the sanctity of the judicial system. The most radical paper, the Charleston *Mercury*, expressed exaggerated surprise, noting that "everyone in the South is disposed to unite in the chorus of congratulations."[104]

Politically, the Northern Democrats gained by the decision, because it was understood as relaxing the controversy over slavery in the territories—perhaps as a final settlement of a tough issue. Northern business interests (as reflected in the New York *Journal of Commerce*) saw the slavery debate as a threat to commerce and hoped the decision would minimize the divisiveness of the issue and let them get on with western settlements.[105]

For the new Republican Party, the decision was a serious threat—it undercut its platform calling for a ban on slavery in the territories.[106] Republicans made clear that their goal was to overturn the case via the presidential appointment powers—and to elect a Republican as the next president in 1860. That approach, of course, aggravated the South's increasing fear of a Republican president.

The excessiveness of the Republican reaction pushed the party closer in the public's mind to the radical abolitionists. The unofficial voice of the Buchanan administration and the mainstream Democratic Party was the Washington *Union*, which noted on March 12, 1857: "Never before . . . has there existed so much bitterness between the North and the South as within the past year. . . . [T]he chief cause of alienation was the unbridled license of a portion of the press . . . . It has been common for some of the ablest journals of the North to misrepresent and vilify the institutions and people of the South."[107] Further driving a wedge between Republicans and Democrats, North and South, were the many Northern clergy who denounced slavery and the Supreme Court, producing conservative protest against the mixing of clergy in politics.

In May and June 1857, the opinions of the lawyers and scholars began to circulate, as the official report of the decision was published. The critiques of the legal community were as divided as the press and political communities. Lincoln and Douglas, in their contest for the Illinois Senate seat, focused on the decision—with opposing perspectives. Lincoln, in his Springfield address of June 26, 1857, noted that he "could no more improve on McLean and Curtis, than [Douglas] could on Taney." Not only did Lincoln think the decision was "erroneous," but he asserted that "we shall do what we can to have it to overrule this." Lincoln focused on Douglas's support of the *Dred Scott* decision in part to paint Douglas as fervently pro-slave. Attacking the decision also positioned Lincoln as the moderate anti-slave candidate—and that was important later in the contest for the Republican presidential nomination, since his opponents, Salmon Chase and William Seward, were considered radicals.

Much of the political attack was against Chief Justice Taney personally; the fact that he was old and feeble and looked like a sour prude, and also the fact that he was a Catholic at a time of strong anti-Catholic feeling, made him an easy target.[108] He was not rehabilitated until the

THE POLITICAL QUADRILLE. MUSIC BY DRED SCOTT. A parody on the 1860 presidential contest highlighting the impact of the *Dred Scott* decision on the race. The four candidates dance with members of their "constituencies" to music played by Scott: Breckinridge dances with Buchanan (depicted as a goat), Lincoln dances with a black woman, Bell dances with an American Indian, and Douglas dances with a ragged Irishman.

1930s: Chief Justice Hughes, in an address in Frederick, Maryland, in 1931 portrayed Taney as "a dignified leader in an age of partisan strife as well as a fitting successor to the great Chief Justice Marshall."[109] In 1937, Felix Frankfurter, then a Harvard law professor, published a book which concluded that Taney "stood second in American constitutional history only to the great Marshall." In 1954, Chief Justice Earl Warren echoed those accolades; Warren defended Taney and hoped to "erase the calumny which Taney's enemies had hurled at him during his lifetime."[110] Taney's portrait hangs in the East Conference Room on the fifth floor of the Supreme Court's building.

What is the bottom line? Since Professor Fehrenbacher's book in 1978, no scholar had attempted a comprehensive examination of the *Dred Scott* case—until 2006 with Professor Mark Graber's illuminating and provocative book, *Dred Scott and the Problem of Constitutional Evil*.[111] The theme essentially is that sometimes, to achieve a greater good, evil (slavery) has to be lived with constitutionally; peace trumps justice, and constitutions are often compromises with the devil. Graber proposes that the Court's conclusion in *Dred Scott* "that slavery could not be banned in the territories and that former slaves could not be American citizens was as plausible as the contrary views detailed in the dissents."[112]

As Graber notes, Taney's constitutional claims were

> well within the mainstream of antebellum constitutional thought. The judicial denial of black citizenship reflected beliefs held by the overwhelming majority of antebellum jurists in both the North and the South. Virtually every state court that ruled on black citizenship before 1857 concluded that free persons of color were neither state nor American citizens.[113]

Graber reports that the "claim that slaves and their descendants did not enjoy distinctive citizenship rights in 1787 and immediately afterward rests on strong historical foundations."[114] With respect to the issue of whether the Constitution protected slaveholders going into the territories, Graber concludes that "mainstream thinkers in both the free and slave states [in 1857] concluded that persons had a constitutional right not to be divested of property rights . . . ."[115] when they moved with their slaves into the territories.

Finally, as to the Missouri Compromise issue, Graber notes that if the framers intended Congress to have the power to ban slavery in every territory, this was "the best kept secret in American politics" at the time: Northerners who pointed to the prospective Congressional ban on the slave trade in 1808 never mentioned legislative power to ban slavery in the territories; Southern opponents of ratification failed to include the power to ban slavery in the territories in the list of the ills of the constitution.[116] The grounding political alliance during the first thirty years after ratification was that moderates in both the North and the South agreed to share the territories. In a political sense, the Congress could constitutionally ban slavery in the territories, but only by a process that secured consent from both sections. "The Taney Court decision came closer than the dissents to the original understanding that national slavery policy [could only] be made in ways that accommodated crucial elites in both North and South."[117]

A superb scholar of the period leading to the Civil War, William W. Freehling, destroys the conventional myth that the seven Justices in the *Dred Scott* majority were Southern diehards, determined to save slavery at whatever cost to the Union. "[I]n reality, these [seven] judges sought to save the Union from sectional storms, partly in hopes that pacified slaveholders might incrementally reform and perhaps end absolute power."[118]

One can easily agree with Professor Graber's analysis and conclusion that the opinion of the Court—the Chief Justice's opinion—was well grounded in the law of the day, and so probably a correct decision, while at the same time not a *wise* decision. It is a good principle for the Court to decide any question on the narrowest possible basis, unless it is clear that the Court is unanimous (or at least not split on a partisan basis). Therefore, it might have been wiser for the Court to have returned the case to the U.S. Circuit Court to deal with factual issues that were unclear at the Supreme Court, such as whether Dr. Emerson and/or Dred Scott were in fact *temporary sojourners* in Illinois and in the Territory or if they were *domiciled* there.[119] Yes, this would have prolonged the matter, but the final decision on the matter would have been clearer and might have been different.[120]

As to the decision to declare the Compromise of 1820 unconstitutional, this is a good example of a correct but unwise action. That Act, in effect, had been repealed by the Kansas-Nebraska Act less than three years earlier. Thus, it was not necessary to challenge a law that was already overthrown. If there could have been a unanimous decision or at least a decision where there were not seven Democrats on one side and two Republicans/Whigs on the other, it might have been useful to declare the Act unconstitutional so that lower court errors were not left standing. The *Dred Scott* decision probably kept the South from seceding earlier, by giving its "domestic institution" renewed legal protection in the territories. But given the partisan split in the charged atmosphere of the time, attacking the Missouri Compromise was a step too far.

One impact of the Court's decision may have been on the economy, and some scholars argue that the decision brought on the Panic of 1857, the first global crisis of modern capitalism. The argument, in essence is this: (a) the decision put the brakes on westward migration as free-soilers feared the spread of slavery in the territories, which (b) reduced land values, which (c) reduced the value of railroad stock, which was keyed to land values and population movements, which in turn (d) led to heightened risk in capital markets and ultimately the financial panic.[121] Of course, it is virtually impossible to prove convincingly that the *Dred Scott* decision was *the* cause of these events; it is difficult to assign appropriate weight to the turmoil in Kansas, the gradual impact of the Kansas-Nebraska Act, or even the ending of the Crimean War, which perhaps produced fewer Europeans interested in immigrating to the United States. Whatever provoked the Panic of 1857, the fact that its impact in the North was far greater than in the South may well have emboldened Southern separatists into believing that an independent South would be better off.

Ableman v. Booth

Exactly two years after the *Dred Scott* decision, on March 7, 1859, the Court rendered a unanimous 9–0 decision in another case relating to slavery, *Ableman v. Booth*,[122] where the opinion of the Court was also written by Chief Justice Taney.[123] The fact that Taney was able to rally all the Justices behind him was in great contrast to the *Dred Scott* case. (Ironically, the case had been docketed in March 1857, exactly when the *Dred Scott* decision was announced.) The case was comprised of emotionally charged facts. And the facts were quite complicated.

In 1852, a slave, Joshua Glover, escaped from Missouri and found work in Wisconsin. In 1854, the slave's "owner" found the slave and obtained a warrant from the Federal Commissioner in Wisconsin for the slave's arrest under the Fugitive Slave Act of 1850. The slave was arrested. On March 11, 1854, a crowd led by abolitionist newspaper editor Sherman M. Booth broke into the Milwaukee jail and released Glover. Booth was charged by a Federal Commissioner with aiding and abetting the escape of the fugitive slave. Booth then applied for a writ of habeas corpus to one of the Justices of the Wisconsin State Supreme Court (A.D. Smith), arguing that his imprisonment was illegal because the 1850 Fugitive Slave Act was unconstitutional. Justice Smith agreed and ordered the federal marshal, Stephen V. R. Ableman, to release Booth. The marshal then went before the Wisconsin Supreme Court charging that the order to release Booth was unlawful. Ableman lost the appeal.

A federal grand jury then indicted Booth on the original charges, and he was convicted and sentenced to one-month imprisonment and a fine. Once again, Booth petitioned the Wisconsin State Supreme Court for release, arguing that the Fugitive Slave Act was unconstitutional.

And once again, the state court found Booth's imprisonment illegal and ordered his discharge. Within two months, the U.S. Attorney General filed a petition with Chief Justice Taney, arguing that the state court had no jurisdiction in this matter.

This repeated defiance of federal authority by the Wisconsin judiciary was not unlike the nullification propositions of Calhoun that President Jackson had confronted twenty years earlier.

At the Supreme Court argument, the United States was represented by Jeremiah S. Black, Buchanan's Attorney General; neither Booth nor the State of Wisconsin was represented by counsel. On March 7, 1859, the Supreme Court overturned the actions of the Wisconsin authorities on the theory of concurrent sovereignty. The Court flatly stated that the Constitution provided for the uniformity of judicial precedent which would be ruined if the states claimed primacy over federal courts.[124] Taney explained that the powers of the federal and state governments reflect "separate and distinct sovereignties, acting separately and independently of each other, within their respective spheres. . . . And the State of Wisconsin had no more power to [act in this matter] than it would have had if the prisoner had been confined in Michigan . . . ."[125] Thus, the Wisconsin *state* court lacked the authority to issue a writ of habeas corpus to remove Booth from *federal* custody.

Analogous to the question of whether the Court should have addressed the constitutionality of the Compromise of 1820 in the *Dred Scott* opinion, the Court explained that since the Wisconsin court addressed the issue,[126] and since the Justices of the U.S. Supreme Court "are not willing to be misunderstood,"[127] it would opine on the constitutionality of the Fugitive Slave Act of 1850—even though it expressly noted that it was unnecessary to do so—and found it was indeed constitutional. Thus, barely two years after *Dred Scot*, the Court spoke on a slavery issue and the constitutionality of a slavery law in a unanimous[128] voice.

Perhaps more importantly, and certainly ironically, it was Jackson in the 1832 crisis with South Carolina who successfully insisted on federal supremacy, and, in the *Ableman* decision, it was Taney—who was Jackson's Attorney General and who was put on the Court by Jackson—who successfully asserted federal judicial supremacy over the states.

Northern Democrats and Southerners supported the decision, while Republicans were split. The Wisconsin legislature, on March 19, 1859, condemned this unanimous decision as "despotism" and called for "positive defiance" by the states.[129] Booth's personal saga was complicated: On March 1 he was rearrested by federal authorities and placed in the Federal Customs House in Milwaukee; on March 23 he had served the term of his sentence, but he remained confined, since he refused on principle to pay the fine that had been imposed; on August 1 armed men stormed the Customs House and removed Booth; and on October 8, 1959, Booth was taken back into custody.

President Buchanan referred to the *Ableman* case in his fourth State of the Union address on December 3, 1860. He said that the "most palpable violations" of the constitutional duty to return fugitive slaves had come from state legislatures trying to defeat the execution of the Fugitive Slave law. Fortunately, Buchanan pointed out, all the courts—state and federal—had declared the Fugitive Slave Act to be constitutional, but for "the single exception" of a state court in Wisconsin. Nevertheless, that was reversed, and the Wisconsin action has been "met with such universal reprobation that there can be no danger from it as a precedent." President Buchanan pardoned Booth exactly three months later, on March 3, 1861, hours before Lincoln was inaugurated.[130]

The case that would have completed the legal stepping stone trail of *Dred Scott* and *Ableman*, *if* it had gotten to the Supreme Court in time, was the New York case of *Lemmon v. The People*.[131]

Lemmon v. People

On November 5, 1852,[132] a steamship arrived in New York from Norfolk, Virginia, and Jonathan and Juliet Lemmon disembarked, along with their eight slaves, all between the ages of 2 and 23. The Lemmons were on a voyage from Virginia to New Orleans, and then on to Texas. Since there were no steamships that ran directly from Virginia to New Orleans, they had to travel first to New York where, after a few days' layover, they would board a ship bound directly for New Orleans. For the layover, they lodged in a boarding house. The next day, an application for a writ of habeas corpus was filed by Louis Napoleon, a free Negro who was an officer of the Anti-Slavery Society.

The judge in the Superior Court of the City of New York was Elijah Paine; he granted the writ, and the slaves were remanded to police custody. Lemmon argued that his wife had inherited the slaves, that they were perfectly legal in his home state of Virginia, and that they were en route to another slave state, Texas. On November 13, Judge Paine found for the slaves and discharged them from custody based on a New York statute adopted in 1841 that freed all slaves in the territorial limits except fugitives.[133]

This provoked a political donnybrook. The governors of Georgia and Virginia denounced Judge Paine's decision, and the Virginia General Assembly appropriated funds to retain appellate counsel to reverse the ruling. In 1855, the New York state legislature appropriated funds for the defense of the ruling. The *Lemmon* case had been moving through the layers of appellate review in New York when the decision in the *Dred Scott* case was announced on March 6, 1857. An Albany newspaper predicted that if and when the *Lemmon* case finally got to the U.S. Supreme Court, the Taney Court would decide for the Virginia Lemmons, and that slavery would be maintained in New York. The lawyers in the case, William Maxwell Evarts for the slaves and Charles O'Conor for the Lemmons, asked the New York Supreme Court—which is not the highest court in New York—for an adjournment so that they could obtain and study the report of the *Dred Scott* case. At the end of 1857, the five judges of that court decided that the slaves were free and that the state intended to exclude slavery completely from New York.[134] O'Conor appealed on January 4, 1858, to the highest state court, the eight-judge Court of Appeals.

Evarts and O'Conor argued the case before the Court of Appeals on January 24, 1860. Assisting Evarts was a young abolitionist lawyer, Chester A. Arthur—later the twenty-first president. The 1772 English case of *Somerset v. Stewart*,[135] which held that slavery was unlawful in England and which was written by the great Lord Mansfield, figured prominently in the argument. O'Conor, whose father had fled Ireland after the 1798 uprising of the Irish against the British, sneered at Lord Mansfield's opinion and taunted the abolitionist North for hypocrisy. Lincoln referenced O'Conor's argument in his famous Cooper Union speech in late February 1860.[136] Evarts argued that the *Dred Scott* case determined that the existence of slavery was a matter for the law of each state.

The New York Court of Appeals announced its decision in March 1860. The court split 5–3 and affirmed the decision of the lower courts: the slaves were free. The dissenting opinion asserted that under Taney's opinion in *Dred Scott*, slaves were property, and their owners had a right to pass through New York with their property.

John Lemmon appealed the decision to the U.S. Supreme Court, but the advent of the War aborted further action. Had the Taney Court had the opportunity to deal with *Lemmon*, it would have been more than interesting—but that dog did not bark, as Sherlock Holmes would say.

Dred and His Owners

What happened to poor Dred Scott and the others personally involved in this case?

In mid-March 1857, the public learned that the real owner of Dred Scott was probably not John Sanford, but rather his sister Irene, who was now the wife of a prominent Republican abolitionist from Massachusetts, Congressman Calvin C. Chafee. The widow of Dr. Emerson, now Mrs. Chafee, lived with her husband in Springfield, Massachusetts. Under attack from the Democrats for hypocrisy—profiting from the Scotts' slave status while simultaneously professing love for the Negro—Chafee denied that he had any control over the case. Not surprisingly, Democrats and others suggested that the entire case of Dred Scott had been contrived—cooked up by the Republicans for political purposes. Chaffee chose not to run for reelection in 1858 and, after serving as librarian of the House for two years, practiced medicine. Mrs. Chafee, formerly Irene Sanford Emerson, lived until 1903.

John Sanford was confined to an insane asylum where he died in May 1857. Three weeks later, on May 26, 1857, Irene Emerson Chafee transferred ownership of the Scotts by quitclaim to Taylor Blow, one of the sons of Scott's original owner. Taylor Blow manumitted Dred Scott and his family the same day. The Scotts remained in St. Louis, where Dred continued to work as a hotel porter, and Harriet worked as a laundress.[137] In accordance with Missouri law, they posted a bond the following year in order to continue to live in the state. Taylor Blow acted as security. Dred Scott was stricken with consumption and died on September 17, 1858; he lived as a free man for less than eighteen months.

* * *

As a practical matter, the *Dred Scott* case died in 1862, when Congress prohibited slavery in the territories,[138] and when Attorney General Bates opined that free blacks should be treated as citizens. As a legal matter, *Dred Scott* became irrelevant with the adoption in December 1865 of the Thirteenth Amendment, which abolished slavery, and the adoption in July 1868 of the Fourteenth Amendment, which declared all persons born in the United States to be citizens of the United States.

The Continuing Debate

On November 29, 1862, Attorney General Edward Bates rendered an Opinion on the question of whether a man is "legally incapacitated to be a citizen of the United States by the sole fact that he is a *colored*, and not a white man?"[139] In this brilliant twenty-seven-page Opinion, Bates provided a discourse on "citizenship," exploring ancient Greece and Rome—including St. Paul's claim of Roman citizenship. As to the *Dred Scott* case, Bates made clear that he was not opining on the rights of slaves, and sharply limited the holding of the case by explaining that it was limited to the plea in abatement, and that whatever the Court said after that point was "of no authority as a judicial decision."[140]

Presciently, Bates noted the objection "not in law, but sentiment only" that "if a negro can be a citizen of the United States he might, possibly, become President."[141] It was almost exactly 146 years later that Barack Obama was elected president.

Attorney General Edward Bates.

CHAPTER 3

Virginia v. John Brown

John Brown Before Harpers Ferry

Born on May 9, 1800, in Connecticut, John Brown moved with his family to Ohio when he was five; his mother died when he was eight. He was brought up by his father as a strict Calvinist with a rigorous sense of right and wrong. Brown's childhood was "as colorful as a Puritan church."[1] Brown worked in his father's tannery, and when he was twenty years old, he married his first wife, Dianthe Lusk, with whom he fathered seven children, five of whom survived to adulthood. The Brown family moved in 1826 to Pennsylvania, where Brown built a tannery. Six years later, Dianthe died in childbirth, and a year later Brown married sixteen-year-old Mary Anne Day, with whom he fathered thirteen children, only six of whom reached adulthood. In a sense, he was an Old Testament patriarch.

During a visit to Boston in 1831, Brown met William Lloyd Garrison, the prominent abolitionist, journalist, and social reformer, and became intensely interested in the antislavery movement. He began to help runaway slaves on the Underground Railroad. In 1835, he moved his family back to Ohio and settled them on a farm. At an abolitionists' meeting in 1837, Brown publicly swore to God that he would devote his life to the destruction of slavery.

Money plagued Brown throughout his life. He borrowed heavily, and, as many others did, Brown speculated in land. The Panic of 1837,[2] which produced a severe financial crisis and high unemployment that lasted for five years, caught Brown with his wallet empty. He was sued in

JOHN BROWN.

four states for his outstanding debts, humiliated, and bankrupt, but he did learn a great deal about courts and the judicial process—knowledge that would serve him well in Virginia years later. In June 1844, the Browns' furniture, farm implements, and livestock were sold at auction. They were evicted from their farm, and Brown was briefly jailed for resisting the eviction.[3] In September 1843, dysentery ravaged his family, and four of his children died. At about that time, Brown claimed to have had a dream: that he was the Messenger of God, predestined to free the slaves.

Brown met a rich merchant, and they decided to go into the wool business together. In 1846, Brown moved to Springfield, Massachusetts, to conduct the business. There, inspired by his dream that he was the

Messenger of God, Brown sought out Frederick Douglass. In February 1848,[4] he told Douglass that slaveholders had forfeited their right to live. In April 1848, Brown presented himself at the home of Gerrit Smith, a New York philanthropist. Two years earlier, Smith had devised a plan to provide 3,000 black men with an independent livelihood and possibly the means to satisfy the $250 property requirement for voting in New York. To each approved applicant, Smith would sign over 40 acres of a huge tract of land at North Elba in the Adirondacks, known later by its residents as "Timbuktu." Brown proposed to Smith that he (Brown) serve as a sort of overseer of the colony, if he could have some land at a fair price. Smith was impressed and agreed to sell him a 244-acre tract, payable over time.[5] Brown then moved his family to North Elba.

Later in 1849, the wool business collapsed; Brown even went to England to generate business but, once again, failed and went deep into debt. In March 1851, he moved his family back to Ohio, with a promise that once the debts were cleared, they would return to North Elba.

The 1854 Kansas-Nebraska Act resulted in great tension in the Kansas Territory. Five of Brown's sons moved to Kansas to homestead and vote against slavery. In March 1855, proslavery forces invaded and voted in their own legislature; the abolitionists were, literally, outgunned. John Brown Jr. wrote to his father in May 1855: persuade Gerrit Smith or another wealthy friend to give them the money to buy high-quality weapons, such as Sharp rifles. In late June, Brown traveled to Syracuse, New York, to visit the convention of an interracial political party, the Radical Abolitionists—with Gerrit Smith presiding. Shortly thereafter, Brown left North Elba for Kansas with a wagonload of guns and knives. Money and guns poured into Kansas from all directions.

The town of Lawrence, Kansas, a center of Free-Soil (antislavery) activism, was sacked by proslavery forces. The news of the caning on the Senate floor of Massachusetts Senator Charles Sumner[6] by Congressman Preston Brooks of South Carolina[7] in May 1856 was deeply upsetting to Brown—"Something is to be done now," he is reported to have said. On the night of May 24th, Brown and his sons dragged five men—proslavery men—from their homes in the area of Pottawatomie Creek and brutally butchered them.[8]

The hunt was on to find the Brown men; Governor Shannon reported to President Pierce of the "excitement" in that portion of the Territory, and he posted a $3,000 reward for Brown, dead or alive. Brown and his band joined other antislavery fighters in Kansas; at the same time, Brown was also careful to enlist the support of willing anti-slave journalists—such as the young Scot, James Redpath,[9] on May 30th and William Phillips from the *New York Herald* in late June.[10] These interviews made the national press, and they made John Brown a hero in the eyes of all antislavery partisans. Violence eased in Kansas, and in October 1856, Brown left Kansas and headed east. His focus was to gather money, men, and guns and take the battle to the heart of the South.

In early January 1857, Brown presented himself at the Boston office of the Massachusetts Kansas Committee, the chairman of which was George Luther Sterns, a wealthy scion of one of the state's first families. In 1854, the National Kansas Committee was formed, mostly to raise funds for the supporters of Kansas as a Free state. State chapters were set up under that umbrella organization, mostly in the northeast. One of those chapters was the Massachusetts [State] Kansas [Aid] Committee. Frank Sanborn was the secretary of the Massachusetts Kansas Committee. In the preceding six months, the Committee had collected $48,000[11] for 200 Sharp rifles and other weapons and supplies for the Free State cause. Brown met at the home of Theodore Parker with other wealthy Committee members. The Committee entrusted the 200 Sharp rifles to Brown. Before the month's end, Brown was at Astor House in New York meeting with the National Kansas Committee. "Yankee intellectuals succumbed to Brown's animalistic force,"[12] noted one scholar. For the next several months, Brown traveled across Massachusetts, Connecticut, New York, and Pennsylvania, asking for funds. Some of the funds he obtained from Smith, Stearns, Samuel Gridley Howe (a prominent Boston physician and abolitionist), and others, however, were designated for the support of his wife and children in North Elba.

HARPERS FERRY. STEREOGRAPH SHOWS VIEW OF TOWN, RAILROAD, BRIDGE, AND RIVER.

In May 1857, Brown left for Kansas and acquired recruits on the way. They assumed their mission would be in Kansas or along the Missouri border. But one evening in Iowa, Brown told them that their destination was Virginia.

> Steeled by faith in God's omnipotence, on October 16, 1859, John Brown set in motion a plan he believed would liberate 4 million slaves throughout the American South. Brown envisioned a biblical flood, not of water, but of people, rising at the confluence of the Potomac and Shenandoah Rivers, as bondsmen rallied to the Harpers Ferry federal arsenal. This army of liberation would break over Dixie in a divine wave, cleansing the region of sin. . . . . [During the raid on the arsenal] he held captive George Washington's great-grandson [sic], proving that, if nothing else, Brown understood symbolic politics."[13]

The infamous raid at Harpers Ferry, Virginia, began late Sunday night, October 16, 1859, when Brown and eighteen men crossed the bridge from Maryland into the village of Harpers Ferry and immediately took possession of the federal armory. (Three other of Brown's men stayed behind at the Maryland farm with additional weapons and supplies to be brought forward when summoned.) Brown also took white slaveholders as hostages, the first of whom was Colonel Lewis W. Washington.

HARPERS FERRY. Interior of the engine house just before the gate is broken down by the storming party. Colonel Washington and his associates are shown as captives, held as hostages by Brown.

Colonel Washington was "Brown's first and principal target among the local slaveholders because of his prestige as a great-grandnephew of the first president.... [F]or symbolic value, Brown had his men carry off two valuable heirlooms: a sword and a pistol reportedly given to George Washington by Frederick the Great and Lafayette."[14]

The first person killed by Brown's men was a free Negro, Heywood Shepherd, who worked as a porter on a train from Wheeling to Baltimore, and who lived in Harpers Ferry. One of Brown's men stopped the train shortly after midnight on the railroad bridge that connected Maryland and Virginia at Harpers Ferry and shot the porter, who had disembarked. The train was later permitted to continue on to Baltimore.

Amazingly, within twenty-four hours of the start of the raid, ninety marines arrived from the Navy yard in Washington, under the command of Colonel Robert E. Lee. Brown and most of his men were under siege in the engine house. Lee ordered Lieutenant J. E. B. Stuart to seek their surrender. (Stuart recognized Brown, since Stuart had served in Kansas in 1856.) When the raiders refused to surrender, Lee ordered a storming party of twelve marines, led by Lieutenant Israel Green, and they captured Brown and his party and freed the hostages. In the fighting, Lieutenant Green stabbed Brown with his sword, but Green had mistakenly brought his dress sword with him to Harpers Ferry, and so the blows were not strong enough to kill Brown. Had this simple mistake not happened, there would have been no trial and hanging of John Brown, and his political impact would have been significantly less.

The Trial of John Brown and His Coconspirators

When the raid at Harpers Ferry ended early in the morning on October 18, 1859, ten of the original band of twenty-three had been killed, and seven had escaped, though two of them were recaptured;[15] Brown and six others were captured.[16]

One of the first questions to arise was whether the prisoners should be tried in a Virginia state court, or in a U.S. federal court. Treating the raid as a federal matter made some sense since it was federal property (an Army arsenal) that had been attacked and since much of the fighting had taken place there, and, as a political matter, it involved national issues. On the other hand, Virginians were killed, and there was virtue in demonstrating that the raiders could get a fair trial in Virginia. Some advised Governor Henry A. Wise that he should declare martial law, convict Brown in a drumhead court, and hang him on the spot. However, Wise felt that a fair trial was essential, since the South's honor was at stake.

The trial ended up in Virginia for a variety of reasons. First, as there was no federal prison nearby and the closest state courthouse—the Jefferson County Circuit Court in Charles Town—was several miles away and was scheduled to begin its fall term on October 20, 1859, there would be no delay in beginning a trial in the local state court in Virginia.[17]

Second, on October 19th, President Buchanan held a cabinet meeting and invited Supreme Court Justice John A. Campbell, believing that "an officer of justice" could perhaps aid in the discussion of Brown's raid. Campbell, originally from Alabama, had been appointed to the Court by President Pierce in 1853, when he was only 41. Campbell was so highly regarded that the members of the Supreme Court had unanimously proposed that the president nominate him, and then the Senate confirmed him unanimously—the only time in history that has ever happened. Campbell advised that Brown's crime was not a violation of federal law, and so Virginia had the sole obligation to prosecute him.[18]

Finally, Governor Wise conferred with President Buchanan, and they both agreed—or Buchanan acquiesced—that the matter should be handled by the Virginia judicial system. Wise and Buchanan were both Democrats, and Wise was an ambitious politician who had his eye on the presidential nomination for the following year.

Governor Wise, Virginia Senator James M. Mason, Ohio Congressman Clement L. Vallandigham,[19] and Charles J. Faulkner, a former

HENRY A. WISE.

Congressman from that district,[20] met with Brown.[21] The four talked for several hours in the office of the Armory. Wise promised Brown a fair trial. One scholar argues that Wise had developed great respect for Brown (despite his assessment that Brown was an overzealous extremist) and that the reason for trying him in a Virginia court was to ensure a speedy trial and prevent Brown and the others from being lynched.[22] On October 19th, the same day as the cabinet meeting in D.C., the captured men were taken to Charles Town and handed off by the military to the civil authorities. The next day, Justice of the Peace Roger Chew formally commanded the county sheriff to commit them to the county jail to be held for trial on charges of murder and conspiracy to cause a slave insurrection.

On the morning of October 25th, the Magistrates' Court assembled[23] and the sheriff brought in the prisoners protected by an armed guard of eighty men. The charges were read—treason and murder[24]—and then the state's attorney asked if Brown had counsel.[25] Brown, after noting that Governor Wise had assured him of a fair trial, used the opening to attack the proceeding: "if we are to be forced with a mere form of a trial to execution, you might spare yourselves that trouble. . . . I ask to be excused from the mockery of a trial."[26] The court then appointed for the defense two local qualified attorneys: Charles James Faulkner and Lawson Botts.[27] Quite properly, Faulkner asked the court to be excused because he had taken part in the fighting at Harpers Ferry as part of the defending forces, had met with Brown in the company of Governor Wise and others, and had openly expressed his opinion that Brown was guilty. Brown ignored the offer of counsel, noting that he had sent for his own attorneys, but the other prisoners accepted Botts.

The Circuit Court met that same afternoon, and the grand jury was called and given a report. The next day, October 26th, the Grand Jury reported "true bills" against each prisoner. The indictment contained four counts: (1) treason against the Commonwealth of Virginia; (2) advising and conspiring with slaves to rebel; (3) first degree murder of the five men (one Marine and four civilians, including Heyward Shepard); and (4) murder of three citizens separately.

Governor Wise appointed a prominent lawyer, Andrew Hunter,[28] to be the Special Prosecutor, and he was assisted by Charles B. Harding, the Jefferson County State attorney. (Hunter may have had a conflict of interest, since he was a relative of the militiaman from Charles Town— Henry Hunter—who admitted on the witness stand during trial that he had murdered a defenseless captured raider.[29]) Brown consulted with Botts and finally agreed to retain him and another local attorney, Thomas C. Green,[30] who happened to be the Mayor of Charles Town (and a cousin of Virginia Senator James Mason) and someone Botts wanted as his assistant. Brown had feared that if he accepted counsel, he would not be allowed to speak, but agreed to cooperate after the court and assigned counsel promised him speaking rights.[31] At that time, courts generally barred defendants from taking the stand in their own defense. The rationale was the assumption that, if guilty, the defendant would lie. Thus, the deal to allow Brown to speak in the courtroom was a major concession and a great victory for Brown.

A jury was selected, composed of a majority of non-slaveholders. The local physician pronounced Brown physically able to stand trial, despite the wounds he had suffered during the raid at the Harpers Ferry arsenal (as noted above, he was stabbed with a dress sword by Lieutenant Israel Green). The trial began on Wednesday, October 26, 1859, and lasted through Monday, October 31. There was little dispute over the basic facts of the case.

As the trial opened, Botts made a critical motion: that Judge Parker should declare that Brown was insane. Botts had received a telegram from someone in Ohio who claimed to have known Brown when the family lived in Akron, and that it was clear to the writer that "insanity is hereditary in that family."[32] (A successful insanity defense would have saved Brown from death, but it is hard to imagine him confined to an insane asylum, perhaps continuing to write letters to supporters, though with substantially less political impact.) However, Brown himself torpedoed the plea. He rose from his cot and said angrily, "I am perfectly unconscious of insanity, and I reject, so far as I am capable, any attempt to interfere on my behalf on that score."[33] (Perhaps undermining his claim to sanity, Brown disrupted the proceedings once each day he was in court, and he chose his moments carefully.[34])

On October 28th, Brown announced that he had no confidence in his lawyers, and so Botts and Green asked the court to be allowed to withdraw. George H. Hoyt, a 21-year-old[35] Boston attorney, volunteered to defend Brown; Botts offered Hoyt his office to prepare the defense. Hoyt had been sent to Charles Town by Brown's New England supporters.[36] There was a rumor that in fact Hoyt had been sent there to arrange for Brown's escape.[37]

The next day, Saturday, October 29th, Hoyt appeared in court with two other defense lawyers, Hiram Griswold of Cleveland and Samuel Chilton of Washington, D.C.[38] Chilton was a Virginia native practicing in Washington. He had been hired (for the very expensive fee of $1,000) by John A. Andrew, a leading Boston abolitionist lawyer who would later become governor of Massachusetts. Lawyers Green and Botts resigned on the arrival of "foreign counsel."[39] The examination of witnesses was concluded the same day.

On Monday, October 31st, Harding presented the arguments for the prosecution, followed by closing defense statements from Griswold and Chilton. Griswold argued that it was absurd to charge Brown with treason against the Commonwealth of Virginia, because Brown was not a citizen of that state and so owed no duty of loyalty to it. Brown's lawyers also argued that since Brown was the commander-in-chief of a provisional army, he should be tried under the laws of war, and not as a common criminal.[40]

In contrast, the prosecutor pointed out that Virginia defined treason broadly, and that as a U.S. citizen seeking residence in the state, Brown had duties to Virginia in the same measure as he received its privileges and immunities.[41] Hunter then concluded the argument for the state.

Judge Parker charged the jury and warned them: "[A]ct upon prejudice or from excitement or passion, and you will have done a wrong to that law in whose services you are engaged. As I said before, those men are now in the hands of justice. They are to have a fair and impartial trial."[42] After about thirty minutes, the jury returned a verdict of guilty of treason, conspiring to incite slave rebellion, and murder. Reporters in the packed courtroom had expected whoops of elation and wild applause, but there was not a sound[43]—Virginia was trying to prove that its decorum matched its justice.[44]

On November 2, 1859, Brown was asked if he had anything to say before sentence was pronounced. Brown said that he never intended murder or treason or the destruction of property. He also said that it was "unjust" that he should suffer penalty, since he took action not for the rich but for the poor and enslaved. He said he was "entirely satisfied with the treatment received at trial. Considering all the circumstances, it has been more generous than I expected, but I feel no consciousness of guilt."[45] This overly generous statement reflected a recalibration of Brown's earlier strategy of confrontation—allowing him to be seen as the guardian of freedom everywhere, rather than as a raider and a nightmare of the South.[46]

Brown concluded with his stirring remarks that galvanized the North:

> I believe that to have interfered as I have done—as I have always freely admitted I have done—in behalf of His despised people, was not wrong, but right. Now if it is deemed necessary that I should forfeit my life for the furtherance of the ends of justice, and mingle my blood further with the blood of my children and with the blood of millions in this slave country whose rights are disregarded by wicked, cruel and unjust enactments—I submit; so let it be done![47]

The Court then sentenced him to be hanged on Friday, December 2, 1859.

The Trial as an Event, and the Aftermath

Brown's trial became the first modern courtroom event, the first to claim daily media validation from newspapers, essayists, poets, orators, and from the great invention of the times, the telegraph.[48] News reports employed the rhetorical flourishes typical of nineteenth-century romantic fiction.[49] Brown was a ne'er-do-well who failed in every major venture of his life, a loner on the fringes of antebellum politics. He bungled his plans and used violent tactics that left innocent blood on his hands. Yet he emerged from his trial an American saint.[50]

The legal process was crucial in shaping this opinion. Brown used his right to be heard at his trial to dramatize a contradiction in the American culture: slavery existed in a society where all men were declared to be equal.[51] Brown knew his way around courtrooms, having been humiliated for years by constant litigation and bankruptcy proceedings relating to more than fifteen business failures. Helpless in previous courtrooms, Brown was a commanding presence in this one. He translated innocence and guilt into good and evil, awakening sympathy and magnifying his cause. One scholar noted that Brown "turned the courtroom into an exploration of whether the ideal and the real should change places and whether the spiritual could supplant the merely legal."[52] If Brown had been killed by Lieutenant Green when storming the engine house, or if Brown had been lynched by a mob, he would have had no opportunity to write political letters, talk to journalists, and he would not have made his impassioned speech in the courtroom that energized most of the North. Brown's impact on history would have been substantially less.

Six days after Brown's sentencing, on November 8th, the leading Transcendentalist and prominent philosopher, Ralph Waldo Emerson, delivered a major lecture in Boston's Music Hall.[53] The eloquent abolitionist said of Brown: "That new saint, than whom none purer or more brave was ever led by love of men into conflict and death, the new saint awaiting his martyrdom, and who, if he shall suffer, will make the gallows glorious like the cross."[54]

Meanwhile, Brown's lawyers were preparing for an appeal to the highest court in the state, the Court of Appeals of Virginia. John Andrew hired the leading lawyer in Richmond, William Green, to handle the appeal. Working under enormous time pressure, Green managed to draft and have professionally printed a sixteen-page brief, which was co-signed by Samuel Chilton.[55] Green filed his petition in *Commonweal v. Brown* on November 18, 1859. He devoted twelve of the sixteen pages to the treason charge. Reaching back to seventeenth-century English law and encompassing a host of opinions (federal and state), Green argued that treason is a breach of allegiance, and since Brown had no allegiance to Virginia, he could not have committed treason against Virginia. This argument had been tried unsuccessfully at the trial, but in the appeals petition, Green developed the point substantially.

Why did Green focus so heavily on this point? Under Virginia law, the governor could not extend executive clemency to someone convicted of treason. Therefore, if Green could persuade the Appeals Court to throw out the treason charge, then Governor Wise would have the legal authority to offer clemency to his client.

Apart from the treason issue, Green also argued that the conspiracy charges were too nonspecific to be acceptable; for example, the particular slaves that Brown was alleged to have advised and conspired with to rebel were not named; and those who were murdered were not named. This introduced an unacceptable element of uncertainty, and so the jurors could not have rendered proper judgment, and the indictment and verdict were defective.

The Attorney General of Virginia, John Randolph Tucker, filed no written response, and there was no oral argument before the Court of Appeals. Nevertheless, on the very next day, November 19th, the court issued a very short statement that it had denied Brown's appeal. Tucker telegraphed Andrew Hunter that Brown's appeal had been unanimously refused.[56]

In the month between the sentencing and execution, Governor Wise received thousands of petitions for mercy. Some were from astute Southerners who argued that Brown's execution would serve to rally the antislavery forces even further. Former President Tyler, a Virginian, urged Wise to commute the sentence to life imprisonment, "so that 'the enemy [would be] disarmed.'"[57] George Hoyt, Brown's young Boston lawyer, returned from Ohio with affidavits supporting the claim of Brown's insanity; Hoyt met with Governor Wise during a visit in Washington.[58] Wise decided not to commute Brown's death sentence.[59]

During the period after the trials (all of Brown's co-raiders were found guilty of various charges[60]), but before the executions, Charles Town hummed with activity. There were mysterious fires that seemed to concentrate on the homes of the former jurors. As a result, the governor asked for volunteer reinforcements to maintain law and order. Volunteers poured in, totaling one thousand men from Wheeling, Richmond, Petersburg, Fauquier, and other companies, including the Richmond Grays—one of whose recent recruits was the actor John Wilkes Booth.

While in Charles Town, Booth entertained the townspeople and troops with dramatic readings from Shakespeare; this diversion from the tension in the air was welcomed by the townspeople.[61] The troops were guarding Brown against the twin terrors of the lynch mob and the rescue party—and perhaps a slave insurrection.

Brown's wife, Mary Ann, arrived from North Elba on December 1st and spent four hours with her husband. Early on December 2nd, Brown called for Andrew Hunter, the prosecutor. Brown said he wanted to make a will, and asked the lawyer to draft it for him. Hunter did Brown that favor.[62]

The next day, just before noon, Brown was hanged. There were a thousand soldiers standing at attention, including cadets from the Virginia Military Institute.[63] John Wilkes Booth was there, as a member of the Richmond Grays militia. Brown's body was taken to Harpers Ferry, and from there his wife took it to their home in North Elba in upper New York State.

Brown's Secret Supporters: Frederick Douglass and the Secret Six

Did Brown act alone? Who financed his raid? The indictments of Brown and the others noted that they acted "together with diverse other evil-minded and traitorous persons to the Jurors unknown . . . being moved and seduced by the false and malignant counsel of other evil and traitorous persons."[64] Brown had spent the summer at a rented farmhouse (the Kennedy farm) in Maryland about four miles from Harpers Ferry. The day after the raid, scouts from the Independent Greys of Baltimore found Brown's hidden arms at a schoolhouse near the farm: 200 Sharp's rifles, boxes of revolvers and 1,000 pikes.[65] The searchers at the farmhouse found a carpetbag full of papers and other correspondence between Brown and some of his backers. This discovery exposed links to Frederick Douglass, and certain men in New England, known as the Secret Six.

Frederick Douglass and Brown first met in the late 1840s, and stayed in touch thereafter. In January 1858, Brown appeared at Douglass's door in Rochester, New York, and stayed for nearly a month.[66] They met again in Philadelphia in March 1858; however, the key meeting took place about three weeks before the Harpers Ferry raid. Brown wrote to Douglass and asked him to meet at an old stone quarry near Chambersburg, Pennsylvania. Brown took his young secretary, John Kagi, and asked that Douglass bring Shields Green, an escaped slave. They debated Brown's planned attack during their weekend together. Douglass asserted that he "at once opposed the measure with all the arguments at my command. It would be an attack upon the federal government, and would array the whole country against us."[67] Brown pleaded for Douglass to join him, but Douglass declined due to his "discretion or [his] cowardice," as Douglass phrased it.[68] Douglass and Brown never saw each other again. Shields Green remained with Brown.

While the Harpers Ferry raid was taking place, Douglass was in Philadelphia, addressing a large audience on the topic of "The Self Made Man." The next day, he got word that Brown's carpetbag had been found, and that it contained documents directly implicating him and others. Rather than confront the matter directly in Charles Town, Douglass immediately went north and made his way into Canada. He believed that if he were found in Virginia, he would be hanged;[69] and in fact, Governor Wise had sought indictments against Douglass (along with Howe and Sanborn) for conspiring to cause murder, even though he knew it would be difficult to get them extradited to Virginia.[70] On November 12, 1859, three weeks before Brown was executed, Douglass sailed from Quebec to England. In April 1860, Douglass returned to the United States via Canada.

In 1881, Douglass gave a speech about Brown at Storer College, a black school set up after the Civil War on a hill overlooking the site of the old armory at Harpers Ferry. On the platform with Douglass was Andrew Hunter, the prosecuting attorney in 1859. Douglass's goal, he said, was "to vindicate in some degree a great historical character . . . a grand, brave and good old man."[71] Once again, Douglass denied that he had "a lot to do with planning Brown's raid," and he closed with the memorable line: "I could live for the slave, but he could die for him."[72]

Then there were the Secret Six—six wealthy and influential abolitionists with ties to John Brown and his raid: Theodore Parker, a graduate of the Harvard Divinity School and a leading Transcendentalist;[73] Dr. Samuel Gridley Howe,[74] a graduate of the Harvard Medical School, who was deeply involved with aiding the blind and who founded the first Braille library; George Luther Sterns, a wealthy manufacturer and philanthropist, who advocated violent resistance to the Fugitive Slave Act; Franklin B. Sanborn,[75] a 28-year-old teacher; the Reverend Thomas Wentworth Higginson, who had been an ordained Unitarian minister until he resigned the pulpit in 1848 after losing a Congressional bid; and multimillionaire Gerrit Smith, who failed in his run for New York governor in 1858.[76] Some of them had worked together in New England to prevent the enforcement of the Fugitive Slave Act of 1850, and in March 1858, Smith recruited the other five to form a secret "committee of six" to advise Brown and to raise money for the Harpers Ferry expedition.[77] These were "men of means who, from the comfort of their studies, admired Brown, but wanted to keep their hands clean."[78]

Two months after forming the committee, and more than a year before the Harpers Ferry raid, Smith delivered a major speech at the Park Street Unitarian Church in Boston to the American Peace Society during which he conveyed the general purpose and design of the raid. The "taking of human life . . . when necessary to take it, is to be classed not with the most degraded, but with the most honored callings."[79] Smith's most outspoken heralding of Brown's raid was in a public letter to a leading abolitionist (John Thomas) on August 29, 1859, less than two months before Brown's raid. He explained that the time had passed for bringing slavery to an end by peaceful means.

In the several days following the Brown raid, the *New York Herald* obtained and reprinted Smith's August letter to John Thomas, along with one of Smith's letters to Brown, which had been found in Brown's carpetbag (along with a draft for $200—to help Brown with his "Kansas

HONORABLE GERRIT SMITH.

work"). That was enough for the *Herald* to charge on October 21st that Smith was an "accessory before the fact" and that he should be arrested and sent to Virginia for trial.

This alarmed Smith. In his earlier actions of support and endorsement of violence, he felt spared from culpability for actual deaths—he had preferred not to know about the precise details of the conspiracy, but only the grand design and intended effects. Now, however, he knew this raid had cost lives and that he had publicly advocated it. He destroyed all the evidence he could find connecting him to the affair.[80] By early November, he was found wandering around his mansion as if in a trance, and became rambling and incoherent in conversation. On November 7, 1859, Smith's family committed him to the state Asylum for the Insane at Utica, New York.[81] Smith's nephew sent a letter to Governor Wise explaining his uncle's situation, to which Wise replied that he found Gerrit Smith's collapse "very touching" and evidence of his innocence.[82] Eight years later, Gerrit Smith posted bail for Jefferson Davis in a Richmond courthouse.

When the news of the raid reached Concord, Massachusetts, Frank Sanborn burned every scrap of paper that bound him to Brown, though later he claimed that his destruction of evidence was solely to prevent others from being compromised. One of Brown's raiders, Francis Merriam, who had escaped, showed up at Sanborn's door, but Sanborn refused to see him. (Not long before, Sanborn had given Merriam money to join Brown's effort.[83]) Sanborn conferred with poets and abolitionists Ralph Waldo Emerson and Henry David Thoreau, then went to Boston to consult with John A. Andrew, a leading abolitionist lawyer and later governor of Massachusetts. Andrew advised them that they were liable to be arrested and extradited to Virginia. Sanborn immediately fled; he took a steamer to Maine and then crossed into Quebec. Later, Andrew offered another legal opinion to Frank Sanborn: that even if he and the others were indicted in Virginia, they would be tried in Massachusetts and presumably found not guilty. Sanborn then returned to Concord.

Dr. Samuel Gridley Howe met with George Luther Sterns and pressed Sterns to join him in fleeing the country. They left for Canada on the same day that Brown appeared in court in Charles Town. The Reverend Thomas Wentworth Higginson did not run. He actually longed to testify, but he did not admit that he had assisted the effort to inspire a slave uprising. The Reverend Theodore Parker was in Rome, Italy, dying of tuberculosis.[84]

Brown's Legacy

Only the deaths of Presidents Washington, Adams, and Jefferson, decades earlier, matched the "paroxysms of emotion" unleashed by the death of John Brown.[85] Brown proved, in death, to have a much greater impact on the nation than he did during his life. The reaction in the South to the Harpers Ferry episode was immediate: the climate resembled that of a separate nation threatened with invasion from without and rebellion from within. The *Richmond Enquirer* of October 25, 1859, stated:

> The Harpers Ferry invasion has advanced the cause of Disunion more than any other event . . . since the formation of the Government; it has rallied to that standard of men who formerly looked upon it with horror; it had revived, with ten-fold strength, the desire of a Southern Confederacy.[86]

Secessionist plotters gloated. Southerners saw Brown as the face of abolitionism, of Republicanism, and of the North.

Outside of the South, there was an unprecedented outpouring of grief over Brown's death: buildings in Cleveland were draped in black. In Haiti, where the first North American slave uprising took place, flags were flown at half-staff. Even in Europe, Brown was admired. The most respected public voice in England, the *Times of London*, was conflicted: it valued British slave emancipation as a great national accomplishment, but it viewed Brown as "a fanatic who had dared to endanger the British-born civilization of America."[87]

A John Brown cult was rising. The Democrats fastened blame on the Republicans. The immediate impact of Brown's raid, one historian has noted, was that it "'sent a shiver of fear to the inmost fiber of every white man, woman, and child' in the South. . . . [And while] antislavery fervor in the North was intensified, Southern solidarity and rhetoric reached a new level of zealotry."[88] In death, "Brown embodied the South's greatest anxiety: that armed slaves would rise up and throw off their chains."[89] The prize-winning novelist Geraldine Brooks put the Southern view simply: "If a Northerner such as Brown was prepared to kill fellow whites, regardless of whether they owned slaves or not, and was canonized for it, then war was as good as declared."[90]

CHAPTER THREE

The Continuing Debate

Brown's legacy continues to resonate today. The Brown story has repeatedly appeared in the theater and movies: in 1950, Seyril Schochen's play, *The Moon Besieged*; in 1953, Stephen Benet's *John Brown's Body*, starring Tyrone Power, Judith Anderson, and Raymond Massey, directed by Charles Laughton; and *The Anvil*, a play based on Brown's trial, written by Julia Davis in 1962. The 1982 *Blue and the Grey* was a TV miniseries featuring Sterling Hayden as Brown. Johnny Cash played Brown in the 1985 film *North and South*. In the 1940 movie *Santa Fe Trail*, Raymond Massey played Brown, Errol Flynn was Jeb Stuart, and Ronald Reagan was George Custer. Massey also played Brown in the 1955 movie, *Seven Angry Men*. In 1998, Russell Banks published his widely acclaimed novel, *Cloudsplitter*, in the form of a fictional biography of Brown.[91] The winner of the 2006 Pulitzer Prize, *March*, a wonderful novel by Geraldine Brooks that re-imagines Louisa May Alcott's *Little Women* from the point of view of the sisters' father fighting in the Civil War, describes the enthrallment with Brown by Mr. and Mrs. March and the attachment to Brown by Frank Sanborn, the young schoolmaster of March's "little women."[92]

The Second Trial: *United States v. Brown*; The Mason Committee

On December 14, 1859—three days after Brown was hanged—Congress met, and the Senate passed a Resolution (55–0) to appoint a Select Committee "to inquire into the facts attending the late invasion and seizure of the armory and arsenal of the United States at Harpers Ferry." It then specified the particular points within the Committee's scope of inquiry:

1) (a) whether the invasion was made "under color of any organization intended to subvert the government of any of the States . . ." and (b) "whether any citizens of the United States not present were implicated therein, or accessory thereto, by contributions of money, arms, munitions, or otherwise."
2) what military equipment did the raiders use and how was it obtained and transported, and
3) whether any legislation might be needed for the future preservation of the peace.

Needless to say, the first of these was the major question and the most controversial. In a sense, this Senate inquiry became the second trial of John Brown and the Harpers Ferry Raid. Instead of a state courtroom in Virginia, the "trial" was conducted in a Senate chamber in Washington, but the lawyerly questioning and judicial rules of procedure and decorum were in evidence.

The Senate selected five members for the Committee: James Mason[93] of Virginia (chair), Jefferson Davis of Mississippi, Dr. Graham N. Fitch of Indiana, James R. Doolittle of Wisconsin, and Jacob Collamer of Vermont. The first three were Democrats, and the last two were Republicans. Mason was known as a hothead; he was a leading advocate of the Fugitive Slave Act of 1850 and was inclined toward secession if a Republican was elected President in 1860. Yet, in the judgment of a leading scholar, Mason had "conducted one of the coolest, most sensible, most impartial congressional investigations in all of American history."[94]

The Select Committee went straight to work, holding their first meeting on December 16, 1859, and worked into June 1860. Altogether they interviewed thirty-two witnesses. On June 15, 1860, the Select Committee produced a Report[95] comprising Majority and Minority views divided on partisan grounds (the three Democrats wrote the Majority, and the two Republicans wrote the Minority), a complete Journal of the Committee's

JAMES M. MASON.

proceedings, an Appendix of documents,[96] and the transcripts of the hearings and testimony of the thirty-two witnesses. This has become known as the "Mason Report."

The Mason Report detailed the substantial amount of weaponry Brown had taken with him to Harpers Ferry and stored at the farm in nearby Maryland. It included 200 Sharp rifles, 200 revolvers, and 1,000 pikes—enough "to have placed an effective weapon in the hands of not less than 1500 men."

Brown had the pikes made in Connecticut (and was given $100 by Gerrit Smith directly in part payment for the pikes[97]), and the carbines were acquired by the "Massachusetts State Kansas Committee," then placed under the control of a "National Aid Kansas Committee," and then under Brown's control in Iowa. Brown acquired funds in New England by giving lectures "patronized by the principal men in the States where they were given."[98] Contributions were made "occasionally in large sums paid directly to Brown, but more usually by collections in the villages and towns."

In a key conclusion, the Committee stated that it did *not* appear

> that such contributions [of money] were made with actual knowledge of the use for which they were designed by Brown, although it does appear that money was freely contributed by those styling themselves friends of this man Brown, and friends alike of that they styled "the cause of freedom" . . . without inquiry as to the way in which the money would be used by him to advance such pretended cause.[99]

The Mason Report summarized the key underlying worry—for men of great social prominence and wealth:

> [A]t work, unchecked by law and not rebuked but encouraged by public opinion, with money freely contributed and placed in irresponsible hands, it may easily be seen how this expedition was got up, and it may equally be seen how like expeditions may certainly be anticipated in the future.[100]

The expedition could have been arrested by the exercise of "ordinary care."[101]

With respect to the charge to determine whether any legislation was needed, the Report sadly noted that there really was not much the Congress was empowered to do; the power in Article I of the Constitution to protect against invasion refers to "an invasion by the public force of a foreign power."[102] Brown's "invasion" was "simply the act of lawless ruffians . . . distinguishable . . . from ordinary felonies . . . by the fact that the money to maintain them, had been contributed and furnished by the citizens of other States of the Union." The Commission was saying that the task of appropriate legislation would fall to the states. The implication was that the South had to protect itself if the North failed to rein in the radical abolitionists.

The Minority Report was issued by the two Republicans, Doolittle and Collamer. Not surprisingly, it took a somewhat more benign view of the situation. The two Republicans acknowledged that "some abolitionists have at times contributed money to what is occasionally called 'practical abolitionism'—that is, in aiding the escape of slaves—and may have placed too implicit confidence in John Brown."[103] However, they asserted that there was no evidence that any of these abolitionists had any complicity in the conspiracy. As to the concern expressed by the Majority about potential future occurrences, the Minority in effect said this was a discrete, one-off event, not likely to happen again. In a nice twist of irony, the Minority agreed that there was too much disregard for the rule of law—as when the laws against the slave trade are breeched,[104] or when lawless armed men invade Kansas and go unpunished.

During the course of the Select Committee's inquiry, three lawyers were called as witnesses: John A. Andrew of Boston, Samuel Chilton of Washington (one of Brown's defense counsel), and Andrew Hunter, the prosecutor at Brown's trial. In interviewing Hunter on January 13, 1860, the Select Committee focused mainly on the facts of his interview with Brown before the trial; he spoke of the "respect and courtesy [Brown and Governor Wise] had for each other. Brown was impressed with a high regard for Governor Wise, and the governor with an estimate of him, in which I at first participated."[105]

Chilton's appearance before the Select Committee was on January 30, 1861. The inquiry was directed at how he became Brown's lawyer, and who paid him. Chilton explained that it was Montgomery Blair of Washington who had approached him on behalf of a prominent lawyer in Boston, John A. Andrew, against whose drafts Chilton was paid. It was on the recommendation of Chilton that Thomas A. Green was also retained for Brown's defense. At one point during the hearing, Senator Mason asked Chilton whether Brown had told him the names of any persons outside of Virginia who had helped him. Senator Collamer immediately questioned the appropriateness of asking counsel about his communications from his client. (Collamer had been a judge in Vermont for a decade, before he was elected to the Senate.) Mason withdrew the question, explaining that he really was not intending to get to private conversations, but Chilton immediately added that, if he felt the question would require him to disclose privileged communication, he would, of course "respectfully decline to answer it."[106]

The exchange with John A. Andrew on February 9th was the most interesting. He acknowledged that he had engaged Chilton through Montgomery Blair. Senator Mason pressed hard to learn who had financed Andrew's actions, but Andrew was agile and never produced a name. Andrew explained that he had learned that the Virginia court planned to move swiftly against Brown—whom he had met once, earlier in 1859, and to whom he had given $25—and he thought that would be "a judicial outrage."[107] As well as being judicially opposed to a swift trial, Andrew said that friends and even strangers in the street, at church, or in court asked him to defend Brown, to which Andrew replied: "If I should go to Virginia, I, a Republican lawyer and a Massachusetts man, should be before a court and jury so little in sympathy with myself that I should be quite as much on trial as my client would be."[108] That's why he wrote to Montgomery Blair, who was renowned as Dred Scott's lawyer.

Senator Mason then pushed Andrew on where the money came from to pay for Brown's defense. Alert and clever, Andrew replied, "the money was furnished by A., B., & C. whom I might happen to meet in business, or in pleasure, or at church. . . . In that way the money came in. Some gentleman would give five dollars, and some fifty dollars. I knew some of the donors; others I did not know."[109] Mason suggested that it was not quite believable that Andrew would donate so much of his own effort and professional time to someone he said he hardly knew. That was a mistake, because it allowed Andrew to reply at length about a huge pro bono case he had taken on involving a man convicted of piracy in Boston: Andrew had come to Washington to meet with the Attorney General and the president to obtain clemency; the first time he met his client was on the happy day that he delivered the clemency commission.

The Chairman then moved to the question of Hoyt: who employed him? Where did the money come from? Again, Andrew explained his assumption that the young lawyer volunteered as a conscientious aspiring professional. Mason and Senator Jefferson Davis tried to pin Andrew down as to whether he respected—sympathized with—Brown's actions of murder in Kansas and at Harpers Ferry. Andrew replied, "My sympathy, so far as I sympathized with Captain[110] Brown, was on account of a good and just cause, and in support of the rights of persons who were treated with unjust aggression."[111]

Of the "secret six"—those men said to be Brown's principal backers—George L. Sterns was the only one who appeared and testified before the Select Committee.[112] The Committee tried to get John Brown Jr. to appear, since he seemed likely to know as much as anyone about the background of the Harpers Ferry raid. However, he surrounded himself with bodyguards in Ohio and defied Senate agents who were sent to arrest him.[113]

Another wealthy Northerner, Thaddeus Hyatt, also defied the summons of the Select Committee, but he ended up in jail anyway. Hyatt, a prosperous New York manufacturer and inventor, had been the chair of the "National Kansas Committee" and a vigorous supporter of the Free-Soil Party in the Kansas Territory, and he became acquainted with John Brown. Hyatt's name appeared in the documents in Brown's carpetbag. He was summoned by the Mason Committee on January 16th, but he was sick by the time he arrived in Washington on February 1, 1860. He requested and received a postponement, but finally declared that the Senate had no power to compel his testimony. Hyatt then went to Boston to consult counsel about his options in this matter—counsel included John A. Andrew. On March 6th, Hyatt returned to Washington; the Senate had adopted a Resolution (49–6) requesting that Hyatt be asked what excuse he had for failing to appear originally, and whether he was now ready to testify.[114] On March 12th, Mason offered a Resolution to commit Hyatt to jail. The Resolution was adopted 44–10. Hyatt remained in jail until June 15th, when the Select Committee disbanded.

Hyatt never availed himself of the writ of habeas corpus to test the legality of his imprisonment and the Senate's power. But this case marked the *first time* that the issue of compulsory process—"a process to compel the attendance in court [or at a legislative hearing] of a person wanted there as a witness or otherwise," according to *Black's Law Dictionary*—had been brought to a head in the Senate.

Hyatt's fervent antislavery position did eventually help instead of hinder him: in August of 1861, Hyatt was appointed by President Lincoln to serve as the American Consul at La Rochelle, France. A few months later, he received a letter from his brother reporting that his former persecutor, James Mason, was confined in Fort Warren in Boston Harbor, having been caught by a U.S. frigate off the coast of Cuba where he was en route to England to serve as Ambassador of the Confederate States of America.[115]

After the Mason Report

The issuance of the Mason Report and the disbanding of the Select Committee in June 1860 concluded the effort to get at all the facts surrounding the Brown raid at Harpers Ferry. But the steam had already gone out of the process: Brown had already been either sainted or demonized, the antislavery forces in the North felt invigorated, and the proslavery South felt confirmed in their worry about the future. The Republicans felt they had dodged a bullet, and the Democrats fractured further into Northern and Southern factions.

Lincoln at first denounced Brown's raid as "wrong for two reasons. It was a violation of law and it was . . . futile as far as any effect it might have on the extinction of a great evil."[116] Months later, Lincoln took offense at the effort to find the root cause among the abolitionists in the North. In his famous Cooper Union speech in February 1860—the speech that propelled him toward his presidential nomination—Lincoln said, "You charge that we stir up insurrections among your slaves. We deny it; and what is your proof? Harpers Ferry! John Brown!! John Brown was no Republican; and you have failed to implicate a single Republican in his Harpers Ferry enterprise."[117]

Perhaps more tellingly, in his Cooper Union speech, Lincoln knew he had to dissociate himself and the Republican Party from John Brown, who was viewed as a radical murderer in at least half the country. On the other hand, Lincoln had to be careful not to insult those in the North who sympathized with Brown. Threading the needle, Lincoln dismissed the Brown raid as "absurd" because it could not work—indeed, even "the slaves, with all their ignorance, saw plainly enough it could not succeed." But Lincoln did not label Brown a fanatic and did not denounce those sympathizing with Brown.[118] In the South, Lincoln's approach must have been read as support for the abolitionists' goals of forced emancipation, but with a better operating plan.

Almost a month before the Select Committee issued its Report, the Republican Convention in Chicago nominated Lincoln for the presidency. Southerners said that if a Republican was elected, they would secede. "For Southerners, John Brown's raid . . . revealed the true intent of the Republican party . . . . [After Harpers Ferry,] the perception [of the Republican Party as a hostile force] became more visceral than thoughtful."[119] In the opening minutes of his Inaugural Address, on March 4, 1861, Lincoln dealt with the John Brown raid: "we denounce the lawless invasion by armed forces of the soil of any State or Territory."[120]

Herman Melville, in a collection of poems he wrote during the Civil War dedicated to the Union dead, acknowledged John Brown's role in igniting the conflict. He called Brown the "meteor" of the war.[121] A scholar more recently noted that Brown changed the mood of the nation such that it went from "compromise to conflict" in a decade.[122]

CHAPTER 4
Secession

Virtually all modern secession or self-determination movements—from the disbanding of federal unions (USSR, Czechoslovakia, Yugoslavia) to independence for constituent parts (East Timor, Kosovo)—were the result of deep religious, ethnic, or linguistic differences. None of these elements were present in the secession of the Southern states that led directly to the American Civil War.

The story of secession in America is long, and it ended in profound sadness.

Early "Secession" Activity

There were efforts made by disgruntled groups to withdraw from the Union prior to the series of state secessions that began in December 1860. Aside from the specific issues that might have caused the dissatisfaction, the argument always reverted to the question of the very nature of the Union: was it a compact, a sort of treaty among coequal independent states, and, if so, could it be altered by any single state? Or, was it a "perpetual union"—a new and indivisible union—that could not be altered without the consent of all states?

The Louisiana Purchase

The first serious threat to the idea of "perpetual union" occurred at the time of the 1803 Louisiana Purchase,[1] which deeply upset some New Englanders and Federalists.[2] They worried that the addition of such a large territory would dilute the political power and economic health of New England and doubted that the United States could double in size without "overloading the still fragile republic beyond its capacity to govern. . . ."[3] John Quincy Adams was the only New England Federalist to vote for the Purchase (though Adams led the opposition to the enabling legislation which he felt gave Jefferson more power than George III had over the American colonies[4]).

Senator Plumer of New Hampshire argued that "the Eastern States must and will dissolve the Union and form a separate government of their own . . . ." Roger Griswold of Connecticut, the Federalist leader in the House, and Senator Timothy Pickering of Massachusetts (a former Secretary of State) promoted what Pickering called "a new Confederacy exempt from the corruption and corrupting influence of the . . . South," a Northern Confederacy including New England, New York, Pennsylvania, and the British provinces of Canada. Griswold and Pickering suggested to Aaron Burr, who, in early 1804, was running for governor of New York, that he might become the new president of this Northern Confederacy—assuming he could bring New York with him. While Burr "refused to make any promises to deliver New York to the secessionists . . . he also would not repudiate the conspiracy."[5] Burr lost the election[6] for governor in a landslide to the Democratic-Republican Morgan Lewis, and the secession effort fizzled.[7]

The Federalist plot to engineer a secession of the northeastern states was "a fateful and ultimately suicidal decision that left Jefferson free to act toward Louisiana with impunity while the Federalists self-destructed."[8] The New England secession threat over Louisiana was serious, but never gained traction, and never reached the level of formal action by any political entity. The next serious threat of secession came a dozen years later, and it was a step further toward formal secession: the Hartford Convention of 1815.

The Hartford Convention

The War of 1812 with Britain—sometimes referred to as the Second War of American Independence—was hard on commercial New England and was very unpopular. Massachusetts and Connecticut had refused to surrender their militias to the orders of the Federal War Department because of fear of British invasion; people complained that the federal government had abandoned New England. Some extremist Federalists talked of secession and a separate peace with Britain. In October 1814, the legislature of Massachusetts issued a call for a delegate convention to be held in Hartford, and it appointed twelve delegates.

When the convention assembled on December 15th, the twelve Massachusetts delegates were joined by seven delegates appointed by the legislature of Connecticut and four from Rhode Island. Vermont and New Hampshire also sent delegates, but they were not appointed by the respective legislatures. Most of the delegates were lawyers. George Cabot, head of the Massachusetts delegation and a moderate Federalist, presided.

A proposal to secede from the Union was discussed and rejected. Some scholars have suggested that the "moderate" Federalists called the Hartford Convention in order to head off New England's secession—rather than to achieve it. The Final Report and Resolutions of the Convention, which were approved on January 5, 1815, proposed a series of constitutional amendments to address what they thought of as unfair advantages held by the South under the Constitution. The first of seven proposed amendments called for eliminating the three-fifths clause of Article I of the Constitution,[9] thereby ensuring that representation and direct taxes would be apportioned "among the Several States . . . according to their respective number of free persons . . . ." Other proposed amendments dealt with limitations on the federal government's ability to declare war and to interfere with international commerce. Interestingly, the seventh proposed amendment limited presidents to a single term.

By the time the Hartford delegation arrived in Washington to present their resolutions, the War of 1812 was over: the Treaty of Ghent had been signed by President Madison, and the news of General Andrew Jackson's victory at New Orleans had reached an excited capital. The position of the delegates was undercut, and they withdrew their recommendations.

The Missouri Compromise

By the end of 1818, the population of the Missouri Territory had grown to a point where it warranted admission to the Union. On December 18, 1818, the legislature of the Territory requested that they be permitted to form a constitution and a state government, on an "equal footing with the original States." Since the Territory had been settled largely by Southerners, and since slavery existed in the Territory, Missouri would be admitted as a slave state. In February 1819, a congressman from New York (James Tallmadge, Jr.) proposed two amendments to the enabling legislation: one would bar future slaves from entering the new state, and the other would provide for gradual emancipation over twenty-five years. These amendments passed in the House by narrow margins (87–76 and 82–78), but failed in the Senate. The debate was bitter. As the great scholar William W. Freehling noted, "The Tallmadge Amendments initially received bipartisan support from the North and bipartisan condemnation from the South."[10]

The anti-slavery North argued that: (a) the slavery compromise reflected in the Constitution related only to the limits existing at that time—i.e., the temporary protection of the slave trade, considering slaves three-fifths of a person for legislative apportionment, and returning escaped slaves was merely a "toleration" of things that existed then, and was not a basis for things that were to be; and (b) the Northwest Territory Act of 1787 prohibited slavery in new states, and Missouri should ban slavery in order to become a state.

The proslavery South argued that: (a) slavery was incorporated into the society when the United States purchased Louisiana (which included the Missouri Territory) from France, and it would violate the rights of the people there now to prohibit slavery. If the treaty was ill-advised, it nevertheless would be manifestly unjust to make its citizens suffer the loss of slavery; and (b) the federal government had no authority to condition admission of a state on the abolition of slavery.

Thus, apart from the unique circumstance of the Treaty of Purchase, the North/South division rested on the fundamental view of the nature of the role of the states and the national government. The acrimonious discussion was resolved by a compromise developed by Henry Clay.

In 1819, Alabama was admitted as a slave state,[11] which brought the slave and free states to equal representation in the Senate. In January 1820, the House passed a bill admitting Maine as a free state. The idea then was that, by pairing Maine and Missouri, the equal balance of slave versus free states would be maintained. Thus, two bills were joined into one in the Senate, with the clause prohibiting slavery in Missouri replaced by a

Henry Clay.

measure prohibiting slavery in the remainder of the Louisiana Purchase north of latitude 36 degrees 30 minutes (the southern boundary of Missouri), except within the boundary of Missouri. While the House initially rejected this approach, the bills were treated separately, and in March 1820, Maine was made a state and Missouri was authorized to adopt a constitution having no restrictions on slavery. Missouri was finally admitted on August 10, 1821, as the twenty-fourth state.

Thomas Jefferson, retired at Monticello, was deeply upset at the "Missouri question," because he was opposed to the assertion of federal power to regulate the "conditions" within the states. He feared that, ultimately, this federal power would lead to emancipation without compensation or removal of blacks to Africa or some location in the Caribbean—both, in his opinion, fundamentally necessary conditions—that in turn would lead to racial war or civil war.[12] "Jefferson believed that [slavery] was akin to an inoperable cancer, and that any effort by government to remove it would only end up killing the patient."[13]

No new states were admitted after Missouri until 1836, when Arkansas became a slave state; it was followed by Michigan in 1837 as a free state, thus maintaining the equal balance in the Senate. As noted earlier, the Missouri Compromise held until 1854 when it was effectively repealed by the Kansas-Nebraska Act; in 1857, the *Dred Scott* case determined that the Missouri Compromise of 1820 was unconstitutional.

South Carolina's Nullification and "Secession" of 1832

A tariff is a tax on imports used to gain revenue for the federal government. But it also can be used as a device to protect certain domestic interests from foreign competition—for example, to protect an important, but infant, industry from more powerful established competition from abroad. The downside of a high protective tariff is that it places consumers of those foreign goods at a disadvantage. The Tariff of 1816 was generally considered moderate in that it reflected a general balancing between the domestic manufacturers (who wanted high tariffs) and consumers (who wanted low tariffs).

In 1828, Congress enacted a highly protective tariff benefiting industry in the Northern states, and President Adams[14] signed it. The tariff was deemed by the South to be the "Tariff of Abominations," because it made imported manufactured goods more expensive than those goods made in the North. South Carolina felt particularly aggrieved. John C. Calhoun anonymously wrote about the states' rights principle of "nullification"—the right of states to nullify acts of Congress—in his essay, *South Carolina Exposition and Protest* of 1828. Andrew Jackson was elected president in late 1828 (with Calhoun as his vice president), and South Carolina hoped that when he took office in 1829, he would act to lower the tariff.[15]

In January 1830, following the opening of the Twenty-first Congress on December 7, 1829, there was a dramatic debate in the Senate over the nature of the Union: issues included slavery, the tariff, allocation of resources, the role of political parties, the role of the Supreme Court, and secession. Sectional discord was sharp: the core debate was between Senators Daniel Webster of Massachusetts and Robert Y. Hayne of South Carolina. Webster and Hayne were both lawyers, and their powers of argument reflected their professional experience.

The debate began with a speech from Hayne on January 19th, and continued with Webster's response the next day; it effectively ended with the speech of Senator Edward Livingston of Louisiana on March 9th. During the debate, twenty-one of the Senate's forty-eight members spoke on the state of the Union. The speeches drew packed galleries to the Senate chambers and attracted national attention.

The great debate began with the relatively innocuous question of the sale of public lands, but Hayne turned it toward the Tariff of 1828. This clash between state sovereignty and national sovereignty turned on the principle of nullification—that states had the right to nullify acts of Congress. For its supporters, nullification was based on the "compact" theory of the Union; it was a procedure for deciding the constitutionality of federal measures in a way that would preserve the Union. In contrast, for Webster the effect of nullification would be to destroy the Union and foment lawlessness and revolutionary violence. Webster argued that the Union was a sovereign national government created by the people of the United States as a whole—not a treaty created by states—with the authority to decide on the constitutionality of its actions. Webster's second reply to Hayne containing the appeal to "Liberty *and* Union, now and forever, one and inseparable" is regarded as one of the most powerful and effective speeches ever given in Congress.

Webster, in effect, accused Hayne of treason and isolated South Carolina. He also removed the onus of disunionist sectionalism from the New England states—where it had been since the War of 1812 and the Hartford Convention—and placed it on the sectional groups within the Democratic Party. (Hayne had expressly referred to the "celebrated assembly . . . known by the name of the 'Hartford Convention.'")

On February 25th, Hayne's colleague from South Carolina, William Smith (another lawyer), laid out the clear question relating to secession: whether, if a state feels oppressed by a law of the federal government, the proper appeal is to the judiciary[16] or whether that state has

> a right to withdraw, and say to the rest of the Union, we no longer belong to you, because you have violated the compact with us; we have decided for ourselves that you have oppressed us; your laws are unconstitutional, and we will no longer continue a member of the Union.[17]

Senator Smith was quite specific in his choice of examples:

> If South Carolina is aggrieved by the Tariff . . . to the extent of great opposition, and the remedy is only to be found in a separation from the Union, it belongs exclusively to the people of that State to meet in convention, examine the subject, weigh the consequences, and settle the mode of operation.[18]

Woodrow Wilson, before he was president, wrote that this debate marked the "formal opening of the great controversy between the North and the South concerning the nature of the Constitution which bound them together."[19] This was the first time that clear statements were presented on the floor of Congress on the constitutional principles over which the North and the South would divide. There was no real outcome to the debate, and no formal steps by South Carolina to move toward secession; it was more of a gentlemanly airing of positions.

The Nullification Crisis of 1832–33

The Tariff Act of 1828 was amended by Congress on July 14, 1832, and was signed by President Jackson. Though it was milder than the 1828 Tariff—lowered from the 50 percent average rate in the 1828 Tariff—it still distressed many in South Carolina. On October 22, 1832, Governor James Hamilton, Jr., convened a Special Session of the South Carolina legislature, which then voted to hold a Convention in November to address the issue.[20] This produced, on November 24, 1832, the South Carolina Ordinance of Nullification.

The Ordinance was relatively clear and simple: Congress passed tariff laws to protect domestic manufactures, which benefited some (the North) at the expense of others (the South). However, Congress had no power to do so, especially in light of the constitutional requirement that there should be equality in imposing the burden of taxation on the states. As a result, the people of South Carolina declared the tariff laws "null, void, and no law, nor binding upon this State . . . ." Further, it was made unlawful for anyone to enforce payment imposed by those tariff acts from February 1, 1833. The Ordinance also prohibited any court from questioning the Ordinance or taking an appeal to the U.S. Supreme Court, and it required all officeholders to take an oath to support the Ordinance.

Then came the hard fist: just to be sure that the determination of South Carolina "may be fully understood by the government of the United States, and the people of the co-States," the Ordinance states:

> [W]e will not submit to the application of force on the part of the federal government, to reduce this State to obedience; but that we will consider . . . any act authorizing the employment of a military or naval force against the State of South Carolina [or any act of closing her ports, etc.] . . . *as inconsistent with the longer continuance of South Carolina in the Union; and that the people of this State will henceforth hold themselves absolved from all further obligation to maintain or preserve their political connection with the people of the other States; and will forthwith proceed to organize a separate government* . . . . (emphasis added).

The die was cast.

President Jackson responded by assembling a small naval force to head to Charleston and put General Winfield Scott in command. Then, he moved the customs revenue collection beyond South Carolina's firepower—quite literally: he instructed Federal Customs officials to move from Charleston to Fort Moultrie, on an island five miles from Charleston's battery. From there, the revenue cutters were to enforce the tariff before imports could reach Charleston. Since South Carolina had no navy, the cutters were not threatened while they enforced the federal tariff law.[21]

Privately, Jackson threatened to hang Vice President Calhoun (it was common knowledge that he had written the *South Carolina Exposition and Protest* of 1828).[22] On December 10, 1832, Jackson issued his nineteen-page Proclamation Regarding Nullification, written by his new Secretary of State, Edward Livingston, a lawyer and former senator from Louisiana. It was a very powerful document. A generation later, the newly elected President Lincoln asked his law partner Herndon to collect some documents to assist him in the preparation of his inaugural address. There were only three documents on Lincoln's list: the Constitution, Clay's speech on the Compromise of 1850, and President Jackson's Proclamation Regarding Nullification.[23]

Jackson's Proclamation began by setting out the South Carolina Ordinance, which, he said, "prescribes to the people of South Carolina a course of conduct in direct violation of their duty as citizens of the United States." "Strict duty" would require him to do nothing more than exercise the powers of the president to preserve the Union, but in light of the importance of the issues, Jackson felt he should provide a "full exposition to South Carolina and the nation" of his views.

Jackson then attacked the idea of state nullification, which he termed "the strange position that any one State may not only declare an act of Congress void, but prohibit its execution . . . ." He reminded his audience that had this doctrine been established in an earlier day, "the Union would have been dissolved in its infancy." After reviewing the history of independence, the Confederacy, and the forming of the Constitution, Jackson concluded with the principle that:

> [T]he power to annul a law of the United States, assumed by one State, is *incompatible with the existence of the Union, contradicted expressly by the letter of the Constitution, unauthorized by its spirit, inconsistent with every principle on which it was founded, and destructive of the great object for which it was formed.* (emphasis added)

The bond of the Union, Jackson said, was "perpetual": "Did we pledge ourselves to the support of an airy nothing—a bubble that must be blown away by the first breath of disaffection?"

Then, Jackson turned from nullification to secession: it is argued that the Constitution is only a compact among sovereign states, and so they can break it. Jackson refuted the "compact" theory. The people, not the states, are represented by the president and vice president. Members of Congress represent the whole United States (not only their respective districts) and are paid by the United States. "[E]ach State having expressly parted with so many powers as to constitute jointly with the other States a single nation cannot from that period possess any right to secede." Interestingly, Jackson acknowledges that "secession, like any other revolutionary act, may be *morally justified* by the extremity of oppression; but to call it a constitutional right, is confounding the meaning of terms . . . ." (emphasis added).

Reminding his audience that he had been born in the Carolinas, Jackson appealed to fellow citizens of "my native State": "you are being deluded by men who are either deceived themselves or who wish to deceive you." Offering an olive branch, Jackson acknowledged that the tariff laws had an injurious effect on South Carolina, but even that was greatly exaggerated by the deceivers. Those laws might have been "unwisely, not unconstitutionally passed." Then Jackson asked South Carolinians what would be their fate if in fact they formed a separate nation. Disunion is treason and "mad"—and South Carolinians would be the first victims.

The Proclamation Regarding Nullification was at once persuasive and powerful. It was a lawyers' product—both Jackson and the Proclamation's author, Secretary of State Livingston, were lawyers—*and* a politician's product. And the threat of force, coming from the hero of the War of 1812's Battle of New Orleans, was backed up by his movement of naval forces. In addition, no other Southern state backed South Carolina, regardless of sympathies. Indeed, on February 1, 1833, the Louisiana legislature formally condemned South Carolina for its nullification efforts; it was no coincidence that Livingston, the author of Jackson's Proclamation, was from Louisiana. "Jackson maneuvered so brilliantly that the whole South massed against the Nullifiers. . . . So South Carolinians backed down . . . ."[24]

Fortunately, the Great Compromiser, Henry Clay of Kentucky, stepped forward. He worked with Calhoun[25] to secure the passage of a new Tariff Act, which provided for the gradual reduction in the tariff over ten years down to the level of the 1816 tariff, which was not controversial.[26] Ironically, Clay was a political rival of Jackson's and a supporter of protective tariffs. On March 2, 1833, the day the Compromise Tariff Act was passed,[27] Congress also passed "The Force Bill of 1833," which authorized Jackson to use armed force to suppress South Carolina if it fired a shot. South Carolina promptly enacted a Nullification of the Force Bill. Jackson wisely ignored this challenging action.

Jackson and his fellow Unionists had won[28] in the sense of committing the federal government to the principle of Union supremacy; a state could not nullify federal law.[29] But South Carolina also won, at least in the sense that it achieved its key immediate goal of reducing the tariff. The nation won in that South Carolina did not secede; but the nation lost in the sense that *the idea of secession* in the face of perceived oppression was now clearly planted, especially in the South.

The Loss of Equilibrium

The tariff issue that provoked the nullification crisis was essentially an economic issue—not an issue that excited passion, except in the hearts of a few theorists and those whose economic interests were directly affected. In contrast, the slavery issue was increasingly exciting passion. The battleground was the expansion of the United States westward and the issue was, in Calhoun's phrase, "equilibrium"—the balance between the North and the South, between slave states and free states. The Missouri Compromise of 1820 settled the issue for almost a generation. But as the nation moved into the mid-1840s, that resolution was no longer satisfactory. Broad sectionalism arose in politics and even in religion—when, for example, the Methodist Episcopal Church divided along sectional lines.[30]

The Annexation of Texas

The annexation of Texas, and the political fallout from it, may have been the critical moment when sectional momentum shifted into high gear.[31]

The Mexican province of Texas revolted in 1836 and declared itself a new republic. Pressured by a congressional resolution, President Jackson extended formal diplomatic recognition to the new Republic of Texas just before he left office in early 1837. The republic pushed to be annexed to the United States. The British government preferred that Texas remain independent in order to block the U.S. expansion into the southwest and perhaps to create a bit of a British protectorate that would be a better source for cotton, and also perhaps to end slavery there.[32]

Until the early 1840s, the issue of Texas's annexation was mainly a partisan issue: the Democrats (both North and South) were in favor, and most Whigs (both North and South) opposed. But then Secretary of State Calhoun[33] stated that annexation was necessary to strengthen slavery, an institution he believed was essential to the safety and prosperity of the South. At this point, the annexation of Texas became a Southern issue, not a partisan one.

The year 1844 was a presidential election year, and so political passions were high. James Polk, a pro-annexation Democrat from Tennessee, was elected.[34] It was clear that the slavery issue would make it impossible for a treaty of annexation to get the required two-thirds vote in the Senate for ratification. However, Tyler and Calhoun decided to bypass the treaty route by proposing a joint congressional resolution.[35] The Twenty-eighth Congress was in its final hours at the end of February 1845—Tyler was still in office until Polk replaced him in early March—and the Senate met in an evening session on February 27th to consider the joint resolution to annex Texas.[36] (The House had passed its version weeks earlier by 120–98.) Late that night, the Senate passed the resolution 27–25. Since some amendments had been made to the House version, the measure had to go back to the House, where, on the next day, the House approved the Senate's amended version, 132–76. President Tyler signed the joint resolution on March 1, 1845, three days before he left office. It was not until October that the people of Texas voted to join the Union. Sam Houston and Thomas Jefferson Rusk, Texas's first U.S. senators, and their two colleagues in the House, took their seats in Congress early in 1846.

David Wilmot, a Democrat from Pennsylvania, entered Congress as the Polk administration was getting underway in early 1846. Polk had requested an appropriation of $2 million to conduct negotiations with Mexico. It was to that measure that Wilmot introduced his famous "Proviso" that prohibited slavery in any territory acquired from Mexico as a result of those negotiations. The Northern Whigs and Northern Democrats were almost unanimously in favor, while the Southern congressmen almost unanimously opposed it. The Proviso passed the House (85–79) on a sectional vote, though it did not come to a vote in the Senate before Congress adjourned.

The Proviso led to an explosion of sectional responses, sparring sectional speeches, and bitter expressions of hostility. Calhoun called a caucus of Southern congressmen—Whig and Democrat—to meet in January 1849 in the capital. Only 48 congressmen of the 121 from slave states agreed on joint action, but this event clearly reflected the rising intensity of sectionalism. The Southerners insisted that the South should have an equal position in the territories, along with better enforcement of the fugitive slave laws. It was in this context that California sought admission as a free state; abolitionists all over the country felt a grave crisis looming.

Undeterred, Calhoun arranged for the state of Mississippi to call a convention for October 1, 1849, the Mississippi Slaveholders Convention, to address the growing threat that the federal government would place limits on the growth of slavery. Delegates denounced the Wilmot Proviso. But a Mississippi Army General, F. C. Wilkinson, set out the fundamental concern: in six to eight years, the Northern states would possess a three-fourths majority needed for a constitutional majority; by then, blacks in the Lower South would outnumber whites, and the freed slaves would precipitate a race war.[37] To avoid that catastrophe, they felt a Southern Convention was needed to counsel together for their common safety; it was agreed to hold such a session in Nashville the following June.

Delegates from nine slaveholding states[38] attended that meeting in early June 1850, just a few miles down the road from The Hermitage, Andrew Jackson's home and graveyard. None of the Border States sent delegates, nor did North Carolina and Louisiana. The delegations from Texas, Arkansas, Virginia, and Florida contained only a few members. Only the South Carolina delegation was full, the state vastly overrepresented. Despite the uneven attendance, this was the first broad gathering of Southern leaders convened to confront slavery and secession.

Radicals urged secession if slavery was restricted in the new territories, but in the end, the moderates (Whigs and Democrats) overruled the radicals. The presiding officer, Judge Sharkey of Mississippi, declared that the meeting had been called "not to prevent, but to perpetuate" the Union. Jefferson Davis was among those delegates calling for secession, and Sam Houston was among the moderates who put a lid on such talk.

The Nashville Convention declared twenty-eight resolutions, the seventh of which reminded the readers that to deny slaveholders the power to enter the territories is to deny a constitutional right, and those who would deny such a right are the "disunionists." The eleventh resolution offered, "as an extreme concession," to acquiesce in extending the Missouri Compromise geographic line westward to the Pacific. This concession contributed to the resolution that became the Compromise of 1850 less than four months later.[39]

One can easily draw a straight line from the 1850 Nashville Convention of those nine slaveholding states to the 1856 Republican Party platform demanding slave-free territories, the election of Lincoln in 1860, and the cascade of state secessions beginning with South Carolina in December 1860.

Senator Jefferson Davis denounced California's free-state constitution, noting that it was to work the California gold mines that the Spaniards first brought Africans to the country.[40] He also made clear his real concern: that for the first time there would be a permanent destruction of the balance of power between the slave and free states. Congressman Robert Toombs of Georgia asserted that if slavery was driven from the territories of California and New Mexico, "I am for disunion." Several Southerners echoed Toombs' threat. Civil War scholar James McPherson has noted: "Secession and perhaps war in 1850 over the admission of California seemed a real possibility."[41]

Henry Clay had emerged from retirement and had just been returned to the Senate by Kentucky's legislature. Concerned about disunion, Clay proposed a series of measures—which became known as the Compromise of 1850—in an omnibus bill, supported by Senator Stephen A. Douglas: admission of California as a free state, the organization of New Mexico and Utah territories without mention of slavery (to be determined by the territories when they were ready for admission), the prohibition of

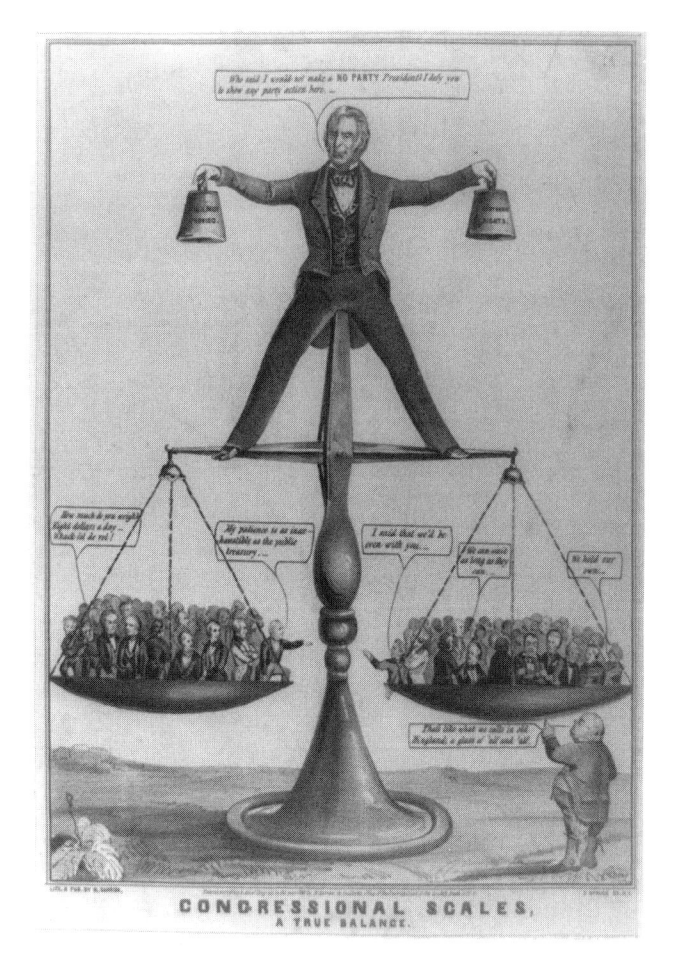

CONGRESSIONAL SCALES, A TRUE BALANCE. A cartoon satirizing President Taylor's attempts to balance Southern and Northern interest on the question of slavery in 1850.

the slave trade in the District of Columbia, and a more stringent fugitive slave law.

Senator John C. Calhoun, a lawyer from South Carolina, gave[42] one of his most famous speeches on March 4, 1850, dealing with the Clay Compromise measures. He began by noting that there is "almost universal discontent" in the South, where the people believe that "they cannot remain, as things are now, consistently with honor and safety, in the Union." The primary cause, as Calhoun put it, was that the "equilibrium between the two sections [North and South] in the government as it stood when the Constitution was ratified . . . has been destroyed." As opposed to the period of the founding, now the North had a "predominance in every department of the government." To exclude the South from the new territories "will effectively and irretrievably destroy the equilibrium which existed when the government commenced." This destruction did not come about by "the operation of time," but by legislation pushed by the North. Calhoun put the potential new imbalance at 75–25 to the South's disadvantage.

Calhoun then turned directly to the slavery issue. In the North, he reported, slavery is viewed as a sin, a crime against humanity, and a blot and stain on the character of the nation. He did not argue with those characterizations, but said that slavery in the South cannot be destroyed without subjecting "the two races to the greatest calamity, and the section [the South] to poverty, desolation, and wretchedness . . . ." If something isn't done to right the balance and to stop the agitation from the North, said Calhoun, the South will be forced to choose between abolition or secession. The only way to hold the Union together is for the North to concede to the South an equal right in the territories, and to restore the equilibrium. Finally, if we can't settle this conflict, said Calhoun, "let the States we both represent agree to separate and part in peace."

It was a powerful speech, ending with the gauntlet of secession having been laid down.

Who better to respond to Calhoun than the warhorse Daniel Webster. Three days after Calhoun's speech, Senator Webster rose in the chamber to support Clay's Compromise; his famous oration is known as the Seventh of March Address. He spoke for more than three hours, and argued that slavery was not going away in the South, and it would not take hold in the arid land of the southwest, where plantation agriculture would not flourish; he agreed that the South's rights to the return of fugitive slaves had been insufficiently protected: "In that respect, the South, in my judgment, is right, and the North is wrong."

Webster lamented the harshness of the slavery debate between the North and South, and specifically attacked the "religious" in the North who, confident of the correctness of their position, attacked the South without mercy.[43] Webster noted that the agitation in the North against Southern slavery by the abolition societies from 1835 onwards caused a backlash in the South, and as a result, "the bonds of the slave were more bound more tightly than before." The example he used was the fact that in 1832, the Virginia House of Delegates thoughtfully and openly discussed a proposal by Thomas Jefferson Randolph for gradual abolition of slavery. But after the "incendiary publications" sent South, Virginia "drew back and shut itself up in its castle"—and now emancipation could not be openly considered in any legitimate public forum.

Webster concluded also with a warning about secession: "I hear with distress and anguish the word 'secession' .... Peaceable secession! ... There can be no such thing as peaceable secession.... [It] is an utter impossibility.... I see that it must produce war ...." Thanks to the introduction of the telegraph, Webster's speech traveled throughout the nation, and won praise—except from New England, where his political base was destroyed. (For his action in support of the Compromise, Webster was included among eight senators honored for bravery and integrity in John F. Kennedy's 1955 Pulitzer Prize winning book, *Profiles in Courage*.)

In July 1850, President Zachary Taylor died unexpectedly, and his successor, Millard Fillmore, offered Webster the position of Secretary of State. Webster resigned from the Senate on July 22nd to take that post, knowing that he was unelectable in any future race for senator from Massachusetts. Webster died two years later.

Webster's speech helped to increase acceptance of Clay's Compromise; Taylor's death and the accession of Fillmore to the presidency made the Compromise more feasible. Finally, Congress passed the Compromise of 1850 as separate bills in September 1850. Both sections hoped that this would be the final solution to the question of slavery in the territories. Both hoped that the threat of secession had been turned away.

The Christiana Riot

One of the cornerstones of the Compromise was the enactment of the Fugitive Slave Act, designed to strengthen the ability of slave owners to recapture escaped slaves. Not long after its passage, its implementation led to the largest treason trial in American history, following the "Christiana Riot" of 1851.[44]

In August 1851, Edward Gorsuch, a farmer from Baltimore County, Maryland, got word that four of his fugitive slaves were living close by, near the town of Christiana, in Lancaster County, Pennsylvania. Pennsylvania had abolished slavery in 1780, and so many slaves felt they would be safe if they crossed the Mason-Dixon Line into Pennsylvania. Christiana became one of the crossroads on the Underground Railroad; many Quakers (the Religious Society of Friends) inhabited the area around Christiana, providing a sympathetic population.

Gorsuch formed a posse of five men and secured in Philadelphia the necessary papers and arrest warrants for his slaves from the Deputy Federal Marshal, Henry Kline, who accompanied the posse to Christiana. Gorsuch was relatively liberal: he had inherited slaves, but freed many and never physically mistreated them. Not atypically, he sought his fugitive slaves as a matter of principle; in exercise of his constitutional right to the return of his slaves (whom he believed had stolen from him before they fled). On the other side, dishonest slave catchers often kidnapped free Negros or freed slaves for profit, and as a result, free Negroes (and some whites, mostly Quakers) in the North formed protective organizations to guard against the dreaded kidnappers.

One of these protective organizations collided with Gorsuch's posse just outside Christiana on September 11, 1851. The one-hour "riot" left Gorsuch dead and his son, Dickinson, badly wounded. Hoping to alleviate public pressure—including the demand by Maryland Governor Louis E. Lowe for swift prosecution—federal prosecutors indicted thirty-four black and four white men in the protective organization for treason against the United States. The indictment charged that the men prevented the execution of the Fugitive Slave Law of 1850 and levied treason against the United States, having conspired to resist the laws of the United States. The trial was held November 24 through December 11, 1851, in the Circuit Court of the United States for the Eastern District of Pennsylvania. Abolitionist Congressman Thaddeus Stevens served as one of the defense counsel; Supreme Court Justice Grier served on the bench (along with District Judge Kane). The jury deliberated for less than fifteen minutes and returned a verdict of not guilty. No one was ever tried for the death of Gorsuch.

Edward Gorsuch's youngest son, Tom, never got over the fact that his father's killer had not been tried. He spoke bitterly of these feelings to his classmate at Milton Academy, a young John Wilkes Booth.[45] An inscription on the "Christiana Riot Monument," erected in the town in 1911, states: "Edward Gorsuch, he died for Law."

The Christiana Riot symbolized the sectional division of the country at that time: the North was outraged that the law favored slave owners, and the South demanded swift punishment for runaway slaves. And it had lasting repercussions; in his Message of April 29, 1861, to the Provisional Congress of the Confederate States of America (CSA), in which he announced the ratification of the Constitution of the CSA, Jefferson Davis cataloged the actions of the North that unfairly aggrieved the South. Without mentioning the Christiana case by name, Davis said:

> [T]he constitutional provisions for [the] rendition [of slaves] to their owners was [sic] first evaded, then openly denounced as a violation of conscientious obligation and religious duty . . . . [O]wners of slaves were mobbed and even murdered in open day solely for applying to a magistrate for the arrest of a fugitive slave . . . .

Secession

The issue of territories and slavery refused to go away. The Kansas-Nebraska Act of May 30, 1854, authored by Senator Stephen A. Douglas of Illinois, repealed the Missouri Compromise of 1820 and opened the way for Kansas to become a slave state and Nebraska a free one—depending on the decision of the territorial settlers themselves. This was termed "popular sovereignty," an ingredient in the package known as Clay's Compromise of 1850.[46]

This Act led to "bleeding Kansas" and to the establishment in 1854 of the Republican Party, founded by opponents of the Kansas-Nebraska Act. This occurred roughly simultaneously with the demise of the Whig Party, which had been split along sectional lines. The new Republican Party filled the vacuum left by the collapse of the Whigs, but so also did the rise of the nativist, anti-Catholic Know-Nothing party.

The election of 1856 rekindled secessionist talk. Captain John Fremont was the first presidential nominee of the new Republican Party. As the election approached, it looked as though Fremont might win, and this produced anxiety in the South. Governor Wise of Virginia suggested that if Fremont won, the South might have to consider secession. Wise called Southern governors to a meeting on October 13th, but only three showed up: North Carolina, South Carolina, and Virginia—and they did nothing. Four years later, another Republican nominee produced different results.

The Republican Party Platform was adopted at the May 16, 1860, convention in Chicago. While it acknowledged that states had inviolate rights to control their own "domestic institutions," and while it denounced "lawless invasion by armed force of the soil of any State or Territory [such as that by John Brown]," it contained a direct attack on the possibility that any of the new territories might be slave. It denounced as a "dangerous political heresy" the idea that the Constitution permits slavery into any of the territories. The "normal condition" of all the territory of the United States is that of freedom, and so "we deny the authority of Congress, or of a territorial legislature, or of any individual, to give legal existence to Slavery in any Territory of the United States."

The Democratic Party was split down the middle into two sectional parties: John Breckinridge of Kentucky represented largely the Deep South; Stephen Douglas of Illinois represented the North and Border

States. The Republicans clearly were a Northern sectional party only. The fourth party was the Constitutional Unionists, led by John Bell of Tennessee and comprised of some old-line Whigs and scattered others. None of the candidates were on every ballot in all thirty-three states. The split in the Democrats virtually ensured a Lincoln victory, and the realization of the South's worst fears.

During the summer and fall, as the campaign wore on, rumors, exaggerations, and hysteria gripped the South. Stories of plans for blacks to murder whites moved some who wavered into the secession camp. That fall, a congressman from Alabama, Jabez Curry, declared that "immediately after a Lincoln election, an abolition army of a half million Republicans planned to invade the South, lay waste its fields, free its slaves, and worst of all, 'amalgamate the poor man's daughter and the rich man's buck-nigger.'"[47] "No abstruse theory can convey the *feel* of the South's visceral hatred of the Yank."[48]

On Tuesday, November 6, 1860, Abraham Lincoln was elected with 1.8 million votes and 180 electoral votes from seventeen of the thirty-three states. (The population of the United States was 31 million, one-tenth the current 2010 population.) Douglas received 1.3 million votes (but only 12 electoral votes); Breckinridge received 0.8 million (and 72 electoral votes, from eleven of the fifteen slave states); and Bell drew 0.5 million and 39 electoral votes. Thus, Lincoln would be a minority president (in popular vote), with just over one-third of the ballots, though he received a majority of the electoral votes. The future Justice John Marshall Harlan later wrote in his reminiscences of this period that: "When the election of Lincoln was settled . . . the work of secession was begun. . . . The country literally *trembled* at the possibility of war between the Unionists and Disunionists."[49]

War

The next day, November 7, 1860, the Civil War began. It began not with a bang, but with a retreat. In today's terms, it might have been called a "cold war"—until the bang took place in Charleston Harbor on April 12, 1861, and it turned into a "hot" war. On the day after Lincoln's election, the federal infrastructure of the city of Charleston, South Carolina, began to crumble, as U.S. judges, tax collectors, and other officials resigned. On November 7th, Judge Andrew Gordon Magrath of Charleston's U.S. Federal District Court pronounced the federal judicial process legally closed. Posters appeared in Charleston showing Magrath[50] tearing off his judicial robes and firing a cannon at a law library.[51] "Here was a great political movement precipitated, not by bloody encounters in the street or upon the field, but by a deliberate and reasoned act in the most unexpected and conservative of all places—the United States courtroom."[52]

The next two months were fateful, and busy.

On November 9, 1860, President Buchanan called a cabinet meeting to consider how to deal with the serious secession threat.[53] He favored calling a general convention of all states to devise a compromise. Secretary of State Cass and Attorney General Black urged a show of force; Treasury Secretary Cobb of Georgia thought disunion was desirable and legal; Secretary of the Interior Thompson of Mississippi said that any show of force would cause Mississippi to secede; Secretary of War Floyd of Virginia opposed secession, arguing that it would not be necessary because Lincoln would be inept and would fail as a president. The *New York Tribune* proposed that the "erring sisters" be allowed to go in peace: "We hope never to live in a republic whereof one section is pinned to the residue by bayonets."

The next day, November 10th, the legislature of South Carolina passed a law calling for a convention to meet in Columbia on December 17th to consider secession. On Monday, November 12th, the New York financial markets experienced heavy selling and a sharp drop in prices. Lincoln remained silent.

In his speech to the Georgia legislature on November 14, 1860, Alexander Stephens pointed to the successful resolution of the tariff issue as a triumph of reason.[54] He argued that the slavery/secession issue in 1860 was as vexing as the tariff/secession issue of 1832. Stephens used that precedent for his argument against secession, since he felt "reason" again could triumph: "If reason and argument . . . produced such changes in the sentiments of Massachusetts . . . on the subject of the tariff, may not like changes be effected there by the same means, reason and argument . . . on the present vexed question [of slavery]?" Stephens became the vice president of the Confederate States of America three months later.

Black's Opinion and Buchanan's Response

Buchanan wrote a letter to his Attorney General on November 17th, asking for a formal legal Opinion on the scope of presidential authority to respond to an act of secession. Buchanan did *not* ask for an Opinion as to whether a state might legally secede.[55] Of course, at that point, no state had taken final secession action, but it was not difficult to foresee that prospect.

Three days later, Attorney General Black[56] provided a ten-page Opinion.[57] He began by explaining that the states and the federal governments are "independent and supreme" in their "respective spheres of action."[58] The federal government cannot "displace" the jurisdiction of a state. The fundamental duty of the president is to see to it that the laws are faithfully executed, but only as Congress directs. "He cannot accomplish a legal purpose by illegal means, or break the laws himself to prevent them from being violated by others." On the other hand, the federal government owns forts, dock yards, customs houses, etc., and the president has a right to take measures necessary to protect that property. The right to defend public property "included also the right of recapture after it has been taken unlawfully by another." Black cited the recapture of the Harpers Ferry Arsenal in late 1859 as an example.

Black then turned to the topic of the "greatest practical importance": use of the military. He told Buchanan: "you may employ such parts of the land and naval forces as you may judge necessary, for the purpose of causing the laws to be duly executed . . . ." But Black quickly cautioned that the operations of a military force "must be purely defensive. It can suppress only such combinations as are found directly opposing the laws and obstructing the execution thereof." Then, Black turned to the even more practical: what if all the federal officers in a state resign and no one is willing to take their place—no federal judges or marshals? (Black must have been aware that, at least in Charleston, the federal legal infrastructure had collapsed the day after Lincoln's election the previous month.) In that event, Black asserted, "troops would certainly be out of place, and their use wholly illegal. . . . [T]o send a military force into any State, with orders to act against the people, would be simply making war upon them."

Finally, the Attorney General got to the matter of secession. "If one of the States should declare her independence, our action cannot depend on the rightfulness of the cause upon which such declaration is based."

Black did not touch on whether secession was permitted under the Constitution, because that was irrelevant to Buchanan's power to act. Black clearly said that whether an act of secession was the "exercise of a right reserved in the Constitution, or a revolutionary movement," Buchanan did not have the authority to absolve a state from its federal obligations; he was expressing the legal opinion that the president cannot "recognize" the secession of a state. Only "Congress, or the other States in convention assembled, must take measures as may be necessary and proper." The only course for Buchanan was to continue to execute the laws by nonaggressive means, and assume that the current state of relations would continue "until a new order of things shall be established wither by law or force."

Thus, Black put the ball squarely in the court of Congress (or an assembly of the states). Does Congress have the right, or duty, to make war upon seceding states? That, said Black, is a question that only Congress can answer—but he gratuitously noted that the Constitution expressly grants no such power. He also noted that the framers of the Constitution were convinced that "military force would not only be *useless*, as a means of holding the States together, *but pernicious*" (emphasis added). Yes, Black said, the right of the federal government to *defend* against aggression upon its property or officers is undeniable, but "this is a totally different thing from an *offensive* war, to punish the people for the political misdeeds of their State Government . . . ." Gravely, Black closed his Opinion: "[T]he Union must utterly perish at the moment when Congress shall arm one part of the people against another for any purpose beyond that of merely protecting the General Government in the exercise of its proper constitutional functions."[59]

In a nutshell, Black told Buchanan, his compatriot from Pennsylvania, that he could take only defensive action, and then only to cause federal laws to be executed (assuming the court's marshals could not).[60]

On December 3rd, the lame duck session of the Thirty-sixth Congress convened.[61] The next day, President Buchanan sent his State of the Union message. Almost thirty pages, the first half is taken up with the secession issue, but then it lapses for the next seven pages into sort of a foreign affairs report (our relations with Britain are good, but not good with Mexico, etc.), and concludes with a long discussion about the territories, the budget, and tariffs. On the key issue, Buchanan's message was: the North is at fault for agitating, the South has no basis to withdraw simply because of an election; and he proposed constitutional amendments that might resolve the crisis.

Buchanan's State of the Union went on to lay much of the fault on "the incessant and violent agitation of the slavery question through-

JAMES BUCHANAN.

out the North for the last quarter of a century" inspiring the slaves with vague notions of freedom, and instilling in the hearts of other Southerners "apprehensions of servile insurrections." This sounds much like Webster's March 7, 1850, speech. As Webster had done a decade earlier, Buchanan referred to the "inflammatory" literature and "abolition sermons." In effect, he told the North to lay off: you have no more right to agitate for abolition in the South than you do for freeing the serfs in Russia or the slaves in Brazil!

Turning to the South, Buchanan said relax—this was only an election; wait for some overt act before you take revolutionary action. "[A]pprehension of future danger is no good reason for an immediate dissolution of the Union." Then he got harsher on the South; referring to Jackson's Proclamation of 1833, Buchanan said that the Union was "perpetual" and not to be annulled at the pleasure of one of the contracting states; otherwise the Union would be a "rope of sand, to be . . . dissolved by the first adverse wave of public opinion in any of the States."[62] Secession would be a "revolution against an established government, not a voluntary secession from it by virtue of an inherent constitutional right."

He referred to the *Dred Scott* decision, though not by name, and noted that the Court "solemnly decided that slaves are property, and . . . their owners have a right to take them into the common territories and hold them there under the protection of the Constitution." As a reflection of the "factious temper of the times," the "correctness of this decision has been extensively impugned before the people, and the question has given rise to angry political conflicts," said Buchanan.

What could be done? Here, one can hear the echo of Attorney General Black's Opinion. Buchanan wrote that if, in the unlikely event South Carolina attempted to expel the United States from its property there, he had ordered the commanders of the forts to act strictly on the defensive. Beyond that, the president has no power. However, said Buchanan, it was his duty to submit to Congress the whole question to decide the "momentous question whether you possess the power by force of arms to compel a State to remain in the Union." Then lawyer Buchanan felt compelled—unwisely—to offer his own opinion as to the power of Congress: none. Congress has no expressly delegated power to use coercive force against a state, and "the power to make war against a state is at variance with the whole spirit and intent of the Constitution." Once again, the voice came from Black's Opinion.[63]

In a memorable phrase, Buchanan summed up: "*Congress possesses many means of preserving [the Union] by conciliation, but the sword was not placed in their hand to preserve it by force.*" This led to Buchanan's proposal to Congress (and to the state legislatures) to provide an "explanatory amendment" to the Constitution concerning slavery. Specifically, the amendment would recognize

(a) the right of property in slaves where it may exist (now or hereafter),
(b) the duty to protect that right in territories until they became states, with or without slavery, and
(c) a clearer statement of the duties under the fugitive slave provisions.

Buchanan acknowledged that not all the Southern states would agree that this would be a satisfactory resolution, but "it ought to be tried in a spirit of conciliation before any of these States shall separate themselves from the Union." The same day, the House established a Special Committee with one member from each state to consider potential compromises.

Two days later, on December 6, 1860, in Springfield, Illinois, Lincoln read a summary of Buchanan's message, and reportedly was displeased that Buchanan had placed too much responsibility for the crisis onto the shoulders of the North. A week later, Lincoln made it clear that there could be no compromise on the question of extending slavery. In the meantime, Buchanan's cabinet was disintegrating: Secretary of the Treasury Howell Cobb of Georgia resigned on December 8th, and 78-year-old Secretary of State Lewis Cass of Michigan resigned on the 12th. In sharp contrast to the 1832–33 Nullification/Secession Crisis when the president was very strong (Jackson, a military hero, had just won reelection), poor Buchanan was at his weakest—an unpopular lame duck, whose cabinet members were jumping overboard.[64]

On December 18, 1860, Kentucky Senator John J. Crittenden, in an effort to resolve the crisis, introduced a series of proposed unamendable amendments to the Constitution.[65] The key element was an amendment that would have revived the line set in the Missouri Compromise of 1820, but extending it westward to the Pacific: slavery would be prohibited in territories north of the line and protected south of the line. One of the proposals also prohibited the abolition of slavery in the District of Columbia, so long as it existed in Maryland and Virginia, without the consent of the inhabitants and without compensation. Interestingly, one of the proposals required the United States to pay compensation to a slaveholder who was blocked by mobs or some other obstruction in his effort to arrest a fugitive slave.

President Buchanan sent a Special Message to Congress dated January 8, 1861, in which he supported the Crittenden proposals and explained that the situation was beyond the control of the Executive, and so the entire responsibility to act to deal with the emergency was in the hands of Congress—quite consistent with his Message in December. The next day, the Mississippi Secession Convention passed a secession ordinance, 84–15, and the Union's steamship, the *Star of the West*, was fired upon by South Carolina batteries as it tried to reinforce Fort Sumter.

It would be interesting to speculate about a radical alternative course that the lame duck Congress might have taken: to recognize the secession of those states of the Deep South, and negotiate arrangements for the withdrawal from federal property in those states. There would have then been no Fort Sumter attack, and perhaps in time the CSA might have rejoined the Union.

After the efforts by Crittenden did not take hold, the second major effort to seek a resolution of the crisis was initiated by the Virginia legislature. It issued a call for a meeting of delegates from all states to convene in Washington on February 4, 1861. Virginia was at that point one of the eight slave states remaining in the Union. The entire Deep South refused to send delegates, and most Northern states also failed to send delegates.

Nevertheless twenty-one states sent delegates, and 71-year-old former President (1841–45) John Tyler of Virginia presided.[66] The Peace Conference met until February 27, 1861. The Conference produced a plan in the form of proposed amendments to the Constitution quite similar to the Crittenden Compromise. The proposals were transmitted to the Congress shortly before it adjourned and the new president was sworn in.

One can wonder what would have happened if those eight slave states from the Upper South—Virginia, North Carolina, Maryland, Delaware, Kentucky, Tennessee, Arkansas, and Missouri—had decided to stay within the Union, but to form a coalition to prevent U.S. forces from attacking the states of the Deep South. Their threat would be that, otherwise, they too would secede and form a separate Confederacy of Middle America—thus partitioning the United States into three nations.

South Carolina Secedes, Then Others

At the 1787 constitutional convention in Philadelphia, Pierce Butler and John Rutledge of South Carolina clearly set forth the position of the Deep South that slavery was absolutely vital. "The implicit but unmistakably clear message underlying their position . . . was the threat to leave the union if the federal government ever attempted to implement a national emancipation policy."[67] South Carolina, in late 1860, traced its position back to the Philadelphia convention and took action.

The South Carolina Convention met on December 17th in a Baptist church in Columbia. The resolution on secession passed 159–0, but, because of an outbreak of smallpox in Columbia, the Convention adjourned to Charleston. Finally, on December 20th, the South Carolina Convention adopted the Ordinance of Secession by a vote of 169–0. That evening, the 169 delegates assembled in "Secession Hall" in Charleston, and one by one, in alphabetical order of their district, they signed the parchment document that made the Palmetto State the first to leave the

SECESSION HALL, VIEW OF INTERIOR.

Union.[68] The Ordinance was one long sentence: "We, the people of the State of South Carolina . . . declare that the Ordinance [ratifying the Constitution] is hereby repealed; and the Union now subsisting between South Carolina and other States . . . is hereby dissolved."

At the time of its secession, South Carolina had substantially more slaves than whites and more slaves than any other state: the white population was 291,722, and the slave population was 402,406 (with 9,914 "free colored"). South Carolina also had a greater percentage of slaveholders (9.2 percent) among its white population than any other state.

In the South, the news was generally received with approval, while in the North the news was received with incredulous resentment. The next day, the South Carolina congressional delegation formally withdrew, and the following day the South Carolina Convention named commissioners to deal with the United States with respect to the federal property in the state.[69] Finally, on December 24th, the Convention issued a proclamation relating the causes of the secession. It began by referring to the action of the Convention of 1832, when South Carolina threatened to secede during the nullification crisis. Essentially, the proclamation resembles a lawyer's brief in a contract law dispute: the other party broke the contract (the Constitution), and so this party has the right to terminate the contract.[70]

On December 26th, the new Union commander at Fort Moultrie in Charleston, Major John Anderson, decided that the fort was a sitting duck, and that night he took his unit to Fort Sumter three miles away in the harbor, well beyond the reach of the militias that had been gathering in the city. Those militias wasted no time in occupying Fort Moultrie and Castle Pinckney the following day. On that same day, December 27th, state authorities captured the U.S. revenue cutter *William Aiken*, and on the 30th of December, state authorities seized the U.S. arsenal at Charleston.

In mid-December Buchanan moved Jeremiah Black from Attorney General to Secretary of State. On December 31st, the British envoy in Washington, Lord Lyons, sent a Note to Secretary Black explaining that the British Consul at Charleston had reported that the U.S. Customs Houses in South Carolina had been converted into Customs Houses of the State of South Carolina, and that all duties collected are now collected for the account of that State. Lyons noted that this would lead to "certain practical difficulties" for British vessels. On January 7th, Lord Lyons told Black that South Carolina had extinguished the lighthouse and destroyed the beacons and buoys that served the entrance to Charleston harbor.

In January 1861, twenty-two forts and other federal properties were taken over by seven Southern states,[71] including seven forts in Louisiana and six in Florida. During the month of February, four more federal installations were seized or abandoned in Texas, Arkansas, and Louisiana. In March, two days before Lincoln's inaugural, a revenue cutter was seized in Galveston by Texas authorities.

Reaction and Rallies

In contrast to the time of the nullification crisis a quarter of a century earlier, when no other state actively supported South Carolina, this time, the Southern political leaders were working closely together, especially in the Deep South. For example, on December 13th—prior to South Carolina's Ordinance—seven senators and twenty-three congressmen from the South issued a manifesto urging secession and the formation of a Southern Confederacy. The advent of the telegraph—not available during Jackson's confrontation with South Carolina—made a huge difference in the ability of the Southern leaders to coordinate their policies.

The reaction in the North was somewhat uneven. There was a deep economic relationship between the South and New York City. New York dominated every aspect of the cotton market: New York banks financed the planters, the cotton was transported on New York ships (some owned by John Jacob Astor), and cotton was insured through New York brokers; Southerners traveled to New York to buy luxury goods, and married into the city's leading merchant families. (Three Lehman brothers were cotton brokers in Alabama before moving North to help establish the New York Cotton Exchange; J. P. Morgan studied the cotton trade.) Thus, New York's merchants were overwhelmingly Democratic, in sympathy with the South and its slavery.

Therefore, it was not surprising that on December 15, 1860, two thousand merchants met at Pine Street in New York City to show solidarity with the South and to seek alternatives to secession. Delegates from among these merchants went to Washington and met with President Buchanan and with Congress. Finally, on January 6, 1861, the mayor of New York City, Fernando Wood, in his annual State of the City address, proposed that New York become a "free city"—an independent city-state called "Tri-Insula."[72] The meeting between Lincoln and Wood on February 20th, when Lincoln was in New York City en route to Washington for his inaugural, was less than warm.[73] Despite the meeting, the idea for Tri-Insula went nowhere fast—it was impractical.

New York City was also the largest and most diverse market for guns, ammunition, and other war material anywhere in the Western Hemisphere. And the South took advantage of it, before hostilities began. In November 1860, months before Georgia seceded, Georgia Governor Joseph E. Brown sent agents—assisted by U.S. Army personnel from the state—to New York on a buying spree for the Georgia militia. The agents stayed at the Fifth Avenue Hotel for almost three weeks before Christmas, meeting openly with a procession of arms merchants. No one in authority interfered with their activities. They bought cannons, rifles, powder, and siege gun carriages. The *New York Times* of December 11th noted the arrival of the arms purchasers. (Commerce out of New York continued largely unobstructed until the Confederacy was formally established in February. Before then, one of the problems in efforts to block this trade was that Southern governors threatened to retaliate by seizing Northern merchant vessels in their ports.[74])

Alarmed by events, President Buchanan, in late December, *finally* called the General-in-Chief of the Army, Winfield Scott, to Washington for consultations. At that point, the military forces of the United States consisted of 1,108 officers and 15,259 men widely distributed to distant frontiers (some allege this distribution was done by Southern sympathizers[75]). It would have taken months to concentrate in Washington a force of three thousand regular troops.[76]

Mississippi Secedes

On January 9th, Mississippi seceded. Mississippi was the only state besides South Carolina that had more slaves (436,631) in its population than whites (353,899). Similarly, second only to South Carolina, Mississippi had the highest percentage of slaveholders among its white population, 8.7 percent. Mississippi's secession was followed quickly by Florida (January 10, 1861), Alabama (January 11th), Georgia (January 19th), Louisiana (January 26th), and Texas (February 1st). By February 9th, the Provisional Congress of the CSA unanimously elected Jefferson Davis as its president.

In an extraordinary speech in the Senate on January 21, 1861, Jefferson Davis[77] said his farewell—and brought tears to the eyes of all his colleagues. He began by clearly stating his view that "an essential attribute of State sovereignty [is] the right of a State to secede from the Union." In contrast, he said that he deplored the idea of nullification, because a state had no right to nullify Union law and at the same time stay in the Union; he agreed with Andrew Jackson's action to "execute the laws" in defiance of South Carolina's nullification action—but not to threaten force to prevent secession.

Davis then dealt with the slavery issue. He noted that the phrase "all men are created equal" in the "sacred" Declaration of Independence had been made the basis of the attack on the South's social system, the inequality of the races. But, he explained, the Declaration's phrase was intended to make the point that "no man inherited the right to govern," and that it obviously had no reference to slavery—since one of the charges against King George in the Declaration was that he endeavored to stir up insurrection among the slaves.[78] Thus, we have to protect the rights we inherited, "which it is our duty to transmit unshorn to our children." Davis concluded with a touching goodbye to his former colleagues in the Senate club.

Texas Secedes

Texas voted to join the Union in 1845; in early 1861, it withdrew. While only 5 percent of Texans owned slaves, the state's economic system was dependent on large plantation crops grown by slaves (although most German settlers grew vast cotton crops without the use of slaves[79]). Moreover, there was great fear of a slave uprising, fanned by Northern preachers and writers. Adding to popular discontent with the Union was the perception that Washington had "almost entirely failed to protect the lives and property of the people of Texas against the Indian savages on our border, and . . . against the murderous forays of banditti from the neighboring territory of Mexico."[80] Secession seemed attractive, even though Governor Sam Houston was strongly against it. Over his opposition, the legislature voted to hold a convention in Austin on January 28, 1861. Then, events moved too quickly for Houston to control them.

On February 1st, the convention adopted an Ordinance of Secession by a vote of 166–8.[81] The Ordinance repealed the Ordinance of 1845, which had accepted admission into the Union. (Shortly after the adoption of the Ordinance, Lieutenant Colonel Robert E. Lee, commanding the Union cavalry at Fort Mason, Texas, boarded a steamer heading for Washington.)

As in 1845, and uniquely among the states that had already seceded, the Texas Ordinance also provided for a popular referendum. That referendum was held on February 23rd, and supported secession by a vote of 34,794 for and 11,235 against.[82] The Secession Convention reconvened on March 5th and took steps for independent Texas to join the Confederacy and, at the same time, required all officeholders to swear an oath of loyalty to the Confederacy. Sam Houston refused. His Governor's Office was then declared vacant, and Houston was removed.[83]

There would be a final step in the story of the secession of Texas: a Supreme Court decision in 1869, discussed later in this chapter.

The Confederate States of America

On February 8, 1861, the Confederate States of America was formed by the six states that had seceded at that time. Montgomery, Alabama, was its capital,[84] and on February 9th, Jefferson Davis was inaugurated provisional president. On February 27th, Davis sent a letter to President Lincoln, who was still several days away from his own inauguration. The letter, "animated by an earnest desire to unite and bind together our respec-

THE DIS-UNITED STATES. OR THE SOUTHERN CONFEDERACY. This cartoon depicts the Confederate leaders as a band of competing opportunists, led by South Carolina governor and secessionist Francis Pickens (far left).

---

tive countries by friendly ties," noted the appointment of three Special Commissioners, John Forsyth (editor of the *Mobile Register*), Andre B. Roman (a former Whig governor of Louisiana), and Martin J. Crawford (a former congressman from Georgia), authorized to negotiate with the United States "all matters and subjects interesting to both nations, and to conclude" treaties.[85] On March 11th, Crawford and Forsyth requested a meeting—"an unofficial interview"—with Secretary of State William Seward, but that was denied the next day. On the 13th, they delivered a sealed document at the State Department in which they—quite amazingly—formally requested the secretary to arrange an appointment with Lincoln so they could present their credentials. Lincoln instructed Secretary of State Seward to refuse.[86]

Lincoln was inaugurated on March 4, 1861. Seven states had already seceded, all in the Deep South. Lincoln's inaugural address had many memorable, moving lines, but also many from his lawyer's pen: he had "no lawful right" to interfere with slavery in the South.[87] He discussed the legalities of the fugitive slave rights and obligations; he addressed the "contract" theory of the Union—"one party to a contract may violate it . . . but does it not require all to lawfully rescind it?"; and he stated that the Ordinances of secession "are legally void" and that "no State upon its own mere motion can lawfully get out of the Union." Just as Buchanan had asserted, and as Black had advised, Lincoln stated that the

> power confided to me will be used to hold, occupy, and possess the property and places belonging to the Government and to collect the duties and imposts . . . [though] there will be no invasion, no using of force against or among the people anywhere.

Finally, Lincoln noted that while "the strict legal right may exist" for him to enforce appointment of local federal officeholders who might have been seen as "obnoxious strangers," he deemed such an attempt to be "irritating," and so he would hold off for the time being.

Lincoln generally supported the idea of amendments to the Constitution, as a reconciliation step, but he refused to endorse any particular proposals. Similarly, he stated his refusal to "fix terms" for the separation of the states, noting that it was the job of Congress, not the president.[88]

Presumably, Lincoln adopted such a relatively noncombative position in his inaugural address because his goal was to confine secession to the Deep South, and to keep the Upper South and the Border States within the Union.[89] Perhaps a Confederacy of only seven states would not be economically viable, and they would in time be required to return to the Union. A young Ohio attorney, Rutherford B. Hayes, noted that the loss of the seven slave states appeared to be an improvement, leaving the remaining twenty-seven states to stand together with firmer strength than the "unfortunate union of thirty-four."[90]

Just seven days after Lincoln's inaugural, on March 11th, the month-long convention in Montgomery, Alabama, formed by delegates from the seven states of the Deep South, concluded and adopted the Constitution of the CSA, and elected Jefferson Davis and Alexander Stephens, president and vice president, respectively. The CSA Constitution was modeled after the U.S. Constitution, but it also reflected some changes that many argue improved upon the original. These include provisions that allowed cabinet officers the privilege of seats on the floor of the Senate and House, and most importantly, a single six-year term for the president. This change, in the words of the new CSA vice president, was to "remove from the incumbent all temptation to use his office or exert the powers confided to him for any objects of personal ambition."[91] On the other hand, the CSA Constitution had as its "cornerstone" the absolute inequality of the races, and that slavery of the African Negro was, as Stephens asserted, "his natural and normal condition."[92]

Fighting Begins

South Carolina fired on Fort Sumter on April 12, 1861.[93] One prominent scholar of the period takes the view that Lincoln's plan to send unarmed supply ships to the fort, and to communicate their innocent status to Governor Perkins, put the CSA in a tough spot without good countermoves. If the CSA let the Union ships into the harbor, it would imply that South Carolina really had not withdrawn from the Union; on the other hand, if President Davis ordered the supply ships sunk—and the men in the fort left to starve—the Upper South fence-sitters would be appalled. Lincoln "now sat at the poker table with a pair of aces, waiting for the Confederate president to fold or to raise the ante. Davis ordered the fort destroyed before the ships arrived."[94] And the rest is history—the U.S. Commander surrendered the fort on April 14, 1861, thirty-four hours after the bombardment began. There were no casualties in this first military engagement of the American Civil War.

A Negotiation Attempt

Prior to those tragic events at Fort Sumter, an odd "back channel" dialogue took place involving two U.S. Supreme Court Justices. At a dinner party on February 10th, Justice John A. Campbell of Alabama and the future Secretary of State William H. Seward talked about their shared desire to preserve the Union. Campbell suggested that a constitutional amendment protecting slavery, coupled with the acceptance of New Mexico as a slave state, would restore the South's confidence in the Union. Seward was interested, but he said that he was not yet in the cabinet, and so he could do little.[95]

A month later, on March 15th, Campbell happened to run into Supreme Court Justice Samuel Nelson of New York, as they were walking on Pennsylvania Avenue not far from the White House. Nelson told Campbell that Jefferson Davis had sent three Commissioners, but neither Lincoln nor Seward would see them. The two Justices then went to Seward to urge him to meet with the CSA Commissioners as a way to ease tensions.[96] Seward said he could not meet with them, but that Lincoln was planning to abandon Fort Sumter in an effort to ease tensions. Campbell then volunteered to act as an intermediary between Seward and the

CSA Commissioners. This began a series of exchanges between Campbell and the Commissioners in which Campbell assured them that Seward promised that Fort Sumter would be abandoned. The two Justices met with Seward on March 22nd, and Seward and Campbell met again on April 1st.

The Commissioners visited Campbell on April 7th, explaining that they had heard enough of Seward's promises and assurances—which they finally came to conclude were a mask to hide Lincoln's real plan to buy time to mount a naval force to defend or supply Sumter.[97] The Commissioners withdrew from Washington on April 11th. Justice Campbell was grief stricken. He sent Lincoln a letter of resignation from the Court on April 26th.

Virginia's Secession and the Formation of West Virginia

In Virginia, Lincoln had the help of a unionist Democratic governor, John Letcher. Letcher was from the northwestern part of the state, which held a majority of Virginia's white population and less than 20 percent of its slaves. Letcher used his inaugural address in January 1860 to urge sectional reconciliation through a national convention. A year later, January 1861, the state legislature accepted Letcher's call for what later became the Washington Peace Conference, and it seemed possible that Virginia could be kept in the Union. His strength began to wane as the Deep South appeared to prepare for war, and as Congress failed to act on significant compromises.

On April 15th, immediately following the Confederate attack on Fort Sumter, Lincoln called for troops—his request of the remaining Union states to provide a combined total of seventy-five thousand men to put down the rebellion was, in effect, a declaration of war. From Virginia's perspective, Virginians had been called to kill South Carolinians. "Only when Lincoln called up the troops, to destroy the people of a state's alleged right to withdraw their consent, did disunion consume Virginia. . . . Southerners' visceral loathing of Yankees turned Lincoln's coercion into a summons to disunion."[98]

Governor Letcher's efforts collapsed. The Virginia Convention met on April 17th and voted (88–55) for an Ordinance of Secession, but those voters from Letcher's northwestern counties rejected secession by a comfortable majority.[99] The Ordinance was put to a popular referendum on May 23rd, and it was confirmed by a vote of 132,290 to 37,451. The referendum voters in the northwestern counties rejected secession 3 to 1.[100] The great Lincoln scholar, David Herbert Donald noted: "The whole process of portioning Virginia was extraordinarily complicated and largely extralegal . . . ."[101]

During Lincoln's inaugural address, in dealing with the "right" of a minority to withdraw, he said:

> [I]f a minority . . . will secede rather than acquiesce [in a decision of a majority], they make a precedent which in turn will divide and ruin them, for a minority of their own will secede from them whenever a majority refuses to be controlled by such a minority. For instance, why may not any portion of a new confederacy a year or two hence arbitrarily secede again . . . .

How prophetic he was—at least in the case of Virginia/West Virginia.

On May 13, 1861, just before the referendum on the Virginia Ordinance of Secession, delegates from the northwestern counties met in Wheeling, West Virginia. Some argued for the formation of a new state, but others properly pointed out that Virginia's secession had not yet been ratified, and so such action would constitute revolution. They met again in the Second Wheeling Convention on June 11th, after the popular referendum confirmed Virginia's secession from the Union. The delegates decided that the Secession Convention was illegal, all its acts were void, and the offices of those who adhered were declared vacant. A referendum in the western counties on October 24th approved all acts of the Wheeling Convention.

A "Restored Government of Virginia" was established, and a new "governor" was elected, Francis H. Pierpont, along with two new U.S. Senators, W. T. Willey[102] and John S. Carlile.[103] All three were lawyers. The Thirty-seventh Congress admitted those "elected" by the Wheeling Restored Government of Virginia, thereby officially recognizing only the Union-led government of seceded Virginia.

As federal armies secured parts of Virginia, the Wheeling "restored" government would replace local Confederate officials with Union men. The Pierpont administration later left Wheeling and spent the rest of the war "under the shelter of federal guns at Alexandria."[104]

A Third Wheeling Convention was held November 1861 to February 1962, and on February 18th, it adopted a Constitution for a new state of West Virginia. A referendum in April approved that Constitution, 18,862 to 514. Governor Pierpont of the Restored Government of Virginia, on May 13, 1862, called the General Assembly into session, and it technically gave its approval for the separation of the western counties and the creation of the new state. Thus, at that point, there were three state governments in Virginia: the Pierpont government in Alexandria loyal to the Union, another in Richmond—a constituent member of the CSA, and a third in West Virginia loyal to the Union.[105]

The new state of West Virginia applied for admission to the Union, and on July 14th, the Senate approved the bill[106] 23–17. On December 10th,[107] the House approved by a similar margin of 96–55. In the Senate, only one Democrat supported the action, and in the House, not a single Democrat. The most contentious part of the admission bill was a requirement that West Virginia change its Constitution, which was vague about the status of Negroes.[108] The proposed revision, known as the "Willey Amendment," named for the U.S. senator from the Restored Government of Virginia who drafted it, provided for gradual emancipation.[109] The Act admitting West Virginia was to come into force sixty days after the president issued a proclamation confirming that the appropriate change had been made to the new state's Constitution.

The legislation landed on Lincoln's desk. He was troubled by the issue, and, on December 23rd, Lincoln formally asked his cabinet members for their written views on the constitutionality and the "expediency" of the bill.[110] Seward, Chase, and Stanton replied affirmatively to the two questions. Welles, Blair,[111] and Bates responded negatively to both questions. Thus, Lincoln's advisers were divided equally on this key issue. Governor Pierpont telegraphed Lincoln urging swift signature of the bill and threatening dire consequences if Lincoln vetoed it.

The idea of recognizing a "restored" government of Virginia was, in part, designed to provide a path or template for the restoration of the seceded states. The western counties of Virginia were also considered important as a route for the Union armies to move into the heart of the Confederacy, and to sever the east–west transportation links of the CSA. But the introduction of separate statehood and the slavery issue that it brought with it made this a delicate and highly controversial issue. The wind was largely out of the sails of the supporters of the new state by the time the statehood bill was introduced in Congress.[112]

On December 27, 1862, Attorney General Bates issued a formal Opinion[113] in response to Lincoln's request. It was quite candid. Bates advised that the "bill in question is unconstitutional; and also by its own demerits, highly inexpedient." Bates reminded Lincoln that the Constitution provides that no new state could be formed within the jurisdiction of a state without the consent of the legislatures of the two states.[114] Congress has no power to *make* states, but only to *admit* states. This had been the clear practice.[115] Bates argued that a state should not "be blotted from the map" by form over substance. He continued by saying that

> everybody knows—that the government of Virginia . . . is a government of necessity . . . intended only to counteract the treacherous

> perversion of the ordained powers of the State . . . . It is a provisional government . . . . That object was not to divide and destroy the State, but to rehabilitate and restore it.

Bates noted that the government of Virginia only represented about one-fourth of the state, and that same population also represented the new proposed state of West Virginia. Bates asked rhetorically: "Is that honest legislation? Is that a legitimate exercise of a constitutional power, by the legislature of Virginia?"

Bates concluded by noting that "no reflecting man will seriously affirm that 'the legislature of Virginia' which, at Wheeling, on the 13th of May, 1862, gave *its* consent (not the consent of Virginia) to the dismemberment of the Old Commonwealth, was, in truth and honesty, such legislature of Virginia as the Constitution speaks of . . . ."[116] Finally, Bates stated:

> It is a very grave and important thing to cut up and dismember one of the original States of this nation . . . ; and if we must do it, it behooves us to *know* that we are acting within the letter of the Constitution, and with decent respect for the forms of law.

This was powerful language from the president's very distinguished lawyer.

On December 31, 1862, the day before he signed the final Emancipation Proclamation, Lincoln signed the West Virginia statehood bill. He issued an explanatory memorandum at the same time and stated that, while the admission was more of a question for Congress than the president, he would not evade his role. The question, he noted, was whether admission would help or hurt the restoration of the Union. Of course, those in Virginia would be happier to consider returning to the Union if their state were not cut up. But the overarching point was that the Union "can scarcely dispense with the aid of West Virginia in this struggle . . . . The division of a State is dreaded as a precedent. But a measure made expedient by a war is no precedent for times of peace."

Then Lincoln closed with his famous line:

> It is said that the admission of West Virginia, is secession, and tolerated only because it is our secession . . . . Well, if we call it by that name, there is still difference enough between secession against the constitution, and secession in favor of the constitution.[117]

Lincoln later told Governor Pierpont that it was the governor's telegram earlier that month that was the turning point for him. Lincoln reportedly said to himself "this is not a constitutional question; it is a political question. . . . I will not trouble myself further about the constitutional point, so I determined to sign it."[118]

On February 17–18, 1863, the West Virginia Convention reconvened and adopted the Willey Amendment to the West Virginia Constitution. On April 20, Lincoln issued his proclamation formally confirming that West Virginia had complied with the condition in the Act, and declaring that the Act would become effective in sixty days.[119] Accordingly, the new state of West Virginia was admitted on June 20, 1863,[120] and on July 4, 1863, a new star was added to the American flag.[121]

West Virginia Secession into the 20th Century

A curious debate took place concerning whether the counties of Berkeley and Jefferson belonged to Virginia or to West Virginia. In January 1863, the Restored Government of Virginia held an election to determine to which state the counties belonged. The dispute ended up in the Supreme Court in the case, *Virginia v. West Virginia*, decided in 1870.[122] Justice Miller, a Lincoln appointee, wrote the opinion of the Court. West Virginia believed those two counties fell within its jurisdiction, and the Court held that they did and that the U.S. Congress had consented to that jurisdiction at the time it admitted West Virginia. The dissent was written by Justice Davis, also a Lincoln appointee, in which Justice Clifford (a Buchanan appointee) and Justice Field (another Lincoln appointee) joined.

When the separation of West Virginia was accomplished, no arrangement was made concerning the respective share of Virginia's pre-war debt that should be borne by West Virginia. Virginia claimed that West Virginia should be responsible for one-third of the debt, since it comprised one-third of the territory of the original state of Virginia; West Virginia offered to assume less of the debt, based on the proportion of the funds that were actually spent in West Virginia. Negotiations failed. Virginia in 1906 brought the first of nine cases to the Supreme Court, *Virginia v. West Virginia*.[123] In the end, the division was made on the basis of property values, excluding slaves, at the time of separation; on this basis, West Virginia owed one-fourth of the debt. It was not until 1919 that West Virginia finally admitted liability and began making payments. It completed its payments in 1939.

Is Secession Legal?

During the buildup to the Civil War, most people in the South and in the North had clear—and totally different—opinions as to whether secession was legal.[124] There seemed to be more common ground on whether a state had a "revolutionary right" to withdraw if the Union or other states were engaged in a gross violation of that state's rights; the only remaining question for those who held that view was whether the actions of the North were oppressive enough to warrant exercising this revolutionary "right." In the end, of course, the issue was permanently settled by the War.

Texas Secession and the Supreme Court

In a case decided well after the War ended, the Supreme Court, unsurprisingly, ruled that secession was illegal. The case was *Texas v. White*,[125] argued on February 5, 1869, and decided five weeks later. The case was brought by the state of Texas to recover bonds that had been transferred to George W. White and others. The issue of the validity of Texas's secession arose because it had a bearing on whether the Court had jurisdiction. The Court decided (5–3) that Texas had no right to secede, its Ordinance of Secession was null and void, and Texas had remained a state of the Union.

The case was a complicated one, involving finance and fraud. In 1851, The United States issued $10 million bonds payable to the state of Texas, or bearer, as compensation for certain boundary claims. Half of the bonds were held in the U.S. Treasury, and the other half were held by the state; the bonds paid interest and were redeemable in 1865. The Texas legislature provided that no bonds should be available in the hands of any holder without the endorsement of the governor. In early 1861, the "insurgent" legislature—as the Court termed it—repealed the Act requiring the governor's endorsement. It also established a "military board" to provide funds for the defense of the state by means of any bonds in its treasury. That board entered into a contract in January 1865 with Messrs White and Chiles for the sale to them of certain of these bonds, and in exchange they were to provide cotton and medicines. None of those bonds had been endorsed by the governor.

In February 1862, the U.S. Secretary of the Treasury—Salmon Chase, who at the time this case reached the Supreme Court, was the Chief Justice and who wrote the majority opinion[126]—learned of the deal in

Texas the year earlier concerning the transfer of the bonds, and thereafter refused to pay on any bonds that had not been endorsed by the governor of Texas. After the War, in October 1865, Texas notified the financial public, via notices in the press,[127] that the transfer of the bonds had been a conspiracy between the rebel government and White and Chiles to rob the state, and that they had fled and in fact had provided nothing to the state in payment. In October 1866, the Texas governor was authorized to recover the bonds, and he then brought suit to enjoin White and Chiles from seeking or receiving payment from the United States, and to deliver the bonds back to Texas.[128]

This relatively mundane commercial dispute brought into the open the issue of the legitimacy of Texas's secession: *if* Texas, at the time of filing its complaint, was *not* a state of the United States, the Court would have no jurisdiction and would have to dismiss the action. Did Texas cease to be a state or a member of the Union when it seceded? The Court was clear in its answer:

> The Constitution . . . looks to an indestructible Union, composed of indestructible States. When . . . Texas became one of the United States, she entered into an indissoluble relation. . . . The act which consummated her admission . . . was something more than a compact . . . . The union between Texas and the other States was as complete, as perpetual, and as indissoluble as the union between the original States. There was no place for reconsideration, or revocation, except through revolution, or through consent of the States.
>
> . . . [T]herefore . . . the ordinance of secession . . . ratified by a majority of the citizens of Texas . . . [was] absolutely null.

The Court found that Texas continued as a state after seceding even though its rights were "suspended" during the War, and the current lawsuit was instituted by competent authority.[129] The Court, therefore, had jurisdiction and could decide the merits. The Court agreed with Texas, and the injunction was issued against the bondholders.

In a strong dissent, Justice Grier said that, politically, Texas was still not a state—Texas and Louisiana constituting the Fifth Military District[130]—but was, during the War and still, akin to a territory. Territories do not have the right to the Supreme Court's original jurisdiction, and so Grier argued the case should be dismissed. Cleverly, Grier noted that Texas sought to annul a contract based on the claim that there was no authority competent in Texas to enter into the contract during the rebellion, but at the same time Texas claims to be a competent state to bring suit in the Court. The Ordinance was "ill-advised," but it was still the act of a sovereign state; Texas cannot now plead insanity and set aside her contracts. Justices Swayne and Miller concurred that Texas did not have the capacity to maintain an original suit in the Supreme Court.

The *Texas v. White* decision is remembered and often cited for finding secession illegal; however, that issue was not really central to the final decision.

Secession in Today's World

Since the decision in *Texas v. White*, the issue of secession has not arisen in any serious way in the United States,[131] and so the Supreme Court has not had an occasion to address the issue. However, another North American court was confronted with the issue in the late 1990s: the Supreme Court of Canada, in its August 1998 decision in the matter of *Reference re Secession of Quebec*.[132]

In 1980, Quebec held a referendum on whether it should negotiate sovereignty for the province and establish an economic union with the remaining Canadian provinces. The referendum was defeated. Quebec held a second referendum in 1995, prior to which the National Assembly of Quebec enacted a bill that laid out Quebec's plan for secession, if it won the referendum: if the negotiations with Ottawa and the other provinces failed, Quebec would simply proceed with secession and seek international recognition. The referendum failed by a slight majority; as the *Economist* put it, the "referendum on independence . . . was lost by a margin as thin as a maple leaf, with 49.4 per cent voting in favour."[133]

As a result of this activity, the governor in Council (the cabinet) submitted a request for an advisory opinion[134] to the Canadian Supreme Court: Can Quebec secede unilaterally under the Canadian Constitution? Under international law, does Quebec have the right to secede unilaterally? And, in case of a conflict between the Constitution and international law on this point, which should govern? No question was submitted relating to whether Ottawa was authorized to use force to prevent unilateral secession.

Quebec refused to take part, but the Court appointed an *amicus curiae* to argue for the secessionist view. The *amicus* lawyers argued "in elegant French" that the procedure of reference was unconstitutional, and that the constitutional question was conjectural, political, and therefore nonjusticiable. On the substance, the *amicus* argued that in extraordinary circumstances there might be a peaceful and lawful but revolutionary change in government, taking the form of secession from Canada, even though the event defied the old constitutional order.[135] The *amicus* lawyers failed.

The Court's fifty-page Advisory Opinion concluded that (1) unilateral secession was *not* legal under the Canadian Constitution:

> Quebec could not, despite a clear referendum result, purport to invoke a right of self-determination to dictate the terms of a proposed secession

to the other parties to the federation. The democratic vote, by however a strong majority, would have no legal effect on its own, and could not push aside . . . the rule of law [or] the rights of individuals and minorities . . . in the other provinces or in Canada as a whole. . . . [But, on the other hand the] other provinces and the federal government would have no basis to deny the right of . . . Quebec to pursue secession . . . so long as in doing so, Quebec respects the rights of others.

The Court also concluded that (2) the right of self determination (the right to secede) understood in international law was meant for "peoples" under a colonial rule or under foreign occupation,[136] and did not apply to component parts of sovereign states wishing to secede from the parent state. The "right of self determination" was expected to be exercised within the framework of existing states, by negotiation, since the state representing the whole of the people is entitled to the protection of its territorial integrity under international law.

The Court did not have to reach to the third question, since it found no conflict between the Canadian Constitution and international law. However, it did conclude with a wise and very practical statement:

> Although there is no right . . . to unilateral secession, the possibility of an unconstitutional declaration of secession leading to a *de facto* secession is not ruled out. The ultimate success of such a secession would be dependent on recognition by the international community, which is likely to consider the legality and legitimacy of secession . . . in determining whether to grant or withhold recognition.

In short, acting lawfully is important, and illegal actions will likely have significant consequences.

Quebec professed to be pleased with the opinion, because it validated the referendum approach, and because it made clear that Ottawa and the other provinces would have to negotiate with Quebec after a winning referendum on secession. Ottawa professed equal pleasure with the opinion, since the Court had made it clear that Quebec could not declare its independence unilaterally.

The decision of the Canadian Supreme Court is, of course, not binding on the United States. But it does reflect modern, clear, and wise thinking with respect to the secession issue, taking into account the last two centuries. Interestingly, the 1998 Canadian Supreme Court's decision sounded eerily similar to the statements of President Buchanan and his Attorney General in December of 1860.

The Continuing Debate

The issue of secession under international law was recently illuminated by the International Court of Justice—the principal judicial organ of the United Nations, commonly called the "World Court"—in an Advisory Opinion rendered on July 22, 2010.

The Serbian province of Kosovo unilaterally declared its independence from Serbia on February 17, 2008. Almost seventy countries recognize that independence, but Russia, China, India, and five European Union countries do not. In the fall of 2008, Serbia proposed a Resolution in the General Assembly to request the Secretary General to seek an Advisory Opinion from the International Court of Justice as to whether Kosovo's declaration of independence was in accordance with international law. The vote was 77 in favor, 6 opposed (including the United States) with 74 abstentions. The question to the Court was not about the legal consequences of the declaration, or whether Kosovo had achieved statehood thereby, or whether the recognition of Kosovo was legal or valid by those countries that had previously recognized it.

The specific question asked was narrow, and so was the answer. The Court decided: (1) unanimously, that it had jurisdiction to render the advisory opinion, (2) by 9 to 5, that it should comply with the request, and (3) by 10 to 4, that Kosovo's declaration of independence did not violate international law.

The case dealt with two cardinal principles of international law: the territorial integrity of states (such as Serbia) and self-determination (for Kosovo's Albanian majority). The principle of territorial integrity has been embodied in international law for several centuries, but it was only in the last sixty years that the international law of self-determination developed to create a right to independence for the peoples of non-self-governing territories and peoples subject to alien subjugation, domination, and exploitation. The World Court decided that it was not necessary in this case—the first secession case before the Court—to resolve the question of whether the international law of self-determination confers upon part of the population of an existing State the right to separate from that State.

While the decision of the International Court of Justice was narrow, it is apt to encourage aspirations among separatists in the Basque County and Catalonia in Spain, Nagorno-Karabakh, Tibetans and Uighurs in China, and others.

CHAPTER 5

The Conflict Between the Chief Justice and the Chief Executive: *Ex Parte Merryman*[1]

***Inter arma silent leges**[2]*

Rarely does the clash of ideas on the scope of governmental authority get reduced to a direct conflict between leaders of the branches of government. However, early in the Civil War period, the Chief Executive and the Chief Justice directly confronted each other. The stakes were high, the issues related to the conflict between national security and personal liberty.

The Beginning

Just before noon on Tuesday morning, the fourth of March, 1861, in the Senate chamber, Vice President Breckinridge[3]—as president of the Senate—called to order the final moments of the Second Session of the Thirty-sixth Congress and made a courteous farewell speech. He then turned the proceedings over to Lincoln's running mate, Hannibal Hamlin, who spoke briefly. Breckenridge then administered the oath of office to Hamlin. The entourage proceeded to the central portico, where Lincoln took his place in the front row; behind him sat President Buchanan, and behind Buchanan sat Chief Justice Taney and the Associate Justices of the Supreme Court. There had been some rain in the morning, but it had cleared.

Edward Dickinson Baker, Lincoln's old lawyer friend from Springfield, now a senator from Oregon, introduced the president-elect.[4] Lincoln rose and spoke to the thousands of people for about thirty minutes. His speech was both a political leader's effort to allay the fears of Southerners, and a lawyer's brief on the application of the Constitution to the issues of the day—from slavery[5] to secession[6]—as well as a statement of determination to preserve the Union.[7] He concluded with the lofty language that has become so famous:

> The *mystic chords of memory*, stretching from every battlefield, and patriot grave to every living heart and hearth-stone all over this broad land, *will yet swell the chorus of the Union when again touched*, as surely they will be, *by the better angels of our nature* (emphasis added).

Midway through his speech, however, Lincoln launched an attack on the Supreme Court. He began in a low key noting "the position assumed by some" that constitutional questions are to be decided by the Supreme Court, and that such decisions must be binding—but then he cleverly confined the binding nature of those decisions only "upon the parties to the suit." Lincoln then cautioned that even erroneous decisions ought to be respected on the chance that they might be overruled later.[8] Having eased his way into a discussion of the Supreme Court, Lincoln then struck at the heart of the Court's authority:

> [T]he candid citizen must confess that if the *policy* of the government upon *vital questions*, affecting the whole people, is to be irrevocably fixed by decisions of the Supreme Court, the instant they are made, in ordinary litigation between parties, in personal actions, *the people will have*

ceased to be their own rulers, having to that extent practically resigned their government into the hands of that eminent tribunal (emphasis added).[9]

> ## The Continuing Debate
>
> Almost exactly a century later, the Supreme Court was confronted with the same proposition: the governor of Arkansas argued that he was not bound by the decision in *Brown v. Board of Education*,[10] and President Eisenhower dispatched troops to Little Rock's Central High School to ensure the admission of Negro students. The legal issue was decided unanimously by the Supreme Court in the 1958 desegregation case of *Cooper v. Aaron*[11] in which the Court quoted three former Chief Justices—John Marshall in 1803, Roger Taney in 1859, and Charles Hughes in 1932—on the proposition that a state cannot ignore the Supreme Court's interpretation of the Constitution.[12] Ironically, Justice Felix Frankfurter, in his concurring opinion in the *Aaron* case, referred to Lincoln's appeal to "the better angels of our nature" in Lincoln's inaugural speech—but Frankfurter conveniently overlooked Lincoln's effort in that same speech sharply to narrow the role of the Court.[13]

Having attacked the Court, Lincoln quickly made a tactful qualification. He said that he intended no "assault" upon the Court or the Justices. It is their duty to decide cases; it is not their fault "if others seek to turn their decisions to political purposes."

The abolitionists and many Northerners could construe Lincoln's remarks as a message that they should keep their powder dry and await some changes on the Court—Justices nominated by Lincoln—that would lead to more agreeable decisions on fugitive slaves and other contested issues. Southerners, on the other hand, could have interpreted his message as a guarantee that prior decisions would be obeyed. And, of course, the clear message to the Court itself was: don't meddle in broad policy; just settle private disputes.

The Associated Press[14] report of the inaugural ceremonies remarked that, during the delivery of Lincoln's remarks, "Judge Taney seemed very much agitated, and his hands shook very perceptibly with emotion." The largest Baltimore newspaper quoted the AP report, and then opined: "Coming events in that solemn hour must have cast their dark shadows before the mental vision of the venerable Chief Justice; and no wonder he trembled with emotion."[15] The same newspaper editorialized that the South had received Lincoln's inaugural as a declaration of war.

Whatever impact Lincoln's inaugural speech had on Taney, both men then stood face-to-face on the steps of the Capitol building—under the partially constructed great dome—and Chief Justice Roger B. Taney administered the oath of office to the new chief executive, Abraham Lincoln. After that solemn moment, Taney congratulated Lincoln amid the loud applause of the crowd.[16]

A World of Difference

In almost every respect, the differences between Lincoln and Taney were striking.

Physically, the president and the Chief Justice could not have been more different. Lincoln had just turned fifty-two a few weeks earlier, while Taney was in his eighty-fourth year. (Taney was a boy of twelve when the federal government came into being.) Taney looked like the incarnation of Old Age: feeble, dark, and hollow, his back stooped. Lincoln, of rail-splitter fame (or fable), was tall and sturdy and looked fit.

In terms of experience, they both had been successful practicing lawyers,[17] but they were at opposite ends of their political careers. Lincoln had been a local politician and an Illinois state legislator. His single term in the Thirtieth Congress was at best undistinguished. Lincoln was elected president with less than a majority of the national popular vote. Taney, in contrast, had been Attorney General of Maryland, Attorney General of the United States, and Secretary of the Treasury. Andrew Jackson appointed Taney in 1836—the year before Lincoln was admitted to the Illinois bar—to serve as Chief Justice upon the death of the illustrious John Marshall. (Taney and Marshall, serving sequentially, presided as Chief Justice for sixty-three years—almost the entire life of the Court.)

Their respective backgrounds were quite different. Lincoln was a Whig turned Republican, whereas Taney was a Jacksonian Democrat. Taney was well educated, a 1795 graduate of Dickinson College—the same college attended by President Buchanan—where he studied Greek, Latin, and science. Lincoln's lack of formal education is legendary, but was best characterized by Lincoln himself: when he went to Congress, he was asked to provide relevant information for the Congressional Directory. After listing his date and place of birth, he indicated that his profes-

CHIEF JUSTICE ROGER B. TANEY.

sion was lawyer, but for the category of "education," he stated simply "defective."

Lincoln was not quite wealthy, but he was clearly well off. His law practice had been successful with a concentration in representation of major western railroads.[18] Taney, after so many years of public service, clearly was not wealthy. Indeed, he continued to work because he needed the income to support himself. (At that time there was no pension for federal judges.[19]) Taney was a devout Roman Catholic; the nature of Lincoln's religious faith is not entirely clear, though he was a believer in God. Lincoln's personal opposition to slavery is beyond question, though he was content to take no action against slavery where it existed, since it was protected under the Constitution. Taney inherited slaves—Maryland was a slave state until near the end of the Civil War—but out of conviction, he freed them, "aided them in their employments, and took care of them when they were in want."[20]

Lincoln was homey and charming. He had a seemingly inexhaustible fund of stories, many of them humorous, often with sharp barbs attached. People seemed to enjoy his company. To those who did not know him, especially in his last years, Taney seemed cold, aloof, distant, too cerebral, and not tender enough. On the other hand, those who knew him closely had a totally different impression. Justice Samuel F. Miller of Iowa[21] was appointed by Lincoln to the Supreme Court in mid-1862. Miller acknowledged that before he came to the bench and personally met Taney, he "hated" him for being the Court's chief spokesman in the *Dred Scott* case and for Taney's role in support of President Jackson's attack against the Bank of the United States. However, Miller stated that "before the first [T]erm of my service in the Court had passed I more than liked him; I loved him. And after all that has been said of that great, good man, I stand always ready to say that conscience was his guide and sense of duty was his principle."[22]

The greatest difference between Lincoln and Taney is apparent in the way they are viewed today: one is deified,[23] while the other is vilified.[24]

Their History

When Lincoln and Taney looked at each other that March morning on the Capitol steps, their thoughts could well have been simple and ordinary: Lincoln assessing how the crowd had taken his inaugural speech, and Taney focusing on the pain in his joints. They had met a week earlier, on February 25th, when Lincoln paid a courtesy call on the Supreme Court in the Capitol Building chambers. That encounter was described as "dignified and free of rancor."[25] Neither man left a record of his thoughts at that moment, but it is possible to speculate.

Lincoln might have turned his mind's eye back more than two decades to the time he first directly encountered the Chief Justice. While he served in the House in the late 1840s, Lincoln continued his law practice back in Illinois with his partner, William Herndon. Just after the end of the Thirtieth Congress, but before returning to Illinois, Lincoln served as co-counsel in an obscure case involving whether litigants in a land transaction were barred from suing because of an amendment to an Illinois statute of limitations. Thus came the opportunity for Lincoln to argue his first case before the U.S. Supreme Court—*Lewis v. Lewis*.[26] Lincoln's side lost. Chief Justice Taney wrote the opinion of the Court.

It is also possible that Lincoln thought about the infamous *Dred Scott* decision,[27] in which Taney wrote the main opinion in the 7–2 split decision. Lincoln used that decision as a bludgeon on the political stump—it had deeply upset the abolitionists in the North—and to temporarily satisfy the South. Lincoln might also have been reminded of the Court's decision in *Ableman v. Booth* almost exactly two years earlier, on March 7, 1859, in which Taney wrote for a unanimous Court that federal enforcement of the Fugitive Slave Act could not be interfered with by state process.[28] (The controversy over the Fugitive Slave Act was so great that Lincoln addressed it at some length in his inaugural speech, even quoting the entire text of the fugitive slave provision in the Constitution.)

Taney might have been thinking of a case then currently before the Court concerning whether the Court should require the governor of Ohio to turn over to the governor of Kentucky a person (a free man of color) indicted in Kentucky for the crime of assisting a slave to escape. (Less than two weeks later, on March 13th, Taney wrote the opinion for a unanimous Court that held that there was no power in the federal government to compel that action.[29])

Being a practical politician, Lincoln likely wondered when the Old Man was going to step down from the Court, or be removed by death, so that Lincoln would have the chance to nominate a Chief Justice of his liking—a Chief who could be relied upon not to throw legal roadblocks into Lincoln's path during these difficult times. An abolitionist senator from Ohio, Ben Wade, is quoted as having prayed every night during the Buchanan administration that Taney's life might be spared until a Republican president had the opportunity to appoint his successor. Wade eventually remarked that he had overdone the prayers, since Taney—with tenacious viability—stayed in office until late 1864.[30]

Taney probably had little, if any, recollection of *Lewis v. Lewis*, and probably no remembrance of the young Mr. Lincoln's role as counsel for the losing side. But Taney too may well have thought of the *Dred Scott* case: he may have been reminded of it by the presence on the Capitol's portico of Lincoln's choice for Postmaster General, Montgomery Blair, who had served as counsel for the slave Dred Scott.

Taney previously had administered the presidential oath of office to eight men: Van Buren, Harrison, Tyler, Polk, Taylor, Fillmore, Pierce and, exactly four years earlier, Buchanan. Some of those had not been very successful as president, but none had had to confront disunion—at the time of Lincoln's swearing in, seven Southern states had already claimed to have seceded from the Union. Taney must have wondered whether this odd-looking man from the West would be up to the job. As an old Maryland politician, Taney knew that Lincoln had received a minority of the national popular vote in the four-way race with Vice President John C. Breckinridge, John Bell, and Stephen Douglas, but also in particular that he had come in a very distant fourth behind those three in Taney's home state of Maryland.

The Arrest of John Merryman

Ten weeks after Lincoln's inauguration, late on Saturday, May 25th, a petition for a writ of habeas corpus was presented to Chief Justice Taney at his rented rooms on Indiana Avenue in Washington by Maryland attorneys George M. Gill and George H. Williams. They explained that they were counsel for John Merryman, and that they had just sworn to the petition in front of the U.S. Commissioner in Baltimore. Gill and Williams further explained that at two o'clock that same morning, Merryman had been abducted from his bed in his home outside Cockeysville, north of Baltimore, by a detachment of soldiers led by a Lieutenant Abel, stationed at Relay House on the Northern Central Railroad. Merryman had been taken by train to Baltimore, and then by hack to Fort McHenry, where by nine o'clock that morning, Merryman was locked up.

The lawyers explained that they had visited Merryman at the fort. Merryman reported to them that, since his arrest, he had been informed

FORT MCHENRY, BALTIMORE, MARYLAND.

that he had been arrested on an order from "one General Keim, of Pennsylvania" whom he did not know. It was alleged that Merryman was the captain of some militia company of Baltimore County, but Merryman said he never heard of that company. Finally, the person now detaining Merryman "in close custody" was Brevet Brigadier General George Cadwalader.

MAJOR GENERAL J.B. CADWALADER.

Merryman had signed his petition for a writ of habeas corpus in front of his lawyers during their interview at Fort McHenry. The petition concluded:

> Your petitioner therefore prays that the writ of Habeas corpus may issue to be directed to the said George Cadwalader commanding to produce your petitioner before you, judge as aforesaid with the cause, if any, for his arrest and detention, to the end that your petitioner be discharged and restored to liberty, and as in duty.

All access to Merryman was denied except for his counsel and his brother-in-law.

The lawyers had come to Taney for relief because at that time, Supreme Court Justices also sat as Federal Circuit Court judges, and Taney's assigned Fourth Circuit included Maryland.[31] That was fortuitous for Merryman, since Taney had deep Maryland roots. It was no small irony that Fort McHenry—in which Merryman was imprisoned—was the setting, during the War of 1812, for the *Star Spangled Banner*, based on a poem written by Taney's late brother-in-law, Francis Scott Key, who had been a prominent Washington lawyer.[32] Merryman's lawyers had assumed that Taney would order that Merryman be brought before him in Washington.

John Merryman, age 37, was from a distinguished Maryland family that had come to Maryland before 1650. He lived on a five-hundred-sixty-acre estate called "Hayfields" near Cockeysville, north of Baltimore. It was a cattle farm that raised Timothy hay; hence the name "Hayfields." (The estate, in 1998, became the Hayfields Country Club and golf course.) Merryman was long active in the Maryland militia, having been a Third Lieutenant of the Baltimore County troops in 1847; and by early 1861, he was a First Lieutenant of the Baltimore County Horse Guards. Tall and handsome, Merryman was a prominent citizen and president of the Maryland State Agricultural Society.

On Sunday, May 26th, the day after Merryman's lawyers met with Taney in Washington, Taney went to Baltimore where he could deal more conveniently with the Merryman petition for the writ, since all the potential parties were there.[33] In particular, Taney recognized that it would be awkward to direct the General to leave Fort McHenry and come to Washington—beyond the limits of his military command. One of Merryman's lawyers, Williams, presented Taney with a sworn statement explaining that he had gone to Fort McHenry earlier that Sunday, and obtained an interview with General Cadwalader. Williams sought permission to see the papers (and to copy them) under which the General was detaining Merryman. Cadwalader replied that he would "neither permit the deponent [Williams], though officially requesting and demanding, as such counsel, to read the said papers, nor to have or make copies thereof."

Taney ordered that a writ of habeas corpus be issued, and the Clerk of the Circuit Court complied. The writ commanded General Cadwalader to appear at the federal courthouse the following morning, Monday, May 27th at eleven o'clock, and that he bring John Merryman with him. At four o'clock that Sunday afternoon, the deputy U.S. Marshal served the writ on General Cadwalader at Fort McHenry.

The Continuing Debate— Habeas Corpus

The writ of habeas corpus was developed early in English common law as an order issued by the courts in the name of the monarch to control public authorities within the kingdom. The full name of the Great Writ in medieval Latin is *habeas corpus ad subjiciendum* (we command that you have the body). By the seventeenth century, "it was recognized as a safeguard of personal liberty. A person arrested was entitled to have a court issue this writ to his custodian, directing the custodian to produce the prisoner in court and explain the reason for his detention."[34]

The common law writ was put into statutory form in the English Habeas Corpus Act of 1671, was included in the list of basic liberties in the Northwest Ordinance of 1787 under the Articles of Confederation,[35] and made its way into Article I, Section 9, of the U.S. Constitution (the Article that dealt with the powers of the Congress), the only common law process mentioned in the Constitution:

> The Privilege of the Writ of Habeas Corpus shall not be suspended, unless when in Cases of Rebellion or Invasion the public safety may require it.

It was then elaborated in U.S. statute form as Section 14 of the Judiciary Act of 1789,[36] The writ of habeas corpus was also enshrined in the Constitution of the Confederate States of America; in 1862, the Confederate Congress empowered President Jefferson Davis to suspend the writ in parts of the Confederate States of America (CSA) endangered by enemy attack.[37] Prior to the Civil War, the writ was also used as a device to free fugitive slaves.

The Supreme Court in June 2008 devoted fourteen pages in an opinion to an account of the history and origins of the writ. Justice Kennedy, speaking for the Court, noted:

> [P]rotection for the privilege of habeas corpus was one of the few safeguards of liberty specified in a Constitution that, at the outset, had no Bill of Rights. In the system conceived by the Framers the writ had a centrality that must inform proper interpretation of the Suspension Clause.[38]

On the morning of Monday, May 27, 1861, Taney entered the old Masonic Hall on St. Paul Street, leaning on the arm of his grandson. At precisely eleven o'clock, he took his seat at the bench in the courtroom. Word had spread quickly throughout the Baltimore area of the impending controversy, and the courtroom was thronged by members of the bar and the public eager to learn of the General's response. Twenty minutes later, an aide-de-camp of General Cadwalader's, a Colonel Lee, appeared in full military regalia, including red sash and sword, under instructions from General Cadwalader.

George Cadwalader, 57, was from a famous Philadelphia family. His grandfather was a brigadier general who had served under George Washington during the Revolution, and his father was a lawyer who also was a major general in the Pennsylvania militia during the War of 1812. George Cadwalader practiced law in Philadelphia, except for a period during the Mexican War in 1846—then he was commissioned Brigadier General of volunteers and received awards for gallantry. After the war, he returned to his law practice. In 1861, the governor appointed him Major General of State volunteers, until May 15th, when he assumed command at Fort McHenry.[39] General Cadwalader's brother John, younger by a year, was also a highly regarded Philadelphia lawyer. During the Buchanan administration, John was appointed to the United States District Court for the Eastern District of Pennsylvania.[40] Judge Cadwalader's grandson many years later was reported to have said, "if Judge John had issued the writ [in the Merryman case], he would have damn well made his brother obey it."[41]

Colonel Lee read a statement from the General to the Chief Justice. Cadwalader explained that *he* had not arrested Merryman, but rather his arrest was on the orders of Major General Keim and a Colonel Yohe, and that Merryman had been brought to Fort McHenry by a Lieutenant Abel acting on their orders. He further explained in his statement that Merryman was charged with various acts of treason and that Merryman was ready to cooperate with those engaged in the "present rebellion" against the government of the United States. Finally, Cadwalader stated that he wanted to inform the Chief Justice that he was "duly authorized by the president of the United States . . . to suspend the writ of habeas corpus, for the public safety." While there is no record of any reaction to that alarming news, one could imagine an audible gasp in the packed courtroom. Cadwalader concluded by requesting that Taney "postpone further action upon this case, until he can receive instructions from the president of the United States . . . ."

His task completed, Colonel Lee handed the General's statement to the court clerk and made a move to sit down. One of Merryman's lawyers (George Gill), however, suggested to Taney that Colonel Lee ought to inform them if he had produced the body of John Merryman, as commanded by the writ.[42] (A good lawyer always wants to ensure that the official record is unambiguous so that there can be no room for speculation later by opposing parties.) Thus, in an almost theatrical step, Taney then interrogated Colonel Lee and asked whether he had brought with him the body of John Merryman. Lee replied that his only instructions were to deliver the General's statement. Taney responded by inquiring: "The commanding officer declines to obey the writ?"[43] Lee, in effect, threw up his hands and noted that his duties and powers ended after providing the General's statement.

Taney noted that the General had been commanded to produce Merryman before him that morning so that the case might be heard, and that Merryman might either be remanded to proper custody or be set at liberty. However, said Taney, the General "has acted in disobedience to the writ . . . ." Therefore, Taney said he would order a writ of attachment for contempt according to which General Cadwalader was to appear before Taney at noon the next day, Tuesday, May 27th.

Of course, there was little expectation that the General would appear before Taney at noon the next day. But there was speculation that the General might do something to Taney. While in Baltimore, Taney stayed at the Franklin Street home of his eldest daughter, Anne, and her husband J. Mason Campbell, a prominent member of the Baltimore bar. On leaving his daughter's house the next morning, Taney said that it was likely he would be imprisoned in Fort McHenry before the day was over.[44]

Taney's anticipation of personal danger was well founded: in the months ahead, the military imprisoned the mayor[45] and chief of police of Baltimore, a member of Congress, thirty-one members of the Maryland legislature, and several newspaper publishers and editors. Five months later, Secretary of State Seward recommended that Judge Richard B. Carmichael, a judge of the circuit court in Easton, Maryland, be arrested. Carmichael's arrest was delayed until the following May, but it was dramatic: federal troops apprehended him in his courtroom, with a trial in progress, beating him over the head with a revolver butt.[46] Judge Carmichael was held at Fort McHenry for five months. Ironically, Judge Carmichael's father had shared rooms in Annapolis with a young Roger Taney.

The Political Context: The Events Between March and May

A great deal had happened between Lincoln's inaugural on March 4th and that Sunday, May 26th, when the writ of habeas corpus was served on General Cadwalader in Fort McHenry. April was a particularly busy month.

On April 14th, Fort Sumter surrendered. The next day, Lincoln issued a proclamation calling for the states to supply seventy-five thousand men, and he summoned a special session of Congress for July 4th.

Marylanders were divided on the slavery issue and on secession, but generally the sentiment was to remain in the Union and to remain a slave state. Marylanders were quite willing to protect the national capital from Southern attack, but at the same time, there was very little support for the notion of launching attacks against their neighbors in Virginia. The notion of "permitting" Maryland to be used by troops from the North as a base for an attack on Virginia also made them uncomfortable—in part because of the fear that Maryland, in turn, would become a battleground. Only a generation before, in the War of 1812, Maryland had been the scene of brutal attacks by British forces.[47]

Most rail traffic to Washington from the North passed through Baltimore. Baltimore, the third largest city in the United States, had a well-deserved reputation for unruly mobs and violence.[48] Lincoln, of course, understood the "problem" of Baltimore. Just two months earlier, as he was on his way to Washington from Illinois, rumors of an assassination effort in Baltimore caused his security advisers to insist that he pass secretly through Baltimore in the middle of the night.[49] Political cartoonists had a field day. Lincoln was depicted hiding in a rail boxcar dressed in a Scotch plaid cap and a long military coat, being frightened by a cat.[50] His stealthy transit through Baltimore remained personally and politically embarrassing to Lincoln. At an address exactly three years later in Baltimore, Lincoln noted "three years ago the same soldiers [who were among the audience] could not so much as pass through Baltimore. The change from then till now is both great and gratifying."[51]

A Baltimore ordinance prohibited locomotives from running through the city. Thus, trains coming south from Philadelphia to Washington on the Philadelphia, Wilmington & Baltimore line terminated at the President Street Station, where the rail cars were hitched to horses and drawn along tracks through the city, along Pratt Street to the Camden Station,

The Conflict Between the Chief Justice and the Chief Executive 139

just over a mile away along the harbor. (The site of the Camden Station is now the home of the Baltimore Orioles baseball team, Oriole Park at Camden Yards.) At the Camden Station, the cars were then attached to a locomotive to head south to Washington on the Baltimore & Ohio line.

On April 18th, a regiment of Pennsylvania troops from Harrisburg changed trains in Baltimore under the eyes of a raucous crowd of thousands.[52] Police Marshal George Kane employed one hundred thirty policemen to escort the soldiers successfully down Eutaw Street from the Bolton Station to the Camden Station, where they headed to Washington. Governor Hicks and Baltimore Mayor George W. Brown immediately wrote to Lincoln—and then sent a telegram—and said "send no troops." Lincoln misunderstood the message, and thought that Hicks and Brown meant that they could manage the handling of more troops passing through Baltimore without the need of federal assistance.[53] Hicks and Brown, of course, meant to say "send no more troops through Baltimore."

On April 19th, as Lincoln issued a proclamation blockading all Confederate ports, the Sixth Massachusetts Volunteer Militia, seven hundred armed men, arrived at the President Street Station in Baltimore and began the horse-drawn transit.[54] The first several rail cars successfully made the haul along Pratt Street westward over to the Camden Station, though growing crowds taunted the soldiers in the rail cars as they were towed along the route. The soldiers were ordered to get off the train and march. Suddenly, all hell broke loose when the taunted soldiers opened fire. George William Brown,[55] the mayor and a staunch antislavery advocate, tried to calm the mob, and even joined at the head of the soldiers' line; Police Chief Kane eventually rescued the soldiers. While the soldiers were firing into the crowd, they were vastly outnumbered—the police surrounded the soldiers and escorted them to safety. When the day was over, at least sixteen were dead, four soldiers and twelve civilians.[56] *These were the first fatalities of the Civil War.*

These events became known as the "Pratt Street Riot," a phrase coined in the North. To Southerners, it might have been known as the "Pratt Street Massacre," since most of the deaths were civilians who were killed in their own city by soldiers from Massachusetts. Those civilians were viewed as martyrs, having given their lives trying to prevent the state of Maryland being used as transit for Northern troops en route to attack the South. The headlines in the *Baltimore Republican* cried: "Our Citizens Shot Down by the Ruffian Black Republicans—Our Streets Drenched with Blood by Lincoln's Hirelings—A Foreign Soldiery Passing Through." When he learned the news from his native state, 22-year-old James Ryder Randall, who was teaching in Louisiana at the time, wrote "Maryland, My Maryland" to the tune of "O Tannenbaum." The lyrics

PRATT STREET RIOT. The sixth regiment of the Massachusetts volunteers firing into the people in Pratt Street, while attempting to pass through Baltimore en route to Washington, April 19, 1861.

imply that Lincoln was a "despot" and a "tyrant," and refers to the "patriotic gore that flecked the streets of Baltimore." (A friend and classmate of Randall's was one of the civilians killed on Pratt Street.) "Maryland, My Maryland" was adopted as the official state song in 1939.[57]

In St. Mary's County in southern Maryland, where the people were not known for their loyalty to the Union, the largest public meeting ever held in the county—upwards of a thousand citizens—convened on April 23rd. One of the resolutions adopted by the assembly noted that:

> [W]e mourn over the graves of our fellow citizens who lost their lives in the City of Baltimore, while heroically and even without arms defending our common rights and the seal of our State from the pollution of the steps of the enemies of both the mercenary soldiers of Massachusetts—and have thus taught that bigoted and fanatical people that there can be a "Lexington" elsewhere than on their soil, which now disgraces its sacred memories.[58]

The "Lexington" reference was a pointed nod to the first military engagement of the American Revolution in April 1775. But a more direct parallel reference might have been to the Boston Massacre, when, in March 1770, a civilian mob of hundreds taunted British soldiers who had been sent to reinforce the local colonial government, and five civilians were killed. (Nine British soldiers were prosecuted for murder, but seven were acquitted, and two were found guilty of manslaughter; John Adams, later the second president, was the chief counsel for the defense of the British soldiers.)

In the end, however, the key event was not the "riot," but rather the actions taken by the civic authorities *after* the shootings.

That same night, April 19th, the governor, the mayor, and other important citizens convened a mass meeting in the center of Baltimore. Mayor Brown then learned that more troops were en route by train— likely from the Maryland militia—and he knew that the explosive mix in Baltimore could produce an even greater catastrophe. As a result, the mayor and the Board of Police Commissioners met and decided to order the burning of railroad bridges north of the city. Isaac Ridgeway Trimble, a West Point graduate, was commissioned by Baltimore Mayor George Brown as commander of the local militia when the Civil War broke out. After the Pratt Street Riot, Trimble "was ordered to 'burn the draws' of the bridges belonging to the Philadelphia, Wilmington, and Baltimore railroads and the Northern Central Railroad so as to prevent further troop movements south through the city. Wisely, he demanded written military orders commanding this action from the Mayor and Governor of Maryland . . ."[59] Pursuant to these orders, John Merryman participated in the burning of the bridges. Armed Marylanders forced a Pennsylvania regiment to turn back at Cockeysville. In the meantime, the mayor rushed to Washington to meet with President Lincoln. General Winfield Scott advised Lincoln that the best immediate solution would be to send troops around Baltimore rather than through it, and Lincoln agreed. On Sunday, April 21st, Lincoln assured Mayor Brown and others from Baltimore that troops coming through Maryland would not be used for any aggressive action against Southern states.

The 8th Massachusetts Regiment, under the command of General Benjamin F. Butler,[60] a Massachusetts lawyer, took the water route around Baltimore to Annapolis and continued by rail to Washington, as proposed by General Scott. Thus, the immediate pressure on Washington was relieved, since troops from the North could get to Washington's defense with relative efficiency. On April 20, 1861, Secretary of the Navy Welles telegraphed the U.S. Naval Academy at Annapolis to defend Old Ironsides (the USS *Constitution*), which served as a floating classroom for the midshipmen; if the venerable ship could not be protected, Welles ordered that it should be destroyed.[61] It was a great symbol of the country, and Welles would rather see it destroyed then fall into the hands of the Confederacy. That instruction produced a comical event: on April 21st, lawyer-turned-General Benjamin Butler arrived at Annapolis with a ferryboat to transport his 8th Massachusetts, when the superintendent of the Academy asked Butler whether he had come to "save the *Constitution.*" Butler, of course, thought he meant the document, the Constitution, and said: "Yes, that is just what I am here for."[62] It took a few moments to clear up the confusion.[63]

On April 22nd, Governor Hicks scheduled a special session of the Maryland legislature to meet on the 26th in Frederick, since General Butler and his troops were occupying the state capital at Annapolis. In Washington, it was feared that the legislature would adopt a secession ordinance, and in Annapolis, General Butler threatened to arrest any secessionist-minded legislator.

On April 25th, Lincoln ordered Commanding General Winfield Scott not to interfere with the Frederick meeting of the Maryland legislature. But, Lincoln added, Scott was to watch to see whether the legislators decided to arm the state against the Union, and in that event, Scott could order: "*the bombardment of their cities—and in the extremist necessity, the suspension of the writ of habeas corpus*" (emphasis added). This is the first Lincoln document in which habeas corpus is mentioned. This order was not made public.

On April 27th, Lincoln issued an order to Scott specifically authorizing him to suspend the writ to protect the military transit line that had been used by General Butler—the water route around Baltimore to Annapolis, continued by rail to Washington. The order stated: "If . . . you find resistance which renders it necessary to suspend the writ of Habeas Corpus . . . , you, personally or through the officer in command at the point where the resistance occurs, are authorized to suspend that writ."[64]

Like the order of April 25th, this letter to General Scott was not made public, and no one informed the courts or other civil authorities.[65]

On May 10th, Lincoln for the first time *publicly* suspended the writ of habeas corpus by formal proclamation, but it was confined to an order to the Commander of the Union forces on the Florida coast. The proclamation noted the existence of an insurrection in Florida, and then directed and authorized the Commander "if he shall find it necessary, to suspend the writ of habeas corpus . . . ." The idea seems to have been that, having seceded, the citizens of Florida no longer had any rights under the Constitution. This first public suspension of the writ caused little comment, presumably because its focus was confined to the remote areas of coastal Florida.

On May 13th, General Butler—acting on his own authority—established occupation of the city of Baltimore with men from the Massachusetts 6th, the same regiment involved in the April 19th riot. (Butler was a flamboyant character, and acting without instructions was not unusual for him.) The following day, General Scott relieved Butler of his command, but Baltimore remained under military occupation for the duration of the War.

On May 14th, just before he was moved out of Baltimore and at the adjournment of the Maryland General Assembly, General Butler ordered the arrest of Ross Winans. Winans was one of the richest men in Maryland, a prominent inventor, who had been elected in April 1861 to represent Baltimore in the Maryland General Assembly. Winans also was an outspoken secessionist. Winans' lawyer, John Latrobe, immediately enlisted the services of Reverdy Johnson, one of America's greatest constitutional lawyers and a former U.S. senator, who, like Lincoln, had been a Whig. Not coincidentally, Johnson later also happened to be a Union Democrat who supported Lincoln—with whom and against whom Johnson had litigated many a railroad case. Johnson rushed from Baltimore to Washington, and within forty-eight hours he had an Executive Order releasing Winans.[66]

On May 23rd, Virginia formally ratified its ordinance of secession, and the next day Lincoln ordered thirteen thousand federal troops to cross the Potomac River and to occupy Alexandria, Virginia.

It was against the background of these events that Merryman's arrest took place on the early morning of May 25th.

Taney's Decision

As reported by Baltimore's largest circulating newspaper,[67] the morning of Tuesday, May 28th saw "an immense concourse of persons assembled on St Paul Street in the neighborhood of the US Courthouse building, all manifesting the most intense anxiety on the result of the case of habeas corpus for Mr. John Merryman."

At the appointed hour of noon, Taney again took his seat in the courtroom and called for the Marshal. The Marshal, charmingly named Washington Bonifant, reported that he dutifully had gone to Fort McHenry earlier that day, but he had not been permitted to enter the gate, and so he could not serve the writ on the General. Taney noted that the Marshal had the power to summon a *posse comitatus* to aid him in bringing the General to court, but he excused the Marshal, since the General clearly had superior power.[68] Faced with this deadlock, Taney said that he had ordered the writ of attachment the day before because it was the duty of the military officer to turn Merryman over to civil authority, and failing that, it was "very clear that John Merryman . . . is entitled to be set at liberty and discharged immediately from imprisonment." Taney explained that he had decided the previous day not to state the full legal reasoning for his position, because he feared that such an oral statement might be misunderstood. He promised to put his opinion in writing and to file it with the Clerk of the Court later in the week. Finally, the Chief Justice said that he would order his written opinion and the papers filed in the case, "to be laid before the president, *in order that he might perform his constitutional duty, to enforce the laws, by securing obedience to the process of the United States*" (emphasis added). Taney did so on Friday, June 1st.

The Written Opinion

The opinion of the Chief Justice, together with the accompanying petitions and writs, comprises about twenty pages. The opinion came from Taney's own hand; at that time there were no brilliant young law clerks to prepare drafts for the Justices. At times, the opinion speaks in the first person; at other times, it reviews English history. But overall, it presents an overwhelming case for the proposition that Lincoln had seriously overstepped his bounds. It is an excellent piece of *legal* analysis and writing. It is also an excellent *political* document.

Taney began with the barest statement of the facts—of course, presented in the way most favorable to his conclusion—which, he noted, General Cadwalader did not deny:

> [A] military officer, residing in Pennsylvania, issues an order to arrest a citizen of Maryland, upon vague and indefinite charges, without any proof.... [H]is house is entered in the night, he is seized as a prisoner, and conveyed to Fort McHenry .... [A]nd when a habeas corpus is served on the commanding officer ... the answer of the officer is that he is authorized by the president to suspend the writ ... at his discretion ... and on that ground refuses obedience to the writ.

Taney then made his statement more personal. As he understood the case, Taney said, the president not only claims the right to suspend the writ of habeas corpus himself—at his sole discretion—but also claims the right to *delegate* that power to a military officer and leave it to that officer to determine whether he will or will not obey judicial process. Then Taney put his finger on one of the key flaws in Lincoln's action: the president never gave notice to the courts[69] or to the public, by proclamation or otherwise, that he claimed that power. Referring to the statement of General Cadwalader conveyed by Colonel Lee, Taney remarked in a near theatrical fashion: "I certainly listened to it with some surprise, for I had supposed it to be one of those points of constitutional law upon which there was no difference of opinion . . . ." Constitutionally, the writ could be suspended only by an act of Congress. Taney reacted, in his opinion, as though the General had said the world was flat.

Taney concluded: "the president has exercised a power which he does not possess under the constitution." However, "a proper respect for the high office" of the president, made it necessary for the Chief Justice to state fully the ground of his opinion—to demonstrate that he had not ventured to question the legality of Lincoln's action without a careful examination of the whole subject.

The Chief Justice's substantive opinion began with an effort to construe the Constitution relying on where, in that document, authority is granted. He concluded that the placement of the suspension power in Congress's hands (i.e., in Article I) is "expressed in language too clear to be misunderstood by anyone . . . ." Then he engaged in a review of English history, quoting Blackstone at length. It was relevant to explain the understanding of the relationship between liberty and habeas corpus by the framers of the Constitution at the time when they were still subjects of the Crown:

> If the president of the United States may suspend the writ, then the constitution of the United States has conferred upon him more regal and absolute power over the liberty of the citizen, than the people of England have thought it safe to entrust to the crown; *a power which the Queen of England cannot exercise at this day*, and which could not have been lawfully exercised by the sovereign even in the reign of Charles the First.

Taney's reference to Charles I might have been calculated irony. King Charles I was brought down in a trial by the presiding judge, John Cooke. Cooke was a man of principle who took the job of prosecuting the King even though no one else wanted it. Cooke's innovation—far ahead of his time in the mid-1600s—was to assert the primacy of the law over all, including the King. (Charles I had brought on two civil wars and was accused of conspiring to start a third.[70])

Turning to American experience, Taney referred to the 1806 Aaron Burr conspiracy and President Jefferson's deferring to Congress, in that instance, the question of whether or not *Congress* should suspend the Writ of Habeas Corpus.[71] "And in the debate which took place upon the subject, no one suggested that Mr. Jefferson might exercise the power himself, if, in his opinion, the public safety demanded it."[72]

Taney quoted at length from Justice Story's definitive *Commentaries on the Constitution*[73]—Story had served with Chief Justice John Marshall and with Taney—and quoted from an opinion in which Marshall says the suspension decision is one for the Congress.

Having established a powerful demonstration of legal authority in support of his position, Taney then broadened his scope and turned somewhat political. He claimed that this was not merely a case of an erroneous suspension of the writ, but rather a situation in which the military thrust aside the judicial authorities, "and substituted a military government in its place, to be administrated and executed by military officers." The courts were open in Baltimore, and the district attorney of Maryland was available. Nevertheless,

> a military officer, stationed in Pennsylvania, without giving any information to the district attorney, and without any application to the judicial authorities, assumes to himself the judicial power in the district of Maryland; undertakes to decide what constitutes the crime of treason or rebellion; what evidence . . . is sufficient to support the accusation . . . and commits the party, without a hearing, even before himself, to close custody, in a strongly garrisoned fort . . . .

These actions, Taney pointed out, clearly violated a number of fundamental personal liberty rights protected under the Constitution.[74]

This led Taney to raise the issue, in effect, of whether a military coup had taken place, or whether the President had created a military dictatorship.[75] He concluded: if indeed these fundamental Constitutional rights can be suspended and disregarded and "usurped" by the military power, "*the people of the United States are no longer living under a government of laws, but every citizen holds life, liberty and property at the will and pleasure of the army officer in whose military district he may happen to be found*" (emphasis added).

Having presented both the legal and the political arguments, Taney rested his case.[76] He confronted the hard reality that he had exhausted all his constitutional power, but noted that his disagreement with Lincoln's order was "a force too strong for me to overcome." Taney then quickly offered an escape route, a face-saving way out for the president: "It is possible that the officer . . . may have misunderstood his instructions, and exceeded the authority intended to be given him . . . ." Lincoln merely had to note that indeed the General had misunderstood his instructions, and the controversy would have disappeared.

Taney explained again that he would arrange for the opinion and other documents of the proceedings to be transmitted to the president—from the Chief Justice to the Chief Executive. Then Taney squarely laid the burden on Lincoln "to determine what measures he will take to cause the civil process of the United States to be respected and enforced." This is so because the president has the constitutional obligation to "take care that the laws be faithfully executed."[77] In effect, Taney exercised his authority to state the law, but it was exclusively in the hands of the Executive to discharge his duty, since Taney had no coercive means to compel the president to act. This was exactly the position that Taney had taken just a few months earlier, when he delivered the opinion for a unanimous Court in *Kentucky v. Dennison*, where Taney explained that the governor of Ohio had a constitutional duty to obey an extradition request from the governor of Kentucky, but that the Court had no power to use "coercive means to compel him" to do so.[78]

It was a masterful performance by the 84-year-old Chief Justice.

An Unavoidable Confrontation?

Was it necessary for Taney to confront Lincoln directly by throwing down the gauntlet? Or did he have other options?

The most obvious alternative course of action would have been for Taney to suspend further action in the case in order to give Lincoln time to provide proper instructions to General Cadwalader. Indeed, in the General's statement to Taney presented by Colonel Lee on May 27th, Cadwalader expressly and respectfully requested exactly that. In Taney's statement of the facts in his written opinion, however, he conveniently neglected to mention the General's request for additional time.

It is not unlikely that Taney chose not to take that temporizing course because he felt it would be pointless. Enough time had already elapsed between the arrest on that Saturday morning and the Court session on Tuesday for Cadwalader to get all the instructions he needed. Moreover, in Taney's view, the clarity and the nature of the wrong—the deprivation of Merryman's liberty, the usurpation of power by the military, and the flaunting of the judicial process—were so overwhelming that the matter simply could not be deferred. Such a wrong had to be stopped dead in its tracks. And Taney, as Chief Justice, was the only person who could legitimately put the issue squarely on the president's shoulders.

Nevertheless, Taney was wrong to act so quickly. Merryman was not in mortal danger. His accommodation at Fort McHenry was not a dank dungeon, but rather an airy room on the second floor. Taney could have waited another week before making his decision; that would have been sufficient time for the General to receive new instructions from Washington and perhaps for the creation of a plausible cover story of misinterpretation of the previous instructions. In short, this would have gotten Lincoln off the hook. Taney's legitimate worry over the powerful danger to constitutionally protected liberties posed by Lincoln's actions could—and should—have been suspended for a week. If Lincoln continued to stonewall, Taney's position would have been even stronger.

Did Taney have any other options? None that were realistic or safe. For example, he had the authority to order the U.S. marshal to gather a force of men to attempt to storm the gate at Fort McHenry. That would have made for dramatic newspaper copy, but it also might have caused a dangerous mob scene with civilians and soldiers battling each other, as had occurred with lethal horror the previous month in the center of Baltimore. In any event, the Union military forces would overwhelm any effort of a marshal. Of course, if Taney had wanted public theater, he could have gone personally to Fort McHenry and nailed the writ of attachment to the gate, as Martin Luther did with his theses. But Taney was not interested in provoking that sort of dramatic confrontation. He did, however, want to make a public statement that would have the effect of not allowing Lincoln to wiggle off the hook.

Lincoln's Response

Silence.
      Not a public word from the Chief Executive.
      Until the Fourth of July.
      On that day, Lincoln sent a detailed written Message to Congress convening in the Special Session that he had called in mid-April. (Without a Special Session, Congress would not be scheduled to meet until December.[79]) Congress heard the President's Message the next afternoon from a clerk who read it in a dull monotone.[80] The Message began with a lengthy review of events since Lincoln's inaugural (Fort Sumter, the establishment of the Confederate "capital" in Richmond, and Lincoln's call for troops), and then asked Congress for more men and more money. The second half of the Message was devoted largely to a detailed and powerful political and legal argument against the legitimacy of secession. Here Lincoln employs pithy phrases, accusing the South of "insidious debauching of the public mind" and engaging in "ingenious sophism." One can sense the hand of a confident politician, a master on the stump.
      About one-third of the way into the Message, Lincoln dealt with the *Merryman* problem, though he never referred to the case by its name. The tone is totally different in this section than the rest of the message: it is strained and awkward and does not suggest confidence. Lincoln brought the recitation of events up to his proclamation of the April 19th, 1861 Blockade, then drew a line at those actions: "So far all was believed to be strictly legal." Then he briefly ventured into a second category of presidential actions: the call for volunteers to expand the military. "These measures, whether strictly legal or not, were ventured upon, under what appeared to be a popular demand, and a public necessity; trusting, then as now, that Congress would ratify them. It is believed that nothing has been done beyond the constitutional competency of Congress." In effect, Lincoln was explaining that all the actions he had taken up to that point were legal (category one), or almost legal and at least not beyond the power of Congress to ratify (category two).
      It was at that point that Lincoln moved to a third category of presidential action—suspending the writ of habeas corpus. He explained in the indirect passive voice that "it was considered a duty to authorize the Commanding General . . . to suspend the privilege of the writ of habeas corpus . . . ." Even though, he argued, this authority had been exercised "very sparingly," the legality and propriety "are questioned"—never identifying the Chief Justice as the questioner—and the country's attention

had been drawn to the proposition that "one who is sworn to 'take care that the laws be faithfully executed,' should not himself violate them." Once again, Lincoln did not attribute the quoted remarks to Taney. It must have pained Lincoln to acknowledge this charge against him.

Lincoln pointed out that there was resistance to the faithful execution of the laws in one-third of the country. Then Lincoln raised some of his famous rhetorical questions, one of which became the title of the late Chief Justice William H. Rehnquist's 1998 book, *All The Laws But One*:[81]

> [A]re all the laws, but one, to go unexecuted, and the government itself go to pieces, lest that one be violated? Even in such a case, would not the official oath be broken, if the government should be overthrown, when it was believed that disregarding the single law, would tend to preserve it?

In a tone that almost pleads for a sympathetic response, Lincoln continued in the passive voice: "But it was not believed that this question was presented. It was not believed that any law was violated." To the point that it is exclusively Congress—not the president—that has the power to suspend the writ, Lincoln notes perhaps disingenuously, though literally correctly, that "the Constitution itself is silent as to which, or who, is to exercise the power," and, in any event the framers would not have wanted the country to be endangered until Congress could be called together. Lincoln concluded his argument right then, and passed the ball to the Congress: "Whether there shall be any legislation upon the subject, and if any, what, is submitted entirely to the better judgment of Congress."

That is all there is to Lincoln's public defense of his actions. This was his "response" to Taney. Lincoln failed to mention that just two days earlier, July 2, 1861, he had authorized General Scott to suspend the writ of habeas corpus along the military line between New York City and Washington.[82] That was the fourth time in as many months that Lincoln authorized the suspension of the writ, each time expanding the geographic scope of the area of potential suspension.[83]

In an odd conclusion to this portion of the Message, Lincoln notes an expectation that an opinion "will probably be presented by the Attorney General." And, indeed, the next day, Attorney General Bates presented his opinion.[84]

The Attorney General's Opinion

The Attorney General of the United States from time to time renders formal legal opinions on matters relating to the function of the federal government. From his appointment on March 5, 1861, to the end of that year, Attorney General Bates published forty-one Opinions. Most were brief and were directed at other cabinet members. They ranged from an interpretation of a procurement contract (for the Secretary of War) to whether the Postmaster General had authority to acquire land for a post office.

Just a few weeks before Bates issued his Opinion on the suspension of the writ of habeas corpus, he published an Opinion on whether the president had the authority to revoke the decree of a General Court Martial held in Texas in November 1860, as a result of which a soldier, John Ryan, was imprisoned. (Ironically, the Court Martial was ordered by Colonel Robert E. Lee, who also confirmed the sentence.) Bates opined that Lincoln could take no action: "it is beyond the power of the President to annul or revoke the sentence of a court-martial which has been approved and executed under a former President . . . ."[85] Bates acknowledged that in some areas, the president was powerless to act, even in his role as the commander in chief. As early as May 20th, Lincoln had asked the Attorney General to confer with the prominent Maryland constitutional lawyer, Reverdy Johnson, in order to "prepare the argument for the suspension of the Habeas Corpus."[86] Bates was "uncomfortable" about confronting Taney on this matter.[87] Welles, the Secretary of the Navy and one of the very few nonlawyers in the cabinet, had fought Lincoln on the suspension of habeas corpus, but had never publicly vented his objections.[88]

Bates' twenty-page formal Opinion is a good example of fine lawyering—when your client does not have a solid case. He ignored Taney's citations of the experience of President Jefferson and Justice Story's *Commentaries on the Constitution*, and he ignored Taney's textural construction of the suspension power in Article I of the Constitution. While he touched on English history, he did so in order to make the point that it was not particularly relevant, since the United States had an entirely different structure of government.

To have taken on Taney directly would have been an uphill battle. Bates' approach was to deal at a high plane of constitutional theory, with a deep focus on the separation of powers and the *implied* authority that flows from it. The syllogism is this: only the president has the obligation to "preserve, protect and defend" the Constitution, and so he is duty bound to put down a rebellion (the courts cannot do that, Bates noted), and, if he locates spies and other supporters of the rebellion, he is obligated to arrest and confine them. The president is the sole judge "both of the exigency which requires him to act, and the manner in which is most prudent for him to employ the powers entrusted to him . . . ."[89]

Having asserted that the president has the power to arrest and detain anyone whom he suspects might be "holding criminal intercourse" with the rebellious forces, Bates confronted the second question: whether the president is justified in refusing to obey a writ of habeas corpus under these circumstances. Once again, drawing on the principle that the three branches of the federal government are fully independent and equal, it is simply unthinkable that a judge could command a president to submit implicitly to the judge's judgment, and to treat the president as a criminal if he disobeys. (Taney, of course, did no such thing.) In any event, Bates argued, the "whole subject-matter is political and not judicial. The insurrection itself is purely political." And, conveniently, the President is "the political chief of the nation . . . ."

Then, in a clever tactical step, Bates cited a Supreme Court decision written by Taney on the question of whether the president properly called up the militia; Taney explained in that case that the president alone has the power to decide whether the exigency exists. (Taney's position was that, while it was within the president's responsibility to decide the exigency exists, it was solely within Congress's power to decide to suspend the writ in light of the situation.) In a quite amazing exercise of legal gymnastics, Bates admitted that only Congress has the power to suspend the writ of habeas corpus to the extent that is understood to mean a repeal of *all* power to issue the writ. Bates asserted, however, that under the circumstances of a dangerous rebellion, where the public safety requires the confinement of persons implicated in that rebellion, the president has "the lawful power to *suspend the privilege* of persons arrested under such circumstances."

Bates concluded with the observation that the power of the president to capture insurgents and imprison their accomplices was so obvious that "I never thought of first suspending the writ of *habeas corpus*, any more than I thought of suspending the writ of *replevin*, before seizing arms and munitions destined for the enemy." In other words, technical, quaint legal writs have to move aside when the country is confronted with the reality of possible national survival. With this observation, Bates also conveniently shifted the topic from the imprisonment of persons (such as Merryman) to the confiscation of munitions.

PRESIDENT, VICE PRESIDENT, AND CABINET. H. Hamlin, A. Lincoln, Edward Bates, E. M. Stanton, W. H. Seward, M. Blair, G. Welles, W. P. Fessenden, and J. P. Usher.

Thus, Attorney General Edward Bates defended the legitimacy of the president's actions. A Missouri native and former slaveholder, Bates had been one of Lincoln's earliest selections for the cabinet, and a rival of Lincoln's—along with Seward and Chase—for the 1860 Republican presidential nomination.[90] At age 68, Bates was the oldest member of Lincoln's cabinet, and was viewed highly in political and legal circles as a man who revered the Constitution. Without question, Bates did a fine job in offering a professional legal defense of the president's actions.

But why did he do so, in light of the overwhelming strength of Taney's legal position and the likelihood that he was personally uncomfortable with Lincoln's action? He had alternatives: he could have remained silent and simply let Lincoln's Message to Congress stand as the definitive statement on the matter (for example: "I can add nothing to what the president has explained in his Message"). That would have had the virtue of withholding his personal stamp of approval, while at the same time not undercutting the president. At the extreme, of course, Bates could have threatened to resign in protest, but that would have been quite damaging to the new president and would have gained applause from only a handful of constitutional purists.

Professor David Herbert Donald, the late Lincoln scholar, suggested that perhaps Bates was extremely appreciative that Lincoln selected him for the cabinet, and for having done so in an especially gracious manner. More directly, Donald also suggested that Bates passionately wanted to be appointed to the Supreme Court, and that such an aspiration made it difficult to take any action that might diminish Lincoln's interest in him.[91] Indeed, in October 1864, upon Taney's death, Bates asked Lincoln for the nomination for Chief Justice; Lincoln declined, believing that Bates was too old.

* * *

Lincoln's written Message to Congress dated July 4th and Bates' formal Opinion of July 5th were the only *public* responses by the Executive Branch to the stern judgment of the Chief Justice at the end of May. Lincoln could have taken the escape route offered by Taney: order General Cadwalader to explain to Taney that he had indeed misunderstood his instructions and that Merryman would be released from Fort McHenry and turned over to Taney's Court. (To help Cadwalader save face, the decorous Colonel Lee could have presented this statement.) But that course risked being seen as a public defeat for Lincoln—despite the covering excuse of mistake—at a critical time and place. Lincoln needed to be seen as a strong leader focused on protecting the Union at all costs. In addition, Lincoln probably worried that if he yielded to the judiciary, and if civilian juries subsequently were left to decide cases of treason, there was a significant risk (at least in Maryland and the other Border States) of jury nullification. Perhaps no jury in Maryland would convict a Marylander for indirectly helping the Confederates, or at least not helping Union forces move south to attack Virginia.

Another alternative for Lincoln would have been to make no direct response to Taney, but to obtain congressional ratification of his action.

He easily could have taken the opportunity of the July 4th Special Session of Congress specifically to request that Congress take action to suspend the writ of habeas corpus, or at least to ratify his previous suspension. Rather, in his Message to the Special Session, Lincoln merely, but explicitly, left it to Congress as to *whether* there should be any legislation and, *if any, what kind* of legislation.

While Lincoln had almost no supporters in Congress for his unilateral action in suspending the writ,[92] Republicans held large majorities in both chambers.[93] However, to ask Congress to ratify his suspensions—thus making Lincoln's actions legally unassailable—might have suggested that Lincoln had acquiesced to Taney, a politically unacceptable position for Lincoln to have taken. On the last day of the Special Session, August 6th, Congress enacted a joint resolution to ratify the acts and proclamations of the president, but only those relating to the army and navy. The resolution was silent on Lincoln's suspensions of the writ.[94] This ratification of the military actions related to the second category of presidential actions that Lincoln referred to in his Message, where he trusted then that Congress would "readily ratify them." Clearly, Congress understood that the president wanted those actions ratified, and the Congress shared that view. However, Congress did not take final action on the third category—the suspension of the writ—until almost twenty months later, not until the last day of the third lame duck Session in March 1863, with the Habeas Corpus Act.

Central to Lincoln's consideration of his options in responding to Taney in the summer of 1861 must have been the raw political fact that Taney was not a formidable political opponent. Taney was widely condemned by the public in much of the North, because of the *Dred Scott* decision at the beginning of the Buchanan administration four years earlier.[95] Few political figures would then want to be seen rallying to Taney's side in a dispute with a wartime president. And the public generally was more concerned about the broad national political/military situation than about a technical legal writ for the detention of a possible Confederate sympathizer from rural Maryland. In short, Taney was unpopular, action against the Confederacy (and its sympathizers) was popular, and the country was rallying to the president.

Another reason that Lincoln decided it was politically possible for him to ignore Taney may have been simply that the Chief Justice was not speaking for the full Supreme Court. Perhaps the situation would have been different if Lincoln had been confronting an opinion of the full Supreme Court (such as in *United States v. Nixon*[96] in 1974), rather than merely an opinion by a single Justice.

In sum, it is likely that Lincoln made the political calculation that he had virtually nothing to lose by failing to offer a response to Taney, and that he would risk unacceptable political (and perhaps military) consequences if he yielded to Taney. Neither legally nor politically did Lincoln have to do anything but let Taney stew.

However, the fact that Lincoln chose to ignore Taney directly and publicly—aside from his stilted and awkwardly written Message to Congress more than a month after Taney transmitted his opinion—does not mean that Lincoln did nothing. In fact, he may well have worked quietly under the table to "fix" the problem of John Merryman.

The Resolution of *Merryman*

On June 19, 1861, a press report in Baltimore indicated that a grand jury investigation was underway that would probably involve an indictment of Merryman. It was learned that there was testimony from witnesses that Merryman had burned down the railroad bridges. (Merryman, of course, never denied destroying the bridges; rather he insisted that he was only doing his duty as an officer of the state militia and following orders from his superiors.) Press speculation was that if Merryman was in fact indicted for treason, since that was a capital offense, the district court would have to remit the case to the circuit court, which would not meet again until November.[97]

On July 4th—the very day Lincoln's Message was sent to the Special Session of Congress—Secretary of War Simon Cameron interviewed Merryman in Fort McHenry. The *Baltimore Sun* reported merely that Cameron had come to the fort with his family and that he reviewed the troops there, leaving by steamer for Virginia. It is more than interesting that General Keim, who issued the order to arrest Merryman at his home, and General Cadwalader, who commanded Fort McHenry at the time of Merryman's arrest, as well as Secretary of War Cameron, were all from Pennsylvania and all had an acute understanding of politics. Is it possible that Cameron was sent to Fort McHenry for the purpose of cutting a deal with Merryman—a promise of good behavior[98] in exchange for his release—and the troop review was merely a convenient "cover" story? It is not difficult to imagine Lincoln working out a "deal" with Bates and Cameron, with Cameron taking the lead in soothing the ruffled feathers of his two fellow Pennsylvanians.

Eight days later, Attorney General Bates sent to the district attorney for Maryland, William Addison, a letter from Cameron directing that Merryman be released from Fort McHenry in the custody of a U.S. marshal.[99] The Register of Prisoners at Fort McHenry simply notes that Merryman "was transferred to civil authority."[100] Addison was successful in indicting Merryman for treason, but Merryman was permitted to post a $20,000 release bond. He was allowed to return to his home on July 25th, almost exactly two months after he had been taken by the troop of Pennsylvania soldiers. Taney repeatedly postponed proceedings because of ill health, but he did not allow another Justice to sit in his place. It is possible that Taney was convinced that the formidable Union military presence in Baltimore would have made a fair trial impossible.[101] In any event, the case against Merryman never went to trial, and the government eventually dropped the charges.

Thus the matter of John Merryman was concluded in *exactly* the way that Chief Justice Taney said the Constitution required—Merryman was handed over by the military authorities, and the case was handled within the civil judicial process. (This was also consistent with the procedure that Congress mandated later, under the 1963 Habeas Corpus Act.) All this took place within weeks of the Lincoln/Bates public defense of the arrest and rejection of the Taney writs of habeas corpus and attachment. But this result was virtually unknown by the general public.

The Habeas Corpus Act

In the meantime, on September 24, 1862, Lincoln issued a broad proclamation subjecting to martial law "all Rebels and Insurgents, their aiders and abettors . . . and all persons . . . guilty of any disloyal practice," and suspending the writ of habeas corpus in respect to all such persons in military custody. This was Lincoln's fifth suspension and the first since the Special Session. In contrast to the previous four suspensions, this was no longer narrow in geographic scope: it applied to the entire United States. And, unlike the prior four, it was not focused on a threat to a relatively narrow military line. It imposed martial law for virtually anyone suspected of disloyal actions. Lincoln was worried about draft resisters and Confederate sympathizers, and presumably he felt free to be bold in light of the absence of any congressional action to take the suspension power from his hands. However, from July 6, 1861, to March 3, 1863, the Thirty-seventh Congress was in fact working on legislation—refining and refining again—dealing with whether the president had acted legally, and whether his action should or could be ratified.[102]

On March 3, 1863,[103] Congress authorized the suspension of the writ of habeas corpus, and the president signed the bill on the same day. In extremely careful language, the Habeas Corpus Act stated that the president, whenever he judged public safety may require it, "is authorized to suspend the privilege of the writ of habeas corpus in any case throughout the United States . . . ."

What was intended by the phrase "the President . . . is authorized"? Does it mean "is now by virtue of the authority we now grant"? Or does it mean "we now ratify the president's previous action which, without this ratification, would be unconstitutional"? Or does it suggest neutrality: "whether the president had his own independent authority to suspend the writ or not, he now has the authority by this grant of Congress"? It is clear only that Congress was *not* stating that it judged that Lincoln's prior suspensions were unconstitutional—that it was not going to opine on whether the president shared with Congress the authority to suspend the writ, or whether the authority to suspend was held exclusively by Congress. That would have pulled the rug out from under the president.

Instead, Congress seemed to be implying that there could well be circumstances in which the president could take this action on his own authority, but by this Act, Congress was asserting its authority to take control of the suspension issue and to moderate the president's action. In the second section of the March 3rd Act, Congress tied the president's hands. It required the Secretaries of State and War to provide to the federal courts a list of all prisoners they held (except prisoners of war). Then, the courts were required to order the release of any persons held in custody who were not indicted by the first available grand jury. Thus, Congress in effect time-limited the suspension of the writ. This second section, therefore, met exactly one of Taney's objections to Lincoln's unilateral action of suspension—the president was now required to inform the courts of the fact of those held in custody, and to turn them over to the traditional nonmilitary criminal judicial process.

The First Proclamation Under the Act

Lincoln's first proclamation under that congressional authority—suspending habeas corpus in cases where the military held deserters, spies, aiders or abettors of the enemy, or draft resisters—was issued on September 15, 1863. The geographic and substantive scope of this September 15, 1863, proclamation was almost the same as Lincoln's proclamation of September 24, 1862, a year earlier. The essential difference was that in 1862, Lincoln proclaimed that he acted under the *sole* authority of the president, while the proclamation of September 15, 1863, expressly cited the authority of the congressional authorization. In short, Lincoln felt strong enough in 1862 to continue to suspend the writ on his own authority, but, by the early fall 1863—in the midst of severe draft resistance—he decided it would be wise to seek some political cover by also pointing to the authorization granted by Congress.

In the early summer of 1863, Lincoln made a very spirited and public defense of his actions. He was sharply criticized in May of that year for infringement of civil liberties in general (and the arrest of former Congressman Clement Vallandigham in particular[104]) by a meeting of Democrats in Albany, New York. The group was led by Erastus Corning, who was the president of the New York Central Railroad. Lincoln sent his reply, dated June 12, 1863, to Corning and also to the *New York Tribune*. Lincoln's legal and political skills were brilliantly on display.

Lincoln flatly asserted that his actions were perfectly constitutional. He pointed out that the constitutional "safeguards" he allegedly violated had been put in place *after* years of English civil war and were adopted in the Constitution at the *close* of the revolution—but that they had not been tested *during* a civil war and *during* the American Revolution. In short, he argued that the New York Democrats were innocents, dangerously naïve about the proper role of the Executive during times of violence. Then, in a not too-veiled jab at Taney, Lincoln explained that the insurgents had been preparing their side for years, that their

> sympathizers [had] pervaded all departments of the government . . . [and that] under cover of . . . Habeas Corpus they hoped to keep on foot amongst us a most efficient corps of spies, informers . . . . They knew that . . . the Habeas Corpus might be suspended; but they also knew they had friends who would make a question as to *who* was to suspend it; meanwhile their spies and others might remain at large to help on their cause.

Leaving aside Taney's role, Lincoln explained that "ordinary courts of justice are inadequate to 'cases of Rebellion'" where at least one member of a jury might be "more ready to hang the panel, than to hang the traitor." Pushing the point, Lincoln explained that had he acted more quickly and seized John Breckinridge and Robert E. Lee, they would have been discharged "on Habeas Corpus, were the writ allowed to operate." Unable to resist an ironic slap at the Democrats, Lincoln recalled that when the Democrat Andrew Jackson was an officer in New Orleans at the time of the War of 1812, he, in effect, suspended the writ of habeas corpus and was fined by a federal judge, but later Congress reimbursed Jackson for the fine.[105]

Lincoln's letter to Corning sums up his view on the flexibility of the Constitution:

> If I be wrong on this question of constitutional power, my error lies in believing that certain proceedings are constitutional when, in cases of rebellion or Invasion, the public Safety requires them, which would not be constitutional when, in absence of rebellion or invasion, the public Safety does not require them . . . .

The Continuing Debate

The conflict between the Court and the president suggests an interesting parallel to the Steel Seizure Case[106] in 1952. President Truman seized certain steel mills, arguing that it was necessary to the Korean War effort. The Supreme Court told Truman that he had acted unconstitutionally, since only the Congress had the power to legislate such an action, and the fact of the wartime conditions did not alter the relative powers of the legislative and executive branch. (This sounds quite like Taney's conclusion that "the president has exercised a power which he does not possess under the constitution.") Chief Justice Rehnquist, who was a Supreme Court clerk in 1952, suggested that the fact that Truman and the Korean War were very unpopular at the time, and that the original position of the administration—that the president's power was absolute unless some provision of the Constitution expressly denied authority to him—was so sweeping and offensive, may well have influenced the Court decision.

Aftermath

In July 1864, the Confederates, led by CSA Lieutenant General Jubal Early, staged a daring raid into Maryland that threatened Washington. CSA Brigadier General Bradley Johnson, before the War, was a lawyer in Frederick, Maryland, and an active delegate to the Democratic conventions in Charleston and Baltimore in 1860. Working under Early, Johnson had brought his Confederate force of fifteen hundred Marylanders near Cockeysville, north of Baltimore, to cut the main trunk line of the Philadelphia, Wilmington & Baltimore Railroad connecting Baltimore with the cities to the north. (The plan then was for Johnson to proceed to the Union prisoner of war camp at Point Lookout in southeast Maryland.) On July 10th, General Johnson stopped for lunch with his friend John Merryman at "Hayfields." Johnson commented that the "charming society, the lovely girls, the balmy July air and the luxuriant verdure of Hayfields, all combined to make the scene enchanting."[107]

Chief Justice Taney died on October 12, 1864, at age 87, at his home in Washington. Lincoln, Seward, Bates, and Postmaster General Dennison attended the memorial service early on the morning of October 15, following which Taney's body was transported in a two-car funeral train to Frederick, Maryland, for burial. Bates traveled to Frederick for Taney's burial. Bates had worked more with Taney than had any other cabinet member, and he had developed "an affection and abiding respect" for him.[108] Lincoln knew that the choice of Taney's successor would be very important, since this would be his fifth Supreme Court appointment, and therefore the next Chief Justice would give Lincoln appointees a majority on the Court. For political reasons, Lincoln waited until after the elections, and then appointed Treasury Secretary Salmon Chase.[109]

Exactly a week before Taney died, Lambdin P. Milligan was arrested in Indiana by U.S. military forces, and was tried for treason by military commission that same month. Milligan was one of the ablest and most prosperous lawyers in northern Indiana. He was also a minor politician who was the Democratic Chairman in his county; he had failed in efforts to run for Congress and for governor. His positions became more radical, and he compared Confederates to the Revolution's patriots; he saw little hope for the restoration of the Union in light of the "suppression of civil liberty" in Indiana.

The military commission sentenced Milligan to death; execution was scheduled for May 1865. His lawyers filed a petition for a writ of habeas

SECRETARY OF THE TREASURY SALMON P. CHASE.

corpus in the federal circuit court for Indiana, and the matter eventually reached the Supreme Court, which held oral arguments on March 5, 1866. On April 3, 1866, the Court decided *Ex parte Milligan*,[110] though it did not release its opinion until December.[111] The Habeas Corpus Act of March 3, 1863, was the foundation of Milligan's claim. The Court decided 9–0 that Milligan must be discharged, and that the writ should prevail, because the military commission had no jurisdiction over the civilian Milligan. Justice Davis wrote the opinion of the Court, in which two previous Chief Justices were cited approvingly, Marshall and Taney.[112] (Chief Justice Chase wrote a concurring opinion for himself and three other Justices.[113])

Justice Davis set the stage for the Court's decision by underscoring the importance of the issue before the Court, which "involves the very framework of the government and the fundamental principles of American liberty." Davis then put the matter into the context of the time, obliquely presenting the Lincoln-Taney conflict over Merryman:

> During the late wicked Rebellion, the temper of the times did not allow that calmness in deliberation and discussion so necessary to a correct conclusion of a purely judicial question. *Then* [in 1861], considerations of safety were mingled with the exercise of power, and feelings and interests prevailed which are happily terminated. *Now* [in 1866] that the

public safety is assured, this question ... can be discussed and decided without passion or the admixture of any element not required to for a legal judgment.

Justice Davis noted that the president had "practically" suspended the writ of habeas corpus and detained suspected persons in custody without trial,

> but his authority to do this was questioned. It was claimed that Congress alone could exercise this power.... The privilege of this great writ had never before been withheld from the citizen, and ... it was of the highest importance that the lawfulness of the suspension should be fully established.

Those were the circumstances, Justice Davis explained, in which the Habeas Corpus Act of March 3, 1863, was enacted, under which "the President was authorized by it to suspend the privilege of the writ...." The Court concluded that Milligan should not have been tried by military commission, since the courts in Indiana in 1864 were "open and their process unobstructed." Davis' statement in this landmark case is famous:

> The Constitution of the United States is a law for rulers and people, equally in war and in peace, and covers with the shield of its protection all classes of men, at all times and under all circumstances.

JUDGE DAVID DAVIS.

In effect, the Court agreed with Taney's *Ex parte Merryman* decision. One of the lawyers representing the government during the argument before the Court in the *Milligan* case—the losing side—was Massachusetts lawyer Benjamin F. Butler, formerly General Butler, who had occupied Baltimore in May 1861. The lawyers representing Milligan at the Supreme Court were James A. Garfield of Ohio—the future president, arguing his first case before the Supreme Court—Jeremiah S. Black, formerly Attorney General and Secretary of State under President Buchanan, and New York lawyer David Dudley Field, brother of Justice Field. Five of the Justices were Lincoln appointees.

The *Milligan* case suggests that Taney was right with regard to the proper interpretation of the Constitution.[114] Ultimately, the Court unanimously decided that a president cannot on his own authority arrest, confine, and subject to military tribunal a civilian while the courts are open and functioning. Constitutional scholar Bernard Schwartz concluded that the "consensus of learned opinion has been that on the purely legal issue involved in *Merryman*, Taney was right and Lincoln was wrong."[115] On the other hand, Taney was wrong in not giving the president a little more wiggle room, a brief period to allow Lincoln to make a face-saving retreat. It is also a matter of fact that no president since Lincoln has suspended the writ of habeas corpus, or otherwise failed to yield to judicial authority, even though there have been wartime emergencies and crises.

It is true that during the Merryman incident, the nation was at war, Maryland's retention in the Union was vital, and the rail link through Baltimore was important (though perhaps not essential, as General Butler proved when he took the water route via Annapolis). It is also clear that Lincoln was new in his job and not fully secure. Lincoln also knew that much of the law and the history of fundamental rights centered on the writ of habeas corpus. He decided that what he saw as risks to the very existence of the Union were more powerful than the risks to the system of laws and protection of personal liberty. Perhaps he concentrated too much on *his* action—knowing that he was a genuine lover of liberty—rather than the precedent for future presidents, by which, unchecked, his action could pave the way for dictatorial powers in the wrong hands.

In short, Lincoln decided that the preservation of the Union was more important than personal liberty—for the duration of the emergency. That decision was wrong. The protection of personal liberty and the protection of national security need not be mutually exclusive or a zero sum game. On the other hand, Lincoln's decision was perfectly understandable. Taney's action was legally correct and personally courageous.

In the end, the nation is very fortunate to have had both Taney and Lincoln. Lincoln alone or Taney alone might have resulted in too great a tendency to have either national security or personal liberty dominate at the expense of the other. Together, Lincoln and Taney provided a perfect balance.

The Continuing Debate

In his address announcing the Proclamation of Emergency on November 3, 2007, President General Pervez Musharraf of Pakistan noted that the Pakistan Supreme Court had released sixty-one confirmed terrorists, and that they were then "roaming around freely." Shifting from Urdu to English, Musharraf pleaded for time from the West: "Please do not demand and expect your level of civil liberties, which you learned over the centuries." He then cited President Lincoln: "Abraham Lincoln had one consuming passion during the time of supreme crisis and this was to preserve the Union because the Union was in danger. Towards that end, he broke laws, he violated the Constitution, he usurped arbitrary power [and] he trampled individual liberties."

On August 18, 2008, Musharraf resigned as president, under pressure of impeachment. On March 16, 2009, Prime Minister Yousaf Raza Gillani announced in a television address that the deposed Chief Justice of Pakistan, Iftikhar Mohammed Chaudhry, would be reinstated. On July 31, 2009, the Supreme Court's full bench struck down the 2007 proclamation and all decrees based on it; Chief Justice Chaudhry also rejected a petition for the registration of treason charges against Musharraf.

CHAPTER 6

The War at Sea: International Law and Diplomacy

The Civil War at sea was a struggle not only of vessels and guns, but also of legal interpretation and lawyers. The first year of the War, 1861, was the most dramatic and conflict-filled year at sea, giving rise to significant legal issues relating to the role and status of privateers and the dramatic trials of Southern "pirates"; the president's authority to impose a blockade; a potentially disastrous diplomatic incident at sea involving international law; and the beginning of the first Supreme Court case dealing directly with the president's war powers.

The Privateers

Lincoln's proclamation of April 15, 1861, following the fall of Fort Sumter, formally announced the existence of an "insurrection" and called for volunteers to assist in the recovery of federal property that had been seized by the seceding states. It was, in effect but not in law, a declaration of war—not legally so because only the Congress has the power to declare war under the Constitution. Nevertheless, it was clear to those in the South that the prospect of an invasion from the North was near.

In response, on April 17th, Confederate States of America (CSA) President Jefferson Davis issued a proclamation, calling for volunteers to defend the new nation: "Whereas, Abraham Lincoln . . . has, by proclamation, announced the intention of invading this Confederacy . . . , it has thus become the duty of this government to repel the threatened invasion . . . by all the means which *the laws of nations* and the usages of civil warfare place at its disposal" (emphasis added). In addition, he invited "all those who may desire, by service in private armed vessels . . . to aid this government" by applying for "letters of marque and reprisal . . . ." These "private armed vessels" were to capture and harass Northern merchant ships at sea, a kind of private naval reserve force.

A *letter of marque and reprisal* was an official warrant or commission from a government authorizing the designated agent to seize or destroy specified assets belonging to another party that had committed some offense under the "law of nations," the term then used for "international law." A letter of marque was usually used to authorize privateers to raid and capture merchant shipping of an enemy nation.[1] "Marque," meaning "frontier" in French, authorized the agent to pass beyond the borders of the nation. It was considered a retaliatory measure short of a full declaration of war. It was part of maritime economic warfare, *guerre de course*, and it was sort of "guerilla warfare at sea."[2] Public navies were expensive, and they had to be maintained in peacetime as well as in wartime, and so governments relied heavily on private initiative and enterprise to fight their wars. The system worked because it was backed by a substantial array of laws, including prize courts and bond requirements.

The first letter of marque issued in England dates from the late thirteenth century, but only after 1585 did the letters make provisions for prizes to be condemned and confiscated by an admiralty court with a subsequent division of the goods made between the crown and the privateer. Privateers had a romanticized[3] history: in the late 1580s, the British Crown issued a letter of marque to Sir Francis Drake and to Sir Walter Raleigh, whose main source of income came from privateering. More than a century later, Edward Teach was a British privateer during Queen Anne's war (1702–1713), but he turned to buccaneering (piracy) after the war, and was then known as the infamous Blackbeard.[4]

During the American Revolution, the colonials were up against the great sea power of the British Navy. In November 1775, Massachusetts legislated an "Act Authorizing Privateers and Creating Courts of Admiralty," which permitted the arming of private vessels to attack and to take into any port in the colony any vessels employed by the enemy.[5] The Continental Congress issued about eight hundred letters of marque, legalizing and commissioning private enterprises to outfit and send out armed merchant ships as commerce raiders. One of the first commissions was signed on October 24, 1776, by John Hancock, as president of the Continental Congress.[6] They were given the legal authority to prey on British shipping. In Boston alone, some 365 vessels were commissioned as privateers during the Revolutionary War. In contrast, the Continental Navy had only about one hundred ships of war. As one scholar put it:

> [The Continental Army] won by not losing; or, in the manner of modern guerilla insurrections, by making the cost of victory too high to seem worth it to a complacent, superior foe. Privateers, on the other hand, carried the war to Britain. Many were plain bandits; some were genuine patriots.[7]

In March 1777, the British Parliament passed the "Pirate Act," which, in denying privateers the legal rights typically granted to prisoners of war, allowed them to be held without trial or prospect of exchange. The Act was very controversial in Britain; many thought it was cruel and shocking. For the next five years, it served as a rallying point for antiwar and humanitarian activists.[8]

After the Revolutionary War, the concept of granting letters of marque was expressly recognized in the U.S. Constitution, in Article I, Section 8, which gives Congress the power "[t]o declare War, grant Letters of Marque and Reprisal" . . . .[9] Article I, Section 10 prohibits any state from granting letters of marque and reprisal.

The apogee[10] of the U.S. issuance of letters of marque occurred during the War of 1812.[11] Congress declared war on Britain on June 18, 1812, and specifically authorized the President "to issue to private armed vessels of the United States commissions of marque and general reprisal, in such form as he shall think proper . . . against the vessels, goods, and effects of the Government of [the United Kingdom] and the subjects thereof."[12] The United States commissioned 526 vessels as privateers, though only about half that number actually went to sea.[13] The U.S. Navy's ships were captured or bottled up in port after 1813, and so it was the privateers that encouraged Britain to terminate the War—since British shipowners and insurance companies suffered heavy losses after American privateers began operating in British waters.

After the War of 1812, particularly after 1814, when King Ferdinand VII was restored to the Spanish throne, Spain tried to stop the revolutionaries in its South American colonies from pressing their independence. Those South American revolutionaries found support in U.S. seaports, especially in New Orleans and Baltimore. Agents from "independent" South American countries would arrive and distribute commissions to privateers: from Cartagena (now Colombia), Buenos Aries (Argentina), or the Oriental Republic (Uruguay). Many of the U.S. seamen were veterans of privateering for the United States against Britain, and looked to South American privateering as a quick way to repair their finances as well as to support the cause of independence. However, the U.S. neutrality laws of 1794 and 1797 made it a crime to engage in hostilities against any nation at peace with the United States. Moreover, in the U.S.-Spanish treaty of 1795, the United States agreed to treat as pirates anyone who violated American neutrality to attack Spain.[14] Enforcement was not very effective, even after Congress revised the Neutrality Act.[15]

In late 1835, on the eve of the U.S.-Mexican War (1846–1848), the Texas Revolutionary Assembly considered how to protect the Texas coast. Since it was not possible to create overnight a Republic of Texas Navy, the Texans issued letters of marque to protect the coast, harass Mexican shipping, and bring in prizes; part of whose proceeds would go to the public treasury.[16]

The issue of privateers consumed a significant portion of the second annual Message to Congress of President Franklin Pierce on December 4, 1854. In discussing the various proposals by European powers to enhance the rules of international law concerning neutral shipping, Pierce noted that the king of Prussia proposed an article renouncing privateering, and explained that this made sense for "nations having naval establishments large in proportion to their foreign commerce." But for a country such as the United States, with a comparatively small naval force, it made no sense. Pierce summed it up:

> The bare statement of the condition in which the United States would be placed, after having surrendered the right to resort to privateers, in the event of a war with a belligerent of naval supremacy will should that this Government could never listen to such a proposition.[17]

Despite this long history of the use of letters of marque, the major powers—especially the mightiest naval powers, Britain and France—decided that its continued practice was an unacceptable threat to their commercial interests. Therefore, seven European powers met in Paris immediately after the Congress of Paris, which ended in the Crimean War in 1856—Great Britain, France, Prussia, Austria, Russia, Sardinia, and Turkey—and formulated the Declaration of Paris. On April 16, 1856, the Declaration Respecting Maritime War was adopted, and in it the practice of privateering under the authority of letters of marque was outlawed. The Declaration had a long preface, but the relevant substantive part had only four short paragraphs, the first of which simply stated: "Privateering is and remains abolished."[18]

Secretary of State William Marcy—a lawyer and former secretary of war under President Polk[19]—argued at the time that if privateering was surrendered, the seas would be ceded to the larger powers, and that was unacceptable to the United States. Marcy pointed out that large navies and standing armies were dangerous to civil liberty, a large force ever ready is a temptation to rush into war, and the expense of maintaining a large standing force is burdensome to the people.[20] Marcy sought modifications to the Declaration, but his requests were ignored. Thus, while the Declaration of Paris banned the use of privateers and the issuance of letters of marque and reprisal, it did not obligate the parties to treat privateers commissioned by non-party nations as outlaws of international criminals. The agreement created no legal obligations for the United States since the United States was not a party to that agreement.[21]

After Jefferson Davis's April 17, 1861 proclamation concerning privateers, Secretary of State Seward asked Britain and France if the United States could then belatedly adhere to the Paris Declaration. The response was, in effect, that if the United States joined, the Declaration's provisions would not apply to the conflict already underway—which meant that the Union would gain nothing by adhering.[22] Seward dropped the matter.[23]

Since the Confederacy had no navy, it made great sense for Davis to propose the issuance of letters of marque. Privateers could challenge the Union immediately, while real war vessels were in the process of being bought or built.[24] Anticipating the likelihood of a Union blockade—in fact proclaimed by Lincoln on April 19th—one goal for the privateers was to help render a blockade ineffective by forcing the Union Navy to draw more and more of its ships off blockade duty to chase privateers. Despite the impact of his proclamation of April 17th, Jefferson Davis was careful to ensure the law was followed exactly. The CSA Constitution provided that Congress had the power to "grant letters of marque and reprisal, and make rules concerning captures on land and water."[25] And Davis did not issue any letters of marque until the CSA Congress passed appropriate legislation. In order to ensure the acceptance internationally of the CSA as a legitimate nation, it was important that its actions be—and be seen to be—in accordance with law. Letters of marque would be issued only to vessels actually present within the borders of the Confederacy; there would be no trading of commissions or thinly veiled piracy. On May 6th, the CSA Congress passed "An Act Recognizing the existence of war between the United States and the Confederate States: and concerning Letters of Marque, prizes, and prize goods." The Act established the administrative procedure for the issuance of letters, requiring, for example, a bond, a list of the investors,[26] and the names of the captain and crew. The Confederate Department of Commerce handled the administrative procedures.

Davis's instructions to the privateers were "to proceed with all justice and humanity" toward Union vessels. All property on neutral ships was exempt from seizure, unless it was contraband. The privateers were the first of the Confederate vessels to put to sea; the very first was the privateer *Savannah*, on May 18, 1861, with Thomas H. Baker in command. The motivation of a privateer, its crew, and supporters was a mixture of patriotism, adventure, and greed. Being a privateer was a risky business: it was close to piracy, and a privateer was held in disdain by professional naval officers.

The risk did not always line up with the profit. Under traditional maritime law, a prize vessel captured by a privateer had to be brought to a properly constituted court for adjudication. To "condemn" a vessel captured as a prize, the privateer had to prove to the court's satisfaction that the enemy owned it; proof was usually found in the ship's papers, including cargo manifests and registers. If the prize was found to be lawful, it was sold at a court-ordered auction. In the case of the Confederacy, the privateer had to get his prize to a Southern port for adjudication, and that soon became very difficult because of the blockade by the Union Navy.[27] If successful, however, the prize (and cargo) would be sold, taxes of 5 percent paid to the CSA, and then the proceeds would be divided among the supporters and crew.

Even though the first letter of marque properly granted by the CSA was not until May 18th, the reaction in the North to Davis's April 17th proclamation was immediate. Quite out of proportion to the actual damage inflicted, there was near panic among the merchants of the North who feared for the survival of their ships and trade. In the end, the vessels that the Confederate privateers (and the commerce destroyers) took "had virtually no effect on the Union war effort. The alarm they provoked in Union shipping circles was their contribution to the Confederate cause."[28]

Two days after Jefferson Davis's proclamation, Lincoln issued a proclamation on April 19th in direct response to the threat of privateering and ordered a blockade. Addressing Davis's proclamation directly, Lincoln's proclamation stated:

And whereas a combination of persons engaged in such insurrection [the CSA], have threatened to grant *pretended letters of marque* to authorize the bearers thereof to commit assaults on the lives, vessels and property of good citizens of the country lawfully engaged in commerce on the high seas . . . . [I]f any person, under the *pretended authority* of the said States, or under any other pretense, shall molest a vessel of the United States . . . , such person will be held amenable to the laws of the United States for the prevention and punishment of piracy. (emphasis added).

Lincoln made it clear that those in the South who wanted to take the risks of entering into privateering also had to weigh the fact that the Union would treat them as pirates. At this time, Lincoln and Davis were hurling proclamation shots at each other every other day: April 15th, Lincoln's proclamation in effect declaring war; April 17th, Davis's proclamation authorizing privateers; and on April 19th, Lincoln's proclamation establishing the blockade and painting privateers as pirates.

By mid-May, the news of Lincoln's proclamation with respect to treating privateers as pirates reached England. On May 13, 1861, Queen Victoria issued a Proclamation of Neutrality which formally commanded all of her "loving subjects to observe a strict neutrality" during the American hostilities. In doing so, as a legal matter, the United Kingdom recognized the belligerent status of the Confederacy, and the CSA was viewed from London as exercising its belligerent rights in commissioning privateers. The following month, France and Spain issued similar Proclamations of Neutrality, followed by the other major European powers.

The reaction in England to Lincoln's message about privateers was sharp. On May 16th, in the House of Lords, there were expressions of outrage at the proclamation. Lord Kingsdown stated that "the enforcement of the doctrine [that the CSA privateers were pirates] of that Proclamation would be an act of barbarity which would produce an outcry throughout the civilized world." The Earl of Derby claimed that the Union must not be allowed to believe that "they are at liberty so to strain the law as to convert privateering into piracy, and visit it with death." The Lord Chancellor opined that if the United States put to death a privateer with a proper letter of marque, it would be "guilty of murder."

Needless to say, the British reaction complicated the Lincoln administration's position. Since the United States had not signed the 1856 Declaration of Paris that outlawed privateering, it was not bound by its terms. Only those countries which had signed on were bound. Therefore, it was perfectly legal for the United States (or the CSA) to commission privateers, and the Europeans were aghast that Lincoln would threaten to hang anyone engaged in a perfectly legal act.

The *Savannah* and the *Enchantress*

Crews from two Confederate privateers with properly commissioned letters of marque, the *Savannah* and the *Jefferson Davis*, were involved in two very important—and very dramatic—trials in October 1861, the results of which had significant impact on both the Union and the CSA.

The *Savannah*, the first privateer commissioned by the CSA, captured the brig *Joseph* with a cargo of sugar on June 3, 1861, and sent its prize to a South Carolina port. But on the next day, the *Savannah* itself was captured by the USS *Perry* off the coast of South Carolina. The U.S. Commander of the Union's Atlantic Blockading Squadron, Silas Stringham, towed the *Savannah* near Charleston harbor to flaunt her capture—sort of like waving a red flag in front of a bull. Then, the *Savannah* was taken to New York as a prize and condemned there by a Federal District Court. It was later sold for $1,200. The sixteen officers and crew of the *Savannah* were arrested and taken to New York City and, in chains, incarcerated in the infamous Tombs Prison in late June.

On June 18th, another Confederate privateer, the *Jefferson Davis*, received approval from the CSA State Department for a letter of marque. The vessel had an interesting history. The ship involved was originally a brig built in Baltimore in 1846, named the *Putnam*. It had been renamed the *Echo* and was in the illegal slave trade when it was captured off Cuba in August 1858 by the USS *Dolphin*. The *Echo* was carrying 318 Africans when captured; the ship was sent to Charleston, and the liberated slaves were returned to Africa. (Lieutenant Maffitt, captain of the USS *Dolphin*, joined the Confederate Navy in 1861 and eventually became naval aide to Robert E. Lee.)

When the *Echo* was brought to Charleston, it was forfeited to the United States, and then was bought at auction in January 1859 by Captain Robert Hunter. He returned her name to the *Putnam*. It was Hunter who, in 1861, organized a group of twenty-seven shareholders and who sought and received the CSA commission as a privateer, under the command of 43-year-old Louis M. Coxetter. Coxetter renamed the vessel the *Jefferson Davis*. She enjoyed a festive send-off from Charleston on June 28th, slipped past the Union blockade, and soon captured several Union merchant vessels along the Atlantic coast.

On July 6th, the *Jefferson Davis* captured the *Enchantress*, a New York–registered vessel bound from Boston to Cuba. Captain Coxetter selected from his crew of ninety a young pilot from Savannah, William Walton Smith, to serve as prize master aboard the *Enchantress* and take her to a prize court in Charleston.[29] There was a free Negro cook, Jacob Garrick, on the captured vessel. At first, Garrick was taken onto the *Jefferson Davis* along with the rest of the *Enchantress* crew. But then, at the last minute, Captain Coxetter ordered Garrick to return to the *Enchantress* to accompany the prize crew to Charleston, because Coxetter was sure that Garrick would fetch a high price as a slave in Charleston. As one perceptive scholar put it:

> Ultimately, Coxetter's decision cost him his prize and put the lives of Smith and his prize crew in jeopardy.... In the eyes of the Union, Smith and his crew became more than merely pirates; they became the nineteenth-century equivalents of the agents of Egyptian pharaoh Ramses II returning the Israelites to bondage.[30]

The Enchantress was then recaptured by the United States on July 22nd off Hatteras Inlet along the Outer Banks of North Carolina and taken to the Navy Yard in Philadelphia. Smith and the small prize crew who were aboard the *Enchantress* were promptly arrested and taken to Moyamensing Prison in Pennsylvania on August 2nd. On August 18th, the *Jefferson Davis* grounded on a bar off the Florida coast near St. Augustine and was lost. She had been extremely successful in capturing prizes, perhaps more than any ship since the War of 1812.

The prize master and small crew from the *Jefferson Davis* who were captured aboard the *Enchantress* on July 22nd, and the crew of the *Savannah* captured June 4th, were tried in Philadelphia and New York, respectively, only days apart, but with different results.

The *Savannah* Trial

On July 6th, two weeks after the crew of the *Savannah* was put in the terrible New York jail, CSA President Jefferson Davis sent a letter to Lincoln about the matter. The letter was carried to Washington by a Confederate officer, Colonel Thomas H. Taylor, under a flag of truce, and delivered to Lieutenant General Winfield Scott—the supreme commander of Union forces, known as "Old Fuss and Feathers"—who assured Taylor that it would get to the White House. Davis's letter contained both a plea and a threat.

Davis explained in his letter to Lincoln that after he had learned of the capture of the *Savannah*, he had arranged on June 19th for a proposal to be put to the commander of the U.S. Atlantic Squadron: let us exchange prisoners. Davis promised to release Union prisoners equal in rank and number to the *Savannah*'s imprisoned crew. The Union commander replied that he did not have the prisoners. Now, Davis continued, it seemed that the *Savannah*'s crew had been taken to New York, treated as criminals rather than prisoners of war, and brought before the courts on charges of piracy and treason. Then, he laid out the threat:[31]

> [T]his Government [the CSA] will deal out to the prisoners held by it the same treatment and the same fate as shall be experienced by those captured on the *Savannah*, and if driven to the terrible necessity of retaliation by your execution of any of the officers or the crew of the *Savannah*, that retaliation will be extended so far as shall be requisite to secure the abandonment of a practice unknown to the warfare of civilized man, and so barbarous as to disgrace the nation which shall be guilty of inaugurating it.

Concluding his letter, Davis then renewed his previous offer: let us exchange for the prisoners taken on the *Savannah* an equal number of those held by the CSA according to rank.

Lincoln never replied to the Davis letter. Instead, a grand jury in New York, on July 16th, indicted the *Savannah* prisoners for piracy in the capture of the *Joseph*. Conviction would carry the death penalty. The line now was drawn by both sides.

The legal defense team in the *Savannah* case in New York was extraordinary:

- Daniel Lord, Jr. was the 70-year-old founder of Lord Day & Lord (for more than a century, one of the great law firms of New York),[32] and the Yale classmate of one of the crewmen;
- Algernon Sydney Sullivan was hired by the Confederate government to represent this crew and any other privateers who might come to New York as prisoners. He was married to a Virginia woman with strong sympathies toward the Confederacy. In 1879, he was a founder of Sullivan & Cromwell, still today one of the great law firms in the nation.[33]
- James T. Brady, the leading criminal lawyer in New York, represented the captain of the *Savannah*, T. Harrison Baker. (The official name of the case was *United States v. Baker*.)

It was not an easy decision to take on the defense of the privateers. In late April 1861, the New York City Bar Association held a special meeting and adopted resolutions relating to the conduct of the bar in wartime. The message was: do not engage in any representation that might compromise the suppression of the rebellion. But courage and preservation of liberty required that lawyers might have to take on unpopular causes.[34]

The prosecutor was E. Delafield Smith, the U.S. district attorney, who also was a law professor at City University.[35] He pushed for a trial as soon as possible, while the defense argued for more time (in part to take testimony in the South).[36] However, since the death penalty was possible, two judges were required to preside. Due to scheduling difficulties with the two judges—Justice William Shipmen was available right away, but due to an injury Justice Samuel Nelson was not available until later—the trial date was put off until the third week in October 1861. Judge Nelson, of New York, was an expert in admiralty law and had served for more than twenty-seven years on the bench.[37]

To prepare the defense, Sullivan felt he needed authenticated documents to prove the formation of the CSA, making the letter of marque found onboard the *Savannah* a valid legal document and in order to show that the letter of marque issued to the *Savannah* was directed narrowly at only one enemy, and was not making war against all nations (as pirates might). To that end, Sullivan wrote on July 19th to the Attorney General of Virginia. The reply to Sullivan came from Judah P. Benjamin, the Attorney General of the CSA. Benjamin said that he was "totally at a loss" to see what he could do to help, that the "question appears to me to be much more of a political than of a legal character." In mid-September, the defense team asked assistance from U.S. Attorney General Bates, who, on October 8th—after consulting with Lincoln—responded that the U.S. government "declines to take any active part, in aid of the accused" and so would not assist in obtaining documents or any other act of facilitation for the defense.

On September 7th, Secretary of State Seward—the de facto Secretary of Internal Security—telegraphed the superintendent of police of New York City (John A. Kennedy), and instructed him to arrest defense attorney Algernon Sullivan and to turn him over to the commander at Fort Lafayette, a grim fortress on a rocky shoal in New York Harbor. Attorney Sullivan was arrested at his home.[38] His fellow defense attorney, Daniel Lord, immediately protested to Seward, who replied dismissively that the "public safety" would not permit Sullivan's release, since he was a "political prisoner" based on Sullivan's "treasonable correspondence." Clearly, Seward was playing hardball.

On October 23rd, the trial of the officers and men of the *Savannah* opened in New York City. The trial of the crew from the *Savannah* would be one of the most passion-filled trials of the early days of the War. Two days before the trial opened, Sullivan rejoined Lord and Brady on the defense team. Seward had finally ordered Sullivan released on October 18th, after ensuring that Sullivan would take an oath of allegiance. The prosecution team had gained another member as well. The original lead prosecutor, Delafield Smith, worried that the defense team was too powerful, on October 10th asked Attorney General Bates to permit the addition to the prosecution team of William M. Evarts—one of the best trial lawyers in New York.

The trial lasted eight days, most of which were consumed by the long arguments of Brady and Evarts. But before the discussion began, Justice Nelson inquired whether defense counsel wished to be seated next to their clients, to which Daniel Lord replied that his clients were in irons, and so, jokingly, they must be dangerous. Justice Nelson turned red, and instructed the marshal to remove the irons from the defendants, commenting "Brother Lord, I think we can risk it."

The defense argued that the South's secession was no more than the original colonies had done in declaring independence from England, and that the CSA was a de facto government, and its letter of marque was a complete defense to a charge of piracy. In any event, the piracy statute required the defendant to have "an intent to steal," and obviously, the *Savannah* crew had no such intent.[39] Evarts, for the prosecution, argued that privateering was barbaric, that the CSA was no government, and that the Union had an obligation to protect its commerce.

The jury deliberated for two days. Finally, it reported that it could not agree—a hung jury. The prosecution filed for an immediate retrial, but Justice Nelson refused.

The *Jefferson Davis* Trial

Meanwhile, Smith and his crew of five from the *Jefferson Davis*, who served as the prize crew on the *Enchantress*, had been held in Philadelphia since the first week in August. At their preliminary hearing, the most damning testimony came from Jacob Garrick, who had been the black cook from the *Enchantress*.[40] The crew was charged with piracy, and the trial was scheduled for the next term of the U.S. District Court for Philadelphia, the third week of October. Thus, even though the Confederate prize crew on the *Enchantress* was captured almost seven weeks after the *Savannah*, the prize crew on the *Enchantress* would be tried at the same time in a different court. The Philadelphia trial in *United States v. Smith* began on October 22nd. Supreme Court Associate Justice Grier was on the bench, along with District Court Judge John Cadwalader (brother of General George Cadwalader, who had commanded Fort McHenry several months earlier when John Merryman was in custody there).

The defense team was composed of Nathaniel Harrison, who had moved from Virginia to Philadelphia only two years earlier and was a Confederate sympathizer; John O'Neill, a prominent lawyer from New York who had been practicing only ten years; and later George Mifflin Wharton, a distinguished and skilled lawyer.[41] This defense team was not as experienced as the defense lawyers in the New York case of the *Savannah*.

The prosecutors were Hubley Ashton (only 25 years old, but who later was to become one of the founders of the American Bar Association) and William Darrah Kelley, a prominent Republican lawyer-politician.

The charge of piracy in the Philadelphia case was not based on common law piracy but, rather, on an 1820 statute that focused on an act of robbery against an American ship. This left the defense with only one argument: this was not robbery, since it took place in the context of a war between belligerents. Wharton tried to establish the existence of the letter of marque (copies of which he could not obtain) duly issued by the competent authorities of the CSA, which at least had to be recognized de facto as an existing and powerful government. They also argued that as a citizen of Georgia, Smith was required to enter the service of the CSA and, in any event, that Smith was a simple man who should be excused for falling into the prevailing sentiment in the South. The defense failed to produce witnesses (Union military officers) who might have testified to the de facto existence of the Union prisoner exchange policy, thereby showing the inconsistency of claiming that a Confederate on land could be treated as a soldier, while a Confederate at sea could not be treated as a naval sailor.

The prosecutors, in contrast, argued that the CSA did not exist and had no lawful authority to turn an act of piracy into legitimate warfare. Jacob Garrick testified for the prosecution that he was to be taken to Charleston to be sold as a slave, and that fact alone seemed to undermine the claim that this capture was an act of war, rather than merely an act for profit—piracy.

On October 25th, Justice Grier charged the jury, and his instructions made it virtually impossible for the jury to find for the defendants. He told the jury that no rebellion can be recognized as a legitimate government; he refused to accept the argument that there are circumstances in which participants in a civil war are entitled to some recognition as prisoners of war and not merely criminals. Essentially, Grier told the jury that privateers in a civil war had no right to be treated in accordance with the laws of war the way that land soldiers might be. The jury considered the case, and in forty-five minutes returned and found Smith and his prize crew guilty of piracy.

The Different Verdicts

Why did the Philadelphia jury convict the prize crew from the *Jefferson Davis*, but the New York jury could not convict the crew of the *Savannah*?

Perhaps it was because Justice Nelson's charge to the jury in New York was softer than Justice Grier's charge in Philadelphia; critically, Grier instructed the jury that the CSA had no recognized legal existence. Another factor may have been that there was no "evidence" in the Philadelphia trial of the CSA documents, including the letters of marque; whereas in New York, copies of the letters of marque were found onboard the vessel and were produced as evidence. In Philadelphia, the court refused even to permit evidence of how other nations viewed the Civil War, whereas in New York, the court permitted evidence of the May Proclamation of neutrality by the Queen of England, and of the fact of the blockade and prisoner exchange. And, at the emotional level, the testimony of Jacob Garrick in Philadelphia—describing how he was destined to be sold into slavery—was powerful, and was absent in New York.

Of course, the different conclusions simply may have been the result of better defense lawyering in the New York case. New York City had a long and close relationship with the South, serving as bankers for the South's cotton trade; as noted earlier, on January 7, 1861, the mayor of New York, Fernando Wood, had proposed that the city should secede from the state and become a "free city" so as to maintain its ties to the South. The New York jurors may have been more sympathetic to the struggling Confederacy, and as residents in a great maritime port, they might have been unsettled at the prospect of sailors (even though privateers) being hanged.

Or, finally, it is possible that the two main defense attorneys in New York—both Irishmen, Sullivan and Brady—touched the not uncommon, anti-Negro prejudice by driving home the point that the War was being fought for the benefit of the Negro.[42] (The Irish were among the leaders of the great Draft Riots in New York in July 1863—the greatest urban riot in American history—the brunt of which fell on Negroes.) The transcript of the argument of James T. Brady reveals that he raised the question of the legitimacy of the Union goals in fighting the secessionist states:

> A war carried on for what? . . . Are we fighting to subjugate the South in the sense in which an emperor would make war upon a rebellious province? . . . Or are we fighting with a covert and secret intention . . . ? Is it to effect the abolition of slavery all over the territory of the United States? . . . [I]f it be . . . designedly waged for the emancipation of all the slaves, our people never will sustain it in the North.[43]

As Brady completed his argument, the court transcript reports that there was "Applause, which was checked by the Court."[44] Brady must have known that the official antislavery stand of the Republican administration

JAMES T. BRADY.

was not fully shared by all New Yorkers—and he hoped that some of them were in the jury in front of him.[45] The hung jury in the piracy trail of the *Savannah* crew may well have been an act of jury nullification.[46]

Aftermath

Despite the hung jury in the *Savannah* trial, Smith and his prize crew from the *Jefferson Davis* remained in jail in Philadelphia after their conviction on October 25th. But help was on the way.

The news of Smith's conviction in Philadelphia hit hard in Richmond. On August 30th, the Confederate Congress authorized President Davis to take whatever measures seemed to him to be "just and proper" to protect Confederate prisoners.[47] On November 9th, the CSA Secretary of War, Judah P. Benjamin,[48] directed that the highest ranking Union prisoners of war confined in Richmond would be held for execution in the same manner adopted by the North for Smith and his crew (and potentially for the crew from the *Savannah*), matching the numbers and ranks. Acting under Benjamin's order, a Confederate general compelled a member of Congress from New York, who had been captured at Bull Run, to draw by lot names of Union officers. Those officers then were taken from Confederate prisoner of war camps to ordinary prisons.

The Lincoln administration had been tough on the idea of prisoner exchanges at the outset of the War, due to the perceived need to avoid any actions that might suggest recognition of the CSA as a separate nation. However, after about a thousand Union soldiers were captured at the First Battle of Bull Run on July 21, 1861, the administration's position began to soften. The forces occasionally exchanged prisoners, usually as an act of humanity between field commanders—sometimes beginning with only an exchange of the sick. Public support for prisoner exchanges grew, and undoubtedly the trial of the privateers added to the pressures. As a result, on December 11, 1861, Congress adopted a joint resolution requesting the president "to inaugurate systematic measures for the exchange of prisoners in the present rebellion." In the preamble, the joint resolution noted that such an action would increase enlistments, serve the interests of humanity, and "such exchange does not involve a recognition of the rebels as a government."[49]

The following February, Smith and the other privateers/pirates were transferred from ordinary prisons to Fort Lafayette in New York Harbor, in the custody of the Secretary of War. Smith and others were released in a general prisoner exchange in May 1862, and were greeted with acclaim in Charleston. But at least two members of the *Savannah* crew died in prison or during the journey home.[50]

Thus, despite the claim that the South was only an organized mob and insurrectionists, the Lincoln administration ended up giving to the Confederacy the rights of a belligerent nation: as members of the armed forces of a belligerent, the crews of captured privateers were treated as combatants, prisoners of war. Granted that the power of the Davis/Benjamin threat of physical retaliation had a great impact on the decision of the Lincoln administration to treat privateers as prisoners of war, the excellent lawyering in the *Savannah* case provided the legal rationale. Henceforth, no jury would convict a privateer of the capital offense of piracy.

The Chapman Piracy Project

In thinking of "pirates" and privateers during the Civil War at sea, one naturally focuses on the Atlantic coast, and perhaps the Gulf of Mexico. However, an interesting case of an unusual privateering effort was decided in the U.S. Circuit Court for the Northern District of California almost exactly two years after the New York and Philadelphia piracy trials. This time, however, the defendants were charged not with "piracy," which carried the death penalty, but with having given aid or comfort to the rebellion, under the Second Confiscation Act of July 17, 1862. The maximum penalty under this Act was ten years' imprisonment and/or a fine of up to $10,000.

Asbury Harpending was an adventurer. As a teenager, he ran away from his native Kentucky to join the "filibuster"[51] of General William Walker in Nicaragua, but U.S. officials interrupted the effort. Harpending eventually made his way to California, where he made a fortune in mining. California was solidly in the Union, but there were Confederate sympathizers there who delighted in conspiracies to undermine the state and the Union. Harpending understood that transport of California gold by Pacific Mail ship to Washington presented a golden opportunity to interrupt those funds vital to the Union—and gave him the opportunity to put some in his own pocket. Not wanting to be labeled a "pirate," Harpending, in the first part of 1862, made a perilous journey from California, across Mexico (where robbers shot his horse from under him), where he boarded a blockade runner, slipped past Union warships into Charleston, and made his way to Richmond.

In Richmond, Harpending met with Jefferson Davis. Davis immediately recognized the value to the CSA of cutting off the Union's supply of gold from California, but he was quite doubtful that Harpending could successfully complete the task, and, finally, Davis was unsure of whether the enterprise could be justified under international law or would simply be viewed as piracy. He put these questions to Judah Benjamin, who had dealt with the New York and Philadelphia piracy trials, and who on March 24th had become the CSA secretary of state. Benjamin opined that the scheme would be legally acceptable as long as no overt act against U.S. commerce was undertaken until a non-U.S. port had been reached and letters of marque exhibited and the purpose openly declared.[52] Harpending was then given letters of marque in blank, with the apparent understanding that he would fill in the names when he secured a ship and crew and got to a non-U.S. port. He was also given a commission in the CSA Navy.

On his return to San Francisco, he found a co-investor in the enterprise, Ridgley Greathouse, and a young English gentleman of fortune with an interest in adventure, Alfred Rubery. Ironically, Rubery was the favorite nephew of John Bright, the great English member of Parliament and leader of the working class who was a key influence in Britain's decision not to recognize the Confederacy. Bright's importance to the Union was demonstrated by the fact that Lincoln kept a photograph of Bright in his upstairs office in the family quarters of the White House; the only other adornment was a portrait of Andrew Jackson.[53]

Harpending, Greathouse, and Rubery arranged to buy a ship, the *J. M. Chapman*, and by February 1863, they had found a captain (William C. Law) and bought a cannon and small arms; engaged a mate (Lorenzo Libby) and crew; and agreed on the division of the expected spoils of their "privateer" escapade. Their plan was to sail from San Francisco on Sunday morning, March 15th, to proceed to Mexico's busiest port, Manzanillo, to enroll the men in the letters of marque and forward a copy of the letters to the CSA in Richmond. But events turned out quite differently: U.S. authorities had become aware of the plot, and that same Sunday morning, the U.S. sloop-of-war *Cyane* trained its guns on the *Chapman* as it cast off from the wharf in San Francisco. The U.S. officials boarded the *Chapman* and took the prisoners to Alcatraz. The "*Chapman* piracy project" became instant news, especially because John Bright's nephew was involved. Greathouse was released on bail, and Law and Libby confessed and became witnesses for the prosecution.

The conspirators were brought to trial in San Francisco on October 2, 1863, before newly appointed Supreme Court Justice Stephen J. Field,[54] who was sitting in the newly created Tenth Circuit. The other judge presiding at the trial was Federal District Judge Ogden Hoffman. Among the eminent counsel was Delos Lake for the defense, who later became U.S. district attorney for California in the Lincoln and Johnson administrations. The defense offered no testimony, but argued, in much the same way as the defense in the New York and Philadelphia piracy trials had, that the CSA was a sovereign state which had received belligerent rights from the United States, and that privateering was a legitimate mode of warfare, and so the court had no jurisdiction.[55] The defense counsel also argued that there had in fact been no commencement of the cruise, so there could not have been any offense since the schooner had not reached the Mexican port and had not commenced hostilities; the mere buying of a pistol did not constitute murder.

The jury took four minutes to bring in a verdict of guilty. The conspirators had been charged not with piracy, but with having given aid or comfort to the rebellion, under Section 2 of the Second Confiscation Act. Justice Stephens took judicial notice of the existence of the rebellion, and he continued:

> If the defendants obtained a Letter of Marque from the president of the so-called Confederate States, the fact does not exempt them from prosecution . . . . As a matter of policy and humanity, the Government of the United States has treated the citizens of the so-called Confederate States, taken in open hostilities, as prisoners of war, and has exempted them from trial for violation of its municipal laws. . . . [The Second Confiscation Act] was passed after captives in war had been treated and exchanged as prisoners of war . . . .[56]

Justice Field underscored that the "allegiance which every one—citizen or alien—owes to the government under which he at the time lives, is sufficient to subject him to the penalties of treason." The defendants were sentenced to ten years in prison and a $10,000 fine, the maximum under the Act.

Most of the prisoners were later released under the general amnesty act after taking the oath of allegiance. Harpending stayed in jail an additional four months, since he had had a commission in the CSA Navy. Alfred Rubery's British uncle, John Bright, contacted Senator Charles Sumner of Massachusetts, the chairman of the Foreign Relations Committee (and an Anglophile) and suggested a pardon. Sumner consulted Justice Field and Senator John Conness of California.[57] President Lincoln issued a pardon of Alfred Rubery on December 16, 1863. The pardon noted that Rubery was "of the immature age of 20," and that "[he] is a subject of Great Britain and his pardon is desired by John Bright of England . . . [and] especially as a public mark of the esteem held by the [United States] for the high character and steady friendship of the said John Bright . . . ." The pardon was to take effect on January 20, 1864, on the condition that Rubery leave the country within thirty days. The *Chapman* was condemned and sold as a prize of war with the proceeds distributed between the United States and the crew that captured it.

The Blockade

While the Union Blockade declared by Lincoln in April 1861 set into motion many of the events discussed in this chapter, the main resulting court case, the *Prize Cases*, was not decided until 1863.

Even before the shelling of Fort Sumter, Lincoln and Seward discussed how they might maintain national sovereignty over the South's coastline without declaring a blockade—which would, in effect, be a declaration of war. Remembering the action of President Andrew Jackson in late 1832, in the face of South Carolina's declared nullification ordinance, when Jackson posted United States ships offshore Charleston to collect tariffs and enforce customs laws, Seward tried out the same idea in late March 1861. Seward floated the idea at a dinner party with several European diplomats. The British Minister, Lord Lyons (Richard B. Pemell), was the host, and he said he thought the idea sounded like a paper blockade, and would put the Europeans in the position of either recognizing the CSA or accepting the interruption of their seaboard commerce.[58] Seward dropped the idea.

The main thrust of Lincoln's proclamation of April 19, 1861, was the creation of a blockade. Having listed the seven states "in which an insurrection has broken out," Lincoln stated that he "deemed it advisable to set on foot a blockade of the ports within [those seven states] . . . in pursuance of the laws of the United States and of the law of Nations." The proclamation noted that a "competent force" would be posted to prevent vessels from entering those ports and that after due notice, any vessel in violation "will be captured and sent to the nearest convenient port, for such proceedings against her and her cargo as prize . . . ." On April 27th, Lincoln extended the proclamation to the ports of Virginia and North Carolina to cover the entire Confederate coast, the four thousand miles from Virginia to the Mexican border.[59] On the same day, Navy Secretary Welles ordered Union ships to seize Confederate privateers.

It was no accident that Lincoln's proclamation referred to international law, "the law of nations." Under the 1856 Declaration of Paris, reflecting customary international law, a blockade must be formally proclaimed, promptly established, enforced, and effective. If any of those elements was missing, the blockade would be illegal and need not be observed. For Lincoln, the blockade was an essential element in the broad Anaconda Plan of General Winfield Scott, designed to encircle and strangle the Confederacy.[60] But despite this plan and great efforts, at first, the blockade was a "tactical failure, and probably hindered other important strategic endeavors by tying down vital Union recourses."[61]

During the course of the War, Confederate blockade runners benefited from more than seven thousand successful runs. The Union Navy failed to capture most of the major Southern ports until late in the war; Tampa, Florida, was still open to blockade-running traffic even after Lee's surrender in April 1865. Clandestine shipments from Nassau, Havana, and Bermuda supported the Confederacy. A ship's captain could receive the equivalent of $150,000 in today's dollars for a successful six-day-round trip from Nassau, the Bahamas, to Wilmington, North Carolina, then back to Nassau.[62]

The goal of the blockade was to stop the export of cotton from the South and the import of munitions and supplies into the South. The South provided three-quarters of the world's cotton; 20 percent of Great Britain's population depended on the textile for its livelihood. The blockade would also force long-distance travel (of goods, horses, or men) within the South to rely exclusively on the CSA's inadequate railway system. For example, the South produced sufficient food for civilians and soldiers, but there was difficulty in moving surplus resources to areas with scarcity. And of course, a congested rail system impaired its use by the Confederate military forces. General Scott advised Lincoln that the cost of transport by water was one-fifth the cost of land transport.

In the period leading to the blockade, and even in the first months, when the North had insufficient ships to fully enforce it, it would have been smart for the South to have anticipated the blockade, and to have delivered to Europe and stored there enough cotton to satisfy the mills of England and France for years, and to acquire arms in exchange. However, the South thought it would be wise to hold its cotton. The idea was that England and other European powers would panic and intervene in the civil war at least enough to acquire badly needed Southern cotton.

But the South's plan didn't work either. There was no serious shortage of cotton on the world market; Egyptian cotton was developing well. The earlier Southern cotton production had been unusually large, and the accumulated stocks carried the Europeans into 1862. By that time, the blockade was relatively effective.

Blockade service was attractive to the Union sailors, though it was boring—sailing back and forth to intercept blockade runners—except when they ran into those blockade runners. The blockading vessels were to stop any vessel leaving or entering the port, notify it of the blockade, and so inscribe it on the ship's log. Thereafter, if the same ship tried to enter or leave, it would be captured and subjected to legal proceedings in a prize court.[63] International law defines the term "prize" as a successful judicial condemnation of a captured vessel. The key for the crew was that the proceeds of the sale of the condemned vessel were apportioned among the officers and crew. That fact made the blockade service more attractive to Union sailors.

The *Prize Cases*

Four vessels got caught up in the blockade during the first months, and their cases made their way to the U.S. Supreme Court, which, in 1863, decided their fate in a decision called the *Prize Cases*.

The schooner *Crenshaw* was leaving Richmond with a cargo of tobacco, bound for Liverpool, when it was captured by the USS *Star* in Hampton Roads at the mouth of the James River on May 17, 1861. The owners of the vessel and the cargo—citizens of Virginia—claimed that they had no notice of the blockade at the time the *Crenshaw* was leaving the port of Richmond. There was some dispute as to the ownership of the tobacco, some of which may have been owned by citizens of New York and some by a British partnership. She was taken into New York City as a prize of war.

The next vessel was a British barque, the *Hiawatha*. She left Richmond on May 17th en route to Liverpool, also with a cargo of cotton and tobacco. She was captured in Hampton Roads on May 20th, and taken to New York City. The owners of the *Hiawatha*, a British company, also claimed insufficient notice of the blockade.

Under the blockade, neutrals were given fifteen days from the date on which the blockade became effective to safely depart; the blockade's effective date was April 30th, and the fifteen days expired on May 15th. The British Consul at Richmond advised the owners of the deadline dates, and on May 8th, the British Minister in Washington took up the matter with the secretary of state. On May 10th, the *Hiawatha* completed discharging her cargo. Instead of leaving then, she started to load cargo for the outbound voyage. On the 16th, she was ready, but the tug had problems, and so it was not until May 20th that she was towed out to sea—and captured.[64]

The third vessel was the schooner *Brilliante*. She was a Mexican ship bound for New Orleans with a cargo of flour, but found the mouth of the Mississippi blocked by the USS *Brooklyn*. The *Brilliante* found another way to New Orleans where she discharged her cargo, and took on another. Then, while anchored in Biloxi Bay on June 23rd, she was seized and taken to Key West for legal proceedings in the U.S. District Court for the District of Florida. She and her cargo were condemned as a prize of war.

The fourth vessel was the brig *Amy Warwick*, owned by citizens of Richmond. She made a voyage from New York to Richmond, and then to Rio de Janeiro where she picked up a cargo of coffee to be delivered to New York, Philadelphia, Baltimore, or Richmond, depending on the orders she would receive at Hampton Roads. While heading to Hampton Roads, she was captured off Cape Henry on July 10th by the USS *Quaker City*. At that time, the *Amy Warwick* was flying American colors, and the captain was unaware of the War. She was carried to Boston and libeled[65] as enemy property.

The legal action relating to these four vessels—spread out from Florida to Boston, and captured between May 20th and July 10th—became the subject of intense interest at home and abroad (as two were owned by Mexican and English interests). Each case touched the issue of the nature of the blockade and Lincoln's authority to impose it. Under international law, a blockade is recognized only between two sovereign nations that are at war. Before proclaiming the blockade in April, Lincoln and his advisers wrestled with the fact that they did not want to take any action that would have the effect of recognizing the CSA as a sovereign nation. This was an "insurrection"—not a "war"—between sovereign powers. On the other hand, the Union needed an effective, internationally recognized blockade—not a mere "closing" of the South's ports. The British government in effect told the Lincoln administration that its action must be a formal blockade if Britain was to recognize it.

The claims of the owners of the four captured vessels—representing purely commercial interests—forced the fundamental question of whether Lincoln had the power to declare a blockade. If not, the capture of these four vessels was illegal, and they would have to be returned or compensation paid. The U.S. district courts in Boston, New York, and Key West condemned the vessels and cargoes, and those decisions were affirmed by the respective U.S. circuit courts; the separate appeals were consolidated and ended up in the Supreme Court as the first case during the Civil War to address the key legal question: Was this a war or an insurrection; did the president have the power to declare a blockade in the absence of congressional authorization? The four appeals were listed on the Court's docket as the *Prize Cases*. Similar cases pending in the lower courts were postponed until the Supreme Court's ruling. The cases were argued and decided in early 1863. We shall return to this case in detail later in this chapter.

International Relations

The blockade, and the capture of these four vessels, also highlighted the difficult diplomatic landscape the new Lincoln administration faced. It was clear that an alliance of European powers and the South—recognition of its independence, and possibly economic and military aid—would ensure victory for the Confederacy. A cut-off of the South's foreign trade might well anger Europe, whose cotton mills and shipping interests would be hurt, and force Europe to side with the South.[66] Most European powers were monarchies, and European conservatives would welcome the break-up of the Union in the hope that it might eliminate an uncomfortable threat of the spread of American "democracy"; many also felt a kinship with the stability and gentility of the South's social system.

At the beginning of the conflict, only Russia stood squarely with the Union, because it looked to the United States to balance any threat to Russia from England, and also to repay the support given by the United States in the Crimean War.[67] Perhaps because of Russia's apparent tie to the Union, the CSA did not appoint a mission to Russia until 1862, and that mission never even made it to St. Petersburg. (Lincoln sent the radical antislavery militant Cassius Clay of Kentucky to St. Petersburg, largely to get him out of Washington.)

The three most important nations for the Union were England and France—the two most powerful nations, and also the largest consumers of the South's cotton—and Mexico, the backdoor for sneaking supplies in and out of the CSA. England and France were divided internally about the American rebellion. English liberals welcomed the democracy and despised slavery, while its conservatives thought that British interests in that hemisphere would be better served if there were two nations, rather than only the United States. In France, Napoleon III despised the Monroe Doctrine, viewing it as an obstacle to rebuilding France's empire centered in Mexico. Mexico was not happy with the United States: the United States had provoked a war in the 1840s and had taken much of its territory. Not surprisingly, Mexico looked to Europe for protection against its powerful neighbor to the north—though in the background was the worry that Mexico's crushing indebtedness to England, France, and Spain might result in a joint military action by those three powers[68] to collect revenue[69] to repay the indebtedness—blowing a hole in the Monroe Doctrine.[70]

Lincoln's diplomatic appointments reflected the importance of these three countries. For Mexico, he chose Ohio Senator Tom Corwin as the American Minister. Corwin had actively campaigned for Lincoln, and, while he served in the House of Representatives with Lincoln in the late 1840s, Corwin had vigorously denounced the war with Mexico—as had Representative Lincoln. Lincoln hoped that the Mexicans would appreciate that touch. Corwin was charming, though he spoke no Spanish.[71] Mexico also understood the importance of its relationship with the United States. Just two months after Lincoln's election, the Mexican leader, Benito Juarez, sent his charge d'affaires in Washington (Matias Romero) to call on Lincoln in Springfield. On January 19, 1861, Lincoln, recognizing a precious ally in Mexico, sent Romero off with a gushing letter of appreciation.[72] Surprisingly, the Mexican was the only diplomatic caller on Lincoln before his inauguration.

Jefferson Davis, in contrast and at the recommendation of CSA Secretary of State Robert Toombs, sent Colonel John T. Pickett, a West Point dropout and a fomenter of revolutions in Cuba and Nicaragua, as the CSA envoy to Mexico. Pickett's activity in Mexico eventually led him to be jailed by the Mexican government—Pickett viewed northern Mexico as ideal for annexation by the CSA. Davis had to recall him to Richmond.

For the key minister to England, Secretary of State Seward pushed for his close friend, Charles Francis Adams. Though Lincoln initially hesitated to name Adams, he acted once he learned that Davis had already dispatched three envoys to Europe. Adams' grandfather, John Adams, had served in a similar position in 1778, taking his son John Quincy with him to London. In 1809, John Quincy, in turn, sailed for Russia to deal with Napoleon and Czar Alexander. He took his son, Charles Francis, with him to Russia. Thus, the American minister to England was the son of the sixth U.S. president and the grandson of the second U.S. president.[73] He arrived in London on May 13th. A skilled diplomat, Adams appeared at the British court in the traditional stockings and lace in order to convey the seriousness of his duty.[74]

William L. Dayton was Lincoln's pick for minister to Paris. He had been a senator from New Jersey, and the first Republican nominee for vice president at the Philadelphia Convention in 1856—beating out Lincoln. He had no previous diplomatic experience, but he proved to be a competent minister in Paris.[75] His task was to keep Napoleon from recognizing the CSA.

These three Union envoys to the most critical diplomatic posts were all lawyers.

In March 1861, Confederate President Davis selected William Lowndes Yancey to be chairman of the commission to Europe to represent the Confederate cause to England and France. (Yancey defended slavery with such a passion that he quickly made himself unpopular in England, and so he did not last long at his post.) Pierre Adolphe Rost was commissioner to Spain, and Ambrose Dudley Mann was commissioner for Belgium and the Vatican. Yancey and Rost were both lawyers. Mann had been a successful U.S. diplomat, and is known as the father of the U.S. consular service; he was the only experienced diplomat in the Confederate service.

The *Trent* Affair

In early November 1861, an incident off the coast of Cuba precipitated the most serious diplomatic crisis of the whole Civil War period, one that brought the United States to the brink of war with Great Britain. It involved an interpretation of international law.

Deciding to substantially enhance the diplomacy of the CSA in Europe, Jefferson Davis in August commissioned two new envoys: James Mason and John Slidell. They would be formidable emissaries. Mason, of Virginia, was the grandson of Founding Father George Mason, a U.S. senator from 1847 until 1861, author of the Fugitive Slave Act of 1850, and of the Senate's Mason Report of 1860 concerning the John Brown

JOHN SLIDELL.

raid on Harpers Ferry. Slidell, originally from New York, was a powerful U.S. senator representing Louisiana from 1853 until 1861. Mason and Slidell were both lawyers.

Mason and Slidell ran the blockade aboard the *Theodora* at Charleston and reached Nassau with their secretaries and Slidell's family, and then went on to Havana. They left Havana on November 7th on the *Trent*, a British mail packet bound for the Danish island of St. Thomas. At St. Thomas, they planned to board a British steamer for Southampton, and then to proceed to London and Paris.

In mid-October, the twelve-gun sloop, the USS *San Jacinto*, under Captain Charles Wilkes,[76] arrived in the Caribbean under orders from Navy Secretary Welles expecting to join the Union expedition against Port Royal, South Carolina. However, Wilkes found out about the Confederate envoys' plan to leave Havana, and became interested in the notion of capturing Mason and Slidell. He consulted his books about the law of nations (international law), but could not find sufficient authority to permit him to capture the two envoys. He found authority to permit his seizure of enemy dispatches, however, and he leaped to the notion—quite creatively—that perhaps he could take the envoys as the "embodiment of dispatches." His first officer, Lieutenant Donald. M. Fairfax, disagreed, fearing war with Great Britain: the *Trent* would be in international waters transiting from one neutral port to another, and stopping it to remove passengers would be a violation of British sovereignty.[77] Wilkes elected to proceed with his plan nevertheless, and awaited the *Trent* in the Old Bahama Channel off the north coast of Cuba. He knew that any vessel bound from Havana to St. Thomas would have to pass that way.[78] Captain Wilkes had known John Slidell as a boy in New York; they had quarreled over a girl, but their paths had not crossed since then. Perhaps that personal history added to Wilkes desire to capture the *Trent*.[79]

At noon, on November 9th, the *San Jacinto* stopped the *Trent* about three hundred miles east of Havana with two shots across its bow. Wilkes told Fairfax to board, demand the ship's papers, arrest the envoys, and seize the *Trent* as a prize. The captain of the *Trent* protested, refused to show the ship's papers, and asserted that force would be needed to take the two CSA envoys. Fairfax disobeyed orders by letting the *Trent* sail on, but he did take the envoys, their baggage, and secretaries onto the *San Jacinto*.[80] Fairfax argued successfully to Wilkes that to take the steamer would have needlessly angered passengers and irritated the British, and that the *San Jacinto* itself would have been weakened by having to place a prize crew aboard the *Trent*. Wilkes proceeded with his captives to Fortress Monroe in Virginia for supplies, and then on to Fort Warren in Boston, arriving on November 24, 1861.

REAR ADMIRAL CHARLES WILKES.

Lincoln first learned of Wilkes' act on November 15th, when a telegram arrived from the U.S. military at Fort Monroe.[81] The next month was stressful for the Lincoln administration.

In the North, the capture of Mason and Slidell was a cause of great jubilation. Captain Wilkes—seen as bold and creative against the British—became a hero overnight. (This was in contrast to the fact that in the navy, Wilkes had been its Peck's Bad Boy[82]—one scholar notes that Wilkes had an "unerring knack for causing trouble."[83]) Massachusetts Governor John Andrew gave the captain a public dinner. Wilkes made a triumphant procession southward to Washington to receive a gold medal awarded by the House of Representatives on December 2nd.[84] After a year of repeated disasters on the battlefield, Unionists finally had a reason to celebrate.

The popular enthusiasm was shared within Lincoln's cabinet. The single exception was Montgomery Blair, postmaster general and former Dred Scott lawyer. Blair believed that the seizure violated the sovereign rights at sea, a position long held by the United States.[85] He urged a preemptive immediate release of the prisoners, before the British could protest. Blair lived across the street from the White House,[86] and staying with him was Gus Fox, the assistant secretary of the navy, the equivalent of today's chief of naval operations (Fox was related to Blair by marriage). Lincoln often dropped in at Blair House to consult Fox. Fox told Lincoln that the superior British Navy could destroy the Union blockade in a month, and therefore Mason and Slidell had to be released.[87]

Lincoln had doubts about the legality of the seizure, but he was assured by legal experts across the North that Wilkes had behaved properly: Harvard Law Professor Theophilus Parsons thought it was as legal

"Policeman Wilkes, noticing . . . that the well-known rogues, Mason and Slidell, were about to pawn some of their late Employer's property at Messrs. Bull, Crapaud & Co.'s shop, kept . . . look-out . . . and nabbed them in the nick of time."

as the blockade of Charleston, and Caleb Cushing (Buchanan's Attorney General) believed every nation had the right to seize enemy dispatches (or their embodiment).[88] Lincoln visited with Attorney General Bates to discuss the issue, and Bates assured him that not only did Wilkes have the right to seize Mason and Slidell, but also the right to seize the ship—that Wilkes had acted as both a naval officer and a prize court. Lincoln acknowledged that he was not much of a prize lawyer, but that it seemed to him that "if Wilkes saw fit to make that capture on the high seas, he had no right to turn his quarterdeck into a prize court."[89]

The British Minister in Washington, Lord Lyons, was certain that this capture was a violation of international law, and that the Lincoln administration would have to surrender Mason and Slidell. Ministers from Italy, Prussia, Denmark, and Russia all called on Lord Lyons to express their opinion that the Union was wrong.

When the news reached Britain on November 27th, it provoked much hostility toward the North, which was believed to have undertaken the action against the *Trent* as a way of compensating for defeats at home (Bull Run, Ball's Bluff, and Wilson's Creek) by bullying innocent English abroad. Prince Albert, the Royal Consort, was gravely ill at the time, but still managed to write in his diary for November 28th about the *Trent* incident, noting: "General indignation. The Law Officers declare the act as a breach of international law."[90] Amazingly, the British cabinet, anticipating such an event as the *Trent* conflict, in mid-November had sought legal advice specifically on what rights the Union could exercise against a British vessel carrying CSA commissioners. As a result of this preparation, the British government acted as soon as the news arrived. The UK charged that the United States had committed a flagrant violation of international law by forcibly removing passengers from a ship of a neutral nation.[91] Foreign Secretary Lord Russell, who was as anti-United States as Secretary Seward was anti-UK, prepared instructions for the minister in Washington. They were bellicose and threatening. The instructions were approved by the cabinet and sent to the Queen. However, Prince Albert reviewed the document on Sunday morning, November 30th, before it went to the Queen. He redrafted it, taking the sting out of it: he noted that it was highly unlikely that the Captain's actions were directed by Washington, and that he was unwilling to believe that the United States "intended wantonly to put an insult" to Great Britain.[92] The Prince died shortly thereafter.

The instructions left Britain on December 1st, though they would not be received by Lord Lyons in Washington until the 18th. The instructions called for the British envoy to demand that Mason and Slidell be released, and that the United States apologize for its breach of international law.[93] If, after seven days, there was not a satisfactory response, Lord Lyons and his staff were to pack up and leave. War would follow. More than eleven thousand British soldiers left the UK for Canada (to repel the assumed American attack), and the British Admiralty beefed up its North American station to forty steam vessels with almost thirteen hundred guns. Even if Britain lost Canada, the British would destroy the Union's blockading fleet, impose a blockade of its own against ports in the North, and hunt down American commerce worldwide.

Despite the popular jubilation, Lincoln had a sense that the British were right, that the capture violated international law. Senator Charles Sumner, the chairman of the Senate Foreign Affairs Committee (and an Anglophile), met with Lincoln to press upon Lincoln the gravity of the situation, and he suggested that perhaps it might be wise to put the issue to international arbitration by a neutral party, such as the King of Prussia. Lincoln was interested, and he began to draft a proposal.[94] But by late November, the administration still had taken no formal position, and both Montgomery Blair and Charles Sumner were advising immediate release of Mason and Slidell. Seward, however, instructed the U.S. minister in London, Charles Adams, to let the foreign secretary know that Wilkes had *not* acted on instructions from the U.S. government—a clever way of distancing the Lincoln administration from the conflict by suggesting that this was a rogue action. On November 30th, Secretary of the Navy Welles sent a congratulatory letter to Wilkes, but wisely, Welles added that Wilkes had erred by not taking the *Trent* to a prize court.[95]

Lincoln elected to use his first annual State of the Union message, on December 3, 1861, to hold out an olive branch to the British. Early in his message—the section dealing with war and foreign relations—Lincoln noted the correspondence between the British minister in Washington and the secretary of state concerning the detention the prior June by a United States steamer of the British vessel *Perthshire* for a supposed breach of the blockade. Lincoln then explained that the detention was occasioned by "an obvious misapprehension of the facts," and that justice required that the United States should commit no belligerent act "not founded in strict right as sanctioned by public law." Lincoln recommended an appropriation to satisfy the reasonable demands of the vessel's owners for her detention. While not mentioning the *Trent* affair, Lincoln had signaled that there were times when the facts were not clear, and that the United States would adhere strictly to international law—and, most importantly, the United States would do the right thing by the British. This was smart public diplomacy: by taking a minor matter like the incorrect detention of a British ship and highlighting it in his speech, Lincoln was demonstrating to the British that he would pay close attention to safeguarding their legitimate maritime interests in the future.

United States Minister Adams wrote from London on December 12th to Secretary of State Seward that "all preparations for warfare are going on at different Depots and magazines with great energy."[96] On December 15th, Seward attended a ball at the Portuguese legation at which, "perhaps under the influence of brandy, he declared that if Britain forced war upon the United States, 'We will wrap the whole world in flames.'"[97] Despite that outward chest-pounding, Seward became more convinced that it was essential to surrender Mason and Slidell, but Lincoln was still uncertain. In the meantime, the British cabinet proclaimed a prohibition on the export to the United States of weapons and saltpeter, the main ingredient in gunpowder. In response, on December 18th, the New York stock market dropped sharply, and the price of gold rose.

Lord Lyons received the instructions from London on December 18th, and on the next day, he visited the State Department. Lyons and Seward diplomatically agreed that Lyons would not formally hand over his ultimatum for several days, in order to delay the start of the seven-day clock. On December 23rd, Lyons officially presented the British ultimatum to Seward.

The Union's Official Response

On Christmas morning, December 25, 1861, Seward formally argued for the release of the CSA envoys in front of President Lincoln and his cabinet. Some cabinet members were still more impressed with the strength of popular opinion and wanted to retain Mason and Slidell. While the meeting was in progress, the French minister to Washington, Henri Mercier, rushed to the State Department with his long-awaited[98] instructions from Paris: the French were in solidarity with the British on this issue. That ended the argument that the North might be able to play Britain and France against each other.[99] At the end of the four-hour meeting, Lincoln told Seward to continue to prepare his position, but that Lincoln in the meantime would "try my hand at stating the reasons why they ought *not* to be given up. We will compare the points on each side."[100] The next morning before the cabinet meeting reconvened, Seward read his twenty-six-page foolscap brief to Treasury Secretary Chase. The two lawyers agreed that Mason and Slidell had to be released.

Seward's elaborated position, designed for presentation to Lord Lyons, offered no apology, but made it clear that Wilkes had not acted properly under international law. Seward noted his pleasure that the British position reflected the American view of the principles over which the War of 1812 was fought.[101] The cabinet unanimously agreed with the position and the release of Mason and Slidell. After the meeting, Seward asked Lincoln why he hadn't presented the opposing argument, as Lin-

SECRETARY OF STATE WILLIAM H. SEWARD.

coln had promised the day before. Lincoln smiled and said that he could not come up with an argument that satisfied him—and that proved to him that Seward's position was right. Lincoln also knew that the Union could not afford a two-front war, one with the Confederacy and the other with Great Britain.

One might speculate about events if Prince Albert, from his deathbed, had not softened the British position, if lawyers close to Lincoln had persuaded him that international law supported Captain Wilkes' action, and if politicians insisted on riding the patriotic fervor: at a minimum, the UK (probably followed by France and Spain) would have recognized the CSA, the blockade would have been broken, and the United States probably would have been forced to negotiate peace with the Confederates.

Once again, the grim prospect of war with Great Britain may well have been the heaviest factor in the decision to release Mason and Slidell, but the lawyers' opinion that the Union's legal position was insupportable under international law had significant influence.

On December 27, Seward presented the United States' position to Lord Lyons, who deemed it satisfactory. In the end, the public reaction in both the United States and in Britain was relief, not anger—though in the South, there must have been great disappointment. On January

1, 1862, Mason and Slidell left Fort Warren for Provincetown, where they boarded the HMS *Rinaldo* and headed to England to seek European recognition of the Confederacy. On January 10, 1862, the British foreign secretary wrote to Lord Lyons that he considered the matter closed.[102]

The close call of conflict between the United States and Great Britain was still in British minds years later. The editors of the London *Economist*, writing in April 1865 about Lincoln's assassination, opined that at the

> very moment when the dread of war between the Union and Western Europe seemed . . . about to die away, a murderer deprives us of the man who had most power and most will to maintain the peace . . . . There is no longer any person in the Union whom the Union dare or will trust to do exceptional acts . . . to act when needful, as in the *Trent* case, athwart the popular instinct.[103]

The *Prize Cases* in the Supreme Court

The owners of the four vessels caught by the Union blockade—the Virginian *Crenshaw* and *Amy Warwick*, the British *Hiawatha*, and the Mexican *Brilliante*—pressed for a quick resolution of the legal issues arising out of their capture during May–July 1861. (This was just before the explosive *Trent* affair in November 1861.) They wanted the lower courts' rulings reversed—the U.S. district courts in Boston, New York, and Key West had condemned the vessels and cargos, and those decisions had been affirmed by the respective U.S. circuit courts—so they could get their vessels and cargo back in their hands, or be compensated for their loss.

At that time, each of the circuit courts was presided over by a Justice of the Supreme Court. Justice Nelson was assigned to the Eastern Circuit, which covered the Southern District of New York. When the *Crenshaw* and *Hiawatha* cases were appealed from that district court, Nelson affirmed both district court decisions without expressing an opinion of his own. Therefore, when those two cases were appealed to the Supreme Court, Nelson would be in the position of reviewing an appeal of his own decision, a situation that seems odd today but that was commonplace then.[104]

All four cases ended up on appeal to the U.S. Supreme Court. At the beginning of 1862, the attorneys for the claimants pressed Attorney General Bates to advance the cases on the Supreme Court calendar.[105] Because of vacancies, there were only six Justices at that time, and Bates understood that those six—who had agreed with the *Dred Scott* decision—reflected an unsympathetic Court. There was nothing to be gained for the administration by trying to accelerate the Court's consideration, and everything to be gained by slowing the process. Lincoln's first appointment to the Court, Noah H. Swayne, was made in late January 1862. In July, Lincoln appointed Samuel F. Miller, and in December, David Davis. The addition of three Lincoln-appointed Justices between January 1862 and January 1863 was critical to the 5 to 4 victory won by the administration in the Court in March 1863.

The Arguments

The oral arguments in the Supreme Court began on February 10, 1863, and continued for twelve days, six days for each side. For the United States, the legal team included William M. Evarts—the very prominent New York lawyer who "lost" the piracy case against the *Savannah* crew sixteen months earlier—and Richard Henry Dana, the Boston expert in maritime law.[106] Counsel for the *Crenshaw* included Daniel Lord, who had been on the successful defense team in the *Savannah* crew's trial.

Lord's argument on behalf of the *Crenshaw* was that the conflict with the South was not an international "war," and so the property of a resident of the South could not be seized as "enemy" property because the South was still part of the United States. Those guilty of the rebellion should be considered traitors, subject to punishment, but mere residence in the South did not constitute hostility or treason. In any event, only Congress had the power to declare war. The president had the power to use force against insurgents, but that step did not carry the legal consequences of war, such as condemnation of vessels.

Counsel for the Mexican owners of the schooner *Brilliante*, James M. Carlisle of Washington, echoed and elaborated Lord's argument.[107] The power of the president as commander in chief did not involve the power to suspend or repeal any law. The temporary powers to repeal invasion or suppress insurrection were not meant to upset the distribution of powers set out in the Constitution—and only Congress had the power to declare war.

> The matter then comes back necessarily to the pure question of the power of the President under the Constitution. . . . [The argument of the United States] makes the President . . . the impersonation of the country, and invokes for him the power and right to use all the force he can command, to "*save the life of the nation.*". . . . This is to assert that the Constitution contemplated and tacitly provided that the President should be dictator, and all Constitutional Government be at an end; whenever he should think that "the life of the nation" is in danger.[108]

In sum, if the seizure of the vessel was claimed under domestic law, it was based on a usurpation of power by the president; if it was based on the belligerent right of blockade under international law, the seizure was invalid because, at the time of the seizure, the United States had not recognized the existence of a war. Congressional acts passed after the seizure could not retroactively legalize the president's actions.

Evarts spoke first for the government's side. He argued that war was a question of actualities: that it was no less a war because it arose without solemnities. To insist that only Congress could declare war would aide and abet the rebellion and help them accomplish the goals of the revolt— the recognition of the rebellious group as a sovereign. As to the argument that there had to be a specific inquiry into whether the particular owners of these vessels or cargo were in fact hostile or loyal to the Union, Evarts insisted that this was totally unnecessary. All commercial property within the area of the rebellion or under its control could be used for the benefit of the insurgency, and therefore had to be seized.

Dana, making only his second appearance before the Court, then took over the government's argument. He quickly acknowledged that the Constitution gives to Congress the power to declare war. But, he then asserted that "War is *a state of things*, and not an act of legislative will."[109] If an invasion takes place while Congress is in recess, can the president act to repel it, Dana asked rhetorically. "It is enough to state the proposition. If it be not so, there is no protection for the State," he answered. He further argued that a declaration of war was not appropriate to civil wars caused by rebels, since that could suggest recognition of sovereignty. Dana's full argument has been described as an unsurpassed display of "eloquence, passion and depth of learning"; and Justice Grier said that it was the best argument he had heard in five years.[110]

Daniel Lord presented a short closing rebuttal on behalf of all the claimants: people who resisted the government were engaging in a criminal act (treason), but that could not be imputed from residence. The only power the president had was to use force to put down the rebellion, but he could not confiscate private property without congressional authority. Oral arguments concluded on February 25th.

The Decision

On March 10th, the Court rendered its decision.[111] The courtroom in the Old Senate Chamber was filled with spectators.

Of the nine Justices, President Jackson had appointed three (Taney, Wayne, and Catron); Presidents Tyler, Polk, and Buchanan had appointed one each (Nelson, Grier, and Clifford, respectively); and President Lincoln had appointed the three newest (Swayne, Miller, and Davis). All of the Justices were from Northern/Western or Border States, except Wayne, who came from Georgia.[112] (Wayne was a slaveholder and felt loyal to Georgia, but he was foremost a Union supporter.) Wayne and Nelson were the two Justices most expert in admiralty law. Grier's majority opinion, which upheld the position of the Lincoln administration, was supported by the three Lincoln appointees and Wayne. It was Grier who presided over the "piracy" trial in Philadelphia of the crew from the *Jefferson Davis* in October 1861 where the jury found them guilty—in part due to the instructions given by Grier.[113]

Grier began by confronting head-on the key issue of the power of the president. He asked whether a state of war existed at the time of the imposition of the blockade.[114] He answered by explaining that:

> The parties belligerent in a public war are independent nations. But it is not necessary to constitute war, that both parties should be acknowledged as independent nations or sovereign States.

Judge Robert C. Grier.

> ... [A] civil war always begins by insurrection ... [and] is never solemnly declared.... [T]he world acknowledges them as belligerents, and the contest a *war*.[115]

As proof, he added that "parties to a civil war usually concede to each other belligerent rights. They exchange prisoners ...." Grier may have been reminded of the fact that the Lincoln administration revisited the question of the status of "criminal prisoners" from the *Jefferson Davis*, and how, after their initial conviction in Grier's court in Philadelphia, the administration declared them "prisoners of war" and ultimately exchanged them for Confederate prisoners. He undoubtedly was also aware of the 1862 formal agreement (the Dix-Hill Cartel) for prisoner exchange, which had been prompted by the congressional joint resolution of December 11, 1861.

Grier readily admitted that Congress alone has the power to declare war, and that the president has no power to initiate or declare a war either against a foreign country or a domestic state. But the president has the power and obligation to resist by force a foreign invasion or a state rebellion. Under international law, Grier pointed out, "It is not necessary that the independence of the revolted province or state be acknowledged in order to constitute it a party belligerent in a war ...." (In support, Grier noted that the Queen of England issued her proclamation of neutrality on

May 13, 1861,[116] a fact introduced by the defense in the New York trial of the *Savannah* crew in the fall of 1861.)

Using brilliant phrasing, Grier wrote that it made no sense to say that the insurgents were not enemies because they were traitors, or that the conflict was not a war because it was an insurrection. Finally, the proclamation of the blockade itself was "conclusive evidence" that a state of war existed. He dealt easily with the issue of the "innocence" of some of the owners of the vessels or cargos: international law recognizes the right of a belligerent to "cut these sinews of the power of an enemy, by capturing his property on the high seas."

In effect, Justice Grier in the 1863 *Prize Cases* adopted the positions taken by the defense in the 1861 *Savannah* and *Jefferson Davis* piracy trials: whether the Union recognized the Confederacy as a nation or not, it had to acknowledge belligerent rights (the CSA privateers were not pirates), and that "facts" could not be ignored. However, since they were at war—as he had just argued—the seizure of the crews and their cargoes was legal.

Grier then turned to each of the four specific cases. All the claimants from the *Amy Warwick* were Virginians, and consequently their property was justly condemned as "enemies' property." With respect to the *Hiawatha*, whose departure was delayed because a steam tug wasn't available, Grier was scornful: "in their eagerness to realize the profits of a full cargo, [the owners] took the hazards of the adventure and must now bear the consequences." The case of the *Brilliante* posed "little difficulty," said Grier: "her condemnation is not for her successful entrance [into New Orleans], but for her unsuccessful attempt to escape." The case of the *Crenshaw* was a bit different as to some of the cargo, since it was hard to ascertain the true owners of the tobacco, but nevertheless, Grier sustained the condemnation.

Justice Samuel Nelson wrote a long opinion dissenting from the Grier opinion. (It was Nelson who presided over the piracy trial of the *Savannah* crew which resulted in a hung jury.[117]) Chief Justice Taney and Justices Catron and Clifford concurred in the Nelson opinion.[118] Nelson's basic point was that there is no constitutional difference between a civil war and an international war. Yes, this war of rebellion is a material war, he said, but with respect to its legal consequences, it is no different from any other kind of war. Thus, the existence of a civil war can only be declared by the Congress. Since Congress did not adopt legislation authorizing the blockade until July 13, 1861, and since that law had no retroactive effect, the seizure of these vessels was illegal. Until that date in July, Nelson insisted, "no citizen of the State can be punished in his person or property, unless he has committed some offense against a law of Congress passed before the act was committed."

JUDGE SAMUEL NELSON.

To support his position, Nelson pointed to the Revolutionary War. Until the Act of King George in 1776 which interdicted all trade, it was a personal war; after that Act, it became a territorial civil war between the contending parties with all the rights of war known to international law. So also, "down to this period [the July 13, 1861, Act of Congress] the only enemy recognized by the Government was the persons engaged in the rebellion, all others were peaceful citizens, entitled to the privileges of citizens under the Constitution." That Act of Congress recognized a state of civil war, but it happened after these ships were caught in the blockade. Nelson concluded that: "the President had no power to set on foot a blockade under the law of nations, and that the capture of the vessel and cargo in this case, and in all cases before us in which the capture occurred before the 13th of July, 1861, . . . are illegal and void and . . . the vessel and cargo restored."

Aftermath

The Supreme Court, in the *Prize Cases*, established that Lincoln, as commander in chief, wielded great plenary powers. The Court granted the Union full belligerent rights from the beginning of the insurrection, while at the same time it did not grant any rights of sovereignty to the South. It represented a major victory for the Lincoln administration. The victory was especially welcomed, since by the beginning of 1863, the Union forces had suffered a series of serious defeats, and the military tide of the South was at its highest.[119] By March, the Confederate military successes had begun to recede, and the gloom in the North was just beginning to lift. An adverse decision in the *Prize Cases* would have been difficult for the administration in many ways: it would have had to compensate the parties whose vessels and cargos had been seized prior to July (when Congress had ratified Lincoln's actions). And, the limiting of Lincoln's war powers would have limited his range of action and emboldened the South.

Justices Wayne and Nelson were the two admiralty law experts on the Court. One might speculate a scenario if they had agreed on the law, in which case Nelson would have written the majority opinion, since the 5 to 4 split would have reversed course.

Congress thought the 5 to 4 decision was too close, and so it added a tenth Justice position, so that Lincoln could appoint someone sympathetic and make for a "safe" Court.[120] The Court had ten Justices[121] from the time of Justice Field's oath of office on May 20, 1863, until the death of Justice Catron on May 30, 1865.[122]

To ensure that the Court's decision was not misunderstood, Richard Henry Dana, the successful author of *Two Years Before the Mast* in 1840, wrote a broadly circulated pamphlet, "Enemy's Territory and Aliens Enemies—What the Supreme Court Decided in the *Prize Cases*." When Dana visited Lincoln at the White House in March 1864, Lincoln told him that he had read and admired the pamphlet.[123]

CHAPTER 7

Ending Slavery

Ending slavery in the United States took a long time. By the early nineteenth century, it had been largely eliminated in the North and the upper areas of the West, but ending slavery in the South and the southern West did not seem possible. At the beginning of the Civil War in 1861, steps to end slavery were taken as military measures. Finally, in January 1863, the Emancipation Proclamation reflected a major shift in the approach to banish slavery, though with little practical results. Slavery was finally ended in 1865 with the adoption of the Thirteenth Amendment. Throughout the effort, the question of the legal authority to end slavery was paramount.

The English Heritage

To understand the path that was taken in the United States toward ending slavery, one must begin with the famous English case of *Somerset v. Stewart*, or *Somerset's Case*. In many ways, this King's Bench[1] case, decided on June 22, 1772, became a rallying cry for the early abolitionists in America.

During the Middle Ages, English peasants had lived in a form of semi-slavery that tied them to a lord and his land, but slavery itself had not existed in England for hundreds of years. Yet, before the *Somerset* case, it was an open legal question whether one could hold slaves in England; slavery in the colonies was based on municipal ordinances, but not in England. Parliament had neither enacted any law establishing slavery, nor any law declaring it unlawful. This was increasingly a problem, as British colonial slaveholders arrived back in England with their slaves.

James Somerset was born in Africa, and was taken by slave traders to Jamaica and then on to Virginia, which, in 1750 when Somerset arrived, was one of the great centers of the slave trade in North America. (In 1756, there were 173,000 whites and 120,000 blacks in Virginia.[2]) His master was Charles Stewart, a young Scot who was a successful merchant and trader in the Virginia Colony, and who was appointed in 1765 by Prime Minister Grenville to be the Receiver General of the Eastern Middle District of his Majesty's customs, an area extending from Quebec to Virginia. In late 1769, Stewart and Somerset sailed to London.

In November 1771, while in England, Somerset fled from Stewart, but he was seized by Stewart's agents and placed aboard a ship bound for the West Indies to be resold. Somerset's godmother obtained a writ of habeas corpus, which released Somerset until his trial before William Murray, first Earl of Mansfield, the Lord Chief Justice.[3] Lord Mansfield was widely considered the greatest English jurist of the eighteenth century.[4] Mansfield—trying to avoid a decision in such a politically charged trial—sought a settlement: why doesn't the godmother buy Somerset from Stewart and then set him free? However, both the antislavery forces behind Somerset and the West Indian slave interests rejected that solution, and they demanded a decision. Lengthy arguments were made before the King's Bench, and there were postponements and rearguments.

Finally, on June 22, 1772, Lord Mansfield delivered the opinion of the Court.[5] The narrow issue before the Court was whether the explanation of the captain of the ship bound for the West Indies, on which Somerset had been placed, was valid, and thus whether the reply to the

Ending Slavery

writ of habeas corpus was valid. The captain had explained the simple facts: Stewart owned Somerset and brought him to England while on a temporary visit with the intent to leave, and Somerset was to be taken to Jamaica and sold as a slave.

Lord Mansfield decided that the applicable law was the law of England: "A foreigner cannot be imprisoned *here* on the authority of any law existing in his own country."[6] He continued that the state of slavery had to be explicitly granted by human law; it derived no power from the law of nature: "Tracing the subject to natural principles, the claim of slavery can never be supported."[7] Since there was no positive law establishing slavery in England, Somerset must be discharged. Mansfield said that "returning a former slave into slavery was an 'odious' and 'high . . . act of dominion' that free-soil judges should not allow in the absence of a strong local custom or a clear legislative command."[8] Wealthier Negroes celebrated at a "Black Assembly" in Westminster, where two hundred guests drank to Mansfield's health before ending the evening with a ball.[9]

For years later, it was argued by antislavery forces that Lord Mansfield had ended slavery in England. Not exactly. In fact, his limited ruling was simply that Stewart had no right to forcibly take Somerset from England to the colonies on the basis of the reasoning supplied in the response to the writ of habeas corpus. Nevertheless, *Somerset's Case* became a rallying cry for the antislavery movement in the UK and in the American colonies. It became also a source of hope for the American abolitionists, especially the Quakers, who led the movement at that time. In 1833, when the British Parliament finally abolished slavery throughout the empire, a provision in the Act made clear that all slaves who, prior to 1833, came to the UK with the consent of their possessors, would be "absolutely and entirely free to all Intents and Purposes whatsoever."[10]

The ruling in the *Somerset* case was modified somewhat in 1827, with the case captioned *The Slave, Grace*, which arose in British Antigua. Lord Stowell decided that a slave who had returned to the colonies from England had not been emancipated by her stay in England. This 1827 English ruling influenced the Missouri state supreme court in its 1852 decision in the *Dred Scott* case.

Slavery and the American Revolution

The American Revolution had a curious impact on the slavery issue. When the British invaded Georgia in 1778, South Carolina proposed in the Continental Congress that some three thousand slaves ought to be freed and armed. The Congress unanimously approved such a plan, which included compensation to the owners of the slaves, and at the end of the War, the slaves who served faithfully would be emancipated.[11] However, the South Carolina legislature kept rejecting the plan, worried that the example of collective emancipation would undermine slavery in the Deep South. Thus, military needs were subordinated to the desire to protect the slave system.

Charles Pinckney of Charleston, an active delegate to the Constitutional Convention and signer of the Constitution, claimed in one of his speeches during the debates over the Missouri Compromise in 1820 that the South had been unfairly disadvantaged by the three-fifths clause. As part of his argument, Pinckney argued:

> [I]n the course of the Revolution the Southern States were continually overrun by the British, and . . . every negro in [the Southern states] had an opportunity of leaving their owners, [but] few did; proving thereby not only a remarkable attachment to their owners, but the mildness of the treatment, from which their affection sprang.[12]

Pinckney spoke with some personal knowledge of the time, since he had been captured by the British in 1780 and held as a prisoner for more than a year. However, he seems not to have recognized that perhaps the slaves elected not to go with the British forces because they were uncertain whether the British might continue their slave status, rather than exclusively the benign view he took—"better the devil you know."

In contrast, the British seized the opportunity to deprive the rebels of their slaves during the Revolutionary War. In November 1775, Lord Dunmore, the royal governor of Virginia, promised freedom to slaves owned by rebels if they would join His Majesty's troops. Dunmore's action was not officially authorized, in part because the British were walking a tightrope: they also wanted to protect the slaves held by those colonials loyal to the Crown. Finally, in 1779, Sir Henry Clinton in New York made a formal offer: all slaves captured while serving the rebels were to be sold for the benefit of the Crown, but slaves who deserted the rebels would be given "full security"—not exactly a clear promise of freedom.[13] Despite that, thousands of slaves assumed the offer meant freedom, and they moved from rebel territory through the British lines. At the end of the War, between fifteen thousand and twenty thousand escaped slaves remained under British protection in the ports that had not yet been evacuated (New York, Charleston, and Savannah). About nine thousand freed slaves accompanied the last British forces to leave.[14] Some of the freed slaves were taken to England, but the largest group was resettled in Nova Scotia and New Brunswick as part of the loyalist population that found refuge there. Some of those were later shipped by the British to Sierra Leone.[15] Many of the slaves taken by the British ended up as slaves in the British Caribbean. In the Bahamas, the influx of British/American Loyalists and their slaves doubled the population and tripled the slave population.[16]

This British action of removing slaves—American property—committed the Continental Congress to sanction racial slavery. The Revolution also had the effect of moving Northern states slowly toward emancipation, and thus to the beginning of the sectionalization of America. In 1777, Vermont became the first region in the New World to outlaw slavery. Other New England states followed slowly with gradual emancipation. Slavery was more deeply entrenched in New York and New Jersey, where even gradual emancipation bills failed until 1799 in New York, and 1804 in New Jersey.[17] (In 1820, New York State had about the same number of slaves as Missouri.[18]) Slavery remained legal in New York until 1827 and in Connecticut until 1848.[19]

One of the reasons that, in August 1839, the U.S. naval officer who had taken custody of the Spanish schooner *Amistad* took her to port in Connecticut rather than in New York where she was found, is that he hoped to profit from an admiralty claim. That claim might have been difficult to make in a New York port since slavery was illegal there. The U.S. Supreme Court, in 1841, decided[20] that the rebellious Africans on the vessel were not slaves, and awarded them their free return to Africa. Justice Story wrote the opinion of the Court in which Chief Justice Taney concurred; lawyer and former President John Quincy Adams successfully argued the case.

Pre- and Post-Revolution

Slavery in America dates back to 1565 in what is now Florida, when Spanish settlers held African slaves at St. Augustine. But it was the English who made slavery such a widespread institution. In 1619, twelve years after the settlement at Jamestown, two English ships sailed into the James River with Africans for sale; they came from what is now Angola, and their captivity had been arranged by the Portuguese.

At the time of the establishment of the new U.S. Government in 1789, there were about seven hundred fifty thousand blacks in the United States, more than 90 percent of whom were slaves.[21] Almost all lived in the South, and almost 40 percent of them lived in Virginia.[22] Slavery was clearly a sectional matter. As Professor Joseph Ellis notes, "there was a direct and nearly perfect correlation between demography and ideology—that is between the ratio of blacks to whites in the population and the reluctance to consider abolition."[23] While no formal proposal for a gradual emancipation came before the Congress, there was a debate over it in the House in March 1790. The antislavery argument was based on the assumption that slavery was a moral and economic problem for which there must be a political solution, and legislators discussed a gradual emancipation (so that costs could be spread over time, perhaps generations), and proposed that the bulk of the slaves would be transported elsewhere to avoid retaliation. The gradual emancipation plans that were adopted in the Northern states did not have to face either of these two elements, since the black population there was relatively small. There was a broad sense that over time—and, as the slave trade shut down—slavery would probably wither away. (Some argue that this view was a convenient illusion.)

Professor Ellis persuasively argues that the acquisition of the Louisiana Territory in 1803 presented a unique opportunity to confront the slavery question *before* the Cotton Kingdom was fully established and the number of slaves multiplied to the millions; revenue from the sale of lands acquired in the Purchase would also provide funds required to make compensated emancipation economically feasible.[24] While Jefferson could have pushed for slavery to be abolished in the new Louisiana Territory, and to make abolition a condition for admission into the Union, and while he could have proposed using the anticipated enormous funds from the sale of lands to compensate slave owners from the South over time, he did not. One of the reasons was that Jefferson came under no pressure from the Federalists, the opposition party, to make slavery in the Louisiana Territory an issue.[25]

However, in the mid-1790s, a young Yankee inventor, Eli Whitney, developed the mechanical cotton gin, which made it possible to harvest enormous quantities of cotton. That, combined with the development of a screw press that permitted cotton to be compressed into bales, led to increased cultivation, which in turn led to greater reliance on slaves. In a few years, the price of slaves had doubled, and manumission was largely forgotten. These technological innovations gave Southern farming a great advantage over Northern farming. The larger Southern plantations were

Ending Slavery

more like the giant agribusinesses of today in terms of size and efficiency.[26] By 1860, two-thirds of the wealthiest Americans lived in the South.[27]

The South also benefited from the introduction of steamboats and the coastal and river system in the South, but, of course, in purely economic terms, what was driving the South was the productivity of the slave system. The westward expansion of the country, especially after the annexation of Texas and other Mexican territories, permitted the spread of this slave-based economy. The demographics were stark: by 1860, there were about 4.4 million blacks in America, about 3.9 million of whom were slaves.[28] While most Southerners were not slave owners,[29] most Southern whites were nevertheless intricately connected to slavery as an institution, and bitterly opposed to agitation against it. Until the early 1830s, it had been possible to discuss and debate the idea of gradual emancipation in the South—and this was in fact done in the Virginia legislature at that time. But after that period, positions had so hardened that it was no longer possible to discuss such an idea openly. By 1860, slavery had sharply declined in the Upper South;[30] for example, there were only two thousand slaves in Delaware.

After the War of 1812 with Britain, the American antislavery movement—mostly in the North, but also thriving in parts of the South (e.g., western Virginia and western North Carolina)—became increasingly absorbed by the colonization movement. The American Colonization Society (ACS) was formed in 1816 on the idea that blacks and whites could not peacefully coexist, so the blacks in America should be sent to have "greater freedom" in Africa.[31] Even though by then most slaves had been born in America the notion of transporting blacks back to Africa was attractive, because it was the "safe and sane approach" to the problems of slavery and racial prejudice.[32] The ACS helped found Liberia in 1822. It was hoped that a flourishing Liberia would induce more slaveholders to manumit their slaves or that state governments would compensate slaveholders. From his retreat at Monticello, Thomas Jefferson estimated in 1824 that it would cost $900 million to relocate the 1.5 million slaves—sixty times the cost of the Louisiana Purchase.[33] Relocation was necessary, Jefferson believed, because blacks and whites could not coexist peacefully.

Most freed blacks attacked the ACS, arguing that colonization actually accentuated and legitimated racism, especially the basic assumption that the blacks' degradation in America was irremediable and permanent. Of course, the Deep South was vehemently opposed to colonization. By 1830, William Lloyd Garrison, the Northern leader of abolitionism, became convinced that the antislavery movement must accept the equal coexistence of blacks and whites.[34]

Nibbling Away at Slavery

Ending the Slave Trade

The first action taken against the slave *trade* by any nation was the 1794 U.S. federal law that made it illegal for anyone (U.S. citizen or foreigner) to prepare any ship to sail from the United States to any foreign port for the purpose of acquiring and transporting slaves.[35] Conviction could result in forfeiture of the vessel and a fine. The first conviction was against a Rhode Island[36] congressman and a member of a leading merchant family, John Brown—no relation to the John Brown of Harpers Ferry fame—for having invested in a slave ship that brought slaves to Cuba. On October 5, 1797, the merchant was forced to forfeit the vessel.[37] Despite this conviction, while the 1794 law was a landmark, it was not vigorously enforced.

In the early morning hours of February 24, 1807, the British House of Commons, by a vote of 283 to 16, passed the Act for the Abolition of the Slave Trade, which ended the British participation in the slave trade[38] effective May 1, 1807. The bill received Royal Assent on March 25, 1807.[39] This ended the legal transport of Africans across the Atlantic on British ships, but it did *not* stop British investment in the slave trade, or the building of slave ships in British dockyards. The Spanish and the Portuguese continued to carry on the slave trade to an even greater extent, and some British subjects became their partners under cover of those flags.

Much of the credit for the end of the British participation in the slave trade was due to the twenty years of effort by the great orator, William Wilberforce.[40] This was a huge political step, since much of British wealth was dependent on the slave trade—the financiers, the shipbuilders, and the importers of the sugar that was produced at slave plantations in the British possessions.[41] One wealthy resident of Bath, England, wrote a poem in the later part of the eighteenth century:

> I own I am shuck'd at the purchase of slaves,
> And fear those who buy them and sell them are knaves;
> What I hear of their hardship, their tortures, and groans,
> Is almost enough to draw pity from stones.
> I pity them greatly, but I must be mum,
> For how could we do without sugar and rum?
> Especially sugar, so needful we see,
> What? Give up our desserts, our coffee, and tea![42]

As early as 1805, efforts were made in the Congress to enact the end of the slave trade, even though the prohibition could not be effective until 1808, due to the Constitutional protection. In December 1806, President Jefferson lent support to the idea of prospective legislation, declaring in his annual Message to Congress that it was possible "to withdraw the citizens of the United States from all further participation in those violations of human rights which have so long continued on the unoffending inhabitants of Africa."[43] While there was agreement on the general principle, there was great debate about the details, such as what should happen to slaves imported in violation of the ban (freedom or forfeiture), or whether violators should be executed. Jefferson signed a bill on March 2, 1807, banning the import of slaves, to go into effect ten months later. The vote in the House had been 113 to 5.[44] One reason Southerners were supportive of the slave trade ban was that the trade threatened to diminish the economic value of slave property already in place.[45]

Getting the details of the slave trade ban right took some time. One of the first dilemmas surfaced in New Orleans in 1809. Thousands of French refugees and their household slaves were expelled from Cuba that year and arrived in New Orleans and other American ports. The Napoleonic conquest of Spain in 1808 had made them undesirable residents—many of whom had originally fled from Haiti to Cuba in the 1790s. Legally, the ships and the slaves faced forfeiture, but Congress excused them due to the extenuating circumstances.[46]

Thirteen years after the effective date of the import ban, a situation arose when a South Carolinian family went to France for a holiday, and took with them a female slave. When the family returned with the slave, the federal revenue collector at the port of Charleston thought the ban on the slave trade barred the slave's reentry into the United States. The matter ended up in the hands of the U.S. Attorney General, William Wirt. Wirt formally opined that the law was not intended to bar returning slaves when they were on a "sojourn" for a short time abroad.[47] They were not being "imported."

In 1820, the United States upped the ante against slave traders. Congress enacted a law that made trade in slaves an act of piracy and provided for the death penalty.[48] The law applied only to American citizens, but included Americans crewing on foreign vessels if they seized "any negro or mulatto" with intent to make him a slave.[49] The enforcement of the 1820 law was not rigorous: in New York City, where most Northern prosecutions took place, only one-sixth of those indicted were convicted; from 1837 to 1861, 125 accused slave traders were prosecuted, but only 20 were given prison sentences, and of those 10 were pardoned and 3 were allowed to plead to lesser crimes.[50] Nathaniel Gordon, from Portland, Maine, was the only man to be hanged—in February 1862—for the crime of slave trading.[51] He had appealed his conviction to the U.S. Supreme Court, but Chief Justice Taney rejected it on the grounds that the Court had no jurisdiction.[52]

In the mid-1850s, a movement began in South Carolina to reopen the slave trade. Yes, it would lower the value of a slave, but it would mean that every non-slaveholding white could become a slaveholder, and it would increase the South's population, which in turn would help to match the growth in the North. To those with sensitive consciences, the trade would employ fair transactions in Africa, healthy conditions on the ships, and Christian salvation in America. Later, as talk of reopening the slave trade spread throughout the South, clever advocates in Louisiana devised a way to avoid a conflict with the federal ban on the slave trade. import "apprentices," based on "voluntary" signatures by the Africans on agreements that suggested a return to Africa after their decades of "apprenticeship" ended.[53] In the end, the various schemes for reopening the slave trade failed.

While the African slave trade was largely stopped, the similar "coolie"[54] trade was not.[55] Poor Chinese were recruited or kidnapped by "coolie agents," made to sign indentured servant labor contracts for an eight-year period, loaded on ships, and taken mostly to Cuba for work in the sugar and tobacco fields. The "contract" was designed to set the coolie trade apart from the illegal slave trade. Upwards of 60 percent did not survive the term of their contract. Between 1847 and 1874, a hundred twenty-five thousand coolies were shipped to Cuba. On February 19, 1862, Congress passed "An Act to Prohibit the 'Coolie Trade' by American Citizens in American Vessels."[56]

British Abolition

At the beginning of the nineteenth century in Britain, democracy was thin, in large part because of the system of "rotten" or "pocket" boroughs under which wealthy landowners controlled members of Parliament. One person in one hundred had a vote; some large towns (such as Manchester) had no representation in Parliament. In 1830, however, the Whigs returned to power after many decades, and they turned to parliamentary reform, beginning with the Reform Bill of 1831, which became law in 1832. This reform dramatically expanded real democracy, and led workers in the cities—long excluded from government—into greater power. Many of the old proslavery members of Parliament were swept away. One scholar noted that "representative government and the tradition of public petitioning as well as the fact that newspapers, pamphlets, sermons, voluntary societies and associations, and a common-law tradition created in Anglo-American societies a degree of public participation unmatched in the rest of the world."[57]

Revolts by at least twenty thousand slaves in Jamaica in 1831 and 1832 were only barely contained by the British Army. A regiment from Barbados and a battalion from Bermuda were brought in to assist in quelling the rebellion.[58] Some five hundred slaves were killed (while fewer than twenty whites lost their lives), and there was great property damage. In 1832, a Select Committee on the Extinction of Slavery throughout the British Dominions was appointed by Parliament to examine the question of how best to effect the abolition of slavery, "whilst ensuring the safety of all classes in the colonies." The Committee issued its report in early 1833, and in August 1833, Parliament decided to abolish slavery in its colonies and possessions with effect one year later.[59] All who had been slaves for under six years were freed immediately, and all others were to be freed gradually over five years.[60] By 1838, the government had paid former slave owners 20 million pounds (about 800 million pounds today).[61] With slavery abolished, many of the plantations in the British colonies were not as profitable and thus shut down. This fact was undoubtedly noted in the American South.

One of the side effects of the British abolition was that slavery in Canada was now clearly outlawed. This, in turn, had the effect of ensuring that Canada would be the main destination of the Underground Railroad. The first major case on the topic to be dealt with in the Canadian courts involved two fugitive slaves, Thornton and Lucie Blackburn, who escaped from Detroit in 1833. The American request for their extradition was denied.[62]

British abolition also played into an incident at sea in late 1841, which resulted in a major U.S.-British diplomatic flap. The American brig *Creole* left Richmond, Virginia, with a cargo of tobacco and slaves bound for New Orleans.[63] On November 7, 1841, 19 of the 135 slaves rebelled as the vessel neared Nassau, in the British colony of the Bahamas. One crew member was killed, and the captain was wounded. The British authorities in Nassau imprisoned the mutineers—led by a slave whose name was Madison Washington—but within a week, the British freed the slaves (two of whom had died while imprisoned). The *Creole* was permitted to sail on to New Orleans, and arrived there on December 2, 1841, with only five slaves on board. (Frederick Douglass later wrote a fictionalized account of the *Creole* incident.[64])

Except for the abolitionists, Americans were outraged at this British action. The U.S.-British tension was so great, and the anti-British rhetoric was so strong, that the celebrated English writer Charles Dickens wrote from his hotel in Baltimore, after he had visited Richmond, that the Southerners are "perfectly frantic about the *Creole* business."[65] Secretary of State Daniel Webster demanded the return of the American "property"—the slaves. Since slavery was illegal in British colonies, the British ignored Webster's demands. In the U.S. House, Representative Joshua Reed Giddings of Ohio introduced resolutions that argued that Virginia's slave law did not apply to slaves outside of Virginia's waters, and so the U.S. government should not act to assist the U.S. slaveholders. The House censured Giddings, who promptly resigned; Giddings was then quickly and overwhelmingly reelected and returned to Congress.

Seven lawsuits were brought in New Orleans by the owners of the slaves against their insurance companies, but the insurers refused to reimburse the slaveholders for their losses, since the policies exempted insurrection as a cause of recovery. The 1853 Anglo-American Claims Commission finally settled the matter by awarding $110,330 to the United States for the owners of the liberated slaves as compensation for their loss of property. After the U.S. Supreme Court in 1841 freed the Africans who had mutinied on the Spanish vessel *Amistad* in 1839, the Spanish government pressed the United States for compensation, but the United States refused.[66]

The District of Columbia

For years there had been wholly unsuccessful attempts to abolish or at least to limit slavery in the District of Columbia. In 1846, the District had become smaller, because Congress retro-ceded the Virginia portion, which was about 30 percent of the whole. Proposals to return the remainder of the District to Maryland—which would have resolved the slavery issue, as the Maryland portion contained all the remaining slaves in the District—had no chance because of Northern opposition. Efforts in the late 1840s to terminate the slave trade within the District were unsuccessful.

It was during a debate over the slave trade on January 10, 1849, that freshman Congressman Lincoln introduced on the floor of the House a proposal for a referendum on slavery in the District of Columbia that could have led to abolition. Under the proposal, if a majority of the free white male citizens approved, slavery would gradually end: owners who agreed to free slaves would be compensated by the U.S. Treasury, and children born to slave mothers after 1850 would be born free. To appeal to proslavery interests, Lincoln's proposal also provided for stricter enforcement of fugitive slave provisions.[67] Support for the proposal vanished after it became public, and, as a result, Lincoln never introduced his proposal as a legislative bill.[68]

The issue of slavery in the District of Columbia arose again in the Compromise of 1850, which led to the admission of California. One of the bills that formed the package of bills that constituted Clay's Compromise was for the suppression of the commercial slave trade in the District—itself a compromise with those wanting abolition. The bill merely prohibited the importation of slaves for sale within the District; it did not forbid local residents from importing slaves for their own use or from selling them within the District. President Millard Fillmore signed the bill on September 20, 1850, after it passed the Senate 33 to 19 and the House 124 to 59.[69] Of the 157 favorable votes, only 10 came from Southerners, and most of them were from the Upper South. Southern hostility was not toward the narrow merits of the bill, but rather toward the principle that this was the "entering wedge" that would lead to more aggressive measures. Slavery in the District remained essentially untouched for another decade.

Southern Worries and Northern Assurances

The establishment of the Republican Party in 1856,[70] with its antislavery platform, greatly worried the South. After Harpers Ferry, and certainly after Lincoln's nomination in May 1860, the South feared that an assault on slavery was imminent if Lincoln was elected. But given the Constitutional protections for slavery, what possible basis could a new antislavery Republican administration have to attack and ultimately to abolish slavery? Clearly, the issue of the expansion of slavery into the territories might be back on the table if a new administration chose to view narrowly or to ignore the *Dred Scott* decision, or if new appointments to the Supreme Court tipped the balance toward overturning that decision. If that happened, slavery might be prohibited, at least in the territories.

Southerners could point to several possible constitutionally legitimate steps that a new anti-slave administration might take. One clever idea had been floated by Frederick Douglass in a speech in early 1860 in Glasgow: if there were a slave insurrection, perhaps an antislavery president might issue an emancipation proclamation, relying on the constitutional authority to protect the states against invasion.[71]

A new antislavery administration might rely on the authority to regulate interstate commerce in order to prohibit interstate slave trade.[72] The worry was not far-fetched: for years, abolitionists had argued that the Congress had unlimited authority over interstate slave trafficking because of the Commerce Clause[73] (slaves were merely articles of commerce), and also because of the use of the word "migration" in addition to "importation" in the provision[74] that had barred Congress from prohibiting international slave trade until 1808. In the latter case, the argument was that, as of 1808, Congress could not only bar the import of slaves into the United States, but could also prohibit their migration from one state to another. During the Missouri Compromise controversy (1819–1820), both John Jay and Daniel Webster argued that Congress had a right and a duty to suppress the domestic interstate trade in slaves.

London's *Economist* noted on November 24, 1860, that Lincoln had not declared himself "as yet in favour of prohibiting the Internal Slave Trade between the different States,—a measure which is the only efficient step towards the extinction of slavery that is constitutionally within the power of Congress to effect." The newspaper, in the same editorial, quoted Lincoln as saying that this was a subject that he had "not given that mature consideration that would make me feel authorized to state a position . . . ." The editorial concluded: "Hearing this, some of our English

Ending Slavery 223

politicians will be tempted not only to wonder at the dismay of the South, but to ask where is the gain to the Anti-Slavery cause in the election of [Lincoln], so very moderate and cautious a Republican."

The Supreme Court never issued a definitive ruling on whether Congress could suppress domestic slave trade, because no act of Congress ever tried to ban that trade. The Supreme Court in 1841 touched on the issue,[75] and three Justices—Taney, McLean, and Baldwin—took the view that Congress did not have that power. One scholar has concluded that if the Court had issued a ruling on whether Congress had the power to ban interstate slave trade, "the Justices who served under Taney would have been unanimous in holding that Congress did not possess the constitutional authority to abolish the interstate slave trade."[76]

Another delicate issue was the use of the postal service to spread antislavery propaganda in the South. In the late 1830s, abolitionists used the mail to good effect. However, under Andrew Jackson's presidency and for many years after it, postmasters agreed that mail in the South was "delivered" when it arrived at a post office—where abolitionist literature stayed undelivered.[77] A new antislavery administration might assign abolitionists to be postmasters in the South and flood the region with insurrectionist tracts. Lincoln, in his inaugural address, specifically dealt with the "mail" issue: "it will continue to be furnished in all parts of the Union."

Lincoln tried to assure Southerners that he had no intention of interfering with slavery in the South. His focus, and that of the Republican platform, had been on preventing the spread of slavery into the territories. In effect, he argued to his party that if slavery was prevented from growing, it would eventually wither and die, and he made it known to the South that he would not abolish slavery. Even at Cooper Union,[78] in February 1860, while shunning his antislavery rhetoric, Lincoln said clearly: "Wrong as we think slavery is, we can yet afford to let it alone where it is, because that much is due to the necessity arising from its actual presence in the nation."[79] On December 22, 1860, after he was elected, but still almost four months before his inaugural, President-elect Lincoln sent a letter to Alexander Hamilton Stephens of Georgia—with whom he had served in the House in the late 1840s—asking whether the

> people of the South really entertain fears that a Republican administration would directly, or indirectly, interfere with their slaves, or with them, about their slaves? If they do, I wish to assure you . . . that there is no cause for such fears.[80]

Lincoln's promise was simply not believed.

In the flurry of activity meant to head off further secession efforts, the Democratic-led Thirty-sixth Congress—which stayed in its second session just until Lincoln was inaugurated—passed a joint resolution on March 2, 1861, proposing a constitutional amendment to prohibit any amendment[81] that would authorize Congress to "abolish or interfere, within any State, with the domestic institutions thereof."[82] Buchanan had asked Congress to propose an "explanatory amendment" to mollify the South. In response, the House established a committee of thirty-three members, chaired by Representative Thomas Corwin of Ohio, to draft such a proposed amendment. The House passed the joint resolution on February 28th by a vote of 133 to 65; the Senate passed the resolution on March 2nd with a vote of 24 to 12. The proposed amendment was signed by Buchanan—though there was no constitutional necessity for his signature—and left for Lincoln to transmit to the state governors for their legislatures to ratify. Lincoln dutifully transmitted an authenticated copy on March 16th, with a cover letter that neither endorsed nor opposed the amendment.[83] Of course, to be effective, this proposed amendment had to be approved by the legislatures of three-fourths of the states. It was not, and the amendment died.

During his March 4, 1861, inaugural address, Lincoln repeated the promise he had made to Stephens, and dealt in the opening minute of his speech with the Southern "apprehension." He made it crystal clear that he had no "intention" to end slavery, and perhaps even more powerfully, he had no *legal* authority to do so: "I have no purpose, directly or indirectly, to interfere with the institution of slavery in the States where it now exists. *I believe I have no lawful right to do so*, and I have no inclination to do so." (emphasis added).

Lincoln's own views on ending slavery can be summarized by the three main ingredients of his "plan": (a) it should be *gradual*, (b) it should be *compensated*, and (c) it should be accomplished *by the vote of the people*.[84] These were the same key elements as were in Lincoln's proposal on the House floor in 1849 relating to slavery in the District of Columbia. Of course, the end of slavery in the United States did not happen that way.

Ending Slavery During the War

Ben Butler, a Massachusetts lawyer turned Major General, was sent to Fortress Monroe, which guarded the mouth of the James River in Virginia, in 1861. Butler was not an abolitionist; indeed, he had supported the nomination of Jefferson Davis as the Democratic candidate in 1860. In late May, three slaves were brought to him at the fort; they had been left behind as Virginia forces drew back. All three slaves had been the property of a rebel colonel from Hampton, Virginia. They had run away because the colonel was planning to take them to South Carolina for military infrastructure work: digging trenches, making fortifications, and performing camp duties.

One could almost imagine the light bulb turning on in Butler's lawyer's mind. Under the Fugitive Slave Law, he might have an obligation to return these slaves to their owner—but the owner had rejected the Union laws, and so clearly, Butler had no such obligation. In the colonel's eyes—

Major General Benjamin F. Butler.

and probably under the Constitution—these slaves were "property." Since this property was being used by the enemy in pursuit of the War, Butler decided that he had the right to seize this "contraband." Once the word spread, the number of "contrabands" swelled; within three days, there were forty-eight slaves at Fort Monroe. Butler wrote out receipts for the seized property, and sent the receipts to the slaves' masters. Butler sought approval of his action from the secretary of war, Simon Cameron, and received it on May 30, 1861.[85] Cameron warned Butler not to begin to snatch slaves from their masters, and to put the contraband "property" to work—and to keep an account of the value of their labor and the cost of maintaining them.

This was a clever and humanitarian idea. But soon it was difficult as a practical matter. By July, Butler had nine hundred contrabands, not enough work for them, and not enough food for them. It was also very hard to distinguish between legitimate contraband—slaves conscripted to work on military projects—as opposed to those who simply saw an easy and safe way to freedom. The "freedom" they sought was not exactly what they got. Their status was unclear: Were they "wards" of the federal government? Were they merely seized, to be returned to their owners after the War? Or were they to be sold and the proceeds forfeited to the United States? Or were they in fact freed? And if so, by what authority?

Congress stepped in. In the report to Congress by the secretary of the treasury on July 4, 1861, Treasury Secretary Salmon Chase proposed that the Union should seize the property of those engaged in insurrection, sell it, and contribute the funds to the war effort.[86] The Union defeat at the first battle of Bull Run (or Manassas), on July 1st, jolted Congress into the

FORTRESS MONROE. BRIDGE AND MAIN ENTRANCE.

Ending Slavery

realization that the War might not be the short, neat confrontation they had assumed, and that disunionists needed to have some liability for their actions. Members of Congress who observed the battle saw CSA slaves at Manassas doing the work of laborers and servants, leaving all the whites available for fighting. Congress struggled with the task, and on August 6, 1861, Congress passed, and Lincoln signed, the First Confiscation Act.[87] Democrats and members from the Border States were generally and strongly opposed to any measure that would touch slavery,[88] while nearly all Republicans in Congress voted for the Act. The House passed the bill by 60–48, and the Senate by 24–11. This was the last action by Congress in that Special Session.

The Act borrowed some of the concepts of maritime law relating to prizes captured at sea, which could be brought into a federal court and condemned. In this sense, it broke little new ground. The Act provided, in Section 1, that all property used

> in aiding, abetting or promoting [an] insurrection . . . is hereby declared to be lawful subject of prize and capture wherever found; and it shall be the duty of the President . . . to cause the same to be seized, confiscated and condemned.

The fourth section of the Act was the key provision. It said that if a slave was required to take up arms or be employed in any fort, ship, etc., against the United States, then the slave owner "shall forfeit his claim" to the slave, any law of a state notwithstanding. Finally, if any slave owner later sought to enforce his claim to his slave, it would be a full answer that the slave had been employed in hostile service. With great drafting skill and elaborate phrasing, as in the Constitution, the terms "slave" or "slave owner" never appeared in the Act.

The Confederate Congress "retaliated" on August 30, 1861, passing the Sequestration Act, which authorized the CSA to forever seize the real and personal property of "enemy aliens"—a term that included every U.S. citizen and all those living in the Confederacy who remained loyal to the Union.[89]

Lincoln had very mixed feelings about the Confiscation Act he had signed. The timing was bad. This was just after the inglorious Union defeat at Bull Run (or Manassas), and Lincoln believed such unprecedented legislation should occur only after military success.[90] And, importantly, the Border States were worried that this was "covert emancipation," and Lincoln was obsessed with the need to ensure that the Border States stayed within the Union, even as slave states. Lincoln may also have worried that there might be a court challenge to the Act, and that the administration might lose such a challenge.[91] In any event, there was little enforcement of the Act.[92] Nevertheless, U.S. attorneys were given wide discretion to instigate proceedings, and they began to seize Confederate property located in the North.[93] In some instances, military commanders in the field carried out some property confiscation. For example, General Ben Butler—where all this started—after conquering New Orleans in April 1962, used the Confiscation Act to seize and sell estates and personal property before Lincoln could replace him with General Nathaniel Banks.[94]

Fremont's Order

A little more than a month after the First Confiscation Act, Lincoln was confronted with another action by the military, but this was not as relatively benign as General Butler's "contrabands" on the Virginia coast. This time, the step was a leap to emancipation in a state within the Union, and the step was taken by a major political figure.

John C. Fremont was a minor hero, known as the "Pathfinder," the great explorer of the West who followed in the path of Lewis and Clark; he became wealthy in California in the gold rush. He was also the first presidential nominee of the new Republican Party in 1856.[95] Lincoln had sought, and lost, the vice presidential nomination at the Philadelphia Republican Convention at which Fremont was nominated; Lincoln campaigned for Fremont during the 1856 campaign. In the summer of 1861, Fremont was appointed a major general, commanding the Department of the West with headquarters in St. Louis, Missouri—a slave state still within the Union.

On August 30th, General Fremont issued an order of martial law throughout the state in order to control the increasing lawlessness and rebel activity. He took the not unreasonable step of declaring that all property (real and personal) of anyone in the state who takes up arms against the United States or who takes "an active part" with the enemy would be confiscated for the public use. But Fremont's order went further: if those people have slaves, those slaves "are hereby declared Free men." *This Order by Fremont was the first federal action to end slavery in the United States*; quite in contrast to the decades of effort at the federal level to deal with the expansion of slavery, this order by Fremont represented an actual rollback of slavery. Its scope was statewide, not confined to a battle line or to slaves employed in rebel, military-related activity.

Surely, one would be justified in assuming that no such measure would have been taken by a general without the authorization of the commander in chief, even if that general was a powerful political figure too. Not so. Fremont had acted on his own. And his action ricocheted throughout the other Border States: even though they were still within

JOHN C. FREMONT.

the Union, they remained slaveholding states, and the idea of emancipation caused deep worry about slave rebellion and personal safety. Kentucky in particular was concerned, perhaps in part due to the proximity of Missouri. The pressure on Lincoln was immediate and strong. He had to act. Lincoln understood this, and he also had to show the nation that he was in charge.

Lincoln handled the problem with delicacy. He dispatched a note on September 2nd to Fremont asking him to modify his order with respect to freeing the slaves, so that it would be consistent with the Confiscation Act, which had been adopted only a few weeks earlier; basically, Lincoln told him to sharply narrow the focus of his order so that it does not free all the slaves of all the rebels and their supporters. Fremont sent his response on September 8th, hand-carried to Lincoln by Fremont's wife Jessie, the daughter of the powerful Thomas Hart Benson of Missouri. (Jessie and John Fremont are sometimes described as the Abigail and John Adams or the Franklin and Eleanor Roosevelt of their day.[96]) Jessie was overconfident when she met with Lincoln at the White House on the evening of September 10th, and Lincoln was cool and impatient during the meeting. He reportedly told her with a sneer, "You are quite a female politician."[97] (Lincoln was always uncomfortable around women, even though he had litigated more than six hundred cases involving women in his law practice, representing women as creditors and debtors, and as landowners and renters.[98])

Fremont's letter said that he knew the local scene better than Lincoln, and that if Lincoln wanted his order to be modified, Lincoln would have to give him a direct and public order to that effect. Fremont, in effect, was telling Lincoln that he, Fremont, was not going to look like a fool by vacillating about the wisdom of his own order.

Lincoln's response was swift and public. On September 11th, Lincoln wrote to Fremont that while he had no "general objection" to the order, the clause relating "to the confiscation of property and the liberation of slaves" appeared to be "objectionable." Lincoln explained that since Fremont wanted "an open order for the modification," he would "cheerfully" do just that. Lincoln then publicly ordered that the offending clause of Fremont's order be modified to conform to the Confiscation Act of August 6th.

Lincoln the lawyer was upset that the slavery portion of Fremont's order was not a legitimate exercise of martial law. It might be permissible to act in the present—to the extent necessary for military reasons to secure a rebel's property—but to take an action that projects into the future (permanently freeing a slave) is an act that cannot be taken under martial law. That is a political act, not an act of military necessity.[99] Lincoln put Fremont in his place,[100] soothed the worrying unionists in the Border States, and did not get ahead of Congress on the issue of dealing with slaves. On the other hand, he angered the radical abolitionists in his own party.

The Cameron Report

Near the end of 1861, Lincoln was surprised again, but this time by the action of his secretary of war, Simon Cameron. (It was Cameron who approved Butler's dealing with contrabands in Virginia.) Cameron prepared a report, dated December 1, 1861, dealing with the issue of property of rebels. The Government Printing Office ran off a thousand copies. The report stated the principle that it would be absurd for the government to spare or protect the property of rebels, "those who are waging war against it."[101] As a factual matter, "the principal wealth and power of the

Ending Slavery

rebel States is a peculiar species of property"—therefore, those who "war against the Government justly forfeit all rights of property," specifically including their slaves. Then, Cameron took a big leap, explaining that the government had "a right . . . to arm slaves when it may become necessary . . . . Whether it is expedient to do so is purely a military question."

When Lincoln learned of the Cameron report, he was aghast. He put his pen to the report, ordered that a sharply revised version be issued instead, and in effect declared inoperative the copies of the original version. The revised report, after Lincoln edited it, was a fraction of its original size. It now simply referred to the problem of slaves abandoned by their rebel masters: they should not be returned to the enemy, and "the disposition to be made of the slaves of rebels, after the close of the war, can be safely left to the wisdom and patriotism of Congress." Short and sweet. There was no question of freeing the slaves, and no action by military authority to make a permanent change in slave status. In a little over a month, Lincoln told Cameron he was appointing him minister in Russia (replacing Cassius Clay)—sending him, literally, out into the cold.

* * *

Thus, there had been (a) the "contraband" approach of Butler, (b) the "property actively used by the enemy" approach of the Confiscation Act, and (c) the "martial law" approach of Fremont. Lincoln was uncomfortable with all of them, in part because of the problem of not knowing what would happen after the War was over—or even over in just a section of formerly rebel territory. These were military measures whose legal ability to survive a court challenge after the "military necessity" was over was at best uncertain. Lincoln understood that the only legally safe and sound way to end slavery was by state action. He also believed that the federal government could assist that process by financing a compensation[102] scheme to induce the states to abolish slavery. This fit with Lincoln's own instincts that emancipation should be gradual, compensated, and accomplished by the votes of the people.

Persuading the States to End Slavery

In the fall of 1861, Lincoln selected tiny Delaware as his test case for ending slavery in the states. In 1847, Delaware had come within a single vote of adopting gradual emancipation, and in 1860, it had only eighteen hundred slaves—less than 2 percent of the state's population. Lincoln was not popular in Delaware; in the 1860 election, he came in third, behind Breckinridge and Bell. But despite Lincoln's loss, the local version of the Republican Party (the People's Party) had won a close race, electing George P. Fisher, a slave owner and Dover lawyer, as Delaware's lone congressman. In November 1861, Lincoln arranged for Montgomery Blair to invite Fisher to the White House to consider a plan for submission to the state legislature that would involve gradual emancipation[103] financed with U.S. bonds that would pay out in thirty-one annual installments. Lincoln even wrote out draft legislation for Delaware providing for the complete elimination of slavery by 1893. The economic message to the slave states would be this: it would be smart to cash in the wealth you now have in your slaves, because after the War they might be worthless. If this worked in Delaware, it might spread to all the Border States, and even become attractive to some of the Deep South.

Fisher returned to Delaware and worked for the plan and rallied sufficient support in the state Senate. However, the idea failed in the Delaware House of Representatives in February 1862. Many members did not believe that Congress would in fact produce the compensation funds, while others thought it was unfair to those who had already freed their slaves without compensation. Thus, compensated emancipation in Delaware was killed, and so were Fisher's chances of being reelected in the fall of 1862.[104]

To remedy this setback, on March 6th, Lincoln sent a special Message to Congress recommending adoption of a joint resolution supporting those states that would move to gradual emancipation:

> Resolved, that the United States ought to cooperate with any state which may adopt gradual abolishment of slavery, giving such pecuniary aid, to be used by such state, in its discretion, to compensate for the inconveniences, public and private, produced by such a change of system.

Lincoln argued in the Message that this would be "one of the most efficient means of self-preservation," and that "in my judgment, gradual, and not sudden, emancipation is better for all." In effect, Lincoln argued

Ending Slavery

that subsidizing emancipation was necessary to suppress the Southern rebellion, because, if the Border States gave up slavery, the CSA would have to conclude that there was no longer any hope that they might join the Confederacy. Lincoln delicately also raised the very practical issue of the present value of slaves:

> I hope it may be deemed no offense to ask whether the pecuniary consideration tendered would not be of more value to the States and private persons concerned than are the institution and property in it, in the present aspect of affairs?

In other words: sooner or later, slavery will end and slaves will have no value, so now is the time to snap up this great offer.

John W. Crisfield of the eastern shore of Maryland was one of the most influential lawyers and slaveholders in the state, and served as a member of the House (1861–1863) from the first congressional district in Southern Maryland. In March, Lincoln asked Crisfield to sound out the Maryland delegation on the idea of emancipation. Crisfield asked Lincoln what would happen if his plan for compensated emancipation were rejected by Congress. Lincoln said he had no other plans.[105] Crisfield doubted the constitutionality of appropriating money for the purpose of freeing slaves, and he sent a report to Lincoln urging that the War be fought only for the restoration of the Constitution to its proper authority; meaning that the War should be about the unity of the country and not about slavery.[106]

On April 10, 1862, in response to Lincoln's request of March 6th, Congress adopted a joint resolution declaring that the United States

> ought to cooperate with any State which may adopt gradual abolishment of slavery, giving to such State pecuniary aid, to be used in its discretion, to compensate for the inconvenience, public and private, produced by such change of system.

This was a good start, but in the end it was ineffective. Delaware would not budge, nor did any of the other Border States. This may have been because of deep racial hatred or fear—slavery may be a curse, but freedom for the Negro might be a greater curse—and it may have been based on the hope of an early Union victory or brokered peace that would leave their system in place. Even in the North, there was hostility from the Democrats who pictured emancipated blacks migrating from the Border States to the North, and the North footing the bill.[107]

On the other hand, congressional action with respect to ending slavery in the District of Columbia was effective. In April, Congress passed the District of Columbia Emancipation Act; Lincoln signed it on April 16,

1862.[108] The Act brought about immediate emancipation, not the gradual emancipation that had taken place in most Northern states; this was cold turkey. The language was taken from the Northwest Ordinance of 1787. While there may have been an argument as to whether Congress could so legislate for the territories,[109] Article I, Section 8 of the Constitution empowered Congress to exercise "exclusive Legislation in all Cases whatsoever over the District . . . ."

The big step was the provision for compensation to loyal slave masters of up to three hundred dollars for each slave, the exact amount to be determined by a board of commissioners.[110] Several members of Congress insisted that the law had to include compensation; otherwise the measure would be an unconstitutional taking of property in violation of the Fifth Amendment.[111] Under this Act, 966 petitioners submitted schedules claiming and describing thirty-one hundred slaves.[112] The law also authorized $100,000 to assist in the voluntary colonization (to Haiti or Liberia or elsewhere) of former slaves and payments of one hundred dollars to each person choosing to emigrate.[113] *This is the only compensated emancipation in U.S. history.* By year's end, more than three thousand slaves in the District were freed. The law resulted in the massive flight of slaves into the District from the two Maryland counties that surround the District—Prince George's and Montgomery—and a political crisis for Maryland's congressional delegation.[114]

The Hunter Order

Less than a month later, Lincoln was again confronted with an errant military commander who stepped on Lincoln's toes, just as had General Fremont. This time, however, Lincoln turned the abortive effort into a pitch for his plan of compensated, gradual emancipation by state action.

After the episode with Fremont in September 1861, Lincoln replaced Fremont with General David Hunter,[115] a West Point graduate who had been severely wounded at the first battle of Bull Run. Hunter was a strong opponent of slavery. In March 1862, Lincoln assigned Hunter to command the Department of the South, comprising Georgia, Florida, and South Carolina, with headquarters at Hilton Head, South Carolina.[116] From Hilton Head on May 9th, Hunter issued General Order No. 11. It noted that two weeks earlier he had declared those states under martial law, as a military necessity. Then, he added this terse sentence: "Slavery and martial law in a free country are altogether incompatible; the persons in these three States . . . . heretofore held as slaves, are thereafter declared forever free." Two days later, Hunter rounded up five hundred blacks and armed them.

Ending Slavery 235

In a local blockade context, Hunter's action was not too surprising. The South Atlantic Blockading Squadron patrolled the waters between Georgetown, South Carolina, and St. Augustine, Florida. Along that coastline, the interaction between the navy and the enslaved persons living along the coast created an awkward situation: the slaves would come to the shore with an expectation of being taken aboard and freed. These slaves created runaway colonies on little islands along the coast with hundreds of displaced former slaves. In September 1861, Navy Secretary Welles authorized the enlistment of these former slaves at a "boys" rating.[117] While Lincoln had repudiated Cameron for announcing a policy of enlisting blacks in the army, he remained silent on Welles' action. Blacks had served in the U.S. Navy since the Revolution, and did not challenge the social order in the same way that arming former slaves as army soldiers did. Historically, free blacks had made up 15 percent of the navy's enlisted force.[118]

One of the great constitutional lawyers and Union Democrat, Reverdy Johnson, implored Lincoln about the Hunter Order: "For heavens sake, at once, repudiate it & recall the officer . . . or it will serve the rebels, nicer than a dozen victories."[119] Treasury Secretary Chase tried to explain that Hunter was facing a military necessity, but Lincoln replied: "No commanding General shall do such a thing, upon my responsibility, without consulting me."[120] Lincoln was angry; having dealt gently with General Fremont nine months earlier for having acted more narrowly, Lincoln felt he had to rein in Hunter. He did so on May 19th.

On that day, Lincoln issued a proclamation that began with a wry comment about "what purports to be a proclamation" of General Hunter, according to the press reports, and quickly added that he was not yet sure such a document was genuine. Then he stated flatly that Hunter was not authorized, and the "supposed proclamation . . . whether genuine or false, is *altogether void.*" (emphasis added). This was no "modification" of an order, as Lincoln had done with Fremont; *this was the broadest possible repudiation.* Then Lincoln made clear that he reserved to himself, as commander in chief, whether to declare slaves free and whether it had become a military necessity; this was expressly not a matter to be decided by commanders in the field.

Having thus repudiated Hunter, and making it clear that he had made no such decision regarding slaves, Lincoln took the opportunity of this proclamation to put forward his real plan: the gradual, compensated emancipation by state action. He noted that the joint resolution of April was adopted by large majorities of both houses of Congress, and that it "now stands an authentic, definite, and solemn proposal of the nation to the States and people most immediately interested"—the slave states in the Union and in the Confederacy. Lincoln begged—literally, begged—for acceptance of this approach: "I beseech you .... I beg of you a calm consideration." In an amazing phrase usually not found in formal proclamations, Lincoln urged: "The change contemplated [the gradual and compensated emancipation] would come *gently as the dews of heaven*, not rending or wrecking anything. Will you not embrace it?" (emphasis added).

Hunter's error was thus turned by Lincoln into an opportunity to deliver a strong political message to all the slave states: the approach of Hunter—immediate and uncompensated emancipation—is *not* my approach or that of the Congress; please, please take my approach, and do it now. Perhaps there was also the underlying message that, unless the states act soon, he might not be able politically to restrain generals like Hunter in the future.

Abolitionists in the North were appalled at Lincoln's repudiation of Hunter, especially on top of the "modification" of Fremont's order the year earlier, and because of the lackluster enforcement of the Confiscation Acts. On August 19th, Horace Greeley, the abolitionist editor of the *New York Tribune*, wrote an open letter to Lincoln defending Hunter and criticizing the president for failing to make slavery the dominant issue of the War and for compromising moral principles. The *Tribune* was the most widely read Republican newspaper in the country, and Greeley's letter was bound to grab Lincoln's attention. Lincoln famously replied on August 22nd that his paramount object was to save the Union:[121]

> If I could save the Union without freeing any slave, I would do it; and if I could save it by freeing all the slaves, I would do it; and if I could do it by freeing some and leaving others alone, I would also do that.

The Territories and Border States

On June 19, 1862, Congress prohibited slavery in the territories[122]—in defiance of the Supreme Court's decision in *Dred Scott*—and in compliance with the original Republican platform in 1856.[123] The original House bills were introduced by two representatives from Illinois (Arnold and Lovejoy). The vote was 28–10 in the Senate and 72–38 in the House.[124] Unlike the measure two months earlier ending slavery in the District, this Act did not provide for compensation—in large part because there were virtually no slaves in the territories, in contrast to D.C. However, the language of emancipation was the same as the District bill taken from the Northwest Ordinance of 1787.

On July 12th, Lincoln called to the White House twenty-nine representatives and senators from Border States (including George Fisher of

Ending Slavery 237

Delaware), with Congress about to adjourn, to urge them to take up the plan for gradual, compensated state emancipation. Once again, he argued that if they would encourage their respective states to accept his plan, it would shorten the War and would secure for them substantial compensation. He made clear that he was not speaking of "emancipation *at* once but of a decision at once to emancipate *gradually*. Room in South America for colonization, can be obtained cheaply . . . ." Lincoln then reminded them of the Hunter episode, and noted that his decision to repudiate Hunter's order caused offense "to many whose support the country cannot afford to lose . . . . The pressure, in this direction, is still upon me, and is increasing." He told them that Hunter had done the right thing in the wrong way. Lincoln was obliquely suggesting that unless the Border States relieved him of the problem, he might be unable to withstand the pressure to immediately free the slaves.

On July 14th, Lincoln urged Congress to pass a bill to compensate states, so that the offer would be fixed in a statute, not merely in a hortatory joint resolution.[125] On the same day, twenty of the Border State congressmen rejected Lincoln's plea.

Congress passed the Second Confiscation Act in mid-July 1862.[126] The Act provided punishment for treason and giving comfort to the rebellion, and authorized the courts to include the liberation of such a person's slaves as part of the punishment. The Act also required the president ("it shall be the duty of the President . . . .") to cause the seizure of all property (from real estate to stocks) of any officer of the CSA or anyone giving aid and comfort to the rebellion if they failed to cease such aid after sixty days; the confiscation would be accomplished through *in rem*[127] condemnation proceedings in federal courts.[128]

The key slavery provisions were in Sections 9 through 12, which provided that all slaves of persons aiding the rebellion who take refuge within Union army lines shall be "deemed captives of war, and shall be *forever free* of their servitude, and not again held as slaves" (emphasis added).[129] (Thus, the Act dealt with the problem that Butler first faced at Fort Monroe on the Virginia coast the year earlier—the status of the slaves who come into the control of Union forces.) This included slaves who escaped, all slaves captured or deserted from the Confederate forces, and all slaves of such persons who were found in territory occupied by Union forces. Union forces were specifically prohibited from returning slaves who came into their control; the president was authorized to "employ as many persons of African descent" as necessary for the suppression of the rebellion; and the president was also authorized to make provisions for "the transportation, colonization, and settlement," "in some tropical country beyond the limits of the United States" for persons of African descent who were made free by this Act. The two provisos were that the government of the "tropical country" had first to consent, and that the freedmen had to be willing to emigrate.

This Second Confiscation Act had quiet a remarkable history—in addition to decades of Supreme Court litigation. The original bill was first introduced in Congress on December 4, 1861, by Radical Republicans. However, it was stalemated by Democrats, as well as conservatives within the Republican Party who felt the proposed Act was a violation of the Fifth Amendment protection of property. When the proposed legislation was debated in March 1862, the Republicans made clear that the intent of this bill was to remake Southern society by destroying the economic and political power of the plantation owners who provoked secession. In May, the entire confiscation issue was sent to a special committee for reconsideration. One issue was whether the confiscation was punishment for a crime, or if it was a non-punishment measure designed to weaken the rebellion. The Senate passed the bill on June 30, and the House passed it on July 12th.

Lincoln was following the congressional debates, and was opposed to the Act; he even prepared a draft veto Message. He was worried, as always, about the reaction in the Border States to the slavery provisions. But apart from the slavery issue, Lincoln believed that the Act was unconstitutional because Congress had no power—under the "attainder" provision of the Constitution, which provided a safeguard against "trial by legislature"[130]—to "prescribe as a punishment for treason the forfeiture of the real property of the offender beyond his natural life."[131] While the Act was sitting on his desk for signature or for a veto, the message was clearly received by the Congress that something had to be done to convince the president that the Act was constitutional.[132]

Congress hurriedly passed a joint resolution on July 16th providing that the Act should not "be so construed as to work a forfeiture of real estate of the offender beyond his natural life"—meaning that slaves could be freed, but land and homes could be passed down from generation to generation. This "explanatory Resolution" was sufficient to allow Lincoln to withdraw his veto threat. The resolution was an odd piece of legislation, since it in effect amended an Act that had been passed but not yet signed into law. When signing the Act and the resolution, Lincoln noted specifically that the Act and the resolution were "substantially one." Aside from Lincoln's legal problem with the Act, his goal in forcing the adoption of the resolution was to "emasculate" the non-slavery provisions of the Act,[133] since only the life estate interest in property could be confiscated.

Lincoln then returned the signed Act and resolution to the Congress, and he attached his proposed veto message that explained his concerns with the Act. The single element that he considered unconstitutional—the attainder issue—was solved by the resolution. But in his proposed veto message, he identified other provisions that troubled him: of particular interest was his comment about the section that provided that slaves of convicted persons shall be free. He generously noted that this was an "unfortunate form of expression," and continued:

> It is startling to say that Congress can free a slave within a State; and yet if it were said that the ownership of the slave had first been transferred to the nation, and that Congress had then liberated him, the difficulty would at once vanish . . . . I perceive no objection to Congress deciding in advance that they shall be free.

In this clever fashion, Lincoln signaled to the slave states within the Union that he still believed that Congress could not act to free slaves in the states.

After the debate over the passage of the Second Confiscation Act,[134] Lincoln returned to his central focus: gradual, compensated emancipation by state action. He again met with Congressman Crisfield of southern Maryland. He assured Crisfield that he would guarantee Maryland slave owners three hundred dollars for each emancipated slave and colonize the freedmen at government expense in Latin America. Lincoln urged acceptance, since the price of a slave would never be higher. Crisfield and his allies remained intransigent, and so lost the opportunity to direct the process of slave liberation in southern Maryland.[135] (Slavery came to a *de facto* end on the Eastern Shore after Union troops arrived in July 1863, and actively enlisted slaves into a regiment of U.S. Colored Troops.)

In addition to the Second Confiscation Act, Congress also enacted on July 17, 1862, the Militia Act which authorized the president to receive into military service persons of African descent, and if they were slaves of rebels, they and their families would be forever free. After the War, Attorney General James Speed issued an Opinion that those blacks who acquired their freedom by virtue of the Second Confiscation Act and were mustered into military service were entitled to receive the same bounty as white volunteers.[136]

The Emancipation Proclamation

While the congressional efforts were underway toward enacting the Second Confiscation Act and Lincoln was pleading with the Border States to accept compensated and gradual emancipation, and even though he publicly reprimanded General Hunter for purporting to emancipate all the slaves in three Southern states, Lincoln seems to have already been mulling over the extent to which he might hold the constitutional power to emancipate slaves as a war measure. Oddly, he sprang this notion on Secretary of State Seward and Secretary of the Navy Welles on July 13th while on a carriage ride to the funeral of Secretary of War Stanton's young son. Seward was "thunderstruck."[137] Lincoln said that a change in policy in the conduct of the War was necessary, and that emancipation was "a military necessity absolutely essential to the salvation of the Union."

Lincoln called a special cabinet meeting for July 21, 1862. It was there that he read his handwritten draft document that later would be termed the Emancipation Proclamation. He explained that he sought a discussion with the cabinet, but he made it clear that he had already decided to take this action. The document began by proclaiming seizure of all property of those in rebellion, expressly referring to the sixth section of the Second Confiscation Act. The next section repeated his plan for federal aid to the states embarking on a gradual emancipation. Finally, the last section was dramatic: "as a fit and necessary military measure . . . I, as Commander-in-Chief—do order and declare that on [January 1st] all persons held as slaves within any state or states wherein the constitutional authority of the United States shall not then be practically recognized . . . shall then, thenceforward, and forever, be free."[138]

In that single, long sentence, Lincoln:

(a) set out his legal authority (his war powers as Commander-in-Chief),

(b) limited the scope of the reach to the Confederacy (since legally it would be a stretch to exercise war powers in the Border States where there was no war),

(c) made it clear that this was a definitive act with future consequences, and that he was not merely seizing slaves and holding them for a future decision as to their status, and

(d) emphasized that it dealt with all slaves in the CSA states, not only those being used in aid of the CSA military or only those owned by people giving aid.

THE FIRST READING OF THE EMANCIPATION
PROCLAMATION BEFORE THE CABINET.

It was of breathtaking sweep, yet technically narrow at the same time. And that sword of emancipation was drawn only after the olive branch of compensated, gradual, and voter-sanctioned state emancipation had been offered many times.

Then the cabinet members spoke. First was Attorney General Bates, who endorsed the document, but conditioned his support with the point that it should be expanded to provide for mandatory colonization. Secretary of War Stanton supported its immediate promulgation; Stanton had immediately grasped the military value of the proclamation and understood the tremendous advantage if the massive workforce of slaves could be transferred to the Union.[139] Then Treasury Secretary Chase expressed concern about legal issues: if there was concern about legal challenges to the Fremont and Hunter approaches, there would be an even greater challenge if this broader action was taken by the president; in any event, wouldn't it be wiser to let the field commanders take similar action within their military districts rather than risking massacre in areas where Union forces were not present? Chase suggested that the army would better control and contain incremental emancipation than an immediate and far-reaching one.[140]

Montgomery Blair, the postmaster general and former lawyer for Dred Scott, worried about the impact on the North as midterm elections approached and as the fear mounted of freed slaves migrating to the North. Blair was vigorously opposed to the proclamation: the Republicans could lose their control of the Congress. William Seward, the secretary of state and the fifth lawyer[141] in the cabinet to speak, endorsed the idea (of course, he had had more time to think about it than the others), but cautioned as to timing: with the current lack of military success, this step might well be seen by foreign powers—especially France and Britain—as an admission by the Union that it could not win the War, and so the foreign powers would be tempted to intervene to prevent "servile insurrection" and to protect the supply of cotton. Therefore, Seward argued, wait until the Union has had a significant military victory, so that this emancipation step could not be perceived as a cry from the defeated Union.

Acting on Bates' suggestion of a colonization provision, Lincoln invited a delegation of freed slaves to the White House—*the first time blacks had ever been invited to the White House* for purposes other than service. Lincoln's goal at this August 14th meeting was to get their cooperation for the idea of colonization.[142] A leading scholar asserts that the real goal was to "soften up the Northern public for an emancipation policy that Lincoln had decided to embrace."[143] Two days later, the delegation wrote to Lincoln with "widespread antipathy."[144] Their very valid point was that the four million slaves in the United States were as much natives of the United States as were their oppressors.

Taking Seward's diplomatic argument to heart, Lincoln did not immediately issue his proclamation. He waited. On September 4th, Lee's troops invaded Maryland. On the 17th, they were repulsed and retreated across the Potomac into Virginia after a bloody battle at Antietam, where, on that single day, six thousand soldiers lost their lives and seventeen thousand were wounded. While it was not an unambiguous Union "victory," it clearly was not a loss for the Union,[145] and so it was sufficiently positive for Lincoln to act on his proclamation.[146] Lincoln locked himself in his office and worked, and re-worked his draft that he had read to the cabinet on July 21st. On September 22nd, Lincoln called a cabinet meeting and read to the members the text of his revised, now preliminary, Emancipation Proclamation that he intended to issue that same day.[147]

The Preliminary Proclamation, which was in all the newspapers the next day, was not quite the same as the July version. Lincoln had tinkered with it, drawing on his lawyer's and politician's skills. It began with a

Ending Slavery

statement setting out the object of the War (to restore the South to the Union), and, as in July, Lincoln then explained his intent "again to recommend" to the next session of Congress the compensation plan, but then he added his intention to continue with the "effort to colonize persons of African descent with their consent." Thus, he added Bates' notion of the importance of the linking of emancipation to colonization, but he rejected Bates' further idea that colonization be mandatory. Those were the first two paragraphs.

The meat was in the third paragraph: On January 1st, "all persons held as slaves in any state, or part of a state, still in rebellion, shall be then, thenceforth, and forever free." Moreover, there were teeth to the statement of freedom for the slaves: the Executive (specifically including the armed forces) "will recognize and maintain the freedom of such persons" and will not impede any steps they might take to make their own freedom. In short, the army will not put down any slave rebellion, and certainly will not enforce the Fugitive Slave Law. The fourth paragraph explained that the president would designate the specific states or parts thereof to be affected by the proclamation on January 1st.

The Preliminary Proclamation then quoted from the Article of War Act of March 13th and the Second Confiscation Act of July 17th. Finally, it closed with a promise that the president will "in due time" recommend that all citizens who have remained loyal will be compensated for all losses "by acts of the United States, including the loss of slaves."

The opening words of the Preliminary Proclamation were also different from those of the original July 21st version: "as a fit and necessary military measure ... I, as Commander-in-Chief ...." The September 22nd Preliminary Proclamation began by referring to "I," President, *and* Commander-in-Chief. Thus, the July version was more of a military directive, issued by the commander in chief "as a fit and necessary military measure," whereas the September version focused more broadly on Lincoln's role as president and commander, without the focus on the "necessary military measure." This reads as a bold statement ("by the person" rather than "of being the person in charge").

Only a lawyer with a very high degree of self-confidence would have attempted to draft such an enormously important document—one with great legal and practical consequences (potentially freeing millions of slaves)—almost entirely on his own. And, as a politician, he must have known that Montgomery Blair's warning about the congressional elections was wise, and yet he issued his Preliminary Proclamation anyway. Clearly, he was set on his course without regard to the political cost.[148]

THE EMANCIPATION PROCLAMATION. The text of the Emancipation Proclamation, with two U.S. flags and an eagle over a portrait of Lincoln and flanked by Justice and Liberty.

The Reaction

The *Times of London*, probably the most powerful newspaper in the world at that time, did not see the proclamation as an attack on slavery, but rather as Lincoln's way of stimulating slave uprisings in the South—an unworthy and morally questionable measure. It bitterly opined that: "Where he has no power Mr. Lincoln will set the Negroes free; where he retains power

Ending Slavery

he will consider them as slaves."[149] (That is not quite accurate in terms of Lincoln's legal power, but it is a forceful statement.) The *Times*, continuing its theme that the proclamation was not about slavery, but rather about winning the War at all costs, concluded:

> Mr. Lincoln will, on the 1st of next January, do his best to excite a servile war in the States which he cannot occupy with his arms . . . and when blood begins to flow and shrieks come piercing through the darkness, Mr. Lincoln will wait till the rising flames tell that all is consummated, and then he will rub his hands and think that revenge is sweet.[150]

The immediate political cost of the proclamation was high. The fall 1862 election results were "devastating to the administration"[151] and "as close to disaster for Lincoln as one could get without actual loss of life."[152] The Preliminary Proclamation had reinvigorated the Northern Democrats; they argued that Lincoln had sacrificed the Constitution for abolition.[153] In the congressional elections, thirty-one Republicans lost. Democratic governors were elected in New York and New Jersey. In Lincoln's state of Illinois, the Democrats took control of the state legislature, and the new congressional delegation contained four Democrats and only one Republican. The "peace Democrats"—those who favored a settlement with the South which would tolerate slavery—were the big winners.[154] While Republicans still retained slim majorities in both Houses, there was no guarantee that there would be a majority for emancipation.

When asked how he felt about the election results, Lincoln replied famously: "Somewhat like that boy in Kentucky, who stubbed his toe while running to see his sweetheart. The boy said he was too big to cry, and far too badly hurt to laugh."[155]

The Amendments and Final Proclamation

The lame duck Congress assembled on December 1st to receive Lincoln's second annual Message to Congress. The first half of the fifteen-page document recited a laundry list of governmental operations such as the new commercial treaty with the Sultan of Turkey,[156] the detailed receipts and disbursements of the Treasury, improvements in the mail system, the establishment of the Agriculture Department, problems with the Indians, etc. The second half of the Message was devoted exclusively and passionately to the plan for compensated and gradual emancipation.

Lincoln proposed three amendments to the Constitution in this Message to Congress: (1) every State will abolish slavery *by 1900*, and shall receive compensation in the form of U.S. bonds equal to the aggregate sum of $___ per slave; (2) all slaves who have gained "actual freedom by the chances of war" shall be forever free, but if they have loyal owners, the owners shall be compensated; and (3) Congress may appropriate money for "colonizing free colored persons with their own consent." Lincoln quickly added the fact that his proposal represented great compromises: emancipation will be unsatisfactory to those who want perpetual slavery, while others who want immediate emancipation will be upset with the thirty-seven years his proposal offered.

After making his sales pitch—including detailed demographics to show how cheap it would be to pay the bonds—Lincoln explained that he proposed his plan "as permanent constitutional law," and that the process would necessarily involve not only two-thirds of the Congress, but also three-fourths of the states, which "necessarily include seven of the slave States." Their concurrence would end the War and save the Union. His message concluded with the lofty words: "In giving freedom to the slave we assure freedom to the free . . . . We shall nobly save or meanly lose the last best hope of earth."

This great proposal was made exactly one month *before* the Emancipation Proclamation was to be made effective. How could it be serious? How did this proposal for constitutional amendments fit with the proposed emancipation? Or, some thought, did this mean that Lincoln intended to delay his proclamation, at least until he could push his constitutional plan further? If he intended to proceed in thirty days with his proclamation, what was the purpose of this constitutional amendment proposal?

The cabinet met on December 29th and again on December 31st to review the proclamation, and to propose final changes. Bates, Seward, Blair, and Chase all suggested changes, many of which found favor with Lincoln. The *final document*, after reproducing the two key paragraphs from the September 22nd Preliminary Proclamation:

a) was from Lincoln, "President of the United States, by virtue of the power vested in me as Commander-in-Chief . . . in time of actual armed rebellion . . . , and as a fit and necessary war measure." In contrast to the earlier versions, Lincoln now squarely put the president at the center, and mentioned his commander role by way of identifying the source of the power he was exercising. The idea of this being a "fit and necessary war measure" was taken from the private July 21st version (dropped in the September version), which, together with the reference to "actual armed rebellion" strengthened Lincoln's claim to be exercising his war powers.[157]

b) set out the ten states, or parts thereof,[158] that were then in rebellion, and thus to which the proclamation would apply.

Ending Slavery

c) ordered and declared that all persons held as slaves in those states "are, and henceforward shall be free." In a major step, Lincoln had dropped from the July version and from the September Preliminary Proclamation the idea that the slaves shall be "*forever* free." Lincoln was not quite sure that a wartime, military measure could survive "forever."[159] This also provided a bit of ambiguity as to the future status of the former slaves, especially if the proclamation were challenged in court. Permanently tearing up the title to property without compensation could well be judged to be unconstitutional, as a violation of the Fifth Amendment protection of property.

d) provided that the Executive, expressly including the military, would "recognize and maintain the freedom of said persons," as did the Preliminary Proclamation; however, this version dropped the earlier provision that the military would take no action to repress the actions the slaves may take for their own freedom. This retreat was pressed hard on Lincoln by Bates, Seward, Blair, and Chase. They argued that the omitted provision might put the army in the position of watching while a slave killed his master in order to escape.

e) added a provision at the strong urging of Blair that "enjoined" the freed slaves to abstain from all violence (except self-defense).[160]

f) added also was a statement that the freedmen—of suitable condition—would be able to join the armed service to garrison forts and to man vessels. The question of armed combat service was at best ambiguous.

g) added also a closing section, drafted by Chase, that declared this to be an "act of justice, warranted by the Constitution, upon military necessity," and invoking the favor of Almighty God. This, then, stressed that the president believed this measure was a constitutionally permissible exercise of war powers: in case anyone might have missed the point, this was a "military necessity."

h) did not include the statement of purpose in the Preliminary Proclamation (to fight the War to restore the Union), or the stated intention to recommend compensation and colonization.

The president had a very busy day on January 1, 1863. Early in the day, he cast his lawyer's eye over the Emancipation Proclamation document that had been "engrossed" by the State Department—put into final form, ready for signature—and he found a clerical error.[161] The document had to be sent back with Secretary of State Seward for repair. In the

PRESIDENT ABRAHAM LINCOLN.

meantime, he entertained the public at the traditional New Year's Day Levee, starting with the diplomatic corps, and then Chief Justice Taney and the Supreme Court. Lincoln also met in the morning, and then again in the afternoon, with the Commander of the Army of the Potomac, General Ambrose Burnside, following the thrashing the army had suffered days earlier at Fredericksburg; Burnside twice that day offered his resignation to Lincoln, who refused it both times.[162] When Seward returned from the State Department with the corrected proclamation document, Lincoln's hand was trembling from shaking so many hands—so his somewhat erratic signature was not due to a quaking acknowledgement of the enormity of the measure he was signing. Thus, on New Years Day 1863, the president signed the Emancipation Proclamation.[163]

Interestingly, Lincoln never gave a speech on the Emancipation Proclamation. There was no stirring eloquence, as in the Gettysburg Address;

in contemporary terms, there was no prime time address from the Oval Office. The document itself is as inspiring as a bill of sale. It was, however, a legal document.

Aftermath

How can one reconcile the Emancipation Proclamation with the flat and solemn statement made by Lincoln in his March 4, 1861, inaugural that "I believe I have no lawful right to [interfere directly or indirectly with the institution of slavery in the states where it now exists]"? The difference, Lincoln would argue, is that in January 1863, the United States was at war, and he could now invoke his war powers, whereas in March 1861, while there was already secession, there was no armed fighting. The statement in the inaugural was more in the nature of a pledge that was based on the assumption that the slave states would remain in the Union. The proclamation only applied behind enemy lines—battlefield measures within the purview of the commander in chief.

How could he reconcile the proclamation with his repudiation of General Fremont and General Hunter, when his proclamation went even further? Lincoln would claim that he had no argument with their good intentions, but rather with their usurpation of a presidential power, a power and a responsibility that he must safeguard. Why didn't Lincoln enhance his position by seeking congressional authorization for his proclamation? Lincoln might have replied that Congress did not have that power; that only the president, drawing on his war powers,[164] could make such a proclamation.

A week after the proclamation, Lincoln wrote to his old political ally from Illinois, General John McClernand, and explained that he "struggled nearly a year and a half to get along without touching the 'institution', and when finally [he] conditionally determined to touch it, [he] gave one hundred days fair notice of [his] purpose . . . within which time they could have turned it wholly aside, by simply again becoming good citizens . . . ." That failure, he went on, forced him to issue the proclamation as "a military necessity."[165]

The reaction to the proclamation was swift, and largely negative. Many expected white Union soldiers to fade away[166] or at least not to reenlist. The new governor of New York, Horatio Seymour, in his inaugural, described the proclamation as a "bloody, barbarous, revolutionary and unconstitutional scheme."[167] New Jersey and Illinois reacted in the same way. The border states reacted the most sharply, fearing that the freed slaves would make their way northward to their states. The greatest challenge to Lincoln's proclamation came from the lawyers. Perhaps the

[APRIL 18, 1868.

BENJAMIN R. CURTIS, OF MASS.—[PHOT. BY WHIPPLE.]

The opening speech on the part of the Managers was made by General B. F. BUTLER on October 30. He very learnedly discussed the right of the Senate as at present constituted to

BENJAMIN R. CURTIS.

most serious and effective assault came from Benjamin Curtis—the lawyer and former Supreme Court Justice from Massachusetts who wrote the long and blistering dissent from Taney's opinion in the *Dred Scott* case, who thereafter resigned from the Court and returned to practice. The fact that Curtis held such clear and public antislavery and pro-war views made his attack even more effective.[168]

Curtis prepared a thirty-two-page pamphlet entitled "Executive Power," and had it published in late 1862.[169] It was a blistering critique of Lincoln's suppression of civil liberties and over-reach of Executive power, focusing chiefly on the Preliminary Emancipation Proclamation. Curtis made clear that he supported the War—"The war in which we are engaged is a just and a necessary war"[170]—but not the proclamation. He argued, "with what sense of right can we subdue them by arms to obey the Constitution as the supreme law of *their* part of the land, if we have ceased to obey it, or failed to preserve it, as the supreme law of *our* part of the land?"[171] Curtis attacked as an illegal assumption of power the use of a mere Executive decree to repeal and annul valid state laws which regulate the domestic relations of their people—a punishment against the entire people of a state. If the president has "an implied right" to disregard positive prohibitions of the Constitution, "he has the same right to disregard each and every provision of the Constitution."[172] The power of commander in chief is a military power, Curtis said, permitting the president to do what generals do "in the sphere of their actual operations." When a general-in-chief disobeys the law of the land, "he super-adds to his *rights* as commander the *powers* of a usurper; and that is military despotism . . . . [A]ll the powers of the President are executive merely. He cannot make a law. He cannot repeal one . . . ."[173]

In a comment quite similar to Taney's charge against Lincoln in *Ex parte Merryman*, Curtis said: "Since Charles I lost his head,[174] there has been no king in England who could make such law in that realm."[175] The military power over citizens is a "power to act, not a power to prescribe rules for future action." Curtis concluded: "It is among the rights of all of us, that the *executive* power should be kept within its prescribed constitutional limits, and should not *legislate*, by decrees, upon subjects [such as freeing four million slaves] of transcendent importance to the whole people."[176]

One can speculate the reaction of most in the South (and some in the North, such as Curtis) if Lincoln subsequently had issued a Second Proclamation giving title to real estate (the plantations) owned by slaveholders to the now-emancipated slaves resident on those plantations in equal shares.[177] Or, to take it one step further: what if Lincoln issued a Third Proclamation that authorized emancipated slaves to treat any resisting slaveholders as criminal resisters and anti-Union agitators; the former slaves would then be authorized to treat them as captives, and, if the former slaveholders resisted, force could be used against them, including deadly force.

* * *

The proclamation, in a sense, did little: it purported to emancipate slaves only in areas in which the Union had no control, and it left slaves in bondage in areas the Union did control. Nevertheless, it did have an impact on the military situation: former slaves joined the Union army; the hope of freedom now held by slaves in the Confederacy sapped the industrial strength of the CSA; it did not, as many feared, set off mass white desertion within the Union army or set off a much-predicted race war; and it did not provoke foreign intervention—indeed, turning the war into a moral war for freedom produced sympathy in Europe (except perhaps in the upper classes in England).

Was the Emancipation Proclamation constitutional? Probably not; former Justice Curtis's arguments seem valid. Would the Supreme Court have declared it unconstitutional? That depends on *when* the Court decided the matter: if *during* the War, probably not, on a close vote; if *after* the War, it probably would—although the issue by then would have been moot in light of the Thirteenth Amendment, and so the Court might have merely dismissed the case.

Emancipation, by state action, followed fairly quickly: West Virginia, when finally admitted as a state; Arkansas on March 16, 1864 (when the new state Constitution was ratified); Louisiana on September 5, 1864 (when its new state Constitution was ratified); Maryland[178] on November 1, 1864 (when its new state Constitution took effect); Missouri on January 11, 1865 (when its state convention abolished slavery); and Tennessee on February 22, 1865 (when its Constitution was amended). In none of these states was abolition accomplished gradually or with federal compensation or with linking to colonization. The plan Lincoln had sought so hard to implement never came to be.

Ending Slavery 253

ʲ⁂ ʲ⁂ ʲ⁂

Emancipation in the South?

The idea of emancipation was also treated in the Confederacy, though the result was quite different. On January 7, 1864, almost exactly a year after Lincoln's Emancipation Proclamation, Major General Patrick Ronayne Cleburne—previously a successful lawyer in Arkansas—used his lawyer's powers of analysis and persuasion to propose the training and arming of the best slaves and setting them free.[179] His proposal, known as the Cleburne Memorial, argued that the CSA Army suffered inferiority in numbers to the Union (three to one), that it had only a single source of manpower, and that slavery had become from a military viewpoint one of the chief sources of weakness.[180] To remedy these problems, he proposed

MAJOR GENERAL PATRICK R. CLEBURNE.

to enlist slaves and guarantee them freedom. The bottom line, Cleburne argued, was that CSA patriots would prefer to lose slavery rather than their own independence. (This Memorial had elements of the proposal in 1779 of Sir Henry Clinton, who promised "full security" to slaves deserting the American rebels and coming over to fight for the British.) Cleburne's superior officer refused to pass on his Memorial to the CSA government in Richmond, but another officer forwarded it to Jefferson Davis, who dismissed the proposition, because of the need to maintain CSA solidarity in the face of the presidential elections in the Union later in the year. In February 1864, however, the CSA Congress did authorize the use of twenty thousand slaves in noncombatant roles.

Davis had a different perspective later in the year. His government officials, including Governor Henry W. Allen of Louisiana and Secretary of State Judah Benjamin, urged arming slaves when Atlanta fell to the Union in September 1864. On November 7, 1864, the day before Lincoln's reelection, Davis proposed to the CSA Congress a dramatic increase in the number of slaves in the army by purchasing them and promising to free them after they rendered faithful service. In short, this was a sort of compensated emancipation. The CSA Congress, however, did not act. For slaveholders and their political allies, the idea of slaves making good soldiers undercut the entire theory of slavery.

Undaunted, Davis, in January 1865, sent Duncan F. Kenner of Louisiana, a lawyer/politician/planter, on a secret diplomatic mission to present a deal to the French and British: if they would recognize the CSA, Davis would emancipate the slaves. Napoleon III deferred to the British, where Prime Minister Lord Palmerston flatly refused—at that point, so very late in the War, the Brits knew that the Union would clearly win and the CSA was doomed, and so the UK would gain nothing by recognizing the CSA. Davis was four years late and the Kenner mission failed. In February, a bill was introduced into the CSA Congress to arm the slaves; Davis and Robert E. Lee endorsed the proposal, and the bill passed on March 13, 1865—but it failed to include the emancipation of those slaves. Nevertheless, later that month, Davis issued an executive order that stipulated that, when a slave agreed to serve, his master had to agree in writing to grant him freedman's rights. The first company of freed slaves was formed in Richmond on March 25, 1865, two weeks before Lee surrendered to Grant. At that point, there were some two hundred thousand free blacks in the Union forces.

The idea of arming and then freeing slaves did not signify a repudiation of the basic goals of the Confederacy.[181] Rather, it was a last ditch effort to prevent defeat, and also a way to preserve the South's plantation system and sharply limit the rights of the Negro. (Remember: only the

JUDAH P. BENJAMIN.

soldier-slave was to be freed, not his family.) It was Secretary of State Judah Benjamin who inspired Davis's about-face on the subject. He laid out a legal status for the post-war former slave that would be sort of a state of serfdom: former slaveholders would still hold all the property, and the former slave would have some new legal protections, such as marital relations, and certain rights of property and of limited personal liberty.[182] The proposition was this: if *we* liberate the slaves, our independence is secured, and we can set the terms to control the free Negro; the continuing penetration of Union forces would eventually destroy slavery in a most pernicious manner.[183]

Slavery was ended in the South not by the South, but by the Thirteenth Amendment to the Constitution.

The Thirteenth Amendment

When the post-proclamation Congress met in December 1863, proposals were floated to abolish slavery by amending the Constitution. On April 8, 1864, the Senate approved the proposed amendment, but the House rejected it in June. On January 23, 1865, the House approved the amendment, and Lincoln, on February 1, 1865, formally sent the amendment to the states for ratification.[184] The text was simple:

> Neither slavery nor involuntary servitude, except as a punishment for crime whereof the party shall have been duly convicted, shall exist within the United States or any place subject to their jurisdiction.

The wording was based on phrases used in the Northwest Ordinance of July 13, 1787, under the Articles of Confederation, which created the Northwest Territory where slavery was specifically forbidden.

Illinois was the first state to ratify, on February 1st. Georgia was the twenty-seventh state to ratify, on December 6th, which was the last ratification needed to allow the amendment to come into force. On December 18, 1865, the secretary of state announced that the Thirteenth Amendment was ratified, and slavery was finally ended. This was the first amendment to the Constitution since 1804, sixty-one years. The amendment was subsequently ratified by other states: Delaware in 1901 (having rejected the amendment on February 8, 1865) and Kentucky in 1976 (having rejected it on February 24, 1865).

Yale Professor Akhil Reed Amar summarized the situation clearly: "A structurally proslavery Constitution became, in a flash, stunningly antislavery . . . . [T]he Founders' Constitution failed in 1861–65. The system almost died, and more than a half a million people did die. Without these deaths, the Thirteenth Amendment's new birth of freedom could never have occurred as it did."[185]

The Continuing Debate

On December 10, 1948, the General Assembly of the United Nations adopted the Universal Declaration of Human Rights. Of the thirty Articles, the first and fourth are relevant:

"Article 1. All human beings are born free and equal in dignity and rights . . . .

Article 4. No one shall be held in slavery or servitude; slavery and the slave trade shall be prohibited in all their forms."

CHAPTER 8

The Revenge Trials

The Trial of the Assassination Conspirators

With the shot that killed the president in the early hours of April 15, 1865, Secretary of War Stanton became the most powerful person in the country. One of his first steps was to launch the most massive manhunt in American history to capture the conspirators. John Wilkes Booth was shot by Union Army Sergeant Boston Corbett on April 26th in a burning barn in the Virginia countryside.

DRAWING OF ABRAHAM LINCOLN'S DEATHBED SCENE.

SECRETARY OF WAR EDWIN M. STANTON.

Captured in the manhunt were:

- on April 17th: Mary Surratt (whose son, John, was close to Booth), Lewis Powell[1] (who tried to assassinate Secretary of State Seward), Samuel Arnold and Michael O'Laughlin (both boyhood friends of Booth's), and Edman Spangler (a stagehand at Ford's who held the reins of Booth's horse)
- on April 20th: George Atzerodt (who admitted to conspiring to kidnap Lincoln, but not to assassinating him);
- on April 24th: Dr. Samuel A. Mudd (who treated Booth's injured leg);
- and on April 26th, David Herold (who was taken alive at the burning barn where Booth died).

Many others were caught in the dragnet,[2] including the Ford brothers—the owners of the theater in which the assassination took place—and Junius Brutus Booth Jr., the brother of John Wilkes, and a prominent actor in his own right and who was performing in Cincinnati, Ohio, at the time of the assassination.[3]

There was a question about how the prisoners should be tried. Secretary of War Stanton wanted them tried before a military court and hanged before the president was buried. Navy Secretary Welles objected.

The Revenge Trials 261

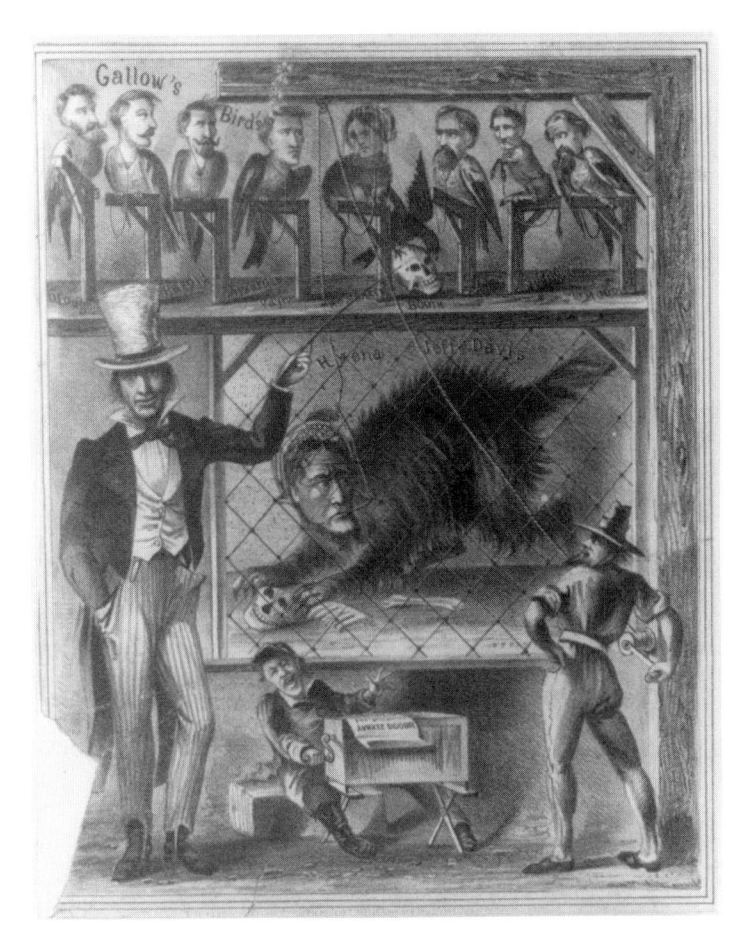

Uncle Sam's Menagerie. Issued in the wake of Lincoln's assassination, this print conveys some of the Northern hostility toward the conspirators, whom the public associated with former president of the Confederacy Jefferson Davis. Uncle Sam stands before a cage in which a hyena with the bonneted head of Jefferson Davis claws at a skull. Davis's neck is in a noose, which will begin to tighten as a man at right turns the crank of a gallows. Below, a man grinds out the song "Yankee Doodle" on a hand organ. Above, the Lincoln conspirators are portrayed as "Gallow's Bird's," with their heads in nooses. From left to right they are: Michael O'Laughlin, David Herold, George Atzerodt, Lewis Payne, Mary Elizabeth Surratt, Samuel Arnold, Edman Spangler, and Dr. Samuel Mudd. Uncle Sam points his stick at a skull, Booth, on which sits a black crow. Booth was killed on April 26, 1865.

Attorney General James Speed, who had been appointed by Lincoln to replaced Edward Bates only five months earlier, agreed that trial by a military commission was desirable. President Johnson and Stanton asked Speed for an Opinion on the legality of trial by military commission. Speed provided a simple one-sentence Opinion on April 28, 1865:[4] "I am of the opinion that the persons charged with the murder of the President of the United States can be rightfully tried by a military court." In July, Speed issued a fifteen-page formal written Opinion[5]—*after* the convictions were announced. On May 1st, President Johnson ordered that they should be tried by a military commission, rather than by a civilian criminal court.

The trial opened on May 9, 1865, at the Old Arsenal Penitentiary. (The Penitentiary was located on the site of today's Fort McNair, on the Potomac River.) Nine U.S. Army officers—seven generals and two colonels—served as the commission; none of the nine were trained as lawyers, except for General Lewis Wallace.[6] Major General David Hunter was the president of the commission. Earlier he had been known as "the abolitionist General." As previously noted, Hunter, exactly three years earlier, had issued a military order that freed the slaves in his Department of the South, which provoked a rebuke by Lincoln. The lead prosecutor was General Joseph Holt, the judge advocate general, who had been postmaster general and then secretary of war in the last few months of the

MILITARY COMMISSION THAT TRIED AND CONVICTED
THE LINCOLN CONSPIRATORS.

Buchanan administration.[7] Holt had been Lincoln's first choice to replace Bates as Attorney General—Lincoln was concerned that his cabinet had "shrunk up North," and so he wanted a Southerner, and Holt was from Kentucky. Lincoln also had worked closely with Holt on court-martial cases. When Holt declined the Attorney General's nomination, he recommended his fellow Kentuckian, James Speed; Speed was the brother of Joshua Speed, Lincoln's friend from Springfield.[8]

Holt was interested in proving that Jefferson Davis and the Confederate government had been involved in the conspiracy. Assisting Holt was a Special Prosecutor, John Bingham, a former congressman from Ohio. Bingham was a tough fighter. His style "was anything but gentle; he scolded, mocked, and intimidated his adversaries, and never yielded an inch of ground."[9]

The trial began in secret on May 9th. On May 13th, Stanton reluctantly yielded to pressure from General Grant[10] and agreed to open the trial to the press and the public—though to attend, one had to have a pass issued by General Hunter.

During their imprisonment, the defendants had had no access to counsel, and had been kept in isolation (in chains and hoods, except for Mary Surratt). Only on the first day of the trial were they asked whether they wanted counsel. The defendants searched for defense lawyers through family, friends and sympathizers: Atzerodt hired the former Provost Marshal of Washington, William E. Doster; O'Laughlin hired Walter S. Cox, a law professor at Columbia College; Herold hired Frederick Stone of Charles County; Dr. Mudd and Arnold shared General Thomas Ewing, a former chief justice of the Kansas supreme court; and Mrs. Surratt initially had only two junior lawyers, Frederick A. Aiken (just completing his first year in practice) and John W. Clampitt,[11] but before the trial began, she added the renowned Maryland Senator Reverdy Johnson. A couple of days into the trial, Spangler and Powell still had no counsel. The assistant prosecutor asked the other attorneys to take them on too. Thus, Doster agreed also to represent Powell, General Ewing added Spangler, and Stone agreed to help Ewing represent Dr. Mudd.

As the proceedings got underway on May 13th, a skirmish took place between one of the members of the commission, General Thomas Harris, and Reverdy Johnson. Harris objected to the admission of Johnson as Surratt's counsel because of statements made by Johnson the previous year during the consideration of a new constitution for Maryland. According to Harris, Johnson's statements suggested that Johnson believed that the oath of loyalty to the Union need not be obeyed.[12] In effect, General Harris claimed that Johnson lacked the moral integrity to appear before the commission. One of the members later recalled Johnson's reaction:

THE HONORABLE REVERDY JOHNSON.

[H]is indignation was very manifest by his flushed face, but his remarks were quiet and dignified, and full of irony, and showed the ill-advised nature of the objection in such a light that Gen'l Harris must have regretted that he made the objection, if he had any sense of the absurdity of . . . raising an objection to a member of the U.S. Senate, appearing before us as a counsel on the ground of disloyalty. Johnson did not do us the honor to appear before us again after this insult to his dignity.[13]

The exchange between the general and the senator grew sharp: Johnson said that the court had no competence "to measure the moral character of the counsel"[14] and that prejudice against him would injure his client. Harris said that the commission had decided an oath by counsel was required; Johnson replied that the court had no right to demand that oath of him, that he had taken it in the Senate, in the circuit court of Maryland, and in the U.S. Supreme Court. General Hunter intervened and called for a recess, after which the commission went into secret session. When the commission reopened, General Harris withdrew his objection to Reverdy Johnson.

(Oath-taking was a hot topic at the time, and the issue was headed toward the Supreme Court. One case involved a Catholic priest in Missouri, and the other involved an Arkansas lawyer seeking reinstatement to practice before the U.S. Supreme Court. Both cases arose in 1865, were argued in 1866, and were decided in 1867. Both cases were decided by 5–4 votes in favor of a lenient approach and against using oath-taking as a punitive measure. Plaintiffs in both cases were represented by Reverdy Johnson: *Cummings v. Missouri*[15] and *Ex parte Garland*.[16])

The Johnson Argument

The substantive confrontation in the trial occurred on June 16th. Reverdy Johnson's written statement argued that the Hunter Commission had no jurisdiction to conduct the trial.[17] (Previous pleas filed with the court objecting to the jurisdiction of the Court were overruled as soon as they were filed.) His argument was recorded in a twenty-five-page document in which the two associate counsel for Surratt expressly concurred. The Johnson argument was read to the tribunal on June 19th by John Clampitt.[18]

The Johnson argument is a brilliant statement on personal liberties and limitations on the power of the president. Johnson argued:

(1) The war power was conferred exclusively on the Congress, and that included making the rules for the army and the navy. The president "possesses no power over the soldier except as Congress may, by legislation, confer upon him"—and Congress had not authorized this military commission. The creation of a court is a legislative function, not an executive function.

(2) A public trial was essential to the protection of the innocent, and it was no answer to say that this particular trial had been in secret only in part.

(3) The crimes alleged were the conspiracy and execution of "traitorous" acts, and so the crime is treason—a civilian crime, not a military crime. The Constitution requires (Article III, Section 3) that no one be convicted of treason except by the testimony of two witnesses. Its trial by military court is clearly illegal. (Even in dealing with the treason of Aaron Burr, Jefferson never proposed a military court, and Burr was tried by a competent civilian court.)

(4) While there was a statute dealing with military tribunals, "persons not belonging to the army cannot be subjected to its jurisdiction." The military court had rules of evidence that have "latitude that no civil court would allow." The "Constitution provides courts consisting of judges selected for legal knowledge, and made independent of executive power. Military

judges are not so selected, and so far from being independent, are absolutely dependent on such power."
(5) How bizarre it was that Jefferson Davis had been indicted by a federal grand jury, according to reports, and yet those charged with being mere instruments of Davis were to be tried by the military (more on the Davis indictment and "non-trial" later in this chapter).
(6) The members of the commission faced personal liability if their actions were held to be void for lack of jurisdiction.
(7) As citizens, the defendants had a constitutional right to be indicted by a grand jury, a right to due process of law (Fifth Amendment), and a right to a public trial by an impartial jury (Sixth Amendment).

Reverdy Johnson concluded by noting that, while he was there defending Mrs. Surratt, he was also defending the Constitution and the laws: "In my view, her cause is the cause of every citizen."

Johnson's presentation was a solid case against trying these civilians in a military tribunal. His argument in defense of Mary Surratt was virtually the same as the position adopted unanimously by the Supreme Court a mere ten months later in the landmark case of *Ex parte Milligan*.[19]

Speed's Opinion

Attorney General Speed's Opinion[20] on the legality of the military tribunal, when it finally appeared *after* the trial in July, was woefully inadequate. He concluded that not only was it legal for the conspirators to be tried by a military commission, but also that they *ought* to be tried by the military.

Speed argued that the laws of war are part of the law of nations, which is part of the law of the United States, and that under this law, an army has a right to protect itself, not only from open belligerents, but also from secret "irregulars." The laws of war authorize commanders to create tribunals for the trial of offenders, whether open or secret participants. Noting the constitutional protections for those charged with crimes, Speed argued that they were not relevant for "offenses"—not crimes—under the laws of war: "Some of the offenses against the laws of war are crimes, and some not." The fact that the civil courts are open does not affect the right of a military tribunal to try a prisoner. Speed concluded:

> [I]f the persons who are charged with the assassination of the President committed the deed as public enemies, as I believe they did, and

ATTORNEY GENERAL JAMES SPEED.

whether they did or did not is a question to be decided by the tribunal before which they are tried, they not only can, but ought to be tried before a military tribunal. If the persons charged have offended against the laws of war, it would be as palpably wrong of the military to hand them over to the civil courts, as it would be wrong in a civil court to convict a man of murder who had, in time of war, killed another in battle.

For Speed, "the war" justified almost everything, and a conspiracy to attack the commander in chief was a military crime properly punished by a military commission. The fact that the defendants were civilians was, in his eyes, irrelevant.

The Verdicts

On June 29th, the commission went into secret session to review the evidence, and on July 5th, the verdicts were presented to President Johnson who approved them at once. All eight were found guilty. Four were sentenced to death, with executions scheduled for July 7, 1865: Lewis

Powell, Mary Surratt, David Herold, and George Atzerodt; three were sentenced to life imprisonment: Dr. Mudd, Samuel Arnold, and Michael O'Laughlin; and Edman Spangler was to be imprisoned for six years. The defense counsel did not learn of the sentences until the newspaper reports on July 6th.

When they read the verdicts in the newspaper, Mary Surratt's young lawyers, Frederick A. Aiken and John Clampitt, wired Reverdy Johnson in Baltimore seeking immediate advice. Johnson wired back that they should seek a writ of habeas corpus, since he was convinced the military tribunal was illegal.[21] Aiken and Clampitt then went to the home of federal Judge Andrew Wylie—in the middle of the night. Wylie came to the door in his nightshirt. Aiken and Clampitt handed Wylie the Application for a Writ of Habeas Corpus on Behalf of Mary E. Surratt. The application asserted that she was a private citizen, not connected with the military, that her alleged crime was not an act of war, and that "the court was and is now open for the trial of such crimes and offenses." The application concluded by noting that she had "a right of public trial by jury" and that the military commission was unlawfully convened. Wylie reportedly said that he would give them his decision after he discussed it with Mrs. Wylie.[22] Judge Wylie returned with the signed writ at three o'clock a.m., ordering Major-General W. S. Hancock to bring Mary Surratt to his civilian court at ten o'clock later that morning, July 7th, execution day. Clampitt later reported that Wylie told them: "I am about to perform an act which before tomorrow's sun goes down may consign me to the Old Capitol Prison."[23] (This is virtually the same fear—imprisonment at Fort McHenry—that Chief Justice Taney expressed almost exactly four years earlier in connection with *Ex parte Merryman*.)

Ten o'clock came and went that morning with no response. Doster came before Judge Wylie on behalf of his clients (Atzerodt and Powell) also seeking a writ, but since the military authorities had ignored the Surratt writ, the judge saw no purpose in issuing another. Then, just before noon, General Hancock[24] and Attorney General Speed appeared in Judge Wylie's courtroom.

The general informed Judge Wylie that he had Mary E. Surratt in his possession under the order of the president,[25] and explained that he was not producing her "by reason of the Order of the President of the United States . . . ." The order was attached to his statement; it declared

> that the writ of *habeas corpus* has been heretofore suspended in such cases as this, and [I] direct that you proceed to execute the order heretofore

given upon the judgment of the Military Commission, and that you will give this order in return to the writ.

Judge Wiley ruled that the court would yield to the suspension of the writ by President Johnson.[26]

The exact authority for this presidential order is unclear. On September 24, 1862, when faced with draft resistance, Lincoln had issued a proclamation ordering that

> all Rebels and Insurgents, their aiders and abettors . . . and all persons discouraging volunteer enlistments . . . or guilty of any disloyal practice . . . shall be liable to trial and punishment by Courts Martial or Military Commission . . . [and that] the Writ of Habeas Corpus is suspended in respect to all persons . . . who . . . during the rebellion shall be imprisoned in any fort, camp, arsenal . . . .

Almost exactly one year later, Lincoln had issued another proclamation virtually the same in scope—in cases where military authorities hold persons in custody as prisoners, spies, aiders, or abettors or otherwise subject to military law—proclaiming that "the privilege of the writ of habeas corpus is suspended throughout the United States in the several cases before mentioned, and that this suspension will continue throughout the duration of the said rebellion . . . ."[27] The key difference in the two suspension proclamations is that the second one was issued under the authority of the Habeas Corpus Act of March 3, 1863, which sharply limited the ability of nonprisoners to be tried by military tribunals when the civil courts were open.[28]

Nine months after the assassination trials in 1866, the Supreme Court unanimously (9–0) decided that a civilian, Lambdin Milligan in Indiana, who was arrested by military authorities and sentenced to death by military commission, should be released. The Court decided that since Milligan was a civilian and the courts in Indiana were open, he should not have been tried by a military commission because he was denied a trial by jury. Thus, if Mary Surratt's application for the writ of habeas corpus had been handled as was Lambdin Milligan's, the arguments of her lawyers might well have been welcomed unanimously by the Court, and she might have been discharged, rather than hanged.

Five of the nine members of the tribunal, including General Hunter, had suggested that President Johnson commute Mrs. Surratt's sentence to life imprisonment in light of her age (mid-forties) and sex. This later became controversial: President Johnson claimed that he never saw this appeal, whereas Judge Advocate General Holt claimed that he had shown it to the president himself.[29] According to some reports, Johnson rejected the appeal for clemency saying that "she kept the nest that hatched the egg" of conspiracy.

Mary Surratt and the other three were hanged in the yard of the prison on July 7th, as ordered.[30] (The yard is now part of the tennis court at Fort McNair, home of the National Defense College.) Mary Surratt and the others were buried in gun boxes, which served as coffins. Four years later, after the pleas of her daughter Anna, Surratt's remains were reburied in Mount Olivet cemetery in Washington; her grave remained unmarked until 1878, when a stonemason donated a simple stone marked "Mrs. Surratt."

THE HANGING, HOODED BODIES OF THE FOUR CONSPIRATORS OF THE LINCOLN ASSASSINATION. FROM LEFT TO RIGHT: MARY SURRATT, LEWIS POWELL, DAVID HEROLD, AND GEORGE ATZERODT.

The Trials of John H. Surratt, Jr.

Mary Surratt's son John was not in Washington at the time of the assassination. He had been in Elmira, New York, on Confederate business, but quickly fled to Montreal, Canada, upon hearing of her arrest. John Surratt, using the name "Charles Armstrong," remained in hiding in the rectory of a Catholic church forty-five miles east of Montreal throughout his mother's trial.[31] He later said that he wanted to come forward to "save" his mother, but he was dissuaded by friends who assured him that there was no evidence against her, and that the government was simply using her to lure him out of hiding. After his mother's execution, Surratt fled to

JOHN A. SURRATT, SON OF MARY SURRATT.

England and then made his way down to Italy, where, under an assumed name he entered the Papal States and, on December 9, 1865, joined the Papal Zouaves at the Vatican—the multinational regiment of volunteers defending the Pope's temporal sovereignty.

United States authorities were tracking information about Surratt from Canada to the United Kingdom and finally to Italy, but Surratt remained elusive. Finally, in April 1866, the resident U.S. diplomat in Rome, Rufus King, learned from one of Surratt's fellow Zouaves from Maryland that Surratt was there. King and Secretary of State Seward exchanged letters about the Surratt problem, which was complicated because the United States had no extradition treaty with the Papal States, and therefore King had no legal basis to request Surratt. In November, because of the gravity of the situation, Pope Pius IX's secretary of state, Giacomo Cardinal Antonelli, reached an agreement with King to deliver Surratt, even in the absence of a treaty. Surratt was ordered to be arrested, but he escaped and jumped on a ship bound for Alexandria, Egypt. In Alexandria, Surratt's luck ran out, and so did his ability to hide behind legal protections. In Ottoman Egypt, citizens of the United States and fourteen other nations enjoyed extraterritoriality, which empowered ambassadors with almost complete legal authority over their citizens.[32] Within days of his arrival in Egypt, Surratt was captured by the U.S. Consul General and placed in an Egyptian jail.[33] On the day after Christmas, 1866, Surratt was on a U.S. Navy ship heading to Washington. Secretary Seward received the good news by telegram on December 29, 1866.

Surratt was delivered in manacles on February 18, 1867, to the marshal of the supreme court of the District of Columbia—from Navy control to civilian control—for trial in a civilian criminal court, charged with assassinating Lincoln.

Two weeks before he returned to Washington, Surratt had been indicted by a grand jury in connection with Lincoln's murder. Shortly after he was brought to court for his arraignment on February 23, 1867, Surratt was offered a "deal" through shady intermediaries: if he would implicate Jefferson Davis or Andrew Johnson in the assassination of Lincoln, his life would be spared. Foes of President Johnson—including former General Ben Butler and Ohio Congressman James Ashley—were desperate to make that connection.[34] Surratt refused to go along; his attorneys had assured him that the government possessed insufficient evidence to convict him.

John Surratt's trial began on June 18, 1867, in Judge George Fisher's courtroom in City Hall. Years earlier, Lincoln had worked closely with Fisher when he was Delaware's sole member of Congress at the time when Lincoln worked to persuade states to emancipate their slaves voluntarily. Fisher lost his seat in the 1862 elections, and in consolation, Lincoln appointed Fisher to the District Supreme Court in 1863.

The prosecution was composed of a team of lawyers, including the district attorney, Edward Carrington (a Johnson appointee), a former Ohio congressman, Albert Riddle, and a former judge from New York, Edwards Pierrepont. The trial recalled as witnesses many of the individuals who had testified against Surratt's mother. The prosecution also drew upon the personnel resources of the War Department's Bureau of Military Justice in order to add depth to its side, including key figures from the trial of Mary Surratt two years before. These included Congressman John A. Bingham (an assistant judge advocate in the 1865 trial) and Joseph Holt (the judge advocate at the earlier trial).

Surratt's defense counsel, Joseph Bradley, Sr., reminded the court that Holt and others from the army had no right to be involved in investigating matters dealing with private citizens.[35] And while the prosecutors persisted in trying to establish that Surratt was in Washington on the day of the assassination, April 14th, rather than in Elmira, New York, as the defense claimed, Surratt's lawyers were able to prove that in fact he had been in Elmira, New York. It would have been physically impossible—due to train schedules and floods—for him to have been in Washington.

As the trial closed, the judge's instructions to the jury were prejudicial to the defense; his charge to the jury, especially his summary of the evidence, clearly favored the government's case. The *New York Times* concluded that the judge had agreed with the prosecution's design to connect the murder of Lincoln with the horrors of the War, and that "Judge Fisher's bias . . . [was] as evident as the bad taste and feeble logic of his final charge."[36] Gideon Welles, Lincoln's secretary of the navy, wrote in his diary: "the Judge was disgracefully partial and unjust."[37] (In fact, almost a decade later, Judge Fisher was forced to resign after mounting complaints about his performance.)

The jury began deliberations on August 7th, but after seventy-three hours of deliberation they could not reach a verdict. They told the judge they were deadlocked at 8–4, with the majority favoring acquittal. The jury was composed of twelve white taxpayers, seven of whom were Southerners; they could easily find Surratt's involvement with Booth's planned kidnapping of Lincoln, but his tie to the assassination plot was not evident, and he had clearly been in New York, not Washington, on the day of the assassination.[38]

The Second Trial

On January 20, 1868, John Surratt's retrial for murder was put on the criminal docket with a trial date in late February, but the retrial was delayed for various reasons. Surratt languished in jail for almost a year until June 18, 1868, when he was indicted again. This time, the charge was aiding the rebellion, under the 1862 Second Confiscation Act. The prosecution decided it was too risky to seek an indictment for murder or conspiracy to murder, and that it was safer to seek a conviction for aiding and abetting the rebellion—even though it carried a sentence of only ten years in prison. A factor in the prosecution's decision was that Judge Wylie had replaced Judge Fisher, and, while Fisher had held that actual presence was not necessary to convict for murder, Wylie believed the defendant had to be physically close to the murder to sustain a conviction. (The "new" judge was the same Judge Wylie who had dealt with the habeas corpus application in July 1865 of John's mother, Mary Surratt.)

The second trial of John Surratt convened on June 22, 1868, but was delayed again until September. On September 21, the prosecution entered a *nolle prosequi*—a formal entry on the record by the prosecuting officer by which he declares that he will not prosecute the case further—for the February 1867 indictment of murder. The next day, Joseph Bradley, Jr., Surratt's defense counsel, argued that the second indictment should be dismissed since it was brought more than two years after the alleged crime—the alleged crime of aiding and abetting had been in March–April 1865, and the indictment for that crime was entered in June 1868; therefore, the proceeding was barred by the two-year statute of limitations. Judge Wylie rather quickly quashed the indictment and discharged Surratt.[39] The government appealed to the supreme court of the District of Columbia, but without success.

In November 1868, Surratt was released.[40] He spent the rest of his life in Baltimore, where he became the general freight agent and auditor of the Baltimore Steam Packet Company. John Surratt died quietly at his home in 1916, never having revealed the full story of his adventures with John Wilkes Booth.[41]

* * *

Did the assassination conspirators get a fair trial before the military commission,[42] or would they have been released—as was John Surratt two years later—if they had been tried by a civilian court? Clearly, there were protections in a civilian court that were not available to the defendants in a military trial, and that might have made a difference for some. Undoubtedly, Powell and Herold would have been convicted; Atzerodt might not have been convicted; Arnold and O'Laughlin might have been acquitted; and Spangler might not have been prosecuted. Dr. Mudd was probably guilty of something, but perhaps only of lying to the commission; Mary Surratt probably knew something about the conspiracy, but how much is not clear. Thus, if the wishes of a majority of the commission had been complied with—including the commuting of Mary Surratt's sentence to life imprisonment—only three of the eight would have been executed, and most observers would have conceded the guilt of those three.

The Continuing Debate

In a sense, it is fair to look at the Hunter Commission as a board of inquiry into the scope of the conspiracy, in the way that the 9/11 Commission or the Warren Commission operated. However, as a method of determining the guilt or innocence of individual citizens—including whether they should be hanged—it is clear that the trial by the Hunter Commission was wrong as a matter of law and of policy, as former Attorney General Edward Bates claimed. It is a lesson that justice is not truly rendered in the enflamed passions of the moment.

Dr. Mudd's Legal Efforts into the Twenty-First Century

The Hunter Commission issued a final judgment against Dr. Mudd on June 29, 1865, convicting him of harboring John Wilkes Booth and another man with the intent to assist them in escaping from justice after the assassination. Dr. Mudd was saved from a death sentence—a vote of at least six of the nine members of the commission was required to sustain a death sentence, but only five thought he should die. Dr. Mudd was sentenced to life at hard labor and imprisoned at Fort Jefferson in the Dry Tortugas, sixty-eight miles west of Key West, Florida.[43] Several months after he arrived there, Dr. Mudd made an unsuccessful attempt to escape, perhaps because the New York regiment serving as security was to be replaced by a regiment of black soldiers, and Mudd feared for his life.[44]

The Supreme Court, on April 3, 1866, unanimously decided the case of *Ex parte Milligan*,[45] which, as mentioned, involved the 1864 arrest and conviction by a military commission of an Indiana lawyer, Lambdin P. Milligan, who was active in the peace movement. Milligan was sentenced to be hanged, and filed a writ of habeas corpus. The Supreme Court decided that Milligan should be released, because the military commission had no jurisdiction over him. Based on the ruling in the *Milligan* case, Mudd filed a petition for a writ of habeas corpus with the Supreme Court. Chief Justice Chase denied the petition on the ground that Mudd had not exhausted his remedies—he had not properly sought relief in the lower courts.

Then in August 1868 Mudd filed with the U.S. District Court for the Southern District of Florida, in Key West. On September 9, 1868, Judge Thomas J. Boynton denied Mudd's petition, which had argued that *Ex parte Milligan* should mean that the military commission had no jurisdiction over him, a civilian in Maryland. The district court distinguished *Milligan*, noting that Lincoln was "assassinated not from private animosity nor any other reason than a desire to impair the effectiveness of military operations . . . . [T]he act was committed in a fortified city which had been invaded during the war . . . [and which] was the headquarters of all the Armies of the United States . . . . It was not Mr. Lincoln [as a person] who was assassinated but [in his capacity as] the commander-in-chief of the Army for military reasons . . . . [T]he offense [was] a military one . . . and the proper tribunal for those engaged in it was a military one."[46] That ruling was appealed, but it became moot due to intervening events—events that were in Dr. Mudd's favor.

In the summer of 1867, yellow fever broke out at the prison on Dry Tortugas, and it lasted for many months. Fellow prisoner O'Laughlin contracted it and died, and so did the prison physician. Dr. Mudd, whose work assignment had been in the carpenter shop, took over the fort hospital and worked tirelessly to save stricken people. Two hundred soldiers and the officer in charge united in petitioning President Johnson for Mudd's release.[47] In addition, thirty-nine members of the House and Senate, and the Medical Society of Hartford County, Maryland, petitioned for Mudd's pardon.

On February 7, 1869, a courier knocked on the door of the Mudd farm, and, when Mrs. Sarah Mudd answered, she was asked to sign a receipt for the delivery of a letter—from President Johnson. That letter reported that the president had drawn up a pardon for her husband, and he invited her to come to his office to receive the document.[48] The next morning, February 8, 1869, President Johnson issued a full and unconditional pardon to Dr. Mudd in recognition of his efforts to assist medical officers during an outbreak of yellow fever.

The pardon noted the broad charge against Dr. Mudd at the Hunter Commission, but made clear that the only guilt found was of receiving and harboring Booth and Herold with the intent to aid them in escaping from justice. Then, Johnson introduced representations made by "respected and intelligent members of the medical profession" arguing that efforts to provide medical assistance were deserving of a lenient construction "as within the obligations of professional duty." The activities of Dr. Mudd in connection with the yellow fever outbreak at the prison were recorded, along with the petitions for pardon. Finally, President Johnson granted "a full and unconditional pardon" to Dr. Mudd. Mudd was released from Fort Jefferson on March 8th and arrived home on March 20th.

More than a century later, Dr. Richard D. Mudd of Saginaw, Michigan, the grandson of Dr. Samuel Mudd, tried to get his grandfather's official record "corrected." On July 24, 1979, President Jimmy Carter wrote to Dr. Richard Mudd in response to many requests. Carter reported that the original 1865 findings of guilt "are binding and conclusive judgment, and . . . there is no authority under law by which I, as President, could set aside his conviction." Nevertheless, Carter continued, the comments by President Andrew Johnson in his pardon declaration substantially discredit the validity of the military commission's judgment: "the Johnson pardon goes beyond a mere absolution of the crimes . . . . President Johnson went on to express his doubt concerning even Dr. Mudd's criminal guilt" of merely aiding an escape from justice. Carter concluded by stating his "personal agreement with the findings of President Johnson."

On October 15, 1990, Dr. Richard Mudd filed a request for the correction of the military files in accordance with a Department of the Army procedure. His argument was that his grandfather was factually innocent of the conspiracy charge, and that the military commission had no jurisdiction. The Army Board for Correction of Military Records held a hearing, and on January 22, 1992, the board issued a decision that the Hunter Commission's jurisdiction did not extend to noncombatant civilians like Dr. Mudd. The board recommended that the secretary of the army alter the necessary records and void the conviction of Dr. Mudd. The secretary of the army, however, declined to follow the Army Board's recommendation.

In June 1997, Democratic Congressman Steny Hoyer[49] and Republican Congressman Robert Ehrlich,[50] both of Maryland, and Congressman Thomas Ewing of Illinois introduced a bill—the Samuel Mudd Relief Act—to "set aside" Mudd's conviction. The bill died.

Mudd's grandson then filed suit in the district court for the District of Columbia, claiming that the army secretary's decision to ignore the Army Board's recommendation was arbitrary and capricious under the Administrative Procedure Act. The district court heard the case twice[51] and ultimately decided in 2001 that the secretary's decision was not arbitrary, and granted summary judgment for the army. Richard D. Mudd's lawyer for the previous nine years' of effort to clear Dr. Mudd's name was Candida Ewing Steel. Her great-great-grandfather was General Thomas Ewing, Jr., who represented Dr. Mudd at the 1865 trial.

Richard D. Mudd died in 2002 at age 101, but his son, Thomas B. Mudd, the great-grandson of Dr. Samuel Mudd and a retired teacher from Michigan, filed an appeal to the U.S. Court of Appeals. (Ten of the Dr. Samuel Mudd's 101 descendants attended the oral arguments.) Finally, on November 8, 2002, a three-judge panel of the court of appeals dismissed the appeal, stating that Thomas Mudd lacked "standing" because the statute that permitted corrections was intended only for the benefit of a member or former member of the armed forces (or his legal representative), and the petition failed because it did not pertain to a member of the armed forces.[52] The Mudd attorney missed the filing deadline for a petition for a writ of certiorari; he admitted that he "blew it," but it would have been a long shot.

The Trial of Captain Henry Wirz: The Andersonville Trial

The next most infamous post-assassination and post-war trial focused on the terrible conditions of the military prisoner-of-war camps. This trial began less that two months after the assassinators' trial ended in July 1865.

A CSA prison camp had been set up in late 1863 near the town of Andersonville in southwestern Georgia, far from the front, and thus easier to protect. Captain Henry Wirz, who was born in Switzerland and immigrated to the United States in 1849, had been assigned to command the camp in March 1864. Conditions were horrible, though how much more horrible than other camps in the North and South is disputed.[53] For example, the death rate at Andersonville was 24 percent, while at the Union camp in Elmira, New York, the death rate was 44 percent.[54] Viewed from a broader perspective, Lincoln, Grant, and Stanton may have contributed to the conditions at Andersonville by their decision in April 1864 to suspend the exchange of prisoners; one rationale for that suspension was that the additional Union prisoners would terribly strain the South's already meager rations and material. It was no secret that the prisoners left in the South were bound to suffer greater hardships.

Union troops took the Andersonville camp in May 1865. Wirz was taken to Washington and imprisoned in the Old Capitol Prison, which is on the site of the present Supreme Court building.

On August 23rd, a military commission was convened by the War Department to try Wirz for war crimes. Secretary of War Stanton, in particular, was interested in staging the trial, because he had failed in the trial of the assassination conspirators to demonstrate a link between them and the Confederate leaders. This new trial provided a second chance for him to make that connection. He also was interested in producing a judicial proceeding that avoided the blatant injustices of the previous trial.

The government wanted to convict not only Wirz, but high-ranking officers of the CSA as well; the original charges against Wirz also named Jefferson Davis, Robert E. Lee,[55] and others as coconspirators with Wirz in the effort to destroy the lives of U.S. soldiers. The day before the commission was to convene, the prosecutor had been instructed by Stanton to prepare new charges against Wirz that omitted Jefferson Davis and his cabinet, substituting the phrase, "and others unknown."[56]

The commission convened in the Court of Claims, a chamber then in the Capitol building.[57] Outside the door of the law library of the current Court of Claims, located near the White House, is posted a copy of *Harper's Weekly* of October 21, 1865,[58] which featured an account of the trial. A typed note under the *Harper's* article states that "Wirz was defended by a law firm of a former judge of the Court of Claims (1860–1864) the Honorable James Hughes of Indiana, also a former Congressman and strong Union man." That is correct, but not complete. In fact, Wirz's first lawyers were Messrs Hughes, Peck, and Denver, a prominent Washington law firm. A young associate, Louis Shade, an immigrant from Germany, was brought in to assist at the last minute. On the first day of the trial, the Hughes lawyers were so frustrated with the commission's hostile attitude that they withdrew. Shade remained alone, due to his sense of obligation to Wirz—a fellow immigrant. However, soon, a New York lawyer, Otis Baker, stepped in virtually out of nowhere, and largely took over the management of the case.

The president of the military commission was General Lewis Wallace, who, before the War, was an attorney. He had served on the commission that tried the Lincoln assassination conspirators. The 31-year-old Judge Advocate General Chipman, the prosecutor, had been seriously wounded at the battle of Fort Donelson in February 1862.

The trial lasted sixty-three days; over a hundred sixty witnesses were called to report on Andersonville's conditions and Wirz's actions; there were nine hundred pages of testimony. The trial concluded on October 24th. Just before the end of the trial, Shade and Baker withdrew because the commission would not grant their request for additional time to prepare the summation. The prosecutor gave an oral summation for Wirz, though Wirz himself had prepared a written statement of summation. Wirz was unanimously found guilty.

At that time, all death sentences issued by a military tribunal had to be presented to the president for final decision, and so the decision and a lengthy statement of the case was sent to President Johnson. The order came from the White House to the War Department that Wirz was to be hanged on November 10th. The night before that date, Wirz was visited in his cell by Louis Shade, who brought with him an eleventh-hour offer of a pardon from an unnamed member of Johnson's cabinet. The condition of the pardon was that Wirz would have to agree to testify that Jefferson Davis was implicated in the deaths at Andersonville.[59] Wirz refused, stating that Davis had no connection with him and Andersonville. Wirz was hanged on November 10th at the Old Capitol Prison. His body is buried only yards away from Mary Surratt's, just outside Washington.

The consensus of scholars seems to be that Wirz was a scapegoat, the victim of a national vendetta and an unjust trial.[60] He clearly did not receive a full defense, the charge of willfully conspiring to murder prisoners was not proved, the charge of murder was based in part on hearsay, and much of prosecutor Chipman's "evidence" was based on exaggerated

THE EXECUTION OF CAPTAIN HENRY WIRZ.

or perjured testimony. Nevertheless, there seemed to be a prima facie case against Wirz.

Wirz was the *only* Civil War figure convicted of war crimes.

> [T]he moral imperative at the end of every war is reconciliation. Without reconciliation there can be no real peace. Reconciliation means amnesty. It is allowable to execute the worst war criminals, with or without a legal trial, provided that this is done quickly, while the passions of war are still raging. After the executions are done, there should be no more hunting for criminals and collaborators. In order to make a lasting peace, we must learn to live with our enemies and forgive their crimes.[61]

* * *

The story of Andersonville was retold in the twentieth century by MacKinlay Kantor in his 1955 Pulitzer Prize-winning novel *Andersonville*. Saul Levitt's play *The Andersonville Trial* opened on Broadway at the end of 1959; Levitt adapted his play to the screen, and it appeared in 1970 as the Emmy Award-winning film *The Andersonville Trial*.[62]

The Non-Trial of Jefferson Davis

While trials were quickly organized for the Lincoln assassination conspirators and for Captain Wirz, the effort to bring the president of the CSA, Jefferson Davis, to trial was not as successful. In the end, however, the revenge trials of Wirz and the assassination coconspirators were conducted in a system outside the traditional expectations of civilian rule of law—by military tribunals—while the resolution of the Jefferson Davis situation took place within the context of the more traditional civilian legal system.

On Sunday, April 2, 1865, the government of the CSA abandoned its capital at Richmond and initially moved to Danville, Virginia, some 145 miles southwest of Richmond, where some Confederate documents and records had already been relocated anticipating such an event.

JEFFERSON DAVIS.

JEFFERSON DAVIS AND HIS CABINET.

Jefferson Davis issued a proclamation on April 4th from Danville, Virginia, declaring his intention to continue the cause. On April 9th, General Lee surrendered to General Grant at Appomattox Court House, and, upon hearing the news, Davis decided to move his government to Greensboro, North Carolina, fifty miles south of Danville. His goal at Greensboro was to devise a plan to win the War,[63] but soon Davis and his "cabinet" had become fugitives, forced to continue moving south. By April 19th, they were in Charlotte, North Carolina, and it was there that Davis learned that Lincoln had been assassinated. By May 2nd, Davis had reached Abbeville, South Carolina; on the 3rd, the secretary of state of the CSA, Judah Benjamin, left the others and made a dash to Florida. The U.S. Army intensified the search for Davis; the Johnson administration accused Davis of complicity in planning Lincoln's assassination.[64] Finally, on May 10th, the federal troops burst into an encampment in the piney woods near Irwinville, Georgia, and captured CSA President Jefferson Davis.

On May 22nd, Jefferson Davis was placed in a cell under heavy guard in Fortress Monroe at the James River entrance to the Chesapeake Bay. (This was the place where, almost exactly four years earlier, General Ben Butler had devised his plan for dealing with escaping "contraband.") Several days later, a prominent New York lawyer, Charles O'Conor, offered to defend Davis on whatever charges might be brought against him.[65] O'Conor was a Union Democrat who believed that secession was not illegal, or at least that the use of force to suppress secession was unconsti-

JEFFERSON DAVIS, IMPRISONED IN FORTRESS MONROE.

tutional. He was a classical strict constructionist, and he worried that the Republicans would rush to punish former Confederates by any means. O'Conor claimed that he took on the defense of Davis on principle, and wanted no fee—though later he agreed to accept funds solely to cover expenses. From London, James Mason informed O'Conor that there were still some Confederate funds in Europe that could be made available.[66]

O'Conor received help from important figures. Former President Franklin Pierce[67] lent his support, in part because Davis had been Pierce's secretary of war.[68] Also supporting O'Conor and his efforts for Davis were Jeremiah Black (President Buchanan's Attorney General and secretary of state), Francis Blair, Sr., Reverdy Johnson, Gerrit Smith,[69] and Horace Greeley—the editor of the leading Republican newspaper in the country, the *New York Tribune*. These men sought to have the country return to a real rule of law, not to having trials within the military structure.

The administration could not decide what to do with its most famous prisoner: On July 18th, Johnson asked his key cabinet members for their opinions. Seward and Stanton wanted Davis tried for murder and treason before a military tribunal as Booth's conspirators were; Welles took the opposite view (predictably), recommending a speedy civilian trial.

Three days later, the whole cabinet agreed that the crime charged should be treason, and most members opted for a civilian trial—except Seward, who continued to favor the more "reliable" military tribunal.[70] Attorney General Speed and others had serious reservations about employing a military court in light of the President's Amnesty Proclamation of May 29th granting pardon to former Confederates.[71] However, Speed also felt that any fair trial would acquit Davis of treason—just one pro-Davis juror could prevent a guilty finding and produce a great embarrassment for the administration. The question of Davis's trial was debated within the cabinet until October, when a consensus formed around a civil trial.

A complicating factor was that any civilian trial would have to be held in Virginia—the scene of the alleged crime,[72] since the Constitution provides (Article III, Section 2) that criminal trials "shall be held in the State where the said crimes shall have been committed." Chief Justice Chase was assigned to the circuit that included Virginia, which was largely occupied by federal troops. The Chief Justice refused to sit where the military authority still ruled—for fear that it would appear as though

CHARLES O'CONOR.

the judiciary was controlled by the military.[73] Ironically, in 1807, former Vice President Aaron Burr was tried for treason in the same federal court in Richmond, and the trial was presided over by Chief Justice John Marshall.[74] Burr was acquitted.

The Senate, on December 21, 1865, passed a Resolution asking the president what the charges were against Davis and why he had not been put on trial. The Attorney General, on January 6, 1866, advised President Johnson that Davis and the other high-ranking CSA officers had been held as prisoners of war, since a legal state of war continued to exist. Speed also noted that trials for treason "cannot be had before a military court." But, he noted, "[n]one of the Justices of the Supreme Court have held circuit courts in those [Southern] States and districts since actual hostilities have ceased." Speed promised that when the courts were open, the persons held as prisoners of war "should be transferred into the custody of the civil authorities of the proper districts."[75]

On May 8, 1866, a federal prosecutor in Norfolk, Virginia, obtained an indictment from the grand jury in Judge John Curtiss Underwood's federal District Court for the District of Virginia against Davis for treason. The Johnson administration requested a continuance, since it was not ready to proceed with the prosecution. In June, Judge Underwood denied O'Conor's request for bail. In August 1866, President Johnson issued a final peace proclamation, officially ending the War.[76] This made it awkward to continue to hold Davis in a military prison.

In the November elections, the Republicans overwhelmingly won in both the House and Senate, laying the foundation for the conflict that led to the impeachment of President Johnson. Jefferson Davis was caught up in that presidential/congressional struggle, and he languished in prison, since neither side knew what to do with him—and, of course, attention was focused on the internal political struggle. The Republicans had depicted Davis as the archfiend of the rebellion, while Johnson (a Democrat) needed Davis in prison to show that he held the head of the Confederacy accountable.[77]

Almost two years after his imprisonment, on May 1, 1867, Davis's lawyers (led now by George Shea, who was assisting O'Conor) applied for a writ of habeas corpus, which they hoped would result in either a trial or bail. On the same day, Judge Underwood issued the writ, returnable on May 13th. Under instruction from the War Department, when the writ was presented at Fortress Monroe, Davis was brought from military control and put into the civilian control of U.S. marshals under the direction of the federal court in Richmond. On his trip up the James River to Richmond on May 11th, and upon entering Richmond, Davis was surrounded by well-wishers.

Trial Preliminaries

At the hearing on May 13th to determine whether Davis could be released under bail, the U.S. special prosecutor, William Evarts—who had been brought in to prosecute the crew of the *Savannah* in New York City in late 1861—did not object to permitting Davis to put up bail, and explained that the government intended no prosecution during that term of the court. Evarts and the new Attorney General, Henry Stanberry, had decided that they simply were not ready for a trial. Judge Underwood set bail at $100,000 and required Davis, as a condition of his bond, to appear back in court in late November.

The bail arrangement required that O'Conor produce the men who would act as sureties. Three men stood up to sign for $25,000 each: *Cornelius Vanderbilt*, the wealthiest man in the United States;[78] *Gerrit Smith*, the financial backer of John Brown a decade earlier; and *Horace Greeley*, the famous editor and abolitionist. Ten others signed on for $2,500 each. That night, Jefferson Davis and his wife left for Montreal, Canada; en route they spent some days resting at the Hudson River residence of Charles O'Conor. While in Canada, James Mason took Davis on a holiday to his cottage in Niagara Falls, Ontario.

On September 7, 1867, President Johnson issued a proclamation extending a full pardon to most people in the Confederacy, by reducing from fourteen to three the classes of persons exempted from the amnesty of the preceding year. However, Jefferson Davis was within the first class of persons to whom the pardon did not apply—the chief executive officers "of the pretended Confederate or Rebel Government."[79]

Davis appeared in Judge Underwood's court on November 26, 1867, in compliance with the conditions of his bail. The government again requested a continuance, and O'Conor readily agreed. The case would be carried over until the spring term of the court, which would begin in late March 1868. After the hearing, Davis visited with Robert E. Lee and then traveled to Mississippi. He returned to Richmond for the next hearing, March 26, 1868. Once again the government requested a continuance, until May 2nd.

In February 1868, President Johnson was impeached in the House of Representatives. His trial in the Senate began in early March. Evarts was retained as one of the president's defense counsel, and of course, Chief Justice Chase presided over the trial. Since Evarts could not simultaneously concentrate on prosecuting Davis and defending Johnson, and since the Chief Justice was consumed by the trial and could not come to Richmond, the Davis matter continued to languish. President Johnson was acquitted in May 1868, and shortly thereafter, O'Conor met with Evarts. They agreed that a trial date could be set for November, though O'Conor was convinced for the first time that a trial would never be held. Davis and his family sailed to England that summer and were warmly accepted by the English social and political elite, although lack of funds sharply limited their participation in the world of England's aristocracy. Judah Benjamin, now a very successful barrister, spent a great deal of time with the Davis family. Later, they went to Paris and had a reunion with John Slidell—the former U.S. senator and ambassador to France from the CSA.

On July 4, 1868, President Johnson issued another proclamation granting a "full pardon and amnesty for the offense of treason against the United States." The sole exception was for any person "as may be under presentment or indictment in any court of the United States . . . upon a charge of treason or other felony . . . ."[80] The prosecution against Davis was now in the hands of Richard Dana—since Evarts had been appointed Attorney General in July. Dana wrote to Attorney General Evarts in August 1868 to warn that there was no possible gain for the government in such a trial. A conviction would do no more than affirm what everyone believed, but there was a great risk that a jury in Richmond would acquit.

Double Jeopardy

The Davis case came before the court in Richmond on November 30, 1868. Chief Justice Chase joined Judge Underwood on the bench. Chase searched for a way out of the legal/political morass of the Davis trial, and he hit upon an idea: the Fourteenth Amendment had gone into effect on July 28, 1868, and Section 3 of the amendment provided that no person who had sworn an oath to support the Constitution and who then participated in the rebellion could hold office. Chase thought this might support an argument of double jeopardy—Davis had already been punished under the Fourteenth Amendment, and so a charge of treason would amount to unconstitutional double jeopardy. In an unusual twist, Chase apparently suggested the argument to Davis's lawyers, who promptly moved for the dismissal of the indictment on those grounds.[81]

Richard Dana contested the point for the prosecution, arguing that the constitutional provision was not a criminal provision, but a political one. On December 5, 1868, the court handed down a divided ruling: Chase accepted the double jeopardy argument, but Underwood did not. The disagreement was certified to the Supreme Court. Attorney General Evarts correctly worried that Chase might persuade a majority on the Court, and that would be a stinging defeat for the administration.

Evarts and O'Conor worked out a deal: if Davis's team agreed to withdraw the Supreme Court appeal, the prosecution would enter a *nolle prosequi.*[82] Shortly thereafter, on Christmas Day 1868, President Johnson issued a proclamation granting "to all and to every person . . . a full pardon and amnesty for the offense of treason against the United States . . . ."[83] The proclamation contained no exception that would otherwise bar Davis from receiving the full pardon. Since there now were no pending charges against Jefferson Davis, after almost four years, he no longer faced federal prosecution.

* * *

After the War and his trials, Jefferson Davis first moved to Memphis, where he ran an insurance company. Then he traveled, and then he wrote books, mostly about the Confederate States of America. He became a bit of a hero again in the South.[84]

290   CHAPTER EIGHT

Revenge Turns to Reconciliation

It took twenty years to successfully resolve a nasty legal battle that was inspired by hatred, which was fanned by the War; this legal battle involved the Virginia estate of Robert E. Lee.

The families of George Washington and Robert E. Lee were closely linked. George Washington's adopted son, "Wash" Custis, built Arlington House between 1802 and 1818, on the large estate on the Potomac given to him by George Washington. Custis was 18 years old when his stepfather died in 1799, and he created at Arlington a sort of museum dedicated to the first president. His daughter, Mary Custis, married Robert E. Lee, the son of "Light Horse" Harry Lee, General Washington's military aide. Mary Custis Lee inherited Arlington House and the eleven thousand-acre estate from her father in 1857 (Robert was the executor of the estate).[85] Lee returned from his military assignment in Texas to manage the restoration of Arlington House; it was from there in October 1859

ARLINGTON HOUSE, JUNE 29, 1864, FORMER RESIDENCE
OF GENERAL ROBERT E. LEE.

The Revenge Trials

that Colonel Lee led the assault on the John Brown attackers at Harpers Ferry.

When the Civil War began, General Lee was in Richmond, and Mary Custis Lee was ordered by a Union officer to pack up and move out of Arlington in May. The estate was taken over by Union military and became the headquarters for the defense of Washington,[86] and later it was used as a hospital and a cemetery (the current famous Arlington Cemetery).[87] Still later, it became Freedman's Village, a camp established for former slaves, including some who had belonged to the Lees.[88]

Congress passed a law on June 7, 1862, entitled "An Act for the Collection of Direct Taxes in Insurrectionary Districts within the United States."[89] The law was designed to raise revenue, but also to punish those who supported the Confederacy. The tax commissioners, appointed under the law, established a rule cleverly designed to lead to confiscation, because it required the payment of taxes in person by "the owner"—then a resident of the Confederacy who might not be able to safely get to D.C. Mrs. Lee sent her cousin, Philip R. Fendall, to pay the taxes in her name. He met with the tax collectors, Frederick Kaufman and Richard P. Strong, and offered on Mrs. Lee's part to pay the taxes, interest, and costs, but he was rebuffed. As a result, the tax commissioners auctioned the land on January 11, 1864, and the U.S. government purchased the estate at that tax sale for $26,800, less than the assessed value. The original tax charge owed by Mrs. Lee was $92.07.[90]

After the War, General Lee refused to entertain the notion of suing the United States for the return of the estate.[91] General Lee died in 1870,[92] and Mrs. Lee died in 1873; five months earlier, she had arranged a farewell visit to Arlington and had toured the estate in a carriage. Upon her death, the Lee's eldest son, George Washington Custis Lee, inherited the Arlington estate. George W. C. Lee was at the time the president of Washington and Lee University in Lexington, Virginia, having succeeded his father. General Lee's son sought legal advice and learned that the federal claim to the Arlington estate was at best tenuous, and, in April 1874, he sought from Congress either the recovery of the property or compensation.[93] Custis Lee claimed that he had been deprived of his property without just compensation, indeed without any compensation.[94] The Radical Republicans ensured that the claim was not acted upon. It languished in the Senate Judiciary Committee, and died quietly.[95]

In 1877, Lee brought an action in the circuit court of Alexandria County against Frederick Kaufman and Richard Strong—the original tax collectors. The case was an action of ejectment to evict the federal government from the Arlington property. The new U.S. Attorney General, Charles Devens—a twice-wounded officer during the War, and then

George Washington Custis Lee, on horseback with staff, reviewing Confederate Reunion Parade in Richmond, Virginia, on June 3, 1907, in front of a monument to Jefferson Davis.

---

associate justice of the Massachusetts Supreme Judicial Court—opposed the suit, and had the matter removed to the Federal Circuit Court for the Eastern District of Virginia. Finally, on January 30, 1879, after a six-day trial, the jury found in favor of Lee.[96] The federal government appealed, and the case ended up in the U.S. Supreme Court.

On December 4, 1882, the Court upheld the lower federal court's decision that the Arlington estate should be returned to Lee as the heir of Mary Custis Lee. The vote in *United States v. Lee* was 5–4.[97] The sixteen-page opinion was written by Justice Miller, who had been appointed by Lincoln in 1862—the same year as the law that was the basis for the confiscation. The only other Lincoln appointee still on the Court was also in the majority; President Grant's two appointees were in dissent.

The Court concluded that the tax commissioners had made an invalid rule, or at least had improperly executed upon it, and that it violated the Fifth Amendment's "taking" provision. Therefore the tax sale was void, and the United States government had not acquired valid title to the estate. Justice Miller noted that if the United States still desires to use the property . . . for the purposes to which it is now devoted, it may purchase such property by fair negotiation, or condemn it by a judicial proceeding, in which a just compensation shall be ascertained and paid according to the constitution.[98]

The law was now clear as to the ownership of the estate, but there was a practical problem in implementing the decision: the eleven hundred acres of the estate contained the remains of thirteen thousand soldiers, as well as the Freedman's Village, which had been created in the spring of 1863 for the emancipated District of Columbia slaves.[99] To return the Arlington property to Lee would mean the disinterment of those remains and the dislocation of the Village.[100]

The task of implementing the Court's decision fell to the secretary of war, a lawyer named Robert Todd Lincoln, the assassinated president's son.[101] Robert T. Lincoln had been present when Lee surrendered at Appomattox Court House, and he also was present at his father's deathbed.[102] Lincoln's son and Lee's son met to resolve the dilemma. They

ROBERT TODD LINCOLN.

each believed that their fathers would have wanted them to take the most honorable course toward resolution. They agreed that the United States would buy the land from Custis Lee for $150,000. On March 31, 1883, Lee conveyed the title to the United States. Congress appropriated that amount for the acquisition of Arlington as a national cemetery.

Robert Todd Lincoln's body is buried at that cemetery in Arlington.

APPENDIX 1

Dramatis Personae: The Lawyers

This Appendix provides brief biographical sketches of one hundred lawyers who were prominent in legal, political, and civic affairs during the Civil War period. They are all white males. The first black member of the Supreme Court bar was John S. Rock, admitted on February 5, 1865, the same day that Congress approved the Thirteenth Amendment. He was admitted to the Massachusetts bar in 1861; he died in 1866, at age 41. The first female member of the Supreme Court bar was Belva Ann Lockwood, who was admitted in 1879. In 1873, the Supreme Court rejected a claim by Mrs. Myra Bradwell that Illinois had violated the Fourteenth Amendment when it refused to admit her to its bar because of her sex.[1]

Charles Francis Adams (1807–1886). Of the Massachusetts bar. Attended Harvard College, was admitted to the bar in 1829, and then practiced law in Boston. Served in the state House and senate, 1831–40, and in the U.S. House of Representatives, 1859–61. He was appointed by Lincoln as U.S. minister to Great Britain in March 1861, and served there until 1868. His father and grandfather were the sixth and second U.S. presidents, respectively.

John Quincy Adams (1767–1848). Of the Massachusetts bar. Attended Leyden University (Holland) and Harvard College, and was admitted to the bar in 1790. George Washington appointed him minister

---

1. *Bradwell v. Illinois*, 83 U.S. (16 Wall.) 130 (1873).

to the Netherlands in 1794, and then to Prussia. Adams was elected to the Senate in 1802, but resigned in 1808. Later, he was minister to Russia and to Great Britain (1815–1817), after which he became secretary of state (1817–1825) under Monroe. Adams was the sixth president, 1825–29, and then was elected to Congress from 1831 to 1848. Adams argued five cases before the Supreme Court, including the landmark *Fletcher v. Peck* (1809) involving the contract clause (the first time the Court declared a state legislative act unconstitutional), and the famous defense of the *Amistad* African captives (1841). Adams was appointed to the Supreme Court by President Madison and confirmed in 1810, but he declined the appointment while he was serving as minister in Russia. He was the first former president to appear before the Court. As a member of Congress he strongly opposed the 1836 "gag rule" aimed at tabling all petitions against slavery, and finally defeated it in 1844.

John Albion Andrew (1818–1867). Of the Massachusetts bar. Graduated from Bowdoin College and practiced law in Boston. He arranged, with assistance from Montgomery Blair, for defense counsel for John Brown. Gave critical legal advice to some of the Secret Six following John Brown's raid, and testified before the Harpers Ferry Committee of the Senate in 1860. Counsel for Hyatt who was jailed by the Senate for failure to testify before the Mason Committee in February–March 1860. Was elected governor of Massachusetts in 1860 and was reelected for four terms. He warmly welcomed Captain Wilkes after the capture of Mason and Slidell. He resumed practice in 1866, and died the following year.

Chester A. Arthur (1829–1886). Of the New York bar. He graduated from Union College, and was admitted to the bar in 1848. Arthur was junior counsel to William Evarts in obtaining the freedom of slaves in New York while in transit from Virginia, in the 1860 *Lemmon v. People* case. He had earlier befriended Gerrit Smith and became active in the antislavery movement. He became Garfield's vice president in March 1881, and then president on September 19, 1881.

Edward Bates (1793–1869). Of the Missouri bar. Born in Virginia, schooled in Maryland, Bates served in the War of 1812. Moved to the Missouri Territory in 1814, and was admitted to the bar in 1817. Served in the state legislature several terms and one term in the U.S. House. Millard Fillmore asked Bates to be his secretary of war, but Bates declined. At the Whig Convention in 1854, Bates came in second for the vice presidential nomination. One of the top three contenders for the Republican presidential nomination in 1860. Attorney General of the United States, 1861–64. Wanted to be nominated to replace Taney, but Lincoln thought he was too old. Died in Missouri in 1869 at age 76.

Judah Philip Benjamin (1811–1884). Of the South Carolina and Louisiana bars. Born in St. Croix in the Virgin Islands, his family moved to Charleston, South Carolina, when he was 2 years old. He attended Yale College for two years. Practiced law in New Orleans. Developed a text book, at age 23, with Tom Slidell (brother of John) that became the standard for lawyers and judges in the state. Elected in 1842 as Whig member of the Louisiana state assembly. He argued cases in the U.S. Supreme Court with Reverdy Johnson. President Millard Fillmore, in 1853, offered Benjamin the nomination to the Supreme Court, but Benjamin declined, because he had been elected to the U.S. Senate as a Whig in 1852, the first acknowledged Jew in the Senate. He was reelected as a Democrat in 1859. He withdrew from the U.S. Senate on February 4, 1861. Was appointed CSA Attorney General in February and then became Secretary of War in August 1861. In March 1862, Benjamin became Secretary of State of the CSA. After the War, he escaped to England where he was admitted to the bar in 1866, became a leading barrister, and was appointed Queen's Counsel in 1872. He was the author of the acclaimed textbook *Benjamin on Sales*, which is still in use in England. When he retired in 1883, he moved to Paris, where he is buried.

John Armor Bingham (1815–1900). Of the Ohio bar. Born in Pennsylvania, he grew up in Ohio, and was admitted there in 1840. He served in the U.S. House 1855–63, after which he was appointed by Lincoln as Judge Advocate of the Army with the rank of major. He served as Special Judge Advocate on the Hunter Commission during the trial of the Lincoln assassination conspirators; he was appointed by his friend from Cadiz, Ohio, Edwin Stanton. He served again in the Congress, 1865–73. Bingham was one of the framers of the Fourteenth Amendment, which was introduced in the House in 1866 and was ratified in 1868. He was a manager in the impeachment trial of President Johnson in 1868, and delivered the closing speech against Johnson. He was minister to Japan, 1873–85.

Jeremiah Sullivan Black (1810–1883). Of the Pennsylvania bar. Though not formally educated, he was admitted to the bar in 1830. After a successful law practice, he was elected Chief Justice of the Supreme Court of Pennsylvania in 1851, and was reelected in 1854. Black was appointed U.S. Attorney General at the start of the Buchanan administration. He vigorously prosecuted fraudulent land claims in California, and hired Edwin Stanton to lead the investigation. His formal opinion of November 20, 1860, was that if a state seceded, the president did not have the power to use military force to coerce the state to return. From December 17, 1860, to March 4, 1861, he was secretary of state (and Stanton became Attorney General). Buchanan appointed Black to the Supreme Court, but he was rejected in the Senate, 26–25, on February 21, 1861 (two weeks before Lincoln's inaugural), because Republicans wanted Lincoln to make the appointment, and some Southerners had resigned. He was appointed Supreme Court Reporter in December 1861 and prepared Black's Reports, Volumes I and II. He was counsel for Milligan in 1866, along with Garfield and Field, and briefly was counsel for Andrew Johnson at his impeachment trial in the Senate.

Francis Preston Blair, Jr. (1821–1873). Of the Missouri bar. Graduated from Princeton and studied law at Transylvania University, and was admitted to the bar in 1842. After service in the Mexican War, he was Attorney General of the New Mexico Territory, practiced law in St. Louis, served in the state legislature, 1852–56, and was a congressman, a general during the War, a senator, and an unsuccessful Democratic candidate for vice president in 1868.

Montgomery Blair (1813–1883). Of the Missouri, Maryland, and D.C. bars. Graduate of West Point. Practiced in St. Louis with his brother, and was U.S. district attorney there (1839–1842); mayor (1842–1843) and judge of the court of common pleas (1843–1849). He moved to Maryland in 1852 and practiced often before the Supreme Court. Counsel for Dred Scott. Arranged counsel for John Brown. Postmaster general of the United States (under Lincoln). He was Lincoln's initial preference for secretary of war to replace Cameron. He was interested in succeeding Taney as Chief Justice, but decided that the Radicals in the Senate would block it. Served as counsel for Tilden in the disputed presidential election of 1876, which was eventually won by Rutherford B. Hayes.

James T. Brady (1815–1869). Of the New York bar. Admitted to bar at age 20, he had worked in his father's law office as an office boy and student. He was a leading member of Tammany Hall and leading criminal defense lawyer. In 1859, he was co-defense counsel (with Reverdy Johnson and Edwin Stanton) in the murder trial of Congressman Dan Sickles and served without charging a fee, since Sickles was a boyhood friend. In 1860, Brady was an unsuccessful candidate for governor of New York on the States Rights ticket, the wing of the Democratic party aligned with John Breckenridge. In October 1861, he was one of the successful defense counsel for the crew of the *Savannah*. During January–February 1865, he was unsuccessful defense counsel at the trial of CSA Captain John Y. Beall for spying, and more before a military commission in Fort Lafayette in New York Harbor. In 1867, Brady was a leading member of the defense team for Jefferson Davis.

John Cabell Breckinridge (1821–1875). Of the Kentucky and Iowa bars. Born in Kentucky, he was educated at the College of New Jersey (now Princeton) and studied law at Transylvania University in Lexington. After admission to the bar in 1840, he practiced in Iowa for two years, then returned to practice in Lexington. Breckinridge served as a major in the Mexican War, then in the Kentucky lower house, and in the U.S. House (1851–1855). He was a slaveholder and was active in getting the repeal of the Missouri Compromise into the Kansas-Nebraska Act. President Pierce nominated him to be minister to Spain, but Breckinridge declined. He was elected vice president under Buchanan, the youngest in history (inaugurated at age 36). In 1860, he was nominated for president by the split Southern National Democratic Party, and came in second in electoral votes, and third in popular votes. He became a U.S. senator on March 4, 1861. Kentucky formally remained with the Union in September 1861, and Breckinridge joined the CSA, where he served as a general. (He was formally expelled from the U.S. Senate on December 4, 1861.) He was the fifth CSA secretary of war, February 6 to May 10, 1865. He fled Virginia with Jefferson Davis, escaped to Cuba, then England and Canada. He returned to Lexington in March 1869, after receiving amnesty, and resumed his law practice.

Aaron Venable Brown (1795–1859). Of the Tennessee bar. Graduated from the University of North Carolina at Chapel Hill, valedictorian of his class. He began practice in Tennessee in 1817, and formed a law partnership with future President James Knox Polk. Brown served in the Tennessee legislature (1821–1835), and in the U.S. House (1839–1845) until he became governor of Tennessee. President Buchanan appointed him postmaster general in March 1857, and in that post he held immense patronage power. He established the overland mail service from Missouri to San Francisco. Before he died in March 1859, Brown claimed that his house off Lafayette Square was haunted by the former owner, Madison's Attorney General William Wirt, and by Chief Justice John

Marshall. He was succeeded as postmaster general by Joseph Holt. A revenue cutter was named after him; it saw service during the Civil War off the North Carolina coast.

Orville Hickman Browning (1806–1881). Of the Illinois bar. Born in Kentucky, Browning began practice in Illinois in 1831, and in the late 1830s served with Lincoln in the state legislature. In July 1861, he was appointed to the Senate by the governor to complete the term of Stephen Douglas. He was appointed interior secretary by Andrew Johnson in July 1866.

James Buchanan (1791–1868). Of the Pennsylvania bar. Dickinson College, Pennsylvania State legislature (as a Federalist); member of the U.S. House as a Democrat (1821–1831) and then senator as a Jacksonian Democrat (1834–1845). A diplomat, he was minister to Russia (1831–1833), secretary of state (1845–1849) under President Polk, and minister to England (1852–1857). Lost the Democratic presidential nomination to Franklin Pierce, who was elected president in 1852. Was the fifteenth president, 1857–61. Argued that secession was unconstitutional, but that he had no power to coerce Southern states. Supported Breckinridge for president, opposed the peace Democrats in 1864. Buchanan is generally regarded by historians as the worst U.S. president. The second largest city in Liberia is named after him.

Benjamin Franklin Butler (1818–1893). Admitted to the Massachusetts bar in 1840. Developed New England's largest criminal law practice. Served in the Massachusetts state House (1853) and senate (1859) as a Democrat. At the Charleston Democratic Convention in 1860, he voted for Jefferson Davis for president, then supported Breckinridge in the Baltimore Convention and ran unsuccessfully for governor on the Breckinridge ticket. As a general, he led the 8th Massachusetts Militia to Maryland, and he occupied Baltimore. General-in-Chief Winfield Scott relieved him of command and transferred him to Fort Monroe. There, he established a precedent by classifying as contraband slaves who escaped to federal lines. In May 1862, he was in charge of occupied New Orleans; in a proclamation of December 23, 1862, CSA President Jefferson Davis formally branded Butler as an "outlaw and common enemy of mankind . . . [who should be] immediately executed by hanging." In 1864, Treasury Secretary Chase offered Butler the vice president position on his ticket; Lincoln sought him too to replace Hannibal Hamlin. Butler refused both. In January 1865, Lincoln again relieved him of command. In 1866, Butler became a Republican member of the U.S. House, where he was a prosecutor in Andrew Johnson's impeachment. In March 1866, he argued the *Milligan* case in the Supreme Court, on the U.S. (losing) side. In 1882, he was elected governor of Massachusetts (as a Democrat).

George Cadwalader (1806–1879). Of the Pennsylvania bar. He was the general in command of Fort McHenry when John Merryman was arrested. His brother John was judge on the federal court for the Eastern District of Pennsylvania, appointed by Buchanan.

John Caldwell Calhoun (1782–1850). Of the South Carolina bar. Graduated from Yale College, and admitted to the bar in 1807. Served in the House for three terms until 1817, when he resigned to become secretary of war under President Monroe (1817–1825). He was elected vice president under John Quincy Adams and also under Andrew Jackson, March 1825 to December 28, 1832, when he resigned in part over the Tariff issue, and to take the Senate seat of Hayne who resigned, until 1843. He was secretary of state under Tyler, 1844–45, and then returned to the Senate until his death.

John Archibald Campbell (1811–1889). Member of the Georgia, Louisiana, and Alabama bars. A child prodigy, he graduated from the University of Georgia at age 14; he spent three years at West Point (having been appointed by John C. Calhoun, a friend of his father's), but had to leave to support his widowed mother. He studied law, was admitted to the Georgia bar when he was only 18, then moved to Alabama where he practiced law and served in the state legislature. He twice refused a seat on the Alabama Supreme Court. In 1851–52, Campbell argued a case (involving decedent's estate) in the circuit court and on appeal to the Supreme Court; his opposing counsel was Daniel Webster. Campbell's presentation was so compelling—even though he lost at the Supreme Court—that the members of the Court unanimously recommended Campbell's appointment to the Court; this was the only time such a request was made by the Court. When President Pierce sent Campbell's nomination to the Senate, he was immediately and unanimously confirmed, and took office on March 25, 1853—at age 41. When Alabama seceded, Campbell remained in Washington, hoping to negotiate a peaceful resolution, but finally resigned from the Court on April 26, 1861. He was vilified by Alabamans for not supporting secession. He moved to New Orleans where he practiced. He served as assistant secretary of war of the CSA, in charge of conscription. Campbell was one of the three CSA commissioners who met with Lincoln at the Hampton Roads Conference (February 3, 1865) on the *River Queen* near Fort Monroe. After Appomattox, he was imprisoned for four months, but was then released and pardoned by order of President Johnson at the request of Justice Samuel Nelson and former Justice Benjamin Curtis. He moved back to New Orleans, established a prosperous practice, and by 1873, he was the undisputed leader of the Southern Bar—and in that year argued the famous *Slaughterhouse Cases* before the Court. He argued his last case before the Court in 1889.

John Snyder Carlile (1817–1878). Of the Virginia and West Virginia bars. Born in Winchester, Virginia, Carlile was admitted to the bar in 1840 and served in the Virginia state senate, 1847–51, and then served one term in the U.S. House. He was a delegate to the Virginia secession convention in 1861, where he was a leader of the anti-secession movement, though he was a slaveholder. On July 13, 1861, he was elected U.S. senator from the Restored Virginia Government at Wheeling, replacing U.S. Senator Robert Hunter who had become CSA secretary of state. Carlile served as U.S. senator until 1865, when his seat was declared vacant; he returned to his law practice in West Virginia.

Richard Bennett Carmichael (1807–1884). Of the Maryland bar. Born on the eastern shore of Maryland, he attended Dickinson College and then Princeton, where he graduated in 1828. He then studied law, and began practice in 1830. Carmichael was a Jacksonian Democrat who served in the state House of Delegates for more than twenty years; he served one term in the U.S. House, 1833–35. He was a delegate to the Democratic National Conventions in 1856, 1864, 1868, and 1876. Carmichael was the president of the State Constitutional Convention in 1867. He was a judge of the state circuit court, 1858–64, in which, in 1862, he was hit on the head and dragged from his courtroom by federal troops and imprisoned in Fort McHenry.

Salmon P. Chase (1808–1873). Of the Ohio and District of Columbia bars. Born in New Hampshire, attended Dartmouth (first in his class). Admitted to the Ohio bar in 1830. Elected to the Senate, 1849–55, then elected governor of Ohio (as a Free-Soil Democrat) and reelected in 1857 (as a Republican). One of the contenders for the presidential nomination in 1860. Elected senator in 1860, but resigned after two days to become Lincoln's secretary of the treasury, and then Chief Justice in late 1864 to replace Taney. He presided over the impeachment trial of President Johnson. He was a contender for president on the Democratic ticket in the summer of 1868 (with the active support of Gerrit Smith), and was interested again as a Liberal Republican in 1872. Died in 1873 at age 65.

Norton Parker Chipman (1834–1924). Of the Iowa and California bars. Born in Ohio, his family moved to Iowa when he was a child. He graduated from law school in Cincinnati in 1859, and was admitted in Iowa and began practice there. He began the war as a major with the Iowa infantry, and at the end was brevetted brigadier general. He was the Judge Advocate General in the successful prosecution of Captain Wirz of Andersonville prison. After the War, he was appointed secretary of the territorial form of government for the District of Columbia, and then was elected as D.C. delegate to Congress (1871–1875). Chipman moved to California and eventually was appointed the first presiding justice of the California Third District Court of Appeal.

Henry Clay (1777–1852). Of the Virginia and Kentucky bars. Studied law at William and Mary, and was admitted to the Virginia bar at age 20. He moved to Kentucky and engaged in a successful law practice, including many Supreme Court cases still cited. He taught law at Transylvania University, and served several terms in the Senate. But his greatest success was in the House where he served as Speaker for five terms, beginning shortly before the War of 1812. Known as the "great compromiser," he helped develop the 1820 Missouri Compromise. In 1833, he brokered a tariff compromise that grew out of the nullification crisis, and was central to the Compromise of 1850, while in the Senate. Clay had a successful law practice and argued twenty-three cases before the U.S. Supreme Court. He served as secretary of state under John Quincy Adams. Clay campaigned unsuccessfully for the presidency five times. Clay was idolized by Lincoln.

Patrick Ronayne Cleburne (1828–1864). Of the Arkansas bar. Born in County Cork, Ireland, Cleburne served in the British Army and then came to the United States in 1849. He settled in Helena, Arkansas, and practiced law. When Arkansas seceded, he became a colonel, and was quickly promoted to major general in December 1862. A year later, in December 1863, he proposed the enlistment into the CSA army of slaves who then could become free. That action prevented further promotion, though he was know as the "Stonewall Jackson of the West," one of the most brilliant soldiers of the CSA. He died on November 30, 1864, at the Battle of Franklin, Tennessee, where he had commanded a division under Major General Benjamin F. Cheatham; 189 Union soldiers were killed and 1,750 CSA soldiers were killed.

Thomas Corwin (1794–1865). Of the Ohio bar. He was admitted to the bar in 1817, served in the Ohio state House, and then as Whig Representative to the House, 1831–40. He was governor of Ohio, 1840–42, then was elected to the U.S. Senate, 1845–50. He was appointed secretary of the treasury by President Fillmore, 1850–53, and then returned to the House, 1859–61. Lincoln appointed him minister to Mexico, 1861–64.

John Jordan Crittenden (1786–1863). Of the Kentucky bar. Born in Kentucky, he was educated at Washington College and the College of William and Mary, after which he studied law and was admitted in Kentucky in 1807. After service in the state legislature, he was elected (Democratic Republican) to the Senate (1817–1819). After further service in the state legislature, he was nominated by President John Quincy Adams for the U.S. Supreme Court, but the Senate failed to act. He returned to the Senate, 1835–1841, and was appointed the fifteenth Attorney General by President Harrison in 1841, and then was again elected to the Senate, 1842–48, when he became governor. President Fillmore appointed Crittenden the twenty-second Attorney General, 1850–53, and he returned to the Senate 1855–61 (American/Know-Nothing), and was elected to the Thirty-sixth Congress, 1861–63, as a Unionist. His son George served with the CSA and his other son Thomas was a Union officer. He was the author of the proposed amendments to the Constitution on December 18, 1860, known as the Crittenden Compromise.

George Ticknor Curtis (1812–1894). Of the Massachusetts bar. Graduated from Harvard College and Law School, he was admitted in 1836, and became a successful patent attorney (representing Goodyear, McCormick, and Samuel Morse). He served as defense co-counsel for Dred Scott; he joined Montgomery Blair as co-counsel for the reargument at the Supreme Court in December 1856. George Curtis was the younger brother of Supreme Court Justice Curtis. He also wrote biographies of Webster and Buchanan and several legal treatises.

Benjamin Robbins Curtis (1809–1874). Of the Massachusetts bar. Graduated from Harvard College and Law School (second in his class), and was admitted to the bar in 1832. He practiced in Boston until 1851 when he was appointed to the U.S. Supreme Court by President Millard Fillmore. Though he earned the label of a "slave-catcher judge" while riding circuit in New England because of his strict enforcement of the Fugitive Slave Act, he is more famous for his lengthy dissent in the *Dred Scott* case. He resigned from the Court in September 1857 and resumed a lucrative law practice. He subsequently appeared as an advocate before the Supreme Court in more than forty cases. In late 1862, Curtis attacked the Preliminary Emancipation Proclamation as having exceeded the power of the president. He opposed Lincoln's reelection in 1864. In 1868, he was the co-defense counsel (with William M. Evarts) in the Senate's impeachment trial of Andrew Johnson. Curtis later declined an appointment by Johnson to be Attorney General. He argued more than forty cases before the Supreme Court.

Caleb Cushing (1800–1879). Of the Massachusetts bar. After graduating from Harvard in 1817, he taught mathematics there, and was admitted to practice in 1821. Cushing served as a Whig member of Congress from 1835 until 1843, and chaired the Foreign Affairs Committee in his last term. President Tyler nominated him to be secretary of the treasury, but he failed Senate confirmation. Tyler then sent Cushing as U.S. envoy to China, where Cushing negotiated the first U.S.-China treaty. Failing twice to be elected (as a Democrat) as governor of Massachusetts, he served on the state's Supreme Judicial Court in 1852, and was President Pierce's Attorney General, 1853–57. He was the first Attorney General to abandon his law practice while in office. Cushing chaired the Democratic Convention that nominated John Breckinridge for president in 1860; later that year, President Buchanan sent Cushing to South Carolina as Confidential Commissioner. President Grant appointed Cushing as one of the U.S. counsel at the Alabama Claims Tribunal, 1871–72, and then nominated Cushing to be Chief Justice in 1874, but then Grant withdrew the nomination in face of Senate opposition. Cushing served as U.S. minister to Spain, 1874–77, having been preceded by Daniel E. Sickles.

Richard Henry Dana (1815–1882). Of the Massachusetts bar. Attended Harvard. Met with John Brown in 1849. Involved in defense of a fugitive slave, Anthony Burns, in a notorious trial in Boston in 1854, as well as defending members of the Secret Six. A member of the Free-Soil Party composed of discontented Whigs. He was appointed by Lincoln U.S. Attorney for Massachusetts. Argued the *Prize Cases* with Evarts as counsel for the U.S. government (for the libellants). He was a friend of Herman Melville's and, in 1840, he published, *Two Years Before the Mast*, based on a diary that he kept while at sea for two years, which also helped him obtain maritime law clients.

David Davis (1815–1886). Of the Illinois bar. Born in Maryland, he went to college at Kenyon, and then to Yale to study law. Upon graduation in 1835, he moved to Bloomington, Illinois, to private law practice. From 1848 to 1862, he presided over the local judicial circuit in which attorney Lincoln practiced. He engineered Lincoln's upset victory at the 1860 Chicago Republican nominating convention. Lincoln nominated him to the Supreme Court in 1862. He was the executor of Lincoln's estate following the 1865 assassination. Davis wrote the opinion of the Court in the *Ex parte Milligan* case in 1866. A registered Independent, Davis was nominated for president by the Labor Reform Convention in 1872, but he withdrew when he failed to receive the Liberal Republican Party nomination. He received one electoral vote in the 1872 election. He served one term as a senator from Illinois, and was elected president pro tempore in 1881. His grandfather was an ancestor of George W. and George H. W. Bush through George Herbert Walker.

William Lewis Dayton (1807–1864). Of the New Jersey bar. Attended the College of New Jersey (now Princeton), and was admitted to the bar in 1825. In 1837, he served in the New Jersey state senate, and was appointed to the U.S. Senate in 1842 and then elected in 1842. Dayton was the first nominee for vice president on the Republican ticket at the Philadelphia convention in 1856—defeating Lincoln who was a candidate too. He served as Attorney General of New Jersey until 1861, when he resigned to become Lincoln's minister to France. He died in Paris.

James William Denver (1817–1892). Of the Ohio, Missouri, and D.C. bars. Attended Cincinnati law school and practiced in Xenia, Ohio, in 1844, and then in Missouri, and later served in the Mexican War under General Scott. He moved to California and in 1852 was a member of the state senate, and was appointed secretary of state of California. He was in the U.S. House 1855–57, and was governor of the Kansas Territory in 1858. A partner in the Washington firm of Hughes, Denver & Peck, he briefly represented Henry Wirz in August 1865.

Charles Devens (1820–1891). Of the Massachusetts bar. Born in Massachusetts, Devens graduated from Harvard College and Law School, and was admitted in 1841. In the 1850s, he was involved in fugitive slave cases while practicing law. He saw great service during the War, being wounded twice, and ended as a general. After the War, Devens served on the Massachusetts superior court, and then was associate justice of the state supreme judicial court, 1873–77, when he was appointed U.S. Attorney General by President Hayes. In that capacity, he arranged for the removal of the Custis Lee suit, involving Arlington, to the federal court. After serving in the two terms of the Hayes administration, Devens returned to the state supreme judicial court for another ten years.

Stephen Arnold Douglas (1813–1861). Of the Illinois bar. Douglas grew up in Vermont where he learned the cabinetmaker's trade, and then he moved to New York and Ohio, finally settling in Illinois. He was admitted in 1834, and two years later was elected to the state House. In 1840–41, he was appointed secretary of state of Illinois, and elected a judge of the state's supreme court. He served three terms in the U.S. House (1843–1847) and then was elected to the U.S. Senate in 1847, where he served until his death. He was the unsuccessful candidate for president on the Democrat ticket in 1852 and 1856, and was the unsuccessful candidate for president in 1860.

William Maxwell Evarts (1818–1901). Of the New York bar. He was born in Boston, the grandson of Roger Sherman, a signer of the Declaration of Independence. He attended Yale, where he was a member of Skull and Bones, and went to Harvard Law School. He was admitted to the New York bar in 1841. From 1849 to 1853, he was Assistant U.S. Attorney in New York, and in 1860, he chaired the New York delegation to the Republican National Convention. Evarts won a victory for the freedom of slaves in the 1860 New York case of *Lemmon v. People*. As the foremost trial lawyer of his day, he was brought in to assist the prosecution in the trial of the *Savannah* crew in October 1861. Served as counsel, along with Dana, for the government (the libellants) in the *Prize Cases*. In 1863, he was sent to England to convince the British not to provide vessels and other war materiel to the CSA. Evarts defended President Johnson (co-counsel with former Supreme Court Justice Benjamin Curtis) in his impeachment trial, and then became U.S. Attorney General under Johnson in July 1868 and served until March 1869. As chief counsel for the Republican Party during the disputed Tilden-Hayes election, he was instrumental in Hayes' election. During the Hayes administration, Evarts was secretary of state (1877–1881), and from 1885 to 1891, he was a U.S. senator from New York. His great-grandson, Archibald Cox, was U.S. solicitor general and special prosecutor during the Watergate scandal in the Nixon White House—thus the great-grandfather defended a president in an impeachment, and the great-grandson prosecuted a president in an impeachment.

Thomas Ewing, Jr. (1829–1896). Of the Ohio, Kansas, and New York bars. Born in Ohio, Ewing attended Brown, and then served as private secretary to President Taylor (1849–1850), while his father was Secretary of the Interior. He then practiced law in Ohio, but then moved in 1856 to Kansas where, five years later, he became Chief Justice of the Kansas Supreme Court. Ewing resigned his position in 1862 and became a successful Union officer, ending as a major general. After the War, he practiced in Washington (1865–1870). He served as counsel for Dr. Mudd and Samuel Arnold during the military commission's trial of the assassination conspirators. He helped secure President Johnson from conviction in the Senate, and turned down Johnson's offer to make him Secretary of War and later Attorney General. In 1870, he returned to Ohio to practice, and later served as a Democrat in Congress, 1877–81. He then moved to New York where he practiced until his death.

Charles J. Faulkner (1806–1884). Born in Martinsburg, Virginia (now West Virginia), he graduated from Georgetown University, and was admitted to the bar in 1829. Active in Virginia politics, he was a member of the House of Delegates (1829–1834), the state senate (1838–1842), and the Constitutional Convention of 1850. He served in the U.S. House, 1851–59 and was appointed by President Buchanan as minister to France in 1859. He was later arrested on charges of buying arms in France for the CSA. After his release, he served in the CSA Army under General Stonewall Jackson. After the War, Faulkner served again in the U.S. House (1875–1877) from West Virginia.

David Dudley Field (1805–1894). Of the New York bar. He was the brother of Supreme Court Justice Stephen Johnson Field. He practiced with his brother Stephen in New York City until 1848. Winning lawyer for Milligan, along with James Garfield and Jeremiah Black, before the Supreme Court in *Ex parte Milligan* (1866). Justice Stephen Field concurred in the opinion.

Stephen Johnson Field (1816–1899). Member of the New York and California bars. Graduated top of the class at Williams College in 1837, and read law at his brother's law office in New York, and then practiced with him until 1848. He was elected to the California state legislature in 1850, and served on the state supreme court in 1857. When Congress created a tenth seat on the U.S. Supreme Court, Lincoln appointed him to the Court, December 1863. He was a unionist Democrat, and his appointment also helped ensure that the new state of California would be cemented to the Union. Field sought the nomination for president in 1880.

George Purnell Fisher (1817–1899). Of the Delaware bar. Born in Delaware, Fisher graduated from Dickinson College, was admitted in 1841, and began practice in Dover. He was a member of the state House in 1843–44, and was secretary of state in 1846 and Attorney General 1857–60. He was Delaware's lone congressman March 1861 to 1863, but was defeated for reelection by thirty-seven votes in 1862. Lincoln met with Fisher in November 1861 and later to try to arrange for compensated emancipation of Delaware's slaves. Lincoln then appointed Fisher a judge on the supreme court of the District of Columbia in March 1863. The climax of Fisher's years on that bench was the trial of John Harrison Surratt in 1867, where Fisher revealed his bias against Surratt. In 1870, Fisher was appointed district attorney for the District, and in 1889, Fisher was appointed by President Harrison as auditor of the U.S. Treasury Department.

James A. Garfield (1831–1881). Member of the Ohio bar. Williams College graduate in 1856, then elected to the Ohio state legislature. In 1861, he became a prominent Union officer, but then was elected to Congress. Lincoln convinced him to resign from the army and to be a congressional Republican ally. He argued the winning side in 1866 in the *Milligan* case before the Supreme Court. Elected the twentieth president in 1880. He was shot four months after his inauguration and died two months later.

Henry Sheffie Geyer (1790–1859). Of the Maryland and Missouri bars. Born in Frederick, Maryland, he was admitted in 1811 and practiced in Frederick. After service as an officer in the War of 1812, Geyer moved to Missouri, practiced in St. Louis, and was for six years a member of the Missouri House, including two years as Speaker. Succeeding the long-serving and powerful Thomas Hart Benson, he was elected as a Whig to the U.S. Senate, serving from 1851 to 1857. He did not run for reelection, but resumed his law practice in St Louis. He was co-counsel for Sanford in the *Dred Scott* case.

Joshua Reed Giddings (1795–1864). Of the Ohio bar. Born in Pennsylvania, Giddings grew up in Ohio, and received no systematic education. He was admitted in 1821, and developed a very successful law practice with future Senator Benjamin F. Wade. He served in the House from 1838 until 1859, first as a Whig then as a Free-Soiler and finally as a Republican. He was strongly antislavery, seeking abolition in the District and territories. During the *Creole* slave ship mutiny incident, Giddings introduced, on March 21, 1842, resolutions in the House declaring that the slaves were free. This brought formal censure, after which he resigned, but then he was reelected by a large majority. He opposed the annexation of Texas (1846), the Mexican War (1846–1848), the Compromise of 1850, and the Kansas-Nebraska Act (1854). He was a founder of the Republican Party. Lincoln appointed Giddings as U.S. consul general in the British North American Provinces in March 1861. Giddings died in Montreal.

Robert Cooper Grier (1794–1870). Of the Pennsylvania bar. Attended Dickinson College, and was admitted to the bar in 1817. He was appointed as a county judge, and then he was appointed in 1846 by President Polk to the Supreme Court. Grier may have been involved in "tipping" off Buchanan to the *Dred Scott* decision. He presided over the "piracy" trial of the *Jefferson Davis* crew, and wrote the majority opinion in the *Prize Cases*.

Henry Wager Halleck (1815–1872). Of the California bar. Born in New York, he attended the U.S. Military Academy at West Point, where he graduated third in his class, and later wrote the first major American book on military strategy. During the Mexican War in the 1840s, Halleck was in the newly annexed territory of California, where he later was appointed secretary of state. He became a lawyer, resigned from the army in 1854, married the granddaughter of Alexander Hamilton, and ran a very successful law practice. In 1861, he wrote a treatise on international law. Lincoln sent him, as a major general, to St. Louis to replace Fremont. In 1862, Lincoln made Halleck general-in-chief of all Union forces, and in 1864, he became chief of staff of the army. He remained in the army until his death.

Hannibal Hamlin (1809–1891). Of the Maine bar. He was admitted to the bar in 1833 and practiced in Maine. Hamlin served in the Maine House of Representatives beginning in 1836, and was Speaker. Elected as a Democrat to the U.S. House in 1848, he resigned in 1857 to become governor. He was elected to the Senate as a Republican, and served until he resigned to become Lincoln's vice president. After a brief time as collector at the port of Boston, he returned to the U.S. Senate where he served until 1881. After that service, he was appointed minister to Spain.

Benjamin Gwinn Harris (1805–1895). Of the Maryland bar. From Leonardtown in St. Mary's County. He went to Yale College

Dramatis Personae: The Lawyers 311

and Cambridge (Harvard) Law School, and was admitted to the bar in 1840. Was a member of the Maryland House of Delegates: 1832–33, 1836, 1849, 1856, and 1861–62; Harris was the U.S. representative from Maryland's fifth district, 1863–67. He was a delegate to the Democratic National Convention in 1864. Harris was censured by the House on April 9, 1864, for utterances on the floor during the debate over censure of Representative Long. He was tried by military commission in May 2, 1865, for harboring paroled Confederate soldiers and was sentenced to three years' imprisonment. He was pardoned by President Johnson on May 31, 1865, after his lawyer met with Johnson through the good offices of Montgomery Blair.

Rutherford B. Hayes (1822–1893). Of the Ohio bar. He graduated from Kenyon College as class valedictorian. Hayes later graduated from Harvard Law School, where Justice Story was one of his instructors. He was admitted to practice in 1845. In the mid-1850s, he handled fugitive slave cases (including a celebrated case with Senator Salmon P. Chase). Just before the War, he was city solicitor for Cincinnati. He was a war hero, suffering five wounds. After the War, he was elected to Congress, and then was elected governor. His election as president in 1877 was disputed, and he finally won over New York lawyer Samuel Tilden by one electoral vote.

Robert Y. Hayne (1791–1839). Of the South Carolina bar. He was admitted in 1812, served in the state House, and was state Attorney General from 1820–22, after which he was elected as a Republican to the U.S. Senate. With Calhoun, he was a radical advocate of state sovereignty. He was a member of the convention that passed the South Carolina Ordinance of Nullification in 1832; during that crisis, he commanded a force of twenty-five thousand South Carolina volunteers. He was governor 1832–34 and mayor of Charleston 1835–37, and was president of a railroad at the time of his death.

Joseph Holt (1807–1894). Of the Kentucky and Mississippi bars. He was born and grew up in Kentucky, where he was admitted in 1828, and became politically active as a Jacksonian Democrat. He was the prosecuting attorney for the Louisville circuit. Holt moved his practice to Mississippi where he was very successful. He turned down the nomination by the Mississippi legislature to serve as a U.S. Senator. In 1842, he returned to Louisville; in 1850, Holt married the daughter or the Kentucky governor, and in 1857, he moved to Washington.

President Buchanan appointed him commissioner of patents in September 1857, and postmaster general in March 1859. On the advice of Attorney General Stanton, Buchanan appointed Holt secretary of war in January 1861, and Holt stayed in that position for several days into the Lincoln administration. Holt worked actively to keep Kentucky in the Union. Stanton appointed Holt in September 1862 to the new office of the Judge Advocate of the army and director of the Bureau of Military Justice. Holt was Lincoln's first choice for Attorney General to replace Bates, but Holt declined, and Lincoln decided on Speed. Holt was the sitting Judge Advocate General for the trial of the Lincoln assassination conspirators, May 8 through July 15, 1865, and he remained in that post for a decade.

Robert Mercer Taliferro Hunter (1809–1887). Of the Virginia bar. Hunter graduated from the University of Virginia, studied law, and was admitted in 1830. He was elected to the Virginia legislature, and in 1837, to the U.S. House of Representatives, serving as Speaker for one term. Elected to the Senate in 1846, he remained there until 1861 when he was appointed CSA secretary of state in July 1861. He resigned in February 1862 to serve as a senator in the CSA, and was president pro tempore. He was a member of the three-person CSA delegation to the Hampton Roads Peace Conference. After the War and his release from prison, Hunter served as treasurer of Virginia, 1874–80.

Duncan Farrar Kenner (1813–1887). Of the Louisiana bar. Born in New Orleans, he became a wealthy sugar planter, served several terms in the state House, and was a member of the state constitutional conventions in 1845 and 1852. He was member of the Confederate Congress, and served as chairman of the Ways and Means Committee. Much of his property was confiscated and his slaves freed after the Union capture of New Orleans in 1862. In very early 1865, Jefferson Davis sent him on a secret diplomatic mission to Europe to propose Confederate emancipation in exchange for formal recognition.

Andrew Jackson (1767–1845). Of the Tennessee bar. Though born in the backwoods of the Carolinas, he became an outstanding young lawyer in Tennessee, where he earned enough to buy slaves. He was the first congressman from Tennessee and served briefly in the Senate. He became a national hero as a major general in the War of 1812, when he defeated the British at New Orleans. He served as president 1829–37, and dealt forcefully and thoughtfully with South Carolina's effort to secede.

Bradley T. Johnson (1829–1903). Of the Maryland and Virginia bars. Born in Frederick County, Maryland, of a prominent family. (Francis Scott Key and Roger B. Taney were distant relatives.) Graduated from the College of New Jersey (Princeton College) and was admitted to the Maryland bar in 1851. He became state's attorney for Frederick County. He was a delegate to the 1860 Democratic Conventions in Charleston and Baltimore, where he staunchly supported Breckinridge. At the time of the Pratt Street Riot in Baltimore in April 1861, Johnson led the Frederick Mounted Dragoons to Baltimore at the request of Police Chief George P. Kane. On May 8th, he led his troops across the Potomac and recruited the 1st Maryland Regiment for the CSA. During the Antietam battle, he was appointed provost marshal of Frederick. As part of General Jubal Early's 1864 effort to take Washington, Johnson was assigned the task of freeing the Confederate prisoners at Point Lookout. After the War, he practiced law in Richmond and served in the Virginia senate. In 1879, he practiced in Baltimore. He wrote a dozen books, including a record of the trial of Jefferson Davis, and a biography of George Washington.

Reverdy Johnson (1796–1876). Of the Maryland bar. Born in Annapolis and educated there at St. John's College, he read law with his father and was admitted to the Maryland Bar in 1815. He was elected a Maryland state senator 1821–29 and a U.S. senator (Whig) 1845–49. President Taylor appointed him Attorney General of the United States, 1849–50. Johnson was counsel for McCormick in the 1855 *Reaper* case involving Lincoln, Stanton, and Harding. He was the winning counsel in the *Dred Scott* case, and consulted in the Key/Sickles murder trial of April 1859. Member of Peace Convention of 1861 in Washington; U.S. Senator (Democrat) 1863–68. He, along with Secretary of War Stanton, was present at the December 15, 1864, swearing in of Chief Justice Chase. Was minister to England (under President Johnson) 1868–69. He served as senior defense counsel for Mary Surratt.

John Letcher (1813–1884). Of the Virginia bar. Born in Lexington, Virginia, and graduated from Washington Academy (now Washington and Lee University). Admitted in 1839. He was the editor of a Shenandoah Valley newspaper, 1840–50, and was a Democratic representative in the U.S. House, 1851–59, and was governor of Virginia, 1860–64. He tried to discourage secession and was prominent in the organization of a Peace Conference in Washington. After the War, he resumed practice, was a member of the House of Delegates, and was president of the board of the Virginia Military Institute for ten years.

Abraham Lincoln (1809–1865). Of the Illinois Bar. Admitted to the bar in 1936. Member of the U.S. House of Representatives (1847–1849), president of the United States (1861–1865).

Robert Todd Lincoln (1843–1926). Of the Illinois bar. He was born and grew up in Springfield, the eldest of Lincoln's three sons (and the only child to live to maturity). He graduated from Harvard College, began studying at Harvard Law School, and then was commissioned a captain in the army, assigned to Grant's staff; he was at Appomattox when Lee surrendered. He resumed his study of law and was admitted in 1867. He was a successful lawyer, representing major companies and railroads (and later was president and chairman of the Pullman Company). President Garfield appointed him secretary of war in 1881, and he remained in that position under President Arthur after Garfield's assassination (witnessed by Lincoln). He served as U.S. minister to Britain, 1889–93. He is buried in Arlington Cemetery.

Edward Livingston (1764–1836). Of the New York and Louisiana bars. Educated at Princeton, he was admitted to practice in New York in 1785. He served in the U.S. House 1795 to 1801, was appointed U.S. Attorney for New York and then elected mayor of New York in 1801. He moved to Louisiana and practiced law there. He was elected to the U.S. House in 1822 and served three terms, and then was elected to the Senate in 1829. Livingston had served on General Andrew Jackson's staff during the War of 1812, and was appointed by President Jackson as secretary of state in 1831, He wrote Jackson's Proclamation on Nullification in 1832. He was minister to France, 1833–35.

Andrew Gordon Magrath (1813–1893). Of the South Carolina bar. Born in Charlestown, South Carolina, he graduated from South Carolina College and briefly attended Harvard Law School; he was admitted to the bar in 1835. Magrath was elected to the South Carolina House at age 25. President Pierce appointed him as federal district court judge in 1856. Two days after Lincoln's election in November 1860, Magrath publicly resigned and in effect closed the federal court in South Carolina. He later served in the secession convention, was named CSA district court judge, and was elected governor in December 1864. After the War, he built a lucrative law practice in Charleston.

William Learned Marcy (1786–1857). Of the New York bar. A graduate of Brown, Marcy was admitted in 1811, and practiced in Troy,

New York, until his service in the War of 1812. He was the Comptroller of New York State, 1823–29, and justice of the New York Supreme Court in 1829. Elected to the U.S. Senate as a Jacksonian Democrat 1831–33. He was governor of New York for three terms (1833–1839), but was defeated for reelection by Whig William H. Seward. Marcy was secretary of war under President Polk, 1845–49, after which he returned to practice. He served as secretary of state under President Franklin Pierce, 1853–57. It was Marcy's decision that the United States should not sign the Declaration of Paris of 1856, prescribing the rules of naval warfare (and prohibiting privateers).

James Murray Mason (1798–1871). Of the Virginia bar. Grandson of George Mason, one of the Founding Fathers. Attended the University of Pennsylvania and studied law at William and Mary. Admitted in Virginia, where he began his law practice in 1820. Elected as a Jacksonian Democrat to the U.S. House 1837–39, and to the Senate 1847–61. Mason was the author of the Fugitive Slave Act of 1850. Was president pro tempore of the Senate in 1857, chaired the Senate Select Committee on the Harpers Ferry Invasion (the Mason Report of June 15, 1860). He was also the chairman of the Senate Foreign Relations Committee for ten years. After secession, he withdrew from the Senate, but did not formally resign; he was expelled in absentia July 11, 1861. Became CSA commissioner to England in August 1861, though delayed due to the *Trent* affair; resided in London 1862–65. After the War, he moved to Canada, and later died in Alexandria, Virginia.

John Alexander McClernand (1812–1900). Of the Illinois bar. Just like Lincoln, he was born in Kentucky and then his family moved to Illinois. He had little formal education and served in the Black Hawk War. A Democrat, he served in the U.S. House of Representatives from 1843–1851 and moved to Springfield and again served in the 36th and 37th Congresses as a Union Democrat, resigning in 1861 to serve as a general in the Army. He served under Grant in the Western Theater. McClernand looked to Stephen Douglass as a mentor, and was a close political ally of Lincoln. He served as a judge in the Sangamon District of Illinois after the war, and later resumed law practice. In 1876, he presided over the Democratic National Convention.

John McLean (1785–1861). Of the Ohio bar. He grew up in Ohio, and at age 26, he was the examiner of the U.S. Land Office in Cincinnati. He served two terms in the U.S. House, 1812–16, and then returned to

Ohio, where he served on the state supreme court. President James Monroe appointed him commissioner of the General Land Office in 1822, and postmaster general (a new cabinet post) the following year. Though he remained in office under President John Q. Adams, he supported Jackson and was rewarded by Jackson's appointment of McLean to the U.S. Supreme Court. He was known as the "Politician on the Supreme Court" during his quest for the presidency. President Tyler offered him the position of secretary of war, but he declined. McLean was openly antislavery. At the 1856 Republican Convention, McLean received 196 votes to John Fremont's 359. His dissent in the *Dred Scott* case made him a possible contender in the 1860 presidential race; he received twelve votes on the first ballot at the Republican Convention. He was close to Salmon P. Chase.

Samuel Freeman Miller (1816–1890). Of the Kentucky and Iowa bars. Born in Kentucky, where he earned a medical degree from Transylvania University, he studied law on his own while engaged in his medical practice, and was admitted to the bar in 1847. He was a Whig supporter in Kentucky, and moved to Iowa where he was active in support of Lincoln's election in 1860. Lincoln appointed Miller to the Supreme Court in 1862, and he supported the administration in the *Prize Cases*. He remained on the Court until his death.

Lambdin P. Milligan (1812–1899). Of the Ohio and Indiana bars. Born in Ohio, he practiced law there for ten years, and then moved to Indiana where he soon became one of the ablest lawyers in the northern part of the state. In 1861, he became chairman of the county Democratic Party, and he began describing Lincoln as a tyrannical usurper and the War as illegal. He was unsuccessful in 1862 and 1864 in his efforts to be elected congressman and governor, respectively. He was arrested for treason on October 5, 1864, at his home in Indiana on the order of the military commandant of the District of Indiana, and was tried by a military commission on October 21, 1864. He was ordered to be executed on May 19, 1865. On May 20th, President Johnson commuted his sentence to life imprisonment. In that same month, he petitioned the U.S. Circuit Court for relief. In the famous case of *Ex parte Milligan*, in a unanimous decision on April 2, 1866, written by Chief Justice Chase, the Supreme Court held that Milligan should be discharged, because the military trial was illegal since civilian courts were open.

Samuel Nelson (1792–1873). Of the New York bar. He attended Middlebury College in Vermont, was admitted to the New York bar in 1817, and quickly developed a successful law practice in upstate New

York. He was appointed to the New York Supreme Court in 1823, and became its chief justice in 1836. President Tyler appointed him to the U.S. Supreme Court in 1845. He served on the New York City panel that tried the Confederate privateers in late 1861, and wrote the minority opinion in the *Prize Cases*. Since Nelson was an expert in admiralty law, President Grant appointed him as one of the U.S. representatives to the *Alabama* Claims Commission in 1871 to resolve the conflict with Great Britain for its support of the CSA.

Charles O'Conor (1804–1884). Admitted to the New York bar in 1824. United States Attorney for the Southern District of New York (1853–1856). O'Conor represented the Virginia slaveholder in the 1860 New York case of *Lemmon v. People*, cited by Lincoln in his Cooper Union Address. (O'Conor spoke at Cooper Union on December 19, 1859, two months before Lincoln.) He presided over the conservative Pine Street Meeting in New York City on December 16, 1860, in an effort to persuade the South to pause in the secessionist movement, which led to the formation of a committee, headed by former President Millard Fillmore, to meet with leading Southerners. O'Conor was a Union Democrat who believed that secession was not illegal. Counsel for Jefferson Davis (without fee) in treason charges, 1865–69. In 1870, he was one of the founders of the Association of the Bar of New York City. He represented Democratic candidate Samuel J. Tilden in 1877, before the special electoral commission that awarded the disputed electoral votes to Rutherford B. Hayes. O'Conor played a major role in the prosecution of the "Tweed Ring" relating to corruption in New York.

Franklin Pierce (1805–1869). Of the New Hampshire bar. Born in New Hampshire, he graduated from Bowdoin College in 1824, studied law, and quickly became the greatest trial lawyer in the state. He became Speaker of the state legislature at age 25 and was elected to the House at 27 and the U.S. Senate at 31. He resigned from Senate in 1842 and returned to New Hampshire in 1843. Pierce served in the Mexican War as a brigadier general. In the 1850s, Pierce supported the Compromise of 1850, and decried slavery while criticizing the moralistic rhetoric from the Northern abolitionists. He was nominated at the Democratic Party Convention in Baltimore in June 1852 as the dark horse candidate, breaking a long deadlock. He won election as president that fall, winning twenty-seven of the thirty-one states. He lost favor with the voters in the North due to his support for the Kansas-Nebraska Act. He became the only president who sought reelection but was denied the nomination (in 1856); the non-controversial Buchanan was nominated instead. During the War, he spoke out against the infringement of civil liberties by the Lincoln administration. In 1861–62, he was the subject of the Hopkins Hoax, involving a false letter that implicated Pierce in treasonable activities. Secretary of State Seward was taken in by the hoax, and was later publicly embarrassed.

Edwards Pierrepont (1817–1892). Of the Connecticut, Ohio, and New York bars. Born in Connecticut, Pierrepont graduated from Yale and the New Haven Law School, and was admitted in 1840. He practiced in Ohio 1840–45, and then moved to New York where he served on the New York Supreme Court, 1857–60. In 1862, Pierrepont was a member of the military commission for the cases of state prisoners in federal military custody. He served as a special prosecutor in the 1867 trial of John Surratt. President Grant appointed him U.S. Attorney for the Southern District of New York, 1869–70, and then was Grant's Attorney General in 1875, and a year later, U.S. minister to Great Britain.

Francis Harrison Pierpont (1814–1899). Of the Virginia and West Virginia bars. Born near Morgantown, he was admitted in 1841 and became the local attorney for the B & O Railroad. In 1861, he was elected the provisional governor of the Restored Government of Virginia. He was an abolitionist. In 1863, when West Virginia was admitted, he moved the capital to Alexandria. In 1865, President Johnson appointed Pierpont as the provisional governor of the reunited Virginia, and the capital was moved back to Richmond. In 1868, he was replaced by a military governor, and he returned to his law practice in West Virginia, where he served one term in the state legislature. In 1910, the state of West Virginia donated a marble statue of Pierpont to the U.S. Capitol's Statuary Hall.

Charles Pinckney (1757–1824). Of the South Carolina bar. Born in Charleston, he followed in the footsteps of his rich father as a lawyer and planter, and began practice in Charleston in 1779. He served as an officer in the Revolutionary War, and was captured by the British and held prisoner for a year. He was a member of the Continental Congress and an influential member of the Constitutional Convention; he worked to achieve South Carolina's ratification. He later was governor three times and a U.S. senator. Jefferson appointed him minister to Spain, where he facilitated the transfer of Louisiana in 1803. He was elected to the U.S. House in 1818, where, as the only member of Congress to have been at the Constitutional Convention, Pinckney fought against the Missouri Compromise.

Pierre Adolphe Rost (1797–1868). Of the Mississippi and Louisiana bars. Born in France and trained as an artilleryman, he emigrated to New Orleans in 1816, and then moved to Mississippi where he studied law under the brother of Jefferson Davis. He then practiced law in Louisiana, and served four years in the state senate. In 1838, Rost was appointed to the supreme court of Louisiana. In March 1861, CSA President Davis appointed Rost as CSA commissioner to Spain. After the War, Rost was pardoned by President Johnson, and practiced law in New Orleans until he died.

Raphael Semmes (1809–1877). Of the Maryland and Alabama bars. Orphaned at age 10, Semmes joined the U.S. Navy, but studied law while on leave, and was admitted to the bar in 1834. After service in the Mexican War, he practiced law in Mobile, Alabama. He resigned his navy commission in February 1861 and became the most successful commerce raider during the War, especially on the *Alabama*, a British-built cruiser he picked up in the Azores. His ship was sunk by the *Keasarge* off the coast of Cherbourg in the last gunnery duel in the era of wooden ships, but he was rescued by a British ship and later returned to the CSA. Arrested by order of Navy Secretary Welles, he was tried in Washington on December 15, 1865, for treason and piracy, but was cleared. In May 1866, he was elected judge of the probate court of Mobile, but President Johnson forbade him to function—due to Northern embittered opinion and his jaunty defiance of the U.S. Navy and the long-term damage he had caused to the merchant fleet. (The SS *Raphael Semmes*, a merchant ship built in 1920, was sunk by a U-Boat in June 1942.)

William H. Seward (1801–1872). Of the New York bar. Attended Union College and then practiced law with his father-in-law. Served as governor of New York, 1839–43, having defeated three-term Governor Marcy (later secretary of war and state). United States senator from New York, 1849–61. He lost the presidential nomination to Fremont in 1856, and was the presumptive nominee for president in 1860. Lincoln appointed him secretary of state; he remained secretary under President Johnson, though he was badly wounded on April 14, 1865, in connection with the Lincoln assassination. Negotiated the purchase of Alaska from Russia on March 30, 1867.

Horatio Seymour (1810–1886). Of the New York bar. Born in New York, he studied at Geneva College (later Hobart College). Was admitted to the bar in 1832, and ten years later was mayor of Utica; by 1845 was Speaker of the state assembly. Seymour served as Governor

1853–54, and he supported Stephen Douglas for president in 1856 and 1860. He was again elected governor in 1862. As governor of the largest state in the Union, Seymour was the most prominent Democratic opponent of Lincoln, especially with the military draft, which led to the Draft Riots of July 1863; Republicans accused him of treason. In 1868, Seymour ran against Grant for the presidency, and was close in the popular vote (3.01 to 2.7 million), but lost the election 214 to 80 in electoral votes.

Daniel Edgar Sickles (1820–1914). Of the New York bar. Member of the New York state assembly in 1847, and then got a Tammany appointment as corporation attorney of New York City. In 1853, Sickles became first secretary to the U.S. legation in London, chosen by Ambassador James Buchanan. In 1856, Sickles won a seat in the U.S. House (when Buchanan was elected president). Worked closely with Senator Slidell and other Democrats for the acquisition of Cuba. In 1859, he killed Phillip Barton Key, and was defended by eight lawyers, including James T. Brady, Reverdy Johnson, and his friend Edward Stanton—just before Stanton became Buchanan's Attorney General. Sickles was a general during the War, and lost his right leg at Gettysburg. (He was notoriously close to Mrs. Lincoln.) After the War, he was military governor of the Carolinas, and later American minister to Spain (1869–1873). (Former Attorney General Caleb Cushing succeeded Sickles in Spain.)

John Slidell (1793–1871). Of the New York and Louisiana bars. Born in New York City, attended Columbia College and practiced in New York City, until he moved to New Orleans in 1819, where he served as U.S. district attorney, 1829–33. He served one term in the U.S. House, 1843–45. In 1845, President Polk sent him to Mexico to negotiate the border and to purchase New Mexico and California, but his mission was rejected by Mexico. (The United States declared war on Mexico the following year.) He practiced commercial law in New Orleans with Judah P. Benjamin. Slidell served in the Senate, as a Democrat, from 1853 until February 1861. Slidell was appointed CSA commissioner to Paris, where he arrived in January 1862. He died in England and is buried in Paris. (Slidell, Louisiana, is named after him.)

William Smith (1762–1840). Of the South Carolina bar. He was admitted in 1784 and later served in the state senate and as a state judge. He served twice in the U.S. Senate, where, in 1828, he participated in the Webster-Hayne debate. Smith declined the appointment to the U.S.

Dramatis Personae: The Lawyers   321

Supreme Court offered in 1829 by President Jackson. He died in Alabama, where he had served in the state assembly.

James Speed (1812–1887). Of the Kentucky bar. Studied law at Transylvania University and was admitted to the bar in 1833. Practiced in Louisville. Was elected to the state House and later the state senate. Leader of the pro-Union forces in Kentucky. Lincoln appointed him Attorney General (on Bates' resignation) in November 1864, upon the recommendation of Holt. (Speed's brother Joshua Fry Speed was Lincoln's close friend from Kentucky, with whom Lincoln lived during the early years practicing law.) In May/July 1865, he provided his opinion that authorized the use of a military commission for the trial of the assassination conspirators. He argued, along with Ben Butler, for the United States (the losing side) in *Ex parte Milligan*. Speed resigned in July 1866 due to conflicts with President Johnson. Speed failed in his attempt to be elected to the Senate in 1867, and returned to practice and teaching law at the University of Louisville. In 1868, he was a candidate for the vice presidential nomination on the Republican ticket, but lost.

Edwin McMasters Stanton (1814–1869). Of the Pennsylvania, Ohio, and D.C. bars. Attorney General of the United States for a few months under President Buchanan. He was a member of the defense team in the famous Sickles murder trial in 1859, along with Reverdy Johnson and James T. Brady. Appointed secretary of war by Lincoln in 1862, while Stanton was practicing law in Washington. He wanted Lincoln to appoint him Chief Justice to replace Taney, but he finally agreed that he was indispensable at war. He refused to leave office when President Johnson asked for his resignation—one of the charges in the Johnson impeachment, that the Tenure in Office Act required Senate consent for removal. He finally resigned when the impeachment failed. He was nominated by President Grant to the Supreme Court on December 20, 1869, confirmed by the Senate (46–11) the same day, but he died four days later, before taking his oath.

Alexander Hamilton Stephens (1812–1883). Of the Georgia bar, admitted in 1834. Served in the state legislature 1836–42. He entered the U.S. House of Representatives in 1843 and served until 1859. In the late 1840s, he worked with Lincoln as a member of the "Young Indians" in the House working for the election of Zachary Taylor. Stephens supported Stephen Douglas in the 1860 election, but Lincoln may have offered him a cabinet position in 1861. He was unanimously chosen by the Provisional Congress in Montgomery as vice president of the CSA, though before then he was an opponent of immediate secession (e.g., his speech of November 14, 1860, to the Georgia legislature). Later he was a leader in the peace movement, and in the summer of 1863, he proposed to go to Washington to meet with Lincoln. He was the CSA leader at the Hampton Roads meeting in February 1865. Believing the Southern cause hopeless, he returned to Georgia in February, and in May was arrested. He was later elected to Congress and became governor in 1882.

Thaddeus Stevens (1792–1868). Of the Pennsylvania bar. He grew up in Vermont, graduated from Dartmouth, and then moved to York, Pennsylvania, where he studied law and was admitted in 1815. He practiced in Gettysburg and then in Lancaster. He was a member of the House 1849–53, and also from 1859 until his death, mostly as a Whig and Republican. He served as one of the defense counsel in the treason trial arising out of the Christiana riot of 1851. During the War, Stevens was one of the most powerful men in Congress: he chaired the Ways and Means Committee and helped draft the Fourteenth Amendment. After the 1866 elections, Stevens was the leader of the Radical Republicans, and proposed the resolution for the impeachment of President Johnson. The public expression of grief in Washington upon his death was second only to that for Lincoln three years earlier; his coffin lay in the Capitol Rotunda.

Charles Sumner (1811–1874). Of the Massachusetts bar. Born in Boston, graduated from Harvard in 1830, and then taught international and constitutional law there. In 1851, he was elected to the Senate to fill the seat of Daniel Webster. In 1856, Congressman Preston Brooks attacked him with a cane on the Senate floor; this became the symbol in the North of the brutality of the South. Sumner traveled frequently and at length to Europe, claiming he needed to recuperate. He was chairman of the Senate Relations Committee and urged Lincoln to settle the *Trent* Affair by freeing Mason and Slidell. Sumner introduced the Thirteenth Amendment to the Senate in 1864. His body lay in honor in the Capitol Rotunda, having been preceded by Thaddeus Stevens (1868) and Abraham Lincoln (1865).

Noah Haynes Swayne (1804–1884). Of the Virginia and Ohio bars. He was born and spent his early adult life in Virginia, where he was admitted in 1823. He was a strong abolitionist, and the slavery issue forced him to move to the free state of Ohio a year later. While practicing law, Swayne served in the state legislature. Jackson appointed him

Dramatis Personae: The Lawyers

U.S. attorney for Ohio in 1830. In that position, he became close friends with Supreme Court Justice John McLean, also from Ohio. Swayne joined the Republican Party when in was formed in 1855. McLean recommended Swayne to Lincoln as a possible Supreme Court nominee, and after McLean's death in 1861, Swayne was appointed in January 1862, since he satisfied Lincoln's criteria: loyalty to the Union, antislavery, and geographically balanced. He was the first of Lincoln's five appointments to the Court. Swayne was undistinguished as a Justice, but was a reliable supporter of the administration, the first Republican and the first Quaker to sit on the Court.

Roger Brooke Taney (1777–1864). Of the Maryland bar. Educated at Dickinson College, first in his class. Admitted in 1799. Practiced in Annapolis and Frederick, and moved from Frederick to Baltimore in 1823. Served in the Maryland Senate and House of Delegates. Attorney General of Maryland, Attorney General of the United States, and secretary of the treasury under President Jackson. Replaced John Marshall as Chief Justice of the United States in 1836.

John Tyler (1790–1862). Of the Virginia bar. Educated at the College of William and Mary, he was admitted to practice in 1809 and soon served in the House of Delegates. Tyler later served as governor (1825–1827) and as a U.S. Senator, where he voted against the tariff bills of 1828 and 1832. He supported the Compromise Tariff of 1833, but voted against the Force Bill (the only senator recorded against). He served for one month as President Harrison's vice president, and then became president in 1841. When South Carolina adopted its Ordinance of Secession in December 1860, Tyler was firmly against disunion: he presided over the Peace Congress on February 4, 1861. Then he was a member of the CSA Provisional Congress in May 1861, and was elected a member of the CSA House, but died before it assembled.

John Curtiss Underwood (1809–1873). Of the Virginia and New York bars. He graduated from Hamilton College, and moved to Virginia where he practiced 1839–56. He was a delegate to the first Republican Convention that nominated Fremont for president. He left Virginia in 1857 out of fear for his abolitionist views. He was appointed by Lincoln to serve as judge in the U.S. District Court for the Eastern District of Virginia, 1863–64. When that court was abolished, he was reassigned as U.S. District Judge for the District of Virginia, 1864–71, which handled the trials of Jefferson Davis.

Clement Laird Vallandigham (1820–1871). Of the Ohio bar. Born in Ohio, he was admitted in 1842, set up a successful law practice, and soon was elected to the Ohio state House. He was elected by small margins to the U.S. House in 1858 and 1860; he supported Stephen A. Douglas. In October 1859, he visited John Brown at Harpers Ferry. He publicly declared on April 20, 1861, that the Union had no right to coerce the South into the Union, and became a leading Copperhead. In April 13, 1863, General Burnside, commander of the Military Department of Ohio issued Order No. 38, which prohibited expressions of sympathy for the enemy. In a speech on April 30th, Vallandigham made derogatory references to Lincoln and the war effort, and was arrested the same night. He was convicted by a military court and sentenced to two years in prison. Lincoln, concerned about making him a martyr, commuted the sentence to banishment to Tennessee. Vallandigham made his way to Canada and, from there, ran for governor of Ohio, losing 288,000 to 187,000. He is best remembered by a Supreme Court case in February 1864, *Ex parte Vallandigham*. He accidentally killed himself while defending a client charged with murder.

Daniel Wolsey Voorhees (1827–1897). Of the Indiana bar. Graduated from Indiana Asbury University (now DePauw University), and admitted in 1850. Practiced law in Indiana and served as U.S. district attorney for Indiana, 1858–60. Member of the U.S. House 1861–66 and 1869–73, and later served in the U.S. Senate 1877–97. Voorhees was defense counsel in 1859 for John A. Cook, who was charged with murder as a member of the Brown raid on Harpers Ferry. Cook was the brother of the wife of the governor of Indiana.

Benjamin Wade (1800–1878). Of the Ohio Bar. Admitted in 1828, and practiced with Joshua Giddings in Ohio; he served as a state judge 1847–51, and served in the U.S. Senate, first as a Whig then a Republican, 1851–69. During the War, Wade was chairman of the Joint Committee on the Conduct of the War. He was nicknamed "the bulldog" due to his appearance and personality. A leader of the Radical Republicans in Congress, he was the cosponsor of a bill in 1864 to establish provisional governments in the seceded states, and to bar CSA officials from participating. Lincoln vetoed the bill. In 1868, Wade voted to impeach Johnson. He was president pro tempore of the Senate during the Johnson administration, and since Johnson did not have a vice president, Wade would have become president had Johnson died. He lost his reelection for the Senate in 1868, and resumed his law practice in Jefferson, Ohio.

Lewis Wallace (1827–1905). Of the Indiana bar. He was born in Indiana, where his father later become governor. Served in the Mexican War. He was admitted to practice in 1849, and in 1856 was elected to the Indiana state senate. During the Civil War, he rose to major general, and was a member of the military commission that tried the Lincoln assassination conspirators. He then served as president of the commission that tried CSA Captain Wirz. Wallace served as governor of the New Mexico Territory in 1878; he was appointed U.S. minister in Istanbul at Ottoman Sultan Abdul Hamid II's court in 1881 and served there for four years. He is most well known for his novels, including *Ben-Hur, A Tale of the Christ* (1880), one of the most popular novels of the nineteenth century.

Daniel Webster (1782–1852). Of the New Hampshire and Massachusetts bars. He was born in New Hampshire and graduated from Dartmouth. He was admitted in 1805 and practiced in Portsmouth. He was elected to the House as a Federalist, 1813–17, but was defeated for reelection. Webster moved to Boston and established a successful constitutional law practice. He served again in the House, 1816–24, and was elected to the Senate in 1827. Webster supported Jackson in the nullification crisis, but later became a Whig. He resigned from the Senate in 1841 to become secretary of state under Harrison and Tyler. He returned to the Senate in 1844 and there supported the Compromise of 1850. Webster was Fillmore's secretary of state, 1850–52.

William Whiting (1813–1873). Of the Massachusetts bar. Whiting was born in Concord, Massachusetts, attended Harvard, and then taught in Concord. He graduated from the law department of Harvard in 1838 and was admitted the same year. He practiced in Boston until he served as solicitor of the War Department, 1862–65. Whiting served briefly as a Republican in the House in 1873.

Waitman Thomas Willey (1811–1900). Of the Virginia and West Virginia bars. He was admitted in 1833 and practiced in Morgantown, Virginia, and was later appointed clerk of the circuit superior court for Monongalia County. Willey was a delegate to the Constitutional Union party convention in 1860 that nominated Bell. He was elected by the Restored Government of Virginia to the U.S. Senate, filling the vacant seat of James M. Mason. Upon the admission of West Virginia in 1863, Willey was elected U.S. senator from West Virginia, and then was reelected, serving from 1863 to 1871, after which he again became clerk of the county court of Monongalia County, West Virginia.

William Wirt (1772–1834). Of the Virginia and Maryland bars. Born in Maryland, Wirt was privately educated and was admitted to the Virginia bar in 1792. Jefferson asked him to be the prosecutor at the treason trial of Aaron Burr in 1807. In 1816, he wrote a biography of Patrick Henry. President Monroe appointed Wirt Attorney General in 1817, and he served for twelve years through the John Quincy Adams' administration—the longest tenure of any Attorney General. In 1830, he defended Cherokee rights before the Supreme Court (cited by Taney in the *Dred Scott* case). In 1832, at the nation's first political party nominating convention, Wirt became the presidential nominee for the third party, the American (or Anti-Masonic) Party. He won only one state (Vermont). He then practiced law. Future Chief Justice Salmon P. Chase tutored Wirt's children in exchange for Wirt's legal direction. (In the 1970s, his skull was stolen from the Wirt Tomb at the Congressional Cemetery in Washington, but it was restored in 2005.)

Henry Alexander Wise (1806–1876). Of the Virginia and Tennessee bars. Attended Washington College (now Washington & Jefferson College) in Pennsylvania, and was admitted to the Virginia bar in Winchester in 1828, but then practiced law in Nashville, Tennessee, for two years. Returning to Virginia, he served in the U.S. House of Representatives from 1833 to 1844. President Tyler appointed him minister to France in 1843, but he failed Senate confirmation. Served as minister to Brazil, 1844–47. Governor of Virginia, 1856–60. He was opposed to secession and the plantation system. Last act as governor was to sign John Brown's death warrant. At February 1861 Virginia State convention, he sought compromise. During War was a brigadier general. (Wise's sister was married to General George Meade, who commanded Union forces at Gettysburg. Wise surrendered to his brother-in-law at Appomattox Court House.) Returned to law practice in Richmond after the War. In 1878, wrote a biography of President Tyler. Counties in Texas and in Virginia are named for him. His great-great-grandson directs the new Civil War Museum in Richmond.

Andrew Wylie (1814–1905). Of the Pennsylvania and Virginia bars. Wylie was born in Pennsylvania, studied law at Transylvania University in Kentucky, and was admitted to the bar in 1837. He practiced in Pittsburgh until 1848 when he opened an office in Washington. He served as a justice of the supreme court of the District of Columbia, 1863–85. He issued the writ of habeas corpus in July 1865 for Mary Surratt, which President Johnson suspended. Wylie served as the judge in the second trial of John Surratt in 1868, and dismissed the charges against Surratt.

His obituary in the *Washington Post* in 1905 recalled his role in the Mary Surratt matter, but failed to mention his role in the trial of her son.

William Lowndes Yancey (1814–1863). Of the Georgia and Alabama bars. Attended Williams College. He was admitted to the Georgia bar in 1834, but two years later moved to Alabama where, in 1839, he resumed practice in Alabama and served in the state legislature. In 1845, he was elected to the U.S. House of Representatives. He was the prime author of the Alabama Ordinance of Secession, and he introduced Jefferson Davis as the president of the new CSA in Montgomery, Alabama, in February 1861. Yancey was the leading "fire-eater." He led the unsuccessful Confederate diplomatic effort in Europe in early 1861. Elected as CSA senator in February 1862, Yancey turned his attention to blocking the enabling legislation to establish a CSA Supreme Court, as a violation of states rights. He died in Alabama in July 1863 of a kidney ailment.

APPENDIX 2

Intersecting Lawyers

Many of the lawyers of the Civil War period had known each other professionally, having tried cases together or against each other. Here are more than a dozen examples.

1) A case originated in Ohio involving fugitive slaves. A civil suit was brought against Van Zandt, a conductor on the Underground Railroad, for the statutory penalty of five hundred dollars, alleging that Van Zandt had harbored and concealed slaves who had escaped from Kentucky to Ohio, where Van Zandt had driven them in his covered wagon. This case was the first opportunity for abolitionists to directly challenge the fugitive slave provision in the Constitution. Van Zandt's lawyers were **Salmon P. Chase** and **William H. Seward**. (Chase's brief was more than a hundred pages, and Seward's was forty pages, the Court noted.) The Supreme Court on March 5, 1847, decided 9–0 against Chase and Seward. *Jones v. Van Zandt*, 46 U.S. (5 How.) 215 (1847). Chase's brief put him in the national spotlight, and he became known as the "Attorney General for Fugitive Slaves."

2) In the summer of 1855, a nationally famous patent infringement trial took place in Ohio, the "Reaper" trial, *McCormick v. Manny*. The leading patent lawyer from Philadelphia, **George Harding**, represented the defendant, Manny. Harding brought in **Edwin Stanton**, who at that time practiced in Pittsburgh.

Harding also brought in **Abraham Lincoln** when he thought the case might be tried in Illinois. Harding's young associate, **Peter Watson**, went to Springfield to enlist Lincoln. Watson later became Stanton's secret intermediary for discussions with Seward during the last days of the Buchanan administration. Lincoln stayed in the same hotel in Cincinnati with Harding and Stanton, and Stanton was very discourteous to Lincoln. **Reverdy Johnson** was one of the attorneys for McCormick. Later, Lincoln appointed Harding to head the Patent Office, and Lincoln got Harding's help in enlisting Stanton to become secretary of war.

3) **Abraham Lincoln** regularly practiced law before Justice **John McLean** in the federal courts in Springfield and Chicago. Lincoln gave McLean his support during the 1856 Republican Party Convention, but John Fremont secured more votes on the first ballot and McLean withdrew. Lincoln was a candidate for vice president at the same convention, but he too lost. McLean wrote one of the two dissents the following year in the *Dred Scott* case.

4) In the famous 1857 *Dred Scott* case, **Montgomery Blair** was counsel for Scott, and **Reverdy Johnson** was counsel for Scott's owners. Lincoln's Attorney General **Edward Bates'** brother-in-law was a justice on the Missouri Supreme Court when that court decided the *Dred Scott* case, the appeal from which went to the Supreme Court. Bates' brother-in-law wrote the dissenting opinion in the Missouri case.

5) In the mid-1850s, there was tough competition between the railroads and the steamboats, and this often led to litigation. In 1857, the case of *Hurd v. Railroad Bridge Company*—involving the problem of railroad bridges across the Mississippi River impeding the passage of steamboats—reached the U.S. circuit court in Chicago. **Abraham Lincoln** represented the railroad bridge company, and he argued that railroads were at least as important as steamboats, and were invaluable when the river froze. The jurors deadlocked. A parallel case took place in Iowa, where a steamboat owner hired **Samuel F. Miller** to bring a case against the railroad arguing that the railroad bridge was an obstacle to steamboat traffic. Miller brought suit in the federal court in Iowa, and the judge agreed, ordering that the bridge be torn down. The railroad appealed, and the case went to the Supreme Court in 1862, when Miller was a Justice appointed by Lincoln. (Miller recused himself from the Supreme Court's

decision.) The Court, filled with former railroad lawyers, overturned the Iowa decision and held for the railroads. *Mississippi & Missouri Railroad Company v. Ward.*

6) The trial in Washington of Congressman Dan Sickles for the murder of **Philip Barton Key** (Chief Justice Taney's nephew, Francis Scott Key's son, and the D.C. district attorney) was held April 4 through April 26, 1859. Among Sickles' eight defense counsel were **Reverdy Johnson** (the winning counsel in the *Dred Scott* case), **Edwin M. Stanton** (became secretary of war in early 1862), and **James T. Brady** (in October 1861 was successful defense counsel of the crew of the *Savannah*, and in 1867 was a leading member of the defense team for Jefferson Davis).

7) In January 1860, the case of *Lemmon v. The People* was argued before the full eight-judge bench of the New York Court of Appeals. The case dealt with whether slaves held by a Virginian who was traveling through New York City en route to Texas should be freed or whether their slave status had to be respected by New York. Arguing for the slaves was **William M. Evarts**. He was assisted by a junior lawyer, **Chester A. Arthur** (later the twenty-first U.S. president). Representing the Virginian slaveholder was **Charles O'Conor**, who later was counsel for Jefferson Davis, who was prosecuted for treason by **Evarts**. The court decided, 5–3, for the freedom of the slaves. The case was appealed to the U.S. Supreme Court, but the Civil War intervened.

8) On December 3, 1860, a committee was formed of the members of the Supreme Court Bar. **Jefferson Davis** was the chair. **Edwin M. Stanton** (then Attorney General) moved that a committee be appointed by the chair to prepare resolutions marking the death of Justice Daniel. Davis appointed **James Mason**. The next day, at the opening of the Court, Stanton spoke about the late Justice Daniel and offered the resolutions of the Mason Committee; **Chief Justice Taney** replied to Stanton with his own laudatory remarks about Daniel. Such were the dignified proceedings of the Court.

9) The two central lawyers in the 1861 New York piracy trial of the crew of the CSA privateer, the *Savannah*, were **William M. Evarts**—brought into the case by the government to strengthen the prosecution—and **James T. Brady**, whose defense co-counsel were Daniel Lord and Algernon S. Sullivan. The result was a hung jury.

10) In connection with the Supreme Court cases consolidated as the *Prize Cases* in 1863, **William M. Evarts** represented the owners of one vessel (the *Hiawatha*), and **Richard Dana** represented the *Amy Warwick*. They argued the cases together. After the War, they both prepared the indictment of Jefferson Davis.

11) The last serious effort to end the Civil War took place on a steamer, the *River Queen*, near Hampton Roads, Virginia, on February 3, 1865. The delegates were as follows: for the United States, President **Lincoln** and Secretary of State **Seward**; for the CSA, Vice President **Alexander H. Stephens**, Senator **Robert M. T. Hunter**, and Assistant Secretary of War **John A. Campbell**. All five were lawyers.

12) The arguments in the Supreme Court in 1866 in the case of *Ex parte Milligan* must have been exciting since the case related to the death sentence of an antiwar lawyer-politician, Lambdin P. Milligan. Successfully defending Milligan were **James A. Garfield**, a young lawyer from Ohio who was arguing his first Supreme Court case and was at the same time a congressman from Ohio (and later a U.S. president); **Jeremiah S. Black** (Attorney General and secretary of state under Buchanan); **Joseph E. McDonald** (former Attorney General of Indiana, and later a U.S. senator); and **David Dudley Field** (a very successful New York lawyer whose brother, **Stephen Field**, sat on the Supreme Court). Leading the losing side was the Attorney General **James Speed** and the infamous Massachusetts lawyer and former political general **Benjamin Butler**. Garfield and Chief Justice **Salmon P. Chase**, both from Ohio, played chess together.

13) The prosecution of Jefferson Davis engaged the talents of many of the great lawyers of the day. Davis's main lawyer was **Charles O'Conor**, but he was assisted at various times by **Jeremiah Black** (Attorney General and secretary of state under Buchanan) and **Reverdy Johnson**. The chief prosecutor was **William Evarts** (who then became Johnson's Attorney General) and **Richard Dana**.

14) During the later part of the War, a Catholic priest in Missouri refused to take a loyalty oath or to cease being a priest. He was fined and sent to jail. In March 1866, **Reverdy Johnson**, **Montgomery Blair**, and **David Dudley Field** argued in the Supreme Court in defense of the priest from Missouri. The Court decided the case of *Cummings v. Missouri* on January 14, 1867, in favor of the priest. The decision was 5–4, with **Justice**

Stephen Johnson Field (David's brother and former law partner) writing for the Court, and the four Republican Justices in dissent.

15) Former Supreme Court Justice **Benjamin R. Curtis**, who wrote the sharp dissent in the *Dred Scott* case, and who later attacked Lincoln over the Emancipation Proclamation, was co-counsel with **Andrew Hunter**, who was the Virginia special prosecutor in the John Brown case in the lawsuit by Virginia against West Virginia to reclaim jurisdiction over Berkeley and Jefferson Counties, *Virginia v. West Virginia* in 1866 and 1870. The opposing counsel was **Reverdy Johnson**.

APPENDIX 3

Chronology

1565: In what is now Florida, Spanish settlers held African slaves.

1619: First Africans imported and sold as slaves at Jamestown, Virginia.

1707: Union Treaty between England and Scotland.

1772: June 22, Lord Mansfield delivers his opinion in *Somerset v. Stewart*, which concluded that a slave brought into England could be set free.

1776: The Declaration of Independence.

1777: Vermont's Constitution outlaws slavery, the first in the hemisphere to do so. The Articles of Confederation are adopted by the Second Continental Congress.

1779: Sir Henry Clinton offers "security" to slaves of American rebels if they cross into British lines.

1780: Pennsylvania adopts a gradual emancipation law.

1781: March: the Articles of Confederation are formally ratified.

1784: Connecticut and Rhode Island enact gradual emancipation laws.

1787: The U.S. Constitution is adopted, providing that three-fifths of a state's slave population may be counted in apportioning representation. Congress is forbidden from ending the slave trade until 1808, and from requiring that fugitive slaves who cross state lines be surrendered to their owners.

1788: June 21, the Constitution comes into force when the ninth state (New Hampshire) ratifies.

1791: The first Bill to abolish the slave trade is introduced into the British Parliament.

1794: The Whiskey Rebellion. An excise tax on distilled spirits was resisted throughout the western frontier, south of New York. On August 7th, President Washington issued a proclamation calling up thirteen thousand militiamen to suppress the rebellion in the western counties of Pennsylvania. On July 10, 1795, Washington issued a pardon to those insurgents arrested but not yet indicted or sentenced.

Eli Whitney invents the cotton gin.

1799: New York State adopts a law for gradual emancipation. Rice production in South Carolina peaks, but soon ebbs as cotton begins to boom.

1802: Napoleon restores both slavery and the slave trade.

1803: Some Federalists in New England threaten secession if the Louisiana Purchase Territory is incorporated into the Union without the approval of every state.

Lower Canada (present-day Quebec and the Maritime Provinces) abolishes slavery.

1804: New Jersey adopts a law for gradual emancipation.

1807: February 23, the British Parliament votes, 283 to 16, to end British participation in the slave trade; the Act passes on March 25th to become effective May 1, 1807.

Chronology

March 7, President Jefferson signs into law the ban on slave trade, effective in 1808.

1812: Beginning of war with Great Britain.

1814: The "Hartford Convention" meets in secret until January 4, 1815, and impliedly advocates the secession of New England. Upper Canada (present-day Ontario) abolishes slavery.

1816: The American Colonization Society is formed.

1817: New York adopts a law that will free all remaining slaves in 1827.

1820: The Missouri Compromise. Missouri was admitted as a slave state, but slavery was prohibited elsewhere in the Louisiana Purchase territory above 36 degrees 36 minutes of latitude; Maine was admitted at the same time, preserving North/South equality in the Senate. South Carolina produces half of the nation's cotton crop.

1821: Opinion of Attorney General Wirt that free persons of color in Virginia are not citizens of the United States.

1822: Charleston is rocked by an ambitious, but thwarted, slave rebellion organized by freed slave Denmark Vesey.

1823: December 2, the Monroe Doctrine is proclaimed.

1827: Lord Stowell delivers his opinion in *The Slave, Grace*, which concludes that a slave who had returned to the British Colony of Antigua had not been emancipated by her stay in England.

1828: Congress enacts the "Tariff of Abomination" benefiting Northern industry, prompting John C. Calhoun to write the principles of nullification.

1830: The Webster-Hayne debate in the Senate on the nature of the Constitution.

1831: August: Nat Turner's rebellion in Southampton, Virginia, sends shock waves through the South: sixty-four whites and more than one hundred slaves are killed.

Revolt by slaves in Jamaica.

1832: December 10, President Andrew Jackson issues his proclamation denouncing South Carolina's attempt at nullification and secession following the high Tariff Acts of 1828 and 1833.

1833: March 2, Congress enacts the Force Bill, authorizing President Jackson to use force to suppress South Carolina.

Slaves Thornton and Lucie Blackburn escape from Detroit to Upper Canada, but the territorial governor of Michigan is refused their extradition, thus firmly establishing Canada as the terminus of the Underground Railroad.

1834: August 1, Britain abolishes slavery in all its colonies, with compensation to owners and an apprenticeship period for slaves.

1837: The Panic produces bankruptcies nationwide.

1839: The *Amistad* slave ship is brought into the United States.

1841: The *Amistad* case is decided by the Supreme Court, after arguments by former President Adams. The *Creole* mutiny involving slaves from Virginia freed in the British colony of the Bahamas.

1845: President Tyler signs the Congressional Joint Resolution to admit Texas to the Union as a slave state on March 1.

1846: April, Dred Scott's lawyers file papers in a Missouri court in St. Louis for his freedom.

1846–48: War between the United States and Mexico. Sweden, France, and Denmark abolish slavery in their colonies.

1847: In the *Van Zandt* case, the Supreme Court unanimously affirms the constitutionality of the fugitive slave laws. Chase and Seward serve as counsel on the losing abolitionists' side.

1849: Congressman Lincoln proposes the termination of slavery in the District of Columbia. Lincoln also argues before the Supreme Court, and loses; the Court's opinion is written by Chief Justice Taney.

1850: In June, delegates from nine slaveholding states meet in convention in Nashville to consider what course to take if the United States decides to ban slavery from the territories.

In September, the Compromise of 1850 is enacted by Congress: California is admitted as a free state, enactment of a strengthened Fugitive Slave Law, and the slave trade is abolished in the District of Columbia.

Brazil, under British pressure, stops African slave imports.

1851: September 11, the Christiana Riot in Pennsylvania, which led to the largest treason trial in U.S. history, involving the Fugitive Slave Act of 1850.

1852: Publication of Harriet Beecher Stowe's book, *Uncle Tom's Cabin*, which she wrote in furious reaction to the Fugitive Slave Act of 1850 (part of the Compromise of 1850), and which had first appeared in serial form the preceding year.

March 22, the Missouri Supreme Court decides that Dred Scott is still a slave.

1853: Anglo-American Commission awards $110,330 to the United States for the loss of its slave property in the *Creole* affair.

November, Dred Scott files case in federal court.

1854: May 30, the Kansas-Nebraska Act becomes law, establishing the territories of Kansas and Nebraska, leaving the question of slavery to the decision of the territorial settlers—thereby repealing the Compromise of 1850.

October 4, Lincoln's first great antislavery speech at annual Springfield State Fair, following Illinois Senator Stephen Douglas.

December 30, the *Dred Scott* case is filed with the U.S. Supreme Court.

1855: Summer, *McCormick v. Manny*, the "Reaper" patent lawsuit in Cincinnati with Stanton, Lincoln, Harding, and Reverdy Johnson.

1856: April 18   The Declaration of Paris outlaws privateering, but the United States does not sign.

May 22 Congressman Preston Brooks, the cousin of South Carolina Senator Andrew Butler who had authored the Kansas-Nebraska Act of 1854, beats with a cane on the Senate floor abolitionist Senator Charles Sumner. Sumner had verbally attacked Butler for having taken "the harlot Slavery" as a mistress.

May 24 The Potawatomie Creek Massacre. John Brown and his sons kill five proslavery settlers in Kansas.

November Buchanan wins (174–114–8 electoral votes); Fremont (first nominee of the new Republican Party) and Fillmore garner more popular votes than Buchanan, who gains only 45 percent of the popular vote.

December 15 The *Dred Scott* case is reargued in the Supreme Court.

1857: March 4 James Buchanan is sworn in as president by Chief Justice Taney.

March 6 Dred Scott decision is read in the Supreme Court by Chief Justice Taney.

Economic Panic begins, perhaps the first global financial crisis.

1859: March 7 Unanimous Supreme Court decision announced in *Ableman v. Booth*; opinion by Chief Justice Taney holds that the Fugitive Slave Act of 1850 is constitutional, and that state judicial authorities have no authority to issue a writ of habeas corpus to remove someone from federal authority. Viewed by abolitionists as the end of hope for the constitutional argument against slavery.

April 4–26 The trial in Washington of Congressman Dan Sickles for the murder of Barton Key (Chief Justice Taney's nephew). He is defended by eight lawyers, including Reverdy Johnson, Edwin Stanton, and James T. Brady.

October 16–18 John Brown's raid on Harpers Ferry, Virginia.

October 26–31 John Brown's trial in Charles Town, Virginia.

November 19 John Brown's appeal to the Virginia Court of Appeals is denied.

December 2 John Brown hanged in a field south of Charles Town.

December 16 The first meeting of the "Mason Commission," the Senate Select Committee investigating the Harpers Ferry raid.

1860: January 24 Arguments begin at the New York Court of Appeals in the *Lemmon* case.

February 27 Lincoln's Cooper Union speech.

March New York Court of Appeals decides 5–3 that Lemmon slaves are free.

March–June First use of compulsory process of the Senate in jailing a nonappearing witness in the Mason Commission.

May 3 Democratic Convention in Charleston, South Carolina, adjourns after Deep South delegates withdraw over slavery plank.

May 9 Constitutional Union Party nominates John Bell of Tennessee for president.

May 16 Republican Party Convention in Chicago; Lincoln nominated; platform declared that slavery in the territories is unconstitutional.

June 15 Report of the Senate Select Committee on the Harpers Ferry raid, the "Mason Report."

June 22, 23 Deep South delegates again withdraw from Convention in Baltimore; "Regular" Democrats nominate Stephen A. Douglas and the Southern wing nominates John C. Breckinridge.

November 6 Lincoln is elected with slightly more than one-third of the popular vote, defeating Douglas, Breckinridge, and Bell.

November 14 Alexander Stephens addresses the Georgia legislature urging against secession, i.e., the mere election of Lincoln does not legitimize secession.

November 20 Attorney General Black issues his formal Opinion on the power of the president to respond to secession.

November 30 Mississippi legislature passes resolutions in favor of secession.

December 2 President Buchanan presents his last State of the Union message to the second session of the (lame duck) Thirty-eighth Congress.

December 18 Crittenden Compromise is introduced in Congress.

December 20 South Carolina formally rescinds its ratification of the U.S. Constitution and secedes by a vote of 169–0 during a convention in Charleston.

December 26 Major Anderson moves the garrison in Charleston from Fort Moultrie to Fort Sumter.

December 27 Castle Pinckney and Fort Moultrie in Charleston harbor are seized by South Carolina.

December 28 Buchanan receives Commissioners Barnwell, Orr, and Adams from South Carolina, but as "private gentlemen."

December 29 Resignation of John B. Floyd of Virginia as secretary of war.

December 30 South Carolina troops seize the federal arsenal at Charleston.

1861: January 3 Georgia seizes Fort Pulaski.

January 4–5 Alabama seizes U.S. arsenal at Mount Vernon and seizes Forts Morgan and Gaines.

January 6–8 Florida seizes Apalachicola arsenal and Fort Marion, and is unsuccessful in its attempt to seize Fort Barrancas. Resignation of Jacob Thompson of Mississippi as secretary of the interior.

January 6 New York Mayor Fernando Wood proposes in his State of the State address that the city secede, and be named Trinsula.

January 8 Buchanan sends Special Message to Congress.

January 9 Mississippi secedes. The *Star of the West*, conveying relief to Fort Sumter, is fired on at the entrance to Charleston harbor and is turned back.

January 10 Florida secedes.

January 11 Alabama secedes.

January 10–14 Louisiana seizes U.S. arsenal at Baton Rouge and Forts Jackson and St. Philip; seizes U.S. Marine Hospital near New Orleans, and Fort Pike.

January 19 Georgia secedes.

January 21 Senator Jefferson Davis delivers his farewell speech in the U.S. Senate.

January 26 Louisiana secedes.

February 1 Texas secedes.

February 4 Meeting in Washington of a Peace Conference, representing thirteen Free and seven Border States, called at the request of the Virginia legislature and presided over by former President Tyler. Convention of seceded states meets in Montgomery, Alabama.

February 5 President Buchanan nominates Attorney General Black to the Supreme Court. Confirmation fails, 25–26.

February 8 Provisional Constitution of the CSA adopted in Montgomery, Alabama, by delegates from six seceded states; Arkansas seizes U.S. arsenal at Little Rock.

February 9 Davis and Stephens elected by the Provisional Congress. February 13, Lincoln and Hamlin officially declared elected.

February 15 Toronto court refuses to extradite the former slave John Anderson, being the last Canadian extradition slave case.

February 18 All U.S. military posts in Texas are surrendered to the state authorities by General David Twiggs. Jefferson Davis is inaugurated CSA president at Montgomery, Alabama.

February 23 Lincoln arrives in Washington.

February 25 Lincoln pays a courtesy call to the Supreme Court Justices in their chamber in the Capitol.

February 27 The Washington Peace Conference closes with proposed amendments to the Constitution.

February 28 The U.S. House adopts (133–65) an amendment offered by the Select Committee of Thirty-three (appointed by the House on December 6, 1860) forbidding any interference by Congress with slavery in the states.

March 2 The Senate adopts (24–12) the proposed Thirteenth Constitutional Amendment offered by the Committee of Thirty-three. Texas is admitted as a member of the CSA.

March 4 Lincoln is sworn in by Chief Justice Taney as sixteenth president, and delivers his inaugural address.

March 11 At the end of a month-long convention in Montgomery, Alabama, the seven Lower South States form the CSA, adopt its final Constitution, and elect Jefferson Davis and Alexander H. Stephens.

March 15 Justice Campbell of Alabama and Justice Nelson of New York meet to seek resolution of the Fort Sumter crisis.

March 16 Lincoln transmits to the states the proposed Thirteenth Amendment.

March 21 Cornerstone speech by CSA Vice President Alexander H. Stephens in Savannah, Georgia.

April 12–14 Fort Sumter is bombed and then surrenders.

April 15 Lincoln issues a proclamation calling for the states to supply seventy-five thousand soldiers.

April 17 Virginia adopts Ordinance of Secession, subject to popular vote. CSA President Jefferson Davis's proclamation calls for letters of marque.

April 18 U.S. armory and arsenal at Harpers Ferry are abandoned and the arsenal is burned. Pennsylvania troops change trains in Baltimore in presence of large crowds.

April 19 Lincoln proclaims blockade of the coastline of six Southern states; in Baltimore, the "Pratt Street Riot/Massacre" involving the 6th Massachusetts Volunteer Militia.

April 25 Lincoln orders Lieutenant General Winfield Scott to monitor the Maryland legislature, and if necessary to bombard and to suspend the writ of habeas corpus.

April 27 Lincoln extends the blockade from Virginia to the Mexican border. Separately, Lincoln authorizes General Scott to suspend the writ of habeas corpus along the military line between Philadelphia and Washington.

April 29 Jefferson Davis's Message to the Provisional Congress of the CSA, outlines the case for secession.

May 6 Arkansas secedes. CSA Congress passes Act Recognizing the Existence of War between the United States and the Confederate States of America, and concerning letters of marque.

May 7 Virginia admitted as a member of the CSA.

May 10 Lincoln's first publicly announced suspension by proclamation of the writ of habeas corpus, relating to the Florida coast.

May 13 Baltimore is occupied by General Butler. The first Wheeling Convention in western Virginia. Queen Victoria issues her Proclamation of Neutrality, treating the CSA as a belligerent power.

May 15 Brevet Major General Cadwalader of the Pennsylvania militia supersedes General Butler in the Department of Annapolis.

May 17 The *Crenshaw*, the first vessel seized under the blockade, is captured at Hampton Roads; its case is combined with seizures to form the *Prize Cases* at the Supreme Court.

May 18 The first CSA letter of marque is granted, to the *Savannah*.

May 20 North Carolina secedes, the last of the Southern states; ironically, North Carolina lost more men, proportionately, during the War than any other. Confederate Congress decides to move the CSA capital from Montgomery to Richmond. General Butler is assigned to Fort Monroe.

May 23 Virginia formally ratifies its Ordinance of Secession.

May 24 General Benjamin F. Butler declares "contraband of war" at Fort Monroe. At two o'clock in the morning, fourteen thousand Union troops cross the Potomac River into Virginia to occupy the Custis Lee Mansion, Arlington, and to occupy Alexandria, Virginia. Resolutions of mediation and neutrality are adopted by Kentucky.

May 25 John Merryman is arrested and imprisoned at Fort McHenry.

May 26–28 Justice Taney issues writ of habeas corpus, holds hearing, issues writ of attachment, and announces decision in *Merryman*.

May 29 Richmond becomes the capital of the CSA.

May 30 Ben Butler receives approval from Secretary of War Cameron for his contraband policy.

June 1 Taney dispatches to Lincoln his written opinion in *Merryman*.

June 4 The CSA *Savannah* is captured by the Union Navy.

June 6 Brigadier General Henry A. Wise (of the CSA army) is ordered to command in western Virginia.

June 8 Tennessee secedes, the last of the four states of the Upper South.

June 11 Unionist delegates from twenty-six counties meet at the Second Wheeling Convention and establish a "Restored" Government of Virginia, and select a governor and two senators.

July 2 Lincoln authorizes General Scott to suspend the writ of habeas corpus along the military line between New York City and Washington.

July 4 Secretary of War Cameron visits Fort McHenry and interviews Merryman.

July 5 Lincoln's Message to Congress is read.

July 5 Attorney General Bates issues Opinion on *Merryman*.

July 6 Jefferson Davis writes to Lincoln concerning the prisoners from the *Savannah*.

July 12 Merryman is released from Fort McHenry to civil authorities in Baltimore.

July 21 The first battle, First Manassas/Bull Run (CSA victory) in Northern Virginia.

July 22 The prize crew from the *Jefferson Davis* is captured aboard the *Enchantress*.

July 25 John Merryman is released on bond to return home.

August 6 Congress enacts the first Confiscation Act, which frees fugitive slaves who had been employed in the CSA war effort.

August 24 CSA President Davis appoints Mason and Slidell as Special Commissioners (ambassadors) to the UK and France.

August 30 General John C. Fremont frees the slaves of pro-Confederate owners in Missouri by issuing his Order of Martial Law; CSA Congress enacts Sequestration Act.

September 7 Secretary of State Seward orders the arrest of Algermon Sullivan, lawyer for the privateers in the New York piracy trial.

September 11 Lincoln orders Fremont to modify his slavery order.

October Spain, Britain, and France decide to launch a joint occupation of the Mexican Gulf coast to force repayment of Mexican debts; in November, troops from the three nations land in Veracruz.

October 23 The trial of the officers and crew of the *Savannah* opens in the U.S. Circuit Court in New York before Supreme Court Justice Nelson and District Court Judge Shipman.

October 24 A referendum in western Virginia approves the prior acts of the Conventions.

October 25 A jury in the U.S. District Court for the Eastern District of Pennsylvania convicts William Walton Smith and his crew of piracy for his part as prize-master of the *Enchantress*.

November 9 The *San Jacinto* (Captain Charles Wilkes) stops and boards the British mail steamer *The Trent* and takes James A. Mason and John Slidell as prisoners.

December 1 Secretary Cameron issues his report on slaves of rebels.

December 3 Lincoln's first State of the Union message.

December 11 Congress adopts resolution requesting Lincoln to arrange for prisoner exchanges.

December 18 The British envoy in Washington (Lord Lyons) receives instructions to demand an apology and release of Mason and Slidell, and, if an apology is not received, he is to leave the United States.

December 25 Cabinet meeting at which Lincoln decides to release Mason and Slidell.

1862: January 1   Mason and Slidell leave Boston, via Provincetown, and board the HMS *Rinaldo* bound for Southampton, England, and they arrive thirty days later.

February 18   The Third Wheeling Convention, which opened in November 1861, concludes and adopts a Constitution.

February 19   Congress enacts a law to ban "Coolie" trade.

February 22   Coinciding with Washington's birthday, Jefferson Davis is sworn in for a six-year term as president of the CSA in Richmond.

March 6   Lincolns sends Special Message to Congress urging support for states electing gradual compensated emancipation.

March 16   Congress enacts the law abolishing slavery in the District of Columbia with compensation to loyal owners.

April 10   Congress adopts joint resolution that the United States ought to cooperate with any state that adopts gradual emancipation, including funds.

April 16   Confederate Congress passes the first national Conscription Act in American history. Lincoln signs the District of Columbia's Compensated Emancipation Act freeing thirty-one hundred slaves, the only compensated emancipation.

May 9   General David Hunter declares all slaves in South Carolina, Georgia, and Florida free.

May 13   The Restored government of Virginia technically gives its assent to the creation of the new state of West Virginia.

May 19   Lincoln issues a proclamation denouncing General Hunter's general order freeing slaves, and pushing his own plan for gradual, compensated emancipation.

June 19   Congress prohibits slavery in the territories.

July   The Senate approves (23–15) the admission of West Virginia, but conditioned upon a change in the state constitution dealing with slavery.

July 12   Lincoln appeals to Border State congressmen to support gradual, compensated emancipation; two days later they reject the proposal.

Chronology

July 17 Lincoln signs the Second Confiscation Act, which frees all slaves of owners who support the CSA, authorizes the employment of freed slaves in the military effort, and authorizes provision for colonization.

July 21 Lincoln tells his cabinet that he intends to issue an emancipation proclamation.

August 22 Lincoln's letter to Horace Greeley.

September 3 Lincoln designates Joseph Holt to the new position of Judge Advocate General in the War Department.

September 17 Union "victory" at Antietam/Sharpsburg.

September 22 Lincoln issues the Preliminary Emancipation Proclamation.

September 24 Lincoln issues a proclamation suspending the writ of habeas corpus for all rebels, aiders and abettors, and draft resisters imprisoned by military authority.

November 4 Democrats gain in Northern off-year elections.

November 29 Attorney General Bates' Opinion on citizenship of free persons of color.

December 1 Lincoln submits his second annual Message to Congress, which focuses on gradual and compensated emancipation, and to that end, he proposes three amendments to the Constitution.

December 10 The House adopts (95–66) the bill for the admission of the new state of West Virginia.

December 27 Attorney General Bates' Opinion on West Virginia statehood.

December 31 Lincoln signs the West Virginia admission bill.

1863: January 1 Lincoln signs the Emancipation Proclamation.

February 10 Arguments begin in the Supreme Court on the *Prize Cases*.

February 17–18 The West Virginia Convention approves the change to its Constitution providing for gradual emancipation.

March 3 Congress authorizes the suspension of the writ of habeas corpus, and passes the Enrollment Act, which institutes a national draft.

March 10 The Supreme Court announces its 5 to 4 decision in the *Prize Cases*, an opinion written by Justice Robert C. Grier.

April 20 Lincoln issues a proclamation providing that West Virginia satisfied the requirement for a change in its constitution, and announcing its admission as a state in sixty days.

June 12 Lincoln writes to Erastus Corning of New York responding to charges of his abridgement of civil liberties.

June 20 West Virginia joins the Union as a new state.

July 1–3 The Battle of Gettysburg.

July 13–16 Anti-draft riots in New York City result in one hundred twenty deaths and $2 million in damages. Troops returning from Gettysburg are brought in to quell the violence.

July 30 Lincoln issues the Order of Retaliation in response to executions by the CSA of black Union soldiers and their white officers.

September 15 Lincoln issues a proclamation suspending habeas corpus in all cases where rebels, draft resisters, and aiders and abettors are held in military custody.

October 2 Trial opens in the San Francisco "Chapman Piracy" case.

December 16 Lincoln pardons Alfred Rubery as a gesture to British Member of Parliament John Bright.

1864: January 7 CSA General Patrick Cleburne proposes freeing numbers of slaves and enrolling many in the army and is met with staunch opposition.

January 11 The auction of the Custis-Lee Mansion (Arlington) is conducted, and the federal government is the sole bidder.

March 16 Arkansas ratifies its new constitution, which ends slavery.

April 8 The Senate debates and passes the Thirteenth Amendment by a vote of 38 to 6. (This was initially rejected by the House.)

Chronology 351

April 17 General-in-Chief Grant ends the prisoner exchange.

June 12 Ferdinand Maximilian Joseph, Archduke of Austria, is crowned Emperor of Mexico, under the control of Napoleon III and with the support of French troops.

June 15 Congress makes pay equal for black and white soldiers.

September 2 Atlanta falls to Union troops.

September 5 Louisiana ratifies its new constitution, which ends slavery.

October 5 Lambdin P. Milligan is arrested at his home in Indiana.

October 12 Chief Justice Taney dies in Washington at age 87.

November 1 A new Maryland state constitution takes effect, ending slavery.

November 7 Jefferson Davis proposes enrolling slaves in the military and freeing all who serve faithfully.

November 8 Lincoln is elected to a second term, winning 55 percent of the popular vote and 221–21 in the electoral college; large majorities of Republicans in both Houses.

December 6 Lincoln appoints Salmon P. Chase to be Chief Justice; Chase takes oath on December 15th. With Chase, Lincoln has now appointed five of the ten Justices (Noah H. Swayne, Samuel F. Miller, David Davis, Stephen J. Field, and Chase).

1865: January 11 The state constitutional convention in Missouri—Dred Scott's state—abolishes slavery.

January 23 The U.S. House of Representatives approves, by a vote of 119 to 56, the Thirteenth Amendment abolishing slavery.

February 1 Lincoln signs the joint resolution, submitting the proposed Thirteenth Amendment; Illinois is the first state to ratify the Thirteenth Amendment, abolishing slavery.

February 3 Lincoln meets with the Confederate peace commissioners aboard the *River Queen* to discuss preliminary terms of surrender.

February 20 The CSA House of Representatives authorizes slaves as soldiers.

February 22 Tennessee's state constitution is amended to abolish slavery.

April 2 The CSA government leaves Richmond and moves to Danville.

April 3 Richmond is captured.

April 4 Lincoln visits Richmond.

April 9 Lee's twenty-six-thousand-man army of Northern Virginia surrenders to Grant at Appomattox Court House.

April 14 Union forces reoccupy Fort Sumter; Lincoln is shot at Ford's Theater and dies the following morning.

April 17 Mary Surratt, Lewis Powell (the attacker of Secretary of State Seward), and Samuel Arnold are arrested.

April 20 Secretary of War Stanton turns over the assassination investigation to Joseph Holt and the Bureau of Military Justice.

April 24 Dr. Samuel Mudd is arrested.

April 26 John Wilkes Booth is shot at the Garrett farm in Virginia; David Herold is arrested. Congressman Benjamin Gwinn Harris is arrested at his home near Leonardtown, in southern Maryland, and is taken to the Old Capitol Prison.

April 28 Attorney General Speed renders his oral Opinion that the assassination conspirators should be tried by military commission.

May 1 President Johnson orders that the assassination conspirators be tried by military commission, not civilian criminal court.

May 2 The military trial of Congressman Harris begins.

May 4 Jefferson Davis in Washington, Georgia, in effect dissolves the government of the CSA. Lincoln is buried in Springfield, Illinois.

May 9 The trial of the eight assassination conspirators begins at the Old Arsenal Penitentiary.

May 10 Jefferson Davis is captured near Irwinville, Georgia.

May 13 The last land battle between sizable forces of the Civil War at Palmetto Ranch, Texas.

May 22 Jefferson Davis is imprisoned in a cell at Fort Monroe.

May 29 President Andrew Johnson grants amnesty and pardon to all who participated in "the existing rebellion" with a few exceptions.

May 31 President Johnson remits the sentence of Congressman Harris, who then returns to Congress.

June 16 Mary Surratt's lawyer, Reverdy Johnson, delivers his civil rights argument to the military commission that it has no jurisdiction.

June 29 The Hunter Commission trying the assassination conspirators goes into secret session to reach a decision.

July 5 The Hunter Commission presents the verdicts and sentences to President Johnson who approves them at once.

July 7 Four of the Lincoln co-conspirators are hanged, including Mary Surratt, the first woman executed in the United States.

August 23 Captain Henry Wirz, former commander of the prison at Andersonville, Georgia, is brought before the Wallace Military Commission.

October 24 The Wirz trial concludes.

November 10 Henry Wirz is hanged at the Old Capitol Prison.

December 9 John Surratt, Jr., joins the Papal Zouaves at the Vatican.

December 18 Secretary of State Seward issues a proclamation verifying that the legislatures of twenty-seven of the thirty-six states had ratified the Thirteenth Amendment, abolishing slavery throughout the United States. Georgia was the twenty-seventh, ratifying on December 6th.

December 21 A Senate resolution asks President Johnson why Jefferson Davis has not been brought to trial.

1866: April 3 Chief Justice Salmon P. Chase announces the unanimous decision of the Court in *Ex parte Milligan* in effect agreeing with Chief Justice Taney's decision in *Merryman*. (The formal opinion of the Court was not given until the opening of the following term on December 17, 1866.)

May 8 Jefferson Davis is indicted for treason in the federal court in Richmond.

August 20 President Andrew Johnson declares the end of the insurrection in Texas. Thus, the final peace proclamation officially ends the War.

1867: January 7 Representative James M. Ashley of Ohio introduces in the House a resolution of inquiry into high crimes of President Johnson leading to impeachment. (The Judiciary Committee decided impeachment was not warranted, Thirty-ninth Congress.)

February 18 John Surratt is delivered to the D.C. court for criminal trial.

May 1 The federal judge in Richmond issues a writ of habeas corpus, transferring Jefferson Davis from military control at Fort Monroe to civil court custody. Bail was arranged on May 13.

June 18 The criminal trial of John Surratt begins in a civilian court.

August 5 President Johnson writes to Secretary of War Stanton and demands his resignation. Stanton refuses, and a week later, Johnson suspends Stanton, transferring power to Grant.

August 10 John Surratt's jury in the first civilian criminal trial deadlocked 8–4 in favor of acquittal, and the jury is dismissed.

September 7 President Johnson issues a proclamation extending pardons to most people in the Confederacy.

1868: Mid-January The Senate Military Committee, on the basis of the Tenure of Office Act, overrules Johnson's suspension of Stanton.

February 21 President Johnson suspends Stanton again. Stanton locks himself in his office. Grant supports Stanton and puts armed guards around the War Department building.

February 25 The House, in a party-line vote of 126–47, impeaches President Johnson.

March President Johnson is tried in the Senate. Evarts is one of Johnson's defense counsel, and so the Jefferson Davis matter is again postponed.

May President Johnson is acquitted in the Senate.

May 26 Stanton resigns.

Chronology

June 22 John Surratt's second trial begins.

July 4 President Johnson issues a proclamation granting full pardon for the offense of treason, except for anyone under indictment.

July 28 The Fourteenth Amendment enters into force.

September 9 Federal Judge Boynton in Florida rejects the petition of Mudd, Arnold, and Spangler to release them in light of the *Ex parte Milligan* case.

November John Surratt is finally released from prison. The Democratic ticket of Horatio Seymour of New York and Francis Blair, Jr. is defeated, but carried eight states. Republicans retain their two-thirds majority in the House and their four-fifths majority in the Senate.

November 30 Lawyers for Jefferson Davis meet in Richmond with Chief Justice Chase and Judge Underwood; Richard Dana opposes.

December 5 The Richmond Circuit Court is divided on whether Jefferson Davis was exposed to double jeopardy.

December 25 President Johnson issues a proclamation for a general pardon for treason, without exception.

1869: February 8 President Johnson issues a full pardon for Dr. Mudd.

April 12th The U.S. Supreme Court decides *Texas v. White*, noting that succession was invalid.

December 20 Grant nominates Stanton as a U.S. Supreme Court Justice, and Stanton is confirmed 46–11.

December 24 Stanton dies.

1870: Spain passes a gradual emancipation act.

July Robert E. Lee meets with his lawyers to see whether Arlington can be regained. Lee dies in October.

1871: Brazil frees all children of slaves when they reach age 21.

1873: Mary Lee pays her final visit to Arlington in June, and she dies in November.

1874: George Washington Custis Lee petitions Congress to compensate him for the confiscation of Arlington.

1879: January 30 Custis Lee wins the trial in Alexandria Federal District Court.

1882: December 4 The Supreme Court holds 5–4 in *United States v. Lee* that the government illegally took the Arlington estate, and that title should be returned to George Washington Custis Lee.

1883: March 31 George Washington Custis Lee formally conveys title of Arlington to Robert Todd Lincoln.

1888: Brazil enacts immediate and uncompensated emancipation of all remaining slaves.

1948: The United Nations Universal Declaration of Human Rights prohibits slavery and the slave trade.

Notes

Introduction Notes

1. Two exceptions are ROBERT BRUCE MURRAY, LEGAL CASES OF THE CIVIL WAR (Stackpole Books 2003), and STEPHEN C. NEFF, JUSTICE IN BLUE AND GRAY (Harvard Univ. Press 2010). Both are fine books. But Murray's book concerns primarily Supreme Court decisions from the unsettled period just *after* the war, where the Court had an eye to the reconciliation of the American legal system. Neff's book tends to have a perspective of international law, especially the laws of war. Neither book treats the great legal issues that arose before the War but that contributed to the creation of the conflict: the *Dred Scott* decision and the trial of John Brown.

2. De Tocqueville noted that lawyers "form the superior political class and the most intellectual portion of society .... The American aristocracy is at the attorney's bar and on the judges' bench." ALEXIS DE TOCQUEVILLE, DEMOCRACY IN AMERICA (University of Chicago Press 2000), translated by Harvey C. Mansfield and Delba Winthrop, at p. 256.

3. The four who were *not* lawyers are George Washington, James Madison, William Harrison, and Zachary Taylor. The twelve who were lawyers are John Adams, Thomas Jefferson, James Monroe, John Quincy Adams, Andrew Jackson, Martin Van Buren, John Tyler, James Polk, Millard Fillmore, Franklin Pierce, James Buchanan, and Abraham Lincoln. See generally NORMAN GROSS, ed., AMERICA'S LAWYER-PRESIDENTS: FROM LAW OFFICE TO OVAL OFFICE (Northwestern Univ. Press 2004).

4. The five who *were* lawyers are Franklin D. Roosevelt, Richard Nixon, Gerald Ford, William Clinton, and Barack Obama. The nine presidents who were *not* lawyers are Herbert Hoover, Harry S. Truman, Dwight Eisenhower,

John F. Kennedy, Lyndon B. Johnson, Jimmy Carter, Ronald Reagan, George Herbert Walker Bush, and George W. Bush.

5. Mark E. Steiner, An Honest Calling: The Law Practice of Abraham Lincoln 26 (Northern Illinois Univ. Press 2006).

6. Congress is composed of 540 individuals, 435 from the states and five delegates and one resident commissioner. At the beginning of the One Hundred Eleventh Congress, 215 listed their occupations as public service/politics, 203 listed law, 202 listed business, and 94 listed education. This reflects a decrease in lawyers and an increase in public service compared with the One Hundred Ninth and One Hundred Tenth Congresses. There was some double-counting because some members listed more than one occupation. Jennifer E. Manning, *Membership of the 111th Congress: A Profile*, CRS Report for Congress R40086, at 2 (Congressional Research Service July 19, 2010).

7. This trend may change, at least if the top six candidates for the presidential nomination of both parties in late 2007 are any indication: Clinton, Obama, Edwards, Giuliani, Romney, and Thompson were all lawyers. And of course, in 2009, those who took the oath as president and vice president were both lawyers.

8. W. H. Brands, Andrew Jackson: His Life and Times 35 (Doubleday 2005).

9. Steiner, *supra* note 5, at 28.

10. Steiner, *supra* note 5, at 28.

11. Steiner, *supra* note 5, at 37.

12. On March 24, 1836, Lincoln was certified as a person of good moral character by a judge of the Circuit Court of Sangamon County. On September 9, 1836, a license to practice law was issued to Lincoln by two justices of the state supreme court. Lincoln later appeared before the clerk of the court and took the oath to support the Constitution. Finally, on March 1, 1837, when the license, with the oath endorsed, was presented to the clerk in accordance with a 1833 statute, Lincoln was formally "enrolled" as a lawyer licensed to practice in Illinois. *See* Albert A. Wolman, Lincoln Lawyer 23 (Carroll & Graf 1936).

13. Alexis de Tocqueville, Democracy in America, vol. I, 351 (Harvey C. Mansfield & Delba Winthrop trans. & eds., Univ. Chicago Press 2001).

14. Lawrence M. Friedman, *Law in Antebellum America*, in America's Lawyer-Presidents 51 (Norman Gross, ed., Northwestern Univ. Press 2004).

15. *See* Appendix 2, *Intersecting Lawyers*.

16. William Blackstone, Commentaries on the Laws of England (1765–1769). By the time of the Revolution, American land, family, and criminal law had drifted away from English concepts of tradition and precedent into instruments of adaptation and innovation. Morton Keeler, America's Three Regimes: A New Political History 19 (Oxford Univ. Press 2007).

17. Winston Churchill famously remarked about one of his political opponents: "He has all the virtues I dislike, and none of the vices I admire."

18. Kermit L. Hall, ed., The Oxford Companion to the Supreme Court of the Untied States 93, 165 (Oxford Univ. Press 1992).

19. De Tocqueville, *supra* note 13, at 252.

20. The secretary of state (Seward), the secretary of war (Stanton), the secretary of the treasury (Chase), the postmaster general (Blair), and the Attorney General (Bates) were all lawyers.

21. The minister to Britain was Charles Francis Adams, the minister to France was William Dayton, and the minister to Mexico was Thomas Corwin—all lawyers.

22. The five were President Lincoln, Secretary of State Seward, CSA Vice President Stephens, CSA Senator Hunter, and CSA Assistant Secretary of War (and former Supreme Court Justice) Campbell—all lawyers. The Conference was inspired by Francis Preston Blair with the notion of the Union and the CSA joining together to dislodge the French from Mexico, and in common cause they might forget their differences.

23. De Tocqueville wisely noted in his *Democracy in America* that there is "almost no political question in the United States that is not resolved sooner or later into a judicial question." ALEXIS DE TOCQUEVILLE, DEMOCRACY IN AMERICA 257 (Univ. Chicago Press 2000).

24. Hepburn v. Griswold, 75 U.S. (8 Wall.) 603 (1870). Legislation in February 1862 created "greenbacks," the first paper money issued by the United States. Before 1862, all debts—private and public—were paid in specie (silver or gold) or with bank notes redeemable in specie. The opinion of the Court upholding the law was written by Chief Justice Chase who had been secretary of the treasury in 1862; his portrait appeared on the face of the one dollar greenback.

25. The tax initially was levied on incomes above six hundred dollars per year at a time when the average annual income was less than two hundred dollars. Apart from simply raising funds for the War, the tax was also designed to raise money in a way that strengthened Northern economic, political, and social cohesion; buying war bonds, as Lincoln did personally, was important.

26. Pacific Ins. Co. v. Soule, 74 U.S. (7 Wall.) 433 (1869).

27. Selective Draft Law Cases, 245 U.S. 366 (1918). The governor of New York, Horatio Seymour, had tried to persuade Lincoln that the conscription law was unconstitutional, and vigorously and publicly attacked Lincoln over his implementation of the draft. In August 1863, Lincoln began writing a public paper that defended the constitutionality of the draft, but in the end, Lincoln decided not to complete his document. DAVID HERBERT DONALD, LINCOLN 450–51 (Simon & Schuster 1995).

28. For a discussion of the problem of Confederate guerrillas who led General Halleck to enlist Dr. Francis Lieber into drafting a code, see Daniel E. Sutherland, *The Missouri Guerrilla Hunt*, AMERICA'S CIVIL WAR, Sept. 2009, at 62–62. *See also* Daniel E. Sutherland, *Abraham Lincoln and the Guerrillas*, 42 QUARTERLY OF THE NATIONAL ARCHIVES & RECORDS ADMINISTRATION 20 (Spring 2010).

29. In the summer of 1862, Major General Henry Halleck became general-in-chief of the Union armies. Halleck was a lawyer—he had published a book on international law—and was troubled by the absence of legal guidelines for dealing with the Confederate forces, especially the irregulars. He invited Francis Lieber, a professor at Columbia College in New York, to prepare a code, and that resulted

in the April 24, 1863, publication of General Orders No. 100, "Instructions for the government of the Armies of the United States in the Field." In political terms, Lieber succeeded by his code in providing for humane treatment of prisoners without recognizing the acts of secession or the legitimacy of the Southern authorities. He did this by implying that granting prisoner-of-war status to CSA soldiers was done not because of legal obligation, but rather out of noble sentiment. *See* Burrus Carnahan, *Lincoln, Lieber and the Laws of War: The Origins and Limits of the Principle of Military Necessity*, 29 AM J. INT'L LAW 213 (1998).

Chapter 1 Notes

1. Brendan Simms, *America's Best Ambassador Is a Piece of Parchment*, WALL ST. J., Jan. 4, 2007, at B11 (reviewing DAVID ARMITAGE, THE DECLARATION OF INDEPENDENCE (Harvard Univ. Press 2007)).

2. WILLIAM H. FREEHLING, THE ROAD TO DISUNION: VOLUME I: SECESSIONISTS AT BAY, 1776–1854, at 7 (Oxford Univ. Press 1990).

3. Abraham Lincoln, Speech at Springfield, Illinois (June 26, 1857). This speech followed Illinois Senator Stephen A. Douglas's by two weeks; it dealt largely with the *Dred Scott* decision.

4. Gordon S. Wood, *Reading the Founders' Minds*, NEW YORK REVIEW OF BOOKS, at 63 (June 28, 2007).

5. AKHIL REED AMAR, AMERICA'S CONSTITUTION: A BIOGRAPHY 26 (Random House 2005).

6. JOSEPH J. ELLIS, AMERICAN CREATION: TRIUMPHS AND TRAGEDIES AT THE FOUNDING OF THE REPUBLIC 88 (Knopf 2007).

7. The Treaty was ratified on January 16, 1707, when the Lord Chancellor touched the document with his scepter. On March 20, 1707, the Scottish Parliament voted to end its own existence. In a sense, there had already been a Union of Crowns in 1603, when the Scots Royalty went to London.

8. PAUL HENDERSON SCOTT, THE UNION OF 1707: WHY AND HOW? 36 (The Saltire Society 2006). The Treaty provided for a single Parliament at Westminster. The restoration of the Scottish Parliament in 1999 technically abrogated the basic provision of the Treaty of Union. *Id.* at 85.

9. AMAR, *supra* note 5, at 28. "Various states failed to honor requisitions, enacted laws violating duly ratified treaties, waged unauthorized local wars against Indian tribes, and maintained standing armies without congressional permission—all in plain contravention of the Articles." *Id.* at 28–29. In 1786, representatives from five states met in Annapolis, Maryland, to deal with a dispute between Maryland and Virginia, and the session sent a resolution to the Congress that a meeting be convened with representatives from all thirteen states. That Annapolis Convention Resolution, drafted by Alexander Hamilton, led the Congress in February 1787 to call for a convention in Philadelphia in order to revise the Articles of Confederation.

10. Rhode Island refused to send a delegate. Its citizens feared the economic and political weight of its neighboring states worse than the uncertainties and inequities they bore at the moment. James Srodes, THE WASHINGTON LAWYER

41 (Mar. 2007) (reviewing DAVID O. STEWART, THE SUMMER OF 1787: THE MEN WHO INVENTED THE CONSTITUTION (Simon & Schuster 2007)).

11. For an excellent discussion of the making of the Constitution, see RICHARD BEEMAN, PLAIN, HONEST MEN: THE MAKING OF THE AMERICAN CONSTITUTION (Random House 2009).

12. Gibbons v. Ogden, 22 U.S. (9 Wheat.) 1, 187 (1824). More than a century later, Justice George Sutherland argued that the foreign affairs power had been transmitted immediately from Great Britain to the united colonies as an essential element of nationhood at the termination of the Revolution. United States v. Curtiss-Wright Export Corp., 299 U.S. 304 (1936).

13. This very practical point is also considered to be a factor in the contemporary failure of the European Union to complete a Constitution, i.e., its massive length and complexity have led to calls to make it much shorter and simpler so that the people might read it. The U.S. Constitution is also shorter than the constitutions of each of the fifty states.

14. Article VII provided: "The Ratification of the Conventions of nine States shall be sufficient for the Establishment of this Constitution between the States so ratifying the Same."

15. Article I of the Articles provided that the Confederacy should be styled "The United States of America." The Preamble of the Constitution states: "We the People of the United States . . . to establish this Constitution of the United States of America."

16. See Srodes, *supra* note 10, at 43–44 (reviewing THE SUMMER OF 1787).

17. AMAR, *supra* note 5, at 52.

18. Article XIII.

19. Ellis notes that the correspondence between Thomas Jefferson and James Madison, much like the text of the Constitution, did not mention slavery, "because it was like a piece of inadmissible evidence with explosive implications capable of blowing up their entire case." ELLIS, *supra* note 6, at 175.

20. "With respect to slavery [in fashioning the Constitution], the federalists had fashioned a silence, not a consensus—or at most a consensus to be silent." DAVID WALDSTREICHER, SLAVERY'S CONSTITUTION: FROM REVOLUTION TO RATIFICATION 153–54 (Hill and Wang 2009). Professor Cass Sunstein noted that Alexander Hamilton, James Madison, and John Jay wrote the "best historical record" of the making of the Constitution, writing under the name of "Publius." But, he further explains, "It is notable how little Publius has to say on the subject of slavery." Cass R. Sunstein, *The Enlarged Republic—Then and Now*, NEW YORK REVIEW OF BOOKS 45–47 (Mar. 26, 2009).

21. Gordon W. Wood, *How Democratic Is the Constitution?*, NEW YORK REVIEW OF BOOKS (Feb. 23, 2006) (reviewing and quoting Akhil Reed Amar, AMERICA'S CONSTITUTION: A BIOGRAPHY).

22. Some scholars argue that delegates from these two states' delegations were playing for time—believing that time was on their side in light of the population trending south and west, and that therefore the future belonged to slavery. See the exchange of views between Lawrence Goldstone and Gordon S. Wood, *"Illusions" of the Founders*, NEW YORK REVIEW OF BOOKS 49–50 (Oct. 11, 2007).

23. Srodes, *supra* note 10, at 43 (reviewing THE SUMMER OF 1787).

24. "The Migration or Importation of such Persons as any of the States now existing shall think proper to admit, shall not be prohibited by the Congress prior to the Year one thousand eight hundred and eight . . . ."

25. Article V provides: "No Amendment which may be made prior to the Year One thousand eight hundred and eight shall in any Manner affect the first and fourth Clauses in the Ninth Section of the first Article . . . ."

26. Article I, sec. 9, cls. 1 and 2 provided: "The importation of negroes of the African race from any foreign country other than the slaveholding States or Territories of the United States of America, is hereby forbidden; . . . Congress shall also have the power to prohibit the introduction of slaves from any State not a member of, or Territory not belonging to, this Confederacy."

27. MORTON KELLER, AMERICA'S THREE REGIMES: A NEW POLITICAL HISTORY 39 (Oxford Univ. Press 2007).

28. Pinckney made the point during the discussion of the Missouri Compromise of 1820, a deal against which he argued forcefully and unsuccessfully. EZRA B. CHASE, THE TEACHINGS OF PATRIOTS AND STATESMEN OR THE FOUNDERS OF THE REPUBLIC ON SLAVERY 251 (J. W. Bradley 1860).

29. Mason was a slaveholder, but he opposed slavery as "a moral evil." "Mason cast a critical eye on slavery, [but] it was an eighteenth century eye' to which the capabilities of blacks were suspect and the rights of blacks were narrow, even nonexistent." Jonathan Yardley, WASHINGTON POST BOOK WORLD 2 (Nov. 4, 2006) (reviewing JEFF BROADWATER, GEORGE MASON: FORGOTTEN FOUNDER (Univ. N.C. Press 2006)). Mason, in the end, could not endorse the new Constitution because of the absence of a bill of rights, but he ultimately secured the Bill of Rights. Mason's grandson, James Mason, was the Confederate Envoy to Great Britain in 1862.

30. AMAR, *supra* note 5, at 91 (reviewing AMERICA'S CONSTITUTION).

31. *Id.* at 95–96.

32. DON E. FEHRENBACHER, THE SLAVEHOLDING REPUBLIC: AN ACCOUNT OF THE UNITED STATES GOVERNMENT'S RELATION TO SLAVERY 299 (Oxford Univ. Press 2002).

33. "Article 6. There shall be neither slavery nor involuntary service in the said territory . . . . Provided, always, That any person escaping into the same, from whom labor or service is lawfully claimed in any one of the original States, such fugitive may be lawfully reclaimed and conveyed to the person claiming his or her labor or service as aforesaid."

34. In June 1864, Congress enacted a brief statute that repealed the Fugitive Slave Acts of 1850 and its 1793 antecedent. "An Act to repeal the Fugitive Slave Act of eighteen hundred and fifty, and all Acts and Parts of Acts for the rendition of Fugitive Slaves." 13 Stat. 200 (June 28, 1864). Opponents argued that repealing the implementing statutes effectively nullified the Fugitive Slave clause of the Constitution—a right without a remedy was a nullity; Congress was duty-bound to carry out the constitutional provision.

35. 46 U.S. 215 (1847). That case presented abolitionists with the first opportunity to direct a challenge to the constitutionality of the 1793 Fugitive Slave Act.

Salmon Chase, then in private practice, argued the case. An earlier case, *Prigg v. Pennsylvania*, 41 U.S. 539 (1842), dealt with the power of the states to legislate on the rendition of slaves, although it also found the 1793 Fugitive Slave Act constitutional. *Prigg* was decided 8–1, with Justice Story writing the opinion.

36. Jones v. Van Zandt, 46 U.S. at 229.

37. 65 U.S. (24 How.) 66 (1861).

38. For an interesting discussion of the arguments of counsel in *Dennison*, see EARL M. MALTZ, SLAVERY AND THE SUPREME COURT, 1825–1861, at 293–95 (Univ. Press of Kansas 2009).

39. JOSEPH J. ELLIS, FOUNDING BROTHERS: THE REVOLUTIONARY GENERATION 93 (Vintage 2002).

40. Gordon S. Wood, *supra* note 4, at 64.

41. Gordon S. Wood, *supra* note 22, at 50.

42. The "Cornerstone" speech of Alexander H. Stephens, delivered at the Athenaeum in Savannah, Georgia, on March 21, 1861.

43. In today's world, 1993 Treaty on European Union (the EU) and the 2009 Treaty of Lisbon, which sets forth the plan for the Economic and Monetary Union) contain no provisions for possible withdrawal by member states. If a member state were to withdraw, there would be serious adverse consequences for the EU and EMU.

44. President Jefferson worried that the Constitution did not provide any authority for acquiring territory and suggested a Constitutional amendment. But in the end, he acquired the territory by treaty, which the Senate ratified on October 20, 1803, by a vote of 24–7. The land acquired comprises 23 percent of the present United States. The trigger for the acquisition was the transfer of power from feeble Spain to mighty France in 1800. In the end, Napoleon decided to sell the territory because he needed money, thought he might lose it anyway in a prospective war with England, and because the French defeat in Haiti reduced French interest in the Americas.

45. Parke Pierson, *Seeds of Conflict*, 22 AMERICA'S CIVIL WAR 25 (Sept. 2009).

46. Professor Amar speculates that the United States could have curled southwest, rather than due west, thereby creating a vast "slavocratic empire" encompassing much of modern Mexico, Central America, and the Caribbean. Amar, at p. 267.

47. President James Monroe addressed the Congress in his seventh annual message on December 2, 1823, and laid out the international policy of the United States with regard to the Americas. In this, Monroe asserted as a principle that "the American continents, by the free and independent conditions which they have assumed and maintain, are henceforth not to be considered as subjects for future colonization by any European powers . . . ."

48. The U.S. population was 10 million, the UK's was 21 million, and France's was 30 million.

49. In reviewing Professor Gordon Wood's book, EMPIRE OF LIBERTY: A HISTORY OF THE EARLY REPUBLIC (Oxford Univ. Press 2010), Professor Susan Dunn noted that "the 'national' culture of the United States . . . had in fact taken hold only in the North. The South . . . stood apart, as many southerners distained

not only work . . . but also commerce and industry. While the North plunged into the future, nostalgic southerners turned to the past, clinging to the agrarian myth. . . . Politically, too, the South remained backward, for the patrician order of slaveholders that dominated the culture and politics of the South took a dim view of an intrusive national government and a restless people who might challenge their authority." Susan Dunn, *When America Was Transformed*, NEW YORK REVIEW OF BOOKS 31 (Mar. 25, 2010).

50. "Speech on the Reception of Abolition Petitions" (Feb. 6, 1837), cited in footnote 46 of Lucas E. Morel, *The Dred Scott Dissents: McLean, Curtis, Lincoln and the Public Mind*," 32 J. SUP. CT. HIST. 133 (Nov. 2, 2007).

51. Before Jackson, only John Adams and John Quincy Adams had served four years; George Washington, Thomas Jefferson, James Madison, and James Monroe had served for eight years. After Jackson, William Henry Harrison and Zachary Taylor served only one year each, while Martin Van Buren, John Tyler, James K. Polk, Franklin Pierce, and James Buchanan served four years. Millard Fillmore served three years.

52. The admission of Texas risked upsetting the delicate political balance between slave and free states. The northern portion of Texas intruded beyond the line of latitude which had been established in the Missouri Compromise. Therefore, the Joint Resolution for Annexing Texas, approved by Congress on March 1, 1845, included a provision which allowed Texas to be subdivided into up to five states—with slavery being banned in the portion of Texas territory north of the Missouri Compromise line, and left to popular sovereignty the slavery issue in states formed south of that line.

53. In 1848, the Treaty of Guadalupe Hidalgo transferred California from Mexico to the United States. Shortly thereafter, gold was discovered near Sacramento.

54. James M. McPherson, *The Fight for Slavery in California*, NEW YORK REVIEW OF BOOKS 13 (Oct. 11, 2007) (reviewing Leonard L. Richards, THE CALIFORNIA GOLD RUSH AND THE COMING OF THE CIVIL WAR (Knopf 2007)).

55. The expansion extended westward across the Pacific: President Polk in 1846 sent Commodore James Biddle on a mission to open Japan; that mission was unsuccessful, but on July 14, 1853, Commodore Matthew Perry carried a letter from President Millard Fillmore, and was more successful.

56. The Compromise was in fact a series of five laws that balanced the interests of the North and South: California was admitted as a free state; Texas was paid for by relinquishing claim to the territory of New Mexico; the New Mexico Territory was organized without prohibition of slavery; the slave trade in the District of Columbia was abolished; and a very strict Fugitive Slave law was enacted.

57. Clay was a very successful lawyer, having argued twenty-three cases before the U.S. Supreme Court. *See* Jeremy M. McLaughlin, *Henry Clay and the Supreme Court*, 34 J. SUP. CT. HIST. 28, 42 (2009).

58. The book was a publishing phenomenon, serialized in an antislavery magazine, the *National Era*, between June 8, 1851 and April 1, 1852. A first edition sold 5,000 copies in four days; within a year more than 300,000 copies had been sold in the United States and more than two million in the world. *See* David

Bromwich, *The Fever Dream of Mrs. Stowe*, NEW YORK REVIEW OF BOOKS 51 (Oct. 25, 2007). Bromwich, an English Professor at Yale, notes how much Stowe borrowed from Dickens. Lincoln was said to have exclaimed to Harriet Beecher Stowe at their first meeting: "So, you're the little woman who wrote the book that started this great war." *See also* George Bornstein, *Best Bad Book: Black Notes and White Notes to the Tale of Uncle Tom*, TIMES LITERARY SUPPLEMENT 3–4 (Mar. 30, 2007).

59. There had been no amendment to the Constitution for more than half a century. The Bill of Rights, the first ten Amendments, was ratified in 1791. The Eleventh Amendment, relating to judicial power, was ratified in 1795, and the Twelfth Amendment (dealing with separate election of the president and vice president) was adopted in 1804.

Chapter 2 Notes

1. Most scholars agree that Scott was born between 1795 and 1805.

2. The statement of agreed facts in the case refers to "the Territory known as the Upper Louisiana."

3. The great-great-great niece of Major Taliaferro wrote that he, as a senior officer, with no minister in the area, performed the marriage of Dred Scott and Harriet Robinson, and suggested that Taliaferro had manumitted her before the marriage, and that Harriet was in any event not sold. The niece acknowledges that this fact would not have changed the outcome of the *Dred Scott* case. Audrey Jordan, CIVIL WAR TIMES 7 (June 2006). The late scholar, Paul Finkelman, asserts that in fact Taliaferro was an Indian agent stationed near Fort Snelling, and that he also was a justice of the peace. In that capacity, Taliaferro married the Scotts. PAUL FINKELMAN, DRED SCOTT V. SANDFORD: A BRIEF HISTORY WITH DOCUMENTS 16 (Bedford/St. Martin's 1997).

4. In the 1855 St. Louis city directory, the Scotts were listed, respectively, as "whitewasher" and "laundress."

5. The Scotts had two other children, but both died in infancy.

6. It was in this same courthouse that St. Louis resident Ulysses S. Grant in 1859 freed his only slave.

7. Also in 1847, Abraham Lincoln represented a Kentucky slaveholder, Robert Matson, in a case involving Matson's demand for the return from Illinois of a women and her four children. Lincoln argued that Matson's slaves had been in Illinois with the consent of Matson, and were not there in transit. Lincoln lost the case, and the former slaves were freed. *See* ALBERT A. WOLDMAN, LINCOLN LAWYER 60–71 (Carroll & Graf 1936).

8. Scott v. Emerson, 15 Mo. 576 (1852).

9. Scott v. Emerson, 15 Mo. 576, 586 (1852), *quoted in* FINKELMAN, *supra* note 3, at 22.

10. AUSTIN ALLEN, ORIGINS OF THE DRED SCOTT CASE: JACKSONIAN JURISPRUDENCE AND THE SUPREME COURT, 1837–1857, at 145 (Univ. of Georgia Press 2006).

11. ALLEN, *supra* note 10, 145.

12. Chief Justice Taney noted in his later 1856 Opinion that if Scott had thought the decision of the Missouri Supreme Court was erroneous, he could have directed a Writ of Error to the State Supreme Court requesting it to transmit the record to the U.S. Supreme Court. However, Taney acknowledged that if that "had been done . . . the writ must have been dismissed for want of jurisdiction." 60 U.S. 393, 453 (1856).

13. There were only narrow circumstances where the U.S. Supreme Court could properly assume jurisdiction to review a decision of a state supreme court. "These circumstances generally required a showing that the state decision denied the validity of a federal statute or constitutional provision, or applied a state law in such a way as to deny the validity of a federal statute or constitutional provision." BRIAN MCGINTY, LINCOLN AND THE COURT 43 (Harvard Univ. Press 2008).

14. Article III, sec. 2, para. 1: "The judicial Power [of the United States] shall extend to all . . . Controversies . . . between Citizens of different States . . . ."

15. Taney wrote in his 1856 *Dred Scott* Opinion: "It would ill become this court to sanction such an attempt to evade the law, or to exercise an appellant power in this circuitous way which it is forbidden to exercise in the direct and regular . . . forms of judicial proceedings." 60 U.S at 454.

16. The plaintiff's Declaration said that the "defendant, claiming to be [the] owner . . . laid his hands upon said plaintiff[s] . . . and imprisoned them, doing in this respect, however, no more than what he might lawfully do if they were of right his slaves," according to the Agreed Facts statement in the later U.S. Supreme Court case. 60 U.S. at 398.

17. FINKELMAN, *supra* note 3, at 25.

18. Blair House, at 1651 Pennsylvania Avenue NW, across the street from the White House, is today the official presidential guest house used for visiting foreign leaders. During most of the Truman Administration, the Trumans lived in Blair House while the White House was being renovated. It was originally built in 1824; Francis Preston Blair bought it in 1836 from the Surgeon General, and his son, Montgomery, moved into it in 1853.

19. ALLEN, *supra* note 10, at 149.

20. FINKELMAN, *supra* note 3, at 26.

21. Reverdy Johnson was also involved in the creation of the great Peabody Institute in Baltimore. In 1857, fresh from his victory in the *Dred Scott* case, he was involved in the drafting of a prospectus for presentation to philanthropist George Peabody. 101(4) *A History of the Maryland Historical Society, 1844–2006,* MARYLAND HISTORICAL MAGAZINE 436 (Winter 2006).

22. Ironically, the Kansas-Nebraska Act, which in effect repealed the Missouri Compromise of 1820, became law in May 1854—just after the Scotts' trial ended in the federal district court in St. Louis.

23. Less than six months before oral arguments, during the previous summer of 1855, Chief Justice Taney suffered a personal tragedy. For years the Taney family had vacationed at Old Point Comfort, near Norfolk, Virginia, but that summer, there were reports of an outbreak there of cholera or yellow fever. Taney's youngest daughter, Alice, wanted to vacation in Newport, Rhode Island, in part due to those reports, but Taney prevailed upon her to

come to Old Point Comfort. Alice contracted cholera/yellow fever and died on September 29th. Taney's wife of forty-nine years, Anne Key Taney, died of a stroke on the same day. Taney was 78. He was devastated by these losses. That December 1855, the distraught Taney sold the family home in Baltimore and moved into rented rooms on Indiana Avenue in Washington. Gregory Wallace, *The Lawsuit that Started the Civil War*, THE CIVIL WAR TIMES 46–49 (Mar./Apr. 2006). Wallace reports that the disease was cholera, while James Simon reports it as yellow fever. Wallace reports that mother and daughter died the same day, while Simon reports that the daughter died hours later, but on the next day. JAMES F. SIMON, LINCOLN AND CHIEF JUSTICE TANEY 96 (Simon & Schuster 2006).

24. The Court continued to meet in the Chamber until 1860, when it moved directly above to the room recently vacated by the Senate, where the lighting was much better.

25. Dred Scot v. Sandford, 60 U.S. 393 (1857), at 399–400.

26. Lincoln later argued that the Court delayed its decision so as to conceal the proslavery intentions of the Democratic Party until after the elections. The preeminent scholar of this case found no evidence to support Lincoln's reading of judicial motives. DON E. FEHRENBACHER, THE DRED SCOTT CASE 290 (Oxford Univ. Press 1978).

27. John McLean of Ohio was appointed to the Court by Andrew Jackson in 1829, as a Jacksonian Democrat, though by the mid-1850s, McLean had become a Republican. By 1868, he had refashioned himself as a Democrat interested in that party's nomination.

28. Under the common law pleading system, a "plea in abatement" is "one, which, without disputing the jurisdiction of the plaintiff's claim, objects to the place, mode or time of asserting it, and it allows plaintiff to renew his suit in another place or form, or at another time, and does not assume to answer the action on the merits, or deny the existence of the particular cause of action on which the plaintiff relies." BLACK'S LAW DICTIONARY 1038 (5th ed. 1979).

29. ALLEN, *supra* note 10, at 150.

30. EARL M. MALTZ, SLAVERY AND THE SUPREME COURT, 1825–1861, at 225 (Univ. Press of Kansas 2009).

31. The new Republican Party had nominated "the egotistical and rash" John C. Fremont to run for president. (Lincoln lost the nomination for vice president to William Dayton of New Jersey.) Millard Fillmore, the Whig president (1850–53), ran as the American or Know-Nothing candidate for president. This split in the antislavery vote (mainly old Whig) gave the election to the Democratic candidate, Buchanan, who supported the proslavery government in Kansas. WILLIAM C. HARRIS, LINCOLN'S RISE TO THE PRESIDENCY (Univ. Press of Kansas 2007). On February 3, 1857, President-elect Buchanan wrote to his friend Justice Catron, asking whether the Court would decide the case such that Buchanan should refer to it in his inaugural address. Catron, on February 10, noted that the Court probably would decide the case at its February 14 conference, and that the issue of the constitutionality of prohibiting slavery in the territories probably would not be reached. *See* MALTZ, *supra* note 29, at 250.

32. David C. Frederick, *Supreme Court Advocacy in the Early Nineteenth Century*, 30(1) J. Sup. Ct. Hist. 12–13 (2005).

33. Prior to 1812, oral argument was unlimited (in the English tradition), but then the rules changed to limit oral argument to two lawyers for each side. In 1832, the rules were changed to permit written briefs. In 1840, the rules required written points and authorities, and limited oral argument to two hours without special leave—as was granted in the *Dred Scott* case.

34. Allen, *supra* note 10, at 151–152.

35. In February 1857, Justice Catron wrote to President-elect Buchanan, urging him to press Justice Grier (a fellow Pennsylvanian) to join a majority opinion. (Buchanan, Grier, and Taney were all graduates of Dickinson College in Carlisle, Pennsylvania, classes of 1809, 1812, and 1795, respectively. Dickinson was founded in 1783 by Dr. Benjamin Rush, a signer of the Declaration of Independence; it was named in honor of John Dickinson, a delegate to the Constitutional Convention in 1787.) Buchanan wrote to Grier who agreed to concur in the majority opinion. Gregory J. Wallace, *The Lawsuit that Started the Civil War*, Civil War Times 47, 50 (Mar./Apr/ 2006). *See also* Maltz, *supra* note 30, at 241.

36. Maltz, *supra* note 30, at 242–43.

37. At least one scholar suggests that it was Justice Wayne who argued that the Court should use this case to address the issue of the expansion of slavery. Professor Michael Powell, Hood College symposium on this case (Mar. 30, 2007).

38. Buchanan, like Lincoln for years later, failed to win a majority of the popular vote. He had 45.3 percent, Fremont (Republican) had 33 percent, and former President Fillmore (Know-Nothing) had 21 percent of the total popular vote of 4,051,470.

39. Jean Baker, James Buchanan 83 (Times Books 2004).

40. Curtis claimed not to belong to any political party, though he earlier had been considered a Whig. *See* Allen, *supra* note 10, at 207.

41. William W. Freehling, The Road to Disunion: Secessionists Triumphant 110 (Oxford 2007). The structure of the court system set by the Judiciary Act of 1837—with its need for geographic balance—also contributed to the geographic balance.

42. Mark A. Graber, Dred Scott and the Problem of Constitutional Evil 36–37 (Cambridge Univ. Press 2006).

43. *Id.* at 36.

44. *Id.* at 38.

45. Fehrenbacher concluded that Curtis was substantially correct in his critique, and that Taney's denial of having made significant changes is inaccurate—though "perhaps not untruthful" according to Taney.

46. *See* Allen, *supra* note 10, at 207.

47. *Dred Scott*, 60 U.S. at 419.

48. The term "Indians" is used rather than the current politically correct term "Native Americans" because that was the term used in the Opinion; similarly,

"Negro" is used rather than the current politically correct "African American," because that was the usage at that time.

49. Article I, sec. 2, of the Constitution provides that representatives and direct taxes shall be apportioned according to the population of the states, "excluding Indians not taxed." In the same provision, slaves were to be counted as three-fifths of a person.

50. On June 13, 1855, Attorney General Caleb Cushing issued an Opinion making clear that the domicile of a slave is that of the master. This was an unusual case involving a Negro slave of a Cherokee, who had committed a crime within the Cherokee nation, but after that was transferred to a citizen of Arkansas. Cushing ruled that the Federal Court in Arkansas was the proper jurisdiction for the trial.

51. Ellen Knickmeyer, *Cherokee Nation to Vote on Expelling Slaves' Descendants*, THE WASHINGTON POST, Mar. 3, 2007, at A-1, and Mar. 4, 2007, at A-7. The Cherokees had fought for the Confederacy, and in defeat, the tribe signed a treaty with the United States committing that its slaves, who had been freed by tribal decree during the War, would be absorbed as citizens of the Cherokee Nation. The Congressional Black Caucus strongly objected.

52. Attorney General Cushing in an Opinion of July 5, 1856, noted that Indians were not citizens of the United States, but were "domestic subjects," and that Indians could be naturalized by a special act of Congress or by treaty.

53. See Judge Charles W. Pickering (retired from the Fifth Circuit Court of Appeals), Letter to the Editor, WALL ST. J. Nov. 4/5, 2006, at A-7. He quoted Joseph Califano as pointing out in 1961 that "the federal courts have become increasingly powerful architects of public policy. . . . Environmentalists, prison reformers and consumer advocates have learned that what can't be won in the legislature or executive may be achievable in a federal circuit court where a sympathetic judge sits . . . ." Pickering also complained that the majority in the *Dred Scott* case went outside the text of the Constitution..

54. This is the opinion of Professor Steven G. Calabresi of Northwestern University. Calabresi, *The Right Judicial Litmus Test*, WALL ST. J., Oct. 1, 2007, at A-23.

55. KERMIT L. HALL, THE OXFORD COMPANION TO THE SUPREME COURT OF THE UNITED STATES 613 (Oxford Univ. Press 1992).

56. *Id.*

57. Lincoln sharply disputed this point in his Springfield speech of June 26, 1857: "It is grossly incorrect to say or assume that the public estimate of the Negro is more favorable now than it was at the origin of the government."

58. This theme is almost exactly the same as stated by Justice Levi Woodbury for a unanimous Supreme Court in the 1847 *Van Zandt* case, which upheld the fugitive slave statute of 1793 and the Constitutional clause. Woodbury, a New Hampshire Democrat, argued that whether slavery laws are "just" or moral is a "political question, settled by each state for itself . . . . [T]his court has no alternative . . . but to stand by the Constitution and laws with fidelity to their duties and their oaths." Jones v. Van Zandt, 46 U.S. 215, 231 (1847). Salmon Chase and

William Seward, counsel for the defendant, argued that slavery was immoral and could not in any form be sanctioned.

59. Several Amendments to the Constitution were designed to overturn decisions of the Supreme Court, such as the Eleventh, which overturned a 1793 decision, and the Thirteenth, which overturned *Dred Scott*.

60. Scott v. Sandford, 60 U.S. at 426 (emphasis added).

61. *Id.* at 407.

62. *Id.*

63. *Id.*

64. FEHRENBACHER, *supra* note 26, at 447.

65. *Scott*, 60 U.S. at 409.

66. *Id.* at 410.

67. In his January 21, 1861, farewell speech in the U.S. Senate, Jefferson Davis noted his view that the "equality" language in the Declaration of Independence was not intended to touch equality of the races (or sexes), but rather that there was no inherited government.

68. *Scott*, 60 U.S. at 410.

69. FEHRENBACHER, *supra* note 26, at 410

70. *Scott*, 60 U.S. at 411.

71. *Id.*

72. *Id.* at 412.

73. *Id.* at 416.

74. One was as late as 1820: the Charter of the City of Washington, in which the city is authorized to restrain nightly meetings of "slaves, free negroes, and mulattoes . . . and to prescribe the terms and conditions upon which free negroes and mulattoes may reside in the city."

75. Wirt was the longest-serving Attorney General in U.S. history, serving from 1817 to 1829. He is described as the great government lawyer of the Marshall Court era. He was also at the same time a private practitioner: of the 138 cases he argued before the Court while he was Attorney General, only 39 were government cases—but no one seemed to have complained about the basic incompatibility of having an Attorney General who spent the bulk of his time on private client matters. See David C. Frederick, *Supreme Court Advocacy in the Early Nineteenth Century*, 30(1) J. SUP. CT. HIST. 7 (2005). Wirt initiated the practice of preserving his official Opinions for use as precedent. In two early Opinions, Wirt made it clear that the official Opinions were authorized only on the call of the president or cabinet officers, not private parties or the Congress. *See* 1 Op. Att'y Gen. 211 (June 12, 1818) and 1 Op. Att'y Gen. 335 (Feb. 3, 1820). In 1832, he ran unsuccessfully for the presidency on the Anti-Masonic ticket. *See also* Galen N. Thorp, *William Wirt*, 33 J. SUP. CT. HIST. 223 (2008).

76. The Wirt Opinion was rendered on November 7, 1821, and concluded that "free persons of color in Virginia are not citizens of the United States." The issue arose because a free Negro in Virginia sought to become a master of a vessel, and the federal statute regulating masters required that they be citizens of the United States. Wirt wrote: "I am of the opinion that the Constitution, by the description of 'citizens of the United States,' intended those only who enjoyed

the full and equal privileges of white citizens in the state of their residence. . . . [F]ree people of color in Virginia are not citizens of the United States in the sense of our shipping laws, or any other laws . . . ."

77. Cushing was the first full-time Attorney General of the United States. He served under President Franklin Pierce (1853–57). President Ulysses S. Grant nominated Cushing to be Chief Justice of the United States, but withdrew Cushing's nomination when it appeared that the Senate would not confirm him due to allegations that Cushing had contact with Jefferson Davis during the War.

78. Much of the Opinion deals with the legal technicalities of pleadings, such as the exact nature of a "pleas in abatement" or the role of a court of law as opposed to a court of chancery or a court of admiralty. These issues are not treated in this book.

79. *Scott*, 60 U.S. at 428, 429.

80. *Id.* at 432.

81. *Id.* at 451.

82. *Id.*

83. DAVID S. REYNOLDS, WAKING GIANT: AMERICA IN THE AGE OF JACKSON 337 (HarperCollins 2008).

84. Roper v. Simmons, 543 U.S. 551 (2005) (Scalia, J., dissenting), *quoted by* Justice Ruth Bader Ginsburg, at the 99th Annual Meeting of the American Society of International Law (Apr. 1, 2005). At the same meeting, Justice Scalia pointed out, for example, that justices cite foreign precedents in capital cases, where European law is far more liberal than American law, but not in abortion cases, where it is more restrictive.

85. One prominent scholar has termed the Taney Opinion "malodorous" and "convoluted." *See* AKHIL REED AMAR, AMERICA'S CONSTITUTION: A BIOGRAPHY 362, 253 (Random House 2005).

86. Grier holds the distinction of being the sole member of the Good Old #5 Club, since President Tyler had made three attempts to fill the seat before President Polk appointed Grier as his second choice in 1846. *See* Artemus Ward, *The 'Good Old #3 Club' Gets a New Member*, 33 J. SUP. CT. HIST. 100, 117 (2008).

87. Professor Graber argues that the Taney Court was very centrist, except for Justice Daniel, who was "fairly characterized as a Southern extremist." GRABER, *supra* note 42, at 37.

88. *Scott*, 60 U.S at 491–922; *see also* GRABER, *supra* note 42, at p. 69–70.

89. Justice Campbell quotes extensively from foreign sources, all of which protect the rights of a master to his slave.

90. In one interesting passage, Campbell explained that: "The American Revolution was not a social revolution. It did not alter the domestic condition or capacity of persons within the colonies, nor was it designed to disturb the domestic relations existing among them. It was a political revolution, by which thirteen dependent colonies became thirteen independent States." 60 U.S. at 502.

91. *Id.* at 511.

92. *Id.* at 527.

93. *Id.* at 529.

94. *Id.*

95. McLean was appointed by President Jackson on March 6, 1829, and confirmed the next day, but he did not take the oath of office until January 11, 1830. He served thirty-two years, until his death on April 4, 1861.

96. Allen Sharp, *Justices Seeking the Presidency*, 29(3) J. SUP. CT. HIST. 286 (2004).

97. McLean cited in detail the reasoning of the dissenting judge to conclude that the Missouri Court overruled settled law influenced "by a determination to counteract the excitement against the institution of slavery in the free States." 60 U.S. at 555–56.

98. *Id.* at 531.

99. *Id.* at 550.

100. *Id.* at 422.

101. *Id.* at 601.

102. *Id.* at 625.

103. MALTZ, SLAVERY AND THE SUPREME COURT, *supra* note 30, at 264.

104. FINKELMAN, *supra* note 3, at 128, 131.

105. FINKELMAN, *supra* note 3, at 127–67.

106. Lincoln was slow to react to the decision. "Not until May did he even refer to the case . . . . An initial examination of the opinions failed to give Lincoln much cause for alarm. . . . [H]e agreed with Taney [that a Negro could not become a citizen]. Nor was he exercised because the Court invalidated the Missouri Compromise; the Kansas-Nebraska Act had already expressly repealed that compromise." DAVID HERBERT DONALD, Lincoln 200 (Simon & Schuster 1995).

107. FINKELMAN, *supra* note 3, at 135.

108. The New York INDEPENDENT, a Protestant paper, pointed out in its denunciation of the decision on March 19, 1857, that Taney was a Roman Catholic ("a member of the Papal church"), playing on anti-Catholic sentiments common to many Northern Protestants. *See* FINKELMAN, *supra* note 3, at 144, 149.

109. D. Grier Stephenson, Jr., *The Judicial Bookshelf*, 31(2) J. SUP. CT. HIST. 207–09 (2006).

110. *Id.* at 208–09.

111. MARK A. GRABER, DRED SCOTT AND THE PROBLEM OF CONSTITUTIONAL EVIL, *supra* note 42. See also the Forward written by Professor Graber in EARL M. MALTZ, SLAVERY AND THE SUPREME COURT: 1825–1861, at ix–xv (Univ. Press of Kansas 2009).

112. GRABER, *supra* note 42, at 4.

113. *Id.* at 28–29. Graber added that Massachusetts was the only court before 1857 to rule that free blacks were state citizens—in an opinion sustaining segregation in schools. That Justice Curtis's opinions were similar to the Massachusetts decision in part may be explained by the fact that he knew that state best.

114. GRABER, *supra* note 42, at 50.

115. *Id.* at p. 65. Graber also notes that it is impossible to determine whether the Framers thought the right not to be divested of property included the right not to be divested when moving into territories.

116. *Id.* at 72

117. *Id.* at 76.

118. WILLIAM W. FREEHLING, THE ROAD TO DISUNION, *supra* note 41, at 109.

119. A current example might be the discussion, during oral argument on October 31, 2006, in a case involving an appeal, from the Oregon Supreme Court, of punitive damages against Philip Morris, when at least one Justice suggested that the case be returned to Oregon for that court to clarify its reasoning. Jess Bravin, *High Court Appears Reluctant to Alter Punitive-Damage Law*, WALL ST. J., Nov. 1, 2006, at A-13.

120. For example, if they were there merely as temporary sojourners, even Justice Curtis might have agreed that Scott was still a slave.

121. See the excellent article by the economic historian Professor Jenny B. Wahl, *Stay East, Young Man? Market Repercussions of the Dred Scott Decision*, 82 CHI.-KENT LAW REV. 361 (2007).

122. 62 U.S. [21 How.] 506 (1859). The case was docketed in March 1857 and was argued on January 19, 1859.

123. There were in fact two cases that were joined, *Ableman v. Booth* and *United States v. Booth*. In one, the Wisconsin Supreme Court annulled the action of the federal officer, and in the other, the Wisconsin court annulled the federal conviction of Booth.

124. See generally the excellent article by Michael J. C. Taylor, *"A More Perfect Union": Ableman v. Booth and the Culmination of Federal Sovereignty*, 28(2) J. SUP. CT. HIST. 101 (2003).

125. *Ableman*, 62 U.S. at 516.

126. The Wisconsin Supreme Court in effect had asserted that the 1850 Act, under which Glover was to be returned to his owner, did not have to be enforced by Wisconsin authorities.

127. *Ableman*, 62 U.S. at 526.

128. Justice Curtis was no longer on the Court at the time of *Ableman*. Nathan Clifford, a Buchanan appointee, took Curtis's seat in early 1858.

129. HALL, THE OXFORD COMPANION TO THE SUPREME COURT OF THE UNITED STATES, *supra* note 55, at 2.

130. MALTZ, SLAVERY AND THE SUPREME COURT, *supra* note 30, at 284–85.

131. 20 N.Y. 562 (1860). Most of the comments about this case are found in John D. Gordon, III, *The Lemmon Slave Case*, 4 THE HISTORICAL SOCIETY OF THE COURTS OF THE STATE OF NEW YORK 1 (2006).

132. Six months earlier, the Missouri Supreme Court had held that Dred Scott was still a slave.

133. *See* MALTZ, *supra* note 30, at 166–67. *Lemmon v. The People ex rel. Napoleon*, 5 Sand. 681 (N.Y. Sup. Ct. 1852).

134. A New York law in 1799 provided for freedom to all children born of slaves after July 4, 1799. An 1817 amendment also permitted nonresidents to enter New York with their slaves for up to nine months, but in 1841, that provision was repealed—and New York became slave-free. By the time of the beginning of the *Lemmon* case in 1852, New York had completed its course of gradual emancipation.

135. See the full discussion of this case in Chapter 7, Ending Slavery.

136. The reference is in note 36 of the formal, printed, and annotated edition that was later published as a campaign document, and is found in the Appendix in HAROLD HOLZER, LINCOLN AT COOPER UNION: THE SPEECH THAT MADE ABRAHAM LINCOLN PRESIDENT 281 (Simon & Schuster 2004).

137. In the 1850s, St. Louis had 82,000 residents, including 2,600 slaves and 1,400 free Negroes.

138. 12 Stat. 432 (1862).

139. Op. Att'y Gen. on Citizenship, at 3 (1862). The Opinion was addressed to the Secretary of the Treasury, November 29, 1862. It was published as a pamphlet by the Government Printing Office, Washington.

140. Bates Op. at 26.

141. Bates Op. at 18.

Chapter 3 Notes

1. *Ari Kelman, Body and Blood: From John Brown's Rebellion to the Redeemers of America*, TIMES LITERARY SUPPLEMENT, Feb. 16, 2007, at 3.

2. As a result of the refusal by President Jackson to renew the Bank of the United States, Jackson transferred government funds to state banks, which in turn began to print money and provide wild loans, causing high inflation. In July 1836, Jackson ordered (in the Specie Circular) that the government would accept only gold and silver in payment for federal land. That produced a rush on banks; the banks did not have sufficient cash on hand, and they were forced to close. Bankruptcies were widespread across the nation.

3. EVAN CARTON, PATRIOTIC TREASON: JOHN BROWN AND THE SOUL OF AMERICA 91 (Free Press 2006).

4. CARTON, *supra* note 3, at 98, 108. However, another scholar puts the date of the first Brown/Douglass meeting in 1847. STAN COHEN, JOHN BROWN: THE THUNDERING VOICE OF JEHOVAH 3 (Pictorial Histories 1999).

5. CARTON, *supra* note 3, at 116–17.

6. Ironically, the commander of U.S. troops at Fort Leavenworth, Kansas, was Colonel Edwin Sumner, a cousin of Senator Sumner's; the Colonel led a force in early June 1856 in an effort to capture Brown. CARTON, *supra* note 3 at 213.

7. Sumner had insulted Senator A. P. Butler of South Carolina by noting, while pointing at Butler's empty seat, that Butler had "chosen a mistress to whom he has made his vows . . . who, though ugly to others is always lovely to him. . . . I mean the harlot Slavery." Brooks was a nephew of Senator Butler's.

8. One author believes that Brown was a "good terrorist": if the "choice of victim is appropriate and the ends serve freedom and justice, then killing in the right cause can be a net 'good.'" David W. Blight, WASHINGTON POST BOOK WORLD, Apr. 24, 2005, at 3 (reviewing DAVID S. REYNOLDS, JOHN BROWN, ABOLITIONIST: THE MAN WHO KILLED SLAVERY, SPARKED THE CIVIL WAR, AND SEEDED CIVIL RIGHTS (Knopf 2005)).

9. James Redpath wrote the first biography of Brown in 1860, THE PUBLIC LIFE OF CAPTAIN JOHN BROWN. After Redpath learned the details of the massacre at Pottawatomie Creek, he repudiated his work.

10. CARTON, *supra* note 3, at 206, 215.

11. This is the equivalent of several million dollars in today's terms.

12. WILLIAM W. FREEHLING, THE ROAD TO DISUNION: SECESSIONISTS TRIUMPHANT 209 (Oxford Univ. Press 2007).

13. Kelman, *Body and Blood*, *supra* note 1, at 3.

14. WILLIAM M. S. RASMUSSEN & ROBERT S. TILTON, THE PORTENT: JOHN BROWN'S RAID IN AMERICAN MEMORY 25 (Virginia Historical Society 2009).

15. Of those killed, eight were white and two were Negroes; four of those who escaped were white, and one was Negro.

16. Those who were captured and taken to Charles Town for trial were John Brown, Aaron D. Stevens, Edwin Coppoc, Albert Hazlett, and John E. Cook (all white), and John A. Copeland and Shields Green (two Negroes).

17. One of the few books to focus exclusively on the trial of Brown is the excellent book, BRIAN MCGINTY, JOHN BROWN'S TRIAL (Harvard Univ. Press 2009).

18. ROBERT SAUNDERS JR., JOHN ARCHIBALD CAMPBELL: SOUTHERN MODERATE, 1811–1889, at 136–37 (Univ. of Alabama Press 1997).

19. On April 13, 1863, General Burnside, commanding general of the Ohio Department, issued General Order No. 38 that outlawed implied treason, including declaring sympathies with the enemy. Former Congressman Clement Vallandigham, a peace Democrat, was arrested on April 30th at his home by 100 soldiers because of a speech a few days earlier in which he termed the war "wicked" and urged voters to hurl "King Lincoln" from his throne. He was convicted by a military court and sentenced to imprisonment for the duration of the War. The Supreme Court declined to hear Vallandigham's appeal for technical jurisdictional reasons. *Ex parte* Vallandigham, 68 U.S. 243 (1864). Embarrassed by the outcry, Lincoln ultimately ordered that Vallandigham be banished and expelled into Confederate territory. From there, Vallandigham made his way to Canada and from there ran unsuccessfully for governor of Ohio. DANIEL FARBER, LINCOLN'S CONSTITUTION 171 (Univ. of Chicago Press 2003).

20. MCGINTY, *supra* note 17, at 59.

21. Mason had come there from his home in Winchester, Virginia, about thirty-five miles southeast; Vallandigham was en route to Ohio from Washington.

22. JOHN STAUFFER, THE BLACK HEARTS OF MEN 246 (Harvard Univ. Press 2002).

23. Peculiar to Virginia, this was an "examining court," composed of at least eight justices of the peace from the county assembled to examine the charges. *See* MCGINTY, *supra* note 17, at 85.

24. Present at the reading of the charges were Brown, Stevens, Coppoc, Green, and Copeland. Hazlett and Cook were not present.

25. MILLARD KESSLER BUSHONG, HISTORIC JEFFERSON COUNTY 189 (Carr Publishing 1972).

26. Bushong, *supra* note 25, at 190 (quoting Brown).

27. Botts, 36 years old, was a graduate of the Virginia Military Institute, and died three years later at the Second Battle of Manassas.

28. Hunter, born in Berkeley County, Virginia, in 1804, argued the case of *Virginia v. West Virginia* in the Supreme Court in 1866 and 1870, dealing with whether the counties of Berkeley and Jefferson were part of West Virginia. See Chapter Four, page 116.

29. Robert A. Ferguson, The Trial in American Life 364 n.59 (Univ. of Chicago Press 2007).

30. Green, age 39, was Collector of Taxes in Virginia during the Civil War. In 1876, he was appointed to the West Virginia Court of Appeals, on which he served for fourteen years.

31. Ferguson, *supra* note 29, at 141.

32. Edward W. Knappman, Great American Trials 135 (Visible Ink Press 1993). Brown's mother had died insane eight years after his birth, just as her mother had before her. At least five of Brown's other close relatives were also insane, including two of the twenty children he fathered by two successive wives. The sender of the telegram, A. H. Lewis of Akron, offered several witnesses from Ohio who would testify as to the hereditary nature of the insanity. The offer was not taken up.

33. Knappman, *supra* note 32, at 135–36.

34. Ferguson, *supra* note 29, at 141.

35. When Hoyt appeared in court, Hunter, the prosecutor, asked for proof that Hoyt was a member of the Boston bar; finally, Judge Parker accepted statements by Green. Thomas J. Fleming, *Verdicts of History III: The Trial of John Brown*, American Heritage Magazine, Aug. 1967, at 67.

36. Hoyt had been hired by Boston abolitionist John W. LeBarnes. According to one scholar, Hoyt's task was to report on the military situation, the opportunities for an attack on the jail, and generally to serve as a communications conduit with Brown. Fleming, *supra* note 35, at 4.

37. Cohen, *supra* note 4, at 79.

38. Fleming, *supra* note 35, at 8.

39. During the six-day trial, Brown was represented by six lawyers, however none of them served as formal defense counsel for more than half of the proceedings. Ferguson, *supra* note 29, at 360 n.12.

40. *Id.*

41. Mark S. Weiner, Black Trials: Citizenship from the Beginnings of Slavery to the End of Caste 177 (Knopf 2004).

42. Cohen, *supra* note 4, at 86.

43. One scholar reports that there was the sound of a single man clapping, which horrified all in attendance. Ferguson, *supra* note 29, at 136.

44. Fleming, *supra* note 35, at 9

45. Bushong, *supra* note 25, at 195 (quoting Brown).

46. Ferguson, *supra* note 29, at146.

47. John Brown's last speech, reproduced in History Resource Center, Farmington Hills, Michigan, Gale Group; also in Annals of America, Encyclopedia Britannica, Inc., cited at PBS.org.

48. FERGUSON, *supra* note 29, at 118. Brown's actions in the courtroom perhaps have a modern echo in the hijinks in the Iraq courtroom by Saddam Hussein.

49. The media sometimes relied on an 1847 daguerreotype portrait of a beardless and steely-eyed Brown. This daguerreotype was acquired by the National Portrait Gallery in October 1996 for $115,000. The photographer, Augustus Washington, was the son of an Asian mother and a former Virginia slave who grew up in New York, but who decided that Africa was the only place a black man could live freely, and so he emigrated to Liberia in 1853.

50. FERGUSON, *supra* note 29, at 118–19.

51. FERGUSON, *supra* note 29, at 123.

52. FERGUSON, *supra* note 29, at 132.

53. American Transcendentalism was the term given to a group of new ideas in literature, religion, and culture that emerged in New England in the early to mid-nineteenth century. It began as a protest against the state of intellectualism at Harvard and the Unitarian church. A core belief was an ideal spiritual state that "transcended" the physical and was realized only through one's intuition. Prominent in this movement was Henry David Thoreau, who supported civil disobedience in protest against the Mexican War. There was a Transcendentalist utopian commune in Massachusetts, Brook Farm, that ultimately failed. "By the 1850's the full horror of slavery took center stage for the transcendentalists, several of whom became eminent abolitionists," noted Michael Dirda in his review in the Dec. 16, 2007, WASHINGTON POST of the book, AMERICAN TRANSCENDENTALISM, by Phillip F. Gurda (Hill and Wang 2007).

54. Douglas O. Linder, *The Trial of John Brown: A Commentary* 13 (2005) (quoting Emerson).

55. The copy of the brief held in the Virginia Historical Society in Richmond is autographed by Green to John A. Andrew, Esquire.

56. MCGINTY, *supra* note 17, at 247.

57. RASMUSSEN & TILTON, *supra* note 14, at 36

58. COHEN, *supra* note 4, at 85.

59. In 1865, Wise sought to evict a schoolmarm from his pre-war farm. "The intruder turned out to be one of John Brown's daughters, come south to educate blacks, including Wise's ex-slaves." FREEHLING, *supra* note 12, at 218.

60. The trials of the other prisoners were even shorter. Coppoc was brought before the court on November 1st and was found guilty. The two Negroes, Green and Copeland, were subsequently tried and also found guilty. The treason charge, however, was dropped for them: the treason statute applied only to "any free person" who committed treason, and it was not definitively established that they were indeed free—and so there was doubt whether the statute applied to them. John E. Cook was captured in Pennsylvania, was indicted in Charles Town on November 7th, and was tried the next day. He had served as Brown's "spy" in Harpers Ferry for twelve months before the raid, and that produced local bitterness. He pled guilty to all charges, except treason, and threw himself on the mercy of the court. His sister was the wife of the governor of Indiana, Ashbel P. Willard. She attended the trial and brought with her Daniel W. Voorhees, the

U.S. District Attorney for Indiana, for Cook's defense. His plea for mercy was based on the argument that Cook was a youth who had been enchanted by the fanatic Brown. After an hour's deliberation, the jury returned a verdict of guilty on all counts except treason. On November 10th, Cook was sentenced to be hanged on December 16th.

Cook and Coppoc attempted a sensational escape on December 15th, but it failed. The next day, they were hanged, preceded by the two Negroes, Green and Copeland. The final two prisoners, Aaron D. Stevens and Albert Hazlett, were tried in February 1860 during a special Circuit Court term for Jefferson County, which had been authorized by the Virginia General Assembly. Stevens and Hazlett were hanged on March 16, 1860.

61. BUSHONG, *supra* note 25, at 197.

62. OTTO SCOTT, THE SECRET SIX: JOHN BROWN AND THE ABOLITIONIST MOVEMENT 304 (Uncommon Books 1979).

63. Standing with the VMI cadets was a 66-year-old veteran of the War of 1812, Edmund Ruffin; two years later, as a member of the Palmetto Guards, he yanked the lanyard that fired the shot at Fort Sumter. COHEN, *supra* note 4, at 92.

64. MCGINTY, *supra* note 17, at 110.

65. After the trial, a leading secessionist and founder of the ultra-patriotic League of United Southerners, Edmund Ruffin of Virginia, sent 15 of Brown's pikes to Southern governors as "evidence of the fanatical hatred borne by the dominant northern party to the institutions [and] the people of the Southern States." Eric Ethier, *I here declare my unmitigated hatred to Yankee rule*, AMERICA'S CIVIL WAR, Nov. 2008, at 23.

66. DOUGLAS T. MILLER, FREDERICK DOUGLASS AND THE FIGHT FOR FREEDOM 89 (Facts on File Publications 1988).

67. FREDERICK DOUGLASS, LIFE AND TIMES OF FREDERICK DOUGLASS 158 (Thomas Y. Crowell Co. 1966).

68. *Id.* at 159.

69. *Id.* at 162.

70. MCGINTY, JOHN BROWN'S TRIAL, *supra* note 17, at 238.

71. MILLER, *supra* note 66, at 92–93.

72. *Id.* at 93.

73. Parker was the "particular hero" of Lincoln's law partner, William Herndon. "Lincoln had carefully avoided contact with Parker, an outspoken abolitionist. But he clearly knew and liked his works." Garry Wills, *Two Speeches on Race*, NEW YORK REVIEW OF BOOKS 8 (May 1, 2008).

74. Dr. Howe's wife was Julia Ward Howe, the poet and playwright. She had met John Brown through her husband. In 1861, she was visiting a military camp near Washington, when she heard the tune "John Brown's Body." She wrote a hymn to its tune, which became the major song of the Union: "The Battle Hymn of the Republic." John Brown's song was not written about the abolitionist, but rather about a young Scotsman of the same name, who was recruited into the Boston Light Infantry. Because of his name, he was the butt of jokes, and other soldiers added a new line to the chorus of "Glory, Glory Hallelujah,"

relating to Brown's body moldering in the grave. The young Scot drowned in the Shenandoah River during the War.

75. In 1860, widow Mary Ann Brown sent her two daughters, Annie and Sarah, to Sanborn's private school in Concord, Massachusetts. Sandra Weber, *Living Legends of Harpers Ferry*, CIVIL WAR TIMES 46 (Feb. 2005).

76. SCOTT, *supra* note 62, at 4.

77. For interesting biographic sketches of the six, complete with photos, see Tim Rowland, *John Brown's Moonlight March*, AMERICA'S CIVIL WAR, Sept. 2009, at 32–33.

78. Kelman, *Body and Blood, supra* note 1, at 3.

79. STAUFFER, *supra* note 22, at 241.

80. Smith sent his son-in-law, Charles D. Miller, to Boston and then to the Ohio home of John Brown Jr. to destroy all Smith letters and any other evidence that would connect Brown to the Secret Six. SCOTT, *supra* note 62, at 293.

81. Gerrit Smith had recovered sufficiently to deliver a major address on "The Country" at the Cooper Institute in New York on December 21, 1862.

82. SCOTT, *supra* note 62, at 245–46.

83. SCOTT, *supra* note 62, at 293.

84. Parker died in Florence in May 1860.

85. FERGUSON, *supra* note 29, at 122.

86. Quoted in STAN COHEN, JOHN BROWN: THE THUNDERING VOICE OF JEHOVAH, *supra* note 4, at 71.

87. RASMUSSEN & TILTON, *supra* note 14, at 63.

88. DORIS KEARNS GOODWIN, TEAM OF RIVALS: THE POLITICAL GENIUS OF ABRAHAM LINCOLN 226–27 (Simon & Schuster 2005). The fear in the South also encouraged the expansion of state militia for protection against further raids, and these strengthened militia also served later as the basis for the rapid deployment of the Confederate States of America's (CSA's) military force.

89. Kelman, *supra* note 1, at 4.

90. GERALDINE BROOKS, MARCH 171 (Penguin Books 1998).

91. RUSSELL BANKS, CLOUDSPLITTER (HarperFlamingo 1998).

92. GERALDINE BROOKS, MARCH 169 (Penguin Books 2005).

93. Note Mason's involvement in the *Trent* affair, *infra* Chapter 6.

94. FREEHLING, *supra* note 12, at 220.

95. *Report of the Select Committee of the Senate Appointed to Inquire into the Late Invasion and Seizure of Public Property at Harpers Ferry*, 36th Cong., 1st Sess., S. Rep. Comm. No 278 (1860) [hereinafter *Mason Report*].

96. Included in the Appendix were a Report by Colonel Robert E. Lee, Brown's "Provisional Constitution," and correspondence of John Brown Jr. and others.

97. *Mason Report, supra* note 96, at 13.

98. *Id.* at 11.

99. *Id.* at 7–8.

100. *Id.* at 13.

101. *Id.* at 16.

102. *Id.* at 18.

103. *Id.* at 28.

104. For example, see the discussion of the hanging of Captain Gordon, the only slave trader to be executed, *infra* Chapter 7.

105. *Id.* at 62.

106. *Id.* at 140.

107. *Id.* at 187.

108. *Id.* at 187.

109. *Id.* at 189.

110. While some called Brown "Captain," he in fact had no military service. His grandfather, however, was a captain in the Revolutionary War.

111. *Mason Report, supra* note 96, at 194.

112. *Id.* at 225.

113. Edgar Langsdorf, *Thaddeus Hyatt in Washington Jail*, 9 KAN. HIST. Q. 234 (Aug. 1940).

114. *Id.* at 229.

115. *Id.* at 239.

116. Quoted in DAVID HERBERT DONALD, LINCOLN 239 (Simon & Schuster 1995).

117. The text of the Cooper Union Address is found in the Appendix of HAROLD HOLZER, LINCOLN AT COOPER UNION: THE SPEECH THAT MADE ABRAHAM LINCOLN PRESIDENT 270 (Simon & Schuster 2004).

118. In a brilliant essay, Professor Gary Wills compared Lincoln's "handling" of John Brown to President Obama's handling of Reverend Jeremiah Wright. Gary Wills, *Two Speeches on Race*, NEW YORK REVIEW OF BOOKS 4–8 (May 1, 2008).

119. DON E. FEHRENBACHER, THE SLAVEHOLDING REPUBLIC: AN ACCOUNT OF THE UNITED STATES GOVERNMENT'S RELATIONS TO SLAVERY 297 (Oxford 2001).

120. First Inaugural Address of Abraham Lincoln.

121. *The Portent*, which is among the 72 poems collectively published in 1866 as BATTLE-PIECES AND ASPECTS OF THE WAR, *quoted in* Wyatt Kingseed, *Herman Melville's Stark Civil War Verses Found Little Favor with Postwar America*, AMERICA'S CIVIL WAR, Jan. 2006, at 10. Melville's refusal to romanticize the War may explain why the book was criticized and sold only 525 copies. Peter Carmichael. *Review*, CIVIL WAR TIMES 65 (Dec. 2008).

122. Professor Paul Finkelman, at the April 25, 2008, Conference of the U.S. Capitol Historical Society, speaking on "A Decade in Crisis: The 1850s."

Chapter 4 Notes

1. President Jefferson worried that he did not have the constitutional authority to acquire territory, but in the end, the treaty was signed on April 30, 1803, and was ratified by the Senate (24–7) on October 20, 1803.

2. The Federalist Party is considered America's first political party, advocating a strong national government. Its prominent leaders included John Adams and Alexander Hamilton. It ceased to be a national party after 1816.

3. Joseph J. Ellis, American Creation: Triumphs and Tragedies at the Founding of the Republic 228 (Knopf 2007).

4. *Id.* at 230.

5. Joseph J. Ellis, Founding Brothers: The Revolutionary Generation 44 (Vintage Books 2002). Jefferson in fact dropped Burr, and selected George Clinton of New York as his running mate in the 1804 election.

6. It was during this election campaign that the Burr/Hamilton feud peaked, and that led to the famous duel outside Weehawken, New Jersey, on July 11, 1804, during which Burr killed Hamilton. The last letter that Hamilton ever wrote was composed the night before the duel with Burr and "was devoted to squelching the still-lingering Federalist fantasies of a separate northeastern confederation . . . ." Ellis, Founding Brothers, *supra* note 5, at 44.

7. Later, when it was proposed to admit Louisiana as a new state, the issue reappeared, and the argument was that the original compact did not envision the admission of new states from beyond the borders of the United States at the time of its formation. (Rep. Josiah Quincy of Massachusetts, on the House Floor January 14, 1811.)

8. Ellis, *supra* note 3, at 235–36.

9. Article I provided that "Representatives and direct Taxes shall be apportioned among the several states . . . by adding to the whole Number of free Persons . . . three fifths of all other Persons . . . ." "Some Northern critics grumbled that three-fifths should have been five-fifths so as to oblige the South to pay more taxes, without noticing that five-fifths would have also enabled the South to claim more House seats." Akhil Reed Amar, America's Constitution: A Biography 89 (Random House 2005).

10. William W. Freehling, The Road to Disunion: Secessionist at Bay 1776–1854, at 149 (Oxford 1990).

11. On March 2, 1819, Congress authorized the Alabama Territory to form a constitution, and on August 2, in a Convention, Alabama formed a constitution and a state government. Congress resolved the admission of Alabama, and President Monroe approved it on December 14, 1819.

12. *See* Ellis, American Creation, *supra* note 3, at 234–39.

13. *Id.* at 239.

14. John Quincy Adams was elected over his rivals Henry Clay, William Crawford, and Andrew Jackson, in an election that was decided by the House of Representatives.

15. Jackson won over Adams as the head of a new political organization, the Democratic Party; his election had a realigning effect on American politics.

16. Smith was clever to present the situation of a divided Supreme Court, where three of the seven Justices would pronounce a law constitutional, while three others would pronounce it unconstitutional—neutralizing each other, leaving the whole weight on the shoulders of a single Justice; "The single Judge would hold the balance, and have the power to decide the fate of the Union, by his single dictum." Herman Belz, Ed., The Webster-Hayne Debate on the Nature of the Union: Selected Documents 300 (Liberty Fund 2000).

17. Belz, *supra* note 16, at 329.

18. BELZ, *supra* note 16, at 330–31.

19. From his 1896 book, WOODROW WILSON, DIVISION AND REUNION 1829–1889 (New York: Logans, Green & Co. 1897) at 43–44, *quoted in* BELZ, *supra* note 16, at xiii.

20. One reason for the delay in convening the Convention was so that it would take place after the elections in early November. In that election, Jackson polled more than 56 percent of the popular vote, and almost five times the electoral vote given to Clay.

21. *See* FREEHLING, THE ROAD TO DISUNION, *supra* note 10, at 279.

22. Jackson was blustering around Washington during that nullification winter, threatening to hang the secessionists from the first tree. Jackson's friend, Senator Thomas Hart Benson of Missouri, told South Carolina's Senator Robert Hayne that "when Jackson begins to talk about hanging, they can look out for the ropes." Quoted in FREEHLING, THE ROAD TO DISUNION, *supra* note 10, at 278.

23. ALBERT A. WOLDMAN, LINCOLN LAWYER 282 (Carroll & Graf 1936).

24. FREEHLING, *supra* note 10, at 352.

25. Robert Hayne (of the Webster-Hayne Debates) had resigned from the Senate to run for governor of South Carolina; John C. Calhoun resigned the vice presidency and took Hayne's seat in the Senate. Thus, Clay worked with Calhoun in the Senate to fashion the Compromise Tariff.

26. In his great DEMOCRACY IN AMERICA, Alexis de Tocqueville believed that the new tariff law represented a defeat for the Union: "Thus Congress completely abandoned the principle of the tariff. For a duty to protect industry it substituted a purely fiscal measure." ALEXIS DE TOCQUEVILLE, DEMOCRACY IN AMERICA 376 (Univ. of Chicago Press 2000).

27. The vote in the House was 119–85, and in the Senate 29–16.

28. De Tocqueville gave Jackson high marks for his handling of the South Carolina threats: "he sustained the rights of the Union with skill and vigor." DE TOCQUEVILLE, *supra* note 26, at 377.

29. In his Farewell Address to the Senate on January 21, 1861, Jefferson Davis drew a sharp distinction between nullification and secession, "so often confounded, are, indeed, antagonistic principles." He argued that Calhoun advocated the doctrine of nullification because it preserved the Union.

30. In his famous March 7, 1850, speech, Senator Daniel Webster specifically referred to that separation, as did Calhoun.

31. This is argued persuasively by Professor Joel H. Silbey of Cornell University in his STORM OVER TEXAS: THE ANNEXATION CONTROVERSY AND THE ROAD TO THE CIVIL WAR xvii (Oxford 2005).

32. See the discussion in the excellent new biography of Henry Clay, DAVID S. HEIDLER & JEANNE T. HEIDLER, HENRY CLAY: THE ESSENTIAL AMERICAN 381 (Random House 2010).

33. Calhoun served as vice president under John Quincy Adams and then Andrew Jackson (1825 to December 1832), then went into the Senate (1832–43). In 1844, President Tyler appointed him Secretary of State, after Webster left. The "team" of Clay, Webster, and Calhoun was extraordinary, without parallel today.

34. Polk defeated Henry Clay by a whisker. The popular vote was 1,339,368 to 1,300,687; the electoral vote was 170 to 105.

35. *See* HEIDLER & HEIDLER, *supra* note 21, at 408.

36. The year before, the Senate had defeated a formal Treaty of Annexation; a two-thirds vote is required for the Senate to advise and consent to a treaty, but only a majority is needed for a resolution.

37. From the conclave's only elaborate address, by General F. C. Wilkinson, noted in FREEHLING, THE ROAD TO DISUNION, *supra* note 10, at 481.

38. Delegates were from Virginia, South Carolina, Georgia, Alabama, Mississippi, Texas, Arkansas, Florida, and Tennessee. A delegation from Louisiana had been blocked by its legislature from attending.

39. After the Compromise of 1850 was enacted in September, a small group of Southern delegates met in November in Nashville to denounce the Compromise and to assert the right of individual states to secede. This Nashville II Convention had little national impact. One scholar noted that this second Nashville Convention was a "fiasco." WILLIAM J. COOPER, JR., JEFFERSON DAVIS, AMERICAN 205 (Knopf 2000).

40. James M. McPherson, *The Flight for Slavery in California* in NEW YORK REVIEW OF BOOKS 13 (Oct. 11, 2007).

41. McPherson, *supra* note 40, at 14.

42. He was, in fact, too ill to deliver it himself, and so another senator read it for him, after which he had to be helped out of the chamber. Calhoun died weeks later, on March 31.

43. Webster said: "They [the Northern religious abolitionists] deal with morals as with mathematics; and they think that what is right may be distinguished from what is wrong with the precision of an algebraic equation. They have, therefore, none too much charity towards others who differ from them."

44. This is more recently referred to as "The Resistance at Christiana."

45. MICHAEL W. KAUFFMAN, AMERICAN BRUTUS 88 (Random House 2004).

46. Samuel F. Miller, appointed to the Supreme Court in 1862, was upset in 1854 at the passage of the Kansas-Nebraska Act. With impressive foresight, he predicted that "the issue would split the national parties along sectional lines and that issues that once united northern and southern Whigs and Democrats, such as banks and internal improvements, would be no match for the divisive slavery issue." MICHAEL A. ROSS, JUSTICE OF SHATTERED DREAMS: SAMUEL FREEMAN MILLER AND THE SUPREME COURT DURING THE CIVIL WAR ERA 27 (Louisiana State Univ. Press 2003).

47. WILLIAM C. DAVIS, A GOVERNMENT OF OUR OWN: THE MAKING OF THE CONFEDERACY 6 (The Free Press 1994).

48. FREEHLING, *supra* note 10, at 531.

49. Peter Scott Campbell, ed., *The Civil War Reminiscences of John Marshall Harlan*, 32(3) J. SUP. CT. HIST. 255 (Nov. 2007).

50. Magrath later sat in the South Carolina secession convention. In 1862, Jefferson Davis appointed him to the CSA District Court in Charleston, and in late 1864, Magrath was elected governor of South Carolina.

51. Mark A. Weitz, The Confederacy on Trial: The Piracy and Sequestration Cases of 1861 65 (Univ. Press of Kansas 2005).

52. Freehling, *supra* note 10, at 399. Magrath went to Harvard Law School where he studied under the great Joseph Story. Within hours, the U.S. district attorney, the U.S. Marshal, and the U.S. collector of customs duties all resigned.

53. Historians usually rank Buchanan in the bottom five of all presidents. The 2009 C-SPAN Historians Presidential Leadership Survey ranked Mr. Buchanan last, number forty-two, with Andrew Johnson at forty-one. Participants in the Survey included sixty-four presidential historians and observers.

54. In November 1860, Governor Joseph Brown called the legislature into session to consider the question of secession. Leading Georgians were heard on the subject. Stephens' speech is considered a response to the speech of Robert Toombs, who later became CSA Secretary of State. Allen D. Candler, comp., Confederate Records of the State of Georgia, vol. 1, 183–205 (Chas. P. Byrd, State Printer 1909).

55. The law, or "legalisms," dominated the discourse in the South in 1860. The great scholar William Freehling noted: "secessionists' . . . states' rights creed started as a legalistic bore [and later] . . . Jefferson Davis and [CSA vice president] Stephens would return to such legalistic hairsplitting in their postwar memoirs." Freehling, *supra* note 10, 346.

56. For six years before he became Buchanan's Attorney General in 1857, Black was a member of the Supreme Court of Pennsylvania. Less than a month after rendering this Opinion, Black became Secretary of State and Edwin Stanton became Attorney General.

57. The Power of the President in Executing the Laws, 9 Op. Att'y Gen. 516–24 (Nov. 20, 1860).

58. Black cited the Taney opinion in *Ableman v. Booth*, which was decided unanimously by the Court on March 7, 1859. *See supra* Chapter 2, at 47–49.

59. One wonders whether Black had read de Tocqueville's *Democracy in America* written three decades earlier: "if one portion of the Union seriously wanted to separate from the other, not only could one not prevent it, but one would not even attempt to do so. The present Union will therefore last only as long as all the states that compose it continue to want to be part of it." de Tocqueville, *supra* note 26, at 355.

60. On February 5, 1861, Buchanan nominated Black for the Supreme Court, but his confirmation failed, 25–26, largely because the Senate felt the appointment should be made by the incoming president.

61. In an ironic scene on the same day, December 3, 1860, a committee was formed of members of the Supreme Court Bar, and Jefferson Davis was called to the Chair. On the motion of Attorney General Edwin M. Stanton, it was resolved that a committee of three be appointed by the Chair to prepare resolutions marking the death of Supreme Court Associate Justice Daniel, who had died earlier. James Mason was appointed by Davis to that committee Chair. The next day, at the opening of Court, Stanton spoke about Daniel and offered the resolutions of the Mason Committee. Chief Justice Taney replied to Stanton

with his own laudatory remarks about Daniel. Such were the courtly proceedings of the nation's Supreme Court.

62. In one of his last official acts as Secretary of State, Jeremiah Black on February 28, 1861, sent a circular message to all American diplomats instructing them to ensure that their host governments took no action to recognize the secession activity. Black referenced Buchanan's December 4th Message to Congress, specifically that "the States have no constitutional power to secede from the Union . . . [and] the grounds upon which they have attempted to justify the revolutionary act of severing the bonds which connect them with their sister States are regarded as wholly insufficient." Of course, much of Buchanan's Message was based on the Opinion written the previous November by then Attorney General Black. On February 5th, Buchanan had nominated Black to the Supreme Court, but on February 25th, the Senate rejected Black's appointment by one vote, 25 to 26.

63. The great Lincoln scholar Harold Holzer devotes much criticism to Buchanan during this period (repeatedly assigning the word "hapless" before his name) but, inexplicitly, does not mentioned the Attorney General's Opinion or even his name. HAROLD HOLZER, PRESIDENT-ELECT LINCOLN: ABRAHAM LINCOLN AND THE GREAT SUCCESSION WINTER OF 1860–1861 (Simon & Schuster, 2008).

64. Most scholars rank Buchanan as the worst President. "What makes a President horribly, immortally bad? Poor luck is not enough. . . . The damage must be largely self-inflicted. And there's another test: The damage to the nation must be substantial." Michael Lind, *He's Only Fifth Worst*, WASHINGTON POST, Dec. 3, 2006, at B-5.

65. On the same day, Supreme Court Justice John A. Campbell of Alabama met with President Buchanan and tried to persuade him to send federal commissioners to each Southern state to placate ill feelings and to stymie further movements toward secession. Buchanan did not take up Campbell's suggestion. Campbell then entered into an exchange of letters with former President Pierce urging him to visit Alabama to calm the secession interest. ROBERT SAUNDERS, JR., JOHN ARCHIBALD CAMPBELL, SOUTHERN MODERATE, 1811–1889, at 140 (Univ. of Alabama Press 1997).

66. In May 1861, Tyler was a member of the Provisional CSA Congress, and then was elected a member of the CSA House of Representatives, but died before its first meeting.

67. ELLIS, FOUNDING BROTHERS, *supra* note 5, at 92–93.

68. A photo of "Secession Hall" can be found in CIVIL WAR TIMES 82 (Nov./Dec. 2006).

69. They met with Buchanan on December 28th. He received them only as "private gentlemen."

70. Why was South Carolina alone in 1832–33 and first in 1860–61? One scholar dealt with the issue of South Carolina's exceptionalism by arguing that (a) South Carolina was not representative of the South early on due to its antidemocratic political structure, statewide plantation belt, and lack of a two-party

system, and (b) South Carolina was not only different, but was ahead of her sister states. By the later 1850s, most of the Deep South started to resemble South Carolina in terms of the disintegration of the party system and the dominance of the slavery issue.

71. South Carolina (1), Georgia (3), Alabama (2), Florida (6), North Carolina (2), Louisiana (7), and Mississippi (1).

72. Tri-Insula" meant "three islands" in Latin: Manhattan, Staten Island, and Long Island. See Chuck Leddy, *New York City's Secession Crisis*, CIVIL WAR TIMES 32 (Jan. 2007).

73. HOLZER, *supra* note 63, at 362–63.

74. For a full discussion of activities of the Georgia agents, see Gerard A. Patterson, *Arming the South with Guns from the North*, CIVIL WAR TIMES 36–39 (Oct. 2007).

75. The Secretary of War, John B. Floyd, was a Virginian who resigned on December 29, 1860.

76. BATTLES AND LEADERS OF THE CIVIL WAR: BEING FOR THE MOST PART CONTRIBUTIONS BY UNION AND CONFEDERATE OFFICERS BASED UPON THE "CENTURY WAR SERIES," edited by Robert Underwood Johnson and Clarence Clough Buel, vol. 1, 8–9 (Castle 1887).

77. Davis had asked his governor whether he should resign from the Senate immediately, or remain in part to head off any possible hostile federal legislation. Governor Pettus instructed Senator Davis to resign. William C. Davis, *supra* note 47, at 14.

78. The Declaration of Independence does indeed state: "He [the King] has excited domestic Insurrections amongst us . . . ." The Declaration does not refer explicitly to slavery or slave insurrections.

79. Most German settlers grew vast cotton crops without the use of slaves. *See* MERLE DURHAM, THE LONE STAR STATE DIVIDED: TEXANS AND THE CIVIL WAR (Hendrick-Long Publishing Co. 1994).

80. The Declaration of the Causes Which Impel the State of Texas to Secede from the Federal Union, Feb. 2, 1861.

81. On March 15, 1866, an Ordinance was adopted that declared the 1861 Ordinance of Secession null and void.

82. The figures are taken from the 1869 Supreme Court case *Texas v. White*, though other sources put the vote at 46,153–14,747. The proportion is roughly the same.

83. The Secretary of State, Eber Cave, was also removed for refusing to pledge allegiance to the Confederacy.

84. The CSA capital was moved to Richmond, Virginia, on May 29, 1861.

85. On February 15th, the CSA Congress formally adopted a resolution calling on the president to appoint a commission of three persons; on February 25th, Davis formally transmitted the names of his three nominees.

86. Seward prepared a memorandum on March 15th that made clear the United States did not recognize the secession or the CSA. The formal delivery of the memo was delayed at the consent of Forsyth and Crawford, but was finally delivered to them on April 8th. Interestingly, Seward, in explaining in the memo

that he was prevented from acknowledging the withdrawal of the "seceded" states, noted in effect that the only way they could properly withdraw would be "with the consent and concert of the people of the United States, to be given through a National Convention, to be assembled in conformity with the provisions of the Constitution . . . ."

87. In his November 14, 1860, speech to the Georgia legislature, in which he urged restraint on secession, Alexander Stephens said: "I do not anticipate that Mr. Lincoln will do anything to jeopardize our safety or security . . . for he is bound by the constitutional checks which are thrown around him, and which render him powerless to do any great mischief. . . . Why, then, should we disrupt the ties of this Union, when his hands are tied—when he can do nothing against us?" Three months later, Stephens became the CSA's vice president.

88. This point is quite in line with the Opinion of Buchanan's Attorney General from the preceding December. On March 14, 1861, the Supreme Court, in a unanimous 8–0 decision written by Chief Justice Taney, declared that Ohio had a "moral duty" to execute an arrest warrant for a crime in Kentucky of assisting a slave to flee, but the United States could not compel that state action. Kentucky v. Dennison, 65 U.S. (24 How.) 66 (1861). The notion of a prohibition that could not be enforced is not dissimilar to the Buchanan position that states were prohibited from seceding, but that the Union could not enforce it.

89. As to the threat of secession in Maryland, see Timothy R. Snyder, *'Making No Child's Play of the Question': Governor Hicks and the Secession Crisis Reconsidered*, 101 MARYLAND HISTORICAL MAGAZINE 304 (Fall 2006).

90. William Marvel, *Martyr Under the Microscope*, AMERICA'S CIVIL WAR, Nov. 2006, at 45. Hayes became the nineteenth president in 1877.

91. The "Cornerstone Speech" in Savannah, Georgia, on March 21, 1861, by Alexander H. Stephens. The text, taken from a newspaper article in the *Savannah Republican*, was reprinted in HENRY CLEVELAND, ALEXANDER H. STEPHENS, IN PUBLIC AND PRIVATE: WITH LETTERS AND SPEECHES, BEFORE, DURING AND SINCE THE WAR 717–29 (National Publishing Company 1886), *available at* http://teachingamericanhistory.org/library/index.asp?documentprint=76.

92. *Id.*

93. At least one serious revisionist scholar, William Marvel, argues that Lincoln viewed Fort Sumter as an asset to heading off the increasing sentiment to simply let the Seven leave—that Lincoln provoked South Carolina to attack Sumter: "the real value of Sumter lay precisely in its vulnerability. . . . Lincoln took provocative action there knowing it would likely lead to violence." Marvel, *Martyr Under the Microscope, supra* note 88, at 45.

94. FREEHLING, *supra* note 10, at 521.

95. SAUNDERS, JOHN ARCHIBALD CAMPBELL, *supra* note 65, at 145.

96. The tie between Campbell and Nelson continued: On December 1, 1864, Campbell (then a CSA official) wrote to Nelson to see whether peace was possible; Nelson replied that another peace effort might be underway And so delay was best. SAUNDERS, JOHN ARCHIBALD CAMPBELL, *supra* note 65, at 161–62. That "other" effort turned out to be the Hampton Roads meeting, at which Campbell was a participant.

97. *Id.* at 147–51

98. FREEHLING, *supra* note 10, at 527–28.

99. The western delegates voted 26–5 against secession on April 17th, and their constituents voted down secession by 3–1 at the May 23rd popular referendum, These thirty-three counties contained one-third of Virginia's white population but only 3 percent of its slaves. FREEHLING, *supra* note 10, at 526.

100. *See* JAMES L. ABRAHAMSON, THE MEN OF SECESSION AND CIVIL WAR, 1859–1861 (Scholarly Resources 2000).

101. DAVID HERBERT DONALD, LINCOLN 301 (Simon & Schuster1995).

102. Willey technically was elected to fill the vacant seat of James M. Mason. In 1863, at the admission of West Virginia, Willey was elected, and reelected to the U.S. Senate from West Virginia, 1863–1871.

103. Robert M. T. Hunter was U.S. Senator from Virginia, 1847–1861, until he became CSA Secretary of State. Carlile was elected to fill Hunter's seat in 1861 and served until 1865, when he returned to his law practice.

104. DONALD, LINCOLN, *supra* note 101, at 300.

105. In his State of the Union message of December 3, 1861, Lincoln's only reference to the state of affairs in Virginia was to the fact that "winter closes on the Union people of Western Virginia, leaving them masters of their own country."

106. CONG. GLOBE, 37th Cong., 2d Sess. 3320 (July 14, 1862).

107. CONG. GLOBE, 37th Cong., 3d Sess. 59 (Dec. 10, 1862).

108. In 1864, Congress passed enabling acts looking toward the admission of three additional states: Nevada, Nebraska, and Colorado. Each of these acts contained a condition that the state was to make an irrevocable commitment to forbid slavery entirely. 13 Stat 30 (Mar. 21, 1864); 13 Stat. 47 (Apr. 19, 1864), and 13 Stat. 32 (Mar. 21, 1864).

109. Children of slaves born after July 4, 1863, were to be born free; all slaves who were under age 10 would be free when they reached 21; and all slaves over 10 and under 21 would be free when they reached age 25; and no slave would be permitted to come into the state for permanent residence.

110. This request for written opinions may have been prompted by the insistence of Attorney General Bates. *See* MICHAEL BURLINGAME, ABRAHAM LINCOLN: A LIFE, vol. II, 460 (Johns Hopkins Univ. Press 2008).

111. Blair arranged meetings between Lincoln and opponents of statehood who tried to persuade Lincoln that the new state would destroy his reconstruction program in Virginia.

112. Finally, the November elections resulted in losses among Republicans in Congress, and it was not at all clear that the new Congress in 1863 would approve statehood. This bill was passed by the old "lame duck" Congress with its strong Republican base. Also, the military situation was not good: the devastating repulse of the Union forces at Fredericksburg shook the nation and added to the gloom. Politically, Lincoln was under pressure from the Radical Republicans, and a veto would deeply upset them. Virginia was winning the war in the field, but with the admission of West Virginia as a state, Virginia would lose her territory.

113. 10 Op. Att'y Gen. 426 (1862).

114. Article IV, sec. 3 provides: "New States may be admitted by the Congress into this Union; but no new States shall be formed or erected within the Jurisdiction of any other State; nor any State be formed by the Junction of two or more States, or Parts of States, without the Consent of the Legislatures of the States concerned as well as of the Congress."

115. Bates noted that Maine was formed from Massachusetts, Kentucky was formed from Virginia, and Tennessee was formed from North Carolina. Op., at 428.

116. Op., at 432.

117. ALLEN C. GUELZO, LINCOLN'S EMANCIPATION PROCLAMATION: THE END OF SLAVERY IN AMERICA 177 (Simon & Schuster 2004).

118. BURLINGAME, ABRAHAM LINCOLN, *supra* note 110, at 461.

119. A bronze statue of Abraham Lincoln graces the steps of the West Virginia capitol in Charleston, commemorating Lincoln's deliberations on making West Virginia a state. In 1867, Lincoln County became the fifty-third county in West Virginia.

120. Two counties (Berkeley and Jefferson) had voted in favor of annexation to West Virginia, but in 1866, Virginia sued West Virginia in the U.S. Supreme Court to have those two counties declared part of Virginia. On March 10, 1866, Congress passed a joint resolution recognizing the transfer. In 1870, the Court, with three dissenting Justices, decided in favor of West Virginia. Virginia v. West Virginia, 78 U.S. (11 Wall.) 39 (1870). The lawyer for the prevailing side, West Virginia, was Reverdy Johnson.

121. Under the Flag Act of 1818, new stars were to be added to the nation's flag on the 4th of July following the admission of a state. Before West Virginia, the previous star had been added for Kansas on July 4, 1861, after Kansas was admitted on January 29, 1861, as the thirty-fourth state. Nevada's star was added on July 4, 1865, after its admission on October 31, 1864, as the thirty-sixth state.

122. 78 U.S. (11 Wall.) 39 (1870). The case was originally argued at the December 1866 term, and then reargued in the December 1870 term. Benjamin R. Curtis, the former Supreme Court Justice who resigned after the *Dred Scott* decision, and Andrew Hunter, the chief prosecutor of John Brown, argued on behalf of Virginia. Reverdy Johnson and others argued for West Virginia, the winning side. Hunter was born in Berkeley County; the John Brown trial was held in Jefferson County.

123. 206 U.S. 290 (1907), decided 9–0.

124. On February 5, 1863, the Senate of the CSA heard a proposed amendment to the CSA Constitution that would allow an aggrieved state to secede from the Confederacy. The departing state would be entitled to its pro rata share of property and be liable for its share of the public debt. The proposal was sent to the Judiciary Committee, where it was dropped as being too dangerous. David J. Eicher, *How the Confederacy Fought Itself*, CIVIL WAR TIMES 55–56 (Jan. 2008).

125. 74 U.S. 700 (1869).

126. There is a question whether Chief Justice Chase should have recused himself from this case since he had been Treasury secretary in 1862.

127. For example, on October 10, 1865, the provisional governor of Texas published a "Caution to the Public" in the *New York Tribune*.

128. Texas v. White, 74 U.S. 700 (1869).

129. Interestingly, Chief Justice Chase cited favorably and at length an opinion written by his predecessor, Chief Justice Taney.

130. In the immediate post-War period, many parts of the South were governed as Military Districts—as occupied territory—before the civil authorities were established.

131. On March 13, 2005, the National People's Congress of the Peoples Republic of China enacted an Anti-Secession Law. (The PRC's official English translation of the law is the "Anti-Secession Law," but the translation of the government of Taiwan is the "Anti-Separation Law," so as not to suggest that Taiwan is part of China. The law provided for the application of "non-peaceful means" in the event that Taiwan tried to secede from China (defined as *de jure* independence).) Clearly, the PRC's goal was to invoke the American Civil War, and to make the PRC position "understandable" to Americans. Taiwan was ceded in perpetuity by China to Japan in 1895, but in 1945, Taiwan was surrendered by Japan to the Kuomintang Administration of the Republic of China.

132. Reference Re Secession of Quebec, [1998] 2 S.C.R. 217.

133. THE ECONOMIST, Feb. 25, 2007, at 43.

134. In the United States, the U.S. Supreme Court does not offer "advisory opinions" since it is empowered by the Constitution to decide only "cases and controversies." However, some ten state supreme courts are empowered to give advisory opinions. The Constitutional Convention of 1787 rejected a proposal for federal Supreme Court advisory opinions; the proposal had been modeled on the Massachusetts Constitution of 1780. *See* Mel A. Topf, *State Supreme Court Advisory Opinions as Illegitimate Judicial Review*, 2001 L. REV. MICH. ST. UNIV. DETROIT C. L. 101. The "World Court," the International Court of Justice (ICJ), is empowered to give advisory opinions within the United Nations system. The court has given twenty-five advisory opinions since 1946. The court's advisory opinions have no binding effect as such, but the authority of the court, as the principal judicial organ of the United Nations, attaches to them. There have been proposals over many years to grant authority to the ICJ to issue advisory opinions on request from the courts of the Member States of the UN. One of the more recent of such proposals came from a former U.S. judge of the ICJ, Stephen Schwebel, in his article *Preliminary Rulings by the International Court of Justice at the Instance of National Courts*, 28 VA. J. INT'L L. 495 (1988). Under Canadian law, in contrast to the United States, the Supreme Court is permitted to offer advisory opinions. The Court decided that the Constitution of 1867 gave Parliament the authority to grant the Court "reference jurisdiction," which includes an advisory role on important questions of law or fact.

135. *See* JOHN REMINGTON GRAHAM, A CONSTITUTIONAL HISTORY OF SECESSION 435–39 (Pelican Publishing 2005), for a discussion of the Canadian Court's advisory opinion.

136. The Court's term was broader, so as to include "where 'a people' is subject to alien subjugation, domination or exploitation; and possibly where 'a

people' is denied any meaningful exercise of its right to self-determination within the state of which it forms a part."

Chapter 5 Notes

1. Portions of this chapter appeared in 31(3) J. SUP. CT. HIST. 262 (2006).
2. Latin for "during war, the laws are silent."
3. Breckinridge had come in second in the electoral votes for president, and would remain in Washington for most of the year as senator from Kentucky.
4. Baker was elected to the Illinois House of Representatives the same year that Lincoln was admitted to the bar, and he defeated Lincoln for the Whig nomination for the congressional seat in 1844. Lincoln named his second son Edward Baker Lincoln. Senator Baker delivered a famous speech on August 1, 1861, in reply to Senator Breckenridge. Eleven weeks later, Baker died at the Battle of Ball's Bluff in Loudon County, Virginia, while leading a Union Army regiment.
5. "I have no purpose, directly or indirectly, to interfere with the institution of slavery in the States where it exists. I believe I have no lawful right to do so . . . ." "There is some difference of opinion whether this [fugitive slave] clause should be enforced by national or by state authority; but surely that difference is not a very material one."
6. "I hold, that in contemplation of universal law, and of the Constitution, the Union of these States is perpetual. . . . It follows from these views that no State, upon its own mere motion, can lawfully get out of the Union . . . ."
7. "In your hands, my dissatisfied fellow countrymen, and not in mine, is the momentous issue of civil war. . . . You have no oath registered in Heaven to destroy the government, while I shall have the most solemn one to 'preserve, protect, and defend it.'"
8. One scholar has noted that *Plessy v. Ferguson* (1896), which upheld a law requiring segregated rail cars in violation of the words of the Fourteenth Amendment, was overruled in 1954. But, a constitutional amendment outlawing segregated schools would never have passed in 1954. Professor Steven G. Calabresi, *The Right Judicial Litmus Test*, WALL ST. J., Oct. 1, 2007, at A-23.
9. The Proclamation of Emergency, declared by Pakistani President General Pervez Musharraf on November 3, 2007, noted, as one of the causes of the emergency, that "some members of the judiciary are working at cross purposes with the executive and legislature . . . [and] there has been increasing interference by some members of the judiciary in government policy . . . [and] some judges overstepping the limits of judicial authority have taken over executive and legislative functions . . . . [T]he honorable judges [must] confine the scope of their activity to the judicial function and not assume charge of administration."
10. 347 U.S. 483 (1954).
11. 358 U.S. 1 (1958). *See* Tony Freyer, Cooper v. Aaron (1958): *A Hidden Story of Unanimity and Division*, 33(1) J. SUP. CT. HIST. 89 (2008).
12. For discussion of the background of the preparation of the opinions, see Freyer, *supra* note 11, at 89.

13. *See* Michael J. Glenmon, *The Case that Made the Court*, WILSON QUARTERLY 20 (Summer 2003). In early 2004, the governor of Massachusetts, Mitt Romney, quoted this part of Lincoln's speech to make the analogy that the Supreme Judicial Court of Massachusetts assumed legislative power in rendering its decision concerning gay marriage. WALL ST. J., Feb. 5, 2004, at A-12.

14. The first associated press group, the New York Associated Press, was founded in 1849. BRAYTON HARRIS, BLUE AND GRAY IN BLACK AND WHITE: NEWSPAPERS IN THE CIVIL WAR 7 (Bradford Brassey, Inc. 1999).

15. DAILY BALTIMORE REPUBLICAN, Mar. 6, 1861. The editorial continued: "It seems to us incredible how anybody can understand the language of the address in any other light. And yet we have journals in our midst professing to look upon it as peaceful and conciliatory, and ready to endorse all its monstrous doctrines."

16. Edward Bates, who would be confirmed as Attorney General, wrote in his diary for that day: "The inauguration of President Lincoln took place in peace without an incident—the day was fine, the crowd immense, thereafter order prevailed everywhere."

17. Taney practiced in Frederick, Maryland, 1801–1823; Lincoln's practice in Springfield, Illinois, lasted only a bit longer.

18. Lincoln represented the Illinois Central Railroad, the Ohio & Mississippi, The Rock Island, the Chicago, Alton & St. Louis, the Tonica & Petersburg, and the Alton & Sangamon railroads. For a discussion of Lincoln's railroad and corporate law practice, see Chapter XV, *Railroad and Big Business Lawyer*, in ALBERT A. WOLDMAN, LINCOLN LAWYER (Carroll & Graf 1936). See also the fine new work, BRIAN DIRCK, LINCOLN THE LAWYER (Univ. of Illinois Press 2007).

19. In 1862, a new law provided for a 3 percent income tax on federal officers, including Court Justices. On grounds of principle (Article III, Section 1 of the Constitution), and probably his financial needs, Taney wrote to Treasury Secretary Chase and declared that he regarded the enactment unconstitutional and void. Chase failed to act, and it was not until 1869, when Treasury Secretary Boutwell put the issue to Attorney General Hoar. The Attorney General agreed with Taney. *See generally* Barry A. Price, *The Question of Diminution of Income for Justices and Judges of the Supreme Court and the Inferior Courts of the United States*, 32(3) J. SUP. CT. HIST. 276 (Nov. 2007).

20. Tribute by senior Associate Justice James M. Wayne upon the death of Taney in 1864, published at 69 U.S. (2 Wall.) (x) (1864).

21. See MICHAEL A. ROSS, JUSTICE OF SHATTERED DREAMS: SAMUEL FREEMAN MILLER AND THE SUPREME COURT DURING THE CIVIL WAR ERA (Louisiana State Univ. Press 2003) for the most complete biography of Miller.

22. William H. Rehnquist, *The Supreme Court in the Nineteenth Century*, 27 J. SUP. CT. HIST. 8–10 (2002). Chief Justice Rehnquist's article provides an excellent overview of the Court during that period.

23. "In the wake of [Lincoln's] assassination, his every act and utterance underwent so deliberate and comprehensive a process of purification and glorification that no mere mortal could satisfy the idealized image of Lincoln we have

inherited." William Marvel, *Martyr Under the Microscope*, AMERICA'S CIVIL WAR, Nov. 2006, at 47.

24. Activists in Maryland have sought to remove the 1872 bronze statue of Chief Justice Roger Brooke Taney from the State House in Annapolis, and a similar one from the Frederick City Hall. The leaders of the effort were the chair of the Democratic Central Committee in Prince Georges County, Maryland. Prince George's County changed the name of the Roger B. Taney Middle School to Thurgood Marshall Middle School. The leaders of the NAACP in Frederick, Maryland, have led a separate movement to remove a 1931 bust of Taney from the front of City Hall in Frederick. WASHINGTON POST, July 23, 2007, at B-1.

25. HAROLD HOLZER, LINCOLN PRESIDENT-ELECT 422 (Simon & Schuster 2008).

26. 48 U.S. (7 How.) 776 (1849).

27. Dred Scott v. Sandford, 60 U.S. (19 How.) 393 (1857).

28. Ableman v. Booth, 62 U.S. (21 How.) 506 (1859). Interestingly, this case involved a writ of habeas corpus issued by a Wisconsin state court with respect to a person in federal custody. The Court said: "No State judge or court, after they are judicially informed that the party is imprisoned under the authority of the United States, has any right to interfere with him, or to require him to be brought before them." 60 U.S. at 524.

29. Kentucky v. Dennison, 65 U.S. (24 How.) 66 (1860). Taney expressly noted the "importance of this case, and of the great interest and gravity of the questions involved in it . . . ." *Id.* at 95.

30. BURTON J. HENDRICK, LINCOLN'S WAR CABINET 539 (Little, Brown & Co. 1946) (Dolphin Books ed. 1961).

31. The petition was addressed to "the Honorable Roger B. Taney Chief Justice of the Supreme Court of the United States and judge of the Circuit Court of the United States in the District of Maryland." An associate of Taney's later asserted that the Chief Justice personally crossed out the reference to "judge of the Circuit Court" to indicate that he was acting as Chief Justice in chambers.

32. Taney's wife Anne was Key's sister. Key was educated at St. John's College in Annapolis and admitted to the bar in 1801. He practiced law in Georgetown with his uncle, Francis Barton Key. Key was the U.S. Attorney for the District of Columbia 1833–1841. In September 1814, he witnessed the British bombardment of Fort McHenry, which inspired him to write his poem, *The Star Spangled Banner*. Key unexpectedly died in January 1843. The Attorney General of the United States, as he was about to begin an argument before the Supreme Court, announced the news of Key's death, and suggested that the Court immediately adjourn; Mr. Justice Thompson readily agreed and ordered adjournment. Obituary Notice at 42 U.S. (1 How.) xi (1843).

33. It is not entirely clear whether Taney went to Baltimore late on Saturday or early on Sunday, but it is clear that the petition was presented to him in Washington on Saturday and that the writ was issued on Sunday in Baltimore.

34. WILLIAM H. REHNQUIST, ALL THE LAWS BUT ONE: CIVIL LIBERTIES IN WARTIME 36 (Knopf 1998).

35. "Article 2. The inhabitants of the said territory shall always be entitled to the benefits of the writ of habeas corpus, and of the trial by jury . . . ."

36. "And that either of the justices of the supreme court, as well as justices of the district courts, shall have power to grant writs of *habeas corpus* for the purpose if an inquiry into the cause of commitment . . . ." Judiciary Act of 1789, Sec. 14, 1 Stat. 73 (1789).

37. William J. Cooper, *Jefferson Davis, American* (Knopf 2000). 386. See also, William C. Davis, *Look Away!* (Free Press 2002) 175–188.

38. Boumediene v. Bush, 553 U.S. 723 (2008). The case, relating to whether aliens detained at Guantanamo had access to the writ, was decided June 12, 2008.

39. General Cadwalader was replaced on June 11th by General Banks of Massachusetts. In December 1862, General Cadwalader was appointed to a Federal Board authorized to revise the military laws of the United States.

40. A year later, Judge John Cadwalader decided the prize case of the vessel *Bermuda*, a blockade runner, and the case was later appealed to the Supreme Court, which in 1865 affirmed Cadwalader's decision in an opinion written by Chief Justice Chase. The Bermuda, 70 U.S. (3 Wall.) 514 (1865).

41. In August 1862, Judge John Cadwalader issued a writ of habeas corpus to secure the release of a Philadelphian, Charles Ingersoll, who was arrested after he gave a speech denouncing the Lincoln administration at a Democratic rally. In mid-1863, the judge was renowned for his use of the writ of habeas corpus to release men conscripted under the new draft law; the riots in New York City that summer reflected the tensions over conscription. *Ex parte Merryman*, 56 MARYLAND HISTORICAL MAGAZINE 386 n.12 (Dec. 1961). *See also* MARK E. NEELY, JR., THE FATE OF LIBERTY: ABRAHAM LINCOLN AND CIVIL LIBERTY 59, 201 (Oxford Univ. Press 1991).

42. Present in the courtroom were Merryman's two lawyers, George M. Gill and George H. Williams, along with the U.S. Attorney for Maryland, William Addison.

43. THE SUN newspaper, Tuesday, May 28, 1861

44. *Ex parte Merryman*, MARYLAND HISTORICAL MAGAZINE, *supra* note 41, at 389–90.

45. Mayor George W. Brown remained in custody in Boston's Fort Warren rather than accept a parole, which implied a crime, when he had committed none.

46. See the excellent article dealing with secession and slavery on Maryland's eastern shore, Brandon P. Righi, *"A Power Unknown to Our Laws": Unionism in Kent County, Maryland 1861–1865*, 103 MARYLAND HISTORICAL MAGAZINE 187, 197–98 (2008).

47. ANTHONY S. PITCH, THE BURNING OF WASHINGTON: THE BRITISH INVASION OF 1814 (Naval Institute Press 1998). Pitch describes the violent rioting in June 1812, just after the Declaration of War against Britain, against the leaders of the antiwar efforts. The sheriff of Baltimore at this time who tried to put down the rioting was William Merryman. *Id.* at 6.

48. *See generally* DAVID GRIMSTED, AMERICAN MOBBING 1828–1861 (Oxford Univ. Press 1998).

49. For an interesting and extended view of the alleged plot, see MICHAEL J. KLINE, THE BALTIMORE PLOT (Westholme Publishing 2008).

50. KRISTEN M. SMITH, THE LINES ARE DRAWN: POLITICAL CARTOONS OF THE CIVIL WAR (Hill Street Press 1999).

51. Address at Sanitary Fair in Baltimore, April 18, 1864.

52. John David Hoptak, *Baltimore, Bricks and First Blood*, AMERICA'S CIVIL WAR, Nov. 2008, at 51. Hoptak describes the injury suffered by an ex-slave who served as an orderly for the commander of the Pennsylvania soldiers.

53. MICHAEL BURLINGAME, ABRAHAM LINCOLN: A LIFE, vol. II, 141 (Johns Hopkins Univ. Press 2008).

54. April 19th also happened to be the anniversary of the battle of Lexington in 1775, where men from Massachusetts were the first to be killed in the Revolutionary War.

55. Mayor Brown was later arrested.

56. There is a major dispute among historians as to the exact number of people killed, and also as to the size of the crowd. *See* Robert Bailey, *The Pratt Street Riots Revised: A Case of Overstated Significance?*, 98 MARYLAND HISTORICAL MAGAZINE 153 (2003).

57. MD. CODE ANN., STATE GOV'T, § 13-307 (1939).

58. From the St. Mary's *Beacon* of April 25, 1861, *quoted in* Edwin W. Beitzell, *Point Lookout Prison Camp for Confederates,* ST. MARY'S HISTORICAL SOCIETY 1983, at 6.

59. William C. Trimble Jr., *Isaac Ridgeway Trimble: One Marylander's Rile in the Civil War.* MARYLAND HISTORICAL SOCIETY NEWS (Fall 2010 at 17–18).

60. Butler was from Lowell, Massachusetts. Two of the soldiers killed in the Pratt Street riot were from Lowell, and a memorial to them stands in downtown Lowell.

61. Mike Clem, *A Port in the Storm*, AMERICA'S CIVIL WAR, Mar. 2010, at 33.

62. Clem, *supra* note 61, at 34.

63. The USS *Constitution* was sent north with the Naval Academy students to Rhode Island, where the Academy was temporally reestablished. The Naval War College was established in 1884 in Newport, Rhode Island.

64. On July 2, 1861, Lincoln issued a formal Order to the Commanding General, Army of the United States which expanded upon this initial Order by authorizing the suspension of the writ in the vicinity of "any military line which is now or which shall be used between the city of New York and the city of Washington" if he or the officer on the line deems it necessary.

65. Law Professor Daniel Farber states that, after the Pratt Street Riot, and before the April 27th suspension order, "Lincoln asked his attorney general for advice about his ability to sidestep normal judicial procedures. Bates delegated the question to an assistant, whose answer was not encouraging." (There is no citation in support of that statement.) DANIEL FARBER, LINCOLN'S CONSTITUTION 158 (Univ. of Chicago Press 2003).

66. Jean Jepson Page, *James McNeill Whistler, Baltimorean, and "The White Girl": A Speculative Essay*, 84 MARYLAND HISTORICAL MAGAZINE 26 (Spring 1989).

67. The DAILY BALTIMORE REPUBLICAN, Tuesday, May 28, 1861, at 3.

68. The Constitution authorizes the use of the militia to execute federal laws. Prior to the Civil War, federal troops were used to disperse abolitionist protestors and forcibly return escaped slaves; in 1957, President Eisenhower used federal troops in Little Rock, Arkansas, to ensure compliance with *Brown v. Board of Education*, 347 U.S. 483 (1954). The case was first argued December 9, 1952, and finally decided unanimously on May 17, 1954.

69. When Congress finally enacted legislation on March 3, 1863, authorizing the president to suspend habeas corpus, it directed the Secretary of State and the Secretary of War "as soon as may be practicable, to furnish to the judges of the circuit and district courts of the United States and of the District of Columbia a list of the names of all persons" who are held as prisoners by the authority of the president. Section 2, An Act Relating to Habeas Corpus, and regulating Judicial Proceedings in Certain Cases, 37th Cong., 3d Sess. (1863) (Habeas Corpus Act of 1863, 12 Stat. 755 (1863)).

70. Julie Reynolds, THE WASHINGTON LAWYER 42–44 (Mar. 2007) (reviewing GEOFFREY ROBERTSON, THE TYRANNICIDE BRIEF: THE STORY OF THE MAN WHO SENT CHARLES I TO THE SCAFFOLD (Pantheon 2006)).

71. Jefferson's Message to Congress on January 22, 1807, was designed to prepare Congress to deal with a motion to suspend the writ of habeas corpus. The Senate voted to suspend with one dissent, while the House voted against suspension 113–19. Peter Charles Hoffer, *The Treason Trials of Aaron Burr* (Univ. Press of Kansas, 2008) at 87–88.

72. While it is not surprising that Taney had access to law books while writing his opinion in Baltimore, one might ask how it was that Taney was able to point to Jefferson's dialogue with Congress a generation earlier. However, around the time of Burr's treason trial in Richmond, Virginia, Taney, as a young lawyer, successfully defended a man accused of conspiring with former Vice President Burr to detach the southern and western states from the Union. So it may not have been difficult for Taney to summon up his memory. Taney did not mention that his mentor, Andrew Jackson, when he was a Major General in New Orleans at the end of the War of 1812, defied a writ of habeas corpus and was fined $1,000 for contempt. Jackson was dogged the rest of his life by the charge that he had acted tyrannically. Well after Jackson had served two terms as president, he lobbied to get the fine refunded. When the Whigs lost control of Congress (March 1842), and the Democrats took control, in January 1844, Congress appropriated funds to repay Jackson the $1,000, plus interest at 6 percent from 1815. The vote was 158–28, with former President John Quincy Adams voting nay. *See* Caleb Crain, *Bad Precedent*, THE NEW YORKER, Jan. 29, 2007, at 78 (reviewing Matthew Warshauer, ANDREW JACKSON AND THE POLITICS OF MARTIAL LAW (Univ. of Tennessee 2006)).

73. JOSEPH STORY, COMMENTARIES ON THE CONSTITUTION OF THE UNITED STATES (Little, Brown & Co. 1851).

74. After Lincoln's suspension of habeas corpus became known, Confederate President Jefferson Davis, a lawyer and former U.S. senator, "exulted that 'we have forever severed our connection with a government that thus tramples on all principles of constitutionality liberty.'" GEORGE C. RABLE, THE CONFEDERATE REPUBLIC 143 (Univ. of North Carolina Press 1994). A Richmond newspaper even proposed that the CSA strike any reference to the ability of the Confederate government to suspend the writ of habeas corpus. *Id.* at 113.

75. After the opinion in the *Merryman* case, former President Franklin Pierce, a New Hampshire Democrat, wrote to Taney to support his decision. In his reply to Pierce dated June 12, 1861, Taney noted the "present state of the public mind inflamed with passion and seeking to accomplish its object by force of arms . . . ." In the same letter, Taney opined that a "peaceful separation, with free institutions in each section, is better than the union of all the present states under a military government . . . ." Clearly, Taney was deeply worried about expanded military powers and the assault on civil liberty.

76. For an excellent treatment of the writ and the courts during the Civil War, see John D. Sharer, *Power, Idealism, and Compromise: The Coordinate Branches and the Writ of Habeas Corpus*, 26 EMORY L.J. 149 (1977). Mr. Sharer notes that on May 2, 1861, Federal District Judge William F. Giles issued a writ for the commanding officer at Fort McHenry, and Judge Giles believed that the power to suspend the writ was exclusively in the hands of Congress. *Id.* at 159–60. Similarly, in August 1861, Federal District Judge Betts in New York took the same position as Taney in ordering the commander of Fort Lafayette to comply with the writ. *Id.* at 162.

77. 17 F. Cas. 144, 153 (1861) (citing U.S. Const., art II, § 3). It was this phrase that Lincoln would throw back at Taney five weeks later.

78. 65 U.S. (24 How.) 66, 109–10 (1861). *Dennison* was overruled by *Puerto Rico v. Branstad*, 483 U.S. 219 (1987). Speaking for an equally unanimous Court, Justice Thurgood Marshall stated that "*Dennison* is the product of another time. The conception of the relation between the States and the Federal Government there announced is fundamentally incompatible with more than a century of constitutional development." 483 U.S. at 230.

79. The First [Special] Session of the 37th Congress met July 4 to August 6, 1861; the Second Session met December 2, 1861, to July 17, 1862, and the Third [lame duck] Session met December 1862 to March 3, 1863.

80. DAVID HERBERT DONALD, LINCOLN 304 (Simon & Schuster 1995). The secretary of the Senate who read the Message was John W. Founey, who was at the same time the publisher of the *Philadelphia Press. See* ERNEST B. FURGURSON, FREEDOM RISING 267 (Knopf 2004).

81. REHNQUIST, ALL THE LAWS BUT ONE, *supra* note 34.

82. It is possible the text of the Fourth of July Special Session Message was being printed for dispatch to Congress at the time that Lincoln issued his July 2nd suspension order to General Scott, and that may explain the absence in the Message of a reference to that action.

83. The first (April 25th) was essentially confined to Frederick, Maryland; the second (April 29th) was confined to the military line from Philadelphia to

Washington; the third (May 10th) was confined to the Florida coast; and this fourth (July 2nd) expanded the line from New York to Washington.

84. Professor Neely notes that Bates' Opinion was not sent to Congress until after the House passed a resolution on July 12th asking for it. The House seemed not to have known about the suspension of habeas corpus, but the Senate apparently did. NEELY, THE FATE OF LIBERTY, *supra* note 41.

85. Ryan's Case, 10 Op. Att'y Gen. 64 (1861).

86. Neely, *supra* note 41, at 11.

87. DORIS KEARNS GOODWIN, TEAM OF RIVALS 673–74 (Simon & Schuster 2005).

88. GOODWIN, *supra* note 87, at 672–73.

89. Opinion of Attorney General Bates, July 5, 1861, at 84.

90. On the first ballot at the nominating convention, Seward received 173½ votes, Lincoln 102, Chase 49, and Bates 48.

91. Conversation with Professor Donald in Washington, November 20, 2003.

92. The sole serious effort to defend Lincoln's suspension was made by Indiana Senator Henry Lane, who accepted Lincoln's argument that if he, the president, could not suspend it when Congress was out of session, there would be times when no one could suspend it. CONG. GLOBE, 37th Cong., 1st Sess. 142–43 (July 16, 1861).

93. The Thirty-seventh Congress had 50 senators of which a majority of 31 were Republicans, and 183 representatives of which 108 were Republicans.

94. 12 Stat. 326, ch. 36, sec. 3 (Aug. 3, 1861).

95. The *New-York Daily Tribune* of May 30, 1861, reminded Taney that the "only man who heartily defended him against the many severe attacks made upon him in the Senate Chamber, because of his decision in the Dred Scott case was Judah P. Benjamin of Louisiana, now the Attorney-General of the so-called Confederate States . . . ."

96. 418 U.S. 683 (1974).

97. The SUN newspaper, June 21, 1981.

98. Within the notion of "good behavior" might well have been a promise by Merryman that he would not file an action for false imprisonment. Such an action could have caused considerable difficulties for the Lincoln administration.

99. Thomas Cotter, *The Merryman Affair*, 24(2) THE HISTORY TRAILS OF THE BALTIMORE COUNTY HISTORICAL SOCIETY (Winter 1989–90) (quoting from the *Attorney General's Letter Books, Edward Bates to William Addison*).

100. Selected Records of the War Department Relating to Confederate Prisoners of War, 1861–1865, Roll 96, vols. 305–310, Fort McHenry, Maryland, Military Prison, Registers of Prisoners and Ledger of Prisoners' Accounts.

101. D. Grier Stephenson, Jr., *Judicial Bookshelf*, 33(2) J. SUP. CT. HIST. 218 n.26 (2008) (reviewing JAMES F. SIMON, LINCOLN AND CHIEF JUSTICE TANEY: SLAVERY, SECESSION AND THE PRESIDENT'S WAR POWERS (Simon & Schuster 2006)).

102. For an extraordinary treatment of this topic, see GEORGE CLARKE SELLERY, LINCOLN'S SUSPENSION OF HABEAS CORPUS AS VIEWED BY CONGRESS, BULL. UNIV. WISC. 149, Hist. Series, vol. 1, no. 3 (April 1907).

103. 12 Stat. 755 (Mar. 3, 1863). The text stated simply that "the President . . . is authorized," leaving it ambiguous whether Congress was conferring the power to suspend or merely recognizing the power in the president's hands. The Act permitted the president to suspend the writ anywhere in the country if he found that public safety required it.

104. The classic book on Vallandigham is Mark E. Neely, Jr., THE FATE OF LIBERTY (Oxford Univ. Press 1991). It was the winner of the 1992 Pulitzer Prize for History.

105. The reimbursement was for the fine ($1,000), but also with interest at 6 percent from March 1815. The congressional action expressly noted that the reimbursement should not be construed as implying censure upon the judge. The vote in the House on January 8, 1844 was 158–28.

106. Youngstown Sheet & Tube Co. v. Sawyer, 343 U.S. 579 (1952).

107. Gordon Berg, *Rebel Raiders Ring Around Baltimore*, AMERICA'S CIVIL WAR, May 2008, at 61. For a more thorough account, see B. F. COOLING, JUBAL EARLY'S 1864 RAID ON WASHINGTON 162–65 (Nautical & Aviation Publishing Co. 1989).

108. JAMES F. SIMON, LINCOLN AND CHIEF JUSTICE TANEY: SLAVERY, SECESSION AND THE PRESIDENT'S WAR POWERS 266 (Simon & Schuster 2006).

109. Not only did Chase want the position, but so also did Stanton, Bates, and Blair.

110. 71 U.S. 2 (1866). The case was argued March 5–13, 1866, and was decided unanimously April 3, 1866; opinions were released on December 17, 1866.

111. For an interesting review of *Merryman* and *Milligan*, see John Yoo, Merryman *and* Milligan *(and* McCardle*)*, 34 J. SUP. CT. HIST. 243 (2009).

112. Taney was quoted in *Holmes v. Jennison*, 39 U.S. 540 (1840), with respect to the procedure of applying for a writ of habeas corpus. *Holmes* substantively dealt with whether the federal government had exclusive authority in foreign affairs.

113. These four Justices, while agreeing that Milligan should be discharged, disagreed that Congress could not authorize military trials of civilians if the civilian courts were open.

114. The Supreme Court of Wisconsin agreed that only Congress could suspend the writ, and it found Taney's reasoning "unanswerable." *In re* Kemp, 16 Wis. 359 (1863). Attorney General Bates advised against taking this case to the U.S. Supreme Court, since an adverse decision would be a blow to the administration. *See* JAMES G. RANDALL, LINCOLN THE PRESIDENT 167–68 (Da Capo 1st ed. 1997). *See also* Joseph A. Ranney, *Wisconsin Law in Wartime*, THE WISCONSIN LAWYER 13, 16 (Feb. 2009).

115. BERNARD SCHWARTZ, THE REINS OF POWER: A CONSTITUTIONAL HISTORY OF THE UNITED STATES 94 (Hill & Wang 1963), *quoted in* Robert Fabrikant,

Review Essay: Some Legal Myths About Lincoln, JOURNAL OF THE ABRAHAM LINCOLN ASSOCIATION 29 (Winter 2008).

Chapter 6 Notes

1. The potential use of letters of marque and reprisal arose in this century in a somewhat different context: Congressman Ron Paul, who ran for president in 2008, introduced a bill, HR 3076, on October 10, 2001, entitled "The September 11th Marque and Reprisal Act of 2001." It authorized the president "to commission, under officially issued letters of marque and reprisal, so many of privately armed and equipped persons and entities as, in his judgment, the service may require, . . . to employ all means reasonably necessary outside the geographic boundaries of the United States . . . the person and property of Osama bin Laden, of any al Qaeda co-conspirator . . . responsible for the air piratical aggressions . . . perpetrated upon the United States . . . ." The bill also provided for the posting of a security bond before a letter of marque could be issued. The bill did not survive the Committee on International Relations. On July 27, 2007, Paul introduced HR 3216, "The Marque and Reprisal Act of 2007," which was essentially the same as the 2001 bill, and it suffered the same fate. In April 2009, Paul suggested the use of Marque and Reprisal as a solution to the Somali pirates.

A professor at the U.S. Naval Academy has suggested that the U.S. might today issue Letters of Marque against non-state actors like terrorist organizations, drug cartels, or even illegal fishing. He suggested a more modern term: "contracts of marque." Lieutenant Claude Berube, "Contracts of Marque" *US Naval Institute Proceedings* (November 2007) at page 10.

2. CRAIG L. SYMONDS, THE CIVIL WAR AT SEA 61 (Praeger 2009).

3. The character Rhett Butler in *Gone with the Wind* was a Confederate privateer.

4. The English tradition in the early nineteenth century was captured brilliantly in Patrick O'Brian's thirteenth novel, *The Letter of Marque*, published in 1988.

5. ROBERT H. PATTON, PATRIOT PIRATES: THE PRIVATEER WAR FOR FREEDOM AND FORTUNE IN THE AMERICAN REVOLUTION 27 (Pantheon Books 2008).

6. Shortly after the outbreak of the Revolution in April 1775, the Provincial Congress—the forerunner of the Continental Congress—authorized the colonies to grant letters of marque to private ships.

7. PATTON, *Patriot Pirates*, *supra* note 5, at xviii–xix.

8. PATTON, *Patriot Pirates*, *supra* note 5, at 142.

9. Letters of Marque were also mentioned in the Articles of Confederation, in Article VI: "nor shall any State grant . . . letters of marque or reprisal, except it be after a declaration of war by the United States in Congress assembled, unless such State be infested by pirates. . . ." Article IX also vested in Congress assembled the sole and exclusive right "of granting letters of marquee and reprisal in times of peace. . . ." However, that Article IX further provides that "Congress assembled shall never . . . grant letters of marque or reprisal in time of peace . . . unless nine States assent to the same. . . ."

Notes

10. As military technology developed, substitution between private and military use became more difficult, and navies became more economical and easier to monitor—and so privateering declined.

11. For a discussion of the laws of war and of prizes and U.S. privateers during the War of 1812, see Frederick C. Leiner, *A Ruse de Guerre Gone Wrong: The Sinking of the* Eleanor, MARYLAND HISTORICAL MAGAZINE 167 (Summer 2006). The situation discussed in the article ended in a unanimous Supreme Court decision in 1817, *The Eleanor*, 15 U.S. (2 Wheat.) 345, 348 (1817). Francis Scott Key was one of the lawyers who argued the case.

12. On June 26, 1812, Congress passed An Act Concerning Letters of Marque, Prizes and Prize Goods to regulate the privateers.

13. A Baltimore schooner, the *Mammoth*, was commissioned on March 7, 1814, AND was one of the most successful privateers, taking twenty-four prizes. Two of her Journals are in the Library of the Maryland Historical Society.

14. The treaty, known as the Treaty of San Lorenzo, which came into force in August 1796, settled the U.S. boundaries, but also provided in Article XIV: "Nor shall any citizen, subject, or Inhabitant of the said United States apply for or take any commissions or letters of marque for arming any ship or ships to act as privateers against the subjects of his Catholic Majesty or the property of any of them from any prince or state with which the said king shall be at war. And if any person of either nation take such commissions or letters of marque he shall be punish as a pirate."

15. Acts of March 3, 1817, April 20, 1818, and May 15, 1820. "Between 1816 and 1820, government agents in Massachusetts, Virginia, Maryland, North Carolina, South Carolina, and Georgia arrested at least 129 men on charges of piracy for commandeering vessels and attacking neutrals . . . . [T]he court found thirty-one guilty of piracy . . . , from April to June 1820 seven of them were executed." See the excellent article, David Head, *Baltimore Seafarers, Privateering, and the South American Revolutions, 1816–1820*, 103 MARYLAND HISTORICAL MAGAZINE 269, 282 (Fall 2008).

16. Texas issued a total of six letters to privateers. Overall, the privateering effort was disappointing, since Mexican shipping was not a rich trade and so relatively few privateers were willing to take the risk. During the U.S.-Mexican war (1846–1848), the United States did not issue any letters of marque; Mexico did, but the result was ineffective. During the Crimean War of 1853–56, neither of the main belligerents (Ottoman Turkey and Russia) issued letters of marque, and the Allied Powers intimated that they would not issue letters of marque.

17. Pierce explained further that the idea of surrendering the right to commission privateers would be akin to surrendering the right to accept volunteers for the land army, and the United States "confidently relies upon the patriotism of its citizens, not ordinarily devoted to the military profession, to augment the Army and the Navy so as to make them fully adequate to the emergency which calls them into action."

18. The other paragraphs stated: "2. The neutral flag covers enemy's goods, with the exception of contraband of war. 3. Neutral goods, with the exception of contraband of war, are not liable to capture under the enemy's flag. 4. Blockades,

in order to be binding, must be effective, that is to say, maintained by a force sufficient to prevent access to the coast of the enemy."

19. Marcy had previously been the three-term governor of New York; he was defeated for reelection in 1839 by William Seward, who became Lincoln's secretary of state.

20. Alexander Tabarrok, *The Rise, Fall, and Rise Again of Privateers*, 11(4) THE INDEPENDENT REVIEW 576 (Spring 2007) (quoting William Marcy).

21. During the U.S.-Spanish War, both countries agreed to abide by the principles of the 1856 Paris Declaration; President McKinley issued such a proclamation on April 21, 1898. As a consequence of merchant vessels being used in combatant fleets during the Russo-Japanese War in 1904—especially the Russian merchant fleet moving through the Bosporus and Dardanelles, the Second Hague Conference of 1907 produced a Convention VII, "Conversion of Merchantships into War-ships," dealing with the problem, for example, by requiring that merchant ships transformed into combatants must bear distinctive signs of their war service. That reflected a more gentlemanly era of naval warfare.

22. CRAIG L. SYMONDS, LINCOLN AND HIS ADMIRALS: ABRAHAM LINCOLN, THE U.S. NAVY, AND THE CIVIL WAR 42 (Oxford Univ. Press 2008).

23. SYMONDS, *supra* note 2, at 63. By mid-August, the British had increased the pressure on Seward. The foreign Secretary, Lord Russell, explained to Charles Francis Adams, the U.S. minister in London, that the UK and other parties to the Declaration of Paris intended to issue a written declaration at the time of any potential U.S. accession. The declaration was to state: "Her Majesty does not intend hereby to undertake any engagement which shall have any bearing, direct or indirect, on the internal differences now prevailing in the United States." Adams viewed this as almost an insult, and all discussions on the topic ended. The timing of this tough British position was significant: just after the news reached London that the Union intended to treat the crews from the *Savannah* and the *Jefferson Davis* as pirates, and after the Union disaster at Bull Run suggested that the rebellion would not be crushed in ninety days, as had previously been assumed.

24. Years after the War, Brigadier General Pierre Gustave Toutant Beauregard, the Southern hero of Fort Sumter, claimed that in May 1861, he presented a plan to Jefferson Davis to buy a fleet of East India steamships, which would form a line to serve as Confederate depots in the Caribbean. This would have undercut the blockade, and also brought recognition from Britain, according to Beauregard. Davis rejected the plan. It is not clear whether this was a real plan or not, and its implementation probably would have bankrupted the CSA Treasury. *See* Keith Miller, *Beauregard's Doubtful Enterprise*, CIVIL WAR TIMES 35 (June 2005).

25. Article I, sec. 8, cl. 11.

26. During the American Revolution, Thomas Paine and George Washington owned stock in privateers.

27. The dashing Confederate raider Raphael Semmes brought seven prizes to Cienfuegos, Cuba, on July 6, 1861, which he planned to leave there until they were adjudicated by a Confederate prize court. But the British, on June 1st,

proclaimed a rule—later adopted by other neutral nations—that excluded prizes from their ports. Therefore, Cuba restored the vessels to their owners. *See* Ari Hoogenboom, Gustavus Vasa Fox of the Union Navy: A Biography 81 (Johns Hopkins Univ. Press 2008).

28. *Id.*

29. Mark A. Weitz, The Confederacy on Trial: The Piracy and Sequestration Cases of 1861, at 23–24 (Univ. Press of Kansas 2005).

30. *Id.* at 25.

31. Ironically, Lincoln made an analogous threat on July 30, 1863. General Order 252 declared retaliation for acts committed against black Union prisoners of war. In the Order, Lincoln referred to the law of nations and "customs of war as carried on by civilized powers" that permit no distinction as to color. Thus, Lincoln declared: "if the enemy shall sell or enslave anyone because of his color, the offense shall be punished by retaliation upon the enemy's prisoners . . . . [F]or every soldier of the United States killed in violation of the laws of war, a rebel soldier shall be executed; and for every one enslaved by the enemy or sold into slavery, a rebel soldier shall be placed at hard labor . . . ."

32. Lord Day & Lord was founded in 1848 and shut down in 1994.

33. Sullivan & Cromwell was involved in the formation of Edison General Electric Company and the U.S. Steel Corporation. It now has offices worldwide.

34. Weitz, *supra* note 29, at 71–72.

35. Smith was one of the dignitaries on the platform when Lincoln delivered his famous Cooper Union speech in early 1860. *See* Harold Holzer, Lincoln at Cooper Union 104 (Simon & Schuster 2004).

36. A full account of the trial is presented in John D. Gordan III, *The Trial of the Officers and Crew of the Schooner "Savannah,"* 1983 Supreme Court Historical Society Yearbook 31.

37. The jurisdiction of the U.S. district court at that time was limited to admiralty, bankruptcy, and minor crimes. The circuit court, at that time was the U.S. court of general jurisdiction; there was no U.S. court of appeal. The circuit court was presided over by the Justice of the Supreme Court allotted for that purpose. A conviction in the circuit court could be reviewed by the Supreme Court only upon the certification of division of the two judges below.

38. Weitz, *supra* note 29, at 80.

39. The United Nations Convention on the Law of the Sea of December 10, 1982 (1833 U.N.T.S. 396) provides a definition of piracy in Article 101: "any illegal acts of violence or detention, or any act of depredation, committed for *private ends* by the crew or the passengers of a private ship . . . ." (emphasis added).

40. Weitz, *supra* note 29, at 84.

41. Weitz, *supra* note 29, at 84–85.

42. "Archbishop John Joseph Hughes of New York . . . urged his flock to help suppress the rebellion. But early in the war he pointedly warned the Lincoln Administration that if Irish-American soldiers had 'to fight for the abolition of slavery, then, indeed, they will turn away in disgust from the discharge of what would otherwise be a patriotic duty.'" Richard F. Welch, *The Green and The Blue*, Civil War Times 24 (Oct. 2006).

43. Quoted in ALAN M. DERSHOWITZ, AMERICA ON TRIAL: INSIDE THE LEGAL BATTLES THAT TRANSFORMED OUR NATION 142–43 (Warner Books 2004).

44. "The abolitionist demand for the end of slavery provoked almost hysterical fear of a flood of liberated slaves marching north and ousting the Irish from their jobs by accepting lower wages." Welch, *supra* note 42, at 23–24.

45. The substantial number of Irish immigrants who came to America due to the Potato Famine of 1845–53 were not welcomed by the Whigs or Republicans, but the Democrats received them with open arms, and so by the 1860s they were a major force in urban Democratic politics.

46. Jury nullification is the phenomenon of turning a blind eye: jurors may refuse to convict criminal defendants because they do not like the law or the use to which it is being put, for reasons wholly unrelated to the strength or weakness of the government's case. The jury has the raw power to acquit defendants notwithstanding the evidence.

47. WEITZ, *supra* note 29, at 195.

48. Benjamin was Attorney General from February to August 1861, when he became Secretary of War. In March 1862, he became Secretary of State of the CSA.

49. The Dix-Hill Cartel, the first formal agreement between the two sides, was signed on July 22, 1862. By June 1863, the exchange had stopped.

50. WEITZ, *supra* note 29, at 196.

51. From the Spanish word *filibustero*, defined as an adventurer who engages in unauthorized warfare against a country at peace with his own, "filibuster" especially applied to nineteenth century U.S. adventurers who led expeditions into Latin American countries.

52. The description of the journey to Richmond and the discussions with Davis and Benjamin may be self-serving, since they come from Harpending's autobiography, edited by JAMES H. WILKINS, THE GREAT DIAMOND HOAX AND OTHER STIRRING INCIDENTS IN THE LIFE OF ASBURY HARPENDING, ch. VI (James H. Barry Co. 1913).

53. MICHAEL BURLINGAME, ABRAHAM LINCOLN: A LIFE, vol. II, 250 (Johns Hopkins Univ. Press 2008). In the famous portrait by Francis Carpenter, *The First Reading of the Emancipation Proclamation of President Lincoln*, the artist substituted John Bright's photo and replaced it with a photo of former Secretary of War Simon Cameron. *See* Harold Holzer, *A Promise Fulfilled*, CIVIL WAR TIMES 33 (Dec. 2009).

54. Field was Lincoln's fourth Supreme Court appointee, on March 6, 1863. Field was confirmed and took his oath on May 20th. Field's brother, David Dudley Field, had been a strong Lincoln supporter at the 1860 Republican Party Convention.

55. The Militia Act became law on July 17, 1862.

56. United States v. Greathouse, 26 F. Cas. 18, 16 (C.C.N.D. Cal. 1863).

57. Conness happened to be with Sumner the night of Lincoln's assassination, and the men rushed to Seward's house upon learning of the attack upon him, and then to the White House. Conness was a pallbearer at Lincoln's funeral on April 19, 1865.

58. Symonds, Lincoln and His Admirals, *supra* note 22, at 39–40.

59. The North Atlantic Blockading Squadron patrolled from Wilmington, North Carolina, north to Virginia. The South Atlantic Squadron patrolled from Wilmington to the tip of Florida. The East Gulf Squadron was responsible for the ports from the Florida tip to New Orleans. And the West Gulf Squadron took New Orleans west to Brownsville, Texas. *See* Jack K. Trammell, *Blockade in Name Only*, America's Civil War, Nov. 2007, at 47.

60. In the spring of 1861, General-in-Chief Winfield Scott advised the president that an effective blockade of southern ports, a strong thrust down the Mississippi Valley, and the establishment of a line of strong federal positions there would isolate the disorganized Confederacy. General McClellan called it Scott's "boa-constrictor" plan. The press ridiculed the plan and renamed it the Anaconda Plan. It was not adopted, though it was utilized in the West and by Grant in 1864. Scott, a national hero, served as a general longer than any other man in U.S. history; he was the Whig nominee for president in 1852. At least one scholar points out that "[i]nitially, at least, Lincoln's blockade declaration was not part of a grand strategy for Union victory—the so-called Anaconda Plan would not emerge for another two weeks [after the April 19th proclamation]." Symonds, Lincoln and His Admirals, *supra* note 22, at 40–41.

61. Trammell, *supra* note 59, at 47.

62. Thomas P. Lowry, *The Big Business of Bahamian Blockade Running*, Civil War Times 58 (May 2007). Large, slow craft brought freight to the Bahamas, and smaller, swifter craft carried the cargo on the final leg of the voyage from the Bahamas to the Confederacy.

63. Generally, a prize court, which in the United States was a U.S. district court, adjudicated the legality of the seizure of ships and cargos, which came into the custody of the court. An attorney for the captor or the government "libeled" the prize, i.e., petitioned an inquest for the purpose of determining the facts. The court made its decision to condemn or to release the vessel. For detailed coverage of these matters, see Stuart L. Bernath, Squall Across the Atlantic: American Civil War Prize Cases and Diplomacy (Univ. of California Press 1970).

64. The British Foreign Secretary consulted the Queen's Advocate General about the merits of the prize case and whether the government should provide representation, since this was the first British vessel to be captured under the blockade. Lord Russell then informed Lord Lyons that the case should go through the prize court without British government intervention.

65. "Libeled" is the technical term, under maritime pleading rules, for the initial step in beginning a proceeding. Similarly, the person who files a libel—the complainant—is known as the "libellant."

66. At that time, one-fifth of the UK made a living from the manufacture of cotton, 80 percent of which came from the American South; France imported 90 percent of its cotton from the South, and it textile factories employed a quarter of a million people. George C. Herring, From Colony to Superpower: US Foreign Relations since 1776, at 226 (Oxford Univ. Press 2008).

67. The United States sold Russia large quantities of coal, cotton, and war supplies; American volunteers fought with Russia, and U.S. doctors served with its army. *Id.* at 228.

68. On July 17, 1861, President Juarez issued a moratorium suspending all foreign debt payments for two years. The French, Spanish, and English invaded Mexico, though the English and Spanish eventually withdrew. Ferdinand Maximilian Joseph, Archduke of Austria, became Emperor of Mexico under Napoleon III. He was crowned in Mexico City on June 10, 1864. The French finally left Mexico in March 1867—in part because of the end of the U.S. Civil War.

69. Ohio Senator Tom Corwin, appointed by President Lincoln as the American Minister to Mexico, understood financial matters, since he had served as President Fillmore's Secretary of the Treasury (1850–1853). Later, Lincoln pushed to make a major loan to Mexico, based in part on a report from Corwin. *See* Lincoln's Message to the U.S. Senate, January 24, 1862.

70. The "Monroe Doctrine" was expressed during President Monroe's seventh annual Message to Congress, on December 2, 1823. He stated: "the American continents, are henceforth not to be considered as subjects for future colonization by any European powers . . . . [W]e should consider any attempt on their part to extend their system to any portion of this hemisphere as dangerous to our peace and safety."

71. Secretary of State Seward proposed a plan that would provide mining concessions in exchange for American loans. In the event that the debts were not repaid, Mexico would agree to the cession of Baja California and other Mexican states. Corwin successfully negotiated a treaty, but Congress rejected it because it would drain funds from Civil War expenditures.

72. HAROLD HOLZER, LINCOLN PRESIDENT-ELECT 229–30 (Simon & Schuster 2008).

73. Charles Francis Adams' grandfather, John Adams, was the second president (1797–1801); his father, John Quincy Adams, was the sixth president (1825–1829).

74. HERRING, *supra* note 66, at 231.

75. HERRING, *supra* note 66, at 237.

76. Wilkes was born in New York City in 1798, the great-nephew of the celebrated late eighteenth-century British politician John Wilkes. Later in the War, he was court-martialed for disobedience, disrespect, insubordination, and conduct unbecoming an officer, due to his comments about the secretary of the navy, Gideon Welles. He was found guilty and sentenced to a public reprimand and suspended for three years, later reduced to one year.

77. SYMONDS, LINCOLN AND HIS ADMIRALS, *supra* note 22, at 74.

78. SYMONDS, LINCOLN AND HIS ADMIRALS, *supra* note 22, at 71.

79. This relationship is described in Jay Monaghan's ABRAHAM LINCOLN DEALS WITH FOREIGN RELATIONS: A DIPLOMAT IN CARPET SLIPPERS (Dobbs-Merrill 1945).

80. Under international law, the Union ship had every right to stop and search the *Trent*, but the *Trent* master had no right to refuse to show the ship's papers.

81. Symonds, Lincoln and his Admirals, *supra* note 22, at 80.

82. *Id.* at 72. Wilkes had been a maverick. Following a long expedition in 1842, there were a series of courts-martial and "a legacy of bitterness and resentment that generated years of unprofessional bickering within the navy." Symonds, Lincoln and his Admirals, *supra* note 22, at 72.

83. Ari Hoogenboom, Gustavus Vasa Fox of the Union Navy: A Biography 106 (Johns Hopkins Univ. Press 2008).

84. David Paull Nickles, at 69.

85. Symonds, Lincoln and his Admirals, *supra* note 22, at 80–81.

86. Today, this is "Blair House," the U.S. official guest house for foreign heads of state. It is also where the Trumans lived while the White House was being renovated.

87. Hoogenboom, *supra* note 83, at 107.

88. *Id.* at 81. Of course, they may have been influenced by anti-British sentiment.

89. Symonds, Lincoln and his Admirals, *supra* note 22, at 82.

90. Richard Hough, Victoria and Albert 182 (St. Martin's Press 1996).

91. James F. Simon, Lincoln and Chief Justice Taney 209 (Simon & Schuster 2006).

92. Prince Albert died not long after. Queen Victoria autographed the instructions document before sending it to the achieves: "This draft was the last the beloved Prince ever wrote."

93. Ironically, in President Buchanan's final State of the Union message to Congress on December 3, 1860, he referred with pleasure to the fact that relations with Britain were good because "the claim on the part of Great Britain forcibly to visit and search American merchant vessels on the high seas in time of peace has been abandoned. . . . This was rendered manifest by the exasperated state of public feeling . . . produced by the forcible search of American merchant vessels by British cruisers on the coast of Cuba in the spring of 1858." The potential collision between the two naval forces was "prevented by an appeal to the justice of Great Britain and to the law of nations as expounded by her own most eminent jurists."

94. Simon, Lincoln and Chief Justice Taney, *supra* note 91, at 209.

95. Symonds, Lincoln and his Admirals, *supra* note 22, at 83.

96. Kathleen Burk, Old World, New World: Great Britain and America from the Beginning 270–71 (Atlantic Monthly Press 2007).

97. Symonds, Lincoln and his Admirals, *supra* note 22, at 83.

98. At that time, a diplomat had to wait for about a month to send a dispatch to Europe and to receive a reply. The first trans-Atlantic cable was laid in 1857 by the USS *Niagara*, but the cable broke. It was spliced together in late July 1858, and Queen Victoria flashed the first cable across to President Buchanan on August 16th. The cable functioned for three weeks only. Telegraphic communication between the United States and Europe was not reestablished until 1866. One scholar concluded that the *Trent* Affair "provides an instance when the use of the telegraph in diplomacy, by eliminating periods of delay, would have created more problems than it solved." David Paul Nicholes, Under

THE WIRE: HOW THE TELEGRAPH CHANGED DIPLOMACY (Harvard Univ. Press 2003) at 77.

99. NICKLES at 72.

100. DORIS KEARNS GOODWIN, TEAM OF RIVALS: THE POLITICAL GENIUS OF ABRAHAM LINCOLN 399 (Simon & Schuster 2005).

101. Indeed, the first naval crisis faced by the new American government was in 1794 when "the British navy began scooping up American merchant ships on the high seas as a part of its naval blockade of France." JOSEPH J. ELLIS, AMERICAN CREATION 194 (Knopf 2007).

102. Wilkes continued to cause problems with the British off Bermuda about which Lord Lyons complained to Seward. Wilkes then angered the Danish government over his provocative actions in the Danish West Indies. Finally, in May 1963, Lyons vigorously complained again about Wilkes, and on June 1st, Wilkes was reassigned to the Pacific.

103. The *Economist*, April 29, 1865.

104. The *Amy Warwick* case in Boston was affirmed at the circuit level, but it is unclear who delivered the opinion, and the *Brilliante* cases from Key West, Florida, seem to have no published opinion at either the district or circuit levels.

105. See the excellent article by Chief Justice (retired) Amestoy. Jeffrey L. Amestoy, *The Supreme Court Argument that Saved the Union: Richard Henry Dana, Jr., and the* Prize Cases, 35(1) J. SUP. CT. HIST. 10, 13 (Mar. 2010).

106. For a superb discussion of the extraordinary role played by Dana, see Amestoy, *supra* note 105.

107. Carlisle also addressed some unique considerations that related to his client's case, such as the fact that the Treaty of Guadalupe Hidalgo required that the port of New Orleans had to be open to trade with Mexico.

108. Prize Cases, 67 U.S. (2 Black) 635, 648 (1862).

109. *Id.* at 659.

110. BERNATH, SQUALL ACROSS THE ATLANTIC, *supra* note 63, at 27–28.

111. On March 6th, just four days earlier, Lincoln nominated Stephen J. Field of California for the new Tenth Circuit of the Supreme Court. His brother, David Dudley Field, had been a strong Lincoln supporter at the 1860 Republican Convention.

112. When the War came, Justice John A. Campbell of Alabama resigned from the Court because of his loyalty to his native state.

113. Grier had fully concurred with the Taney opinion in the *Dred Scott* case; President-elect Buchanan (a fellow Pennsylvanian) had written to Grier to urge him to side with the majority. President Polk nominated Grier in 1846.

114. In an interesting article defending the Israeli legal position with respect to its blockade of Gaza starting in 2007, Professor Eric Posner referred to the *Prize Cases*, though not by name. He suggested that it endorsed the proposition that an armed conflict existed even though one side—the CSA—was not a sovereign state, just as Gaza is not a sovereign state. Eric Posner, *The Gaza Blockade and International Law*, WALL ST. J., June 4, 2010, at A-19.

115. 67 U.S. at 666–67.

116. Following the British recognition of the South's belligerency, this was followed by Spain on June 17, France on June 30, and Portugal on July 29.

Notes

117. Nelson was appointed to the Court in 1845 by President Tyler. Nelson concurred in the *Dred Scott* case, but expressed no opinion on whether the Missouri Compromise was constitutional.

118. The official Supreme Court Report of the *Prize Cases* states that these three Justices concurred in the Nelson dissent, and the written opinion deals only with the *Hiawatha* case. However, one scholar takes the position that the dissents of Taney, Catron, and Clifford were not in concurrence with that, but rather with the *Brilliante* case, which had the special feature of the Treaty with Mexico. However, those dissents were not supported by written opinions. ROBERT BRUCE MURRAY, LEGAL CASES OF THE CIVIL WAR 17 (Stackpole Books 2003). If Murray is correct, then the vote in the other three cases was 8 to 1, not 5 to 4.

119. See EDWIN C. BEARSS & J. PARKER HILLS, RECEDING TIDE: VICKSBURG AND GETTYSBURG—THE CAMPAIGNS THAT CHANGED THE CIVIL WAR (National Geographic 2010).

120. On February 25, 1863, the day after the oral arguments ended in *Prize Cases*, the Senate approved a bill to add a tenth Justice, and on March 2nd, the House followed suit. Lincoln signed the bill on March 3rd, one week before the announcement of the decision in the *Prize Cases*. The *New York Times* noted approvingly that the new Justice would be assigned to the Pacific Circuit, and that he "will speedily remove the control of the Supreme Court from the Taney School." Quoted in MICHAEL A. ROSS, JUSTICE OF SHATTERED DREAM: SAMUEL FREEMAN MILLER AND THE SUPREME COURT DURING THE CIVIL WAR ERA 85 (Louisiana State Univ. Press 2003).

121. Field (Lincoln), Davis (Lincoln), Miller (Lincoln), Swayne (Lincoln), Clifford (Buchanan), Grier (Polk), Nelson (Tyler), Catron (Jackson), Taney (Jackson), and Wayne (Jackson).

122. Congress originally set the number of Justices at six in the Judiciary Act of 1789. It was then decreased to five Justices by the Judiciary Act of 1801, but that Act was repealed in 1802, and the number was increased to seven Justices in 1807. After the great western expansion of the nation, Congress in 1837 increased the size to nine in the Judiciary Act of 1837. In 1863, Congress increased it to ten in the Tenth Circuit Act of March 3, 1863. The Judiciary Act of 1866 reduced the number of Justices to seven from ten by attrition (to prevent President Andrew Johnson from making appointments). Finally, the Judiciary Act of 1869 increased the number to nine, where it has remained ever since. Thus, the Court had ten Justices from Justice Field's oath on December 7, 1863, to the death of Justice Catron on May 30, 1865, except for the two-month period between Chief Justice Taney's death and Chief Justice Chase's oath in 1864.

123. See Amestoy, *supra* note 105, at 22–23.

Chapter 7 Notes

1. The King's Bench (or the Queen's Bench, during the reign of a female monarch) dates back to the thirteenth century in England. It was the senior court of common law with civil and criminal jurisdiction. In 1875, it was abolished by the Supreme Court of Judicature Act, and was replaced by the new High Court of Justice.

2. Mark S. Weiner, Black Trials: Citizenship from the Beginnings of Slavery to the End of Caste 73 (Knopf 2004).

3. Murray (1705–1793) studied at Oxford and at Lincoln's Inn, and entered the House of Commons in 1742. He was immediately appointed Solicitor General at the age of 37. In 1754, Murray was appointed Attorney General, and two years later he was appointed Chief Justice of the Court of King's Bench and was raised to peerage as the first Earl of Mansfield. His portrait hangs in "Kenwood," his former estate near Hampshire Heath.

4. Julius Bryant, Kenwood: The Iveagh Bequest 1 (Kate Jeffrey, ed., English Heritage Press 2001).

5. *See* Steven M. Wise, Though the Heavens May Fall: The Landmark Trial that Led to the End of Human Slavery (Da Capo 2005).

6. Weiner, *supra* note 2, at 85.

7. Id.

8. Akhil Reed Amar, America's Constitution: A Biography 258 (Random House 2005).

9. For an interesting discussion of the Somerset case, especially the "Mansfieldian moment," see David Waldstreicher, Slavery's Constitution: From Revolution to Ratification 39–42 (Hill and Wang 2009).

10. Article III of the "Act for the Abolition of Slavery throughout the British Colonies" of August 28, 1833.

11. David Brion Davis, Inhuman Bondage: The Rise and Fall of Slavery in the New World 148 (Oxford Univ. Press 2006).

12. Ezra B. Chase, Teachings of Patriots and Statesmen; or, the "Founders of the Republic" on Slavery 253 (J. W. Bradley 1861).

13. *Id.* at 150

14. George M. Fredrickson, *Redcoat Liberation*, 53(13) The New York Review of Books 51–53 (Aug. 10, 2006).

15. It was Britain's small colony of freed blacks in Sierra Leone that helped to inspire the later American settlement of Liberia. Davis, *supra* note 11, at 173. By the late 1790s, the colony had lost most of its original humanitarian character and had become a commercial venture directed from London. Fredrickson, *supra* note 14, at 51. *The Book of the Negroes* by Lawrence Hill (HarperCollins LTD: Toronto: 2007) presents the fictional life of an African woman who was abducted into slavery in South Carolina, but who then took advantage of the British offer and was taken to Nova Scotia—and then taken by the British to Freetown, Sierra Leone. The "Book" of the title was taken from the name of the British military ledger in which escaped slaves were enrolled, and which formed the basis for Black Loyalists to gain passage on British vessels from New York to Nova Scotia. A British-American scholar wrote a nonfiction account of the same situation, and asked the revealing question: If you were a black in America at the start of the Revolution, who would you want to win? Simon Schama, Rough Crossings: Britain, the Slaves and the American Revolution (HarperCollins: 2007).

16. John D. Burton, *American Loyalists, Slaves and the Creation of an Afro-Bahamian World*, 26 Journal of the Bahamas Historical Society (October 2004) #13, at 14.

17. *Id.* at 152.
18. DAVIS, *supra* note 11, at 275.
19. DAVIS, *supra* note 11, at 255.
20. The Amistad, 40 U.S. (15 Pet.) 518 (1841). The events surrounding the *Amistad* were presented in movie version in 1997, directed by Steven Spielberg, and starred Anthony Hopkins as former President John Quincy Adams.
21. According to the 1790 Census, there was a total U.S. population of 3,893,635, of which 694,280 were slaves and 59,150 were freed blacks. There were no slaves in two states: Maine and Massachusetts. JOSEPH J. ELLIS, FOUNDING BROTHERS: THE REVOLUTIONARY GENERATION 102 (Vintage Books 2002).
22. WEINER, *supra* note 2, at 92.
23. ELLIS, FOUNDING BROTHERS, *supra* note 21, at 103.
24. JOSEPH J. ELLIS, AMERICAN CREATION: TRIUMPHS AND TRAGEDIES AT THE FOUNDING OF THE REPUBLIC 268 n.53 (Knopf 2007).
25. *See* ELLIS, AMERICAN CREATION, *supra* note 24, at 235.
26. DAVIS, *supra* note 11, at 181.
27. DAVIS, *supra* note 11, at 184.
28. WEINER, *supra* note 2, at 158. In 1820, there were about 1.5 million slaves; by 1840, that number had jumped to 2.5 million.
29. "In 1860, out of a white population of some eight million, roughly ten thousand families belonged to the planter 'aristocracy.' Fewer than three thousand families could be counted as owners of over one hundred slaves. Only one out of four white Southerners owned a slave or belonged to a family that did." DAVIS, *supra* note 11, at 197.
30. Slavery was declining for many reasons, including the nature of agriculture and the rise of industry, which did not need slaves. The big slave movement was slaves from the Upper South (e.g., Virginia) being sold farther south to the giant plantations in Mississippi, Louisiana, and Alabama.
31. Years later, Lincoln was involved with the Illinois chapter of the ACS. ALLEN C. GUELZO, LINCOLN'S EMANCIPATION PROCLAMATION: THE END OF SLAVERY IN AMERICA 24 (Simon & Schuster 2004).
32. DAVIS, *supra* note 11, at 256.
33. ELLIS, AMERICAN CREATION, *supra* note 24, at 238–39.
34. WILLIAM LEE MILLER, ARGUING ABOUT SLAVERY: THE GREAT BATTLE IN THE UNITED STATES CONGRESS 513 (Knopf 1996).
35. An Act to Prohibit the Carrying on the Slave Trade from the United States to any Foreign place or Country ("Slave Trade Act of 1794"), 1 Stat. 348, 3d Cong., 1st Sess. 72 (Mar. 22, 1794).
36. Rhode Island alone sent out more than two hundred slaving expeditions between 1794 and 1804. RON SOODALTER, HANGING CAPTAIN GORDON 3–4 (Atria 2006).
37. DON E. FEHRENBACHER, THE SLAVEHOLDING REPUBLIC: AN ACCOUNT OF THE UNITED STATES GOVERNMENT'S RELATIONS TO SLAVERY 135, 140 (Oxford Univ. Press 2001).
38. An Act for the Abolition of the Slave Trade, 1807, 47 Geo. 3, Sess. 1, c. 36 (Eng.).

39. The King did not come to the House of Lords to endorse the Act in person, but the Royal Assent was noted at the top of the engrossed Act, "Le Roy le vault" (the King wishes it).

40. Howard Temperley, *March of the Saints*, TIMES LITERARY SUPPLEMENT 8–9 (Aug. 17, 2007). For a piercing review of the American film, *Amazing Grace*, which centered on Wilberforce, see Adam Hochschild, *English Abolition: The Movie*, TIMES LITERARY SUPPLEMENT (June 14, 2007).

41. "The 1807 abolition act came at a time when Britain not only led the world in plantation production but had the opportunity, thanks to naval power and the wartime conquests of . . . Caribbean colonies—of nearly monopolizing the slave trade and gaining a preponderant share of the growing world market for sugar and coffee." David Brion Davis, *Universal Attractions of Slavery*, NEW YORK REVIEW OF BOOKS 73 (Dec. 17, 2009). Davis is the Sterling Professor of History Emeritus at Yale. He was reviewing SEYMOUR DRESCHER, ABOLITION: A HISTORY OF SLAVERY AND ANTISLAVERY (Cambridge Univ. Press 2009).

42. "Pity for Poor Africans," William Cowper (1731–1800), was displayed at the museum at No. One Royal Crescent, Bath, Bath and the Slave Trade project, April–July 2007.

43. FEHRENBACHER, THE SLAVEHOLDING REPUBLIC, *supra* note 37, at 144.

44. FEHRENBACHER, THE SLAVEHOLDING REPUBLIC, *supra* note 37, at 43.

45. Ironically, later abolitionists argued that the words "migration or importation" in Article I, section 9 of the Constitution—the provision that barred Congressional action until 1808—gave to Congress the right (in 1808) to ban the import of slaves, but also to prohibit their migration from one state to another. *See* David L. Lightner, *The Supreme Court and the Interstate Slave Trader: A Study in Evasion, Anarchy, and Extremism*, 29(3) J. SUP. CT. HIST. 229 (Nov. 2004).

46. FEHRENBACHER, THE SLAVEHOLDING REPUBLIC, *supra* note 37, at 150.

47. Attorney General Wirt's Opinion of November 5, 1821.

48. "An Act to Continue in force 'An Act to Protect the Commerce of the United States, and to punish the Crime of Piracy' and also to make further provision for Punishing the Crime of Piracy," III Stat. Cap. CXIII of May 15, 1820. Only Sections 4 and 5 applied to the slave trade.

49. Carefully excepted were Negroes who were slaves by the law of U.S. states or territories.

50. RON SOODALTER, HANGING CAPTAIN GORDON 9 (Atria 2006).

51. *Id.* at 1.

52. *Id.* at 196. The jurisdictional problem arose because there was no "division" between the two judges who heard the case, i.e., they both agreed.

53. For an excellent discussion of this, see WILLIAM W. FREEHLING, THE ROAD TO DISUNION: SECESSIONISTS TRIUMPHANT vol. 2, 168–84 (Oxford Univ. Press 2007).

54. "Coolies" were unskilled laborers, usually from the Far East, who were hired for meager wages.

55. See generally Robert J. Plowman, *The Voyage of the "Coolie" Ship* Kate Hooper, PROLOGUE MAGAZINE (Summer 2001).

56. 12 Stat. 340 (1862).

57. Davis, *The Universal Attractions of Slavery*, supra note 41, at 74. Davis added: "By 1833, when public demands succeeded in achieving the emancipation of 800,000 slaves, the number of petition signers had risen to 1.3 million, about 30 percent of whom were women."

58. British National Archives, Colonial Office 137/186, 1832.

59. Slavery Abolition Act, 1833, 3 & 4 Will. 4, c.73 (Eng.).

60. Recent discoveries have implicated the founders of Rothschild and Freshfields—the great British banking and law firms—in slavery, including holding mortgages where slaves were collateral or obtaining compensation for the loss of slaves. *See Rothschild and Freshfields founders had links to slavery, papers reveal*, FINANCIAL TIMES, June 27–28, 2009, at 1 & 4.

61. One scholar has argued that the South overreacted in the 1830s and 1840s to the threat of the abolitionists, and that the explanation for the overreaction was Britain's abolition of slavery—since Britain was by far the largest market for Southerner's slave-grown cotton. *See* DAVID BRION DAVIS, CHALLENGING THE BOUNDARIES OF SLAVERY (Harvard Univ. Press, 2003).

62. The last Canadian slave extradition case involved a Missouri slave, John Anderson, who had escaped to Canada and whose return was sought in early 1861. The Canadian judges decided—on a technicality, not on principle—that Anderson should not be returned. Both the Blackburn and Anderson cases were awkward, because there were allegations in each case that the fugitive slaves had committed murder.

63. By 1840, the westward flow of planters and slaves helped make New Orleans the nation's largest slave market and its third largest city. Robert Behre, *King Cotton*, AMERICA'S CIVIL WAR, Jan. 2010, at 37.

64. FREDERICK DOUGLASS, THE HEROIC SLAVE (Penguin Books 2003).

65. Jon Acheson, *Charles Dickens in America: The Baltimore Letters*, 102(4) MARYLAND HISTORICAL MAGAZINE 331 (Winter 2007).

66. The great scholar Earl M. Maltz notes that "the Southern-dominated Committee on Foreign Affairs of the House of Representatives not only recommended that the demands [of the Spanish Government] be honored but also excoriated the decision itself in the strongest terms." EARL M. MALTZ, SLAVERY AND THE SUPREME COURT, 1825–1861, at 66 (Univ. Press of Kansas 2009).

67. PAUL FINDLEY, A. LINCOLN: THE CRUCIBLE OF CONGRESS 137–40 (James Stevenson 2004).

68. DAVID HERBERT DONALD, LINCOLN 136–37 (Simon & Schuster 1995).

69. *Id.* at 87.

70. The first proto-Republican Party meeting was in early 1854 in Ripon, Wisconsin, but the first full organizing convention was held in Pittsburgh in February 1856, and the party's first nominating convention was in Philadelphia on June 17, 1856—the date of the birth of the party as a unified political force.

71. FEHRENBACHER, THE SLAVEHOLDING REPUBLIC, supra note 37, at 299. Fehrenbacher refers to the authority to protect against "domestic violence," but the provision is clear that such federal authority only applies when requested by the state authorities.

72. *See* Lightner, *The Supreme Court and the Interstate Slave Trade, supra* note 44. *See also* David L. Lightner, Slavery and the Commerce Power: How the Struggle against the Interstate Slave Trade Led to the Civil War (Yale Univ. Press 2006).

73. Article I, sec. 8 provides: "The Congress shall have Power . . . To regulate Commerce with foreign Nations, and among the several States . . . ."

74. Article I, sec. 9 provides: "The Migration or Importation of such Persons as any of the States now existing shall think proper to admit, shall not be prohibited by the Congress prior to [1808] . . . ."

75. *Groves v. Slaughter,* 40 U.S. (15 Pet.) 449 (1841), involved a Mississippi law that prohibited the bringing in of slaves as merchandise—not as an antislavery device, but rather because the price of slaves in Mississippi was being undercut by slaves brought in by commercial traders.

76. Lightner, Slavery and the Commerce Power, *supra* note 72, at 251. Eight of the Justices had indicated their view: Taney, McLean, Baldwin, Woodbury, and Campbell were explicit, and Wayne, McKinley, and Grier were strongly implied. However, there might not have been uniformity on *why* the interstate commerce clause did not give Congress such authority; by the time of the *Dred Scott* decision, a majority had coalesced around the doctrine that the right to property in slaves was untouchable.

77. "In 1835 abolitionists began to mail their literature to prominent Southern whites who they hoped might be open to persuasion. Jackson interpreted their action as inciting the slaves to rebellion; he expressed his loathing for the abolitionists vehemently, both in public and in private. With the President's full support, Postmaster General Amos Kendall encouraged local postmasters to censor the mails." Daniel Howe, *Goodbye to the "Age of Jackson"?* New York Review of Books 35 (May 28, 2009). Howe is the Rhodes Professor of American History Emeritus at Oxford and UCLA.

78. One month before Lincoln's speech at Cooper Union, the South's only antislavery Congressman, Frank Blair, Jr., of St. Louis, spoke at Cooper Union on January 25, 1860. He proposed that the United States should acquire tropical areas in Central America open only to slaveholders who signed an emancipation pact. Freehling, The Road to Disunion, *supra* note 53, at 327.

79. Harold Holzer, Lincoln at Cooper Union: The Speech that Made Abraham Lincoln President 283 (Simon & Schuster 2004).

80. Fehrenbacher, The Slaveholding Republic, *supra* note 37, at 301.

81. This idea of a prohibition on future amendments is not unlike that in Article V of the Constitution, which prevented any amendment that would change the date of 1808 as the earliest for the prohibition of the slave trade.

82. The full text of the resolution, which did not use the words "slavery" or "slave" provides: "No amendment shall be made to the Constitution which will authorize or give to Congress the power to abolish or interfere, within any State, with the domestic institutions thereof, including that of persons held to labor or service by the laws of said State."

83. The Lincoln letter was recently discovered among the governor's papers in North Carolina. It was called the "evil twin" of the Thirteenth Amendment

that abolished slavery four years later. The proposed amendment was approved by only two states (Maryland and Ohio) before the War broke out. WASHINGTON POST, Oct. 26, 2006, at A-23.

84. GUELZO, LINCOLN'S EMANCIPATION PROCLAMATION, *supra* note 31, at 22.
85. GUELZO, LINCOLN'S EMANCIPATION PROCLAMATION, *supra* note 31, at 30.
86. *Id.* at 37.
87. "An Act to Confiscate Property Used for Insurrectionary Purposes," approved, August 6, 1861.
88. Former Kentucky Senator John J. Crittenden, then in the House, introduced a resolution that the purpose of the War was *only* to preserve the Union, not to interfere with the "established institutions" of the states. The House vote on July 22, 1861, was 117–2. The companion measure in the Senate was introduced by Tennessee Senator Andrew Johnson. The Senate vote on July 25, 1861, was almost equally lopsided.
89. "An Act for the Sequestration of the Estates, Property and Effects of alien Enemies and for the indemnity of the citizens of the Confederate States and Persons aiding the same in the existing war with the United States."
90. There is great irony that a year later, as Lincoln considered issuing the preliminary Emancipation Proclamation, he failed to factor in the political value of military success until Secretary of State Seward called it to Lincoln's attention.
91. Guelzo asserts that the Supreme Court was "dominated" by the Chief Justice, though how one Justice of nine had the power to dominate is not explained. He also asserts that the confiscation effort would not survive a court test due to the Bill of Attainder—though he fails to explain this. GUELZO, LINCOLN'S EMANCIPATION PROCLAMATION, *supra* note 31, at 39.
92. An Ohio Senator later noted that the Act was more of a declaration of policy than an Act to be enforced. GUELZO, LINCOLN'S EMANCIPATION PROCLAMATION, *supra* note 31, at 65.
93. Daniel W. Hamilton, *A New Right to Property: Civil War Confiscation in the Reconstruction Supreme Court,* 29(3) J. SUP. CT. HIST. 254, 261 (Nov. 2004).
94. *Id.*
95. Fremont's wife, Jessie (the daughter of the powerful Missouri politician, Thomas Hart Benson), and Francis Blair were the chief engineers of Fremont's nomination, according to GUELZO, LINCOLN'S EMANCIPATION PROCLAMATION, *supra* note 31, at 43.
96. Mimi Swartz, *Manifold Destiny,* NEW YORK TIMES BOOK REVIEW, July 1, 2007, at 16 (reviewing SALLY DENTON, PASSION & PRINCIPLE: JOHN AND JESSIE FREMONT, THE COUPLE WHOSE POWER, POLITICS, & LOVE SHAPED NINETEENTH-CENTURY AMERICA (Bloomsbury 2007)).
97. *Id.* She also was quite attractive, having been sought after by President Martin Van Buren.
98. BRIAN DIRCK, LINCOLN THE LAWYER 128–37 (Univ. of Illinois Press 2007).
99. GUELZO, LINCOLN'S EMANCIPATION PROCLAMATION, *supra* note 31, at 52–53.

100. On November 2, 1861, Lincoln replaced Fremont with General David Hunter and then on November 9, Hunter was succeeded by Major General Henry Halleck as head of the Department of the Missouri at St. Louis. Lincoln ordered Halleck to clean up the mess left behind by his predecessor. Halleck had been a lawyer in California a year earlier.

101. On March 13, 1862, Congress enacted an Article of War that prohibited any U.S. officer from returning fugitive slaves. It provided for a court-martial for any officer violating the Article.

102. While compensation might seem to as abolitionist as "blood money," in a practical sense, it also meant putting money into the hands of the former slaveholders, money they could use to employ their former slaves. *See* GUELZO, LINCOLN'S EMANCIPATION PROCLAMATION, *supra* note 31, at 55.

103. Lincoln in 1863 appointed Fisher to the supreme court of the District of Columbia, where, in 1867, Judge Fisher presided over the trial of John Harrison Surratt.

104. Under the plan, slavery would finally end in 1893, with all children of slaves born after the plan to be automatically free; alternatively, Delaware might end it in 1872 with compressed bond payments. GUELZO, LINCOLN'S EMANCIPATION PROCLAMATION, *supra* note 31, at 57–58.

105. John R. Wennersten, *John W. Crisfield and Civil War Politics on Maryland's Eastern Shore, 1860–1864*, 99 MARYLAND HISTORICAL MAGAZINE 5, 9 (Spring 2004).

106. *Id.* at 10.

107. GUELZO, LINCOLN'S EMANCIPATION PROCLAMATION, *supra* note 31, at 95.

108. The Senate passed the Act on April 6th (29–14), and the House passed it on April 11th (93–39).

109. Article IV authorized Congress only to "make all needful rules and regulations respecting the territory or property belonging to the United States."

110. The notion of compensating slave owners, whose "property" would be "taken," is in contrast to the Freedman's Act after the War, which compensated the freed slaves for their prior deprivations. On the other hand, it might be argued that "compensation" to the former slaveholder was ultimately designed to provide him with the funds to hire the former slave and so to provide employment for the former slave.

111. There were arguments that the Fifth Amendment not only required compensation, but also that the government "taking" must be for a "public use"—not a "public purpose."

112. Damani Davis, *Slavery and Emancipation in the Nation's Capital*, 42 Q. NAT'L ARCHIVES & RECORDS ADMIN. 54 (Spring 2010).

113. Delaware Senator Willard Salisbury denied that Congress had the authority to spend money to ship blacks from the District to "colonies" outside the United States, and no one appeared to contradict him. CONG. GLOBE, 37th Cong., 2nd Sess. 1333 (Mar. 24, 1862).

114. Wennersten, *supra* note 105, at 9.

115. It was the same General Hunter who became the president of the military commission that tried and convicted the Lincoln assassination conspirators in the summer of 1865.

116. On March 13, 1862, Congress passed a law amending the Articles of War by prohibiting U.S. military forces from returning fugitive slaves. Thirty-seventh Congress, Sess. II, Ch. XL.

117. CRAIG L. SYMONDS, LINCOLN AND HIS ADMIRALS: ABRAHAM LINCOLN, THE U.S. NAVY, AND THE CIVIL WAR (Oxford University Press 2008) at 159–61.

118. *Id.* at 165.

119. GUELZO, LINCOLN'S EMANCIPATION PROCLAMATION, *supra* note 31, at 73–74.

120. *Id.* at 74.

121. The great scholar of the Civil War period, Professor James Oakes, asked rhetorically, "What, then, was Lincoln up to? It's impossible to be sure, but the letter to Greeley has all the earmarks of a skillful public relations ploy.... By making it appear as though he had options to choose from regarding emancipation, and that he would choose the option most likely to restore the Union, Lincoln tried to nudge Northern public opinion along the path he had already decided to take." James Oakes, *A Different Lincoln*, NEW YORK REVIEW OF BOOKS 45 (Apr. 9, 2009).

122. "An Act to secure Freedom to all Persons within the Territories of the United States," 12 Stat. 432 (June 19, 1862).

123. The other of the "twin relics of barbarism" that were condemned in the 1856 platform was polygamy. Congress acted to prohibit polygamy in the territories shortly after banning slavery there. 12 Stat. 501 (July 1, 1862). The Senate vote on June 3, 1862 was 37–2; there was no division in the House.

124. Maryland Congressman John W. Crisfield condemned the bill as an unwarranted interference with private property. CONG. GLOBE, 37th Cong., 2nd Sess. 2049 (May 9, 1862).

125. GUELZO, LINCOLN'S EMANCIPATION PROCLAMATION, *supra* note 31, at 108.

126. "An Act to suppress Insurrection, to punish Treason and Rebellion, to seize and confiscate the Property of Rebels, and for other Purposes," 12 Stat. 589 (July 17, 1862).

127. A judgment, disposing of a matter in dispute, may be either *in personam* or *in rem*. In the former case, the judgment determines the rights and duties of the parties (as in a contract or tort dispute), and the court must have jurisdiction over the parties. In the latter *in rem* instance, the judgment determines the ownership of property, typically the claimant's ownership against the world. KERMIT L. HALL, ed., THE OXFORD COMPANION TO AMERICAN LAW 438–39 (Oxford Univ. Press 2002).

128. On August 15, 1863, a seizure was made of considerable real estate in New Orleans owned by John Slidell—the CSA envoy involved in the Trent Affair in late 1861. That seizure was made by the marshal under authority of

the district attorney in accordance with instructions given by the U.S. Attorney General. After notice, the district court decreed a condemnation of Slidell's property. The Supreme Court agreed in *The Confiscation Cases*, 87 U.S. (20 Wall.) 92 (1873). The Court stressed that the proceedings were *in rem,* and "in no sense criminal proceedings." 87 U.S. at 104. To Slidell's claim that the Proclamation of Amnesty in 1868 amounted to a repeal of the Second Confiscation Act, the Court explained that the president had no power to repeal an act of Congress, and, in any event, the property had become vested in the United States by 1865, and so no subsequent amnesty could have the effect of divesting vested rights.

129. The text of Section 9: "That all slaves of persons who shall hereafter be engaged in rebellion against the government of the United States, or who shall in any way give aid or comfort thereto, escaping from such persons and taking refuge within the lines of the army; and all slaves captured from such persons or deserted by them and coming under the control of the government of the United States; and all slaves of such persons found on [or] being within any place occupied by rebel forces and afterwards occupied by the forces of the United States shall be deemed captives of war, and shall be forever free of their servitude, and not again held as slaves." Thus, "property" became "person" upon the treason of the property's owner.

130. Bills of attainder are legislative acts that inflict punishment without a judicial trial; legislative bodies are to enact general rules, while the function of the judicial branch is to decide the guilt of a specific person. In the UK in the seventeenth century, the attained party's property could not pass to his heirs. The attainder issue is treated three times in the Constitution: (1) Article I, sec. 9, in dealing with the powers of Congress, provides: "No Bill of Attainder or ex post facto law shall be passed"; (2) Article I, sec. 10, dealing with restrictions on states, provides "No State shall ... pass any Bill of Attainder, ex post facto law or Law impairing the Obligation of Contracts, or grant any Title of Nobility"; (3) Article III, sec. 3, dealing with the judiciary, provides: "The Congress shall have Power to declare the Punishment of Treason, but no Attainder of Treason shall work Corruption of the Blood, or Forfeiture except during the Life of the Person attained."

131. Miller v. United States, 78 U.S. (11 Wall.) 268, 272 (1870).

132. Immediately after the War, the Court dealt with attainder in the context of loyalty oaths. *See* Cummings v. Missouri, 71 U.S. (4 Wall.) 277 (1867) and *Ex parte* Garland 71 U.S. (4 Wall.) 333 (1867). A century later, the Supreme Court dealt with an attainder issue in *United States v. Brown,* 381 U.S. 437 (1965). The case involved legislation that made it a crime for one who belongs to the Communist Party to serve on the board of a labor union. The purpose of the law was to protect the national economy by minimizing the danger of political strikes. The Court ruled, 5–4, that the bill of attainder clause is to be liberally construed in light of its purpose to prevent legislative punishment of designated persons or groups. The Court held that the law constituted a bill of attainder and thus was unconstitutional.

133. Hamilton, *supra* note 93, at 271.

134. During the War, one state court invalidated the Act: in the summer of 1863, the Kentucky Court of Appeals held that the Act was unconstitutional. The court found that the Act was a straightforward violation of the Fifth Amendment's guarantee of due process and uncompensated takings. Litigation under the Act first reached the Supreme Court in 1870, where the constitutionality of the Act was sustained on a 6–3 vote. The case involved the confiscation in 1864 of shares owned by a CSA Virginian in two Michigan railroads. The Court, in effect, decided that the confiscation was "not a congressional power at constitutional law [a criminal law], but a belligerent power at international law [an emergency war measure]." The dissent was written by Lincoln appointee, Justice Field, who decided that the Act violated international law and that it was an unconstitutional deprivation of individual property without trial.

135. Wennersten, *supra* note 105, at 10–11. Crisfield's political career also came to an end shortly thereafter. Following a January 3, 1863, speech on the House floor in which Crisfield accused Lincoln of using emancipation for selfish political purposes, Crisfield became *persona non grata* at the White House. Later that year he also lost his reelection in significant part due to interference by Union troops. Wennersten, at 12–13.

136. Speed's Opinion, in response to questions put by the Secretary of the Treasury McCulloch, was dated October 17, 1865. (11 Ops Atty. Gen. 365–69.)

137. GUELZO, LINCOLN'S EMANCIPATION PROCLAMATION, *supra* note 31, at 112.

138. GUELZO, LINCOLN'S EMANCIPATION PROCLAMATION, *supra* note 31, at 119–20.

139. DORIS KEARNS GOODWIN, TEAM OF RIVALS: THE POLITICAL GENIUS OF ABRAHAM LINCOLN 465 (Simon & Schuster 2005). In contrast, Allen C. Guelzo asserts that Stanton "remained silent." LINCOLN'S EMANCIPATION PROCLAMATION, *supra* note 31, at 122.

140. GOODWIN, TEAM OF RIVALS, *supra* note 139, at 467.

141. There is a scholarly dispute whether a fifth lawyer, Secretary of War Stanton, spoke. Guelzo suggests that Stanton remained silent, whereas Goodwin explains that Stanton declared himself in favor, grasping the military value of the tremendous advantage it would be to transfer the workforce of the slave from the South to the Union side.

142. As early as March 1861, Lincoln had directed the American minister to Guatemala to begin looking for possible colonization sites in Central America. GUELZO, *supra* note 31, at 141.

143. James M. McPherson, NEW YORK REVIEW OF BOOKS 66 (Apr. 26, 2007). McPherson also points out that Lincoln's rhetoric at that meeting was "tactless and insulting to his immediate black audience, however effective it may have been with the larger white audience to which it had really been directed."

144. GOODWIN, TEAM OF RIVALS, *supra* note 139, at 469.

145. For the two-day battle of Antietam, or Sharpsburg, 2,108 Union soldiers were killed (with 9,549 wounded and 753 missing), and 2,700 Confederate soldiers were killed (and 9,024 wounded and 1,800 missing). THE PHOTOGRAPHIC HISTORY OF THE CIVIL WAR 142 (Portland House 1997).

146. Lincoln apparently made a "deal" with God, that if the rebels were repelled from Maryland, he would free the slaves. GUELZO, *supra* note 31, at 153.

147. The original manuscript of Lincoln's was donated for sale as a fundraising premium at the Albany Army Relief Bazaar in 1864, and was purchased by Gerrit Smith. A year later, it was acquired by the New York State Library.

148. In an address at the Cooper Institute in New York on December 21, 1862, Gerrit Smith said that "the price of slaves declined in Cuba as soon as the news of the President's Proclamation reached that island."

149. TIMES OF LONDON, Oct. 7, 1862.

150. *Id.*

151. GOODWIN, TEAM OF RIVALS, *supra* note 139, at 485.

152. GUELZO, *supra* note 31, at 167.

153. *Id.* at 166 (referring to the campaign in Iowa).

154. For a thorough and new treatment of the Peace Democrats and others in the North, see JENNIFER L. WEBER, COPPERHEADS: THE RISE AND FALL OF LINCOLN'S OPPONENTS IN THE NORTH 66–70 (Oxford Univ. Press 2006), and especially the impact on the 1862 elections.

155. GOODWIN, TEAM OF RIVALS, *supra* note 139, at 485.

156. Included within the section on foreign relations is a section relating to colonization of "free Americans of African descent." Some Latin countries were apprehensive, and so Liberia and Haiti were the only countries where colonists could go knowing that they would be received and adopted as citizens.

157. During the Hampton Roads conference in early February 1865, Seward was quoted by two of the Southern participants as suggesting that the proclamation (and the Thirteenth Amendment which had just been passed in Congress) were war measures, and that if the South returned to the Union, it was probable that the measures of war would be abandoned. Lincoln seemed to agree, but he noted that the disposition of the slaves (as property) would have to be resolved by the courts. *See* ROBERT SAUNDERS, JR., JOHN ARCHIBALD CAMPBELL: SOUTHERN MODERATE, 1811–1889, at 169 (Univ. of Alabama Press 1997).

158. For example, the proclamation exempted twelve parishes in Louisiana, as well as the forty-eight counties of Virginia designated as West Virginia.

159. GUELZO, *supra* note 31, at 180–81

160. *See* GUELZO, *supra* note 31, at 178–79.

161. During Lincoln's regular reviews of execution orders for soldiers, one scholar reports that Lincoln "brought a lawyer's eye view to the task, parsing each document carefully for mistakes." DIRCK, LINCOLN THE LAWYER, *supra* note 97, at 120.

162. EDWIN C. BEARSS & J. PARKER HILLS, RECEDING TIDE: VICKSBURG AND GETTYSBURG—THE CAMPAIGNS THAT CHANGED THE CIVIL WAR 43–44 (National Geographic 2010).

163. The final document had undergone the most careful scrutiny by the key lawyers in the administration: Lincoln, Seward, Chase, Bates, and Blair. Some were worried that there could be a legal challenge. While it is not clear exactly how—as a technical matter—such a challenge could successfully be mounted, it is possible to imagine a former slaveholder (ideally, a loyal Unionist, or one inca-

pable of disloyalty due to age or disability) in a part of a state recently taken over by the Union army getting into a federal court, arguing that this proclamation could not constitutionally deprive him of his property right in his slaves who had just been set free.

It would take some time, however, for a case to reach the Supreme Court. At the time of the Emancipation Proclamation in 1863, Lincoln had appointed three Justices (Swayne, Miller, and Davis), Jackson had appointed three (Taney, Wayne, and Catron), and Tyler, Polk, and Buchanan had appointed one each (Nelson, Grier, and Clifford). It probably would have been a good bet that if the constitutionality of the proclamation had immediately come to the Court, Lincoln would have won, though by a close vote. In mid-March 1863, the Lincoln administration won a major victory in the *Prize Cases* matter, in a 5–4 vote. On the other hand, he had lost a confrontation with Chief Justice Taney in late May 1861 over Lincoln's effort to rely on his war powers to suspend habeas corpus; however, there was no actual war in Maryland then, while there was a real war in the Confederacy.

By May 1863, still well before any case would get to the Court's docket, Lincoln had appointed his fourth Justice, Stephen J. Field. With the Chief Justice well into his 80s, it is likely that Lincoln felt there was good reason to believe that he would have the opportunity to appoint a new Chief Justice, and that would clearly give him a solid five votes. So Lincoln probably thought the legal risks inherent in the problematic constitutionality of the proclamation were worth taking—especially since it was possible that a Court challenge would not take place until after the War was over and the Union had won—and the slavery issue would have been rendered moot. In any event, Lincoln probably sensed that the courts generally give a president some extra leeway during wartime.

164. It will be argued that the president has no "war" powers, since only Congress is granted the power to declare "war"; that the president's only related powers are "military" powers within the scope of his role as commander in chief.

165. Letter to Major General John McClernand, January 8, 1863.

166. The largest number of desertions Illinois regiments faced during the War was immediately after the proclamation was published.

167. GUELZO, *supra* note 31, at 187.

168. Before the end of 1862, Curtis rushed into print a pamphlet entitled "Executive Power." GUELZO, *supra* note 31, at 190.

169. The pamphlet was published by Little, Brown & Co, and was dedicated to "all persons sworn to support the Constitution, and to all citizens who value principles of civil liberty for the preservation of which is our only security."

170. "Executive Power," at 11.

171. *Id.* at 12.

172. *Id.* at 17.

173. *Id.* at 20.

174. King Charles I of England was tried in 1649. His prosecutor was barrister John Cooke, the author of the legal theory that heads of state are not above the law. This case was the first modern legal argument against tyranny, based on a universal right to punish a tyrant. Cooke himself would die brutally, executed by

the Restoration government of Charles II, the son of the executed King, in 1660. See GEOFFREY ROBERTSON, THE TYRANNICIDE BRIEF (Pantheon 2006).

175. *Id.* at 23–24.

176. *Id.* at 28. Curtis was not alone. Even stronger criticism came from Judge Joel Parker, a Massachusetts judge and law professor, an old Whig. He asserted that this was a "paper emancipation" only and that no court in the United States would uphold it. *See* GUELZO, *supra* note 31, at 191–92.

177. The Radical Republicans, in putting forth the original Second Confiscation Act of 1862, had in fact planned the confiscation of planter lands and their division among freedman. The Freedman's Bureau Act of early 1865 provided that Southern lands abandoned by their owners, and property subject to confiscation, be set aside for the use of the emancipated slaves.

178. *See* CHARLES LEWIS WAGANDT, THE MIGHTY REVOLUTION: NEGRO EMANCIPATION IN MARYLAND, 1862–1864 (Maryland Historical Society 2004)

179. BRUCE LEVINE, CONFEDERATE EMANCIPATION: SOUTHERN PLANS TO FREE AND ARM SLAVES DURING THE CIVIL WAR 2 (Oxford Univ. Press 2006). In 2008, a graphic novel was published, *Cleburne*, that centered on Cleburne's plan to free the slaves so they could fight for the South.

180. Paul D. Escott, *We Must Make Them Free*, CIVIL WAR TIMES 46 (June 2010). This fine article was adapted from Professor Escott's book, "WHAT SHALL WE DO WITH THE NEGRO?": LINCOLN, WHITE RACISM, AND THE CIVIL WAR (Univ. of Virginia Press 2009).

181. *Id.* at 15.

182. *Id.* at 99.

183. The idea of "quasi-serfdom" was not entirely new: in 1778, Jefferson wrote that he was thinking of importing German farmers and mixing them with slaves as tenants on his lands in a diluted form of serfdom; the Germans would teach the slaves good habits, and the children would grow up free. Jefferson's Polish colleague, Colonel Tadeusz Kosciuszko, had hundreds of serfs, but he freed them upon his death. And in 1825, when the Marquis de Lafayette visited Monticello and kidded Jefferson about his slaves, Lafayette's secretary proposed transforming the slaves into serfs.

By the spring of 1865, when only a handful of black soldiers were enlisted, there were nearly two hundred thousand blacks in the Union Army.

184. There was an initial question as to whether the constitutional requirement of approval by "three-fourths of the several states" meant, in this instance, three-fourths of the thirty-six states admitted to the Union, or three-fourths of the twenty-five states that had not attempted to secede. In the end, the amendment was proclaimed ratified when the legislatures of twenty-seven of the thirty-six states ratified, Georgia being the twenty-seventh on December 6, 1865.

185. AMAR, AMERICA'S CONSTITUTION, *supra* note 8, at 360.

Chapter 8 Notes

1. Lewis Powell also used as an alias Lewis Payne, sometime spelled as Paine.

2. On April 26th, Representative Benjamin Gwinn Harris (Democrat from Maryland's fifth District) was arrested at his home (Ellenborough) near Leonard-

town, and imprisoned in the Old Capitol Prison. He was charged with aiding the enemy because, on April 23rd he had given two dollars to two paroled CSA soldiers from Maryland, and was tried on a charge of a violation of the 56th article of war by a military Commission on May 2nd. He was convicted and sentenced to three years' imprisonment and was forbidden ever to hold office. Through the good offices of Montgomery Blair, Harris's counsel John Camiliar of Leonardtown met with President Johnson on May 26th. President Johnson remitted the sentence on May 31st, and Harris returned to his seat in Congress. Frederick Stone was one of Harris's lawyers at his trial; Stone was also counsel for Mudd and Herold, and his appearance for them was delayed until the end of the Harris trial.

3. Mrs. Surratt was held for two weeks at the Old Capitol Prison (on the site of the present Supreme Court building) before she was transferred. Anna Surratt was held there for forty-five days, along with a Surratt boarder and the three Ford brothers. For an interesting discussion of that prison, see Joan L. Chaconas, *The Old Capitol Prison*. 35(4) THE SURRATT COURIER (Apr. 2010).

4. The full text is: "Sir: I am of the opinion that the persons charged with the murder of the President of the United States can be rightfully tried by a military court." Opinion, at 215.

5. "Opinion on the Constitutional Power of the Military to Try and Execute the Assassins of the President," July 1865, 11 Op. Att'y Gen. 215, 297–317 (1865).

6. Wallace, later in the summer, was the head of the military commission that tried Captain Henry Wirz of Andersonville.

7. Stanton was close to Holt during those last days of the Buchanan administration when Stanton was Attorney General. In 1862, Stanton appointed Holt to the new office of the judge advocate general of the army and director of the Bureau of Military Justice. Holt may have been Lincoln's first pick to succeed Cameron as secretary of war, but in the end, Lincoln chose Stanton.

8. Doris Kearns Goodwin, TEAM OF RIVALS: THE POLITICAL GENIUS OF ABRAHAM LINCOLN 675 (Simon & Schuster 2005). James Speed was the brother of Joshua F. Speed, who was an early and important friend of Lincoln's when Lincoln opened his practice in Springfield. Joshua Speed was also a friend of the father of Justice John Harlan, both of Kentucky. Peter Scott Campbell, ed., *The Civil War Reminiscences of John Marshall Harlan*, 32(3) J. SUP. CT. HIST. 249 (Nov. 2007).

9. MICHAEL W. KAUFMAN, AMERICAN BRUTUS: JOHN WILKES BOOTH AND THE LINCOLN CONSPIRACIES 349 (Random House 2004).

10. General Grant was called as a witness on May 12th, and reporters approached him as he was leaving and pressed him to open the trial. He then went to the White House and talked to President Johnson. James H. Johnson, *The Trial of the Nineteenth Century*, LEGAL TIMES, June 18, 2001, at 23.

11. KAUFMAN, *supra* note 9, at 340.

12. During the referendum debate on the proposed new Maryland state Constitution, Reverdy Johnson sent a letter to voters challenging the constitutionality of the oath requirement, and argued that otherwise-qualified voters were not bound by such an oath. EDWARD STEERS, JR. & HAROLD HOLZER, eds.,

THE LINCOLN ASSASSINATION CONSPIRATORS: THEIR CONFINEMENT AND EXECUTION, AS RECORDED IN THE LETTERBOOK OF JOHN FREDERICK HARTRANFT 36 (Louisiana State Univ. Press 2009).

13. Reminiscences of General August V. Kautz, the third-ranked member of the tribunal, who sat on the left of General Harris. Quoted in THE SURRATT COURIER 4–5 (Oct. 2008).

14. HARPER'S WEEKLY, June 3, 1865, 342.

15. 71 U.S. (4 Wall.) 277 (1867). In this case, the new Missouri Constitution of 1865 required any attorney or "bishop, priest, deacon, minister, elder or other clergyman of any religious persuasion" to take an oath before such persons could teach, preach, solemnize marriages, and so forth. The required oath included statements the oath-taker had not had sympathy with the rebels or harbored them. A young priest, Cummings, refused to take the oath and he was arrested and confined in jail. In addition to being represented at the Supreme Court by Reverdy Johnson, Cummings also was represented by Montgomery Blair and David Dudley Field, the brother of Justice Stephen J. Field, an 1863 Lincoln appointee. The case was argued in March 1866 and decided on January 14, 1867. The opinion of the Court was written by Justice Stephen J. Field; the four dissenters were all Republicans.

16. 71 U.S. (4 Wall.) 333 (1867). Augustus J. Garland was an Arkansas lawyer. When the state seceded, he became a member of the Confederate House and later the CSA Senate. On January 24, 1865, Congress passed a law requiring an oath for any person to practice before the Supreme Court; the oath required a statement that the person had never given aid or comfort to the rebels. On July 15, 1865, President Johnson granted Garland a personal full pardon and amnesty. Garland petitioned the Supreme Court for the right to practice before it without taking the oath—which he could not honestly take. Garland argued the case himself, along with Reverdy Johnson. The majority opinion, by Justice Field, held the act of Congress unconstitutional, and admitted Garland to practice.

17. According to Kaufman, Johnson had withdrawn from the trial just before the 16th, and he had asked one of the other lawyers to read his prepared jurisdictional statement in his place. Johnson never returned. KAUFMAN, *supra* note 9, at 346.

18. Professor Kate Clifford Larson suggest that Johnson was unhelpful to Surratt by allowing two inexperienced lawyers to handle most of the court appearances, by rarely being present, and then by foolishly challenging the jurisdiction of the tribunal knowing that these arguments had failed repeatedly in the past. "The court was unimpressed by his efforts, and the public knew it." LARSON, THE ASSASSIN'S ACCOMPLICE: MARY SURRATT AND THE PLOT TO KILL ABRAHAM LINCOLN 190 (Basic Books 2008). "Overwhelming evidence, coupled with an incompetent defense team, destroyed any possibility of acquittal." *Id.* at 196.

19. Former Attorney General Bates was strongly opposed to the commission, believing it unconstitutional. He was bewildered that his successor Speed had approved:

[H]e must know better. Such a trial is not only illegal, but it is a gross blunder in policy . . . . [I]f the offenders be done to death by that tribunal, however truly guilty, they will pass for martyrs with half the world."

Bates was prophetic: when President Johnson's enemies were engaged in the impeachment process, one of the claims was that he might have been involved in the assassination of Lincoln, and that Johnson used the military trial to enforce silence on his coconspirators.

20. "Opinion on the Constitutional Power of the Military to Try and Execute the Assassins of the President," July 1865.

21 LARSON, *supra* note 18, at 206.

22. Remarks of Chief Justice William H. Rehnquist to the Historical Society of the District of Columbia Circuit (on its 200th anniversary), March 9, 2001.

23. LARSON, *supra* note 18, at 206–07.

24. General Winfield Scott Hancock was the commander of the Middle Military District, to whom General Hartranft, who was in charge of the prisoners, reported. Years later, Hancock ran for president, as a Democrat, against James Garfield; in 1880, he became president of the National Rifle Association.

25. JAMES L. SWANSON & DANIEL R. WEINBERG, LINCOLN'S ASSASSINS: THEIR TRIAL AND EXECUTION 25–26 (Arena Editions 2001). The authors offer no citation for this statement, but Swanson claims it is detailed in the papers of Andrew Johnson.

26. A year before he was appointed President Johnson's Interior Secretary, Illinois lawyer and Lincoln confidant, Orville Hickman Browning, happened to witness the brief proceeding in Judge Wylie's courtroom. Browning noted in his diary:

> The Judge said he was powerless and could do nothing further, and let the Genl go. He [Wylie] should have proceeded against him [Hancock] for contempt, and have seen whether the President would have taken him forcibly from the hands of the court.

The scene has interesting parallels to a situation four years earlier when Chief Justice Taney too felt "powerless" in the face of a general being ordered by the president not to comply with a judge's order—involving then, John Merryman.

27. Proclamation of September 15, 1863.

28. "An Act Relating to Habeas Corpus, and regulating Judicial Proceedings in Certain Cases," 37th Cong., Sess. III, March 3, 1863.

29. This may have symbolized "gender marking," which lowered the standards of proof required to execute an unfortunate, middle-aged landlady who found herself in the wrong place at the wrong time. In 1873, Andrew Johnson accused Holt of concealing the clemency petition from him, and Holt responded indignantly with a letter campaign and a "vindication" published in a pamphlet. KAUFMAN, *supra* note 9, at 382.

30. *The Judicial Murder of Mrs. Surratt*, by Richard Amada, won first place in the 2007 Nathan Miller History Play Contest.

31. An extraordinarily detailed account of John Surratt's flight and return to the United States appears in ANDREW C. A. JAMPOLER, THE LAST LINCOLN CONSPIRATOR: JOHN SURRATT'S FLIGHT FROM THE GALLOWS (Naval Institute Press 2008).

32. JAMPOLER, *supra* note 31, at 131.

33. There is some doubt about whether U.S. "authorities" in fact wanted John Surratt to be returned. William Hanchett, in *The Lincoln Murder Conspiracies*, suggests that Surratt's arrest in Egypt came about because of "zealous consular officials" who did not understand how desperately their superiors in Washington wanted Surratt to disappear. WILLIAM HANCHETT, THE LINCOLN MURDER CONSPIRACIES (Univ. of Illinois Press 1983).

34. Joseph George, Jr., *The Trials of John H. Surratt*, 99 MARYLAND HISTORICAL MAGAZINE 17 (Spring 2004). Butler claimed he had proof that the conspirators never meant to include Vice President Johnson among their victims. *Id.* at 24. In mid-year, Congressman Butler was named chair of the new House Select Committee on the Assassination of President Lincoln, from which position he had the power to offer immunity to the likes of John Surratt.

35. Joseph George, Jr., *supra* note 34, at 32.

36. Quoted in Joseph George, Jr., *supra* note 34, at 41.

37. Quoted in JAMPOLER, *supra* note 31, at 217. Though Welles had a legal education, he was never admitted to the bar. He was no friend of Seward's and viewed Pierrepont as one of Seward's close associates from New York.

38. JAMPOLER, *supra* note 31, at 246. In a dramatic conclusion to the proceedings, on August 10th, after the deadlocked jury had been dismissed, the judge announced that he had the "unpleasant duty to discharge." Due to a nasty conflict earlier in the trial between the judge and Surratt's defense counsel, Bradley, Sr., the judge ordered Bradley disbarred and ordered that his name be stricken from the roll of attorneys practicing in the court. Bradley appealed to the District's Supreme Court and lost, but his appeal to the U.S. Supreme Court was successful.

39. Technically, the dismissal was based on a 1799 law that provided that no person should be prosecuted for any non-capital offense unless indicted within two years from the alleged crime, and the new indictment for aiding the rebellion was more than two years after the rebellion.

40. KAUFMAN, *supra* note 9, at 389–91.

41. John H. Surratt, Jr., married Mary Victorine Hunter, a relative of Francis Scott Key; they had seven children. Mary Surratt's oldest child, Isaac, returned from service as a Confederate soldier and moved to Baltimore to try to save the family's holdings. He worked for the Old Bay Steam Packet Company, and died in 1907. Mary Surratt's third child, Anna, married a former army chemist, and died in 1904. 32(6) THE SURRATT COURIER 5 (Aug. 2007).

42. Defense counsel had insufficient time to prepare to consult with their clients, the defendants had no right to take the stand, none of the judges were lawyers, a simple majority of the nine-member tribunal was sufficient for a con-

viction, a two-thirds majority was sufficient for death sentence, the prosecution was not obliged to reveal the existence of the Booth diary, and there was no right of appeal.

43. The eleven-acre fort is now a national park. The seven small islands comprising the Dry Tortugas are the tops of coral reefs, and they lack water. Tortuga is the Spanish word for turtle.

44. Joseph George, Jr. *"This Horrible Place": Dr. Mudd's Prison Years in the Dry Tortugas*, 102 MARYLAND HISTORICAL MAGAZINE 276 (No. 4, Winter, 2007).

45. *Ex parte* Milligan, 71 U.S. (4 Wall.) 2 (1866). Lambdin P. Milligan was a lawyer and teacher in Indiana who became active in the peace movement during the War to the point of encouraging draft resistance and smuggling to the CSA. He was arrested on October 5, 1864, and tried by a military commission. He was sentenced to hang on May 19, 1865. There is some evidence that Lincoln might not have approved the execution, but rather ordered Milligan confined until the War was over; however, President Johnson did not intervene. Milligan filed for a writ of habeas corpus on May 10, 1865, and the case ended up in the Supreme Court, which held unanimously on April 3, 1866, that Milligan should be released, because the military commission had no jurisdiction to try him. James A. Garfield defended Milligan in his first appearance at the Court; his co-counsel was Jeremiah S. Black, who had been Buchanan's Attorney General and secretary of state.

46. *Ex parte* Mudd, 17 F. Cas. 954 (S.D. Fla. 1868).

47. Professor Joseph George notes that 199 soldiers and the officer in charge signed the petition, and that Mudd reported that every noncommissioned officer at the post also signed it. George, *supra* note 44.

48. Johnson apparently was inclined to release Mudd relatively early, but he decided that prudence dictated that he delay so that "radicals" did not use it as a weapon against him. Reverdy Johnson, in June 1866, warned Johnson that it would not be wise for the president to act while Congress was in session. George, *supra* note 44, at 288.

49. In January 2007, Representative Hoyer became the Majority Leader of the House.

50. Ehrlich later became governor of Maryland.

51. Mudd v. Caldera, 26 F. Supp. 2d 113 (D.D.C. 1998), and Mudd v. Caldera, 134 F. Supp. 2d 138 (D.D.C. 2001).

52. Thomas B. Mudd v. Thomas A. White, Secretary of the Army, No. 01-5103 (D.C. Cir. Nov. 8, 2002).

53. For a new study of conditions in the prisons, see JAMES M. GILLISPIE, ANDERSONVILLES OF THE NORTH: THE MYTHS AND REALITIES OF NORTHERN TREATMENT OF CIVIL WAR CONFEDERATE PRISONERS (Univ. of North Texas Press 2008).

54. According to Secretary Stanton's 1866 Report, there were two hundred seventy thousand Union soldiers in Confederate camps (with an average death rate of 8.7 percent) and two hundred twenty thousand Confederate soldiers in Union camps (with an average death rate of 12 percent. *See* Edwin W. Beitzell, *Point Lookout Prison Camp for Confederates*, ST. MARY'S COUNTY HISTORICAL

SOCIETY 1983, at 181. Before the War, the area of the Point Lookout camp was to be a major resort comprising four hundred areas with cottages leased to subscribers. Among the subscribers by 1859 were Chief Justice Taney and Benjamin G. Harris, later a congressman from St. Mary's County tried by military commission in 1865. Beitzell, *supra* at 2.

55. For an excellent novel detailing a military trial—at Arlington—of General Lee, see THOMAS FLEMING, THE SECRET TRIAL OF ROBERT E. LEE (Tom Doherty Associates 2006).

56. SUSAN BANFIELD, THE ANDERSONVILLE PRISON CIVIL WAR CRIMES TRIAL 39–40 (Enslow Publishing 2000).

57. The Court of Claims is now located on Lafayette Square, across from the White House.

58. Vol. XII, No. 460.

59. BANFIELD, *supra* note 57, at 78–79.

60. *See* Darrett B. Rutman, *The War Crimes and Trial of Henry Wirz*, 6 CIVIL WAR HISTORY 117 (1960).

61. Freeman Dyson, *Rocket Man*, NEW YORK REVIEW OF BOOKS 12 (Jan. 17, 2008). Dyson, a professor emeritus of physics at the Institute for Advanced Study in Princeton, acknowledged his role in working with the British Bomber Command during World War II in collaboration with those who planned the raid on Dresden, in the context of von Braun's role with the Nazi SS.

62. While the play was taken largely from the transcript, there were several factual errors: Baker was from New York, not Baltimore; the original lawyer withdrew at the outset, but Shade continued with Baker until nearly the end of the trial; unlike the play, Wirz never attempted suicide; and Wirz never took the stand.

63. WILLIAM J. COOPER, JR., JEFFERSON DAVIS, AMERICAN 525 (Knopf 2000).

64. President Johnson had issued a proclamation calling for Davis's arrest and offering a reward of $100,000 in gold.

65. On May 31, 1865, O'Conor wrote to Secretary of War Stanton explaining that he intended to represent Davis, and requesting permission to inform his client. Stanton agreed that O'Conor could send an open letter to Davis through the U.S. attorney in Washington. COOPER, *supra* note 64, at 539.

66. COOPER, *supra* note 64, at 540. Davis's wife, Varina, was in close touch with all these supporters who tried to intercede with President Johnson and otherwise assist in Davis's defense. *Id.* at 544–45.

67. Pierce visited Davis at Fortress Monroe in the spring of 1867. COOPER, *supra* note 64, at 552.

68. Pierce also knew something about treason charges. In late 1861, Republican newspapers published a letter that suggested Pierce was engaged in treasonable activities. Secretary of State Seward informed Pierce of the charges and of his planned arrest. However, the alleged Pierce letter was a hoax, Seward was publicly embarrassed, and Pierce was vindicated.

69. In the summer of 1866, Smith informed President Johnson that Davis's long confinement without trial had brought "deep dishonor" to the government. COOPER, *supra* note 64, at 561.

70. JAMPOLER, *supra* note 31, at 233.

71. Amnesty Proclamation of May 29, 1865. Amnesty was offered to those who took an oath; however, there were fourteen classes of people exempted from the amnesty, e.g., all who left seats in Congress to aid the rebellion.

72. The Attorney General rejected the argument that Davis could be tried in the North, on the basis that he had been "constructively" present when CSA troops invaded Northern territory. COOPER, *supra* note 65, at 559. Ironically, one of the arguments in the treason trial in Virginia of Aaron Burr decades earlier was that Burr had been "constructively" present when the alleged treasonous activity took place.

73. COOPER, *supra* note 64, at 541–42. The presiding federal district court judge in Virginia was John Underwood, who was not a judicial heavyweight, and that was another reason to ensure that Chase would be present. When Congress reduced the number of Justices to seven, it failed to provide for the assignment of Justices to circuit courts; that gave Chase another argument for why he could not sit in the Virginia circuit. It was not until the spring of 1867 that Congress passed legislation to assign Justices.

74. President Jefferson appointed William Wirt as prosecuting attorney in the trial of Burr. President Monroe appointed Wirt U.S. Attorney General in 1817.

75. Opinion of Attorney General Speed, at 413 (Jan. 4, 1866).

76. Proclamation of August 20, 1866. The final step had been the restoration of Texas, and so President Johnson proclaimed that "the said insurrection is at an end and that peace, order, tranquility and civil authority now exist in and throughout the whole of the United States."

77. COOPER, *supra* note 64, at 558.

78. Cornelius Vanderbilt, whose businesses included steamboats and railroads, is the second wealthiest man in American history. Converted to current dollars, he was worth $143 billion at the time. The wealthiest man in U.S. history, John D. Rockefeller, was worth $192 billion; in contrast, Bill Gates, the contemporary wealthiest American, is worth "only" $82 billion. N.Y. TIMES, July 15, 2007, at 1 & 18–19. At the time of his death in 1877, Cornelius Vanderbilt "possessed, at least on paper, one-ninth of all the American currency in circulation . . . . [His substantial gift to seed a university in Nashville was from] a desire to reconcile the South and the North so that, under the leadership of a new elite, the whole nation might prosper." Michael Kazin, *Ruthless in Manhattan*, NEW YORK REVIEW OF BOOKS 24 (May 10, 2009), (reviewing T. J. STILES, THE FIRST TYCOON: THE EPIC LIFE OF CORNELIUS VANDERBILT (Knopf 2009).

79. Proclamation 167, Offering and Extending Full Pardon to All Persons Participating in the Late Rebellion, September 7, 1867.

80. Proclamation 170, Granting Pardon to All Persons Participating in the Late Rebellion Except Those Under Indictment for Treason or Other Felony, July 4, 1868.

81. COOPER, *supra* note 64, at 581.

82. Latin for "we shall no longer prosecute." It is an entry made on the record by a prosecutor stating that he will no longer pursue the matter. Essentially, it is an admission by the prosecution that some aspect of the case has fallen apart.

83. Proclamation 179, Granting Full Pardon and Amnesty for the Offense of Treason Against the United States During the Late Civil War, December 25, 1868.

84. A very well-reviewed biography of Davis, written by William Cooper, Jr., and published by Knopf, came out in 2000, JEFFERSON DAVIS, AMERICAN.

85. George Washington Parke Custis provided in his will that within five years of his death, all slaves (more than two hundred) on his three plantations should be freed. As executor of the estate, General Robert E. Lee accomplished the manumission task by December 29, 1862.

86. JAMES EDWARD PETERS, ARLINGTON NATIONAL CEMETERY: SHRINE TO AMERICA'S HEROES 17–19 (Woodbine House 2000).

87. General Montgomery C. Meigs had served under Lee in the engineer corps, but he turned against Lee. In the spring 1864, Meigs decided that a graveyard should be established at Arlington, and on May 13, 1864, the first soldier was laid to rest there.

88. ROBERT M. POOLE, ON HALLOWED GROUND: THE STORY OF ARLINGTON NATIONAL CEMETERY 53 (Walker Publishing 2009). The community grew to fifteen hundred, and "was applauded by those who believed that slavery was a sin and Lee a traitor." Id.

89. 37th Cong., Sess. II, Ch. 97, 98 (1862)

90. The Arlington property had been assessed at $26,810, against which the tax was levied. Since the property was declared delinquent in taxes, on January 11, 1864, Arlington was offered for public sale, with the tax commissioner the only bidder; they purchased the property for the assessed value. PETERS, *supra* note 87, at 20

91. Lee had consulted attorney Francis Smith of Arlington to investigate the status of the property. Lee took no legal action because, until the general amnesty of Christmas 1868, he believed his status to be that of a paroled prisoner of war without civil rights (thus having no power to bring a law suit), and more important, because he wanted to "accept" the outcome of the War as a healing gesture. PETERS, *supra* note 87, at 27–28.

92. For an interesting review of Lee's journey South in the year of his death, see Noah Andre Trudeau, *Lee's Last Hurrah*, CIVIL WAR TIMES 28 (Feb. 2010). The author notes that for Southerners, "there had been no real closure to the tragic experiment in independence . . . [and so Lee's] 1870 journey, undertaken for purely personal reasons, would in fact trigger an unprecedented outpouring of emotion by white Southerners toward one of the enduring figures of their lost cause."

93. Shortly after her husband's death, Mary Custis Lee petitioned Congress in an indelicate fashion—by urging an estimate of the cost to remove the bodies. It was defeated in the Senate 54 to 4.

94. POOLE, *supra* note 89, at 89.

95. Robert M. Poole, *The Battle at Arlington*, THE SMITHSONIAN, Nov. 2009, at 56.

96. PETERS, *supra* note 87, at 31.

97. United States v. Lee, 106 U.S. 196 (1882).

98. *Lee*, 106 U.S. 196, 222.

99. The Freedman's Village was dedicated on December 4, 1863. PETERS, *supra* note 87, at 25.

100. The U.S. Army vacated the Freedman's Village in 1888.

101. Robert Todd Lincoln had studied law in Chicago and was admitted to the bar in 1867. He became secretary of war under President James Garfield in 1881, and remained in that position under President Chester Arthur. He was U.S. minister to Britain from 1889 to 1893, after which he resumed his law practice until he became president of the Pullman Company.

102. *See* Jason Emerson, *In His Father's Shadow*, CIVIL WAR TIMES 55 (Oct. 2008).

In Appreciation

The idea for this book initially began to take shape a decade earlier, and its development was assisted by a great many people. My family members provided much needed encouragement, and I am grateful to each of them. In that context, I must single out my son Tom, also a lawyer, who read every page of the manuscript, and who always offered helpful specific and refreshingly candid comments.

At a somewhat more professional level, my dear friend Professor John F. Murphy was unceasing in his support and direction. Professor Donald Dowd, who taught me law decades ago, heroically read an early draft, despite his eyesight difficulties, and provided tough love. The award-winning author of *American Brutus: John Wilkes Booth and the Lincoln Conspiracies*, Michael W. Kauffman, read chapters and gave me hope. Professor Ed Smith, founder of the Civil War Institute at American University, was also my teacher and supporter.

The legendary Civil War historian, Edwin Bearss, taught me a great deal about the Civil War, as I tramped with him through battlefields from Vicksburg, Mississippi, to the suburbs of Washington, D.C. Our mutual friend, Chris Bradley, always offered sage advice.

I am grateful to Melody Curtis of the Smithsonian Associates, who arranged from me to present the essence of this book in a series of lectures at the Smithsonian. It was a helpful learning experience to present similar lectures at the Osher Lifetime Learning Institute at American University and at Johns Hopkins University.

More directly related to this publication, I wish to thank Niko Pfund, who gave generously of his time and insights, and my lawyer at my former law firm, Elisabeth A. Langworthy of Sutherland, Asbill & Brennan. And finally, I salute Erin Nevius, Executive Editor at ABA Book Publishing, who repaired all the mistakes in the manuscript, and who was a delightful collaborator.

Joseph Fox shared not only his wisdom, but also a part of his Civil War library.

Finally, my greatest debt, as always, is to my wife, Mary, who joined me in visiting endless Civil War sites, from Fort McHenry to Vicksburg, who read and edited every word of the manuscript, hid her boredom and surrounded me with tolerance, encouragement, and enthusiasm.

Index

Notes are designated with *n*.

A

Aaron, Cooper v., 127
Ableman, Stephen V. R., 41
Ableman v. Booth, 41–43, 131, 373*n*, 384*n*
Abolition, British, 210–211, 219–220
Abolitionism, 65, 69, 215
Abolitionists
   Brown and, 47, 49, 62, 69, 73, 377*n*, 378*n*
   Chief Executive/Chief Justice conflict and, 127, 131
   Dred Scott case and, 37, 41, 44
   ending slavery and, 210, 211, 222, 223, 230, 236, 412*n*–414*n*
   Fugitive Slave Act and, 362*n*
   Radical, 49
   secession and, 88
   from 1776-1857, 2, 9, 11
Adams, Abigail, 230
Adams, Charles Francis, 191, 197, 198, 295, 359*n*, 402*n*, 406*n*
Adams, John, 141, 191, 230, 357*n*, 364*n*, 380*n*, 406*n*
Adams, John Quincy, 213, 357*n*, 364*n*
   ending slavery and, 411*n*
   as prominent Civil War period lawyer, 295–296
   secession and, 76, 81, 381*n*, 382*n*
Addison, William, 156, 157, 394*n*

Administrative Procedure Act, 278
Africa, 9, 174, 210, 213, 217, 218, 377*n*
Africans, 25–26, 89, 174, 213, 216, 218, 220
Aiken, Frederick A., 263, 268
Alabama
   secession and, 106, 110
   admitted as state, 381*n*
Alabama, 319
Albert (Prince), 196, 199, 407*n*
Alcott, Louisa May, 66
Alexander II, Czar, 13
Alexander (czar), 191
All the Laws But One (Rehnquist), 150
Allen, Henry W., 254
Amada, Richard, 426*n*
Amar, Akhil Reed, 256, 360*n*, 363*n*
American Bar Association, 179
American Colonization Society (ACS), 9, 215
American Revolution, 27, 140, 159, 169, 212–215, 371*n*, 402*n*. *See also* Revolutionary War
Amestoy, Jeffrey L., 408*n*
Amistad, 213, 220, 296, 411*n*
Amnesty, 185, 285, 287, 288, 289, 429*n*, 430*n*
Amy Warwick, 188–189, 201, 205, 332, 408*n*
Anaconda Plan, 405*n*
Anderson, John, 104, 413*n*

435

INDEX

Anderson, Judith, 66
Andersonville in plays and novels, 279–281
Andrew, John Albion, 56, 58, 64, 70, 71, 194, 296
Anglo-American Claims Commission, 220
Annapolis Convention Resolution, 360*n*
Annexation, of Texas, 87–92
Antislavery movement, 8, 47, 223
Anti-Slavery Society, 43
Antonelli, Cardinal Giacomo, 272
Arguments
　in *Dred Scott* case, 21, 22
　oral, 368*n*
　in *Prize Cases*, 201–203
　in revenge trials, 265–266
Arkansas, 80, 89, 102, 105, 252, 369*n*
Arlington Cemetery, 291, 294
Arlington estate/property, 292, 293, 430*n*
Arlington House, 290
Arnold, Samuel, 260, 261, 263, 268, 274
Arthur, Chester A., 44, 296, 331, 431*n*
Articles of Confederation, 3, 4, 7, 27, 35, 36, 135, 256, 360*n*, 361*n*, 400*n*
Ashley, James, 272
Ashton, Hubley, 179
Assassination, 138, 200, 271–274, 276, 283
Assassination conspirators, 259–270, 279, 280, 282
Astor, John Jacob, 105
Atzerodt, George, 260, 261, 263, 268, 270, 274

B

Bahamas, 213, 220, 405*n*
Baker, Edward Dickinson, 126, 391*n*, 428*n*
Baker, Otis, 280
Baker, Thomas Harrison, 172, 176
Baker, United States v., 176
Balance. *See also* Equilibrium
　Compromise of 1850 and, 11
　Dred Scott case and, 24
　secession and, 80, 87, 89, 90, 91
　Southern worries and, 222

　Texas and, 364*n*
　Union blockade and, 190
Baldwin, Henry, 223, 414*n*
Baltimore Republican, 139
Baltimore Sun, 156
Bankruptcies, 374*n*
Banks, Nathaniel, 228
Banks, Russell, 66
Barbados, 219
Bates, Edward, 359*n*
　Chief Executive/Chief Justice conflict and, 150–161, 392*n*, 395*n*, 399*n*
　Dred Scott case and, 45, 46
　Emancipation Proclamation and, 241, 243, 246, 247
　ending slavery and, 420*n*
　as intersecting Civil War period lawyer, 330
　legal issues and, xiv
　as prominent Civil War period lawyer, 296–297
　revenge trials and, 262, 275, 424*n*, 425*n*
　secession and, 114, 115, 389*n*
　War at sea and, 177, 178, 196, 201
Bell, John, 38, 95, 131, 232
Benet, Stephen, 66
Benjamin, Judah Philip, 177, 181, 182, 183, 254, 255, 283, 288, 297, 398*n*, 404*n*
Benson, Thomas Hart, 230, 382*n*, 415*n*
Bermuda, 219, 408*n*
Bermuda, 394*n*
Berube, Claude, 400*n*
Beuregard, Pierre Gustave Toutant, 402*n*
Biddle, James, 364*n*
Bingham, John Arnold, 263, 273, 297
Black Codes, 8
Black, Jeremiah Sullivan, 96–102, 104, 110, 164, 284, 297–298, 332, 384*n*, 385*n*, 427*n*
Blackbeard, 169
Blackburn, Lucie, 219, 413*n*
Blackburn, Thornton, 219
Blackstone, William, xiii, 145
Blair, Francis Preston, Jr., 20, 298, 359*n*, 366*n*

Index

Blair, Francis Preston, Sr., 19, 284
Blair, Frank, Jr., 414*n*
Blair House, 19, 195, 407*n*
Blair, Montgomery P., 359*n*, 366*n*
   Brown and, 70
   Chief Executive/Chief Justice conflict and, 131, 153, 399*n*
   Dred Scott case and, 19, 20, 21
   Emancipation Proclamation and, 242, 243, 246, 247
   ending slavery and, 232, 420*n*
   as intersecting Civil War period lawyer, 330, 332
   as prominent Civil War period lawyer, 298
   revenge trials and, 423*n*, 424*n*
   secession and, 114, 388*n*
   War at sea and, 194–195, 197
Bleeding Kansas, 12, 94
Blow, Peter, 15, 17
Blow, Taylor, 45
Board of Education, Brown v., 127, 396*n*
Bonifant, Washington, 144
Book of the Negroes, The (Hill), 410*n*
Booth, Ableman v., 41–43, 131, 373*n*, 384*n*
Booth, John Willkes, 59–60, 93, 259, 260, 261, 273, 274, 276, 277, 284, 427*n*
Booth, Junius Brutus, Jr., 260
Booth, Sherman M., 41, 42, 43
Booth, United States v., 373*n*
Border States, 94–95, 110, 227, 228, 230, 232, 233, 236–240
Botts, Lawson, xvi, 55, 56, 376*n*
Boumediene v. Bush, 394*n*
Boutwell, George S., 392*n*
Boynton, Thomas J., 276
Bradley, Joseph, Jr., 274
Bradley, Joseph, Sr., 273, 426*n*
Bradwell, Myra, 295
Bradwell v. Illinois, 295*n*
Brady, James T., 176, 177, 180, 181, 298–299, 331
Branstad, Puerto Rico v., 397*n*
Breckinridge, John Cabell, 38, 94, 95, 126, 131, 159, 232, 299, 391*n*
Breyer, Stephen, 31
Bright, John, 183, 184, 185, 404*n*

Brilliante, 188, 201, 202, 205, 408*n*, 409*n*
Britain. *See* Great Britain
British abolition, 210–211, 219–221
Bromwich, David, 365*n*
Brooks, Geraldine, 65, 66
Brooks, Preston, 49
Brown, Aaron Venable, 299–300
Brown, Annie, 379*n*
Brown, Commonweal v., 58
Brown, George W., 139, 141, 394*n*
Brown, John, xiv, xv, xvi, 47–74, 357*n*, 374*n*, 375*n*, 378*n*, 380*n*, 389*n*
   biography of, 375*n*
   ending slavery and, 216
   before Harpers Ferry, 47–52
   insanity and, 55, 56, 376*n*
   legacy of, 65–66
   Mason Report, 73–74
   media and, 377*n*
   in plays, movies, and novels, 66
   secession and, 94
   supporters of, 61–64
   trial of, 53–60, 67–72
Brown, John, Jr., 49, 71, 379*n*, 380*n*
Brown, Joseph E., 105, 384*n*
Brown, Mary Ann, 60, 379*n*. *See also* Day, Mary Anne
Brown, Sarah, 379*n*
Brown, United States v., 67–72, 418*n*
Brown v. Board of Education, 127, 396*n*
Browning, Orville Hickman, 300, 425*n*
Buchanan, James, 357*n*, 364*n*
   Brown and, 53
   Chief Executive/Chief Justice conflict and, 126, 128, 131, 136, 155
   Dred Scott case and, 21–23, 38, 43, 367*n*, 368*n*, 373*n*
   ending slavery and, 224, 421*n*
   as prominent Civil War period lawyer, xvi, 300
   revenge trials and, 263, 284, 427*n*
   secession and, xv, 96–102, 104–106, 110, 116, 121, 384*n*, 385*n*, 387*n*
   War at sea and, 407*n*, 408*n*, 409*n*
Burnside, Ambrose, 248, 375*n*
Burr, Aaron, 76, 146, 265, 286, 381*n*, 396*n*, 429*n*
Bush, Boumediene v., 394*n*

Bush, George Herbert Walker, 358*n*
Bush, George W., 358*n*
Butler, Benjamin Franklin
   Chief Executive/chief Justice conflict and, 141, 142, 143, 164
   ending slavery and, 225, 226, 228, 230, 231, 237
   as intersecting Civil War period lawyer, 332
   as prominent Civil War period lawyer, xv, 300–301
   revenge trials and, 272, 283, 426*n*
Butler, Pierce, 103
Butler, Rhett, 400*n*

C

Cabot, George, 77
Cadwalader, George, 133–138, 145, 147–148, 154, 156, 178, 301, 394*n*
Cadwalader, John, 178
Calabresi, Steven G., 369*n*
Calhoun, John C., 9, 10, 42, 81, 84, 85, 87, 88, 90, 91, 301, 382*n*, 383*n*
Califano, Joseph, 369*n*
California, 11, 89, 183, 221
Cameron Report, 230–231
Cameron, Simon, 156, 226, 230, 231, 235, 404*n*, 423*n*
Camiliar, John, 423*n*
Campbell, Anne, 137
Campbell, J. Mason, 137
Campbell, John Archibald
   Brown and, 53
   Dred Scott case and, 22, 24, 33, 371*n*
   ending slavery and, 414*n*
   as intersecting Civil War period lawyer, 332
   as prominent Civil War period lawyer, 301–302
   resignation and, 408*n*
   secession and, 111, 112, 385*n*, 387*n*
Campbell, Peter Scott, 423*n*
Canada, 61, 62, 64, 76, 219, 272, 413*n*
Carlile, John S., 113
Carlisle, James M., 202, 408*n*
Carmichael, Richard B., 137, 302
Carpenter, Francis, 404*n*

Carrington, Edward, 273
Carter, Jimmy, 277, 278, 358*n*
Cash, Johnny, 66
Cass, Lewis, 96, 101
Catron, John, 22, 24, 34, 203, 205, 207, 368*n*, 409*n*, 421*n*
Cave, Eber, 386*n*
Chafee, Calvin C., 17, 44, 45
Chafee, Irene Emerson, 17. *See also* Emerson, Irene; Sanford, Eliza Irene
Chapman piracy project, 182–185
Charles I (king), 146, 421*n*
Chase, Salmon P., 359*n*, 363*n*
   Chief Executive/Chief Justice conflict and, 153, 161, 162, 392*n*, 399*n*
   Dred Scott case and, 38
   Emancipation Proclamation and, 241, 246, 247
   ending slavery and, 226, 235, 420*n*
   as intersecting Civil War period lawyer, 329, 332
   as prominent Civil War period lawyer, 302–303
   revenge trials and, 276, 285, 287, 288, 429*n*
   secession and, 114, 117, 389*n*, 390*n*
   War at sea and, 198, 409*n*
Chaudhry, Iftikhar Mohammed, 165
Cherokees, 26, 369*n*
Chew, Roger, 54
Chickasaw, 26
Chief Executive/Chief Justice conflict, 125–165
   aftermath of, 161–165
   Attorney General's opinion in, 151–160
   beginning of, 126–137
   debates regarding, 127, 135, 160, 165
   events between March/May in, 138–143
   Habeas Corpus Act in, 157–158
   Lincoln's response in, 149–150
   political context of, 138–143
   Taney's decision in, 144–148
Chilton, Samuel, 56, 58, 70
China, 122, 123, 390*n*
Chipman, Norton Parker, 280, 303

Index

Choctaws, 26
Cholera, 367n
Christiana Riot, 92–93
Churchill, Winston, 358n
Cicero, xiii
Citizenship, *Dred Scott* case and, 26, 27, 28, 29, 35
Civil War
  chronology regarding, 335–356
  intersecting lawyers of, 329–333
  prominent lawyers of, 295–327
Clampitt, John W., 263, 265, 268
Clay, Cassius, 190, 231
Clay, Henry, 10, 11, 78, 79, 85, 89, 303, 364n, 381n, 382n, 383n
Clay's Compromise, 84, 89, 91, 92, 94, 221
Cleburne, Patrick R., 253, 254, 303–304
Clifford, Nathan, 116, 203, 205, 373n, 409n, 421n
Clinton, George, 381n
Clinton, Sir Henry, 212, 254
Clinton, William, 357n, 358n
Cloudsplitter (Banks), 66
Cobb, Howell, 96, 101
Collamer, Jacob, 67, 69
Colonies
  British abolition and, 219
  Dred Scott case and, 27, 29, 33
  slavery in, 2, 210, 211
Colonization, 215, 243
Colorado, 12, 388n
Commentaries on the Constitution (Story), 146, 151
Commerce Clause, 222, 414n
Commonweal v. Brown, 58
Compromise of 1850, 11, 92, 221
Compromise Tariff Act, 85, 382n
Compulsory process, defined, 72
Concurring opinions, in *Dred Scott* case, 22, 31–34
Confederacy
  Articles of Confederation and, 361n
  Dred Scott case and, 369n
  emancipation and, 254
  Emancipation Proclamation and, 240, 251, 252

  ending slavery and, 205, 227, 236, 421n
  revenge trials and, 286, 287
  secession and, 84, 106, 108, 109, 110, 114, 389n
  War at sea and, 168–173, 176, 182, 183, 186, 187, 190, 199, 200, 405n
Confederacy of Middle America, 102
Confederate Congress, 135, 181, 227. *See also* CSA Congress
Confederate Constitution of 1861, 5, 135
Confederate Department of Commerce, 172
Confederate States of America (CSA)
  emancipation and, 253, 254
  Emancipation Proclamation and, 240, 251
  ending slavery during war and, 227
  persuading states to end slavery and, 237
  revenge trials and, 279, 282, 288, 289, 427n, 429n
  secession and, 93, 96, 101, 106, 108–110, 111, 114
  Trent affair and, 192, 193, 196, 198
  Union blockade and, 186, 189, 190, 191
  War at sea and, 168, 174, 178, 179, 180, 182, 183, 184
Confederates
  revenge trials and, 284, 285
Confederation of States, 4, 33
Confiscation Act
  First, 227–231, 236
  Second, 182, 184, 237–240, 243, 274, 422n
Congress
  American Revolution/slavery and, 214
  British abolition and, 220
  Brown and, 67, 69
  Chief Executive/Chief Justice conflict and, 128, 145, 146, 149, 150, 155–159, 396n–399n
  composition of, 358n
  Confederate, 135, 181, 227 (*See also* CSA Congress)
  Constitution and, 5

Congress, *continued*
  Continental, 169, 212, 213
  CSA, 172, 254, 386n (*See also* Confederate Congress)
  Dred Scott case and, 21, 22, 25, 27–36, 40, 45
  Emancipation Proclamation and, 242, 243, 245, 246, 249
  ending slave trade and, 217, 218
  ending slavery and, 412n, 414n, 416n, 417n, 418n, 420n, 421n
  ending slavery during war and, 226, 227, 230, 231
  Fugitive Slave Act and, 362n
  lawyers and, xii
  Monroe and, 363n
  persuading states to end slavery and, 232, 233, 234, 235, 237, 238, 239
  Prize Cases and, 202, 203, 204, 205, 207
  revenge trials and, 265, 291, 294, 423n, 427n, 429n, 430n
  Southern worries and, 222, 223, 224
  tariffs and, 81
  Thirteenth Amendment and, 256
  three-fifths clause and, 6
  War at sea and, 168, 170, 182, 401n, 406n, 407n, 409n
Congress of Paris, 171
Connecticut, 6, 50, 68, 77, 213
Conness, John, 185, 404n
Conscription law, xvii, 359n
Constitution
  acquiring territory and, 363n
  amendments to, 5, 13, 365n
  American Revolution/slavery and, 212
  CSA, 110, 171
  Dred Scott case and, 19, 25–35, 369n
  Emancipation Proclamation and, 245, 247, 250, 251, 252
  ending slavery and, 255, 412n, 414n
  ending slavery during war and, 226, 227
  EU and, 361n
  founders and, 12
  fugitive slave clause and, 7–8
  lawyers and, xvii
  making of, 361n
  overview of, 4–5
  persuading states to end slavery and, 233, 234, 238
  Prize Cases and, 202, 203, 206
  revenge trials and, 265, 266
  slave trade and, 5
  Thirteenth Amendment and, 256
  three-fifths clause and, 6–7
  War at sea and, 168, 169
Constitution of the CSA, 110
Constitutional Convention, 6, 212, 368n, 390n
Constitutional Unionists, 95
Continental Congress, 169, 212, 213
Continental Navy, 169
Cook, John E., 375n, 377n, 378n
Cooke, John, 146, 421n
Coolie trade, 218
Coolies, 412n
Cooper Union speech, 44, 73, 223, 403n, 414n
Cooper v. Aaron, 127
Copeland, John A., 375n, 377n
Coppoc, Edwin, 375n, 377n, 378n
Corbett, Boston, 259
Cornerstone speech, 363n, 387n
Corning, Erastus, 159, 160
Corwin, Thomas, 190, 224, 304, 359n, 406n
Cotton, 187, 190, 214, 405n, 406n
Cotton gin, 9
Cotton market, 105
Cowper, William, 412n
Cox, Walter S., 263
Coxetter, Louis M., 174, 175
Crawford, Martin J., 109, 386n
Crawford, William, 381n
Creeks, 26
Crenshaw, 188, 201, 202, 205
Creole, 31, 220, 309
Crimean War, 41, 171, 190, 401n
Crisfield, John W., 233, 239, 417n, 419n
Crittenden, John J., 101, 304, 415n
CSA. *See* Confederate States of America (CSA)
CSA Congress, 172, 254, 386n. *See also* Confederate Congress

Index 441

CSA Constitution, 110, 171
CSA prison camp, 279
Cuba, 174, 191, 192, 216, 217, 218, 402n, 403n, 407n, 420n
Cummings v. Missouri, 265, 332
Curry, Jabez, 95
Curtis, Benjamin Robbins
  Dred Scott case and, 20, 22, 24, 25, 34–38, 368n, 372n, 373n
  ending slavery and, 250, 251, 422n
  as intersecting Civil War period lawyer, 333
  as prominent Civil War period lawyer, xvi, 304–305
  secession and, 389n
Curtis, George T., xvi, 20, 304
Curtiss-Wright Export Corp., States v., 361n
Cushing, Caleb, 29, 196, 305, 369n, 371n
Custis, George Washington Parke, 430n
Custis, Mary, 290

D
Dakotas, 12
Dana, Richard Henry, 201, 203, 207, 288, 305, 332
Daniel, Peter V., 24, 32, 371n, 384n, 385n
Davis, David, 116, 162–163, 201, 203, 306, 409n, 421n
Davis, David Brion, 412n, 413n
Davis, Jefferson, xvi, 2, 135, 225, 279, 331, 397n
  Brown and, 63, 67, 71
  Dred Scott case and, 370n, 371n
  emancipation and, 254, 255
  non-trial of, xiv, 282–289
  revenge trials and, 261, 266, 272, 280, 282–289, 292, 428n, 429n
  secession and, 89, 93, 106, 107, 108, 110, 111, 384n, 386n
  Trent affair and, 192
  Union blockade and, 191
  War at sea and, 168, 171, 172, 173, 175, 182, 183, 402n, 404n
Davis, Julia, 66
Davis, Varina, 428n

Day, Mary Anne, 47. *See also* Brown, Mary Ann
Dayton, William, 191, 306, 359n, 367n
de Lafayette, Marquis, 422n
De Tocqueville, Alexis, xiii, 357n, 359n, 382n, 384n
Death penalty, 176, 177, 182, 217
Death sentence, 276, 280
Debates
  regarding Brown, 66
  regarding Chief Executive/Chief Justice conflict, 127, 135, 160, 165
  regarding *Dred Scott* case, 26, 31, 45–46
  regarding ending slavery, 257
  over slave trade, 221
  regarding revenge trials, 275
  regarding secession, 82, 116, 122–123
  regarding tariffs, 81
  regarding West Virginia, 116
Debts
  Brown and, 48, 49
  Juarez and, 406n
  West Virginia/Virginia, 116
Declaration of Independence, 2, 3, 27, 28, 29, 106, 368n, 370n, 386n
Declaration of Paris, 171, 173, 186, 402n
Declaration Respecting Maritime War, 171
Deep South, 94, 101, 102, 103, 105, 109, 110, 112, 212, 215, 232, 386n
Delaware
  ending slavery and, 215, 232, 233, 416n
  secession and, 102
  Thirteenth Amendment and, 256
Democracy, 190, 219
Democratic Party, 9, 10, 20, 24, 37, 82, 94, 367n, 381n
Democrats
  Brown and, 53, 65, 67, 73
  Chief Executive/Chief Justice conflict and, 159
  Dred Scott case and, 24, 31, 37, 40, 42, 45
  Emancipation Proclamation and, 245
  ending slavery during war and, 227
  persuading states to end slavery and, 233

442 INDEX

Democrats, *continued*
  revenge trials and, 286
  secession and, 87, 88, 89, 114, 383*n*
  War at sea and, 404*n*
Denmark, 196
Dennison, Kentucky v., 7, 147, 363*n*, 387*n*, 393*n*, 397*n*
Dennison, William, Jr., 161
Denver, James William, 280, 306
Devens, Charles, 291, 306–307
Dickens, Charles, 220, 365*n*
Dickinson, John, 368*n*
Diplomacy, 167. *See also* International law; War at sea
Dirda, Michael, 377*n*
Dissents, 23, 34–36, 409*n*, 419*n*
District of Columbia, 11, 90, 101, 220–221, 224, 233, 272, 274, 278, 293, 416*n*
District of Columbia Emancipation Act, 233
Disunionists, 95
Diversity, *Dred Scott* case and, 19
Dix-Hill Cartel, 404*n*
Donald, David Herbert, 112, 154
Doolittle, James R., 67, 69
Doster, William E., 263
Double jeopardy, 288–289
Douglas, Stephen, 11, 37, 38, 89, 94, 95, 131, 307
Douglass, Frederick, 7, 49, 61–64, 220, 222
Draft, xvii, 359*n*
Draft Riots, 180
Drake, Francis, 168
Dred Scott and the Problem of Constitutional Evil (Graber), 39
Dred Scott Case, The (Fehrenbacher), 22
Dred Scott case/decision, xiv, 1, 15–46, 80, 100, 357*n*, 360*n*. *See also* Scott, Dred
  after, 37–46
  Chief Executive/Chief Justice conflict and, 130, 155, 398*n*
  debates regarding, 26, 31, 45–46
  dissents in, 23, 34–36
  Emancipation Proclamation and, 250
  ending slavery and, 414*n*
  facts of, 15–23
  intersecting Civil War period lawyers for, 330
  opinions in, 22, 25–34
  persuading states to end slavery and, 236
  Prize Cases and, 201
  prominent Civil War period lawyers for, 305, 309, 310, 313, 316, 326
  secession and, 389*n*
  Somerset case and, 211
  Southern worries and, 222
  Supreme Court and, 19–23, 24–36
  War at sea and, 408*n*, 409*n*
Dred Scott v. Sanford, 13, 393*n*
Dunmore, Lord, 212
Dunn, Susan, 363*n*
Dyson, Freeman, 428*n*

E
Early, Jubal, 161
East Timor, 75
Echo, 174
Economist, 200, 222
Edison General Electric Company, 403*n*
Ehrlich, Robert, 278
Eisenhower, Dwight D., 127, 357*n*, 396*n*
Eleanor, The, 401*n*
Eleventh Amendment, 365*n*
Ellis, Joseph, 3, 8, 214, 361*n*
Emancipation
  American Revolution/slavery and, 213, 214, 215
  ending slavery during war and, 229, 231
  persuading states to end slavery and, 232, 233, 234, 235, 237
Emancipation Proclamation, xiv, xv, xvi, 115, 240–252, 253, 415*n*, 421*n*
Emerson, Irene, 19, 45. *See also* Chafee, Irene Emerson; Sanford, Eliza Irene
Emerson, John, 15, 17, 36, 40, 44
Emerson, Ralph Waldo, 58, 64
Emerson, Scott v., 18, 34. *See also Dred Scott* case
Enchantress, 174, 175, 178
England
  acquiring territory and, 363*n*

Index

American Revolution/slavery and, 213
Articles of Confederation and, 3
Brown and, 49, 65
Douglass and, 62
Dred Scott case and, 17
revenge trials and, 288
slavery in, 210–211
Surratt and, 272
Trent affair and, 200
Union blockade and, 187, 190, 191
Equilibrium, loss of, 87-93. *See also* Balance
European Union, 122, 361*n*
Evarts, William M., 44, 178, 201, 202, 287, 288, 307, 331, 332
Ewing, Thomas, 263, 278
Ewing, Thomas, Jr., 278, 308
Ex parte Garland, 265
Ex parte Merryman, xiv, 164, 251, 268. *See also* Merryman, John
Ex parte Milligan, xvi, 162, 266, 276, 308, 316, 321, 332, 427*n*. *See also Milligan* case; Milligan, Lambdin P.
Ex parte Vallandigham, 324
Expansion
 American Revolution/slavery and, 215
 from 1800-1855, 11
 secession and, 87
 of slavery into territories, 222
 westward, 364*n*
Extradition Clause, 7

F

Fairfax, Donald M., 193
Farber, Daniel, 395*n*
Faulkner, Charles J., 53, 55, 308
Federal Constitution, 33
Federal War Department, 77
Federalist Papers, The, 32
Federalist Party, 380*n*
Federalists, 76–77, 214, 361*n*
Fehrenbacher, Don E., 22, 39, 368*n*, 413*n*
Fendall, Philip R., 291
Ferdinand VII (king), 170
Ferguson, Plessy v., 391*n*

Fessenden, W. P., 153
Field, David Dudley, xvi, 164, 308, 332, 404*n*, 408*n*, 424*n*
Field, Roswell M., 19
Field, Stephen Johnson
 ending slavery and, 419*n*, 421*n*
 as intersecting Civil War period lawyer, 332, 333
 as prominent Civil War period lawyer, xvi, 308
 revenge trials and, 424*n*
 secession and, 116, 164
 War at sea and, 184, 185, 207, 404*n*, 408*n*, 409*n*
Fifth Amendment, 30, 234, 238, 247, 266, 292, 416*n*, 419*n*
Filibuster, defined, 404*n*
Fillmore, Millard, 21, 92, 131, 221, 357*n*, 364*n*, 367*n*, 368*n*, 406*n*
Finkelman, Paul, 365*n*, 380*n*
First Confiscation Act, 227–231, 236
Fisher, George Purnell, 232, 236, 272, 273, 274, 309, 416*n*
Fitch, Graham N., 67
Flag Act of 1818, 389*n*
Fletcher v. Peck, 296
Florida
 American Revolution/slavery and, 213
 Chief Executive/Chief Justice conflict and, 142
 Dred Scott case and, 16
 persuading states to end slavery and, 234
 revenge trials and, 283
 secession and, 89, 105, 106, 386*n*
 Union blockade and, 187
Floyd, John B., 96, 386*n*
Force Bill of 1833, 85
Ford brothers, 260, 423*n*
Ford, Gerald, 357*n*
Foreign Relations Committee, 185
Forsyth, John, 109, 386*n*
Fort Armstrong, 15
Fort Donelson, 280
Fort Jefferson, 276, 277
Fort Jessup, 16
Fort Lafayette, 397*n*

Fort McHenry, 132–138, 144, 148, 156, 178, 268, 393*n*, 397*n*
Fort McNair, 262, 270
Fort Moultrie, 104
Fort Snelling, 15, 16, 365*n*
Fort Sumter, 101, 104, 111, 112, 138, 149, 168, 186, 378*n*, 387*n*, 402*n*
Fort Warren, 394*n*
Fort/Fortress Monroe, xv, 226, 237, 283, 284, 286, 428*n*
Founders/Founding Fathers, 1, 4, 6, 8, 9, 11, 12, 13, 192
Founey, John W., 397*n*
Fourteenth Amendment, 13, 45, 288, 295, 391*n*
Fox, Gus, 195, 407*n*
France
  acquiring territory and, 363*n*
  cotton in, 405*n*
  Declaration of Independence and, 2
  Dred Scott case and, 30
  Emancipation Proclamation and, 242
  Indian independence and, 13
  minister to, 359*n*
  revenge trials and, 288
  secession and, 78
  Trent affair and, 198, 199
  Union blockade and, 187, 190, 191
  United States and, 9
  War at sea and, 170, 171, 173, 408*n*
Frankfurter, Felix, 127
Frederick the Great, 52
Free states
  Brown and, 50
  change/polarization and, 9, 11
  secession and, 80, 87, 94
  Texas and, 364*n*
Freedman's Act, 416*n*
Freedman's Bureau Act, 422*n*
Freedman's Village, 291, 293, 431*n*
Freedom suit statute, 17
Freehling, William W., 40, 78, 384*n*
Free-soil activism, 49, 71
Free-soil wing, 20
Fremont, Jessie, 229, 230, 415*n*
Fremont, John C., 21, 94, 228–231, 234, 236, 241, 249, 367*n*, 368*n*, 415*n*, 416*n*

Fremont's Order, 228–230
Fugitive Slave Act, 11, 41–43, 62, 67, 92, 93, 131, 192, 225, 243, 362*n*, 363*n*, 364*n*
Fugitive slave clause, 7–8
Funds
  for Brown, 50, 68
  for ending slavery, 232

G

Garfield, James A., 164, 309, 332, 425*n*, 427*n*, 431*n*
Garibaldi, Giuseppe, 13
Garland, Augustus J., 424*n*
Garrick, Jacob, 175, 178, 179, 180
Garrison, William Lloyd, 47, 215
Gates, Bill, 429*n*
Geneva Conventions, xvii
George, Joseph, Jr., 426*n*, 427*n*
George (king), 76, 107, 206
Georgia
  American Revolution/slavery and, 212
  Dred Scott case and, 24, 32, 34
  Lemmon v. People and, 43
  persuading states to end slavery and, 234
  secession and, 105–106, 386*n*
  War at sea and, 401*n*
Gettysburg Address, 248
Geyer, Henry, 20, 21, 309
Gibbons v. Ogden, 361*n*
Giddings, Joshua Reed, 220, 309–310
Giles, William F., 397*n*
Gill, George M., 132, 136, 394*n*
Gillani, Yousaf Raza, 165
Ginsburg, Ruth Bader, 31, 371*n*
Glover, Joshua, 41, 373*n*
Goodwin, Doris Kearns, 423*n*
Gordan, John D. III, 403*n*
Gordon, Nathaniel, 218, 380*n*
Gorsuch, Edward, 92, 93
Gorsuch, Tom, 93
Graber, Mark, 39, 40, 371*n*, 372*n*
Grant, Ulysses S., 254, 263, 279, 283, 292, 365*n*, 371*n*, 405*n*, 423*n*
Great Britain
  Articles of Confederation and, 3

Index

Declaration of Independence and, 2
Dred Scott case and, 31, 33
Emancipation Proclamation and, 242
ending slavery and, 410*n*, 412*n*, 413*n*
Indian independence and, 13
legal issues and, xv
minister to, 359*n*
secession and, 77, 98
Trent affair and, 192, 193, 196, 198, 199
Union blockade and, 187
United States and, 9
War at sea and, 169, 170, 171, 407*n*
Greathouse, Ridgley, 183, 184
Greeley, Horace, 236, 284, 287
Green, Israel, 52, 55, 56, 58
Green, Shields, 61, 375*n*, 377*n*, 378*n*
Green, Thomas C., 55, 70, 376*n*
Green, William, 58, 59
Greenbacks, 359*n*
Grenville, George, 210
Grier, Robert Cooper
  Dred Scott case and, 22, 24, 32, 368*n*, 371*n*
  ending slavery and, 414*n*, 421*n*
  as prominent Civil War period lawyer, 310
  secession and, 93, 118
  War at sea and, 178, 179, 180, 203, 204, 205, 408*n*, 409*n*
Griswold, Hepburn v., 359*n*
Griswold, Hiram, 56
Griswold, Roger, 76
Groves v. Slaughter, 414*n*
Guelzo, Allen C., 415*n*

H

Habeas corpus
  Chief Executive/Chief Justice conflict and, 134–138, 142, 144–152, 155, 161–162, 164, 394*n*, 396*n*, 397*n*
  English heritage and, 210, 211
  revenge trials and, 268, 269, 274, 276, 286, 427*n*
Habeas Corpus Act, 155, 157–158, 162, 163, 269
Hague Conventions, xvii
Haiti, 5, 65, 217, 234, 363*n*, 420*n*
Halleck, Henry Wager, 310, 359*n*, 416*n*

Hamilton, Alexander, 361*n*, 380*n*
Hamlin, Hannibal, 126, 153, 310
Hampton Roads conference, xiv, 351, 420*n*
Hanchett, William, 426*n*
Hancock, John, 169
Hancock, Winfield Scott, 268, 425*n*
Harding, Charles B., 55
Harding, George, 329
Harlan, John, 95, 423*n*
Harpending, Asbury, 183, 185
Harpers Ferry, xvi, 47–53, 55, 60, 61, 62, 65, 67, 68, 71, 73, 97, 222, 291, 377*n*
Harper's Weekly, 280
Harris, Benjamin Gwinn, 310–311, 422*n*, 423*n*, 428*n*
Harris, Thomas, 263, 264, 424*n*
Harrison, Nathaniel, 178
Harrison, William Henry, 131, 357*n*, 364*n*
Hartford Convention, 77, 82
Hartranft, John Frederick, 425*n*
Hayes, Rutherford B., 110, 311
Hayne, Robert Y., 81, 82, 311, 382*n*
Hazlett, Albert, 375*n*, 378*n*
Hepburn v. Griswold, 359*n*
Herndon, William, 84, 130, 378*n*
Herold, David, 260, 261, 263, 268, 270, 274, 277, 423*n*
Hiawatha, 188, 201, 205, 332, 409*n*
Hicks, Thomas, 139, 142
Higginson, Thomas Wentworth, 62, 64
Hill, Lawrence, 410*n*
HMS Rinaldo, 200
Hoar, George F., 392*n*
Hoffman, Ogden, 184
Holmes v. Jennison, 399*n*
Holt, Joseph, xv, 262, 263, 270, 273, 311–312, 423*n*, 425*n*
Holzer, Harold, 385*n*
Hoover, Herbert, 357*n*
House of Representatives
  American Revolution/slavery and, 214
  British abolition and, 220, 221
  Chief Executive/Chief Justice conflict and, 130

House of Representatives, *continued*
  ending slavery and, 416n, 417n
  ending slavery during war and, 227
  persuading states to end slavery and, 232, 236, 238
  political power in, 11
  revenge trials and, 286, 287
  secession and, 78, 88, 110, 114, 381n
  Southern worries and, 224
  Thirteenth Amendment and, 256
  three-fifths clause and, 6
  Trent affair and, 194
Houston, Sam, 88, 89, 108
Howe, Julia Ward, 378n
Howe, Samuel Gridley, 50, 61, 62, 64, 378n
Hoyer, Steny, 278
Hoyt, George H., 56, 59, 71, 376n
Hughes, Charles, 39, 127
Hughes, James, 280
Hughes, John Joseph, 403n
Hunter, Andrew, 55, 59, 60, 62, 70, 333, 376n, 389n
Hunter Commission, 265, 275, 276, 277, 278
Hunter, David, 234, 236, 240, 241, 249, 262, 263, 264, 265, 269, 416n, 417n
Hunter, Henry, 55, 56, 376n
Hunter, Mary Victorine, 426n
Hunter Order, 234–236, 237
Hunter, Robert Mercer Taliferro, 174, 312, 332, 359n
Hurd v. Railroad Bridge Company, 330
Hyatt, Thaddeus, 71, 72

I

Illinois
  Dred Scott case and, 15, 17, 18, 32, 34, 40
  Emancipation Proclamation and, 245, 249
  Matson and, 365n
Illinois, Bradwell v., 295n
Inaugural address
  of Buchanan, 23
  of Davis, 2
  of Letcher, 112
  of Lincoln, 7, 73, 84, 105, 109–113, 127–131, 138, 149, 223–224
Independence, 13, 84, 122
Indian independence, 13, 122
Indiana, 161, 162
Indians, 25–26, 369n
Ingersoll, Charles, 394n
Insanity, 55, 56
Internal Slave Trade, 222
International Court of Justice, 122, 123
International law, 359n. *See also* War at sea
  ending slavery and, 419n
  legal issues and, xv
  Prize Cases and, 202, 204
  secession and, 121, 122
  Trent affair and, 192, 196, 197, 198, 199
  Union blockade and, 186, 188, 189
  war and, 357n
International relations, 189–191
Interstate slave trade, 222, 223
Iowa
  Brown and, 68
  Dred Scott case and, 15, 16, 17
Irish imigrants, 404n
Italy
  Garibaldi and, 13
  Parker and, 64
  Surratt and, 272
  Trent affair and, 196

J

J. M. Chapman, 183
Jackson, Andrew, 9, 10, 357n, 364n
  Brown and, 374n
  Chief Executive/Chief Justice conflict and, 128, 130, 159, 396n
  Dred Scott case and, 42, 367n, 372n
  ending slavery and, 414n, 421n
  lawyers and, xii
  as prominent Civil War period lawyer, 312
  secession and, 77, 81–87, 89, 99, 101, 105, 106, 381n, 382n
  Southern worries and, 223
  War at sea and, 183, 186, 203, 409n
Jamaica, 210, 211, 219
Japan, 364n, 390n

Jay, John, 222, 361*n*
Jefferson County Circuit Court, 53
Jefferson Davis, 174, 175, 178–179, 181, 203, 204, 205, 402*n*
Jefferson, Thomas, 2, 357*n*, 361*n*, 363*n*, 364*n*
   American Revolution/slavery and, 214, 215
   Chief Executive/Chief Justice conflict and, 146, 151
   ending slave trade and, 217
   ending slavery and, 422*n*
   revenge trials and, 265, 429*n*
   secession and, 76, 79, 80, 380*n*, 381*n*
Jennison, Holmes v., 399*n*
John Brown, Virginia v., 47. See also Brown, John
Johnson, Andrew
   lawyers and, xii
   revenge trials and, 262, 267–273, 277–280, 283, 286–289, 423*n*–429*n*
   secession and, 384*n*
   War at sea and, 184, 409*n*, 415*n*
Johnson, Bradley T., 161, 313
Johnson, James H., 423*n*
Johnson, Reverdy
   Chief Executive/Chief Justice conflict and, 143, 151
   Dred Scott case and, 20, 21, 22, 366*n*
   as intersecting Civil War period lawyer, 330, 331, 332, 333
   persuading states to end slavery and, 235
   as prominent Civil War period lawyer, xvi, 313
   revenge trials and, 263–266, 268, 284, 423*n*, 424*n*, 427*n*
   secession and, 389*n*
Jones v. Van Zandt, 7, 329, 369*n*
Joseph, 174, 176
Joseph, Ferdinand Maximilian, 406*n*
Journal of Commerce, 37
Juarez, Benito, 191, 406*n*
Judicial Murder of Mrs. Surratt, The (Amada), 426*n*
Judiciary Act of 1789, 135, 409*n*
Judiciary Act of 1801, 409*n*
Judiciary Act of 1837, 368*n*, 409*n*
Judiciary Act of 1866, 409*n*
Judiciary Act of 1869, 409*n*
Jury nullification, 404*n*
Justices, number of, 409*n*

K

Kagi, John, 61
Kane, John K., 93
Kane, Marshal George, 139
Kansas
   Brown and, 49, 50, 51, 52, 69, 71
   Dred Scott case and, 21, 30, 41
   secession and, 94, 389*n*
   slavery in, 12
Kansas-Nebraska Act of 1854
   change/polarization and, 11, 12
   Dred Scott case and, 30, 40, 41, 49, 366*n*, 372*n*
   secession and, 80, 94, 383*n*
Kantor, MacKinlay, 281
Kaufman, Frederick, 291, 424*n*
Kautz, August V., 424*n*
Keasarge, 319
Keim, William High, 133, 136, 156
Kelley, William Darrah, 179
Kendall, Amos, 414*n*
Kennedy, Anthony, 135
Kennedy, John A., 177
Kennedy, John F., 92, 358*n*
Kenner, Duncan F., 254, 312
Kent, William, xiii
Kentucky
   ending slavery during war and, 229
   fugitive slave clause and, 7
   secession and, 102, 389*n*
   Thirteenth Amendment and, 256
Kentucky v. Dennison, 7, 147, 363*n*, 387*n*, 393*n*, 397*n*
Key, Francis Barton, 393*n*
Key, Francis Scott, 134, 401*n*, 426*n*
Key, Philip Barton, 331
King, Rufus, 272
King's Bench, 409*n*
Kline, Henry, 92
Knickmeyer, Ellen, 369*n*
Korean War, 160
Kosciuszko, Tadeusz, 422*n*
Kosovo, 75, 122

L

Lafayette, Marquis de, 52
Lake, Delos, 184
Lane, Henry, 398*n*
Larson, Kate Clifford, 424*n*
Latrobe, John, 143
Law
   admiralty, 203
   conscription, xvii, 359*n*
   domestic, 202
   international (*See* International law)
   maritime, 227
   martial, 228, 230
   naturalization, 28
   neutrality, 170
Law, William C., 183, 184
Lawyers
   Congress and, 358*n*
   intersecting Civil War period, 329–333
   larger-than-life, xv–xvi
   leadership and, xi
   in mid-nineteenth century, xi–xiv
   presidents as, 357*n*, 358*n*
   prominent Civil War period, 295–327
   as superior class, 357*n*
LeBarnes, John W., 376*n*
Lee, George Washington Custis, 291, 292, 294
Lee, Harry, 290
Lee, Mary Custis, 290, 291, 292, 430*n*
Lee, Robert E.
   Brown and, 52
   Chief Executive/Chief Justice conflict and, 136, 137, 145, 147, 151, 154, 159
   ending slavery and, 242, 254
   revenge trials and, 279, 283, 287, 290, 291, 430*n*
   secession and, 108
   War at sea and, 174, 187
Lee, United States v., 292
Legal Tender Cases, xvi
Legality
   Chief Executive/Chief Justice conflict and, 145
   secession and, 117–119
Leiner, Frederick C., 401*n*

Lemmon, John, 44
Lemmon v. People, 32, 43–44, 296, 307, 317, 331, 373*n*
Letcher, John, 112, 313
Letter of marque, 168, 169, 170, 171, 172, 174, 177, 179, 180, 184, 400*n*, 401*n*
Letter of Marque, The (O'Brian), 400*n*
Levitt, Saul, 281
Lewis, A. H., 376*n*
Lewis, Morgan, 76
Lewis v. Lewis, 130, 131
Libby, Lorenzo, 183, 184
Libel, defined, 405*n*
Liberia, 9, 215, 234, 377*n*, 420*n*
Lieber, Francis, 359*n*
Lincoln, Abraham, 4, 7, 10, 357*n*, 359*n*
   British abolition and, 221
   Brown and, 72, 73, 378*n*
   character of, 358*n*
   Chief Executive/Chief Justice conflict and (*See* Chief Executive/Chief Justice conflict)
   Dred Scott case and, 37, 38, 43, 44, 367*n*, 369*n*, 372*n*
   emancipation and, 253
   Emancipation Proclamation and, 240, 242–248, 251, 252
   ending slavery and, 416*n*, 417*n*, 419*n*, 420*n*, 421*n*
   ending slavery during war and, 227, 228, 229, 230, 231, 411*n*
   as intersecting Civil War period lawyer, 330, 332
   lawyers and, xii, xvi
   legal issues and, xiv, xv, xvii
   Matson and, 365*n*
   persuading states to end slavery and, 233, 234, 235, 238, 239
   Prize Cases and, 201, 203, 204, 206, 207
   as prominent Civil War period lawyer, 314
   revenge trials and, 259–263, 269–273, 276, 279–282, 292, 423*n*–427*n*
   secession and, 84, 95–97, 100, 101, 105, 108–114, 116, 385*n*–389*n*
   Southern worries and, 222, 223, 224
   Stowe and, 365*n*

Index   449

Thirteenth Amendment and, 256
Trent affair and, 194, 195, 196, 197, 198, 199, 200
Union blockade and, 186, 187, 189, 190, 191
War at sea and, 168, 171–175, 177, 182–185, 402*n*–406*n*, 409*n*
Lincoln, Edward Baker, 391*n*
Lincoln Murder Conspiracies, The (Hanchett), 426*n*
Lincoln, Robert Todd, 293, 294, 314, 431*n*
Little Women (Alcott), 66
Livingston, Edward, 81, 84, 85, 314
Lockwood, Belva Ann, 295
Lord, Daniel, 76, 177, 178, 202, 203
Lord Day & Lord, 176
Loss of equilibrium, 87–93
Louisiana
  Dred Scott case and, 16
  Emancipation Proclamation and, 252
  ending slave trade and, 218
  ending slavery and, 411*n*, 420*n*
  secession and, 78, 89, 104–105, 105, 106, 118, 381*n*, 386*n*
  Trent affair and, 193
Louisiana Purchase, 9, 22, 76–77, 79, 215
Louisiana Territory, 214
Lovejoy, Owen, 236
Lowe, Louis E., 93
Lowry, Thomas P., 405*n*
Lusk, Dianthe, 47
Luther, Martin, 148
Lyons, Lord, 104, 186, 196, 198, 199, 405*n*, 408*n*

M

Madison, James, 32, 77, 357*n*, 361*n*, 364*n*
Maffitt, John Newland, 174
Magrath, Andrew Gordon, 95, 314, 383*n*
Maine
  as free state, 9
  secession and, 78, 79, 389*n*
Maltz, Earl M., 413*n*
Mammoth, 401*n*

Mann, Ambrose Dudley, 191
Mansfield, Lord, 44, 210, 211. *See also* Murray, William
March (Brooks), 66
Marcy, William, 171, 314–315, 402*n*
Maritime law, 227
Marshall, John, xiii, 4, 39, 127, 128, 146, 286
Martial law, 228, 230
Marvel, William, 387*n*
Maryland
  Articles of Confederation and, 3
  Brown and, 51, 60, 68
  Chief Executive/Chief Justice conflict and, 134, 138–143, 146, 151, 154, 155, 161, 164, 393*n*
  Dred Scott case and, 20, 24, 34, 39
  ending slavery and, 221, 234, 239, 242, 252, 415*n*, 420*n*, 421*n*
  revenge trials and, 423*n*
  secession and, 101, 102, 387*n*
  Virginia *vs.*, 360*n*
  War at sea and, 401*n*
Mason Committee, 67–72, 384*n*
Mason, George, 6, 192
Mason, James, 53, 362*n*, 388*n*
  Brown and, 53, 55, 67, 68, 70, 71, 72
  as intersecting Civil War period lawyer, 331
  as prominent Civil War period lawyer, 315
  secession and, 384*n*, 388*n*
  War at sea and, 192–200, 284, 287
Mason Report, 68, 69, 73–74, 192
Massachusetts
  Andrew and, 64
  Brown and, 49
  Dred Scott case and, 17, 19, 20, 24, 35, 44, 372*n*
  Sanborn and, 64
  secession and, 77, 92, 96, 389*n*
  three-fifths clause and, 6
  War at sea and, 169, 401*n*
Massachusetts Kansas Committee, 50
Matson, Robert, 365*n*
McClellan, George B., 405*n*
McClernand, John, 249, 315
McCulloch, Hugh, 419*n*

McDonald, Joseph E., 332
McKinley, William, 402*n*, 414*n*
McLean, John, 21, 22, 24, 34, 38, 223, 315–316, 330, 367*n*, 414*n*
McPherson, James, 89, 364*n*, 419*n*
Meigs, Montgomery C., 430*n*
Melville, Herman, 74
Mercier, Henri, 198
Mercury, 37
Merriam, Francis, 64
Merryman, John, 132–137, 141, 143, 144, 148, 152, 154, 156–157, 161, 162, 178, 425*n*. *See also Ex parte Merryman*
Merryman, William, 394*n*
Methodist Episcopal Church, 87
Mexican War, 136, 170, 377*n*, 401*n*
Mexico, 10, 11, 88, 98, 108, 183, 184, 190, 191, 359*n*, 401*n*, 406*n*, 408*n*
Michigan, secession and, 80
Military court/tribunal, 260, 262, 265, 266, 268, 269, 280, 282, 284, 285, 286
Militia Act, 239, 404*n*
Miller, Charles D., 379*n*
Miller, Samuel Freeman, 116, 119, 130, 201, 203, 292, 316, 330–331, 383*n*, 421*n*
Milligan case, 309. *See also Ex parte Milligan*
Milligan, Lambdin P., 161, 162, 164, 269, 276, 316, 399*n*, 427*n*. *See also Ex parte Milligan*
Minnesota, *Dred Scott* case and, 15
Mississippi
  ending slavery and, 411*n*, 414*n*
  secession and, 89, 96, 106–107, 386*n*
Mississippi & Missouri Railroad Company v. Ward, 331
Mississippi Secession Convention, 101
Mississippi Slaveholders Convention, 88
Missouri
  American Revolution/slavery and, 213
  Brown and, 51
  Dred Scott case and, 15, 17–18, 19, 20, 30, 32, 34, 41
  Emancipation Proclamation and, 252
  ending slavery during war and, 229
  secession and, 102
  as slave state, 9
Missouri cases, *Dred Scott* case and, 17, 34
Missouri Compromise of 1820, 362*n*, 364*n*, 409*n*
  American Revolution/slavery and, 212
  change/polarization and, 9, 11
  Dred Scott case and, 15, 18, 21, 22, 30–40, 42, 366*n*, 372*n*
  secession and, 78–80, 87, 94, 101, 383*n*
Missouri Constitution, 424*n*
Missouri, Cummings v., 265, 332
Missouri Railroad Company v. Ward, Mississippi v., 331
Mobile Register, 109
Monaghan, Jay, 406*n*
Money
  Brown and, 47
  ending slavery and, 233
Monroe Doctrine of 1823, 9, 190, 406*n*
Monroe, James, 357*n*, 363*n*, 364*n*, 381*n*, 406*n*, 429*n*
Montana, 12
Moon Besieged, The (Schochen), 66
Morgan, J. P., 105
Morris, Philip, 373*n*
Mudd, Richard D., 277, 278, 423*n*, 427*n*
Mudd, Samuel A., 260, 261, 263, 268, 274, 276–278
Mudd, Sarah, 277
Mudd, Thomas B., 278
Murdock, Francis Butler, 17
Murray, John. *See* Dunmore, Lord
Murray, Robert Bruce, 357*n*
Murray, William, 210, 410*n*. *See also* Mansfield, Lord
Musharraf, Pervez, 165, 391*n*

N

Napoleon, 191
Napoleon III, 190, 406*n*
Napoleon, Louis, 43
Nashville Convention, 89
Nassau, 220
National Assembly of Quebec, 120

Index 451

National Kansas Committee, 50, 71
National Rifle Association, 425*n*
National security
   Chief Executive/Chief Justice conflict and, 164, 165
   Constitution and, 4–5
   importance of, 12
National sovereignty, 81, 186
Naturalization law, 28
Nebraska
   Dred Scott case and, 30
   secession and, 94, 388*n*
   slavery in, 12
Neely, Mark E., Jr., 398*n*, 399*n*
Neff, Stephen C., 357*n*
Nelson, Samuel
   Dred Scott case and, 21, 22, 24, 29, 32, 34
   ending slavery and, 409*n*, 421*n*
   as prominent Civil War period lawyer, 316–317
   secession and, 111, 387*n*
   War at sea and, 177, 178, 180, 201, 203, 205, 206, 207
Neutrality Act, 170
Neutrality laws, 170
Nevada, 388*n*, 389*n*
New Brunswick, 213
New England
   Brown and, 56, 61, 62, 68
   Dred Scott case and, 28, 35
   ending slavery and, 213
   secession and, 76, 77, 92
New Hampshire
   Constitution and, 4
   Dred Scott case and, 35
   secession and, 77
New Jersey
   American Revolution/slavery and, 213
   Dred Scott case and, 35
   Emancipation Proclamation and, 245, 249
   slavery in, 2
New Mexico, 11, 89, 111, 364*n*
New Orleans
   British abolition and, 220
   ending slavery and, 413*n*
   Mexico and, 408*n*

New York
   American Revolution/slavery and, 213
   Brown and, 49, 50, 61
   Dred Scott case and, 16, 19, 22, 24, 32, 34, 35, 37, 373*n*
   Emancipation Proclamation and, 245, 249
   Lemmon v. People and, 43, 44
   secession and, 76, 78, 105–106
   slavery in, 2
   Smith and, 63
   War at sea and, 180
New York Central Railroad, 159
New York City Bar Association, 176
New York Cotton Exchange, 105
New York Court of Appeals, 44
New York Herald, 49, 62, 63
New York State Library, 420*n*
New York Supreme Court, 44
New York Times, 106, 273, 409*n*
New York Tribune, 96, 159, 236, 284, 389*n*
New-York Daily Tribune, 398*n*
Nicaragua, 191
9/11 Commission, 275
Nixon, United States v., 155
North
   in 1820, 9
   American Revolution/slavery and, 215
   assurances regarding slavery and, 222–224
   Brown and, 57, 58, 65, 69, 73
   Chief Executive/Chief Justice conflict and, 131, 155
   Dred Scott case and, 24, 34, 37, 40, 41
   Emancipation Proclamation and, 242, 251
   ending slave trade and, 218
   fugitive slave clause and, 8
   persuading states to end slavery and, 233
   population growth in, 11
   Prize Cases and, 207
   revenge trials and, 279
   secession and, 78, 81, 82, 83, 87, 91, 93, 98, 99, 101, 104, 105, 117

452   INDEX

North, *continued*
   three-fifths clause and, 6
   Trent affair and, 195, 196, 198
   Union blockade and, 187
   War at sea and, 168, 181
North and South, 66
North Carolina
   American Revolution/slavery and, 215
   Dred Scott case and, 35
   ending slavery and, 414*n*
   secession and, 89, 94, 102, 386*n*
   Union blockade and, 186
   War at sea and, 401*n*
Northern Central Railroad, 141
Northwest Ordinance of 1787, 7, 32, 36, 78, 135, 234, 236, 256
Nova Scotia, 213
Nullification, 81–86, 87, 101, 105, 106, 154, 186, 382*n*, 404*n*

O

Oakes, James, 417*n*
Oath-taking, 264–265
Obama, Barack, 46, 357*n*, 358*n*, 380*n*
O'Brian, Patrick, 400*n*
O'Connor Sandra Day, 31
O'Conor, Charles, xvi, 44, 283, 284, 286, 287, 288, 317, 331, 332, 428*n*
Ogden, Gibbons v., 361*n*
Ohio
   Brown and, 47, 49, 55, 71
   Dred Scott case and, 18, 24
   ending slavery and, 415*n*
   fugitive slave clause and, 7
O'Laughlin, Michael, 260, 261, 263, 268, 274, 277
Old Ironsides, 141
O'Neill, John, 178
Oral argument, 368*n*

P

Pacific Ins. Co. v. Soule, 359*n*
Paine, Elijah, 43
Paine, Thomas, 402*n*
Pakistan, 165
Panic of 1837, 47
Panic of 1857, 40–41

Papal States, 272
Pardon, 185, 277, 280, 289
Paris Declaration, 171, 402*n*
Parker, Joel, 422*n*
Parker, Richard, 55, 56, 376*n*, 378*n*
Parker, Theodore, 50, 62, 64
Parliament, 219
Parsons, Theophilus, 195
Paul, Ron, 400*n*
Payne, Lewis, 261
Peabody, George, 366*n*
Peace Conference, 102
Peck, Fletcher v., 296
Pemell, Richard B., 186. *See also* Lyons, Lord
Pennsylvania
   Brown and, 50, 61
   Chief Executive/Chief Justice conflict and, 156
   Dred Scott case and, 24, 32, 34
   secession and, 76, 92, 93
Pennsylvania, Prigg v., 363*n*
People, Lemmon v., 32, 43–44, 296, 307, 317, 331, 373*n*
Perpetual Union, 3
Perry, Matthew, 364*n*
Perthshire, 197
Pettus, Edmund, 386*n*
Philadelphia Press, 397*n*
Philadelphia Republican Convention, 228
Phillips, William, 49
Pickering, Charles W., 369*n*
Pickering, Timothy, 76
Pickett, John T., 191
Pierce, Franklin, 357*n*, 364*n*
   Brown and, 49, 53
   Chief Executive/Chief Justice conflict and, 131, 397*n*
   Dred Scott case and, 371*n*
   as prominent civil War period lawyer, 317–318
   revenge trials and, 284, 428*n*
   secession and, 385*n*
   War at sea and, 170, 401*n*
Pierpont, Francis H., 113, 114, 115, 318
Pierrepont, Edwards, 273, 318, 426*n*
Pinckney, Charles, 6, 212, 318, 362*n*

Index   453

Piracy, 176, 178–185, 203, 205, 217, 401*n*, 403*n*, 412*n*
Pirate Act, 169
Pius IX, 272
Plessy v. Ferguson, 391*n*
Plumer, William, 76
Polarization, from 1800-1855, 9–12
Political context, of Chief Executive/Chief Justice conflict, 138–143
Politics
  Chief Executive/Chief Justice conflict and, 156
  sectionalism in, 87
Polk, James, 87, 88, 131, 171, 357*n*, 364*n*, 383*n*, 408*n*, 409*n*, 421*n*
Polygamy, 417*n*
Popular sovereignty, 23, 30, 364*n*
Population
  in North, 11
  slave, 7, 104, 106, 112, 214, 232, 411*n*
  of slaveholders, 104
  in South, 11
  white, 104, 106, 112, 388*n*, 411*n*
Portugal, 408*n*
Posner, Eric, 408*n*
Postal service, 223
Potato Famine, 404*n*
Powell, Lewis, 260, 263, 267–268, 270, 274, 422*n*
Pratt Street Massacre, 139
Pratt Street Riot, 139, 140, 141, 395*n*
Preliminary Proclamation, 242, 243, 245, 246, 247
Prigg v. Pennsylvania, 363*n*
Prisoners of war, 169, 176, 181, 204, 286
Privateers, 168–185, 401*n*, 402*n*
Prize Cases, xiv, 188–189, 201–207, 307, 310, 316, 317, 408*n*, 409*n*, 421*n*
Prize court, defined, 405*n*
Proclamation of Amnesty, 418*n*
Proclamation of Emergency, 165, 391*n*
Proclamation of Neutrality, 173
Proclamation Regarding Nullification, 84, 85
Profiles in Courage (Webster), 92
Proto-Republican Party, 413*n*
Provisional Congress of the CSA, 106
Prussia, 196, 197

Publius, 361*n*
Puerto Rico v. Branstad, 397*n*
Putnam, 174

Q

Quakers, 92, 93, 211
Quasi-serfdom, 422*n*
Quebec, 120, 121
Queen's Bench, 409*n*

R

Racism, 215
Radical Abolitionists, 49
Radical Republicans, 238, 291, 388*n*, 422*n*
Railroad Bridge Company, Hurd v., 330
Raleigh, Walter, 168
Randall, James Ryder, 139, 140
Randolph, Thomas Jefferson, 91
Reagan, Ronald, 66, 358*n*
Reaper case, 313, 329
Reconciliation, 290–294, 357*n*
Redpath, James, 49, 375*n*
Reform Bill of 1831, 219
Rehnquist, William, 31, 150, 160, 392*n*, 425*n*
Religion, sectionalism in, 87
Republic of Texas, 87
Republican Convention, 73
Republican Party, 10, 37, 73, 89, 94, 222, 228, 232, 238, 367*n*
Republican Party Convention, 404*n*
Republicans
  Brown and, 65, 67, 69, 73
  Chief Executive/Chief Justice conflict and, 155
  Dred Scott case and, 24, 31, 40, 42, 45, 367*n*
  Emancipation Proclamation and, 242, 245
  ending slavery during war and, 227
  Radical, 238, 291, 388*n*, 422*n*
  revenge trials and, 284, 286, 424*n*
  secession and, 95, 388*n*
  Southern worries and, 223
  War at sea and, 404*n*
Restored Government of Virginia, 113, 114, 116

454 INDEX

Revenge trials, xv, 259–294
   Andersonville, 279–281
   of assassination conspirators, 259–270
   debates regarding, 275
   double jeopardy in, 288–289
   Mudd's legal efforts and, 276–278
   non-trial of Davis and, 282–289
   to reconciliation, 290–294
   of Surratt, Jr., 271–275
   of Wirz, 279–281
Revolutionary War, 169, 206, 212, 380n, 395n. *See also* American Revolution
Rhode Island, 77, 216, 360n, 395n, 411n
Richmond Enquirer, 65
Riddle, Albert, 273
River Queen, 332
Robinson, Harriet, 15, 16, 365n. *See also* Scott, Harriet
Rock, John S., 295
Rockefeller, John D., 429n
Rocket Man (Dyson), 428n
Roman, Andre B., 109
Romero, Matias, 191
Romney, Mitt, 358n, 392n
Ronayne, Patrick, 253
Roosevelt, Eleanor, 230
Roosevelt, Franklin, 230, 357n
Roper v. Simmons, 371n
Rost, Pierre Adolphe, 191, 319
Rothschild and Freshfields, 413n
Rubery, Alfred, 183, 185
Ruffin, Edmund, 378n
Rush, Benjamin, 368n
Rusk, Thomas Jefferson, 88
Russell, Lord, 196, 402n, 405n
Russia
   ending slavery during war and, 231
   secession and, 122
   serfs and, 13, 99
   Trent affair and, 196
   Union blockade and, 190, 191
   War at sea and, 171, 406n
Rutledge, John, 6, 103
Ryan, John, 151

S

Salisbury, Willard, 416n
Samuel Mudd Relief Act, 278
Sanborn, Frank, 50, 61, 62, 63, 64, 66
Sanford, Dred Scott v., 13, 393n
Sanford, Eliza Irene, 16, 44. *See also* Chafee, Irene Emerson; Emerson, Irene
Sanford, John F. A., 16, 17, 19, 20, 44, 45
Santa Fe Trail, 66
Sardinia, War at sea and, 171
Savannah, 172, 174–179, 181, 182, 202, 205, 287, 299, 307, 331, 402n
Scalia, Antonin, 31, 371n
Schwartz, Bernard, 164, 399n
Scotland, Articles of Confederation and, 3
Scott, Dred, 15, 16, 19, 22, 25, 29–34, 38, 40, 44–46, 70, 131, 194, 242, 365n, 373n. *See also* Dred Scott case
Scott, Eliza, 16
Scott, Harriet, 16. *See also* Robinson, Harriet
Scott, Lizzie, 16
Scott v. Emerson, 18, 34. *See also* Dred Scott case
Scott, William, 18
Scott, Winfield, 83, 106, 141, 142, 143, 150, 175, 186, 187, 405n
Seceding/secessionist states, 2, 8
Secession, 75–123
   Black and, 97–102
   Buchanan and, 97–102
   Chief Executive/Chief Justice conflict and, 143
   Christiana Riot and, 92–93
   debates regarding, 116, 122–123
   early activities regarding, 76–80
   explanation of, 75, 94–96
   Hartford Convention and, 77
   legality of, 117–119
   loss of equilibrium and, 87–93
   Louisiana Purchase and, 76–77
   Mississippi and, 106–107
   Missouri Compromise and, 78–80
   negotiations regarding, 111–112
   persuading states to end slavery and, 238
   South Carolina and, 81–86, 103–107
   South Carolina's nullification and, 81–86

Index   455

Texas and, 87–92, 108–116, 117–119
 in today's world, 120–123
 Virginia and, 112–116
 West Virginia and, 112–116
Second Confiscation Act, 182, 184, 237–240, 243, 274, 418n, 422n
Second Continental Congress, 3
Second Hague Conference, 402n
Second War of American Independence, 77. *See also* War of 1812
Second Wheeling Convention, 113
Secret Six, 61–64, 71, 379n
Sectionalism, 87
Security bond, 400n
Self-determination/self-determination movements, 8, 75, 120, 122, 391n. *See also* Secession
Seminole War, 16
Seminoles, 26
Semmes, Raphael, 319, 402n
Senate
 acquiring territory and, 363n
 Brown and, 67, 70, 71, 72
 Campbell and, 53
 ending slavery and, 415n, 416n, 417n
 ending slavery during war and, 227
 persuading states to end slavery and, 232, 236, 238
 political power in, 11
 revenge trials and, 286, 287, 430n
 secession and, 78, 80, 81, 87, 88, 106, 107, 110, 114, 380n, 383n, 385n, 386n
 Southern worries and, 224
 Thirteenth Amendment and, 256
Sequestration Act, 227
Serbia, 122
Serfs, 422n
Seward, William H., 359n
 Chief Executive/Chief Justice conflict and, 137, 153, 161
 Dred Scott case and, 38, 370n
 Emancipation Proclamation and, 240, 242, 246, 247, 248
 ending slavery and, 415n, 420n
 as intersecting Civil War lawyer, 332
 as intersecting Civil War period lawyer, 329

 as prominent Civil War period lawyer, 319
 revenge trials and, 260, 272, 284, 285, 426n, 428n
 secession and, 109, 111, 112, 114, 386n
 Trent affair and, 197, 198, 199
 Union blockade and, 186, 191
 War at sea and, 171, 177, 402n, 404n, 406n, 408n
Seymour, Horatio, 249, 319–320, 359n
Shade, Louis, 280, 428n
Shannon, Wilson, 49
Sharer, John D., 397n
Sharkey, William Lewis, 89
Shea, George, 286
Sherman, Roger, 6
Shipman, William, 177
Sickles, Daniel Edgar, 320
Sierra Leone, 213, 410n
Simmons, Roper v., 371n
Simon, James, 367n
Sixteenth Amendment, xvii
Sixth Amendment, 266
Slaughterhouse Cases, 302
Slaughter, Groves v., 414n
Slave Grace, The, 17, 211
Slave population, 7, 104, 106, 112, 214, 232, 411n
Slave states
 change/polarization and, 9, 10, 11
 Dred Scott case and, 16
 ending slavery during war and, 227, 228
 persuading states to end slavery and, 232
 secession and, 80, 87, 94, 110
 Texas and, 364n
Slave trade
 Constitution and, 5, 8
 Dred Scott case and, 28
 ending, 216–218
 international, 222
 interstate, 222, 223
 Southern worries and, 222
Slaveholders, population of, 104, 106
Slavery
 American Revolution and, 212–215
 Articles of Confederation and, 3

Slavery, *continued*
  assurances in North regarding, 222–224
  British abolition and, 219–221
  Constitution and, 5–8
  debates regarding ending, 257
  Declaration of Independence and, 2, 3
  District of Columbia and, 220–221, 224, 233
  Dred Scott case and (See *Dred Scott* case)
  from 1800-1855, 9–12
  emancipation in South of, 253–256
  Emancipation Proclamation and, 240–252
  ending during war, 225–232
  ending slave trade for, 216–218
  English heritage and, 210–211
  explanation of end of, 209
  persuading states to end, 232–239
  Thirteenth Amendment and, 209, 256–257
  worries in South regarding, 222–224
Slidell, John, xv, 192, 193, 194, 195, 196, 197, 198, 199, 200, 288, 320, 417n, 418n
Smith, A. D., 41
Smith, Francis, 430n
Smith, Gerrit, 49, 50, 62, 63, 284, 287, 379n, 381n, 403n, 420n, 428n
Smith, United States v., 178
Somerset, James, 210, 211
Somerset v. Stewart, 17, 44, 210
Soule, Pacific Ins. Co. v., 359n
South
  American Revolution/slavery and, 212, 214, 215
  British abolition and, 219
  Brown and, 50, 53, 57, 65, 69, 73
  Chief Executive/Chief Justice conflict and, 128, 131, 149
  cotton and, 405n
  Deep, 94, 101, 102, 103, 105, 109, 110, 112, 212, 215, 232, 386n
  Dred Scott case and, 24, 28, 34, 37, 40, 41
  in 1820, 9
  emancipation in, 253–255, 255
  Emancipation Proclamation and, 243, 244, 245, 251
  ending slave trade and, 218
  ending slavery and, 413n, 420n
  fugitive slave clause and, 8
  population growth in, 11
  Prize Cases and, 202, 206, 207
  revenge trials and, 279, 289
  secession and, 76–78, 81–83, 86–95, 98, 104, 105, 106, 111, 117, 381n
  three-fifths clause and, 6, 7
  Union blockade and, 187, 189–190
  Upper, 24, 102, 110, 111, 215, 221, 411n
  War at sea and, 168, 173, 178, 179, 180, 408n
  worries regarding slavery in, 222–224
South Carolina
  American Revolution/slavery and, 212
  Brown and, 49
  Dred Scott case and, 42
  ending slave trade and, 218
  ending slavery during war and, 225
  persuading states to end slavery and, 234
  secession and, 81–86, 89, 90, 94–96, 100, 103–107, 382n, 383n, 385n, 386n
  three-fifths clause and, 6
  War at sea and, 401n
South Carolina Convention, 103, 104
South Carolina Exposition and Protest, 81, 84
South Carolina's nullification, 81–86, 186
Sovereignty
  under Articles of Confederation, 4
  Dred Scott case and, 23, 30, 34
  national, 81, 186
  popular, 23, 30, 364n
  Prize Cases and, 206
  state, 81, 106
  Trent affair and, 193
Spain
  acquiring territory and, 363n
  Declaration of Independence and, 2
  ending slave trade and, 217
  secession and, 123

Index

Trent affair and, 199
Union blockade and, 190, 191
War at sea and, 170, 173, 408*n*
Spangler, Edman, 260, 261, 263, 268, 274
Speed, James, 239, 262, 266–267, 268, 285, 286, 321, 332, 419*n*, 423*n*, 424*n*
Speed, Joshua F., 423*n*
SS Raphael Semmes, 319
St. Louis, *Dred Scott* case and, 16, 17, 19
Stanberry, Henry, 287
Stanton, Edwin McMasters, 359*n*
   Chief Executive/Chief Justice conflict and, 150, 399*n*
   ending slavery and, 240, 241, 419*n*
   as intersecting Civil War period lawyer, 329, 331
   as prominent Civil War period lawyer, 321
   revenge trials and, 259, 260, 262, 263, 279, 284, 423*n*, 427*n*, 428*n*
   secession and, 114, 384*n*
Star of the West, 101
Star Spangled Banner (Key), 134, 393*n*
State Sovereignty, 81, 106
States
   Border, 94–95, 227, 228, 230, 232, 233, 236–239
   Confederation of, 4, 33
   constitutions of, 361*n*
   to end slavery, 232–239
   free (*See* Free states)
   seceding, 2
   slave (*See* Slave states)
   three-fifths clause and, 6
States v. Curtiss-Wright Export Corp., 361*n*
Stearns, George, 50
Steel, Candida Ewing, 278
Steel Seizure Case, 160
Stephens, Alexander Hamilton, 8, 96, 110, 223, 321–322, 332, 359*n*, 363*n*, 384*n*, 387*n*
Sterns, George Luther, 50, 62, 64, 71
Stevens, Aaron D., 375*n*, 378*n*
Stevens, Thaddeus, 93, 322
Stewart, Charles, 210, 211
Stewart, Somerset v., 17, 44, 210

Stone, Frederick, 263, 423*n*
Story, Joseph, 146, 151, 213, 363*n*
Stowe, Harriet Beecher, 11, 365*n*
Stringham, Silas, 174
Strong, Richard P., 291
Stuart, J. E. B., 52
Sullivan & Cromwell, 176, 403*n*
Sullivan, Algernon Sydney, xvi, 176, 177, 180
Sumner, Charles, 49, 185, 197, 322, 374*n*, 404*n*
Sumner, Edwin, 374*n*
Sunstein, Cass, 361*n*
Supreme Court
   Ableman v. Booth at, 42
   American Revolution/slavery and, 213
   British abolition and, 220
   Campbell and, 53
   Chief Executive/Chief Justice conflict and, 126, 127, 130, 152, 154, 155, 160, 161, 162
   Dred Scott case in, 13, 18, 19–23, 24–36, 37, 366*n*, 370*n*
   Emancipation Proclamation and, 251
   ending slavery and, 415*n*, 419*n*, 421*n*
   fugitive slave clause and, 7
   lawyers and, xvi
   Lemmon v. People and, 44
   persuading states to end slavery and, 236
   Prize Cases in, 201–207
   revenge trials and, 264–265, 266, 269, 276, 288, 292, 424*n*, 427*n*
   secession and, 81, 117–119, 120, 389*n*, 390*n*
   Southern worries and, 222, 223
   Texas and, 117–119
   Union blockade and, 188, 189
Surratt, Anna, 270, 423*n*, 426*n*
Surratt, Isaac, 426*n*
Surratt, John H., Jr., 260, 271–275, 416*n*, 426*n*
Surratt, Mary, xvi, 260, 261, 263, 265, 266, 268, 269, 270, 271, 273, 274, 275, 280, 423*n*, 424*n*, 426*n*
Sutherland, Daniel E., 359*n*
Sutherland, George, 361*n*

Swanson, James L., 425*n*
Swayne, Noah Hayes, 119, 201, 203, 322–323, 409*n*, 421*n*

T

Taiwan, 390*n*
Taliaferro, Lawrence, 15, 365*n*
Tallmadge, James, Jr., 78
Taney, Alice, 366*n*, 367*n*
Taney, Anne Key, 367*n*, 393*n*
Taney, Roger
   American Revolution/slavery and, 213
   Chief Executive/Chief Justice conflict and (*See* Chief Executive/Chief Justice conflict)
   Dred Scott case and, xvi, 19–32, 34, 35, 38, 39, 41, 42, 366*n*, 367*n*, 368*n*, 372*n*
   Emancipation Proclamation and, 248, 250
   ending slave trade and, 218
   ending slavery and, 414*n*, 421*n*
   as prominent Civil War period lawyer, 323, 331
   revenge trials and, 268, 425*n*, 428*n*
   secession and, 384*n*, 387*n*, 390*n*
   Southern worries and, 223
   War at sea and, 203, 205, 409*n*
Tariff, 81, 83–86, 87, 96, 98, 186, 382*n*
Tariff Act of 1828, 82
Taylor, Thomas H., 175
Taylor, Zachary, 90, 92, 131, 357*n*, 364*n*
Teach, Edward, 168
Tennessee
   Dred Scott case and, 24, 34
   Emancipation Proclamation and, 252
   secession and, 102, 389*n*
Territories
   Border States and, 236–239
   slavery expansion into, 222
Texas
   admission of, 364*n*
   American Revolution/slavery and, 215
   annexation of, 87–92
   Dred Scott case and, 16
   Republic of, 87
   revenge trials and, 429*n*
   secession and, 87–92, 105, 106, 108–116, 117–119
   as slave state, 10, 11
   War at sea and, 401*n*
Texas Revolutionary Assembly, 170
Texas v. White, 117, 119, 120, 386*n*
Theodora, 193
Third Wheeling Convention, 113
Thirteenth Amendment, 13, 45, 209, 252, 255, 256–257, 295, 370*n*, 414*n*, 420*n*
Thomas, Clarence, 31
Thomas, John, 62
Thompson, Jacob, 96
Thoreau, Henry David, 64, 377*n*
Three-fifths clause, 6–7
Times of London, 65, 244
Toombs, Robert, 89, 191, 384*n*
Transcendentalism, 62, 377*n*
Treason
   Brown and, 56, 59, 375*n*, 377*n*, 378*n*
   Chief Executive/Chief Justice conflict and, 156, 157, 396*n*
   persuading states to end slavery and, 237
   revenge trials and, 265, 284, 285, 286, 288, 289, 428*n*
   secession and, 93
   War at sea and, 165, 176, 185
Treaty of Ghent, 77
Treaty of Guadalupe Hidalgo, 364*n*, 408*n*
Treaty of Lisbon, 363*n*
Treaty of San Lorenzo, 401*n*
Treaty of Union of 1707, 3
Treaty on European Union, 363*n*
Trent affair, xv, 192–200, 201, 322, 406*n*, 407*n*, 417*n*
Trials of John H. Surratt, (George), 426*n*
Tri-Insula, 105, 386*n*
Trimble, Isaac Ridgeway, 141
Truman, Harry S., 160, 357*n*, 366*n*, 407*n*
Tucker, John Randolph, 59
Turkey, War at sea and, 171
Turner, Nat, 9
Twelfth Amendment, 365*n*

Index 459

Two Years Before the Mast (Dana), 207
Tyler, John, 59, 87, 88, 102, 131, 323, 357*n*, 364*n*, 371*n*, 409*n*, 421*n*

U

Uncle Tom's Cabin (Stowe), 11
Underground Railroad, 47, 92, 219
Underwood, John Curtiss, 286, 287, 288, 323, 429*n*
Union
　American Revolution/slavery and, 214
　Articles of Confederation and, 3
　Chief Executive/Chief Justice conflict and, 126, 154, 157, 161, 164, 165
　Civil War beginning and, 13
　Constitution and, 4, 8
　defined, 3
　Dred Scott case and, 18, 40
　emancipation and, 253, 254, 255
　Emancipation Proclamation and, 240, 241, 242, 243, 246, 247, 249, 251
　ending slavery and, 415*n*, 420*n*, 421*n*
　ending slavery during war and, 225, 226, 227, 228, 229
　Louisiana Purchase and, 9
　perpetual, 3
　persuading states to end slavery and, 233, 236, 237
　Prize Cases and, 205, 206, 207
　revenge trials and, 263, 279, 291
　Trent affair and, 196, 198–200
　War at sea and, 171, 172, 173, 174, 179, 180, 183, 402*n*, 406*n*
Union blockade, 171, 172, 174, 186–191, 197, 201, 205, 206
Union camps, 427*n*
Union Navy, 171, 172, 187
Unionists, 95
United Nations, 122, 257
United States
　acquiring territory and, 363*n*
　British abolition and, 220
　Brown and, 67
　Douglass and, 62
　Dred Scott case and, 20–22, 25–27, 29–31, 34–36, 41

　Emancipation Proclamation and, 242, 243, 249
　ending slave trade and, 217
　ending slavery and, 418*n*
　European powers and, 9
　lawyers in, xi–xii
　Mexico and, 11
　national security in, 12
　Prize Cases and, 201, 202
　revenge trials and, 272
　Southern worries and, 222
　Trent affair and, 194, 198, 199
　War at sea and, 170, 171, 173
United States v. Baker, 176
United States v. Booth, 373*n*
United States v. Brown, 67–72, 418*n*
United States v. Lee, 292
United States v. Nixon, 155
United States v. Smith, 178
Universal Attractions of Slavery (Davis), 412*n*, 413*n*
Universal Declaration of Human Rights, 257
Upper South, 24, 102, 110, 111, 215, 221, 411*n*
U.S. Steel Corporation, 403*n*
Usher, J. P., 153
USS Brooklyn, 188
USS Constitution, 141
USS Dolphin, 174
USS Niagara, 407*n*
USS Perry, 174
USS Quaker City, 189
USS San Jacinto, 193
USS Star, 188
USSR, 75
Utah, 89

V

Vallandigham, Clement L., 53, 159, 324, 375*n*, 399*n*
Van Buren, Martin, 131, 357*n*, 364*n*
Van Zandt, Jones v., 7, 329, 369*n*
Vanderbilt, Cornelius, 287, 429*n*
Vermont
　American Revolution/slavery and, 213
　secession and, 77

Victoria (Queen), 173, 407*n*
Virginia
    American Revolution/slavery and, 214, 215
    British abolition and, 220
    Brown and, 51, 53, 56, 57, 59, 62, 67, 70
    Chief Executive/Chief Justice conflict and, 138, 143, 154, 156
    Dred Scott case and, 24, 31, 34
    Emancipation Proclamation and, 242
    ending slavery and, 225, 420*n*
    Lemmon v. People and, 43
    Maryland *vs.*, 360*n*
    Nat Turner slave rebellion in, 9
    revenge trials and, 285
    Sanborn and, 64
    Scott and, 15
    secession and, xiv, 89, 94, 101, 102, 112–116, 388*n*, 389*n*
    slavery in, 2
    Somerset and, 210
    three-fifths clause and, 6
    Union blockade and, 186, 188
    War at sea and, 401*n*
Virginia Convention, 112
Virginia v. John Brown, 47. See also Brown, John
Virginia v. West Virginia, 116, 333, 376*n*, 389*n*
Voorhees, Daniel W., 324, 377*n*

W

Wade, Benjamin, 131, 324
Walker, William, 183
Wallace, George, 367*n*
Wallace, Lewis, 262, 280, 325, 423*n*
War
    Crimean, 41, 171, 190, 401*n*
    Declaration Respecting Maritime, 171
    international law and, 357*n*
    Korean, 160
    Mexican, 136, 170, 377*n*, 401*n*
    prisoners of, 169, 181, 204, 286
    Revolutionary, 169, 206, 212, 380*n*, 395*n* (*See also* American Revolution; Revolution)
    Russo-Japanese, 402*n*
    at sea (*See* War at sea)
    Seminole, 16
    slavery ending during, 225–232
    Spanish, 402*n*
War at sea, 167–207
    Chapman piracy project and, 182–185
    international relations and, 189–191
    Jefferson Davis and, 174, 175, 178–179, 181, 203, 204, 205
    privateers and, 168–185
    Prize Cases and, 188–189, 201–207
    Savannah and, 172, 174, 175–178, 179, 181, 182, 202, 205
    Trent affair and, 192–200, 201
    Union blockade and, 171, 172, 174, 186–191, 197, 201, 205, 206
War of 1812, 9, 77, 82, 85, 134, 136, 138, 159, 169, 170, 175, 215, 396*n*, 401*n*
War powers, 421*n*
Warren Commission, 275
Warren, Earl, 39
Washington, Augustus, 377*n*
Washington, George, 52, 65, 136, 290, 357*n*, 364*n*, 402*n*
Washington, Lewis W., 51–52
Washington, Madison, 220
Washington Peace Conference, 102, 112
Watson, Peter, 330
Wayne, James M., 22, 24, 32, 203, 207, 368*n*, 392*n*, 409*n*, 414*n*, 421*n*
Webster, Daniel, 10, 11, 81, 82, 91, 92, 99, 220, 222, 325, 382*n*, 383*n*
Welles, Gideon
    Chief Executive/Chief Justice conflict and, 141–142, 151, 153
    ending slavery and, 235, 240
    revenge trials and, 260, 273, 284, 426*n*
    secession and, 114
    War at sea and, 186, 193, 197, 406*n*
West
    Dred Scott case and, 24
    slavery in, 11
West Indies, 210
West Virginia
    Emancipation Proclamation and, 252
    ending slavery and, 420*n*

secession and, xiv, 112–116, 388n, 389n
West Virginia Convention, 116
West Virginia, Virginia v., 116, 333, 376n, 389n
Wharton, George Miflin, 178–179
Wheeling Convention, 113
Whig Party, 94
Whigs
  British abolition and, 219
  Chief Executive/Chief Justice conflict and, 128, 143, 396n
  Dred Scott case and, 20, 24, 31, 40, 367n
  secession and, 87, 88, 89, 94, 95, 383n
  War at sea and, 404n
White, George W., 117
White House, 175, 183, 195, 207, 230, 232, 236, 242, 279, 280, 407n
White population, 104, 106, 112, 388n, 411n
White, Texas v., 117, 119, 120, 386n
Whites, 28–29, 104, 215, 219, 414n
Whiting, William, 325
Whitney, Eli, 9, 214
Wilberforce, William, 216
Wilkes, Charles, 193, 194, 195, 196, 197, 198, 199, 406n, 407n, 408n
Wilkes, John, 406n
Wilkinson, F. C., 88, 383n
Willard, Ashbel P., 377n
Willey Amendment, 116
Willey, W. T., 113, 325, 388n

William Aiken, 104
Williams, George H., 132, 134, 394n
Wills, Gary, 380n
Wilmot Proviso, 88
Wilson, Woodrow, 82
Winans, Ross, 143
Wirt Opinion, 29, 370n
Wirt, William, 29, 217, 326, 370n, 429n
Wirz, Henry, 279–281, 282, 423n, 428n
Wisconsin
  Ableman v. Booth and, 41, 43, 373n
  Dred Scott case and, 15, 17
Wise, Henry A., 53, 54, 55, 59, 61, 63, 70, 94, 326
Witnesses
  Brown and, 56, 67, 70, 376n
  in revenge trials, 280, 423n
  War at sea and, 179, 184
Wood, Fernando, 105
Woodbury, Levi, 369n, 414n
World Court, 122
Wright, Jeremiah, 380n
Writ of habeas corpus. *See* Habeas corpus
Wylie, Andrew, 268, 274, 326–327, 425n
Wyoming, 12

Y

Yancey, William Lowndes, 191, 327
Yellow fever, 277, 367n
Yohe, Samuel, 136
Yugoslavia, 75

About the Author

Arthur T. Downey has lectured at the Smithsonian on Civil War legal issues and on Abraham Lincoln, and at American University's Civil War Institute. He has taught at Georgetown University Law Center, and is a member of the bar of the District of Columbia.